Cambridge Studies in International Relations is a joint initiative of Cambridge University Press and the British International Studies Association (BISA). The series will include a wide range of material, from undergraduate textbooks and surveys to research-based monographs and collaborative volumes. The aim of the series is to publish the best new scholarship in International Studies from Europe, North America and the rest of the world.

Cambridge Studies in International Relations

NATIONAL CHOICES AND INTERNATIONAL PROCESSES

ZEEV MAOZ

Department of Political Science
University of Haifa, Israel

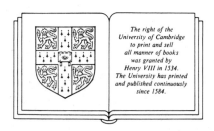

The right of the
University of Cambridge
to print and sell
all manner of books
was granted by
Henry VIII in 1534.
The University has printed
and published continuously
since 1584.

CAMBRIDGE UNIVERSITY PRESS
Cambridge
New York   Port Chester   Melbourne   Sydney

Published by the Press Syndicate of the University of Cambridge
The Pitt Building, Trumpington Street, Cambridge CB2 1RP
40 West 20th Street, New York, NY 10011, USA
10 Stamford Road, Oakleigh, Melbourne 3166, Australia

First published 1990
Printed and bound in Great Britain by
Redwood Press Ltd, Melksham, Wiltshire

British Library cataloguing in publication data

Maoz, Zeev
National choices and international processes. –
(Cambridge studies in international relations; 8).
1. Foreign relations. Policies. Formulation
I. Title
327

Library of Congress cataloguing in publication data

Maoz, Zeev.
National choices and international processes/Zeev Maoz.
    p.   cm. – (Cambridge studies in international relations: 8)
Includes bibliographical references
ISBN 0-521-36595-3
1. International relations – Research.   I. Title.   II. Series.
JX1291.M3795 1990
327 – dc20   89-17314 CIP

ISBN 0 521 36595 3

To Zehava
my smartest choice

CONTENTS

LIST OF FIGURES

LIST OF TABLES

PREFACE

This book started to take shape quite a long time ago. As a graduate student at the University of Michigan, I wrote a long paper reviewing the decision making approach to world politics. While working on this paper I was impressed both by the tremendous progress in this field and by the significant degree of cumulative research. However, I was also struck by the large number of conflicting models, propositions, and inconclusive empirical findings. The paper concluded with a plea for an integrative framework that would attempt to put together the main ideas of the various approaches under a single theoretical view.

As time went by, and as I became involved in empirical research on foreign policy decision making, I became increasingly convinced that an integration of decision making theories – though a significant contribution – would not solve the main problems of the approach as a whole. The rationale for studying international politics from a decision-theoretic perspective is the notion that the world is shaped by people and their choices rather than by a hidden hand operating above and beyond the nation state. Yet, decision theories – no matter how sophisticated – fall short of providing adequate theoretical bridges between people, their choices, and long-range international processes.

This book is my response to what I see as a fundamental challenge in international political research: to bridge the gap between microlevel approaches focusing on individual decision makers or on collective decision making bodies, and macroaspects of international politics, such as prolonged and multilateral international processes.

In a nutshell, this is an effort to develop an integrative theory of international processes. It starts out with assumptions about individual decision makers, and goes on from there to describe how national decision makers establish preferences for various courses of action or inaction concerning the relations between their state and other actors in the international system. It explores the processes leading to the aggregation of individual preferences into national

xvii

decisions. It examines the relations between national choices and international outcomes. Finally, it speculates on the patterns which long-term international processes may assume.

This is a "bottom up" approach. It is predicated on the notion that international politics is but a chain of interdependent and temporally related intersections of national choices. Its implication is also that, no matter how complex and insurmountable international problems may seem, they were made by ordinary people; they can also be unmade by people.

The book is addressed primarily to the serious student of international politics, who is interested in theoretical aspects of the field and is willing to put in the time and effort to comprehend a complex theory of a complex problem. I assume some basic familiarity with theories and concepts of international political analysis. However, it being an integrative book, I go step by step through theory and research on decision making and bargaining. Both bodies of literature are thoroughly surveyed before the original ideas of the present theory are discussed. Hence, those who are interested in learning about decision making and bargaining approaches will find this a fairly comprehensive source.

I have designed the book in a manner that would be readable by both scientifically oriented and more traditional readers. Extensive mathematical material is contained in chapters 4, 6, and some limited sections in chapter 8. Most of the material presented in chapter 4 is discussed in chapter 3; most of the material presented in chapter 6 is discussed in chapter 5. The mathematics in chapter 8 are rather elementary, but they are essential to the arguments and cannot be skipped without substantial loss.

Several individuals have influenced, through their writings, this work. These influences will be recognized by everyone who reads this book. I wish to thank, in particular, Steven Brams, Michael Brecher, and Ben Moore, and the anonymous referees of Cambridge University Press whose comments have helped make this a better book. The final part of the writing was supported by a Research Challenge Fund grant at New York University. Last, but not least, I wish to thank my children Inbal and Omry who accepted with understanding my absence from home "to finish my book." My wife, Zehava, who was busy with her own work and studies was always there when I needed advice and encouragement. She was always able to see the light at the end of the tunnel when I could see none. To her this book is dedicated.

1 TOWARD A THEORY OF INTERNATIONAL PROCESSES

1.1 INTRODUCTION

What makes history move? What are the forces that determine what we will read in the newspapers tomorrow? What factors do we examine if we want to predict whether, given a crisis in the Middle East or Southeast Asia, there will be another war or not? The answer to all these questions and the major rationale of this essay is simply: people and their choices.

What follows is a theoretical statement about the unfolding of international processes viewed from the perspective of the people who participate in them and the decisions which – I believe – determine when such processes start and end and what they tend to look like. Because international processes are extremely complex, especially when viewed from a human – rather than systemic – perspective, the theory that follows is not a simple one. This study attempts to bring together our seemingly disparate pieces of theoretical and empirical knowledge within a synthesized and empirically testable framework of interdependent choices.

The complexity of international processes and the diversity of available explanations require that the interdependent choice framework be constructed gradually. We must discern step-by-step the maze of theory and research on the relationships between people, their choices, and world politics. We must show why the resulting framework is needed and how it emerges from, and improves upon, other images of international politics. This is, indeed, the guiding principle behind the organization of the study. The present chapter provides a general overview of the theory of national choices and international processes, including the definitions of the basic terms, the major research questions, and the major implications.

1

1.2 INTERNATIONAL PROCESSES

An international process represents any long-term interaction among states or non-state actors in the global system; from processes of political and economic integration to war. However, a more formal definition views an international process as *a chain of temporally related and spatially interdependent intersections of decisions made by two or more actors in the global political system, which pertain to a particular set of issues, over a relatively long period of time.*

An international process is longitudinal; it evolves over time. As such, it is composed of a set of elements – let us call them international outcomes – that may vary from one point in time to another, but which share three common properties. First, each international outcome is an observed event which results from the joint (but not necessarily coordinated) choices of the participants directed at each other. In an international process that involves two actors, such an outcome is composed of a decision of actor **A** toward actor **B** and of a decision of actor **B** toward actor **A**. To illustrate this point, let us consider the Arab–Israeli peace negotiations 1973–1979. Events such as the Geneva peace conference of December 1973, the disengagement agreement between Israel and Egypt (January 1974) and between Israel and Syria (May 1974), the suspension of the Kissinger Middle East mission in April 1975 and the Egyptian–Israeli interim agreement of September 1975, Sadat's trip to Jerusalem in November 1977, the Camp David accord of September 1978, and the Egyptian–Israeli peace treaty of March 1979, are all examples of international outcomes. Each of these events represents a result of the joint choices of two or more actors.

Observable outcomes in the international system are not always products of the interdependent choices of several actors. Outcomes can be shaped by unilateral decisions. If I choose to cross the street against a red light, then the outcome is determined solely by my decision. However, such an outcome is less significant and probably less interesting from a social perspective than the outcome of a similar decision to cross the street against a red light when a car is approaching. In the second case, the observable outcome is a result of both my decision to cross the street and of the willingness and ability of the driver to press the brakes. The most significant and scientifically interesting events in a densely-populated international system are products of multiple national choices.

The second element in the definition of international processes concerns the factors that link together seemingly discrete international outcomes over time. Two factors determine whether a set of inter-

2

national outcomes is part of the same international process: commonality of issues, and the existence of a temporal relationship. The onset of international processes (as well as their termination) is marked by the concentration of national choices on a certain set of issues which seems to overshadow in terms of perceived salience and importance other areas of their external affairs. The shift from war-related choices to peace-related choices in the aftermath of the 1973 war marked the beginning of a new international process in the Middle East. The predominance of peace-related issues in the considerations and resulting actions of many key actors in the Middle East suggests that these seemingly unrelated events formed a coherent chain of interrelated outcomes to which we can refer as an international process.

By a temporal relation between distinct intersections of choices, I mean that a chain of national choices displays a certain logical flow over time. Specifically, the notion of temporal relation implies a causal association among international outcomes over time. Each intersection of choices is, at least partially, a function of the previous intersection of choices. The choices of Nations **A** and **B** that are involved in an international process will be, at any given point in time, at least partially affected by the nature of the previous international outcome (i.e., by the previous intersection of their choices). External changes have a significant effect on subsequent decision processes. They shape the motivational and situational framework within which the choice process takes place. Granted, no decision maker has complete control over the surrounding system in which he or she operates. Yet every decision in a foreign policy context has some effect on the surrounding system. The notion of temporal relation suggests that the product of multiple choices determines the nature of the international outcome at time t. This outcome constitutes the environmental change which sets into motion decision processes from t to $t+1$, and the international outcome at $t+1$ induces subsequent decision processes from $t+1$ to $t+2$, and so on. This perspective of national choices, international outcomes, and subsequent national choices as a continuous process is the heart and soul of the theory of international processes.

Consider the Israeli and Egyptian decisions to participate in the Geneva conference of December, 1973. Each of these choices was at least partially affected by the previous outcome of the bargaining: the technical agreement to provide supplies to the encircled Egyptian Third Army, and the agreement on prisoners exchange. The outcome of the Geneva Conference, inconclusive as it may have been, affected nonetheless the subsequent Israeli and Egyptian choices and helped

3

bring about the First Disengagement Agreement. Likewise, the mutual suspension of the Kissinger Middle East mission in April of 1975 affected the next observable international outcome of the bargaining process: the Egyptian decision to open the Suez Canal and the almost simultaneous Israeli decision to reduce the size of its forces stationed at the Canal area. This outcome, in turn, led to the renewal of Kissinger's mission which culminated in the September 1975 Interim Agreement.

1.2.1 Interdependence

Another important component of the concept of international processes is the term "spatial interdependence." By spatial interdependence I mean that national decisions are based upon decision makers' anticipation of decisions made at the same or some future point in time by other actors.[1]

Israel's decision to participate in the 1973 Geneva Conference was based on an anticipation of Egypt's, Jordan's, and Syria's responses to the UN invitation, as well as on what it hoped to achieve given the anticipated choices of the Arab states (Golan, 1976: 124–132). A similar set of considerations was probably involved in the Egyptian and Jordanian decisions to participate and in Syria's decision not to participate in the conference. The idea that interdependence is a crucial feature of international relations has generated a substantial literature in the field (e.g., Keohane and Nye, 1977; Mansbach and Vasquez, 1981; Snidal, 1985). However, the implications of interdependence at the international level for the choices of individuals and groups within national settings are not self-evident. Nor is the notion of interdependence developed in the theoretical and empirical literature of foreign policy decision making. This study suggests that the explicit incorporation of interdependence into our explanations of international relations may serve two important functions. First, it may enhance the external validity of our theories and improve their explanatory power. Second, it may provide a powerful tool for normative evaluation of the quality of foreign policy decisions.

The concept of interdependence forms a bridge between microlevel analyses of foreign policy decisions and macrolevel analyses of international outcomes. It provides for the analysis of international events

---

[1] Decisions within elements of an international process are not necessarily simultaneous. They are, by and large, sequential. However, the notion of interdependence as defined above applies because, at any given point in time, an actor faces some degree of uncertainty regarding the subsequent choices of its adversaries.

as products of choices that are reached within a setting where no single participant entirely controls the outcome of its choice. Hence, interdependence suggests that, when analyzing foreign policy decision making processes, we must consider the effects of decision makers' expectations regarding the possible courses of action open to other states. Within domestic settings, the choices of an individual decision maker addressing a foreign policy problem will depend to some extent on the preferences he or she attributes to other decision makers taking part in the same problem-solving process. This point is recognized and is given considerable attention by students of foreign policy decision making. However, theories of foreign policy decision making suffer from relatively little external validity in the sense that we rarely develop multilevel explanations of decision processes, and our explanations tend to focus on a single level of analysis. Hence, we know a great deal about, say, personality effects on individual choice. But we know relatively little on the effects of personality structures on group decisions. Similarly, we have a vast body of literature on the dynamics of group decision, but there is relatively little written on the process by which individual preferences are transformed into group choices.[2] The idea of interdependence can thus provide a conceptual and analytical bridge across levels of analysis.

Beyond this contribution, the notion of interdependence can prove instrumental in the normative evaluation of choice processes. One often hears decision makers justifying the most absurd decisions by saying: "we did the best under the circumstances." Yet, even our most sophisticated analytic tools do not provide us the means for reliably judging such statements. It is impossible to determine whether the factors perceived by the decision makers to compose the "circumstances" are indeed the factors that compose the "objective" reality. Unless we treat choices retrospectively, it is impossible to evaluate the relationship between the quality of choice and the quality of outcomes. But retrospective evaluations of choice are not only unfair to decision makers; they tend to be methodologically unsound on at least two grounds. The first and obvious one is that we use the wisdom of hindsight as a vehicle for normative evaluation of choices. The second is embedded in the tendency to attribute to decision makers more control over events than they normally have. One could claim that there is no "objective" reality beyond what is perceived by decision

[2] This is an interesting puzzle because there is a vast body of literature dealing with problems of preference aggregation in policy groups. I am referring particularly to the social choice literature. Unfortunately, theories of foreign policy making have rarely taken advantage of this rich and analytic literature, as we shall see in the following chapters.

makers. Hence, it is extremely difficult – if not impossible – to separate perception from misperception, without resorting to methodologically suspicious *ex post facto* evaluation.

Awareness of these problems led scholars to resort to evaluations of the procedural aspects of choice processes rather than the evaluation of substantive choice outcomes (Holsti and George, 1975; Brecher, 1979a; Janis and Mann, 1977). The underlying assumption of this approach was that there is a strong association between the quality of decisions and the quality of their outcomes. Yet there is no empirical guarantee that high-quality choice procedures would yield adaptive or successful outcomes. Furthermore, such an approach may lead to a tendency to fit process-explanations to consequences, that is, to analyze decisions whose outcomes were proven *ex post facto* to be adaptive, in terms of optimal decision theory. Similarly, there is a tendency to analyze disastrous choices in terms of systematic deficiencies in the preceding process. Consider for example studies of surprise attacks (Wohlstetter, 1962; Ben-Zvi, 1976; Handel, 1976; Whaley, 1973). The general theme emerging from these studies is that decision makers had all the relevant information for an accurate estimate of the imminent attack. Yet, for a variety of reasons, their estimates proved to be incorrect. As long as we deal with estimates and predictions – which are, by definition, probabilistic – rather than with prophecies which are deterministic by nature, it becomes almost impossible to judge quality. Can we say that Israel's intelligence analysts who estimated the probability of war as "extremely low" on the eve of the 1973 war were wrong? The answer is no. There is a tremendous difference between low probability and zero probability. Low probability events are still apt to occur. Evaluating probabilistic estimates in terms of a one-shot success or failure is highly unreliable, and likely to result in biased substantive inferences.

These points illuminate the problem of normative evaluation of choice processes. If reality is formed by the transformation of individual preferences into national choices, then we need an objective frame of reference, a picture of reality, against which evaluation of national choices can be done. Foreign policy choices are based, among other things, on the perceptions of foreign policy decision makers of the options open to, and the preferences of, external actors. This fact requires decision makers to establish estimates regarding the likely courses of behavior of external actors, and regarding events which are beyond the control of the decision maker.

Whether such estimates are accurate or not is the central issue that may separate a good decision from a bad one, because this is the context in which misperception may arise. However, to analyze the extent to which decision makers correctly perceived reality, we must have a better picture of reality than the one available to decision makers at any given point in time. In other words, we must be able to see not only things beyond any decision maker's control, but also the way in which the preferences of any given decision making unit relate to the preferences of other decision making units.

The interdependent intersection of preferences of several actors and the outcomes of their interactive choices form the *objective* reality. It forms a coherent and complete picture of a situation, and hence allows for a substantive evaluation of individual choices. It allows us to distinguish between perception and misperception in the sense that we can tell whether a specific estimate of decision making unit **A** regarding the intentions and preferences of decision making unit **B** are indeed compatible with **B**'s intentions and preferences. If not, we can judge how far off-target were **A**'s estimates of **B**. Without the application of interdependence into our evaluations of choices, we may be just like one of the blind persons and the elephant, each of whom is trying to guess the identity of the object standing in front of them, unaware that each is holding part of the picture, and that the perceptions of all provide a more complete picture than the separate perceptions of each. Without this realization we can never say that we have an elephant (North, 1969).

The notion of interdependence, as used here, may also provide a set of quality criteria against which choices can be judged. Even if we are able to provide an accurate picture of the circumstances at a time a given decision was made, we must still judge the actual decision against some quality standard. The representation of reality as an interdependent intersection of preferences and outcomes via a game-theoretic setting allows for the determination of such quality standards. This approach allows us to compare actual decisions to a theoretical benchmark of quality, and to answer intriguing questions concerning the relationship between national choices and international consequences, between individual preferences and international outcomes.

1.2.2 Definition-related caveats

Several caveats which stem from the preceding discussion of international processes must be enumerated before we go on. First, I have labeled such processes international in search of a better term. Although my primary interest in this study is with the interaction among states, the framework that follows is not confined to interstate processes. In the Arab–Israeli peace process one can count as occasional participants the UN (with its various organs), and the PLO (with its various factions). The main point, however, is that while the nature and number of actors is not fixed, each element in such a process involves, by definition, at least two actors, of which at least one is a nation-state. This criterion renders such processes both international and interdependent. What makes international processes central to the understanding of history and world politics is both their longitudinal nature and the variations in the international outcomes of which they are composed.

The complexity of the definition raises a number of issues regarding empirical feasibility. First, there are easier ways to define and classify international processes. Instead of viewing them as sets of intersections of decisions, one can define international processes as aggregations of events, that is, as a chain of observable transactions among states. Events are easier to discern, observe, and classify than decisions. Events tend to be also more quantifiable than decisions. The event-data literature is guided by such considerations, and has provided us with a significant body of knowledge regarding the relations among states (e.g., McLelland, 1968; Azar, 1980). However, the focus on events tends to obscure the mechanisms by which they were produced. Moreover, the notion of intersections of decisions covers both observable events as well as their causes. Finally, the study of international processes as event-aggregation tends to ignore or downgrade the interdependent and continuous nature of world politics.

The purpose of theory is to simplify reality by capturing its most important aspects, not to duplicate reality in its entirety. One of the desirable properties of a good theory is parsimony, that is, its ability to use as few explanatory concepts as possible to explain as many phenomena as possible. The complexity of the concept of international processes suggests that parsimony may be beyond reach in the context of this study. I believe, however, that this is not the case. The set of ideas that will be developed below emphasizes the fact that relatively few variables explain the ups and downs in international processes. The same set of explanatory factors operates on several levels of analysis, and the challenge is to explore the ways in which these variables are transformed from one level of analysis to another. The factors that determine the preferences and choices of individual decision makers tend to be the same factors that determine the preferences and choices of decision making groups. Similarly, the same set of factors accounts for international outcomes within an interdependent and multiple actor setting. But the context in which these factors operate does make a difference. Thus, we must account for the processes through which such factors are transformed from the individual level to the group level, and from the single group level to the international level. These are the major underlying ideas of the theory presented below.

Hence, the main complexities in the theory arise not from the number of variables which are used to explain international processes but rather from the interrelations among the few variables which, regrettably, must be employed. Furthermore, complexities arise from the transformation of the few variables across levels of analysis. If we say that choice behavior is influenced by the degree of antecedent stress that decision makers experience, we have made a simple empirically testable statement about the relations between stress and choice behavior. However, these relations may become increasingly complex as we move across levels of analysis. Each individual considering a given policy problem may be influenced by antecedent levels of stress. However, the degree of stress may differ for any two individuals considering the same problem, hence their choice behavior and their consequent preferences will also vary. Exactly how the relations between stress and choice will be expressed once these two individuals jointly deliberate on the problem is not only a function of the individual perceptions of stress and of their preferences. It is a function of the fact that, in the second case, we are dealing with group decision and with interpersonal interaction. Thus, the components that account for the preferences of individuals are transformed into group-level determinants of choice, and this transformation makes for complexity.

1.3 WHAT ARE WE AFTER? RESEARCH QUESTIONS

This study is predicated on a certain view of world politics. The major assumptions of this view are that international relations consist of a continuous and interdependent flow of national choices, and that people are not only the nuclear unit in world affairs but also the most important one. Accordingly, the main theoretical aim of this research is to explore the implications of this particular view for the study of world politics in terms of the relationship between individuals and aggregates in world politics.

Three major research questions guide the study.

1 *What is the relationship between the preferences of individual decision makers and the aggregate outcomes which are observed at the international*

9

level? How can we explain the process through which the preferences, beliefs, and dispositions of individuals are aggregated and transformed into events observed at the international level of analysis?

2 *What is the relationship between choice and consequences? More specifically, do high-quality choice processes tend to yield high-quality consequences? Are low-quality choice processes frequently associated with disasters or counterproductive consequences?*

3 *How do international processes evolve over time? Can we explain their evolution in terms of a causal chain linking aggregate, international-level occurrences and micro, that is, individual and group-level choices? If such a relationship exists, can we gain some insights with regard to general evolutionary patterns of international processes in terms of what Schelling (1978) termed "micromotives and macrobehavior?"*

These questions are logically interconnected in that they cover various aspects of the definition of international processes discussed above. The first question requires exploration of the process leading to the generation of distinct international outcomes. It also suggests the emphasis on the notion of interdependence in world politics. The answer to this question requires exploring the descriptive properties contained in the concept of interdependence. The second question has a built-in normative connotation. As such, it touches upon a long-standing debate in the social sciences between proponents of rational choice models of human behavior and (what I would label for the lack of a better term) behavioral and cognitive decision theorists. Much of this debate revolves around the question of the empirical potency and validity of rationality as an explanatory concept of human, social, organizational, and national behavior. Can behavior be accounted for in terms of the postulates of rationality? Are people and groups indeed rational?

Perhaps less salient is the normative facet of this debate which revolves around the question: "should people be rational?"[3] A theory that accounts for the relationship between choice and consequences may provide us with an appropriate frame of reference for converting this debate into an empirically answerable form. But such a question cannot be answered unless our theory addresses the evolution of outcomes from the preferences of the participating actors. This is the logical link between the first and second questions. The evaluation of

---

[3] For a good statement of this debate as it relates to world politics see Stein (1978) and Stein and Tanter (1980: ch. 1). Mandel (1987: 13–14, 105–108) argues explicitly that sometimes irrational behavior may yield better outcomes from the perspective of the national interest than prudent, rational behavior.

consequences can be done only at aggregate levels of analysis; in our case, at the level of international outcomes. To relate choice to consequences, we must explore the features of the various paths to choice. But we need more than that; we need a theoretical benchmark of quality that will tell us both what a good choice process looks like and how to differentiate among consequences in terms of quality.

The third research question concerns the nature of the dynamic and continuous features of world politics. It takes the answers we have been able to develop for the previous two questions as a point of departure and requires us to apply them to long-term interactions among states and other actors in the global political system. The answer to this question requires the abandonment of approaches that treat events and decisions occurring at distinct points in time as discrete and independent. It requires an evolutionary perspective and a dynamic analysis of change (Axelrod, 1984; Gilpin, 1981; Handel, 1981).

Two distinct approaches to the dynamic analysis of international processes are discussed in this study. The first views the evolution of international processes in terms of an interrelated chain of outcomes, each of which has a strictly *ad hoc* foundation. Specifically, each outcome within a process is seen as a function of two factors: the nature of the previous outcome and the choice processes taking place within the political systems of the various participants. The second approach views the evolution of international processes in primarily strategic terms, that is, as a confrontation among a set of long term strategies adopted by the various players. Perhaps the best way to explain the differences between these approaches is through an analogy to a game of chess. One approach to chess is of a strictly *ad hoc* nature. A player moves on the basis of the specific configuration of the game at any given juncture. One makes no effort to develop long term combinations of moves but rather responds to the specific threats or opportunities that emerge at any given point in time. Another approach views chess as a clash of strategies, that is, as a confrontation between complete plans for playing the game from beginning to end. The third question attempts to examine which of these approaches best characterizes the international chess game. The following sections provide a general overview of the theory of international processes.

1.4 THEORY OF INTERNATIONAL PROCESSES: AN OVERVIEW

The theory of international processes consists of four interrelated blocs or layers of ideas. Each of these layers builds upon the

11

previous one in the sense that it takes the outcome variables of a previous layer as a point of departure for generating an explanation of its own. But each of these layers focuses on a different level of analysis, hence the unique features of the level or unit of analysis become an important component in its explanation. Taken together, these models describe stages in the evolution of international processes combining different levels of analysis. This section provides a general overview of these stages and the interrelations among them. This theory offers: (*a*) a general synthesis of the various schools of thought within the decision making approach to world politics, (*b*) a general synthesis of the various schools of thought within the interactive approach to world politics, and (*c*) a theory of international processes in terms of a synthesis of decision making and interactive approaches. These ideas are based on a broad survey of the theoretical and empirical literature on foreign policy decision making and international bargaining whose aim is to identify some logical and empirical links among them.

1.4.1 Individual choice

The units of analysis on which foreign policy decision making approaches focus their attention are heads of states and their close circle of advisers, ministers, and high-level government officials. Decision making is basically a problem-solving process, a process of selecting among several courses of action (or inaction) one which is designed to address a particular issue or set of issues concerning the relations between one's state and other actors in the global system. In a foreign policy context, problems arise when an individual perceives that external or internal developments create a discrepancy between a desired or expected state of affairs and an observed one. Such discrepancies may arise abruptly, due to the occurrence of significant events, or develop gradually as the perceptions of individuals regarding expected courses of events change slowly over time. Discrepancies create a need for decision; their perceived features affect the procedural and substantive nature of the decision process that follows. In particular, the perceived nature of the stimulus defines for decision makers specific situational factors that influence their choice processes. Two such frequently mentioned factors are decisional stress and perceived situational ambiguity. Decisional stress taps the motivational and practical parameters under which decision makers operate. Stress is conceived here as a combination of three essential concepts: perceived threat, perceived opportunities, and time

12

pressure. Threat and opportunity perceptions represent the motivational antecedents of decisions; time pressure represents the practical constraint under which decision makers operate.

Threat perception refers to a perceived danger of depreciation in, or loss of, some assets or values under the nation's control. The magnitude of threat perception is a function of: (a) the nature and scope of assets perceived to be affected, (b) their relative importance to the decision maker, (c) the perceived extent of loss to each of these assets or values, (d) the likelihood of loss, and (e) the scope of currently possessed assets. Opportunity perception refers to perceived gains in some currently unpossessed assets or values. The magnitude of perceived opportunities is a function of the nature and scope of the expected gains, their relative importance, and the likelihood of gain. Decisions are motivated by mixtures of threats and opportunities; but they are also affected by the practical context within which the problem is to be addressed. In particular, the form and substantive content of a choice process are a function of the perceived time pressure under which a decision maker operates.

Time pressure is defined as a ratio of the optimal time needed for decision to the practically available time. But since the optimal time needed for decision is a function of the motivational cues a problem generates, that is, of the interaction between threat and opportunities, decisional stress is a combination of threat, opportunity, and time pressure. Perceived situational ambiguity refers to the extent of clarity of the situation and to the degree of confidence decision makers think they can place on their judgments and predictions. There may be a strong association between decisional stress and perceived situational ambiguity. As stress levels approach their limiting upper and lower boundaries, ambiguity will diminish. Only when decision makers experience moderate stress will they perceive high situational ambiguity due to the uncertainty surrounding the perceived threats and opportunities.

The effects of decisional stress and perceived situational ambiguity on individual choice processes are mediated by two factors: the psychological posture of the decision maker and his or her organizational role. The psychological posture of an individual refers to personality and belief-system-related factors which affect the definition of the situation. It is equivalent to what Brecher *et al.* (1969) label an "attitudinal prism," to what Holsti (1962) calls a "belief system," to what George (1969; 1979) calls an "operational code," and to what Axelrod (1973) referred to as a "schema." All these concepts denote a general cognitive structure or lens through which people interpret

13

events in their environment. Such cognitive structures are composed of both subconscious, personality-based dispositions and of explicit beliefs and world views. However, since the substantive contents of belief systems are individual-specific, and since my aim here is to generalize across individuals and situations, I shall focus on the structural properties of the cognitive posture.

The psychological posture of an individual is defined in terms of cognitive complexity (Hermann, 1978). A rather loose definition of cognitive complexity is the degree of interdependence and inconsistency contained in a belief system. Operationally, measures of flexibility can be derived from cognitive structures via systematic comparisons of cognitive maps (Axelrod, 1976, 1977; Hart, 1977; Levi and Tetlock, 1980; Maoz and Shayer, 1987). Varying levels of cognitive complexity serve to magnify or modify the effects of decisional stress and ambiguity on the decision making process. Cognitively complex individuals will be less susceptible, on the average, to the biasing effects of stress and ambiguity on decision making than cognitively simple individuals. This is to suggest that stress and ambiguity will have different influences on different individuals, and the mechanism explaining these different effects is the concept of cognitive complexity.

The interaction between stress, ambiguity, and cognitive complexity reflects the psychological notion that human behavior can be understood in terms of an interaction between personality and environment. As such, this framework is applicable to decision making in any realm. However, in a foreign policy context, our unit of analysis is not just any individual addressing a wide array of more or less routine problems. The context and the type of problems confronted by foreign policy decision makers also intervene between decisional stress and the choice process. At the level of individual choice, the context in which problems are addressed is organizational in nature. Because principal foreign policy decision makers are leaders of large-scale organizations, threats and opportunities will be perceived not only in relation to personal values, but also in relation to organizational goals and interests.

The organizational role of an individual represents both substantive areas of expertise and structural areas of responsibility. It is an additional lens through which the effects of stress and ambiguity on choice processes are filtered and changed. Individuals occupying different organizational roles will experience differing levels of stress and ambiguity even under the same circumstances and given identical cues. An event may be perceived by one individual to generate threat

14

or opportunity to the organization which he or she represents. Yet, another individual who is preoccupied with another domain of issues may consider this event to be insignificant insofar as his or her organizational responsibilities are concerned. In contrast to the quantitative interaction effect that is implied by the notion of cognitive complexity, the interaction effect entailed in the concept of organizational role is essentially qualitative. It suggests substantive differences in the interpretation of decisional stimuli among individuals occupying different organizational roles.

Now we can turn to a delineation of the major features of the dynamics of choices. The decision making part of the theory considers three alternative models of decision making at the individual and group levels. Each such model consists of a body of interrelated propositions concerning the substantive and procedural characteristics of various stages in the process. The models are not mutually exclusive, and probably not exhaustive. Yet, each model advances a relatively distinct set of propositions which are derived from a different set of assumptions about human behavior and about the workings of the human brain. The three choice models that are included in our framework are labeled: the analytic model, the cybernetic model, and the cognitive model. Here I shall briefly discuss the relations between the various exogenous variables and these models. The analytic model's postulates require considerable calculational and cognitive capacities from individuals because the entire complexity of the problem is to be included in the solution algorithms. The cybernetic and cognitive models are based on assumptions regarding limited cognitive capacities, or regarding situational and emotional needs to reduce decisional complexity. The essential features of these models are given in table 1.1.

These assumptions suggest that the empirical applicability of these models is context-dependent. That is, the likelihood of observing a given model at work in real-world decisions will depend on a number of situational or psychological preconditions. The purpose of the decision making theory is to specify the relationships between the situational, psychological, and organizational factors and the kind of process models these factors tend to produce. First, the kind of procedures individuals apply to solve foreign policy problems vary with the level of stress the problem invokes. Specifically, low levels of stress tend to be associated with cybernetic choice processes; moderate levels of stress tend to be associated with analytic choice processes, and high levels of stress tend to be associated with cognitive choice processes. Individuals confronted by low-stress problems tend to

15

Table 1.1. *Three models of decision*

Stage	Analytic	Cybernetic	Cognitive
Search	Exhaustive: across all relevant options	Sequential: programmed consideration of a preselected number of options	Deductive: through the general system of beliefs
Revision	Optimal: combination of base-rate information with current indicators	Incremental and conservative	Deductive and categorical: unequal reliability weights assigned to evidence compatible with prior beliefs relative to discrepant items
Evaluation	Comprehensive: cost-benefit analysis of outcomes across all value-dimensions; multiple value integration	Single-value analysis: sequential elimination by aspects for additional value-dimensions	Conflict-reducing: unidimensional analysis of costs and benefits to avoid value conflict
Choice	Maximizing: incorporation of utilities and probabilities for SEU maximization	Satisficing: application of acceptability thresholds for choice	Analogizing: single value maximization
Main fearures of group process	Weighted aggregation of preferences: argumentation and coalition formation; exercise of formal and informal influence	Elimination by aspects: sequential elimination by aspects; limited argumentation; limited exercise of influence	Groupthink: concurrence-seeking; little dissidence; limited or no argumentation; leader's preferences or group norms major determinants of outcomes

Source: Maoz (1981: 685), partially adapted from Stein and Tanter (1980).

adopt routine, incremental, and semi-mechanical procedures to the search for alternatives, to data collection and processing, evaluation of options and the trading-off of various values. Problems are seen as familiar and hence routine procedures tend to be available and are perceived as suitable for standard coping. Moreover, the expected gains or losses involved in choices of this sort are not extreme, and hence no serious threats or opportunities are perceived. Thus, decision makers will not invest much time and thought in finding a solution. They search for an alternative which is satisficing, accessible, and easy to implement. When such solutions are at hand, they are usually the ones chosen even if they may not be the optimal ones.

Moderate levels of stress arise when the decisional problem raises noticeable threat or opportunity and when the decision must be made within a well-defined but not extremely short time-span. The problem is considered sufficiently serious and pressing to warrant close investigation. The time-frame for decision is not overly restrictive and the problem is perceived to contain both familiar and novel features. Routine coping procedures are perceived to be inadequate, and sufficient time is available for rather extensive exploration of options, extensive information processing, and multiple value-integration during the evaluation stage. Since the values threatened or promised are important, yet threats or opportunities are not extreme, value tradeoffs are being made, and maximizing choice may become possible.

High levels of stress are perceived when extreme threats or opportunities to central values arise, and when time for decision becomes extremely short. Such problems are perceived as extreme departures from routine conditions, and in a foreign policy context they usually entail a major crisis.[4] The novelty of the situation and the extreme stress impose on decision makers a need for complexity-reduction and invoke cognitive mechanisms designed to eliminate value-conflict and to facilitate information processing tasks. There is a need to minimize search for options; yet the novelty of the situation precludes utilization of standard solutions. Information overflow and shortage of time require the utilization of biased cognitive selection criteria. Value tradeoffs become both practically and cognitively difficult to accept, hence decision makers resort to conflict-reducing tactics such as unidimensional evaluation of options. Satisficing or optimizing choice principles are replaced by single-value maximizing principles.

---

[4] The term crisis, as referred to here, is a situation which involves extreme threats or opportunities. This conception departs radically from crisis literature which views crisis as a high-threat situation (Maoz 1982b).

This analysis suggests that there exists a curvilinear inverse U-shape relationship between stress and choice quality at the individual level. Choice quality is used here as a procedural characteristic of the process rather than as an evaluative expression derived from its consequences. Specifically, choice quality increases as the procedural features of individual choice processes approach or approximate the postulates of the analytic model.

The theory also postulates a positive linear relationship between perceived situational ambiguity and choice quality. At low levels of ambiguity the situation facing decision makers seems to be clear and non-ambivalent, either because it is perceived to be non-novel, or because it is extremely novel. In an entirely novel situation which generates high stress, the importance of the values threatened or the perceived gains render the situation clear due to the perceived imminence of their occurrence. The clarity of high- or low-stress situations may yield low-quality choices. Under highly ambiguous circumstances decision makers are unable to come up with clear-cut definitions of the situation. Competing and equally-plausible inter-pretations of the environmental conditions dominate the analysis of problems. Decision makers cannot make high-confidence judg-ments of events and therefore cannot come up with quick-and-easy estimates and solutions. Hence the search for options and for information becomes extensive and the quality of the choices is enhanced.

The relationship between stress and choice processes is not a direct one; it is mediated by cognitive complexity and organizational role. The cognitive complexity factor suggests that, for any given level of stress and ambiguity, a cognitively complex individual would display, on the average, a greater disposition toward analytic decision making than a cognitively simple individual. Cognitively complex individuals tend to have flexible (i.e., non-deterministic) belief systems, and are not committed to dogmatic policy positions. Such individuals may be able to explore multiple options and to accept value tradeoffs. In addition, cognitively-complex individuals may be more tolerant of environmental uncertainty and complexity and willing to accept them as characterizing features of the political reality in which they operate. Such dispositions make cognitively-complex individuals susceptible to rational choice processes. Cognitively-simple individuals, on the other hand, tend to have black-and-white images of reality, firm and clear-cut views of friends and foes, and non-ambivalent value systems. They are intolerant of uncertainty and complexity, and normally have strong and deterministic theories of human behavior

18

and of world politics. Such individuals operate under tremendous normative and interpretative constraints when making choices, and these ingredients of their belief systems strongly affect their decision making style. Thus, for any given level of stress and ambiguity, there will be systematic differences in the decision making styles of cognitively-complex and cognitively-simple individuals (Maoz and Shayer, 1987).

The interaction between stress, ambiguity, and cognitive complexity concerns mainly the procedural features of individual choice processes. The notion of organizational role as an intervening variable raises a number of issues regarding the substantive aspects of individual choice. The operational implications of the proposition regarding individual differences due to variations in cognitive complexity are that complex individuals may, on the average, explore *more* options, process *more* information, make *more* sophisticated choice calculations than cognitively-simple individuals. The implications of organizational role for individual choice are qualitative in nature. The proposition here is that individuals occupying different organizational positions will tend to look at *different* options, will review and analyze *different* information, and will assign *different* weights to certain values. Specifically, individuals are apt to judge problems in terms of their organizational frame of reference. Hence, given the same kind of policy problem, any individual within a decision making group will tend to limit the search process to such options which conform to the concerns and interests of the organization he or she represents. The distribution of preferences within a decision making group will reflect, to some degree, the role distribution of the participants. The individual choice process is summarized in figure 1.1.

A few words about the contents of this figure are in order. First, the decomposition of choice processes into distinct stages is a heuristic device which helps increase the internal validity of the explanation. This is particularly useful for discriminating among the propositions of the three decision making models in that it allows for variations in decision strategies even within single decisions. Since the three decision making models are not mutually exclusive, we may observe situations wherein decision makers employ a mixture of strategies across decisional stages (Stein and Tanter, 1980). For example, a decision maker may explore multiple response options, and yet in the evaluation of these options he or she would consistently avoid value tradeoffs. By decomposing decision processes into distinct stages we minimize the likelihood of making unsound inferences that are based on overly general judgments regarding the kind of model that fits a

19

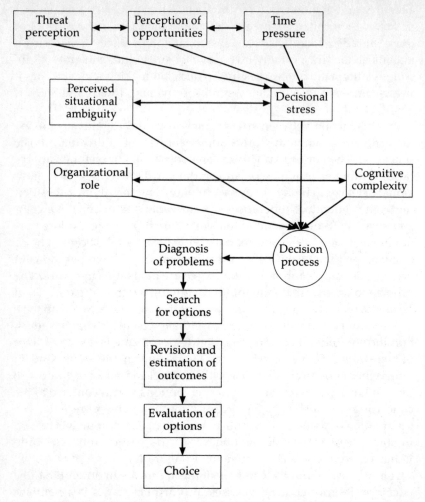

Figure 1.1 The dynamics of individual choice

certain decision process. We also increase our ability to analyze decision making as a dynamic process by studying it as a sequence.

Second, when tracing the decision behavior of a single individual over time and across problems, the intervening variables would add very little insight to our explanation. Both the cognitive capacity of an individual and – to a lesser extent – his or her organizational role display little variability over time or across problems. While perceptions of threat and opportunity may change dramatically across policy problems and issue-areas, personality structures and belief systems tend to be stable over time (Holsti, 1962; Bonham and

Shapiro, 1976; Hermann, 1978; but see Maoz and Shayer, 1987 for a different view). Foreign policy decision makers do not change roles very often, and even when they do, they are likely to carry over previous role-perspectives into their new administrative positions. Role-related influences are also stable across problems and issue-areas. The general idea here is that these two mediating variables point to rather persistent decisional and behavioral dispositions of individuals which cut across problems and over time. As such, they are of little use in explanations of individual choice if our unit of analysis is a single individual acting across issue-areas and over time. These variables become crucial, however, in cross-individual comparisons of choice behavior. Hence, cognitive complexity and organizational role are seen as major factors which allow systematic comparison of different individuals confronted with identical policy problems under rather similar environmental circumstances.

Third, the final element in our causal chain of individual decision making is the concept of choice. Choice is defined as a preference ordering of policy options by an individual. What we wish to explore in analyzing choice processes is not only that option which is eventually selected by an individual, but also how such an option is preferred to those options that were not selected. This point is crucial because the distribution of individual preferences across options forms the bridge between individual choice and group decision making.

1.4.2 Group decision making

Three assumptions serve as the logical basis of the part of the theory dealing with group decisions. First, the vast majority of foreign policy decisions are products of group processes. The setting in which such processes take place is interorganizational. Even in personalist political systems, the leader must solicit information and advice from his or her subordinates. This is even more true for cabinet-type executives. Policy groups are interorganizational in the sense that individual participants represent various organizations that are customarily responsible for various aspects of a nation's external and internal affairs (Allison, 1971; Allison and Halperin, 1972).

Second, individuals enter group discussion with pre-established preferences. The treatment of foreign policy problems in governmental settings is typically preceded by discussions and deliberations in intraorganizational settings. Even when the time frame for decision is extremely short, decision makers tend to be familiar with the general class of cases to which the specific decision problem falls, and tend to have pre-established positions and preferences. While initial preferences may change during the course of group discussions, they nonetheless form the basis for explaining group outcomes.

Third, even the most democratic and egalitarian groups in the context of foreign policy decision making are not just voting machines. While individuals may enter group discussion with pre-established preferences, these preferences may change during group deliberations. Hence, the product of group discussions, i.e., group decisions, will not necessarily reflect the initial distribution of preferences across individuals. The processes that take place in group discussion have a significant effect both on the distribution of preferences across individuals and on the final outcome. The focus of this section is thus on the process by which individual preferences are transformed into national decisions within group settings. The dependent variable is a group preference ordering of options and the explanation consists of two factors: individual preferences and group structure. The first factor is derived from our explanation of individual choice. Each individual enters the group discussion with pre-established preferences which represent the outcome of his or her choice process. Thus, at the opening stage of the group decision, we have a certain distribution of preferences across participants.[5] The essence of group processes is the transformation of this distribution into a single preference ordering of options. How is this done?

First, the initial distribution of preferences contains some important information beyond the mere description of the array of options facing the group. It indicates, for example, the degree of initial group polarization, thus hinting at the degree of difficulty of reaching a final ordering of options by the group. The second factor affecting group choice is formal group structure. Foreign policy groups may vary with respect to the diversity of roles represented in them, from "kitchen cabinets" which consist of a small and homogeneous circle of ministers and advisers, to broad panels of politicians and lower-ranked administrative aides. The distribution of roles within groups indicates the degree of their structural hierarchy. We may distinguish between highly hierarchical and homogeneous groups, on the one hand, and pluralistic groups, on the other. The interdependent decision making framework suggests that group structure, defined in terms of role-distribution and hierarchy, has an important bearing on the dynamics of group choice.

[5] It is important to note that not all participants will have pre-established preferences for all the options represented in this distribution. This is due to the fact that certain individuals did not consider at all certain options which have been considered by other individuals.

Group decision making is a bargaining process in which individual preferences are changed, modified, and aggregated according to certain generalizable rules. The rules that guide the bargaining and determine the decisional outcome vary, however, according to the kind of model we adopt for explanation. The analytic model postulates a process of argumentation, exchange of information, and persuasion based on substantive considerations that guided individual choices. Group discussion, according to this model, is fairly extensive across the range of options considered by individual participants, and the decisional outcome reflects some sort of weighted aggregation of preferences. The cybernetic model postulates a more restricted degree of bargaining. Options are reviewed sequentially until one option satisfies enough individuals to be selected by the group. The cognitive model posits a very limited degree of bargaining and a groupthink pattern according to which individual preferences shift rather rapidly to what is perceived to be the emerging group consensus or the leader's preference.

Which model would best fit the observed group dynamics in a particular case is a function of the initial distribution of individual preferences and of the group structure. A highly polarized distribution of individual preferences and a pluralistic group structure tend to lead to an analytic decision process. In moderately polarized groups whose structure is still fairly pluralistic, we are likely to observe a process whose features are consistent with the ones postulated by the cybernetic model. Finally, homogeneous groups in terms of preference distribution and highly hierarchical in terms of (formal or informal) structure are likely to engage in groupthink decision modes. The group preferences are seen as a consequence of the kind of process taking place during the deliberations. These ideas are depicted schematically in figure 1.2

Two points of clarification ought to be made regarding this figure. First, the notion of interdependence which was raised in the broader context of international outcomes reveals itself in the context of group choice. The overlapping areas in the circles represent a certain degree of interdependence among the preferences of individual participants within groups. Substantively, this interdependence reflects overlapping preferences among individuals and indicates an initial level of group homogeneity or polarization with respect to preferences. It also suggests that group discussions may be characterized by processes in which preferences are being traded-off among individuals. That is, individuals may be willing to coordinate choices and positions during group discussion in order to promote mutual interests, or to block mutually undesired group decisions.

23

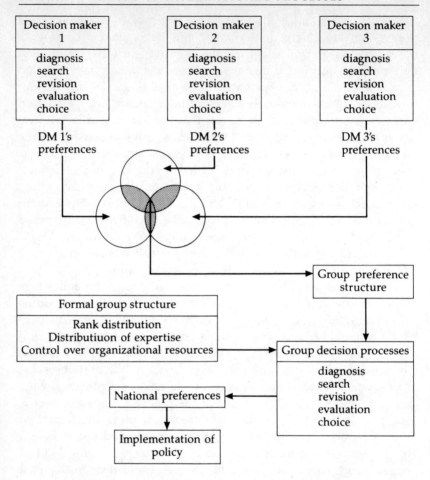

Figure 1.2 Group decision making

Second, the stages of group decision are, with slight modifications, a replica of the stages of individual choice processes. Groups are engaged in search of options, but the options they search come from a predetermined array: the set of options explored by individual participants prior to the group session. Under some cases, however, the group may explore additional options. This happens when the group cannot devise an acceptable decision from the predetermined array. Estimates regarding the possible occurrence of outcomes are revised as information is exchanged among group members. Individuals who are considered experts on the general issue-area of the decision problem have a relatively high influence on group estimates of possible outcomes. Search for options and revision of opinions and estimates may be more or less extensive as a function of the initial distribution of preferences and of group structure. The evaluation stage consists of the transformation of the initial distribution of individual preferences into a group preference ordering of options according to the processes and the transformation rules specified by each of the models. The outcome of each stage in the group decision process affects the process and outcome of subsequent stages. Limited search for, and exploration of, options are likely to result in limited and conservative revision of opinion; limited revision of opinion is likely to lead to biased evaluation of options, and so forth. Finally, the net product of group decision processes is a group preference ordering of options, rather than the act of selecting the most preferred option by the group. The reason for this specification is the wish to use the group preference ordering as a point of departure in the explanation of higher-level processes.

1.5 INTERNATIONAL OUTCOMES

International outcomes are viewed as interdependent inter-sections of national choices. As we move from individual choice to collective decision making, the preferences of foreign policy decision makers form an interdependent group-level distribution whose features affect the form and substance of group decision processes. The same principle applies to the movement from the single-nation choice process to the international level. The preference orderings of national policy groups become elements of the international puzzle. The combination of national preferences over policy options which relate to a specific problem forms the foundation of the international outcome. There is, however, one important difference between the interdependent transformation of individual preferences to group decisions and the interdependent transformation of national prefer-ences to international outcomes. The distribution of individual prefer-ences is only a point of departure for group decisions. This distri-bution may change considerably during the discussion and deliberations of the group. Although the initial distribution of indi-vidual preferences affects the final group ordering of options, it does not predetermine the final group decision. The dynamics of group discussion make a major difference. At the international level, the distribution of national preferences predetermines the international outcome. Individuals in the context of foreign policy formation are not autonomous units. Their power derives from their role, and their preferences affect – but do not shape deterministically – national decisions. On the other hand, states in the international system are autonomous units, hence their decisions carry a certain stamp of finality. Since the end-product at the national level is a national commitment to a certain course of action, the intersection of such commitments at the international level yields directly an international outcome. No process of transformation is involved, and all we need to know in order to determine the nature of the international outcome is how distinct choices intersect.

Why, then, do we examine the entire preference ordering of options by national decision making groups if all that counts is their actual choices? There are two reasons for studying links between national preference orderings and international outcomes. First, this analysis is essential for substantive evaluations of choice quality at the national level. Second, the distribution of national preferences is a major element in the analysis and explanation of long-term international processes. What we seek to explain is not only how distinct international outcomes emerge out of the choices of the participants in the game of nations, but also how they are related to each other over time. Analyses of the link between national preferences and international outcomes provides a set of theoretical criteria for choice evaluation. This set of criteria derives directly from the normative postulates of game theory which becomes our major theoretical basis at this point.

Suppose that nations **A** and **B** are engaged in interaction revolving around a certain set of issues. At some point in time, a problem arises and both nations must decide about resolving it. The decision making process within each nation includes perceptions as to the options available to, the preferences and intentions of, the other nation. Game theory as a model of such interactions has a number of rather restrictive assumptions which limit its descriptive applicability. Much of game theory assumes universal rationality, complete information, and strategic thinking which may or may not characterize real-world decision makers. Games are formed by intersecting the options available to the players. Each intersection becomes an outcome. The structure of games is determined by three factors: a) the number of players, b) the number of alternatives available to each player, and c) the distribution of players' preferences over all the possible intersection of their alternatives. In real-life situations a player usually does not know which courses of action are available to one's counterparts, let alone what are the preferences of other players across these alternatives. Thus, while foreign policy decisions are truly interdependent, they involve a considerably larger amount of guesswork than what is required according to game theory.

26

The analysis of international outcomes is based on a fundamental distinction between "objective" and "subjective" games. Briefly, an *objective* game is an image of all the possible outcomes in a given situation, along with the actors' preferences over these outcomes. This "image" is formed by intersecting all the policy options perceived by the participants. The preferences each participant has over the outcomes it has perceived form the content (or substantive aspect) of the objective games. The idea is that the researcher, as an external observer, can superimpose a game structure on international interactions if he or she can determine the distribution of national preferences across alternatives. Once the choice process in each of the participating nations has been analyzed, the researcher can intersect the preferences of the participants and construct an *objective* game. Hence, the researcher has at his or her disposal information which could never be known to the real participants in this "game." Obviously, objective games are purely theoretical constructs, they represent a complete picture of the "objective reality," which may or may not actually exist.

On the other hand, a *subjective* game represents a perception of an international environment as seen through the lenses of a given participant in an international process. It includes the policy options that a player attributes to itself, and its preferences over those policy options. It also includes the policy options that a player attributes to other players, and the preferences attributed by the former to the latter. Obviously, objective games may coincide with subjective games or differ from them. In the latter case, a player is seen to have some degree of misperception of reality. This misperception may be structural or substantive. A structural misperception consists of under, over, or partially-correct estimation of the structural aspects of the objective game: the number and identity of other players and the number and identity of the policy options available to them. Substantive misperception consists of misperception of the preferences of other players over the outcomes of the game. The comparison between subjective and objective games forms the basis for the substantive evaluation of national choices which is based on the outcomes of national decisions rather than on the procedures by which these decisions were made.

To make such a comparison theoretically meaningful, I develop the concept of *theoretical outcome*. A theoretical outcome is the outcome of the objective game assuming that each of the participants is rational and endowed by full information regarding the structure and contents of the objective game. This outcome is seen as what would have happened in a certain strategic situation, had the participants in this

27

situation made the best choices they could do. Since each objective game has a certain fixed or expected value for each participant, we have a criterion of what we may call decisional quality. We can compare the utility that each player has derived from the actual international outcome, i.e., the outcome that had actually occurred, to the theoretical outcome.

This research strategy creates a basis for a "fair" and theoretically sound evaluation of choices in terms of substantive quality. It allows us to judge whether decision makers really did "the best under the circumstances." It allows for examination of the relationship between the procedural and substantive aspects of choice processes and their consequences defined in terms of "good" or "bad" outcomes. It allows for a systematic examination of why and under what conditions misperception, misjudgment, and inept decisions arise. Finally, it creates a major theoretical basis for the analysis of chains of inter-national outcomes. A schematic illustration of the transformation of national preferences into international "games" is given in figure 1.3.

Each of the three states represented in figure 1.3 forms a subjective game, which is made up of the options it sees as feasible for itself and of the options it sees as open to other players. Each nation evaluates the outcomes of the subjective game and forms preferences over these outcomes. The options each of the national decision making groups attribute to their own state, and the preferences they form over the outcomes of the respective subjective games are taken to form the objective game. The "solution" of the objective game is the theoretical outcome. The outcome that arises out of the actual choices of the various states represents the actual outcome. The difference between the valuation of the actual outcome and the valuation of the theoretical outcome by a given state is the criterion by which the substantive quality of national choices is judged. Specifically, in terms of its outcome, a national decision is a "good" one if the actual outcome was valued by the decision makers of that state at least as highly as the theoretical outcome of the game. Obviously, a defective decision is one wherein the theoretical outcome is valued by decision makers more than the actual one. In this case, it could be reasonably argued that decision makers could have done better than they actually did.[6]

Note that the components of this interdependent transformation of national preferences may change from one "game" to another. For

---

[6] An actual international outcome can be valued more than a theoretical outcome. The theoretical international outcome is by no means the highest-valued outcome of a given strategic configuration. In fact, in many cases, the theoretical outcome of an objective game can be one which is valued very negatively by all players involved.

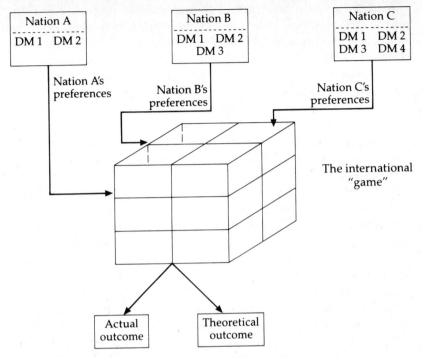

Figure 1.3 The analysis of international outcomes

example, the number of nations involved, the size and personal composition of decision making units, the number of alternatives considered by each, all may change over time. However, the fundamental nature of the process remains the same over "games." National decisions also entail expectations regarding their outcomes. An *expected international outcome* is defined as that outcome that national decision makers expect to arise as a result of their own choice and the predicted choices of other states (whether that outcome is what they want to arise, is another issue). Expected outcomes may differ from actual outcomes and from theoretical outcomes. The discrepancy between expected outcomes and theoretical ones is of secondary significance. However, the discrepancy between expected and actual outcomes is very important for the analysis of international processes.

1.6 THE UNFOLDING OF INTERNATIONAL PROCESSES

The analysis of international processes seeks to explore the fundamental logic of the evolution of international relations over time.

29

This logic rests on the structure of international outcomes and the relations among them over time. As mentioned above, international processes can be studied from two different perspectives. One perspective views such processes as a causal chain linking microlevel occurrences to international outcomes, international outcomes to subsequent microlevel occurrences, and so forth. According to this view, nations respond flexibly and in an *ad hoc* manner to the immediate circumstances in their external environment. No overarching strategic logic is required to explain their behavior. The focus of this perspective is on the unfolding of international processes as a chain of temporally related international outcomes, each of which is a function of the choice processes taking place within the political systems of the participating states.

The other perspective views state behavior as essentially predetermined by a grand strategy, that is, by a complete plan that specifies how the state would react in a variety of situations, and how it uses its foreign policy instruments to manipulate, modify, and change its environment in a manner that would advance its goals.

The differences between these perspectives are illustrated by some of the most acute debates in world politics. For instance, the literature on the superpower behavior during the cold war is divided into traditional and revisionist. Traditional explanations of US foreign policy view it as a set of necessary reactions to a seeming "master plan" of the Soviet Union. According to this view, American behavior was a set of *ad hoc* responses to a variety of situations which emerged due to a Soviet master plan. Revisionist explanations portray a diametrically opposed picture in which the US plays the role of master strategist and Soviet behavior is seen as a set of *ad hoc* responses to American challenges.

Another case in point is the literature on the origins of the Second World War. A. J. P. Taylor's (1963) controversial book portrays Adolf Hitler as an opportunistic leader whose behavior is seen as a series of attempts to capitalize upon opportunities which emerged due to the confusion in the foreign policies of, and lack of coordination among, the Western powers. While other historians and political commentators (e.g. Churchill, 1948; Bullock, 1952; Shirer, 1960; Martel, 1986) accept Taylor's view about the ineptitude and incompetence that characterized the foreign policies of Britain and France for much of the period, they strongly reject the claim of a lack of a master plan on Hitler's part. One of the major sources of disaster, according to the traditionalist conception, was the failure of the Western powers to detect the presence of a Nazi master plan. Be that as it may, these two approaches have different implications regarding the appropriate characterization and analysis of international processes.

The point of departure of the *ad hoc* perspective is the final brick of the previous stage: the actual and expected international outcomes. It was noted that actual outcomes of distinct international games are related to each other over time. Yet, this relationship is neither a direct nor a simple one. This relationship involves a linkage between an international outcome at one point in time and decision processes which yield a new outcome at a later point in time.

The occurrence of an international outcome creates an environmental change which raises a need for decision among individual participants in the process. Discrepancies between actual and expected international outcomes serve to alter decision makers' prior perceptions of threat, opportunity, and ambiguity, thus invoking new choice processes. Once these new choice processes evolve, they breed a new international outcome, which itself evokes new situational conditions leading to new choice processes, and so forth.

This chain of choice-outcome-choice-outcome, depicted in figure 1.4, is the product of the relationship between individual preferences and group decision, between group decision and international outcomes, and between international outcomes and individual preferences. This is the essence of the conception of international relations as a continuous and interdependent interflow of national choices. It also represents the prime rationale underlying the application of decision-related approaches to world politics. The analysis of international processes, seen in these terms, may provide the bridge between what Schelling (1978) referred to as "micromotives and macrobehavior." Although dealing with a different issue, Schelling's words succinctly tap the realm of international relations, because it involves

> situations in which people's behavior or people's choices depend on the behavior or the choices of other people . . . [These situations] usually don't permit any simple summation or extrapolation to the aggregates. To make that connection we usually have to look at the *system of interaction* between individuals and their environment, that is, between individuals and other individuals or between individuals and the collectivity. And sometimes the results are surprising. Sometimes they are not easily guessed. Sometimes the analysis is difficult. Sometimes it is inconclusive. But even inconclusive analysis can warn against jumping to conclusions about individual intentions from observations of aggregates, or jumping to conclusion about the behavior of aggregates from what one knows or can guess about individual intentions.　　　　　　　　　　(Schelling, 1978: 14)

31

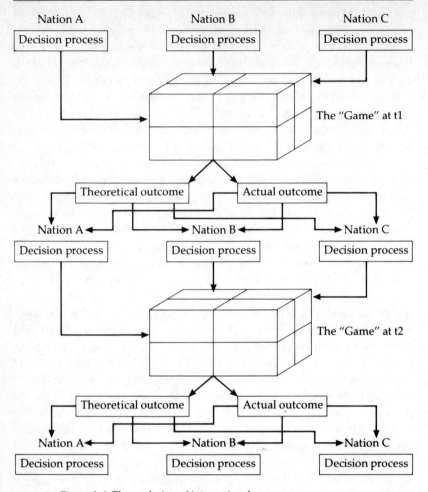

Figure 1.4 The evolution of international processes

But this kind of analysis requires a different approach from the game-theoretic approach suggested in the previous section. In inquiring about the long-term unfolding of international processes, we seek the factors that determine variations in international games over time. Specifically, we attempt to locate the factors that may account for the entry into and the exit from international processes of certain actors at certain points in time. We search for factors that explain why actors revise not only their preferences for a constant set of alternatives, but why and under what conditions actors change the alternatives included in that set. My assumption is that none of the factors that determine game structures remain constant over time: the number of actors changes; the number and substantive content of the array of alternatives at each actor's disposal change; and the preferences of actors change. The changes in actors' behavior over time given a fixed set of alternatives is analyzed by game theorists in terms of mixed strategies. However, to observe mixed strategies when they are employed by actors, one must observe iterated versions of a game with a constant structure. This is rarely the case in world politics. What is needed, in short, is a model that specifies how preferences change as a result of environmental feedback.[7]

The strategic approach posits several identifiable patterns of relations among international outcomes over time. First, if parties to an international process are seen to employ well-calculated, long-range strategies, then their preferences will not change significantly over time. This implies two things: (*a*) We will find little or no variation in both individual and group preferences over time. (*b*) We will find little or no relationship between preferences and choices, or regarding a relationship between procedures and outcomes.

In fact, both points suggest that decision making theories and bargaining theories that operate on an *ad hoc* basis are not very useful in explaining the evolution of international processes for several reasons. Specifically, the dependent variable, the structure of international games, displays little variability over time. Moreover, specific choices of national actors do not make sense given the preference order of the participants. Regardless of the processes by which individual preferences were established, and regardless of how individual preferences were transformed into national choices, there will be many instances in which actual choices do not follow logically from the preferences of the individual or group. The sacrifice of a queen during a game of chess cannot be understood within the context of a given game configuration when players assume that other players operate in terms of an *ad hoc* logic. However, it may make perfect sense in the context of a long-range strategy.

Schelling's point is that in some cases the disaggregation of a system of interactions into distinct parts may disable an analyst from capturing the overall picture. The strategic approach to the analysis of international processes requires two essential items of information:

[7] The foregoing discussion focused only on the general process depicted by the *ad hoc* approach. The content of the process by which outcome discrepancies affect subsequent choice processes entail some counterintuitive implications: For example, national choices that yield low quality outcomes may lead to substantial improvements in the process and substance of subsequent national choices. However, national decisions yielding high-quality outcomes might cause gradual deterioration in the quality of subsequent national choices. A detailed discussion of these issues is given in chapter 9.

(*a*) the fundamental preferences of the actors, (*b*) their strategies. The preferences of actors are based on their fundamental goals and on their risk-taking orientations. The strategy of the player is the "master plan" for playing the game. In some cases, preferences dictate strategies, but this is not true in general. In many instances, a given set of goals and preferences can give rise to a multitude of strategies: there are many logical ways to accomplish a set of goals, and not always can one find a unique optimal strategy. The choice of a strategy by an actor is, therefore, something that must be explored even by those who view the strategic perspective as the best model of international interactions.

The strategic perspective suggests that an approach could be developed to explain the general patterns of actors' behavior during an international process.[8] Such an approach would allow description of international processes in general terms, once preferences of the players and their strategies are given. The problem is that long-term strategies are difficult to detect even if they exist. Thus, only when all the distinct elements of a process have been laid out in a sequence does it become possible to determine whether the *ad hoc* decision-theoretic approach or the strategic approach provide a more accurate account of what has actually happened.

Yet, these difficulties do not preclude theory. On the contrary, they may lead to a richer and more profound theory of international processes than one which is simply game-theory-based. The conception of international processes, which links game outcomes with subsequent decision processes and which traces decisional origins of international games, allows a certain flexibility in theorizing that game theory, by itself, cannot offer. It allows us to address a series of questions concerning the relations between micromotives and macrobehavior. It also allows us to address a number of questions about the relations between macrobehavior and micromotives. For example, how do changes in international outcomes affect the size and personal composition of national decision making units over time? How do they affect domestic bargaining structures? Can we discern patterns of learning and adaptation by decision makers over time, when the events they perceive are not independent of previous events or of their own actions? Which decision makers tend consistently to rely on certain bargaining strategies? Which decision makers tend to develop *ad hoc* approaches to international problem-solving? The list of questions is long, but the point should be clear by now. The study of

---

[8] The analog of this approach is supergames in the jargon of game theory (Snyder and Diesing, 1977; Taylor, 1976; Axelrod, 1984).

international processes is a study in the relations between individuals and social aggregates. In our case, it is a study of the relations between individual decision makers and national foreign policy groups, and between national units and an interdependent international system.

The strategic approach, on the other hand, is based on a holistic interpretation of international interactions. The comparative study of these two approaches provides, therefore, for a potential set of insights which could not be obtained if the analysis is based strictly on any one approach. For example, both perspectives suggest that an international process may stabilize in some cases while in other cases international interactions will display significant variability from one point in time to another. It is not generally true that *ad hoc* perspectives envision international interactions as being subject to considerable fluctuations over time and leading to considerable instability. Nor is it generally true that stability necessarily arises when actors use long-term strategies.

1.7 SOME CONCLUDING NOTES ABOUT INTERNATIONAL PROCESSES

It could be reasonably argued that while this study promises an extensive and complicated explanation of the evolution of international processes, it says very little about the macroaspects of such processes. For example, the theory of international processes offers little insight into the general characteristics of prolonged and multi-actor processes beyond their mere conceptualization as a chain of spatially interdependent and temporally interrelated national choices. Given the traditional separation between microlevel, decision-related approaches (or foreign policy analysis) and macrolevel (systemic) investigations of world politics, we have a vast body of knowledge on decision making processes and on the structural aspects of the international system. We do not know how these two bodies of knowledge relate to each other. This study offers one way of systematically addressing the relationship between these two bodies of literature. It does not offer a quick-and-easy solution to the level-of-analysis problem. The solution will have to emerge from the empirical application of the theory of international processes, as well as from more detailed theoretical analyses which explore the implications of the strategic perspective in more detail and examine various combinations of the *ad hoc* and strategic perspectives.

It is important to note that the *logic in use* and the *reconstructed logic* (Kaplan, 1964: 8–11) of this study emerge out of a long tradition of

35

research on decision making and bargaining in a variety of disciplines, and on a wide variety of issues in international relations. The basic philosophy of this study closely resembles the philosophy guiding microeconomists, public choice theorists, and game theorists, namely the relations between individuals and social aggregates. However, the ideas presented here depart from the conventional wisdom of the current literature in these fields in two important respects. First, the assumptions about ever-present rationality are replaced in this study by a set of hypotheses concerning rationality as a context-dependent mode of behavior. Second, this study is not a single-shot analysis of some social problem. Rather, it offers a general theory for the analysis of long-term relations among states on a variety of issues. By avoiding simplifying assumptions and by focusing on long-term international relations, this framework requires a rather comprehensive synthesis of the knowledge gained in two central fields of social inquiry: decision making and international interactions. By combining these research fields, I hope to produce a basis for a theory of international relations which is more than the sum of its components. This study focuses on the theory, not on the empirical analysis, of international processes. However, my hope is to convince the reader both of the validity of the abstract theoretical logic, and of the empirical applicability of its product.

2 FOREIGN POLICY DECISION MAKING: ASSUMPTIONS AND CHARACTERIZATION OF THE APPROACH

2.1 INTRODUCTION

Foreign policy decision making analyses are viewed as microlevel approaches to world politics (Dougherty and Pfaltzgraff, 1971: 315; K. Holsti, 1988: 7–9). This is due to (a) the focus of these approaches on relatively limited and well-defined decisional units, (b) the focus on discrete and limited sequences of events rather than on global processes, trends, or patterns over an extended domain of time and space, and (c) the limited set of issues they seek to explain. Decision making approaches offer a limited, but very useful, outlook of politics as a problem-solving process.

Despite their limited scope and their seeming reductionist nature, foreign policy decision making approaches are essential to a thorough examination of world politics. As Bueno de Mesquita and Singer (1973: 238) put it: "no matter how many types of predictor variables we use in our model, or how many levels of analysis we embraced, we fall short of explanation until we demonstrate how the individuals who made (or acquiesced in) the key decisions served as the 'causal' link in the sequence [of events or processes to be explained]."

Decision making is often assumed to have an intervening rather than an exogenous role in explanations of international relations and national behavior. It is the glue that connects basic explanatory factors at the systemic, national, and societal levels to national and international behavior. System structure and national attributes may be associated with war, conflict, or international integration, but such empirical relationships cannot have a substantive meaning which is detached from the people who participate in such processes and the choices they make. To transform these empirical associations into causal relations, one must explain how system structure and national attributes affect the perceptions, beliefs, and values of national decision makers. In addition, one must explain how these perceptions,

37

beliefs, and values of national leaders "produce" the observed phenomena or behavior.[1]

The study of decision making might enable us to generate propositions which transcend the dynamics of choice. It might generalize to the exogenous factors that shape international processes and to the unfolding of the processes themselves in a truly causal fashion. The dynamics of choice within national settings, and their behavioral consequences within international ones allow for the explicit inclusion of human intent and perception which is central to the establishment of causality in social science research (Moon, 1975). The following chapters will examine the factors – external and internal – that motivate choice, the processes of choice, and their consequences. The first part attempts to provide a broad critical survey of the major theoretical and empirical works in the area of foreign policy decision making. On the basis of this survey, I develop a synthesis of the main contribution of this approach. The review of the literature serves to identify the ingredients of a two-step model that includes substantive and procedural elements of decision making processes (Holsti and George, 1975).

Before we start the review of foreign policy decision making, some introductory remarks are in order. First, we need a working definition of decision making. Second, the units of analysis on which the discussion focuses ought to be specified. Third, the emphasis on the descriptive rather than the normative aspects of decision theory must be defended. Fourth, the structure of the literature review must be outlined, and the selection and evaluation criteria of specific works must be introduced.

2.2 DECISION MAKING: DEFINITIONAL ELEMENTS

Decision making is a problem-solving process by which an individual, group, or organization chooses among alternative courses of action (or inaction) one which is designed to solve a particular problem or set of problems (Frankel, 1963: 1–5; Snyder, Bruck, and Sapin, 1962: 90). Foreign policy decisions are those in which the problems addressed involve the relations between a nation-state and its external environment. Decision problems arise when a certain unit (individual or group) perceive "a situation . . . [which] is discrepant from an ideal or

---

[1] The linkages between systemic or national attributes and foreign policy behavior are discussed typically with only sporadic reference to choice processes. See for example Waltz (1979) and Choucri and North (1975: 9). A good exception is the work of Bueno de Mesquita (1981a, 1981b).

38

expected state" (Burnstein and Berbaum, 1983: 536). Situation-related stimuli for decision are categorized according to the kind of pressure they exert on the deciding unit (Mintzberg *et al.*, 1976), as follows:

1 *Opportunities* Situations which are posited to exert minimal pressure for decision,
2 *Problems* which invoke intermediate pressure for decision because they involve a mixture of threats and opportunities, and
3 *Crises* which generate intense pressure by threatening central values of the decision maker, hence demanding prompt resolution.

This classification, though of little theoretical value, suggests that decision-related stimuli involve shifting perceptions of the environment by decision makers due to events or situations that evolve in the "real world." The emergence of the need for decisions may be abrupt, as a result of rapid changes in the environment, or gradual due to incremental changes in attitudes and perceptions.

Decision making is a process, not merely an act of choice. This process entails a dynamic which links the identification of the problem, to the selection of a certain mode of resolution. This process is divided into several stages that may or may not accurately describe actual choice dynamics. They do have, however, a significant heuristic value. These stages are:

1 *Diagnosis*. The identification of a problem and its classification as an occasion for decision. This stage includes a definition of the situation in terms of the extent of threat or opportunity the problem is perceived to evoke, and in terms of the novelty it is perceived to possess. Similar to medical diagnoses, decision makers tend to make an initial analysis of the features of the problem before prescribing treatments or solutions.

2 *Search*. The process of exploring policy options and determining the array of outcomes associated with each of the identified options.[2] The search stage structures possible solutions in two ways. First, decision makers explore solutions which are perceived relevant to the problem. Second, each of the identified courses of action is presumed to yield one or more outcomes, that is, events or states of affairs which are partially – but not exclusively – a result of the implementation of a particular course of action or inaction. The structuring of solutions in

[2] I am using the term "options" instead of the standard decision-theoretic term "alternatives" because alternatives refer to mutually exclusive courses of actions whereas options do not.

terms of linkages between options and outcomes[3] is the main task of the decision maker at this stage.

3 *Revision*. The process of data collection for the estimation of probabilities associated with each outcome, and the updating of likelihood estimates in light of incoming information. This stage applies only to options with multiple outcomes. For such options there is a need to assess which of the outcomes would eventually occur, and to assign them qualitative (e.g., "highly unlikely" or "better than even") or quantitative (e.g., "there is a 20% chance") estimate. Decision makers collect and process information which is judged indicative of the conditions under which a given outcome is hypothesized to take place. Such estimates are updated as new information is collected and processed.

4 *Evaluation*. The identification of goals or values affected by the decision problem and the cost-benefit (or preference) analysis of options on these goals. Decision makers determine preferences for options on the basis of the degree to which each option is seen to mitigate or alleviate those goals. Each option is evaluated according to the extent it maximizes or satisfies certain criteria or values that the decision maker pursues, or minimizes the danger to other values that need to be preserved. The feasibility of each option is judged in terms of the expenses associated with its implementation. Finally, since certain options are perceived to yield multiple outcomes, the evaluation process is done with respect to each outcome and while incorporating the likelihood estimates for outcomes established in the previous stage.

5 *Choice*. The selection of an option for response to the problem. This process rests on certain criteria that determine the ways in which preferences are ordered; the nature of acceptable or unacceptable options, as well as a degree of commitment to a certain policy option.

6 *Implementation*. The process of transforming the verbal commitment entailed in the decision into observable action. A decision is a mental or verbal commitment to a certain course of action. To be realized, the decision must be actually carried out. In foreign policy making, this stage applies mostly to group or governmental levels rather than to individual choice because foreign policy decisions are carried out only after they are finalized within institutional settings.[4]

---

[3] This is equivalent to structuring choice problems in terms of act and event forks within a decision tree or a game matrix (Raiffa, 1968).

[4] The formally-trained reader may want to consider the analogy between these stages and steps in scientific investigation processes. Diagnosis is equivalent to specification of research problems. Search is equivalent to identification of alternative explanatory models and research design specification. Revision is equivalent to data-collection and processing. Evaluation is equivalent to determination of falsification criteria and data-analysis. Choice is equivalent to result-interpretation. Implementation is equivalent to actual treatment of problems on the basis of the empirical findings.

Decision making processes have two aspects: procedural and substantive. Procedural aspects refer to the observable and quantifiable features of the process such as the number of options explored, the quantity of the information that was processed, and the number of goals identified and explicitly incorporated in the evaluation process. Substantive aspects refer to the content of, and the logic used within, each of these stages. Substantive aspects are seemingly qualitative. They refer to the nature of the options that were explored, the nature of the information considered in relation to all available data, the goals that were identified by decision makers and the treatment of conflicting goals; the types of choice criteria that were employed, and the extent to which implementation captured the "spirit" of the decision.

The distinction between procedural and substantive aspects allows examination of the extent to which decision making procedures are related to behavioral tendencies of states: for example, is aggressive behavior of states related to defective decision making procedures of their leaders? It allows examination of the relations between the procedural properties of decision making processes and the substantive adaptiveness of their outcomes: are "good" decisions related to "good" decision making? Finally, this distinction provides a powerful criterion for evaluation of the progress in the field over time. The extent to which decision-related approaches have been able to blend these two aspects is a good indication of the progress and maturity of the literature in the field.

2.3   UNITS OF ANALYSIS

Decision making may well be the most interdisciplinary topic in social research. It is studied by economists, psychologists, statisticians, sociologists, political scientists, and even by mathematicians. This requires a tangible unit of analysis which is of common interest to these disciplines. This requirement can be satisfied only by the most nuclear agent of social, political, and economic action: the individual. A topic such as Robinson Crusoe's coping with problems on his island may be of interest to a psychologist, but it is of little interest to a political scientist or sociologist due to the lack of a social and political context. Yet, the way the psychologist would go about investigating Robinson Crusoe's problem may exhibit strong similarities to the ways sociologists go about investigating community problem solving, or to the ways political scientists go about investigating election campaigns. Furthermore, the psychologist's findings may entail impor-

41

tant implications for the study of decision making in a communal or political context.

While the study of individual choice behavior is indispensable, the kind of social behavior which is unique to each discipline transforms the nature and form of investigation. The substantive context wherein choice behavior takes place alters the substance of research in terms of the realm of decisional issues and its methodology. The study of foreign policy decision making at the individual level of analysis is to a large extent the study of elite behavior. The "iron law of oligarchy" (Michels, 1962) may be more reflective of foreign policy decisions than of decisions in any other political domain. The importance of the issues involved, the secrecy of information, the expertise required for dealing with these issues, and the traditional view of diplomacy and foreign affairs as an "art of aristocrats" (Eban, 1983: 342–345), which is still rooted in most societies, all impose severe restrictions on participation. Thus, the study of individual choice in a foreign policy context focuses on the relatively few national leaders who are authorized, by virtue of their formal roles or by convention, to make decisions concerning the relations between their nation and other nations. While these national leaders may constitute the tip of a gigantic iceberg which includes institutions, interest groups, and public opinion, they are nevertheless above the water in terms of formal authority and responsibility. Disastrous decisions almost never lead to the elimination of organizations, but they often lead to the overthrow, dismissal, or resignation of political leaders.

However, national leaders do not operate in a vacuum; their authority is defined in part by the kind of organizations they represent (Allison, 1971; Neudstadt, 1964; Hilsman, 1964). The mechanisms of preference generation in organizations have an important impact on the decisional outcomes at the national (i.e., interorganizational) level. Organizational norms, interests, and operating procedures affect the process and substance of preference-generation of their leaders, and the positions that these leaders present in interorganizational settings. The Secretary of Defense presents positions concerning the defense budget which reflect to a large measure the needs and interests of the Defense Department, and which are net results of considerable consultations within the defense establishment. Discussions of military or diplomatic options during an evolving crisis necessitate the use of knowledge and expertise of professional soldiers or diplomats in order to assess their feasibility and their implications. Organizational choice behavior reflects the institutional aspects of foreign policy making. As such it adds a political layer to the more general basis of individual choice behavior of political leaders.

National decisions on foreign affairs are political in that they are rarely limited to intraorganizational levels. Although in certain political systems the authority for such decisions is formally accorded to a single individual, in practice foreign policy decisions can be best described as group outcomes. Even in the most authoritarian political system the leader must solicit advice and information from subordinates. Such consultations take place in interorganizational settings. The complexity and importance of the problems require multiple representatives of various organizations. Such groups may vary over political systems in terms of size or hierarchy. The final decisional outcome reflects some aggregation or transformation of the preferences of individual participants.

Thus, explanations of foreign policy decision processes must include three major units of analysis: individuals, organizations, and interorganizational groups. Moreover, such explanations must account for the dynamics by which individual preferences are transformed through organizational and group dynamics into national choices. The extent to which decision theories transcend a single level of analysis in accounting for national choices is an additional evalution criterion for the literature review. Explanations that integrate several units of analysis should be seen as both internally more valid and externally more generalizable than single-level explanations. Concomitantly, dynamic explanations that account for processes of preference-transformation should be preferred to static ones.

2.4 DESCRIPTIVE AND NORMATIVE ASPECTS OF DECISION MAKING

There is a tendency in much of the theoretical and empirical literature on decision making to blend together descriptive and normative aspects on the basis of less-than-conclusive evidence. In particular, it is commonly assumed that a strong association exists between process and outcome; that is, between good decision making and good decisions, between defective choice and disastrous consequences.

This study shares the conviction of some scholars who feel that we still lack commonly accepted criteria of choice-quality, and hence it would be premature to prescribe decision strategies before such normative issues have been resolved (Janis and Mann, 1977: 10; Brecher, 1980: 26). In fact, one of the main aims of this study is to

43

construct a framework that may allow us to examine the nature and magnitude of the relationship between choice processes and their consequences. But since description is a precondition for prescription, I shall focus the analysis on the descriptive aspects of foreign policy decision making, rather than on the normative ones. In order to make prescriptive propositions about foreign policy decision making, one has to be beyond strict decision making approaches and to incorporate the concepts, methodology, and substantive knowledge of international interaction theory. Only within the interdependent setting of international interaction is it possible to develop scientifically-sound criteria of choice-quality. Only within this setting, empirical examinations of the relationship between choice and consequences can yield fruitful and insightful results.

But normative aspects of foreign policy decision making cannot be completely ignored simply because they capture a large part of scholarly discussions. Sometimes the incorporation of such normative aspects is done implicitly in the literature; it peeks between lines. Sometimes it explicitly influences empirical investigations or theoretical discussions of decision-related topics. Debates among proponents of competing decision making models involve a mix of normative and descriptive arguments. In addition, it is important to examine the implications of premature normative closure for our understanding of the subject matter. While the emphasis in the review is on the descriptive aspects of the decision making literature, we will take notes of the underlying normative elements contained in some explanations.

2.5 SELECTION AND EVALUATION CRITERIA

The diversity of foreign policy decision making literature imposes upon the reviewer a need for selection. Obviously, no single person can do justice to all that has ever been written on foreign policy decision making; certainly not within a single volume. At the very least, a review which is supposed to be both informative and critical must rest on relatively explicit selection and evaluation criteria. We must explicitly state which considerations guided the review; what criteria were used for evaluation of certain works, and how the review served the broader theoretical aims of this study.

The literature review is designed to provide the basis for a broad synthesis of the literature into a coherent set of propositions about the evolution of international processes. Given this aim, the process of reviewing the foreign policy decision making literature is very much

44

like the filling up of a puzzle. Seemingly distinct, unrelated, and even contradictory theories and empirical investigations are placed side-by-side until a picture emerges. The search for an overall picture requires that many items that are not part of that puzzle be left aside even if they are of theoretical significance. Thus, the first selection criterion is that of relevance to the purpose of the study. To be reviewed, a certain theoretical or empirical study must fit into what I think is a fairly evolutionary and cumulative pattern of decision making research over the last 30 years. For example, since I am interested in choice as a conscious and intentional process, biological or physiological approaches to foreign policy behavior (for example, Hopple, 1980; Wiegele, 1979, 1973) will be mentioned only in passing.

The second criterion is that of importance. To be selected, a certain study must be influential in the sense that it contains important insights into the ways foreign policy units make choices. Empirical studies must illuminate (either in terms of empirical support or refutation) theoretical ideas about choice processes. The emphasis is on the relationship between abstract concepts, models, and theoretical frameworks, on the one hand, and empirical evidence, on the other. This renders the importance criterion more tangible and less subjective than it appears to be at first glance. The influence of a set of theoretical propositions on foreign policy decision making can be measured in relation to the amount of empirical research it has evoked or to the extent of criticism it has generated.

The third selection criterion refers to literature that examines choices in non-foreign policy settings. Here we will consider items that had a pronounced impact on foreign policy research, or items that illuminate special problems in the research on foreign policy making. Of particular relevance in this regard are formal decision theory (which is frequently associated with microeconomics); the literature on organizational behavior, the literature on human inference and judgment; and the literature on group dynamics and interpersonal bargaining, all of which are subfields of social or organizational psychology. Obviously, these selection criteria are more than somewhat vague. Nevertheless, they impose on the review an historical and evolutionary perspective.

If the selection criteria enumerated above have a somewhat subjective flavor, the evaluation criteria are decidedly subjective. The notion of "good" or "bad" research is clearly in the eye of the beholder. But since evaluation is indispensable given our aim of integration, the criteria by which specific works are evaluated must be made explicit.

The first is the process criterion. It suggests that studies that address

45

multiple decisional stages will be considered more valuable than studies that are limited to the analysis or description of single decisional stages. Moreover, studies that discuss the dynamic nature of choice processes – that is, the transition from problems to solutions across distinct stages – are judged more insightful than simple input-output models of decision making.

Second, studies that encompass multiple units of analysis would be considered more valuable than those focusing on a single unit. Moreover, studies that explicitly link units of analysis to one another will be considered more valuable than those that do not. For example, studies that establish the links between individual preferences and group decisions would be given more credit than those which focus strictly on group dynamics or group structures as determinants of decisional outcomes at this level.

Third, studies that combine the substantive and procedural aspects of choice processes will be, in general, considered more insightful theoretically than those which restrict themselves only to one of these aspects. Optimally, we would seek for studies that contain a comprehensive characterization of the choice processes in terms of the interaction between the procedures used by decision makers and the substantive contents of these procedures. However, as will become clear, we will find very few of those.

Fourth, we would want to grant credit to those studies that (a) clearly distinguish between description and prescription, (b) establish a normative benchmark for the evaluation of real-world decisions, (c) base their evaluations of actual decisions, not on the quality (i.e., success or failure) of the outcome, but on the fit between some theoretically-derived criterion and the actual choice process. Thus, we credit those studies that use some normative standard which is independent of the empirical consequences of the decision(s) under analysis as a means of evaluating the decision making processes, and as a basis for prescribing structural or behavioral modifications in foreign policy decision making.

From these evaluation criteria it seems that we credit generality at the expense of precision. The reason for this is twofold. First, integration involves finding a common denominator for very diverse approaches, methodologies, and case-histories. Hence, studies that are broad in scope might be more helpful for our integrative task than those that are precise and internally valid due to their self-imposed restriction on single cases, units of analysis, decisional stages, and so forth. Second, our focus on evolutionary patterns in the development of the decision making approach which guides the selection of studies for the review grants credit to work that creates an impression of existing order in the chaos of approaches, assumptions, and methods.

2.6 INTELLECTUAL STAGES OF KNOWLEDGE

The last dilemma concerns a choice between a review based on a topical perspective and one based on a historical perspective which describes the evolution of the approach over time. Fortunately, in the case of foreign policy decision making we can rely on Kuhn's ideas regarding the evolution of science as guidelines for the structure of our review. Kuhn (1970) argued that the evolution of scientific knowledge is characterized by both monotonous growth and by revolutionary leaps. A shared paradigm in a scientific field leads to a phase labeled "normal science" in which the process of knowledge acquisition is monotonous, gradual, and cumulative. Progress during the "normal science" phase is accumulated in a manner analogous to the gradual filling of a puzzle whose structure is essentially given and defined by the shared paradigm. A scientific "revolution" occurs when cracks are observed in the puzzle, that is, when scientists discover that the paradigm is either defective or unsuitable for the solving of previously unanticipated problems. In such cases, search for new paradigms begins, competing new paradigms emerge, and once one is developed and accepted by the scholarly community, science returns to its normal, monotonously growing mode.

The adoption of a Kuhnian line of thinking may prove useful in several important respects. First, it calls for an historical outlook on the field of foreign policy decision making. Second, it may facilitate our task of identifying distinct stages of conceptual, theoretical, and empirical development in the field. Third, it provides a set of epistemological criteria for comparing among them. Moreover, such an approach requires that we relate distinct historical stages to one another and examine how and to what extent the scholarly product of the t_1 stage has built upon the theoretical work and the empirical findings of the t_0 stage. One can also explore causes for interstage differences. Finally, an evolutionary approach may prove helpful for the selection of material and for its evaluation and critical appraisal. It allows us to examine explanations of decision making in relation to available knowledge at the time they were developed. It also enables us to assess the impact of various theories and other explanatory schemes on subsequent developments in the field.

Having adopted the Kuhnian line of thinking, we may as well borrow from him the classification-criteria by which we distinguish

47

among stages of theoretical development. The emergence of a paradigm in science is accounted for in sociological terms. A paradigm is accepted as such when the scientific community forms a consensus about some set of theoretical propositions, and when this set of ideas is accepted as a guiding framework for subsequent research. Clearly, we do not have anything resembling the notion of a shared paradigm in world politics. Hence, research almost never resembles the kind posited by Kuhn in terms of "normal science." However, a crude criterion for the identification of developmental stages in a preparadigmatic field may well be embedded in the notion of "fashionable" theories. A developmental stage can be identified to have emerged when there is an apparent emphasis on specific theoretical frameworks, and when empirical research tends to adopt the paths prescribed by those frameworks both in terms of the substantive domain of issues under examination and in terms of concepts and methodologies used. A developmental stage decays or collapses when a new fashion develops, when the theoretical emphasis and the subsequent empirical works shift to different domains of issues, or to the use of different approaches, variables, methodologies, etc. There is no specific time-frame for each of the developmental stages in the foreign policy decision making literature; important work which clearly belongs to one stage is still being done in a later stage. Yet, these criteria allow the identification of three major developmental stages in foreign policy decision making research.

The first stage can be labeled as *input-identification and conceptualization*. This stage goes back as far as the mid fifties and extends into the late sixties. As its name indicates, this stage focused on the identification of the major substantive and procedural inputs that affect foreign policy decision making processes. Both theory and empirical research have been largely influenced by the pioneering work of Richard Snyder and his associates (Snyder, Bruck, and Sapin, 1954), a work that provided the basic epistemological rationale for the application of decision-related approaches to the study of world politics. Two major theoretical emphases characterized this stage. One was the identification of exogenous inputs that impinge upon decision making in a foreign policy context. Such factors were both structural (personality traits and role variables), and situational (threat perception, time pressure, and ambiguity). The other emphasis was on the construction of fairly comprehensive frameworks which combined distinct factors into overarching schemes for the analysis of foreign policy decisions or foreign policy behavior.

The second stage is labeled *process-model specification*. The theoretical preoccupation during this stage, which extends from the late sixties to the mid seventies, was on the development of, and the discrimination among, "conceptual models" of decision processes. The major models that have emerged in this stage are the rational (analytic) model, the cybernetic model, the cognitive model, and the bureaucratic model. Empirical research revolved around the critical examination of these models in an effort to determine which of them provides the "best" approximation to real-world decision processes.

Although a lot of theorizing and empirical research based on these models is still being done at the present, there seems to be emerging – as of the late seventies – a new stage in foreign policy decision making research. This is the stage of *synthesis*. Its main features consist of attempts to integrate the models developed at the previous stage into: (*a*) a single model which is more tolerant to the differences among the original component-models, while – at the same time – assuming some degree of compatibility among them, and (*b*) a broader body of theory in international relations such as international bargaining and international systems theories (e.g., Snyder and Diesing, 1977).

Thus, my main tasks in this part of the book are to survey the major works associated with each stage, and appraise the various stages in terms of the evaluation criteria set above. In addition I will attempt to evaluate the decision making approach as a whole both in terms of the evolution of knowledge in the field and in terms of the value of the knowledge we have (or lack) on decision making processes with respect to the broader understanding of international relations. Finally, the literature review is conducted not only for the sake of assessing existing knowledge, but also for expanding upon it. Hence, my input to this approach consists of an attempt to incorporate decision making approaches into the theory of international processes. To accomplish this objective, each chapter of the review will be followed by a theoretical chapter which develops a section of the framework of international processes. The aim is to develop the part of the framework that deals with decision making processes within states. The second part of the book will do the same with respect to interdependent decision making, that is, it will extend this framework to include processes of strategic interaction among states.

3 THE INPUTS OF DECISION MAKING: IDENTIFICATION AND CONCEPTUALIZATION

3.1 DECISION MAKING AND WORLD POLITICS: THE EPISTEMOLOGICAL LINKAGE

World politics is a discipline in which one studies how states interact with one another. There are numerous approaches to the study of this interaction. One can assign universal motivations and rules of behavior to all states and relate these attributes to patterns of interaction, systemic structures, and a variety of observed phenomena and processes (Morgenthau, 1973; Kaplan, 1957; Bueno de Mesquita, 1981a). One can also infer from observed patterns of interaction the kind of domestic attributes of states that might account for these patterns (Rummel, 1963; Tanter, 1966; Wilkenfeld, 1968). The significance of the decision making approach lies in its contention that world politics cannot be explained by theories that are independent of, and therefore insensitive to, the beliefs, values, and expectations of national decision makers. International relations are shaped by people with highly idiosyncratic interests, values, and ambitions (Moon, 1975; Almond and Genco, 1977).

Theodore Abel made two important observations which were to have a profound impact on the "founding fathers" of the decision making approach to world politics: (1) war is the result of conscious, carefully-calculated decisions of national foreign policy elites to engage in sustained combat against other states, and (2) decisions to engage in war are made much prior to the actual outbreak of military hostilities (Abel, 1941: 855). Whether these observations are empirically valid is arguable. What is important, however, is the "element of decision"; the idea that recurring phenomena in the international system can and should be explained as outcomes of national decisions, and that we can make meaningful generalizations about those seemingly discrete choices of national governments.

This idea was further developed by Snyder and his associates. The major epistemological theme underlying their study was that international relations can be understood in terms of the interflow of decisions and subsequent actions among national units (Snyder, Bruck, and Sapin, 1962: 62, 65). They suggested that events and factors in the external and internal environment serve as stimuli to decision makers in a rather subjective manner, and that they are transformed into a network of values, beliefs, and images concerning the real world. These images, combined with more specific information which is processed and analyzed within organizational channels, are the major ingredients of the decision process which triggers national action. The decision of one nation, translated into operational terms, i.e., action, becomes in turn a stimulus to one or more nations and generates within those nations a similar process of choice.

This theme was, by and large, accepted by students of international relations both within and outside the decision making framework (Caldwell, 1977: 87; Yaranella, 1977: 104; Rosenau, 1967a: 202, 211). While this theme may be classified as a trivial aspect of contemporary international relations research, at the time this essay was published it was the first explicit rationale for the mode of investigation which Schelling (1978: 13) subsequently termed "micromotives and macro-behavior." At a time when the focus of international relations research was on grand theories specified at the systemtic level, or on relatively mythical explanations of foreign policy behavior in terms of "national character" (Snyder, 1955), such a statement was quite revolutionary.

Two specific research strategies characterized the first generation of foreign policy decision making studies. The first was an attempt to identify core variables that affect decision making, with a focus on the exogenous domain of factors that serve as inputs to decision makers. The second strategy focused on the compilation of these variables into fairly comprehensive frameworks so as to facilitate empirical research. The present chapter discusses these two strategies in greater detail.

3.2 THE INPUTS OF DECISION MAKING

Almost any variable one can possibly think of has been, at one point or another, identified as an exogenous input to decision making. This section discusses the major exogenous variables, grouping them into three general categories: (1) personality traits and belief systems, (2) situational variables, and (3) role variables.

3.2.1 Personality traits and belief systems

Greenstein (1969: 142) classified research on personality and politics under three headings: (1) the psychological analysis of single political actors, (2) the analysis of types of political actors, and (3) the aggregate analysis of individuals and types of individuals related to political processes and institutions.

Psychopathological studies of political leaders were not a new thing at the time that Snyder and his colleagues published their study. Langer, a psychiatrist who served at the Office of Strategic Services, wrote a psychological analysis of Adolf Hitler based on Hitler's own writings and on secondary sources. Langer's conclusion in 1943 was that Hitler was most likely to commit suicide (Langer, 1972). Most intelligence agencies have departments specializing in psychopathological analyses of key leaders of foreign states, but this material is usually classified and hence inaccessible for evaluation.

The study by Alexander and Juliette George (1956) of Woodrow Wilson is considered a classical example of this genre. This psychobiography of Wilson emphasized his childhood traumas due to a highly dominating and demanding father and a weak but loving mother. These traumas created a competitive and uncompromising personality which affected Wilson's approach to politics, in particular his pursuit of the ratification of the Versailles Treaty and the League of Nations Charter in Congress. They argued that the uncompromising positions that Wilson adopted in his pursuit of ratification of the Versailles Treaty in Congress can be traced back to the impact of his father's dominating influence.

Similarly, Mongar (1969) asserts that the mental characteristics of John Kennedy's behavior during the Cuban missile crisis can be traced to a sense of insecurity and feelings of physical and intellectual inferiority vis-à-vis his older brother as a child and as a college student. Rogow's (1963) account of James Forrestal goes along the same lines.

Although highly suggestive, these studies are marked by a major methodological problem: they have limited generalizability. Past experience and personal traumas differ significantly from one person to another. Unless one is able to group these experiences, traumas, and mental propensities into a more general framework of personality traits, the explanatory power of personality-based variables with regard to decision making cannot be assessed either theoretically or empirically (Greenstein, 1969: 93–95).

Awareness of this difficulty motivated researchers to identify general personality traits that entail a greater theoretical potential. Kissinger's (1966) classification of types of political leadership rests on the premise that the relationship between personality and foreign policy is defined to a large extent by prevailing societal and political structures. Different political systems produce different types of leaders and hence different policy orientations. Social structures and the various types of political systems define not only what kind of people would hold leadership positions, but also the general attitudes of these people and, consequently, their behavioral patterns in foreign affairs. Kissinger identified three general types of leadership:

1 *Bureaucratic-pragmatic leadership* is shaped "by a society without fundamental social schisms . . . and [is] the product of an environment in which most recognized problems have proved soluble, its approach to policy is *ad hoc*, pragmatic, and somewhat mechanical" (pp. 514–515). This kind of leadership is most commonly found in Western, developed, and bureaucratic societies.

2 *Ideological leadership* is a product of societies that are shaped by an all-encompassing ideological dogma. This dogma defines the leaders' basic world-view and thus their ideologically-based behavioral orientation. The tendency of such a leadership is to interpret patterns and events in terms of this dogma and to base its responses on the prescriptive propositions of this dogma. This kind of leadership is most commonly found in Communist states.

3 *Charismatic-revolutionary leadership* is a product of rapidly-changing societies that lack institutionally-shaped bureaucratic structures, and in which basic societal norms and values are undergoing a process of disintegration and transition. Revolutionary leaders attempt to create values, define goals, and develop new political orientations. Because the social structures that shape this kind of leadership are so elusive, the behavioral patterns of the charismatic-revolutionary leader are difficult to predict. In general, however, charismatic-revolutionary leaders are most likely to take risks and to initiate major foreign policy shifts (Handel, 1981). The personal traits and experiences of such leaders are apt to have a major effect on their behavior.

Implicit in this classification is the assumption that the unique personality traits of political leaders are – with the exception of the charismatic-revolutionary type – almost irrelevant for the understanding of foreign policy. Because leaders are products of societal structures, their own personalities matter very little in the process of policy making. The *ad hoc* and pragmatic approach to problem solving in Western societies suggests that it is almost impossible to generalize about the relationship between leaders' personalities and decision making. In Communist states, the prevailing doctrines determine both patterns of elite recruitment and the dominating value-systems of decision making elites. Given the dominating influence of the prevailing doctrine on Communist leaders, there is very little variation in actual behavior despite different personal traits across individuals. Thus, it may be more useful to understand foreign policy behavior by generalizing on societal structures than on the personality traits of the incumbent decision makers.

Although this classification is highly speculative, some of its more specific propositions seem to be supported empirically. For example, Kissinger asserts that with regard to the charismatic-revolutionary type of leadership, there is "a high incentive to use foreign policy as a means of bringing about domestic cohesion" (p. 523). Wilkenfeld (1968) provides some support for this proposition. He found that in "personalist" political systems, foreign conflict behavior is significantly related to domestic conflict in preceding periods. In "centrist" polities (i.e., ones that according to Kissinger give rise to ideological leadership), there is no relationship between domestic and foreign conflict. In "polyarchic" polities, however, domestic conflict tends to follow foreign conflict. This study also supports the idea that there are significant differences in terms of foreign policy behavior across political systems.

However, several accounts of Kissinger's own performance as a policy maker suggest that his own political experience refutes the idea that leaders' personalities make little difference in decision making. Students of American foreign policy during the 1969–1976 period agree that Kissinger's background as an historian had a profound impact on his view of the world and on his attempts to restructure the international system in general and the American foreign policy process in particular (Hoffmann, 1978: 33–80; Kalb and Kalb, 1974: 623–625; Starr, 1984). Two important points are worth noting in this regard. First, there is a very interesting convergence between the kind of system that Kissinger studied in his *A World Restored* and the "pentagonal" system he attempted to shape, or at least his attempts to form a "trilateral" system by the opening to China (Hoffmann, 1978: 249; Starr, 1984). Second, bureaucratic constraints on national leaders in a democratic society created a major obstacle for an effective pursuit of Kissinger's foreign-policy goals. Thus, as George (1980: 155) points out "the foreign policy-making system that Kissinger . . . developed during the first year of Nixon's administration is generally regarded as by far the most centralized and highly structured model yet employed by any president."

Much of the work on personality traits was influenced by Rokeach's (1960) book. Rokeach linked general personality profiles to explicitly articulated belief systems using psychological tests based on general attitude questions. He concluded that closed-minded people have rigid, dogmatic, and simplistic beliefs; they tend to be intolerant of ambiguity, and seek consistency among separate beliefs. Open-minded people have wide and sometimes undefined belief-structures. Their belief systems normally encompass a broad time-horizon and possess ambiguous boundaries. Barber's (1977) study of presidential character related personality traits to foreign policy behavior. This study developed a two-dimensional classification of personality traits: the motivational (i.e., active-passive) dimension and the attitudinal (i.e., positive-negative) dimension. Barber placed various presidents in the categories formed by the classification, explaining their behavior and performance in office. In contrast to the sociologically-based classification of Kissinger,[1] Barber's typology is psychologically-based. Etheredge (1977, 1978) identified two other dimensions of personality: dominance over subordinates and extroversion. He found that in terms of individual orientation towards foreign policy, competitive people tend to favor use of force as a solution to foreign policy problems. In addition, using hypotheses derived from interpersonal generalization theory, Etheredge found that interindividual differences in foreign policy debates can be accounted for by personality differences. Specifically, individuals that score high on the dominance and introversion dimensions display a higher conflict-related tendency than individuals who score low on these dimensions.

Using survey research comparing elites to a wide cross-sectional mass sample, McClosky (1967) derived both personality traits and foreign policy orientations. He found that isolationism which is similar to Etheredge's notion of introversion is "characteristically xenophobic and belligerent in its posture toward foreign affairs. It represents, for the most part, a rejection of other men rather than a concern for them, a disavowal of responsibility and a strong urge to disengage oneself from obligations towards others" (p. 107).

The most comprehensive set of studies linking personality traits to foreign policy behavior was conducted by Margaret Hermann (1974, 1976, 1978, 1979, 1980). Hermann employed a multifaceted classification of personality traits and suggested a consistent set of associations between such traits as nationalism, dogmatism, cognitive complexity, and foreign policy orientation and behavior. She suggested that such relationships tend to hold across problems and specific situations.[2]

---

[1] Which draws on Weber's three types of legitimacy: traditional, revolutionary-charismatic, and rational-bureaucratic.

[2] However, several studies have challenged Hermann's premise that personality traits are invariant over time and across political circumstances. See Rasler, Thompson, and Chester (1980) and Maoz and Shayer (1987).

Two qualifications must be made about the linkage between leaders' personalities and their decision making styles since the evidence available can be misleading in at least two important respects. First, personality traits affect general behavioral orientations, attitudes, and predispositions; they are not likely to shape specific coping strategies with specific problems. These studies do not explicate the constraints imposed by personality traits on the diagnosis of problems, the search for, and evaluation of, options, decision rules, and information processing (Jervis, 1980).

Second, personality traits and belief systems are stable over time. At most, they display very slow variation over time for any single decision maker. However, decision makers may use different coping strategies for different problems and in different situations. Thus, while the personal profile of a given decision maker is generally related to his or her foreign policy attitudes and behavior, its explanatory power is limited with respect to the analysis of the decision making process in a particular case. This implies that personality-based variables are most useful in two kinds of decision-related investigations: (a) in cross-individual comparisons, and (b) when used as mediating variables between rapidly-changing exogenous factors and decision process variables.

Third, personality traits operate on a subconscious level. Decision making, on the other hand, is a highly conscious process. One does not openly express dogmatism, isolationism, or dominance traits when confronted by a threat from an opponent state. Thus, unless we are able to transform personality traits into an empirically observable form, it is virtually impossible to assess whether and how they affect problem-solving processes. Two related concepts that have been used to resolve this problem are belief systems (Holsti, 1962; 1967) and operational codes (George, 1969; 1979). A belief system includes "all the accumulated, organized knowledge that the organism has about itself and the world. It may be thought of as the set of lenses through which information concerning the physical and social environment is received. It orients the individual to his environment, defining it and identifying for him its salient attributes" (Holsti, 1962: 245). A belief system contains both descriptive and normative i.e., value, elements. It is an organizing framework that transforms both subconscious personality traits and past experience into specific beliefs and attitudes on a variety of issues. It is also a scanning and processing device for information relating to specific problems.

The operational code refers to a more limited set of beliefs whose functions is to "simplify and channel the task of processing information, inventing and appraising options, and choosing the action that seems best in the circumstances" (George, 1980: 45). While belief systems affect general behavior propensities, operational codes contain relevant subsets of beliefs and choice propensities for particular problems.

What makes these concepts more useful than personality traits for decision making analyses? First, they are more operative and observable. Second, they can be decomposed in relation to specific choice problems, while at the same time, they can be used in their entirety to account for general behavior propensities. Third, they link subconscious traumas, experiences, and traits to explicit and conscious beliefs. Fourth, they allow theorizing about the constraints imposed by a person's psychological posture on the observable aspects of one's decision making style. Holsti's (1962; 1967) studies of Dulles suggests that such beliefs tend to form a consistent system which is stable over time. Other studies (e.g., Axelrod, 1976; Bonham and Shapiro, 1976; Shapiro and Bonham, 1973; Hart, 1976a; Levi and Tetlock, 1980) used cognitive mapping techniques applying belief systems to specific policy problems. The concept of belief system was shown to be useful to other areas of political investigation as well. Converse (1964) showed that belief systems impose considerable constraints on voting behavior of elites, whereas at the mass level, voting inconsistency can be accounted for in terms of ambivalence and inconsistency of beliefs.

Belief systems and operational codes share two analytic dimensions: substantive and structural. Substantive variables refers to the contents of belief systems. They specify the concepts used by a person for the definition of the situation, the goals that are perceived to be affected by the decision problem, and the overall view of the world that the system conveys. Structural variables describe the organization of beliefs within the system. They refer to such things as the number of concepts employed, the causal links among them, and, in general, the overall complexity of the system and the degree of consistency within it.

The focus of most studies in this stage was on the definition and delineation of the substantive dimension of belief systems. The major value of this dimension is that it can be directly related to the substantive aspects of individual choice processes. Given a set of beliefs and a problem for decision, we can construct hypotheses regarding which options would be identified by an individual, what kind of information would be perceived as relevant and what kind of information would be discredited and ignored, what kind of values would be

57

invoked, and what would be the general choice dispositions of the focal decision makers.

The shortcomings of the substantive aspects of belief systems stem from their rather subjective nature. Since people have different beliefs, they employ a different set of concepts and values to diagnose and analyze problems, or to the extent that people employ similar concepts, these are organized differently within the system hence generating different evaluations and choice propensities. What this point suggests is that the substantive dimension entails problems of comparability and generalizability in a systematic analysis of decision making processes across people and problems. Additional difficulties arise when the concept of belief systems is applied to the analysis of group decision processes.

The structural dimension can be used to compare belief systems across people in terms of cognitive complexity and cognitive consistency, and can be applied to the analysis of group decisions (Axelrod, 1977). Belief systems, while different and incomparable in terms of substantive content, can be systematically compared to one another not in terms of which concepts they contain, but rather in terms of how the various concepts they employ are organized and in terms of how these concepts relate to one another. Such comparisons provide insights regarding the underlying personality attributes of the decision maker. Variations in structural organization of belief systems tap interpersonal differences in terms of cognitive complexity.

The following points summarize the review of the literature on the effects of personality variables on decision making.

1 There is consistent evidence that decision makers' personalities affect their behavior.

2 Personality variables are associated with general behavior propensities and with global world views, but it is unclear how such associations are expressed in terms of the coping strategies of individuals faced with particular decision problems.

3 General personality classifications are most useful for cross-individual comparisons. We cannot assess how personality affects variations in an individual's coping strategies over time and across problems.

4 Belief systems and operational codes are useful in that they allow transforming general personality attributes that operate on a subconscious level into explicit and conscious views of the world.

5 The substantive dimension of belief systems has the same

problems as the more general personality traits. The structural dimension, however, is highly sensitive to particular problems and is useful for interindividual comparison on cognitive complexity and cognitive consistency.

6 The methodological difficulties concerning the relationship between slowly changing personality variables of belief systems and rapidly changing decision strategies suggest that personality can be best used as an intervening variable, rather than an independent one, in explanations of decision making processes.

Underlying proposition six is an assumption that while people are indeed victims of their psychological posture, they operate under very practical constraints when making decisions. These constraints which consist of situational variables, role variables, and issue-areas, display a higher degree of variation across problems and over time. Personality traits mediate between the objective properties of a problem and its perception and treatment by decision makers. This requires a closer examination of the various situational constraints under which decision makers normally operate (M. Hermann, 1978: 64; Brecher *et al.*, 1969; Brady, 1978: 175–176; Pruitt, 1965).

3.2.2 Situational variables

Before we discuss specific situational variables, a general remark on types of decisions is in order. There are three general types of decisions: decisions under certainty, decisions under risk, and decisions under uncertainty (Lave and March, 1975; Coombs, Dawes, and Tversky, 1970). Decision analysts distinguish between options (or alternatives) which are courses of action or inaction open to an organism, and outcomes which are states of the world or events that may or may not occur given a choice.

1 *Decisions under certainty* are those in which we know for sure which outcomes will occur given our choice. For example, when one must decide whether to buy a hamburger or a book, one knows for sure what outcome would occur given a choice. The choice of a hamburger results in eating a hamburger. The choice of a book results in reading a book. The choice problem is to rank these two outcomes on a utility function; not to estimate the probabilities associated with them.

2 *Decisions under risk* are those in which the decision maker perceives that more than one outcome is possible given a choice, and

one is uncertain as to which outcome would actually occur. However, the decision maker knows (a) the range of all possible outcomes, and (b) their probability distribution. For example, when having to decide whether to undergo a particular operation, one is often given the odds associated with the success and failure of the operation, and a set of statistics on possible complications. These probabilities are "known" because they are based on empirical studies of the outcomes associated with this particular operation. Gambling choices are also examples of decision under risk since the probability of obtaining a given number when rolling a (fair) die or when playing roulette is statistically known.

3 *Decisions under uncertainty* are those in which the set of all possible outcomes is known, but the probability distribution of the outcomes is unknown. Decision makers face not only uncertainty about the outcome that would occur as a result of their choice, they also lack objective knowledge about the probability of each outcome. In such cases, controlled experimentation and sampling techniques that allow determination of an "objective" probability distribution are replaced by intuitive devices of information processing resulting in the generation of a subjective probability distribution across outcomes.[3]

Most foreign policy decisions are made under conditions of uncertainty. Foreign policy makers lack scientifically-based predictions regarding the likelihood of outcomes and hence must rely on subjective probability estimates provided by intelligence agencies (Maoz, 1984a).

Why is the distinction among decision-types important? The situational context in which decision makers operate has a direct bearing on the ways in which they make choices. But there is also an often-neglected indirect effect: the situational context defines the magnitude of the decision problem; the magnitude of the decision problem affects both the substance and the quality of the choice process. As one moves from decisions under certainty to decisions under risk and to decisions under uncertainty, complexity increases, the reliability of information decreases, and the likelihood of defective choice increases. Decision under certainty requires no prediction. It requires merely ranking outcomes on a preference scale and

---

[3] There is, actually, a fourth type of decision: decisions under fuzziness. This type relaxes the assumption of known boundaries of outcome-sets. Substantively, this means that the decision maker does not know, or is unable to define all the possible outcomes associated with a particular option (Kickert, 1978). While this type of decision is not discussed in the present study, it is potentially relevant for the study of foreign policy.

choosing the option leading to the most preferred outcome. Decision under risk requires prediction, but the information and the decision-aids for intelligent choice are readily available. Choice becomes merely an analytic – or technical – process, and while more complex than decision under certainty, is certainly manageable. The technology for making gambling decisions is known and usable; whether people actually rely on such technology is another matter. In decision under uncertainty not only do we lack adequate information for intelligent choice, we also lack scientifically-sound and practically-manageable criteria of efficient information processing for prediction. There is also less agreement about, and knowledge of, optimal decision aids and choice criteria. The task of decision under uncertainty is enormously complex and most susceptible to error.

How does the situational context define the types of decision problems? Under certain situational conditions, decision makers may feel free to explore more options, process more information, and apply more analytic tools than under different conditions. Certain situations impose severe limitations on search, revision, and evaluation of options. While we may know very little about automobiles, if we have enough time and money, we can do extensive research on a variety of brands and thereby reduce the choice of a car from one under uncertainty to one under risk, or even under certainty. However, if our old car breaks down suddenly, we have no temporary transportation alternatives, and we have only a small amount of money for the purchase of another car, the problem is much more difficult. There are fewer alternatives we can explore, we do not have the time for extensive research, and the chances of error are much greater than in the former case.

It is the situational context in which problems occur that defines whether the problem is actually a big one – and thus difficult to resolve – or a small and manageable one. This section is about the specific variables that form the situational context in which foreign policy decision makers usually operate.

Snyder *et al.* (1962: 80–85) explored at some length the situational context of foreign policy decisions. Their framework discusses state behavior as an "actor in a situation," but the authors do not specify concrete situational variables that affect decision making. Yet this very general discussion has yielded a considerable amount of theoretical and empirical investigation on situational factors over the years (Pruitt, 1965; C. Hermann, 1969a, 1969b, 1972; Lanzetta, 1965; Holsti, 1972a, 1972b; Holsti and George, 1975; Brady, 1978; Eldrige, 1979; Brecher, 1977a, 1979a, 1980). Surprisingly enough, this particular research area seems to be characterized by a fair degree of cumulation, and by general agreement with regard to: (*a*) the major situational variables that are relevant for foreign policy decision making, and (*b*) the ways in which these variables affect decision making.

The three major situational variables that seem to be relevant for foreign policy decision making are: (1) threat perception, (2) perceived time pressure, and (3) perceived ambiguity.[4] Note that the word *perception* accompanies each of these variables. This is due to the fact that these variables assume subjectively defined values. That is, they become significant in decision making processes only when identified and assigned subjective scores within the psychological environment of the decision maker. It is assumed, for example, that decision makers are motivated by their perception of threat; not by the "actual" threat that a certain situation seems to entail.[5]

Since the discussion at this stage is on a generally abstract level, we need not concern ourselves with the ways in which decision makers identify and evaluate the magnitude of threat, time pressure, or ambiguity.[6] All we need to assume is that these variables are considered by decision makers as essential components of their situational context. As such, a definition of the situation involves almost invariably the assignment of intuitive and subjective scores to each of these variables by decision makers.

3.2.2.1 *Threat perception*

Threat perception is defined by Lazarus (1968) as "the anticipation of harm of some kind, an anticipation that is created by the presence of certain stimulus cues signifying to the individual (or group) that there is to be an experience of harm." Threat reflects an anticipation of loss to some currently possessed values or assets as a result of some observed environmental cue. The magnitude of threat perception is a function of the magnitude of anticipated losses and of the importance of the values or assets affected to the organism. In addition, since decision makers may be uncertain whether the actual conditions leading to losses on each of the values or assets would actually be incurred, the magnitude of threat perception is also a function of the probability of loss to those values. A person who

---

[4] Another variable – anticipation – was initially considered as relevant for decision making (C. Hermann, 1969a; 1969b) but was devaluated in subsequent research (Hermann, 1972; Brecher, 1977a). However, perceived ambiguity taps some of the properties of anticipation.

[5] The implications of the difference between "objective" aspects of a situation and "subjective" ones will be further explored in chapters 8 and 9.

[6] For a perceptive discussion of the determinants of threat perception in international crises and some historical evidence, see Cohen (1979).

possesses a large sum of money in his wallet would not feel as threatened if he walked in a relatively crime-free neighborhood, as a person possessing the same amount of money but walking in a high crime-rate neighborhood. Finally, the magnitude of threat perception is also affected by the ratio of the perceived loss on those values to the sum of the values that an organism possesses. A farmer whose only cow gets sick will feel more threatened than a farmer who possesses, say, seven cows and only one of them gets sick. The first farmer may lose all his dairy-related income as opposed to only a small fraction of the dairy-related income that may be lost to the second.[7]

3.2.2.2 *Perceived opportunities*

Because threat perception is central to the study of crisis decision making and because crisis theory tended to be defender-oriented (Maoz, 1982b), the opportunity element as a stimulant to decision making was largely ignored in the literature. A certain change in the external environment may signal to decision makers that initially unforeseen opportunities have arisen. For example, the Bay of Pigs fiasco may have signaled (by way of the Cuban requests for Soviet weapons) to Soviet decision makers that there may be a cheap way to reverse the strategic gap in that it was possible to place strategic weapons on the threshold of the United States (George and Smoke, 1974: 464–466). Similarly, Acheson's statement that excluded South Korea and Taiwan from the American defense perimeter in the Pacific, may well have increased North Korean perceptions of opportunities by suggesting that the US might not intervene in a Korean war (George and Smoke, 1974: 160–162). An opportunity perception typically involves anticipation of an imminent gain to some currently possessed assets or the acquisition of new ones. A person might not consider replacing his used car by a new one. However, an upcoming sale or a newly available low-interest loan may create incentives for decision.

The dimensions which determine the magnitude of perceived opportunities are similar to those of perceived threat. The number of values affected by the environmental cue, the perceived magnitude of gains on those values, the relative importance of these values, the likelihood of gains and the value of currently possessed assets all determine the perceived opportunity score. This suggests, contrary to the conventional wisdom of crisis decision making theories, that 'no threat' is not the end point of a continuum but rather its center point. The relevant continuum is one which extends from high threat to high

---

[7] The Biblical story of David, Bat-Sheva, and Uriah is a nice illustration of this dimension of threat (II Samuel 11–12).

63

opportunity. It also suggests that mixed perceptions of threats and opportunities may be a more adequate measure of decision-related motivations than any of them considered independently.

3.2.2.3 Time pressure

Threats and opportunities provide a substantive rationale for decision. They answer the question: why make a decision? Time pressure and ambiguity determine the structural parameters of the process. The perceived time for making a decision imposes practical constraints on the process. It imposes external (as opposed to psycho-logical constraints entailed in the preceding discussion of personality and belief systems) limits on the search for policy options, on the amount of information that can be effectively processed, on the evaluation of costs and benefits, and on careful choice and implemen-tation. But the time available for decision cannot be adequately represented in terms of "clock time" (Brecher, 1979a: 454); it is a function of the magnitude of the decisional problem. Small problems do not require much time to resolve; large ones do. Since threat or opportunity perceptions define the nature of the problem as well as its magnitude, the perception of available time for decision should be combined with these other inputs.[8] Indeed, the combination of threat perception and time pressure forms the concept of psychological stress (Holsti and George, 1975). This concept is equally applicable to a combination of perceived opportunities and time pressure.[9]

A very effective sale-strategy involves creating an opportunity with a deadline. Very often, such opportunities are more apparent than real. For example, a department store announces a 50 percent discount on a particular product effective for only a week. The reduced price of the product may still be substantially higher than its regular price in other places or than the price of available alternatives. The discount invokes incentives; the deadline on the sale imposes constraints on exploration of alternatives.

The outbreak of the Jordanian civil war in September of 1970 created for Syrian decision makers several opportunities. First, there was a real opportunity to overthrow King Hussein and gain control over Jordan. Second, the Syrians saw a chance of increasing their prestige

[8] Allan (1983: 26–31) argued that decision makers in crisis situations have a subjective perception of time which is based primarily on the volume of environmental cues considered relevant for the problem at hand.

[9] Many psychologists tend to equate stress with perceived threat. See, for example, Holroyd and Lazarus (1982: 23), Endler and Edwards (1982: 39). In this sense, the present conceptions of stress as a combination of threats and opportunities deviates from the mainstream literature on the topic.

in the Arab world by appearing as a champion of the Palestinian cause. There were also risks; namely, a possibility of an Israeli and/or American intervention. The deadline was defined by the perceived termination of the conflict. A Jordanian victory would have terminated Syria's dream of controlling Jordan; a Palestinian victory without Syrian aid would have terminated Syria's dream of controlling the PLO. Decisional stress was thus a consequence of the invoked opportunities and the perception of limited time for realizing them (Dowty, 1984; Yaniv, 1985).

The most obvious effect of stress on decision making is realized at the search stage. Under the conditions of high stress decision makers tend to explore few policy options. Moderate stress leads to more extensive exploration of options. But low stress tends to reduce the number of options that are explored. This suggests a curvilinear relationship between stress and the extensiveness of search processes (Brecher, 1980: 380–405; Stein and Tanter, 1980; Holsti, 1979). Since the extensiveness of search processes strongly affects the extensiveness of all other decisional stages, the curvilinear relation between stress and search is likely to be similar to that between stress and revision, evaluation, and choice.

Why is that the case? Low levels of stress imply that decision makers are confronted by routine situations. Such situations are characterized by low levels of perceived threats and opportunities and by generally low time pressure. If a decision needs to be made, it is neither difficult nor pressing. Routine situations are handled routinely. In a national context this means that the need for high-level involvement is not too great and that there usually exist bureaucratic standard operating procedures that specify how one can cope with such minor problems. The absence or the relative remoteness of deadline for decision does not force decision makers to spend much mental energy in exploring the best possible solution to the problem.

The evidence for routine, non-innovative, and incremental handling of low-stress situations is overwhelming. Cyret and March's (1963) study of firms, Davis, Dempster and Wildavsky's (1966) study of budgeting processes at the national level and Crecine's (1967) study of budgeting at the municipal level are cases in point; but they represent mostly domestic decision processes. Both Brecher (1980) and Stein and Tanter (1980) found that low levels of stress generated little decisional innovation and a lot of reliance on standard operating procedures. The readings in Halperin and Kanter (1973) provide numerous illustrations of this tendency.

At moderate stress levels, the problems become sufficiently serious and important for involvement of high-level decision makers. Time is restricted yet sufficient for extensive exploration. Standard operating procedures are perceived to be inadequate, primarily because the situation departs from its previously routine mode. Such situations require decision makers to work hard on analyzing the problem and on generating an acceptable response. Thus, the search for policy options is extensive; the amount of information processed by the decision makers is relatively large; and the evaluation of options is comprehensive. Again, Brecher (1980) and Stein and Tanter (1980) provide compelling evidence for vigilant tendencies under moderate levels of stress.

Most of the theorizing and empirical research on the relationship between stress and foreign policy decision processes covered the extreme portion of the stress distribution – that of high stress levels. Because of the generally accepted definition of crisis as a high stress situation, and thanks to the voluminous literature on crisis decision making, we know a lot about the effects of high stress of foreign policy decision making. High stress is a combination of high decisional incentives which are a product of either high threats or high opportunities, and objective constraints, i.e., high time pressure. The magnitude of the problems requires intensive participation and control by high-level decision makers. Organizational involvement in the decision making process is limited to the introduction of preselected contingency plans that address crisis situations. Thus, highly stressful conditions tend to give rise to cognitive dynamics and the time component imposes severe limits on people's ability to engage in extensive search for policy options and in acquisition and processing of information (Holsti, 1976, 1979). The inverse U-shape relationship between stress and the quality of individual and group-level choice processes has been supported by numerous social psychological and organizational studies (Holsti, 1979; Holsti and George, 1975; Janis and Mann, 1977; McLean, 1979; Shaw, 1976; Steers, 1981; Staw et al., 1981; Mandler, 1982).

The crisis decision making literature confirms the proposition that high stress reduces the amount of search and the extent and quality of revision, evaluation, and choice (C. Hermann, 1969a, 1972; Holsti, 1972a; Snyder, 1978; Stein and Tanter, 1980; Brecher, 1980). Allison (1971) and Tuchman (1962) show that contingency plans introduced by organizations provide rigid choice criteria which are not suitable for the specific problem, yet restrict the flexibility of the decision makers. Shlaim and Tanter's (1978) analysis of the Israeli deep-penetration bombing of Egypt in 1970 suggests that high stress, once routinized, increases the impact of contingency plans on decision makers, thereby reducing their capacity to observe subtle environmental changes and adapt to them.

3.2.2.4 Ambiguity

Snyder *et al.* (1962: 81) distinguished between structured and unstructured situations, the latter being "situation(s) for which the decision makers find it difficult to establish meaning . . . [these situations] may be characterized by change as well as intrinsic obscurity." Situational ambiguity denotes the extent to which decision makers are able to understand what is happening in their external environment, and the degree of confidence they have in their estimates of future developments. Ambiguous situations make it difficult to interpret current events and to estimate future developments. Unambiguous situations are those in which decision makers have a clear grasp – though not necessarily a correct one – of their environment, and are highly confident in their estimates. Although it is empirically known that people are generally overconfident in their estimates (Fischoff *et al.*, 1977; Nisbett and Ross, 1980: 119–120), the extent of overconfidence may differ from one situation to another. It is known, for example, that overconfidence increases when people are confronted with non-novel as opposed to novel situations.

The effects of perceived ambiguity on decision processes can be understood as a result of the relationship between perceived ambiguity and the other situational variables, threat and opportunity perceptions. There is a curvilinear relationship between perceived ambiguity and threat/opportunity perceptions. Acute threats to basic values imply a belief that there is a strong likelihood that some assets or values currently possessed are in real danger of being lost. Such a perception involves an estimate of a fairly high likelihood that currently possessed values would be affected in the future. If an individual (**A**) believes that another individual (**B**) is either very hostile or very friendly, situations involving **B** entail little ambiguity when they confirm **A**'s beliefs. **A** may even tend to disregard or discount discrepant evidence concerning **B**'s attitudes in order to maintain cognitive consistency (Jervis, 1976: 119–142; Axelrod, 1973). However, when there is a lot of evidence contradicting **A**'s beliefs about **B** and when **A** realizes a need to revise her beliefs, ambiguity will increase. This is also the case when **A** has an initially moderate threat or opportunity perception, or when **A** is unsure about whether **B** is a friend or an enemy. Moderate threat or opportunity perceptions entail substantial ambiguity in that they imply multiple definitions of the situation, each of which may be equally plausible.

Thus, as situational ambiguity increases, the search for policy options tends to intensify, the need for information increases, and the decision maker is more vigilant in processing the available information and in evaluation of the identified policy options. Because decision makers are confronted with competing definitions of the situation, none of which is perceived as dominantly plausible, high-ambiguity situations require increased flexibility of search, revision, and evaluation (Pruitt, 1965: 411–414).

However, there are significant disagreements regarding specific identification of situational ambiguity. Schelling (1966: 97) asserts that crisis involves increased situational ambiguity. He writes that "the essence of crisis is its unpredictability." McClelland (1968) argues along the same lines, when he suggests that crises are characterized by an increased event-variety. Others who see crises as situations of high threat, short duration, and high probability of war suggest that ambiguity is relatively diminished (Hermann, 1969a, 1969b; Brecher, 1979a; Snyder and Diesing, 1977). Still others emphasize changes (rather than increase) in the values of the situational variables during crises. This implies that situational ambiguity may vary from one crisis to another, depending on its pre-crisis value (Maoz, 1982b). Pre-crisis periods marked by low levels of perceived situational ambiguity may produce crises in which ambiguity is enhanced to the extent that the triggering events are unanticipated by the decision makers and inconsistent with their previously established definition of the situation. High levels of pre-crisis ambiguity may produce, however, a sharp decrease in perceived ambiguity by the decision makers. This is so because the triggering events render a certain definition of the situation more plausible than others.

Throughout the summer of 1962, the US received ample information indicating that the Russians were sending large amounts of weapons to Cuba. Some reports from Cuba suggested that Soviet nuclear missiles had been placed on the island. These reports created substantial ambiguity both due to the speculative nature of much of the information and to the fact that the administration was not sure what the Soviets were up to in Cuba. These reports led President Kennedy to state that the US would view placement of offensive weapons in Cuba as a highly provocative move, but it was unclear to the US decision makers what precisely were the "gravest issues that would arise" if the Soviets place such weapons in Cuba (Hilsman, 1964: 171). When it became clear that the Soviets had indeed placed strategic missiles in Cuba, much of the ambiguity surrounding the Soviet intentions in Cuba was cleared away. Allison (1971: 39–56) shows how the various hypotheses concerning Soviet intentions were dropped by a process of elimination. The placement of strategic, as opposed to tactical, missiles was inconsistent with the defense of Cuba hypothesis; the magnitude and the character of these missiles was inconsistent with the "bargaining barter" hypothesis, and so on.

The North Korean attack on South Korea of June 24–25, 1950 reduced sharply the previously perceived ambiguity by American decision makers regarding Soviet intentions. George and Smoke (1974: 162–172) note that US decision makers had intelligence reports indicating an imminent Soviet move during the summer of 1950, but these reports did not indicate where and of what nature this move would be. Although the North Korean attack could have led to a number of rival interpretations concerning Soviet intentions (George, 1955), it did, in fact, yield a single dominating interpretation consistent with the prevailing assumptions about Soviet's design to "fill every nook and cranny in the basin of world power" (Kennan, 1947).

Low levels of pre-crisis ambiguity increase the likelihood of unanticipated crises. Throughout the winter and spring of 1967 there was an intense border conflict between Israel and Syria. Yet, despite the fact that Egypt signed a defense pact with Syria in late 1966, Israeli decision makers were pretty certain that Egypt would not intervene in the conflict. This estimate was based primarily on the fact that Egypt was deeply involved in the Yemen civil war, and that it "did not have the capacity of starting a war" (Brecher, 1980: 48). The entry of the Egyptian troops into the Sinai on May 15, 1967 was clearly inconsistent with this belief and hence substantially increased the level of perceived ambiguity.

3.2.3 Situational inputs: a summary

The main contribution of the "first generation" literature was the mere identification of these inputs; little was done to specify their effects on decision processes. This was one of the main tasks confronting students of the third developmental stage. I found it necessary to discuss these effects because it seems difficult to understand why variables like stress and ambiguity are relevant unless one hypothesizes on their effects on the process of decision.

Psychological stress is generated by changes in the decision maker's environment. It is a combination of perceived threat, perceived opportunities, and time pressure. In sharp contrast to threat perception, opportunity perception is a largely neglected concept. My own inclination is to argue that this neglect is due, to a large extent, to the tendency of Western scholarship to view decision processes as generally reactive ones (Maoz, 1982a). Threat and opportunity perceptions are essentially about values, thus affecting both the process and the substance of foreign policy decision making. Time pressure is an element that highlights the practical constraints on decision making, but it also involves values in the sense that it defines the magnitude of decision problems as a function of substantive and practical parameters.

While perceived ambiguity is not a factor in decisions under certainty, it is, however, a major problem in decisions under risk and under uncertainty. It highlights the difficulty of decisional tasks as a function of the amount and clarity of information one has about the substantive problem to be solved. It is hypothesized to be curvilinearly related to decisional stress. However, because stress emphasizes values rather than estimates, it is unclear how strong such an association would be.[10]

Finally, our discussion up to this point has focused on the effects of situational variables on individual choice behavior. It seems obvious, however, that stress and ambiguity are also important determinants of group decision making. But before we can discuss the relations between individually perceived stress and ambiguity and group shared stress and ambiguity, we must consider another input to decision making at the individual level: organizational role. The concept of organizational role is not only an important input to individual choice processes; it is the major link between the individual level and the group level analysis of decision processes.

3.3 ORGANIZATIONAL ROLE

The concept of organizational role represents the political context of individual choice processes. It emphasizes the fact that individuals work within an organizational and thus hierarchical setting when making foreign policy decisions, and that their institutional affiliation has an important impact on their choices. Snyder *et al.* (1962) recognized the importance of the organizational setting in foreign policy decision making, but never discussed the

---

[10] The concept of issue areas is undoubtedly one of the major inputs to decision making. However, it seems that the issues that are perceived to be evoked by a given environmental cue constitute an essential part of both threat and opportunity perceptions.

implications of this setting for individual choice processes. It was not until the emergence of the bureaucratic politics model during the second stage that such implications were explicitly discussed. Although the bureaucratic politics model is primarily concerned with group or interorganizational decision making, it has at least one important proposition regarding individual choice: "where you stand depends on where you sit" (Allison, 1971: 176). In other words, preferences are a function of the decision maker's organizational role.

In other schools of thought, it is implicitly assumed that the major commitment of individual decision makers in a foreign policy context is to an efficient and adaptive solution of the problem at hand. Although cognitive and situational factors may constrain the efficiency of observed decisions, such a commitment implies that foreign policy decision makers are concerned with safeguarding and advancing the national interest, or whatever they perceive this concept to mean. The main assumption of the bureaucratic school is that since individuals operate in an organizational setting, they may be committed also to the well-being of their organizations. This implies that organizations may have interests and goals of their own which are not always consistent with those implied in the "national interest." The potential discrepancy between what is good for one's organization and what is good for the nation as a whole may create a psychological conflict in individual choice processes, and thus will affect a decision maker's diagnosis of the problem, and the process of individual preference generation. This is the psychological effect of one's role on one's choice processes.

But there are practical constraints as well. A decision maker receives information about a problem through organizational channels. These channels are likely to interpret the nature of the problem and its possible implications from a parochial and relatively biased perspective. The Secretary of Defense may have been less concerned with the diplomatic implications of Soviet missiles in Cuba than with their strategic implications. In addition, decision makers are more disposed to policy options which secure for their respective organizations a participatory role than to options which exclude their organization from implementation. Thus, the specific propositions made by the bureacratic school with regard to individual choice processes are the following:

1 The diagnosis of problems will reflect the threats or promises to the organization which a decision maker represents, as well as to the nation as a whole.
2 Search processes are affected by organizational interests,

feasibility constraints, and organizational goals relating to participation in the execution of decisions. More specifically, search is limited to options that advance organizational interests, and assure the organization a major role in their implementation. Options that threaten to weaken one's organization or reduce its role in the implementation process are likely to be discounted or ignored altogether.

3 Revision processes reflect organizational perspectives of future events and are influenced by standard operating procedures (SOPs) concerning information processing.

4 The evaluation of options is influenced by organizational goals and interests. Decision makers weight more heavily values that are consonant with their organizational interests than those that are consonant with the interests of other organizations.

5 The implementation of decisions depends on the interpretation of the operational implications of the decision. Such interpretations are heavily influenced by organizational interests and standard operating procedures (Allison, 1971; Allison and Halperin, 1972; Neudstadt, 1964).

Organizational influences on individual choice processes are a matter of degree, however. The nature of the problems, defined by the decisional context, determine to a large extent how much influence will be exerted by a person's role on the substance and structure of his or her decision process. That role-related influences interact with situation-related influences seems obvious. What is less obvious, however, is the varying degrees of influence that organizational role has on different people choosing under relatively similar situational conditions (Rosati, 1980: 248–249).

Organizations have two dimensions: structural and substantive. The structural dimension of an organization is defined by the hierarchical relations among its members. The substantive dimension is defined by the areas and issues that organizations as a whole, and individuals within them, are responsible for.[11] For individual decision makers, role consists of the same properties: rank and responsibility. Rank designates the person's locus within the organization's hierarchy. Responsibility designates the scope of issues and tasks a person is occupied with. Obviously, there is a strong association between rank and responsibility: the higher a person's rank within an organization, the broader and more profound is the range of issues and tasks he or she is responsible for.

[11] This is what Thompson (1967) calls the task environment of organizations.

The implications of these two dimensions for individual choice processes are quite simple: the higher the rank of a person within an organization and the broader a person's responsibility, the smaller the impact of his or her role on his or her decision making style. Why is that the case? First, the higher a person's rank within the organization and the broader his or her responsibilities, the less compartmentalized the perspectives such a person has. O'Donnell (1979) showed in his study of State Department officials that the higher their rank, the more complex is their dimensional classification of Middle East nations. Reduced compartmentalization reduces the impact of organizational interests on the treatment of decisional problems. Even within organizations there are likely to exist competing interests among the various departments (Simon, 1976: 110–122; Walton and McKersie, 1965). The higher a person's rank within the organizational hierarchy, the more interests he or she needs to aggregate when making decisions. The Secretary of Defense must aggregate the requirements of the four services when making budget recommendations. He is concerned with the overall resources for defense and with their allocation; not only with the amount of resources available to each of the separate branches. In fact, he may often serve as an arbitrator in departmental budget negotiations. Thus, as we move up the organizational hierarchy, the more comprehensive is the decision process.

Second, the higher the rank and the broader one's responsibility, the more information a decision maker is exposed to, the broader the sources of this information, and thus the less biased is the information processing.

Let us now try to understand why the concept of organizational role provides the link between individual choice processes and group decision making. Foreign policy decision making is an interorganizational process because most decisions are reached by groups whose members represent different organizations that take part in the shaping of foreign policy. A person becomes a part of the key policy group by virtue of his or her rank within the interorganizational hierarchy, and by virtue of his or her responsibilities. Who participates in a particular decision process is, to a large extent, a function of the decision problem. The joint Chiefs of Staff would probably not participate in decisions on commercial agreements, but they are almost certain to be members of the core group trying to make decisions on military affairs. Moreover, the commonly invited participants to foreign policy making groups are of relatively high rank within their own organizations.

The elite decision making group can be viewed as the management

73

or board of directors of an organization. Within this group, there exist both hierarchical relations and a division of responsibilities among individuals equal in rank. Each individual in the decision making group contributes a unique organizational perspective to the decision process. The Secretary of Defense brings to the discussion the strategic aspects of the decision problem; the Secretary of State is concerned with its diplomatic aspects; and the Secretary of the Treasury focuses on its financial aspects. The President (or the Prime Minister in cabinets) will try to aggregate all these perspectives into an overall analysis of the problem; but in order to do so, he or she needs the small parts of the big picture.

A problem that poses a high threat to a certain organization would not necessarily pose a similar threat to another organization. In order to assess the group-shared stress given a decision problem, we must aggregate across the perceptions of stress of the individual participants. But this does not necessarily imply that group-shared stress is a simple sum of individually-felt stresses. Rather, group-shared stress is more likely to be a function of individually perceived levels of stress weighted by each person's score on the organizational role scale. A high perception of stress by the President or Prime Minister is more likely to have an impact on the group-shared stress than a high perception of stress by the Undersecretary of State. Group level threat perceptions appear therefore to be some form of weighted aggregation of the varying levels and types of individual threat perceptions.

Consider an episode that occurred during the Cuban missile crisis. When it was discovered that the Soviets had installed nuclear missiles in Cuba, the Executive Committee began deliberations on ways to cope with this problem. But quite early in the discussion, it became evident that not everyone in the policy group agreed on the nature of the Soviet threat. Robert McNamara, the Secretary of Defense, argued that: "A missile is a missile . . . it makes no great differences whether you are killed by a missile fired from the Soviet Union or from Cuba" (cited in Hilsman, 1964: 195). For others, including Paul Nitze, the Assistant Secretary of Defense for International Security Affairs, Soviet missiles in Cuba posed an unprecedented threat on two counts. First, they reduced the warning time from twenty to five minutes, and second, they almost doubled Soviet strategic power. As it turned out, Nitze's assessment of threat prevailed over that of his superior. But this example demonstrates that differences over the magnitude of the various inputs may exist in groups. In this particular case, the numerical superiority of participants who felt highly threatened by the presence of the Soviet missiles in Cuba outweighed the role-based impact of McNamara's argument. Another point is that other factors beside organizational role may be operative in the process by which inputs are transformed from the individual to the group level.

The distribution of roles within groups, which can be referred to as role differentiation (Guetzkow, 1968), defines the formal group structure. Groups can be classified on a continuum ranging from completely uniform to authoritarian. At the uniform end of the continuum, there is no hierarchy, and each participant counts equally. No participant is superior to other participants in terms of rank or responsibility. At the other extreme, a single individual occupies a dominant position of leadership by virtue of his or her rank and responsibility. Between these two ends, groups may differ in terms of role differentiation or hierarchy.

The informal dimension of group structure is also important in explaining the ways in which roles affect group choices. This dimension is best represented both by the characteristics of policy groups in terms of diversity and by the preferences of their members. There is consistent evidence that role differentiation is correlated with decisional efficiency of groups (Fisher, 1974: 52–56; Shaw, 1976: 248–250; Cartwright and Zander, 1968: 489–491; Collins and Guetzkow, 1964; Guetzkow, 1968). Shaw (1964) showed that groups lacking dominant leadership tend to solve problems faster than groups containing a central person because they allow for better exchange of information among participants. Janis (1982) argues that pressure for uniformity and groupthink patterns is more likely to be observed in highly hierarchical groups. De Rivera (1968) and Paige (1968) highlighted the dominating influence of both President Truman and Dean Acheson, the Secretary of State, on the group that decided on American entry into the Korean War and argued that only few options were considered overall. The question was not whether to intervene, but how to intervene.

The preceding discussion suggests two points. First, group structure is of profound importance in political settings. Second, the values of the various situational variables at the group level are a weighted combination of their individually perceived values. The major problem with these ideas is that there is only indirect evidence for their empirical validity. Furthermore, there seems to be a marked difference between social psychologists and political scientists with regard to their perception of the relationship between group structure and the quality of group outcomes (Gaenslen, 1980). This is an inevitable consequence of a failure to specify the relationship between individually perceived stress and group shared stress, let alone the process by which group shared stress is generated.

We also seem to lack precise definitions of the various situational and cognitive inputs at each level, as well as a clear specification regarding the interaction among various inputs in a decision situation. Is there a relationship between stress and ambiguity? It seems reasonable to argue that there is, but the literature we have reviewed thus far is not sufficiently clear on this issue. With the exception of one study (O'Donnell, 1979) we know very little about the relationship between role and cognitive complexity. All these problems are exacerbated when we consider the various conceptual frameworks that have been developed by students of the stage of input identification and conceptualization.

3.4 DECISION MAKING FRAMEWORKS

Because of the basically inductive nature of theorizing that characterized the input identification stage, a need arose for the clustering of the various inputs into broad frameworks that impose some order on the large set of variables considered as relevant for decision making processes. The Snyder *et al.* (1954; 1962) framework is perhaps the best known and the one that inspired the construction of subsequent decision making frameworks during this stage. It consists of an external setting of inputs, an internal setting of inputs and a mediating social structure and behavior cluster of variables. These two sets of inputs interact with the social structure of the decision maker's environment and affect the decision making process. But beyond the identification of relevant factors for decision making, this framework is essentially a long checklist of variables one has to take into account when thinking about foreign policy decision making processes. It is, at best, a taxonomy of inputs; not a theory of decision making (Rosenau, 1967a; McClosky, 1962: 199–200).

Despite its extensiveness, this framework tells us very little about what happens during the decision process itself; it does not distinguish between individual choice and group decision making; it does not specify the relationship between inputs and outcomes or the interaction among inputs. Most importantly, it lacks a set of logically deducible and empirically testable propositions about decision processes. It is not surprising, therefore, that students of foreign policy decision making have found this framework to be of little empirical utility. Only one case study applying this framework has been published (Snyder and Paige, 1958; Paige, 1968). And even some of the major conclusions of this study were reversed subsequently as a result of a change in the normative orientation of its author (Paige,

1977). However, bearing in mind the fact that there was no comparable framework on foreign policy decision making at the time, the impact on the field was quite impressive. As most reviews of the field have argued (e.g., Robinson and Snyder, 1965; Rosenau, 1967a; Caldwell, 1977; Yanarella, 1977), the Snyder *et al.* framework served as a standard and as a guide for subsequent framework construction.

Another notable decision making framework is that of Brecher and his associates (Brecher *et al.*, 1969). Building largely on the Snyder, Bruck and Sapin taxonomy, this framework further developed the distinction between the operational and the psychological environments of decision makers, which had been proposed by Joseph Frankel (1963: 105–122). The operational environment consists of a set of "real world" factors, that is, the "objective reality." The psychological environment represents the transformation of these factors into images within decision makers' minds. Changes in, and the values of, the factors in the operational environment pass a process of transformation into perceptions of the real world by decision makers. Two major variables mediate between the operational environment and the psychological one: communication channels and "attitudinal prism." Channels of communication determine the amount and nature of the information that decision makers receive about real world events. The attitudinal prism, which is equivalent in large measure to the concept of belief systems, incorporates such elements as ideology, historical legacy, and personality traits.

The factors in the operational and the psychological environment are divided into external and internal elements: five of each. This distinction between the operational and psychological environment leads these scholars to hypothesize that the narrower the gap between images of real-world events and their objective values, the higher the quality of the decision process (Brecher *et al.*, 1969: 81). However, given the absence of descriptive propositions regarding the decision process itself, such an hypothesis is non-verifiable within the Brecher *et al.* framework. While it is possible to determine through content analysis the perceived values of the various factors within the psychological environment of individual decision makers (e.g., Brecher, 1974b), how does one define their real-world values? It is also unclear whether this framework focuses on individual choice, group decision making, or both, due to the lack of discussion of the decision process itself. We are not told how these inputs are related to diagnosis of problems, search for options, information processing, and choice, but merely given a static picture of the substantive and procedural factors that are presumably present in a given solution. This is also the way in which the framework has been applied in a series of case studies of Israel's foreign policy (Brecher, 1974a). To explain particular decisions, and especially changes in decisions over time, Brecher had to enter into explanations of interaction between inputs and process which went beyond the original structure of this framework. The static description of Israel's foreign policy system (Brecher, 1972) is, nonetheless, by far the most insightful account of this state's foreign policy to date.

The Brecher *et al.* framework has some clear advantages over the Snyder *et al.* framework. First, correctly emphasizes on the substantive dimension of foreign policy decision processes. It allows the researcher to identify both the operational and the psychological factors that are active in any given situation. Second, it has a useful division of decisions into substantive issue areas. Third, it acknowledges the importance of the differences between decision and implementation. Fourth, it incorporates the notion of feedback at both the operational and the psychological level.

The framework guided a considerable number of empirical investigations on Israeli foreign policy (Brecher, 1972, 1974a, 1980) as well as on India's foreign policy (Brecher, 1977b; Verztberger, 1978). This framework serves also as a primary guide for the more ambitious effort to study international crisis behavior (Brecher, 1977a, 1980). But the development of the crisis behavior model required – as we shall see in chapter 7 – a fundamental extension of the original framework in terms of process specification.

The third framework is one that attempts to account for foreign policy behavior rather than for decision processes (Rosenau, 1966). However, it may be useful to compare it to the previously reviewed frameworks for a number of reasons. First, because it focuses on behavior rather than on decision processes, it is interesting to observe the fact that Rosenau's framework identifies independent variables that are similar to those identified by the frameworks dealing with decisions. This suggests that when we attempt to account for observed actions of states, we tend to look at roughly the same explanatory variables that we have identified as instrumental in explanations of foreign policy decision making.

Second, it is interesting to compare the relationship between theory and research on foreign policy behavior to theory and research on foreign policy decision making. Third, it would prove very useful, for evaluation purposes, to examine what foreign policy decision making approaches can learn from foreign policy behavior approaches, and, perhaps, vice versa.

Rosenau identifies five sets of variables that presumably affect foreign policy behavior of nations.

1 *Idiosyncratic variables* are the personal traits of the decision makers that include values, talents, and prior experience.

2 *Role variables* correspond to organizational influences on decision makers.

3 *Governmental variables* refer to the interorganizational aspect of a state's foreign policy.

4 *Societal factors* concern the interaction between the formal (or interorganization) aspects of foreign policy and its informal ingredients such as public opinion, interest groups, societal cohesion, etc.

5 *Systemic variables* are the events and processes taking place in a state's external environment, including the behavior of other states directed at the state, the structure of the international system, etc.

As can be easily seen, these factors are almost identical to those identified in both the Snyder *et al.* framework and in the Brecher *et al.* framework and in this sense they convey no news. However, Rosenau argues that it is not enough to enumerate the independent variables explaining foreign policy behavior; one must specify their relative potency, that is, their relative influence on observed behavior. He suggests that the relative potency of these five sets of variables may differ from one state to another based on three major structural attributes of the state: its size, the type of political system, and its level of economic development. Third, even within a single state the relative potency of these sets of variables may differ across issue-areas, albeit to a lesser extent than across states.

Thus, the Rosenau framework adds to the insights of the other frameworks a notion of interaction among the various independent variables, as well as a qualification concerning the generalizability of foreign policy explanations. While the relative ranking of the independent variables across types of states suggests implicitly what kind of policy making processes are likely to be observed in each type, little is said about the nature of the processes. It is also difficult to discern the levels of analysis one should adopt in empirical research. Another important feature of the Rosenau framework is that it puts heavier emphasis on domestic sources of foreign policy behavior than on external ones: four out of the five sets of independent variables are clearly domestic. Thus, although this framework goes beyond the previously reviewed ones in terms of theory-building, its basic neglect of the foreign policy making process and the inherent ambiguity concerning level of analysis resembles the liabilities of the Snyder and Brecher frameworks.

Despite these liabilities, the impact of the Rosenau framework on empirical foreign policy research is clearly incomparable to that of the other two frameworks. The Rosenau (1966) article can be seen as the "Bible" of a whole generation of scholars engaged in the scientific study of foreign policy. The most noticeable characteristic of the empirical research based on this framework is that it is rigorous, quantitative, and cross-national. Yet, the results are somewhat sobering. Let us review some of this research. Rosenau (1968) found that role-variables have a higher relative potency than individual (i.e., idiosyncratic) variables on US Senators during the Acheson and Dulles era. Rosenau and Hoggard (1974) found that cross-national differences in terms of international conflict and cooperation are accounted for in terms of the three national attributes (i.e., size, type of political system, and level of economic development) of the framework. However, the relationship turned out to be the inverse of what was initially expected. Large and developed countries tended to be both more conflict-prone and cooperation-prone than smaller and less developed countries. Rosenau and Ramsey (1975) showed that this relationship holds across data-sets. Dyadic characteristics of pairs of nations did not seem to fit a discernible pattern.[12]

Wilkenfeld et al. (1980) have expanded on the Rosenau framework in two important respects. First, they have refined the classification of inputs by dividing the systemic variables into an interstate component and a global component. Second, they developed a more sophisticated and empirically-based classification of foreign policy behaviors. This framework was tested first by relating each cluster of independent variables – mediated by the static national attributes – to foreign policy behavior, and then by testing the framework as a whole. The findings suggest that most of the variance in the foreign policy of states during the 1966–1970 period is accounted for by systemic variables (both global and interstate), but psychological factors seem also to be a significant determinant of foreign policy behavior. There are also significant differences across types of states in terms of the effects of various clusters of independent variables on foreign policy behavior.

One of the major recommendations of these authors supports my previous point about the neglect of decision making processes in the various frameworks. Observing the gap between input-output approaches and decision approaches in research on foreign policy,

---

[12] For a more extensive survey of findings on foreign policy behavior see McGowan and Shapiro (1973); East et al. (1978).

Wilkenfeld *et al.* (1980: 252) argue that "process analysis should receive priority on future research agendas. Source analysis is similar to a snapshot of an area; process analysis is indispensable for fleshing out the details of the terrain on the foreign policy map. With the proliferation of both decision process frameworks and case studies . . . the terrain has been provided."

In a field of study that involves an inherent complexity such as foreign policy decision making, the art of framework construction is an indispensable step in theory building. The enormous number of variables that must be considered requires an organizing scheme that would provide an adequate representation of the forest, rather than that of individual trees within it. Such a representation usually involves defining the locus of individual variables within the framework, specifying their relative potency, as well as outlining the features of the large picture. This also entails a coherent specification of the process.

While the three frameworks that I have discussed are not the only ones on the market,[13] they provide a good illustration of both the strengths and weaknesses of the framework construction studies of the first stage. Their strength lies mainly in the identification of variables, partly in their organization within an overall structure, and only minimally in the specification of their relative impact on the decision making process. The main weaknesses of these frameworks are indicative of the problems asociated with the research of the first generation. Therefore, I will evaluate these frameworks in conjunction with other types of foreign policy studies.

3.5 A BRIEF APPRAISAL OF THE FIRST STAGE

The exploratory nature of most of the studies that belong to this stage renders the task of critical evaluation especially difficult. It seems obvious that the main value of these studies lies in the fact that they opened new avenues for investigation and suggested a radically different outlook on international affairs. In particular, they provided a solid epistemological foundation for the incorporation of decision making approaches into the more general field of world politics. Second, the first generation of foreign policy decision making research identified the main ingredients of the exogenous domain of factors impinging on decision process. Third, the treatment of the field of study was truly interdisciplinary in that these studies adapted concepts and theories from disciplines which – until then – were not

[13] See Wilkenfeld *et al.* (1980: 25–32) for a critical review of the existing frameworks.

considered particularly relevant for the understanding of world politics. And finally, they were remarkably useful as ground-clearing tools in the sense of helping minimize the number of instrumental variables to be considered in subsequent decision making research, or in grouping these variables in meaningful yet manageable clusters.

But such an exploratory research orientation has some inherent problems. These problems can be summarized by the following points.

1 *Lack of parsimony*. The number of decision-related inputs that were identified during this stage is enormous. While parsimony is an admirable goal in any scientific enterprise, it is presumptuous to expect that such a complex research field would yield parsimonious theories. We can expect, however, that there will be an effort to specify the associations among the decision-related inputs and examine areas of convergence that would allow a meaningful reduction of the number of exogenous variables. The concept of decisional stress is a good illustration of how such a goal could be achieved; but this concept was developed only during the stage of synthesis. The problem of the research in the first stage was that it focused on the diversification of decision-related inputs, rather than on integration. Consequently, we have a very long laundry list of exogenous variables, and only a vague notion of how they should be incorporated into a comprehensive theory of foreign policy decision making. This point was common to most of the critiques of the Snyder *et al.* framework (McClosky, 1962; Rosenau, 1967a; Brecher *et al.*, 1969). Yet the frameworks that the very same critics have developed suffer from the same liability.[14]

2 *Lack of formal specification*. There is an inherent ambiguity regarding the precise operational meaning of many of the identified inputs. In addition, the basically inductive nature of most of the first stage product made it difficult to assimilate the various inputs into an interrelated body of theoretical propositions concerning the inputs and structure of foreign policy decision making. For example, not only are the definitions of concepts such as threat perception, belief-system, and perceived ambiguity preoperational, it is difficult to understand the precise locus of, and relations among, the various

[14] The problem of parsimony, or lack thereof, is exacerbated when one considers substantive decision related inputs such as issue-areas (Rosenau, 1967b; Zimmerman, 1973; Lowi, 1964). I chose to ignore the Pandora's box of issues at this point because it is a major obstacle to generalization about foreign policy decision making. The next chapter will provide numerous examples of how we can meaningfully reduce the number of exogenous variables, including an integration of substantive and procedural aspects of decision-related inputs.

inputs. Do situational and cognitive factors display an additive effect on decision making, or is there, as Jervis (1980: 98) argues, an interaction between cognitive and situational factors? The piecemeal process of identification of inputs made it difficult to determine the shape and size of the forest given the individual trees within it. The frameworks that we have reviewed above are only half-way useful in this regard. Although they introduced some structure into the array of identified inputs, they added neither formal rigor nor operational definitions beyond those that had already existed for these inputs.

3 *Neglect of process-dynamics.* This is probably the most serious liability of the first stage research product. Most of the research was of an input-output nature. Studies failed to specify an interrelated body of propositions regarding the internal dynamics of choice processes. Although there are several discussions on the degree of rationality in foreign policy decision processes (e.g., Robinson and Snyder, 1965; Pruitt, 1965; Verba, 1961), the net product of the first stage research was a disjointed body of bivariate hypotheses or propositions linking various inputs to various decision making aspects. For example, we have several hypotheses linking threat perception and time pressure to the extensiveness of search for options or the processing of information, and the size of the decisional unit. We have several propositions regarding the variations in the relative potency of input domains across types of states. Finally, we have some empirical findings concerning the effects of personality and cognitive factors on the substance of decisional outcomes. What is missing, however, is an in-depth account of what really happens from the moment a problem is identified to the point where a decision is made and implemented. The dynamics of choice processes were obscured rather than illuminated by the implicit view of decision making as a mediated stimulus response process (Jervis, 1969: 204).

4 *Confusion regarding units of analysis.* The failure to explore the characteristics of choice processes resulted in major gaps on central issues in decision making, in particular, with respect to the processes by which individual preferences are transformed into national decisions. For example, personality traits and belief systems were appropriately treated at the individual level of analysis. Yet, beyond the general proposition that differences in personalities within groups yield disagreement on policy options there is very little we can learn about group choices. The same applies to the various situational variables. A threatening situation to one person is not necessarily threatening to another person; what one may perceive to be a very clear situation, may be perceived by another as highly ambiguous. As

some scholars (e.g., Singer, 1961; Schelling, 1978: 14) have pointed out, moving across levels of analysis requires more than an aggregation of units at the lower level. A group is not merely a collection of individuals, and its decisional product does not necessarily reflect the sum of individual preferences. Thus, moving from the individual level to the group requires us to investigate principles by which individual preferences are transformed into national decisions. Not only has research in the first stage failed to recognize this fact, but it also did not make it clear what its units of analysis really are, and whether inputs that are considered influential at the individual level are also operative at the group level.

Despite this criticism, the first generation of decision making studies made a major contribution to the study of world politics. This initial journey into the maze of foreign policy decision making provided the basis for a rough mapping of the terrain. A detailed account of what the terrain really consists of was a challenge left for later "generations" of foreign policy researchers. But before we discuss how these later generations dealt with this challenge, I will attempt to formalize the concepts that were developed during this stage.

4 THE ESSENTIAL MATHEMATICS OF INPUTS

This chapter attempts to conceptualize formally the decision-related inputs that were discusssed in the previous chapter, and to specify the interrelations among those inputs. This effort is stimulated by three points I raised at the end of chapter 3. First, I attempt to show how the domain of decisional inputs can be made more parsimonious by developing composite measures of seemingly distinct variables. Secondly, I show that these concepts are not only substantively meaningful but also mathematically precise and operationally tractable. Thirdly, I show how these individual level inputs can be transformed into group level inputs.

Three comments about the contents and structure of this chapter are in order. First, the discussion will be purely abstract. I do not go into details regarding operationalization procedures of the various concepts, though the examples I use should give some ideas regarding empirical measurement. To be sure, there are a lot of problems requiring resolution when one transforms purely abstract concepts into empirically observable variables, and I definitely do not wish to ignore them. However, in order not to confuse abstract concepts with their empirical referents, I will stick to mathematics rather than to statistics. The puzzled empiricist is referred to some of my earlier work (Maoz, 1981, 1986) for a discussion and illustration of measurement procedures and solutions to problems of validity and reliability.

Second, any attempt to transform the nominal definitions of the inputs of decision making into mathematical relations requires a subjective interpretation of these concepts on the basis of one's reading of the literature of the input-identification stage. I certainly do not expect readers to agree with my interpretation, but I ask them to bear with me and try to understand what I am attempting to develop in this chapter. At the very least, this work might be a source of some alternative ideas on how these concepts can be formalized. The

85

mathematical transformation of these concepts requires some assumptions, and I try to make these as few and as explicit as possible.

This chapter is organized as follows. I begin with an individual-level specification of distinct situational variables, some of which are subsequently transformed into composite concepts such as decisional stress. The formal definitions are supplemented by empirical examples from cases of crisis decision making. I continue with the definition of personality and role variables. Finally, I specify the relationship between decision-related inputs at the individual level and the same inputs as they appear at the group level. This is done by introducing the concept of formal group structure through the incorporation of role-related variables.

4.2 THREAT PERCEPTION

Two important assumptions must be stated prior to any formal definition of threat perception. The first assumption is that threat is predicated on inaction. The magnitude of threat perception given some environmental cue is *independent* of the response one sees as adequate to this cue. Since threat perception is a motivational antecedent of decision, it is an element of the definition of the situation (or, to use our terminology, of the diagnosis stage) that precedes actual decision making. Second, given the conceptual definition of threat perception as a sense of imminent loss to some currently possessed assets or values, the formal notion of threat must have strict upper and lower bounds. A no-threat situation constitutes the lower limit of threat perception. At the other extreme, the maximal magnitude of threat cannot be larger than the total value of the currently possessed assets; an organism cannot lose more than it has.[1]

The notion of threat perception as a sense of imminent loss to certain values is quite ambiguous. To be more specific, we must address several questions.

1 What specific values or assets are affected by a given cue? This question requires enumeration of the values that are believed to be at stake. It enables distinction between threat situations that are broad in scope, in that the sense of loss covers multiple values, and those which are narrow in scope.

2 How important are those values or asssets to the decision maker? Clearly, we must distinguish between a sense of

---

[1] This point is problematic because losing more than one has means being in debt or deficit. Yet in most policy-related cases such an assumption seems reasonable. For example, in terms of security, one cannot lose more than one's life. For discussions on the parameters of threat perception see Lazarus (1968: 44); Whitey (1962: 94–95); and especially Breznitz (1984: 3–6).

loss to different values in terms of their relative importance to the decision maker. A person confronted by a ransom demand from a kidnapper will feel a different sense of threat if the person kidnapped is one's distant relative or one's son. Presumably, one may be willing to translate the value of life into monetary terms on the basis of the importance of (or degree of affection to) the person whose life is at stake.

3   How much is at stake? this is the extent of threat perception. Substantial loss on a relatively unimportant value may generate equivalent magnitudes of perceived threat to a small loss on a highly important value.

4   How likely is the event entailing losses? Perceptions of threat are affected by the prospect of loss, that is, by the perceived likelihood that the environmental cue will indeed lead to a situation whereby values or assets are to depreciate. Only rarely are decision makers confronted by situations implying certainty of losses.

5   Loss in relation to what? Clearly, a millionaire facing the loss of 1,000 dollars will not feel as threatened as a person for whom 1,000 dollars constitute one's life-savings, even if both assigns a similar utility to money in relation to other values. Thus, threat perception must be defined in relation to what one possesses at present, that is, in relation to the degree to which a decision maker values the status quo.

The foregoing discussion emphasized the multidimensionality and the complexity of this concept. It also suggests that the formal derivation of this concept will not be simple. I will begin the definition process by introducing a simple example and then turning to a more formal discussion.

4.2.1   A simple example of threat perception

Suppose you are a farmer who has some fruit stored in an open box outdoors. The box contains ten apples, five oranges and one banana. The market price for the fruit is 0.50 dollar per apple, 0.80 dollar per orange and 1.00 dollar per banana. Let us present two vectors, one labeled A_c (A is for assets), whose entries, a_1, a_2, a_3, represent the number of apples, oranges, and bananas in the box, respectively, and the other vector labeled W (for weight) whose entries are w_1, w_2, w_3, for the market prices of the fruit. To determine the total value of your assets, we multiply each element of the A vector by its respective market price (i.e., the corresponding entry in W).

If you define the total value of your current assets as U_c, then U_c can be obtained by:

Assets	A		Price per	W
Apples	10		Apple	0.5
Oranges	5		Orange	0.8
Bananas	1		Banana	1.0

Figure 4.1 The farmer's assets

$$U_c = \mathbf{A'} \times \mathbf{W} = \sum_{i=1}^{3} a_i w_i = 10 \times 0.5 + 5 \times 0.8 + 1 \times 1 = 10.0 \qquad (4.1)$$

So if nothing happens, you own 10 dollars' worth of fruit. However, since the fruit is stored outside, you are worried about the prospect of rain. If it rained while nothing was done to preserve the fruit (this is the assumption of inaction-related threat), you expect that five apples, three oranges and the banana would become uneatable. Let the vector $\mathbf{A}_{dr}$ be the vector of assets destroyed given rain, and let $\mathbf{A}_{ir}$ be the assets with which you are left following the rain. Obviously, $\mathbf{A}_{ir} = \mathbf{A}_c - \mathbf{A}_{dr}$. This is given in figure 4.2.

Now, we can combine the $\mathbf{A}_c$ and $\mathbf{A}_{ir}$ vectors into a single matrix, $\mathbf{SE}$, whose columns represent different assets and whose rows represent different circumstances. This matrix allows us to present different magnitudes of assets (or values) under different circumstances. We can use this matrix to get a feel for the alternative values of our assets under different circumstances. To obtain this, we multiply the $\mathbf{SE}$ matrix by the $\mathbf{W}$ vector and get the product-vector $\mathbf{U}$. This is given in figure 4.3.

The $\mathbf{U}$ vector represents both the value of current assets and the projected value of assets in case of rain. However, since neither the continuation of the present weather nor the state of rain are seen as certain, we must deal with some probabilities before we can determine the magnitude of threat to the fruit. The weather forecaster on the radio says that there is a 30 percent chance of rain. This allows you to construct the probability vector $\mathbf{P}$ in which an entry represents the likelihood of a certain state of the world.

Now we can calculate the expected value of the assets given inaction, that is, under the assumption that you do nothing to preserve your fruit. This is given by,

	A_c			A_{dr}			A_{lr}	
Apples	10		Apples	5		Apples	5	
Oranges	5	$-$	Oranges	3	$=$	Oranges	2	
Bananas	1		Bananas	1		Bananas	0	

Figure 4.2 Current, destroyed, and remaining assets

	SE			W		U	
Assets	Apples	Oranges	Bananas	Price per		Value of assets	
Circumstances							
No rain	10	5	1	Apple	0.5	No rain	10.0
Rain	5	2	0	× Orange	0.8	= Rain	4.1
				Banana	1.0		

Figure 4.3 Values of assets under different circumstances

$$EU_{na} = \sum_{i=1}^{n} u_i p_i = \mathbf{U'} \mathbf{P} \tag{4.2}$$

Or, in matrix algebra, we define the probability vector $\mathbf{P} = [.70, .30]$ for no rain and rain, respectively. Thus, we have

$$EU_{na} = \mathbf{U'} \times \mathbf{P} = 10.0 \times 0.70 + 4.1 \times 0.30 = 8.23 \tag{4.3}$$

If you do nothing to preserve your fruit, and given the expected losses under rain and the likelihood of rain, you expect to get a value of 8.23 dollars on the average. To finalize our definition of threat perception, we need to relate what we expect to get given our inaction to what we have at present. This is done in equation (4.4).

$$T = \frac{U_c - EU_{na}}{U_c} \tag{4.4}$$

In our example, the magnitude of threat perception (T) is:

$$T = \frac{10 - 8.23}{10} = 0.177$$

As can be seen from this example, threat perception is defined as the *percent depreciation in assets or values given a set of circumstances and under the assumption of inaction.* Now we must examine how threat perception varies from case to case as a function of changes in environmental cues. This could be done by adding some complexity to our fruit example. Suppose the weather forecaster predicts that there is a 30 percent chance of showers and a 20 percent chance of a hailstorm. This requires revising your estimates in two ways. First, you must consider the effects of hail on your fruit. Second, you must incorporate the probability of a hailstorm into your threat calculation. In the event of a hailstorm you expect to lose seven apples, four oranges and the banana. The revised probabilities are now: 0.50, 0.30, and 0.20 for no rain, rain, and hailstorm, respectively. Thus, your calculus of threat is as follows:

Assets	SE			W		U	
	Apples	Oranges	Bananas	Price per		Value of	
Circumstances						assets	
No rain	10	5	1	Apple	0.5	No rain	10.0
Rain	5	2	0	× Orange	0.8	= Rain	4.1
Hailstorm	3	1	0	Banana	1.0	Hailstorm	2.3

Figure 4.4 Values of assets under No Rain, Rain, and Hailstorm

$$\mathbf{A}_c - \mathbf{A}_{dh} = \mathbf{A}_{lh} = [10, 5, 1] - [7, 4, 1] = [3, 1, 0] \qquad (4.5)$$

The expected values of your possessions given a hailstorm is given in figure 4.4.

$$EU_{na} = \mathbf{U}'\mathbf{P} = 10 \times 0.5 + 4.1 \times 0.3 + 2.3 \times 0.2 = 6.69$$

And the new value of threat perception is

$$T = \frac{U_c - EU_{na}}{U_c} = \frac{10 - 6.9}{10} = 0.331$$

The magnitude of perceived threat has more than doubled as a result of the introduction of the uncertain yet gloomy prospect of a hailstorm. In more general terms, threat perception may increase in magnitude when estimates of loss become more severe, when new situations involving losses become apparent, or when the probability of losses increases. These examples also suggest conditions of minimal or maximal threats. A no-threat situation is one in which the probability of rain approaches zero. In such a case, the farmer expects that the future value of the fruit will be identical to its present value. On the other hand, if the expected utility of inaction had equaled zero, our farmer would have faced a maximum level of threat. Let us now become more general.

4.2.2 A formal definition of threat perception

To derive a formal definition of threat perception, we need to formalize the notations of the terms used in the preceding discussion.

T = threat perception

$\mathbf{A}_c \rightarrow [c_j = 1, 2, \ldots, m]$ = the set of values or assets currently possessed by a decision maker.

$\mathbf{A}_{do} \rightarrow [d = 1, 2, \ldots, n]; [o = 1, 2, \ldots, m]$ = the set of values or assets destroyed, damaged or lost, given a circumstance, where $\mathbf{A}_{do} \subset A_c$ (read as $\mathbf{A}_{do}$ is a proper subset of $\mathbf{A}_c$).

$\mathbf{A}_{lo} \rightarrow [l = 1, 2, \ldots, m]; [o = 1, 2, \ldots, n]$ = the set of values or assets left to an organism given a circumstance, where

SE

Outcome	Assets				
	a_1	a_2	$\cdots$	a_{m-1}	a_m
o_1	$o_1 a_1$	$o_1 a_2$	$\cdots$	$o_1 a_{m-1}$	$o_1 a_m$
o_2	$o_2 a_1$	$o_2 a_2$	$\cdots$	$o_2 a_{m-1}$	$o_2 a_m$
o_3	$o_3 a_1$	$o_3 a_2$	$\cdots$	$o_3 a_{m-1}$	$o_3 a_m$
o_4	$o_4 a_1$	$o_4 a_2$	$\cdots$	$o_4 a_{m-1}$	$o_4 a_m$
..	$\cdots$	$\cdots$	$\cdots$	$\cdots$	$\cdots$
..	$\cdots$	$\cdots$	$\cdots$	$\cdots$	$\cdots$
..	$\cdots$	$\cdots$	$\cdots$	$\cdots$	$\cdots$
o_{n-1}	$o_{n-1} a_1$	$o_{n-1} a_2$	$\cdots$	$o_{n-1} a_{m-1}$	o_{n-1_m}
o_n	$o_n a_1$	$o_n a_2$	$\cdots$	$o_n a_{m-1}$	$o_n a_m$

a = asset

o = outcome

Figure 4.5 A general-form search-evaluation matrix

$\mathbf{A}_{lo} \subseteq \mathbf{A}_c$, and $\mathbf{A}_{lo} = \mathbf{A}_c - \mathbf{A}_{do}$.

$\mathbf{O} \rightarrow [o = 1, 2, \ldots, n]$ = the set of all possible circumstances.

$\mathbf{P}_o \rightarrow [o = 1, 2, \ldots, n]$ = the set of probabilities assigned to the elements in $\mathbf{O}$.

$\mathbf{W} \rightarrow [w = 1, 2, \ldots, m]$ = the set of importance weights assigned to elements in $\mathbf{A}$.

Given these definitions we can specify the operations in our example. First, equation (4.6) computes the weighted value of the current assets, taking into account the magnitude of the assets and their relative importance weights.

$$U_c = \mathbf{A}'_c \mathbf{W} = \sum_{j=1}^{m} a_j w_j \tag{4.6}$$

Second, equation (4.7) computes the value of the remaining assets given a certain outcome o.

$$\mathbf{A}_{lo} = \mathbf{A}_c - \mathbf{A}_{do} \tag{4.7}$$

The general structure of the search-evaluation matrix which combines assets and outcomes is given in figure 4.5.

The algebraic definition of the search-evaluation matrix is:

$$\mathbf{SE} = se_{ij} = o_i a_j; \quad i = 1, n; \quad j = 1, m$$

Third, equation (4.8) shows how we compute the integrated utility vector of the assets

$$\mathbf{U} = \mathbf{SE} \times \mathbf{W} \tag{4.8}$$

The probability vector has one entry for each outcome: $\mathbf{P} = [p_1, p_2, \ldots, p_n]$. The expected value of inaction, or what one expects to get if one does not react to the cue, is given in equation (4.9).

$$EU_{na} = \mathbf{U'} \mathbf{P} = \sum_{=1}^{n} u_i p_i \tag{4.9}$$

Finally, the general formula of the threat perception is given in equation (4.10).

$$T = \frac{U_c - EU_{na}}{U_c} \tag{4.10}$$

where (as assumed): $0 \leqslant T \leqslant 1.0$.

4.2.3 A real-world example of threat perception

Let us now examine an application of this definition to data taken from a study on crisis decision making (Maoz, 1981). This study examined the Israeli decision process during the 1976 Entebbe crisis. The Israeli government, confronted by the hijacking of 103 Israeli citizens, and with an ultimatum demand to release 52 Palestinians held in Israeli jails felt that four essential values were affected by the hijacking: human life, the credibility of Israel's anti-terrorist policy, domestic support for the government, and Israel's international standing. During its deliberations, the government considered briefly a "do-nothing" option. However, the principal decision makers felt that it was inferior to all other "do-something" options on almost every value. Hence, the "do-nothing" option was not scrutinized in detail during the process. However, to illustrate the threat perception of the Israeli decision makers, it is necessary to look into the "do-nothing" option in some detail.

The hypothetical "do-nothing" option could have resulted in either of the following two outcomes: success, meaning the eventual release of all hostages held at Entebbe, or failure, meaning the massacre of all hostages. From figure 6 of the Entebbe study (p. 700) we can extrapolate all of the data needed for the estimation of threat perceptions of the principal decision makers.[2]

The following analysis shows levels of threat presumably perceived by each of the principal decision makers: Prime Minister Yitzhak Rabin, Defense Minister Shimon Peres, and Foreign Minister Yigal Allon.

Several points are worth noting about this analysis. First, the

[2] The following presentation differs from the one in the Entebbe article in two important respects. First, it uses the data on the case to extrapolate a non-considered option. Second, negative utilities are transformed into positive ones. These two differences create some methodological problems, but the problems are not severe as we shall soon see.

a. Rabin's threat perception

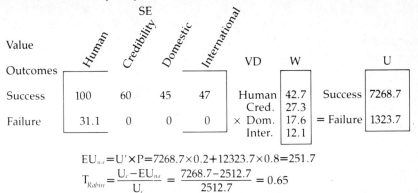

$$EU_{nd} = U' \times P = 7268.7 \times 0.2 + 12323.7 \times 0.8 = 251.7$$

$$T_{Rabin} = \frac{U_c - EU_{nd}}{U_c} = \frac{7268.7 - 2512.7}{2512.7} = 0.65$$

b. Peres's threat perception

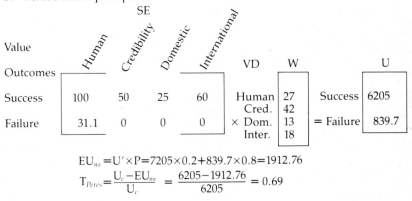

$$EU_{nd} = U' \times P = 7205 \times 0.2 + 839.7 \times 0.8 = 1912.76$$

$$T_{Peres} = \frac{U_c - EU_{nd}}{U_c} = \frac{6205 - 1912.76}{6205} = 0.69$$

c. Allon's threat perception

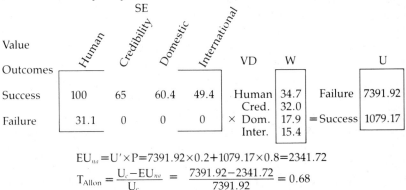

$$EU_{nd} = U' \times P = 7391.92 \times 0.2 + 1079.17 \times 0.8 = 2341.72$$

$$T_{Allon} = \frac{U_c - EU_{nd}}{U_c} = \frac{7391.92 - 2341.72}{7391.92} = 0.68$$

Figure 4.6 The Entebbe hijacking and Israeli threat perceptions, June 27 – July 3, 1976

possibility of loss given by the hijackers ultimatum was perceived as a very real prospect. This is reflected in the high likelihood assigned by all three decision makers to the outcome defined as failure, which implied a real possibility of massacre. But the threat was not only to human life; it included an estimated loss in credibility; a marked decrease in domestic support to the government,[3] and a marked deterioration in Israel's moral standing.[4] Thus threat rises when loss becomes both imminent and extensive. Second, an objective observer may want to put threat perceptions in correct proportion – after all, in the Entebbe case Israel's existence was clearly not at stake. Yet, for the decision makers who viewed the crisis in a rather subjective light, things may have looked quite out of proportion. Decision makers usually do not consider things that are clearly not affected by the environmental cue. For, in a given crisis, the specific values that are evoked by decision makers in their definition of the situation become an isolated set, separated from the "pool" of values that they wish to preserve in general. Part of the diagnosis stage consists of isolating relevant from non-relevant factors in a highly subjective (and perhaps biased) manner. It is thus quite difficult to impose any rational framework that would yield clear-cut prescriptions concerning diagnosis strategies.

Third, an important feature of this analysis is the lack of significant differences in the perceptions of threat across decision makers. This is due to the fact that all three individuals agreed on both the scope of threat (i.e., on the value dimensions affected by the hijacking), and on the prospect of threat (the likelihood of failure). The slight differences in threat perception are due in large measure to the relative importance of various value dimensions which differed across decision makers and to different perceptions regarding the extent of losses on each of those values. The higher degree of threat exhibited by Peres's perceptions resulted from his tendency to emphasize both the credibility and international value dimensions, in contrast to Rabin who placed prime emphasis on the human dimension.

The foregoing analysis suggests that this definition captures both procedural and substantive features of the diagnosis stage. The procedural aspects reflect generalizable factors affecting threat perceptions: number of assets affected by the environmental cue, extent of losses relative to current assets, and so forth. The substantive aspects refer to the precise contents of those component-perceptions, e.g., which values are affected, what is their relative importance, etc.

[3] The zero value of the domestic support in case of failure indicates a shared belief that had hostages been massacred, the government would have had to resign.
[4] Both because of the self-image of Israel as the leading fighter of international terrorism, and because of a negative reaction to a seeming insensitivity of human life.

It is clear that the procedural aspects of threat perception exhibit greater susceptibility to theorizing. Yet the substantive aspects add considerable richness to this concept in that they represent the uniqueness of the case under analysis.

4.3 PERCEIVED OPPORTUNITIES

The formal definition of perceived opportunities exhibits both conceptual similarities and conceptual differences compared to the notion of threat perception. The magnitude of perceived opportunities is also a function of components such as scope, extent, prospect, and is relative to currently possessed assets. Yet, the concept of perceived opportunities rests on a rather different set of assumptions from the ones used to derive the formal measure of perceived threat.

First, perceptions of opportunities are predicated on action. An environmental cue cannot evoke perceptions of opportunities unless some action is considered by the decision maker. A tempting job offer cannot be perceived as an opportunity situation if a person does not contemplate applying for it. Second, while the magnitude of threat perception was defined to possess strict mathematical boundaries (i.e., $0 \leqslant T \leqslant 1$), perception of opportunity does not have a strict upper limit. A certain action can be estimated to double or triple a person's assets. This difference can be illustrated by percent changes in stock prices. A drop in stock prices implies a certain percent depreciation in currently possessed assets, and can thus range between 0 and 100 percent (in which case stocks are valueless). However, an increase in stock prices is, in theory, limitless at its upper bound.

The first assumption raises an important problem. Since both threat perception and perceptions of opportunity are motivational antecedents to decision making processes, they must be defined in terms of factors that precede actual choice. Threat perception fulfills this requirement because it is based on an inaction assumption. However, perceptions of opportunity refer to an action-based expectation of gain and hence their definition must rest on factors that result from actual choice. It looks as if perceived opportunities is a rather tautological term. On the one hand, perceptions of opportunity are said to precede and motivate choice. On the other hand, the magnitude of perceived opportunities is a consequence of whichever action a person elects. Let us illustrate this problem. Suppose a person has just graduated from college. She is being offered two jobs, one with a 25,000 dollars annual income and the other with a 27,000 dollars annual income. To complicate matters, suppose that the first job entails a 7 percent salary

95

raise per year, while the second job entails only a 5 percent raise per year. Obviously, this person faces an opportunity situation, but *how much* of an opportunity is a result of whichever job offer this person elects to accept. Moreover, how would her perceptions of opportunity vary if another job offer arises, entailing a 26,000 dollars annual income with a 6 percent raise? Obviously, her decision will be affected by the magnitude of opportunities she perceives when defining the situation. Yet, how she will go about making the decision given the definition of the situation, and hence, which job she will eventually accept, should be a *result* of the definition of the situation and not vice versa.

The first step toward a solution of this problem is to make the definition of perceived opportunities independent of at least some of the subsequent aspects of the decision process. For example, perceptions of opportunity must be independent of the actual course of action selected eventually. Moreover, when analyzing the decision process we would be obviously interested in the *number* of alternatives that are being considered, and in their precise content. Thus, we must control for the number of alternatives considered by the decision maker, for the nature of those alternatives, and for the actual choice.

Recall that perceived opportunities was defined as a *perception of expected gains to either currently possessed values or assets, or as an expected acquisition of currently unpossessed values or assets*. This definition suggests that perceptions of opportunities must include the nature of gains (i.e., which assets are to increase), the extent of gains (i.e., by how much do we expect to increase our assets), the prospect of gains (i.e., how likely are these gains to be realized), and the relation of gains to currently possessed assets. So, perceptions of opportunity entail all those elements that were incorporated into the definition of threat perception. Let us illustrate the measurement procedure of perceived opportunities through some examples.

4.3.1 A formal definition of perceived opportunities

In the case of threat perception, we had to solve for a scalar EU_{na} representing the expected value of a (real or hypothetical) inaction alternative. For the definition of perceived opportunities we need to define several such scalars, each of which is denoted by EU_a; $a = 1, 2, \ldots, r$. Each scalar represents the expected value of a given action alternative, a. Each of these scalars can be solved for using the same method as was used for the solution of EU_{na} with the adjustment of terms referring to the consequences of a specific action alternative. Together, these scalars form a vector **D**; $d = 1, 2, \ldots, r$. Obviously

$EU_{na} \notin \mathbf{D}$ (that is, EU_{na} is not an element of $\mathbf{D}$). The expected utility of action is defined as the mean entry of $\mathbf{D}$, that is:

$$EU_a = \frac{1}{a} \sum_{i=1}^{a} d_i \qquad (4.11)$$

Defining EU_a in such a manner, we control for the number of elements in $\mathbf{D}$ (that is, we control for the number of action alternatives considered by the decision maker). We also control for the nature of the elements in $\mathbf{D}$ and look only at their associated utilities. Since each entry in $\mathbf{D}$ refers to the expected utility of a given action alternative, it incorporates almost all of the factors we mentioned in the definition of perceived threat, that is, scope of gains, extent of gains, and prospects of gains. To complete the definition, we need to relate the expected utility of action to the magnitude of currently possessed assets. Hence, perceived opportunity (OP) is defined as:

$$OP = \frac{EU_a - U_c}{U_c} = \frac{\frac{1}{a} \sum_{i=1}^{a} d_i - U_c}{U_c} \qquad (4.12)$$

Substantively, this implies that perceived opportunity refers to *a proportional expectation of gain relative to currently possessed assets*. Before turning to the illustrations, it must be shown how our assumption regarding the absence of strict mathematical boundaries is reflected in this definition. First, since perceptions of opportunity are action-based, they can get a negative value. This will happen if the mean expected utility of action is lower than the utility of currently possessed assets. This does not imply, of course, that all action-alternatives are expected to yield actual losses, but rather that the present state of affairs is perceived as better than the average gains expected from action. Likewise, no opportunities are perceived in cases where the mean expected utility of action is equal to the utility of currently possessed assets. Finally, given that there is no upper limit on EU_a, the magnitude of perceived opportunities is greater than 1. Thus, contrary to threat perception, the magnitude of perceived opportunities is unstandardized, and this creates some methodological problems. We will come back to these problems later, but now let us demonstrate this definition.

4.3.2 How to preserve fruit? A simple example of perceived opportunities

The farmer whose fruit-related income is threatened by the weather can obviously do something about it. Suppose the farmer perceives that he has two options for preserving the fruit: (1) to cover the fruit box with a disposable plastic cover that cannot be used after rain. Thus if it rains the farmer is left with 10 dollars worth of fruit but he loses 1.50 dollars (the price for the cover), whereas if it does not rain, the farmer's assets are left intact (he can use the cover another time); (2) bringing the fruit box into the house would result in a certain loss of two apples and one orange (the farmer's kids love apples and his wife loves oranges). Thus the expected utility of covering the fruit is $EU_{cover} = 10 \times 0.5 + (10 - 1.5) \times 0.5 = 9.25$, and the expected utility of storing the fruit in the house is $EU_{store} = 10 - 2 \times 0.5 - 0.8 = 8.2$. The average expected utility of action is, $EU_a = 8.725$. Finally, the magnitude of perceived opportunities is:

$$OP = \frac{EU_a - U_c}{U_c} = \frac{8.725 - 10}{10} = -0.1275.$$

So it can be seen that in this case the farmer perceives negative opportunities. And it is easy to see why. Both action alternatives are perceived to yield an expected utility which is less than what he gets given the status quo, that is, given nothing is done to preserve the fruit and it does not rain. The alert reader will notice, however, that, on average, action is preferred to inaction when all possible circumstances are being considered. We will take notice of this point when combining threat and opportunity perceptions in the discussion of decisional stress. But now we can turn to a real-world example of perceived opportunities.

4.3.3 Perceived opportunities in the Entebbe crisis

During the Entebbe crisis, the Israeli decision makers explored three action alternatives: military rescue of the hostages, negotiation with the hijackers on the exchange of Palestinian prisoners held in Israeli jails for the hostages, and inducing Idi Amin, Uganda's President, to bring about the release of the hostages. Figure 4.7 depicts the derivation of perceived opportunities by the three principal decision makers at two distinct stages of the crisis: on Thursday, July 1, 1976 and on Saturday, July 3. This figure draws on figure 6 in Maoz (1981: 700), but differs from the original figure in that all negative utilities have been transformed into positive numbers. This figure suggests several interesting things. First, perceptions of opportunity for all three decision makers were negative throughout the crisis. This implies that, relative to the pre-crisis phase, decision makers felt that any action to be taken entailed some cost.

a. Rabin's opportunity perception

SE

Value / Outcomes	Human	Credibility	Domestic	International	VD	W		U	P
Mil.-Suc.	86.7	100	100	100	Human	42.7	M.-S.	9402.1	0.32 (0.62)†
Mil.-Fail	0	16.4	0	2.4	Cred.	27.3	M.-F.	476.8	0.68 (0.38)
Neg.-Suc.	100	29	34	51.2	×Dom.	17.6	= N.-S.	6279.6	0.77
Neg.-Fail	31.3	0	4	15.2	Inter.	12.1	N.-F.	1582.3	0.33
Admin-Suc.	100	56.3	44	51.2			A.-S.	7200.9	0.20
Admin-Fail	31.1	6.9	14	24.8			A.-F.	2910.3	0.80

$EU_{mil} = 3341.9$ (6015.5); $EU_{neg} = 5199.2$; $EU_{Amin} = 3768.4$
Thursday's $EU_a = 4103.2$; Saturday's $EU_a = 4994.4$
Thursday:

$$OP_{Rabin} = \frac{4103.2 - 7268.7}{7268.7} = -0.435$$

Saturday:

$$OP_{Rabin} = \frac{4994.2 - 7268.7}{7268.7} = -0.313$$

b. Peres's opportunity perception

SE

Value / Outcomes	Human	Credibility	Domestic	International	VD	W		U	P
Mil.-Suc.	86.7	100	100	100	Human	27.0	M.-S.	9640.9	0.32 (0.62)†
Mil.-Fail	0	30	8.7	11.1	Cred.	42.0	M.-F.	1572.9	0.68 (0.38)†
Neg.-Suc.	100	38	37.5	31.2	×Dom.	13.0	= N.-S.	5345.1	0.77
Neg.-Fail	31.3	0	0	0	Inter.	18.0	N.-F.	3130.0	0.33
Admin-Suc.	100	58.0	26.3	54.5			A.-S.	6458.9	0.20
Admin-Fail	31.1	30	5.1	1.6			A.-F.	2194.8	0.80

$EU_{mil} = 4154.7$ (6575.1); $EU_{neg} = 4835.6$; $EU_{Amin} = 3046.0$
Thursday's $EU_a = 4012.1$; Saturday's $EU_a = 4818.9$
Thursday:

$$OP_{Peres} = \frac{4102.1 - 6205}{6205} = -0.353$$

Saturday:

$$OP_{Peres} = \frac{4818.9 - 6205}{6205} = -0.223$$

c. Allon's opportunity perception

Value	SE Human	Credibility	Domestic	International		VD	W		U	P
Outcomes										
Mil.-Suc.	86.7	100	100	100	Human	34.7	M.-S.	9538.5	0.32 (0.62)†
Mil.-Fail	0	15	5.6	0	Cred.	32.0	M.-F.	580.2	0.68 (0.38)†
Neg.-Suc.	100	37.5	41.2	51.6	× Dom.	17.9	=N.-S.	6218.2	0.77
Neg.-Fail	31.3	0	0	14.2	Inter.	15.4	N.-F.	1297.9	0.33
Admin-Suc.	100	65.0	66.4	49.4			A.-S.	7499.3	0.20
Admin-Fail	31.1	35	46.8	26.2			A.-F.	3440.4	0.80

$$EU_{mil}=3446.9 \ (6134.4); \ EU_{neg}=5086.5; \ EU_{Amin}=4252.2$$

Thursday's $EU_a=4261.9$; Saturday's $EU_a=5157.7$

Thursday:

$$OP_{Allon} = \frac{4261.9-7391.9}{7391.9} = -0.423$$

Saturday:

$$OP_{Allon} = \frac{4261.9-7391.9}{7391.9} = -0.302$$

†Saturday's probabilities

Figure 4.7 The Entebbe hijacking and Israeli opportunity perceptions, June 27 – July 3, 1976

· Second, similar to the analysis of the inaction options in terms of threat perception, perceptions of opportunities varied only marginally across the decision makers. Moreover, the difference in perceptions of opportunity among the three individuals are suggestive of their different definitions of the situation. Peres, whose threat perception was the highest, felt at each stage of the crisis that action offered more opportunities than the other two decision makers. Rabin was relatively more reserved, and Allon was somewhere in the middle, sharing both Rabin's reservations and Peres's enthusiasm. However, the negative value of perceived opportunities cannot be isolated from the foregoing analysis of perceived threat. Rather, negative opportunities imply that the extent of decisional stress, that is, the degree of motivational and practical pressure for decision, should have been stronger than what one could infer merely by the definition of threat perception.

Before proceeding, an important caveat seems to be in order. The way in which I calculated the magnitudes of perceived threat and perceived opportunity in the hypothetical and historical examples corresponds to a certain approach which is called analytic decision making, that will be discussed in chapter 5. Since it is not at all clear that this particular approach truly models the way in which foreign policy elites go about making choices, our definitions of threat and opportunity perception may be biased in the sense that they are computed through the utilization of an unrepresentative choice model. This point requires a brief explication of the underlying logic of the definitions of these concepts.

Threat and opportunity perceptions represent the basic motivational sources of choice. They also provide an important set of guidelines for subsequent decision making processes. The measurement procedures attempted to demonstrate the most complex scheme of measurement for these concepts; a scheme which corresponds to sophisticated analytic attempts to define decision-related inputs. Simpler forms of calculating perceived threat and perceived opportunities can be deduced directly from this framework without loss of generality. For example, a unidimensional definition of the situation, that is, a decision maker focusing on a single value dimension as a relevant criterion for threat or opportunity assessment, would convert the **SE** matrix used to define threat and opportunity into a column vector. The inaction alternative as well as the various action alternatives will be evaluated on a single criterion rather than on multiple ones. Moreover, this framework can incorporate any number of action alternatives, any number of contingent outcomes, and so forth. Thus the resulting calculus is independent of the scope and complexity of the diagnosis process. It can encompass both very simple and very complex definitions of the situation.

4.4 TIME PRESSURE

As was the case with the former concepts defined above, the concept of time pressure takes on a subjective form. This suggests that time pressure cannot be measured in terms of clock-time. Rather, the extent of time pressure was defined by Brecher (1979a) as some relational form of optimal time required for decision to practically available time. This is represented by equation (4.13)

$$TP = \frac{\textit{Optimal time} \text{ for } \textit{decision}}{\textit{Available time} \text{ for } \textit{decision}} \tag{4.13}$$

where TP denotes time pressure

Thus, if one can measure empirically these two subjective time perceptions, such a definition would become meaningful. Yet, it

101

seems clear that the numerator of this ratio is a theoretical construct which can rarely (if at all) assume a concrete form. Hence, to measure optimal time for decision we must be able to find indirect indicators that tap its theoretical meaning. On the other hand, the available time for decision may well have a real and concrete meaning, which is determined objectively or subjectively. Decision makers may feel that there exists a certain deadline which their decision must meet. For example, in the Entebbe case the available time for decision was determined objectively by the hijackers' ultimatum. In the Cuban missile crisis, time pressure was determined subjectively by the American decision makers in the sense that they felt that any response selected would have a meaningful effect only if implemented before the Soviet missiles in Cuba became operational. Facing the North Korean attack on the South in 1950, American decision makers felt a need to respond before South Korea was completely overrun by the North.

The difficulty in deriving the perception of optimal time required for decision is due in large measure to the fact that this perception is a function of the magnitude of the problem that the decision maker faces. Big problems require more time to resolve than small ones; unanticipated developments require more time for digestion than routine ones for which solutions are readily available. Thus, if we assume that the optimal time for decision is a linear function of the motivational scope of the problem then we reach to the following definition:

$$OT = f(T, OP); \quad f = (T + OP)^2 \tag{4.14}$$

Coming back to the original definition of time pressure, we have:

$$TP = \frac{(T + OP)^2}{AT} \tag{4.8}$$

where TP = Time pressure: T = Threat perception; OP = Perception of opportunities; and AT = Available time for decision

This definition brings us directly to the composite concept of decisional stress.[5]

4.5 DECISIONAL STRESS

Decisional stress taps the motivational and practical constraints imposed by the decision problem. It is a composite concept which attempts to bind together these two types of inputs in a manner

[5] The reason that the sum of threat and opportunity scores is squared will be discussed below.

that represents the kind of pressure under which decision makers operate in various circumstances. The motivational inputs invoked by an internal or external cue are perceived threat and perceived opportunities; the practical input is time pressure. The formal definition of time pressure suggests that these two types of inputs are closely linked to one another. Hence, a complete formal definition of decisional stress requires connecting the motivational inputs to the measure of time pressure.[6]

4.5.1 Integrating motivational inputs

Kurt Lewin (1948) in a classical study has distinguished among three types of decisional conflict:

1 *Approach-approach conflict* occurs when an organism is confronted by two or more alternatives which are equally attractive.
2 *Avoidance-avoidance conflict* occurs when an organism must choose among several, equally unattractive, alternatives.
3 *Approach-avoidance conflict* occurs when positive and negative tendencies are simultaneously evoked by all available alternatives, that is, when each alternative entails both positive and negative features (cf. Weiner, 1972).

This conceptualization of decisional conflict resembles notions of threat and opportunity situations in foreign policy settings. Since both threats and opportunity perceptions motivate decision makers, and since both these concepts have clear situational features, the total motivational effect that certain environmental cues have on decision makers can be defined formally as follows:

$$ME = (T + OP)^2 = \left[\frac{U_c - EU_{na}}{U_c} + \frac{EU_a - U_c}{U_c} \right]^2 = \frac{(EU_a - EU_{na})^2}{U_c^2} \qquad (4.15)$$

where ME = motivational effect.

The motivational effect measure as depicted in equation 4.15 suggests that both perceptions of threat and perceptions of opportunity tap decision related motivation. Yet, the different assumptions used to derive each of the components of this integrated measure have some implications for the substantive interpretation of the mathematical

---

[6] For a review of cognitive measures of stress see Haan (1982). It must be noted that stress is mostly measured in terms of physiological indices of hormonal and other body reactions that are typically assumed to be associated with certain forms of physiological arousal. See Siegman (1982) for a review. Situational-based perceptions of stress are discussed by Mangusson (1982).

results. They also explain why the $T + OP$ score must be squared. First, we emphasized that while the T measure has a zero-to-one range of values, the OP score can vary, in principle, from minus infinity to plus infinity. Thus the non-squared sum of these two concepts can be either positive or negative. A positive sum indicates opportunity-dominated motivation. It can be realized when various courses of action are perceived as preferred on the average to inaction, or formally, when $EU_a > EU_{na}$. In such cases, the decision maker is driven by a strong incentive to act. This is a type of drive that corresponds either to a pure approach-approach motivation, or to an approach-avoidance motivation in which the mixed tendencies of action are perceived to dominate the mixed tendencies of inaction.

However, the non-squared sum of threat and opportunities can be negative in either of two cases. One case is that in which, while positive, opportunities entailed in action alternatives are smaller than the expected value of inaction. In that case, the fact that positive opportunities are perceived to exist diminishes somewhat the sense of threat, yet the motivational effect is still negative indicating that the decision maker is driven by the prospect of diminishing assets. Action may be seen to mitigate that fear somewhat but to an insufficient extent. The second case of negative motivational effects is that in which the value of perceived opportunities is negative. This case suggests that the sense of fear associated with inaction is compounded by a concomitant sense of fear associated with action, thereby corresponding to a pure avoidance-avoidance type of decisional conflict.

A certain situational stimulus may invoke no motivational effects ($ME = 0$) to the extent that the average expected value of action equals the expected value of inaction (i.e., when $EU_a = EU_{na}$). In that case the magnitude of perceived opportunities compensates for the sense of depreciated values associated with inaction. In other words, a decision maker feels that the situation offers equal threats and opportunities and that these opposite drives cancel each other out. This arises when decision makers feel that a clearly adequate response to the decisional problem is both readily available and feasible. Thus the sign of the non-squared sum of threat and opportunity perceptions conveys important information concerning the nature of decision-related motivation; it indicates whether the decision maker is driven by fear-related motivation, or by opportunity-related motivation. However, it is obvious that the extent to which a certain situational cue evokes motivational pressure for decision is reflected in the size of the difference between the expected payoffs from action and the expected payoffs of inaction. In other words, irrespective of sign, the moti-

Decisional stress

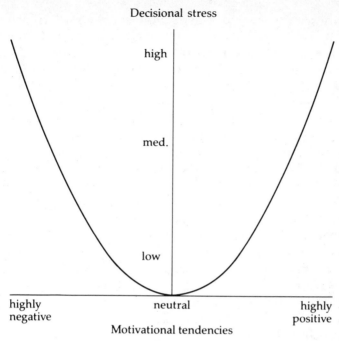

Figure 4.8 Stress, threat perception, and perception of opportunity

vational pressure for decision increases as the sum of threat and opportunity perceptions deviates from zero in either direction. Both strongly positive and strongly negative drives create motivational pressures for decision. Thus, to take this point into account, we must square the $(T + OP)$ measure. This is depicted in figure 4.8.

4.6   DECISIONAL STRESS

To complete our formal definition of decisional stress, we need to combine the motivational effects evoked by the situation with the practical constraints denoted by the concept of time pressure. This has already been done in equation (4.8).

$$DS = \frac{ME}{AT} = \frac{(EU_a - EU_{na})^2}{U_c^2 AT} \tag{4.16}$$

where DS = Decisional stress

This is a composite measure which takes into account the perceptions of threat and opportunity as motivational pressures for decision and the practical, time-related, limitations raised by the

105

problem. This definition of decisional stress integrates through its component-parts the notion of issue-areas as well. Clearly, problems concerning the commercial relations between a nation and other nations will generate different kinds of decisional stress from problems concerning national security issues. Yet, this point is represented by the kind of threats and opportunities that will be perceived by decision makers confronting multiple issue domains, that is to say, by the kind of values or assets that are at stake. Thus the important contribution of students of foreign policy making concerning issue-areas into which such decisions fall is incorporated into the formal definition of decisional stress. This implies, of course, that the definition of decisional stress encompasses both the procedural and substantive aspects of the diagnosis stage. Decisional stress, then, is seen as a composite concept which summarizes the effects of defining the situation on subsequent steps in the decision process. Individual decision makers can be systematically compared in terms of the way they define a certain problem via the utilization of this formal definition of decisional stress as one whole, or via certain components of the definition such as threat perceptions, or perceptions of opportunity. The usefulness of comparing individual definition of the situation through threat and opportunity perceptions was demonstrated by the examples drawn from the Entebbe case. We can now demonstrate the concept of decisional stress for each decision maker in this case.

4.6.1 Decisional stress in the Entebbe crisis

Time pressure was perhaps the only directly observable input for the definitions of the situation in each of the two decisions of the Entebbe crisis. The available time for decision was defined by the hijackers' ultimata. The first ultimatum was set for Thursday July 1 at 2 pm. It was delivered to the Israelis on Tuesday, June 29 at noon. That left two days for decision. The second ultimatum of the hijackers followed the Israeli decision of July 1 to negotiate with the hijackers, and was set for Sunday July 4 at 2 pm. This seemingly allowed three days for the second decision. However, a military rescue operation would have been feasible only if carried out on Saturday night July 3, or more precisely if the raiding force were to leave Israel on Saturday afternoon. The meaning of this was that the available time for the second decision was determined subjectively by the decision makers as two days. Having defined available time we can now measure decisional stress at each decisional juncture, and compare the resulting individual pressures for decision. This is done in table 4.1.

Table 4.1. *Decisional stress in the Entebbe crisis*

Decision maker	Decision 1 (July 1, 1976)				Decision 2 (July 3, 1976)			
	Threat	Opportunity	AT	DS	Threat	Opp.	AT	DS
Rabin	0.65	−0.435	2	0.023	0.65	−0.313	2	0.057
Peres	0.69	−0.353	2	0.056	0.69	−0.223	2	0.109
Allon	0.68	−0.423	2	0.033	0.68	−0.302	2	0.171

Threat = Threat Perception
Opp. = Perception of opportunities
AT = Available time
DS = Decisional stress

This analysis of the motivational inputs for the Entebbe decisions and the practical constraints under which decision makers operated offers several theoretical insights regarding the concept of decisional stress. First, we can compare variations in decisional stress over time and across decisions for each individual participant in the decision making process. It can be readily ascertained that decisional stress increased from the first decision (to start negotiations with the hijackers) to the second one (to launch the military rescue operation). The reason for this increase is that perceptions of opportunity increased over the two days that elapsed between decisions. The increasing feasibility of a military rescue operation which was manifested in a considerably higher likelihood of success, raised the tension involved in the situation and the drive for decision. The approach-avoidance conflict intensified, hence forcing decision makers to reconsider their previous choices. Second, a comparison of distinct components of decisional stress indicates that most of them remained constant over time. This is not an intrinsic feature of the decisional stress construct but rather a characteristic of the specific case under analysis. The non-variation in threat perception across decisions was due to the fact that the stakes and consequences of inaction were seen to have been the same on Thursday and Saturday. The fact that the hijackers decided to extend their initial ultimatum was not interpreted by Israeli decision makers to indicate a lower likelihood of massacre, or a decline in the hijackers' commitment to carry out their threat if negotiation failed. The available time for decision remained the same over time, but as noted above, for different reasons. The way deadlines were defined in both decisional case sheds light on the concept of time pressure. The nature of certain action alternatives imposes important constraints on decision makers. This is evident from the crucial aspect of timing in the execution of the military operation which forced decision makers to reduce subjectively the amount of time for deliberation.

Another example which may shed further light on this problem is the manner in which the American Executive Committee defined the situation during the Cuban missile crisis. A surgical air-strike on the missiles was seen to be strategically and politically feasible only if carried out by surprise and prior to the operationalization of the Soviet missiles. A blockade of Cuba, on the other hand would have rendered a surgical air strike (involving relatively little cost to human life) unfeasible, yet would have gained time for subsequent consideration of other ways to resolve the crisis.

Third, decisional stress, both as a distinct concept and as a composite of several factors, can be used to compare diagnoses of problems across decision makers. For example, Rabin's perception of stress increased by 148 percent from July 1 to July 3. This is a considerably higher shift when compared to Peres's shift (95 percent) and Allon's shift (115 percent). The reason for this difference is that Rabin was more inclined to negotiate with the hijackers than either of the two other decision makers, and his shift to the military option was more reluctant than that of the others. This is a subtle point because in absolute terms, Peres's decisional stress was the highest among all three at each point in time. His relatively strong commitment to a military option made him perceive both the stakes of inaction and the prospects of military rescue as higher than the other decision makers, hence creating an extremely intense approach-avoidance conflict.

The conclusions stemming from this elaborate discussion of decisional stress are two-fold. First, seemingly distinct situational variables that were seen by students of the first stage in decision making research as instrumental factors affecting decision processes, can and should be integrated into composite concepts in order to make our models more compact and parsimonious. Second, these composite concepts indicate that the whole is more than the sum of the parts. Namely, decisional stress is composed of several factors, each of which has received considerable attention from students of foreign policy decision making. Yet it is the *interaction* among these factors which makes the notion of stress so important for the understanding of subsequent processes.

4.7 PERCEIVED SITUATIONAL AMBIGUITY

The clarity with which the problem at hand can be diagnosed by decision makers, the possible consequences stemming from the change in environmental conditions which alert policy makers to the fact that decision time is up, all form the notion of situational ambiguity. When defining international crises, Charles Hermann (1969a, 1969b) noted that one of the attributes of crisis situations is the fact that they come as a surprise to decision makers. In delimiting foreign policy crises from other environmental cues, Hermann distinguished between anticipated and unanticipated events. The surprise element as a necessary attribute of foreign policy crises has been criticized by most students in the field. It has been argued that foreign policy crises can be anticipated as well as unanticipated events (Brecher 1977, 1979a; Snyder and Diesing, 1977: 8–9; Maoz, 1982b: 217–219). Yet the distinction between anticipated and unanticipated environmental cues is useful not only in the context of international crises but – more generally – in the broader foreign policy making context.

Anticipated events are those that conform to, or can be interpreted as being consistent with, some prior expectations that decision makers develop about their environment. Such events are seen to support certain predictions and hence tend to reinforce decision makers' confidence in their views of other actors or of their general view of the world. These events tend to lead to relatively clear definitions of the situation by the perceiver, and – as will be suggested in subsequent chapters – to simplifying choice processes.

Unanticipated events require a drastic revision of the definition of the situation, of previous expectations, images of the environment, and so forth. Such events drastically reduce decision makers' confidence in their ability to forecast future trends and developments and hence make the task of diagnosing the problem and prescribing solutions comparatively difficult. Yet the distinction between anticipated and unanticipated cues should be seen as a matter of degree, not as a clear-cut dichotomy. Although certain events might be expected by decision makers, one may still be surprised by their timing or locus. Moreover, while the discrepancy between an environmental cue and prior expectations does indicate the degree of perceived situational ambiguity (Burnstein and Berbaum, 1983: 536), it does not exhaust this concept. Drastically unanticipated events may lead to extreme alterations of prior expectations whereby a certain view of the environment is changed not from a highly deterministic view to a highly non-deterministic one, but rather from one extreme of determinism to another. For example, President Carter's view of the Soviet Union shifted from one extreme to another following the Soviet invasion of Afghanistan in December 1979. The notion of perceived situational ambiguity reflects not only the degree of anticipation of certain external events, but also the degree to which decision makers can use such events as a basis from which future developments can be extrapolated.

As was assumed when defining threat perception, situational ambiguity is an attribute of the environment which is independent and beyond the control or intervention of the perceiver. The decision maker's actions may reduce such ambiguity in that they imply changing the environment and hence imposing some degree of control – however limited – upon it. Thus, the extent to which a decision maker can make reliable judgment of the nature of the problem to be decided about should be exogenous to the prescribed solutions to the problem. Likewise, the formal definition of situational ambiguity should be made independent of the decision maker's values and normative beliefs because it is based on his or her ability to predict future developments. These points imply that the information we need for our formal definition of perceived ambiguity rests with the – real or hypothetical – "do nothing" alternative, that is, with an attempt to predict the environment in which the decision maker's actions do not play a controlling role.

Recall that when defining threat perceptions we pointed out that one of the aspects of threat refers to the *prospect of loss*. Since loss implies value judgments which we want to ignore at this point, we must define perceived ambiguity in terms of the likelihood of events stemming from the occurrence of the environmental cue. More specifically, the question here is how predictable are future events given the occurrence of this cue. Hence the focus of our definition is on the probability distribution of outcomes in the "do nothing" option, and specifically on the variance of this distribution. A highly ambiguous situation is one in which decision makers are uncertain which of the possible outcomes of the "do nothing" alternative will eventually occur. Thus, if two outcomes are perceived to emerge from this alternative and decision makers think both of them are equally likely, then the environmental cue does not convey diagnostic information enabling reliable prediction. The more certainty is involved in assigning probabilities to the various outcomes, the less ambiguity is perceived. Information theorists have long realized the importance of this conceptualization. For example Argote (1982) discussing the effects of "input uncertainty" on group decision making has defined the concept in terms of the distribution of patients across illness categories. Similarly, Ray and Singer (1973) discussing the concept of power distribution in the international system and relating it to structural clarity (see also Singer, Bremer and Stuckey, 1972) have defined their concepts in similar terms.

Viewing situational ambiguity as the variance of a probability distribution assigned to the discrete outcomes of the "do nothing" option leads to the following formal definition:

$$SA = IQV = \frac{\left(1 - \sum_{i=1}^{n} p_i^2\right) n}{n-1} \tag{4.17}$$

where SA = situational ambiguity, IQV = Index of Qualitative Variation (Bohrnstedt and Knoke, 1982: 75–78), P_i = probability of outcome i, n = number of outcomes.

The Index of Qualitative Variation, IQV, is a standardized measure of dispersion for categorical variables. It ranges from zero, when one category contains all the cases and other categories contain no cases (no dispersion) to cases of maximum dispersion which occur when all categories contain the same number of cases (Bohrnstedt and Knoke, 1982). In our case, this index assumes the value of zero (when the probability of one outcome is 1.0 and other outcomes' probabilities are estimated at zero) and one (when all outcomes are judged equally likely). Situational ambiguity is related to decisional stress by an inverse U-shape function. Under very low or very high levels of stress decision makers normally perceive low levels of uncertainty. This is so because threat and opportunity perceptions are at their extreme. In such cases decision makers perceive the prospects of losses (due to inaction) or gains (resulting from some sort of action) as very clear and unambiguous. On the other hand, at moderate stress levels decision makers are unsure whether losses or gains would indeed materialize, hence perceived situational ambiguity increases.

This inverse U-shape relationship between decisional stress and perceived situational ambiguity is illustrated by the data derived from two studies of Israel's decision making processes during the May–June 1967 crisis (Wagner, 1974: 86–118; Stein and Tanter, 1980: 269–305). Stein and Tanter analyzed four distinct Israeli decisions during this crisis: the May 19 decision to mobilize the entire reserve force following the transfer of Egyptian troops from Yemen to the Sinai; the May 23 decision to delay an attack and to attempt a diplomatic route to solving the crisis; the May 28 decision to further delay an attack to allow time for international maritime action; and the June 4 decision to launch a pre-emptive attack. Wagner's analysis combines all four decisions analyzed by Stein and Tanter sequentially into one decisional

Table 4.2. *Decisional stress and situational ambiguity in the 1967 crisis*

Date	Decision	T	OP	TP	DS	SA
May 19	Mobilize	0.25	− 0.17	?	0.17	0.75
May 23	Delay	0.28	− 0.40	?	0.59	0.96
May 28	Delay	0.30	− 0.97	?	0.45	0.95
June 4	Attack	0.94	− 0.97	?	3.67	0.64
May 19–June 4†	—	0.63	0.18	?	0.65	0.94
Mean		0.48	− 0.47	?	1.11	0.85

† Wagner's (1974) data

T = Threat perception
OP = Perceived opportunities
TP = Time pressure
DS = Decisional stress
SA = Situational ambiguity

problem.[7] Table 4.2 depicts the values of the concepts defined formally thus far as they are derived from the Stein–Tanter and Wagner studies. From these figures, we can discuss the relationship between perceived situational ambiguity and decisional stress.[8]

Although the number of decisions for this illustration is very small we can clearly see that in cases of low decisional stress (e.g., the May 19 decision) and in cases of very high decisional stress (the June 4 decision) perceived situational ambiguity assumes relatively low values. In cases of moderate stress levels, the values of situational ambiguity increase markedly. Of course this relationship is not clear of noise or residual effects. Since stress is a consequence of value estimates as well as probability estimates related to losses and gains, it might fluctuate more rapidly than the measure of situational ambiguity which relies strictly on likelihood estimates. However, the two concepts are intimately related to one another insofar as they depict the value-related and uncertainty-related burdens imposed on the decision makers by certain environmental cues about which they must decide.

The shift from decision under certainty to decision under uncertainty is an important aspect of the diagnosis stage. It indicates the extent of need for information relevant to subsequent decision

[7] Both studies perform their analysis on the decision making collectivity as if it were a single individual. As I shall argue later, this is an important liability. However, for our illustrative purposes we can use the same approach.

[8] While both studies emphasized the considerable time pressure under which decision makers operated throughout the crisis, specific values for the time pressure variable are unavailable from their data. Thus an arbitrary unit-value was assigned to this variable across decisions.

stages. At extreme levels of uncertainty regarding the nature of the problem at hand and its future implications for goals pursued by the decision maker, one typically opts for an extensive amount of information. At low levels of uncertainty, decision makers feel highly familiar with the problem and tend to invest little energy in exploring information beyond what is readily available. It is important to emphasize that the actual degree of situational ambiguity may or may not be identical to its perceived nature. Moreover, its effects on subsequent structuring of the problem and strategies of decision may be modified by the degree of tolerance for uncertainty and ambivalence possessed by an individual or group. Put differently, whether or not a decision maker fits the approach used to solve decisional problems to the degree of uncertainty involved in the definition of the situation depends primarily on the cognitive style of the decision maker. This is the issue to which we turn next.

4.8 COGNITIVE COMPLEXITY

The ability of an individual to cope with stressful and uncertain situations, to absorb, process and consider large magnitudes of information, and to confront incompatible values is reflected in the substantive and structural aspects of his or her cognitive system. Personality-related variables have a marked mediating effect on decision making processes. They connect the perception and diagnosis of problems with prescribed approaches to solutions. As Jervis (1980: 98) argues, the *interaction* between the decision maker's personality and the situation forms the context in which decision processes take place. Indeed, decision making frameworks that have attempted to compile and integrate distinct inputs used personality-related variables in a mediating role between situational variables and decision process (or other outcome) variables (Rosenau, 1966 and especially Brecher *et al.*, 1969).

Cognitive systems are constructs which lie in the interface between subconscious personality traits and explicit, substantive beliefs on life in general and politics in particular. In chapter 3 we discussed some of the literature using such constructs in relation to political behavior and decision making processes. Here we focus on the methodological derivation of these constructs. Contrary to the previous situational concepts such as threat and opportunity perceptions which have not been formally defined in the literature, attempts to tap cognitive systems systematically have been made by students of foreign policy making. The available data on these issues allow us to focus on two

Table 4.3. *Types of beliefs about the nature of political life*

	Fundamental nature of the political universe	
Fundamental sources of conflict	Harmonious (conflict is temporary)	Conflictual (conflict is permanent)
Human nature	A	D
Attributes of states	B	E
International system	C	F

specific approaches to the measurement or classification of such systems: operational code analysis and cognitive mapping.

4.8.1 Operational code approaches

The operational code approach was originally developed by Nathan Leites (1951) in his seminal study of the collective beliefs of the Soviet Politburo. It has been further refined by Alexander George (1969) who has also suggested systematic means of tapping and classifying general types of operational codes. Following these works, Ole Holsti (1977) developed a six-fold typology of operational codes based on a breakdown of possible responses to two questions: what is the fundamental nature of political life (answers are either conflictual or harmonious, where conflict is a temporary characteristic), and what are the fundamental sources of conflict (human nature, attributes of states, and the nature of the international system). In order to apply this framework in a manner allowing empirical differentiation of individuals in terms of master beliefs, Holsti used a qualitative content analysis scheme of documents and other writings. This scheme consisted of the breakdown of master beliefs into specific topical components and matching documents with these components. Walker (1983) analyzed the motivational antecedents of the various operational code types. For the purpose of his analysis, Walker followed Holsti's distinction between master beliefs, i.e., overarching, stable, and abstract ones, and instrumental beliefs, that is, derivative beliefs used to interpret specific events in a variety of contexts. In general, Walker found that three of Holsti's types of operational codes can be collapsed into a single category (see table 4.3). This refers specifically to categories **D**, **E**, and **F**. Moreover, Walker suggested that the different ranking of motivational antecedents such as Need for Achievement, Need for Power, and Need for Affiliation, on the

Table 4.4. *Philosophical and instrumental questions for determining operational code types*

Philosophical questions

P.1 What is the essential nature of political life? Is the essential nature of the political universe one of harmony or conflict? What is the fundamental character of one's political opponents?

P.2 What are the prospects for the eventual realization of one's fundamental political values and aspirations? Can one be pessimistic on this score or optimistic, and in what respects is one and/or the other?

P.3 Is the future predictable? In what sense and to what extent?

P.4 How much control or mastery can one have over historical development? What is one's role in "moving" or shaping history in the desired direction?

P.5 What is the role of chance in human affairs and historical development?

Instrumental questions

I.1 What is the best approach for selecting goals or objectives for political actions?

I.2 How are the goals of action pursued most effectively?

I.3 How are the risks of political action calculated, controlled, or accepted?

I.4 What is the best "timing" of action to advance one's own interests?

I.5 What is the utility and role of different means for advancing one's interests?

Source: Walker (1986). Adapted from George (1969) and Holsti (1977).

remaining four operational code types is sufficiently distinct to suggest that these types are qualitatively different.

How can one derive a certain operational code from a written or oral address made by a decision maker? Holsti (1977) developed a set of questions pertinent to the aspects of the typology, and discussed typical answers that are to be expected from individuals with a specific operational code type to these questions. The list of these questions (as given by Walker, 1986) appears in table 4.4.

The analyst's task is to match statements with typical answers to these philosophical questions, given each type of operational code. Obviously, a decision rule is needed in the not improbable case that the belief system of an individual will be consistent with more than one box in this typology. Walker's approach was to compute the frequencies of beliefs consistent with each operational code type and to determine the operational code type of a decision maker on the basis of the modal belief exhibited by that person. This procedure, then, mixed qualitative and quantitative (i.e., frequency-count) approaches to discriminate between individuls in terms of types of belief systems.

These approaches to the measurement and classification of cognitive systems place a predominant emphasis on the substantive contents of political beliefs. Hence, the generalizations one can derive from these classifications are nominal in nature; namely, such approaches are geared at identification, rather than at quantitative scaling, of cognitive systems. They are useful for our decision-related purposes in that they allow qualitiative prediction or explanation of substantive aspects of the decision making processes. In other words, the typology of cognitive systems may enable researchers to relate operational code types to the substantive content of alternatives that are being reviewed, to the nature of information that is being considered, to the kind of goals or evaluation criteria that are being evoked for the appraisal of these options, and so forth. The procedural aspects of decision making such as the number of alternatives considered, the amount of information processed, the scope and difficulty of evaluation of options, cannot be directly and meaningfully linked to the qualitative operational code typology.

4.8.2 Cognitive mapping and measures of cognitive complexity[9]

A cognitive map is a mathematical or graphical representation of a segment of a belief system. More specifically, a cognitive map represents all explicit or implicit causal assertions contained in a belief system (Bonham and Shapiro, 1986: 30). Since the cognitive mapping approach has been applied to a wide variety of substantive contexts, I will restrict my discussion to the derivation of cognitive complexity indices. Recall that a belief system is defined as a "more or less integrated set of beliefs about a man's physical and social environment. In the case of political leaders, beliefs about the history and the nature of politics may be especially important" (Holsti, 1976: 20). Let us denote such a set of beliefs as $\mathbf{B} = [b_1, b_2, \ldots, b_m]$ where each element b_i is a single belief.

It is readily apparent that this definition is not terribly precise. Nevertheless, the ideas underlying cognitive mapping allow for a more precise, albeit somewhat narrow, conceptualization of belief systems. Briefly, let $\mathbf{B}' \subseteq \mathbf{B}$ be the set of all causal assertions contained in a belief system. $\mathbf{B}'$ consists of a set of n elements, each of which is related to at least one other element. Specifically, concept i is said to be an element of $\mathbf{B}'$ if and only if there exists at least one other concept $j \neq i \in \mathbf{B}'$ such that either $i \rightarrow j$ or $j \rightarrow i$, where $\rightarrow$ represents a causal relation. A system of assertions containing a set of concepts and

[9] The following discussion draws on Maoz and Shayer (1987).

symbols representing the direction and nature of causal relations among the concepts can be represented in a graphical (*extensive*) form or in matrix (*normal*) form. A belief can be either descriptive, i.e., consisting of a factual statement regarding the relationship between concepts, or normative, i.e., consisting of a value statement regarding a causal relationship.

To illustrate, consider two statements made by Henry Kissinger during his famous detente speech before the Senate Committee on Foreign Relations, September 19, 1974. Kissinger stated that "Soviet foreign policy . . . is conducted in a gray area heavily influenced by the Soviet conception of the balance of forces" (Kissinger, 1974: 506). This statement reflects a descriptive belief concerning one of the factors affecting the conduct of Soviet foreign policy. Graphically, this statement can be depicted as follows:

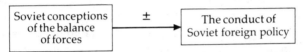

where the arrow indicates the direction of the causal relationship, and the ± sign indicates a non-zero relationship (meaning that this statement does not contain sufficient information to determine whether the relationship between these concepts is strictly positive or strictly negative).

An example of a normative belief is the following statement: "Our approach proceeds from the conviction that, in moving forward across a wide spectrum of negotiations, progress in one area adds momentum to progress in other areas" (Kissinger, 1974: 508). This statement entails a belief about how negotiations should be conducted. Its graphical interpretation is as follows:

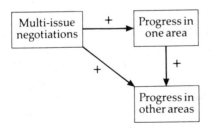

The system of causal relationships contained in the last statement differs from the system of causal relationships contained in the first statement in two additional respects: (*a*) the nature of the causal

117

relationship in the first statement is somewhat ambiguous as implied by the ± sign. We cannot reliably infer the precise nature of the effect of the Soviet conception of the balance of forces on their foreign policy. In the second statement, the relations between concepts are strictly positive. (*b*) The causal relationship in the first statement is of a qualitative nature. In other words, Kissinger implies that the *type* of Soviet conception of the balance of forces affects the *type* of Soviet foreign policy. In the second statement, the causal relationships among concepts are of a *quantitative* nature. Kissinger seems to be saying that the *larger* the number of issues in a negotiation, the *more likely* are the parties to make progress on any single issue, and hence, the *more likely* they are to accomplish progress on other issues.

Moving from single beliefs to the broader context of systems of beliefs, we seek to connect distinct beliefs such as those illustrated above to one another in a comprehensive fashion. Moreover, to describe belief systems we must develop a standardized set of measures across individuals, contexts of statements from which beliefs are derived, and scope of each of the documents on which the empirical derivation of cognitive maps is based. Most of the works employing the cognitive mapping approach focus on decision or policy making domains. The empirical derivation of such maps is based on individual or collective problem solving contexts (e.g. Axelrod, 1976; 1977; Shapiro and Bonham, 1973; Bonham and Shapiro, 1976; 1986; Roberts, 1976, Hart, 1976a). However, a few works focusing on broader philosophical statements can guide or search for the systematic connection of cognitive maps to belief system (Ross, 1976; Hart, 1977).

In order to trace the broad, permanent, and central aspects of belief systems, we need general statements that are not directly related to specific policies, but rather reflect as broad an articulation of the decision makers' world-view as possible. Such statements maximize the inventory of concepts and causal relations used by the decision maker, and hence increase the likelihood of a reliable derivation of his or her belief system. To validate the cognitive map derived from such a statement we must analyze other texts written by the same decision maker to examine whether concepts and causal relations appearing in one text would also appear in another text. In addition, deriving a general belief system requires some modifications of the cognitive mapping technique developed by Axelrod and his associates. Yet several basic concepts and mathematical operations introduced in the original formulation of the approach must be outlined.

First, when distinct beliefs are combined, we move from causal

		A^1	
	1	2	3
1	0	1	0
2	0	0	1
3	0	0	0

		A^2	
	1	2	3
1	0	0	1
2	0	0	0
3	0	0	0

Figure 4.9 Adjacency matrices of Kissinger's multi-issue negotiation statement

paths connecting two concepts to paths connecting several concepts. For example, Kissinger's beliefs about the benefits associated with multi-issue negotiation has as one of its paths the connection: (*a*) between the form of negotiation (multi-issue) and the likelihood of agreement on any *one* issue, and (*b*) between agreement on a single issue and agreement on other issues. So we have in this case two effects, a direct one and an indirect one.

Axelrod and his associates have developed an adjacency matrix (**A**) of order $n \times n$ representing all the direct causal relations contained in a cognitive map. This matrix is a signed binary matrix whose entries can assume the values of $+1$, 0, -1, or other, special signs (such as the $\pm$ sign). To illustrate the construction of the adjacency matrix consider Kissinger's statement about the benefits of multi-issue negotiation. The A^1 matrix one can construct from this statement is of order 3×3 because the statement contains three concepts (variables) and is given in figure 4.9.

Matrix A^1 represents all the first-order (direct) effects of row-concepts on column-concepts. Concept 1 in figure 4.9 affects concept 2 positively, hence entry $a_{12}^1 = 1$. Likewise, concept 2 in figure 4.9 positively affects concept 3, hence entry $a_{23}^1 = 1$.

Matrix A^2 represents all the second-order indirect effects of row-concepts on column-concepts. From the graphical representation of the negotiation statement we can readily ascertain that this portion of the cognitive map contains only one indirect effect: that of concept 1 on concept 3 (through concept 2). This is entry a_{23}^2 in A^2. Matrix A^2 is obtained by squaring matrix A^1 ($A^2 = A^1 \times A^1$).

The analysis of the multi-issue negotiation statement is simplistic. First, it represents a belief which was taken out of context. Any relationship between concepts included in that statement and other concepts which are included in Kissinger's speech are not reflected in the cognitive map constructed above. Second, the causal relations among concepts in this little segment of Kissinger's belief system are

a. A graphical (extensive) form representation

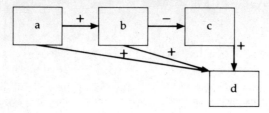

b. A matrix (normal) form representation

	A^1 (1)	(2)	(3)	(4)		A^2 (1)	(2)	(3)	(4)		A^3 (1)	(2)	(3)	(4)
	a	b	c	d		a	b	c	d		a	b	c	d
(1) a	0	1	0	1	(1) a	0	0	−1	1	(1) a	0	0	0	−1
(2) b	0	0	−1	1	(2) b	0	0	0	−1	(2) b	0	0	0	0
(3) c	0	0	0	1	(3) c	0	0	0	0	(3) c	0	0	0	0
(4) d	0	0	0	0	(4) d	0	0	0	0	(4) d	0	0	0	0

c. Summary matrix

$$\text{CON} = \sum_{k=1}^{n-1} A^k$$

	(1) a	(2) b	(3) c	(4) d	
(1) a	0	1	−1	±1	$\sum_{j=1}^{4} \lvert 1j \rvert = 3$
(2) b	0	0	−1	±1	$\sum_{j=1}^{4} \lvert 2j \rvert = 2$
(3) c	0	0	0	1	$\sum_{j=1}^{4} \lvert 3j \rvert = 1$
(4) d	0	0	0	0	$\sum_{j=1}^{4} \lvert 4j \rvert = 0$
	$\sum_{i=1}^{4} \lvert i1 \rvert = 0$	$\sum_{i=1}^{4} \lvert i2 \rvert = 1$	$\sum_{i=1}^{4} \lvert i3 \rvert = 2$	$\sum_{i=1}^{4} \lvert i4 \rvert = 3$	$\sum_{j=1}^{4}\sum_{j=1}^{4} \lvert ij \rvert = 6$

Source: Maoz and Shayer (1987).

Figure 4.10 A graphical and matrix representation of a cognitive map

relatively straightforward. However, it is quite conceivable that cognitive maps may exhibit more complex associations among concepts. To exemplify a more complex cognitive map, consider the hypothetical belief set in figure 4.10.

The graphical form of the cognitive map in figure 4.10a was

converted into a matrix form in figure 4.10b. Matrix $\mathbf{A}^1$ represents again all the first-order (direct) effects contained in the map. For example, entry a_{12}^1 suggests that concept 1 affects concept 2 in a positive way. Likewise, entry a_{23}^1 shows the direct (negative) effect of concept 2 on concept 3, and so forth. Matrix $\mathbf{A}^2$ represents all the second-order causal effects contained in the map. Entry a_{13}^2 reflects the indirect (negative) effect of concept 1 on concept 3 through concept 2. Entry a_{24}^2 reflects the indirect negative effect of concept 2 on concept 4 through concept 3, and so forth.

In general, two matrices $\mathbf{A}$ and $\mathbf{B}$ can be multiplied if and only if the number of columns in $\mathbf{A}$ equals the number of rows in $\mathbf{B}$. If that is the case, the product matrix $\mathbf{C}$ is given by

$$\mathbf{C}_{(m \times k)} = \mathbf{A}_{(m \times n)} \times \mathbf{B}_{(n \times k)}$$

and each element in $\mathbf{C}$, c_{ik} is obtained by

$$c_{ik} = \sum_{j=1}^{n} a_{ij} b_{jk} = a_{i1} b_{1k} + a_{i2} b_{2k} + \ldots + a_{in} b_{nk}$$

where i, j, k are any row and column numbers in matrices $\mathbf{A}$, $\mathbf{B}$, and $\mathbf{C}$. Since all adjacency matrices are square (that is, they have an equal number of rows and columns), they could be raised successively to various powers to represent indirect effects derived from the pattern of direct relationships contained in a first-order matrix. Thus, the notation $\mathbf{A}^1$, $\mathbf{A}^2$, $\mathbf{A}^3$, $\mathbf{A}^4$ in figure 4.10 represents the matrices generated as a result of raising $\mathbf{A}^1$ to various powers. (For example, $\mathbf{A}^3 = \mathbf{A}^2 \times \mathbf{A}^1$; $\mathbf{A}^4 = \mathbf{A}^3 \times \mathbf{A}^1$.)

Since causal relations in a cognitive map can take on special form – such as the $\pm$ sign characterizing the relationship between Soviet conception of the balance of forces and Soviet foreign policy – the operations of matrix multiplication and matrix addition have to be modified to take account of those special signs. To describe the revised arithmetic of matrix operations we have to look first at the possible causal forms that can exist between any two concepts a and b (Axelrod, 1976: 343).

+ positive
− negative
0 zero, i.e., no relationship
⊕ non-negative, i.e., zero or positive: $[0 \cup +]$
⊖ non-positive, i.e., zero or negative: $[0 \cup -]$
± non-zero, i.e., positive or negative: $[+ \cup -]$
⊕ universal, i.e., either negative, zero, or positive: $[- \cup 0 \cup +]$.

In order to allow the incorporation of the special types of causal

121

a. Rules of multiplication

	−1	0	+1	⊕1	⊖1	±1	⊞1
−1	1	0	−1	⊖1	⊕1	±1	⊞1
0	0	0	0	0	0	0	0
+1	−1	0	+1	⊕1	⊖1	±1	⊞1
⊕1	⊖1	0	⊕1	⊕1	⊖1	⊞1	⊞1
⊖1	⊕1	0	⊖1	⊖1	⊕1	⊞1	⊞1
±1	±1	0	±1	⊞1	⊞1	±1	⊞1
⊞1	⊞1	0	⊞1	⊞1	⊞1	⊞1	⊞1

b. Rules of addition

	−1	0	+1	⊕1	⊖1	±1	⊞1
−1	−1	−1	±1	⊞1	⊖1	±1	⊞1
0	−1	0	+1	⊕1	⊖1	±1	⊞1
+1	±1	+1	+1	⊕1	⊞1	±1	⊞1
⊕1	⊞1	⊕1	⊕1	⊕1	⊞1	⊞1	⊞1
⊖1	⊞1	⊖1	⊞1	⊞1	⊖1	⊞1	⊞1
±1	±1	±1	⊞1	⊞1	±1	±1	⊞1
⊞1	⊞1	⊞1	⊞1	⊞1	⊞1	⊞1	⊞1

Entry ij is the product (sum) of the row-entry times (plus) the column entry

Figure 4.11 Rules of multiplication and addition in cognitive maps

relations into matrix operations, Axelrod (1976: 354–346) posited the rules of multiplication and addition as shown in figure 4.11.

Using these rules, we can obtain from the hypothetical cognitive map in figure 4.10a all the first, second, and third-order effects contained in the belief system represented by this map. As a general rule, a non-cycled first-order adjacency matrix A^1 can be raised successively to the A^2, A^3, ..., A^{n-1}th power to represent all the direct and indirect effects contained in the map. Note that matrix A^n is empty (that is, all of its entries are zero), meaning that all the causal relations contained in the map have been exhausted. The final introductory note about cognitive maps concerns two important concepts: cognitive imbalance and cognitive cycles.

An imbalanced cognitive path exists if the relations between two concepts takes on contradictory forms. Consider, for example, the following statement: "A clear and unambiguous deterrent threat will make it clear to our opponent that the costs of aggression outweigh whatever benefits it hopes to derive, and hence will reduce the opponent's incentives to violate the status quo. On the other hand, such a threat might be interpreted by the opponent as an impending attack on our part, hence increasing its incentives to pre-empt due to miscalculation." This implies a belief that a deterrent threat affects the opponent's incentives to attack in two different ways, and that these effects are contradictory. The first causal path linking deterrent threats to the opponent's incentives to attack is negative: the clearer the threat, the less the incentive to attack. However, the second path between these two concepts is positive: the clearer the threat the higher the incentive to attack. In figure 4.10a, there are three paths leading from concept a to concept d; two of them are positive ($a \rightarrow d$ and $a \rightarrow b \rightarrow d$) and one is negative ($a \rightarrow b \rightarrow c \rightarrow d$). This relationship between concepts a and d entails some measure of cognitive imbalance. Cognitive imbalance is an important feature of complexity. Cognitively-complex individuals are willing to entertain some degree of ambivalence and indecisiveness in their world-views, whereas cognitively-simple individuals try to depict their environment in relatively clear-cut unambiguous terms. Thus, the extent of imbalance in belief systems is an instrumental indicator of cognitive complexity.

The second special aspect of cognitive maps concerns the notion of cycles. A cognitive cycle is a causal path leading from a concept to itself through at least one other concept. Consider, for example, the following statement: "An increase in our defense expenditures will be perceived by our opponent as a threatening move. This will force the opponent to increase its defense expenditures, which will be interpreted by us as a threatening move, necessitating an additional increase in our defense budget." This is a self-amplifying cycle because it implies a belief that an initial increase in our defense budget will result in ever-growing allocations to defense through a spiral process. Cyclical arguments are also taken to represent an important dimension of cognitive complexity.

The various measures of cognitive complexity are derived from a matrix labeled **CON**. This is a summary matrix of a cognitive map and is defined as:

$$\mathbf{CON} = \sum_{k=1}^{n-1} \mathbf{A}^k = \mathbf{A}^1 + \mathbf{A}^2 + \ldots + \mathbf{A}^{n-1} \tag{4.18}$$

where $\mathbf{A}^k$ is a k-order adjacency matrix, and the summation is based on the arithmetic rules discussed above. To exemplify this, figure 4.12 represents two **CON** matrices: one derived from Kissinger's statement

123

a. Summary matrix derived from figure 4.9

	1	2	3	Total
1	0	+1	+1	2
2	0	0	+1	1
3	0	0	0	0
Total	0	1	2	3

b. Summary matrix derived from figure 4.10

	1	2	3	4	Total
1	0	+1	-1	±1	3
2	0	0	-1	±1	2
3	0	0	0	+1	1
4	0	0	0	0	0
Total	0	1	2	3	6

Figure 4.12 Summary matrices of cognitive maps

on multi-issue negotiations (figure 4.9), and the other derived from the hypothetical cognitive map introduced in figure 4.10.

The row and column marginals in the **CON** matrix represent, respectively, the total number of concepts that are causally reachable from the row and column concepts. The aggregate total reflects the number of distinct causal relations contained in a map irrespective of sign. Imbalanced causal paths are tapped by entries either the ± or the ⊕ sign in the **CON** matrix. Cycles are denoted by any non-zero entry in the main diagonal of the **CON** matrix.

4.8.3 Dimensions of cognitive complexity

These measures of cognitive complexity have been developed by Maoz and Shayer (1987). The assumption underlying the approach of these authors has been that cognitive complexity reflects the structural organization of, the interdependence among, expressed beliefs. Thus, cognitive complexity measures should be based primarily on the manner in which beliefs are organized within a system, rather than on their substantive content. Maoz and Shayer reasoned that structural aspects of beliefs are less susceptible to conscious manipulation than their substantive aspects.[10] The four dimensions of cognitive complexity developed by Maoz and Shayer are:

1   *Causal connectedness (CC).* This measures taps the extent of interdependence among concepts within a belief system. Operationally, causal connectedness is defined as the number of distinct causal relations per concept in the **CON** matrix. Formally,

[10] For a related approach to the measurement of cognitive complexity see Tetlock (1985, 1984, 1983a, 1983b).

124

$$CC = \frac{1}{n} \sum_{i=1}^{n} \sum_{j=1}^{n} |con_{ij}| \tag{4.19}$$

2   *Cyclicality (CY)*. Measures the proportion of cycles (indirect effects of concepts on themselves) contained in a map. Operationally, cyclicality is measured as the ratio of the non-zero values in the main diagonal of the **CON** matrix to its dimension. Formally,

$$CY = \frac{1}{n} \sum_{i=1}^{n} |con_{ii}| \tag{4.20}$$

3   *Cognitive imbalance (CI)*. This variable measures the extent of imbalance contained in a map, where imbalance refers to contradictory associations between concepts. Operationally, cognitive imbalance is defined as the ratio of imbalanced paths in the **CON** matrix to its non-zero entries (that is, the proportion of imbalanced causal links between concepts). Formally,

$$CI = \frac{\sum_{i=1}^{n} \sum_{j=1}^{n} |con_{ij}^{*}|}{\sum_{i=1}^{n} \sum_{j=1}^{n} |con_{ij}|} \tag{4.21}$$

where $con_{ij}^{*} = \pm 1$, $\oplus$, a (a is the empty set).

Maoz and Shayer developed another measure of cognitive complexity labeled *substantive variation*. This measure reflects a tendency of decision makers to distribute their causal assertions across different concept-categories. Substantive variation was designed to reflect a content-based dimension of cognitive complexity, as opposed to the previous measures which are structure-based. However, in their analysis of the cognitive structure of peace and war argumentation, these researchers found that substantive variation failed to discriminate among individuals. They concluded, therefore, that this variable did not represent a valid indicator of cognitive complexity.

The measures of cognitive complexity discussed thus far are based on a summary description of the entire system of beliefs. They do not allow the characterization of single elements within the system. To tap the relative importance of specific elements of a belief system, two additional measures must be briefly discussed. Bonham and Shapiro (1986) used the notion of cognitive centrality of specific concepts as a device for the elimination of inconsistent causal paths. Whenever they confronted an imbalanced causal path, Bonham and Shapiro measured the relative centrality of the concepts belonging to each of the contradictory paths, and eliminated the less central one (Bonham, Shapiro, and Trumble, 1979). Maoz and Shayer argued that this procedure serves to artificially eliminate cognitive imbalance and hence may lead to biased interpretations of belief systems. However, the notion of cognitive centrality is important in that it allows tracing the relative importance of beliefs within a system.

Two types of cognitive centrality measures represent, respectively, the antecedent and consequent centrality of specific concepts. Since the logic of cognitive mapping approaches follows closely the logic of causal modeling (Blalock, 1964), it is useful to discriminate among concepts used by decision makers in terms of (a) their primary explanatory power, and (b) their importance as dependent variables, that is, as ideas to be explained. For any given individual, variation over time in the antecedent or consequent centrality of certain concepts may be taken to indicate shifts in one's cognitive concerns, as well as broader changes in the belief systems.

The explanatory (antecedent) centrality of concept i is defined as the proportion of all concepts which it serves to explain. Formally,

$$EC_i = \frac{\sum_{j=1}^{n} |con_{ij}|}{\sum_{i=1}^{n} \sum_{j=1}^{n} |con_{ij}|} \tag{4.22}$$

The consequent centrality of concept j is defined as the proportion of concepts in the map that explain it. Formally,

$$C_j = \frac{\sum_{i=1}^{n} |con_{ij}|}{\sum_{i=1}^{n} \sum_{j=1}^{n} |con_{ij}|} \tag{4.23}$$

where $i = [1, \ldots, n]$ and $j = [1, \ldots, n]$ are, respectively, the row and column indexes in the **CON** matrix.

Finally, a cognitive system can be characterized by the distribution of explanatory and consequent centrality over concepts. Cognitive systems in which relatively few concepts are used to explain many other concepts are called *parsimonious*. They are characterized by few concepts with high explanatory centrality and many other concepts with low explanatory centrality. An index of parsimony is based on the complement of the index of qualitative variation (IQV) discussed above, and is defined as,

126

$$IP = \left[1 - \frac{(1 - \sum_{i=1}^{n} EC_i^2)n}{n-1} \right]^{1/2} \qquad (4.24)$$

This index is bound between zero and one. It approaches its maximal value when the explanatory centrality of one concept approaches unity (that is, when one concept explains nearly all other concepts contained in a cognitive map). Conversely, the index of parsimony approaches its minimal value when the absolute row distribution of matrix CON is nearly uniform.

On the other hand, a cognitive system is called *complex* if it uses many explanatory concepts to explain relatively few dependent concepts. Such a system has the' property of containing complicated causal assertions in that its causal paths tend to be rather elaborate (Hart, 1977). Again, the index of qualitative variation can be used to derive the index of explanatory complexity (IEC). Formally,

$$IEC = \left[1 - \frac{(1 - \sum_{j=1}^{n} C_j^2)n}{n-1} \right]^{1/2} \qquad (4.25)$$

where i and j represent, respectively, rows and columns of the **CON** matrix.

The substantive interpretation of this index is similar to that of the index of parsimony (IP). Specifically, a complex system of causal assertions is one in which there are few concepts with high consequent centrality scores and many other concepts with low consequent centrality scores. A "simple" system is one in which most causal assertions are of a first-order nature, hence the marginal column distribution of the **CON** matrix is nearly uniform.

4.8.4 The belief system of Henry Kissinger: substantive and structural dimensions

In order to illustrate the applicability of the operational code analysis and the cognitive mapping approaches and the relations between these approaches, I use a portion of Kissinger's detente speech (Kissinger, 1974) as a case example in the next section.

Kissinger's operational code[11]

The focus of the operational code analysis of Henry Kissinger was on two questions: First, which of the six categories of operational

[11] The operational code analysis presented below draws from Walker (1986). I am indebted to Professor Walker for his permission to reproduce this material.

Table 4.5. *Interpretation of statements in terms of operational code types*

Page	Question type	Statement
505	**P.1**	Throughout history men have sought peace but suffered war; all too often, deliberate decisions or miscalculations have brought violence and destruction to a world yearning for tranquility. (Nature of political life – types **DEF**, causes of war – type **B**.)
505	**P.1**	Deep differences in philosophy and interests between the United States and the Soviet Union . . . do not spring out from misunderstanding or personalities or transitory factors; they are rooted in history and in the way our countries have developed. (Nature of political life – type **E**.)
505	**I.1**	If peace is pursued to the exclusion of any other goals, other values will be compromised and perhaps lost; but if unconstrained rivalry leads to nuclear conflict, these values, along with everything else will be destroyed in the resulting holocaust. (Approach to goals – types **EF**.)
506	**I.2**	We seek, regardless of Soviet intentions, to serve peace through a systematic resistance to pressure and conciliatory responses to moderate behavior. (Pursuit of goals – type **DEF**.)
506	**I.3**	We must oppose aggressive actions and irresponsible behavior. But we must not seek confrontations lightly. (Risk taking – type **E**.)
506	**I.5**	We must attain a strong national defense while recognizing that in the nuclear age the relationship between military strength and politically usable power is the most complex in all history. (Utility of different means – type **E**.)
506	**P.1**	Soviet foreign policy . . . is conducted in a gray area heavily influenced by the Soviet conception of the balance of forces. (Character of opponent – type **E**.)
506–7	**P.1**	For Moscow, East–West contacts are in part designed to promote Soviet influence abroad, especially in Western Europe, and to gain formal acceptance of those elements of the status quo most agreeable to Moscow. (Goals of opponent – types **ABCDEF**.)
507	**P.3, P.5**	Contradictory tendencies contested for preeminence in Soviet Policy; events could have tipped the scale toward either increased competitiveness or toward conciliation. (Predictability/chance – types **ADEF**.)
508	**I.1**	We sought to explore every avenue toward an honorable and just accommodation while remaining determined not to settle for mere atmospherics. (Approach to goals – types **ADEF**.)
508	**P.1**	We did not invent the relationship between issues in the so-called linkage concept; it was a reality because of the range of problems and areas in which the interests of the United States and the Soviet Union impinge upon each other. (Nature of political life – type **BD**.)

Source: Walker (1986: 15–17).

code types best describes Kissinger's belief system? Second, is there a correspondence between Kissinger's operational code and his typical behavioral style with respect to some general policy issues? To answer the first question, Walker matched statements drawn from Kissinger's detente speech with a list of typical answers that would have been given by a person with a certain operational code type to the set of philosophical and instrumental questions given in table 4.4. To see how statements from the detente speech were matched with the typical answers that would have been given by people with different operational code-types to these questions, a sample of statements derived from Kissinger's speech is given in table 4.5.

A close inspection of this table reveals two interesting things. First, a given statement may encompass a typical answer to several different operational code types. Second, a precise match between a given statement and a specific belief type is not always feasible. Walker is careful to point out the difficulty of deriving precise classifications of operational code types using essentially qualitative content analytic methods. Despite this caveat, several reliability tests conducted by Walker – consisting of matches between the codings derived from the detente speech with a previous analysis of Kissinger's operational code which had been based on other sources (Walker, 1983), as well as with the result of a quantitative content analysis of Kissinger (Stuart and Starr, 1981–82) – suggested a high degree of both intra-coder temporal reliability and cross-method reliability. Walker derived the frequencies of the types of operational codes as exhibited by Kissinger's speech, concluding that Kissinger's operational code type is best characterized by type E. Thus Kissinger's belief system is characterized by a view emphasizing the conflictive nature of international politics, and by the idea that the attributes of states seem to be the prime cause of conflict. This classification led Walker to suggest that Kissinger's instrumental beliefs.

> [P]rescribe negotiations and conciliatory tactics as preferable to the use of force, but the use of force is preferable to surrender of vital interests or loss of credibility. The timing of political action is important, and one should avoid high-risk policies except in the defense of the most basic goals . . . The actual bargaining strategy that Kissinger prefers is a reciprocating strategy in which the decision maker should pursue negotiations throughout a conflict; use threats and force only to counter their use by an opponent; apply sufficient force in combination with generous terms of agreement so that the opponent's alternatives are either a costly continuation of hostilities or a beneficial settlement. (Walker, 1986: 19–20)

129

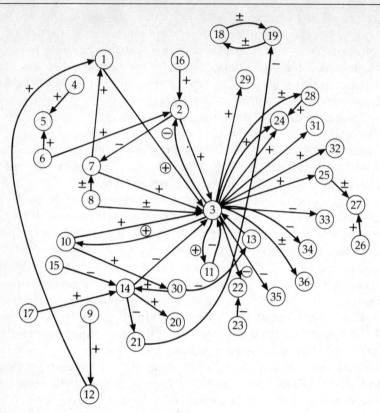

Figure 4.13 Kissinger's cognitive map

Several features of Kissinger's belief system must be discussed before analyzing its structural aspects. First, US–Soviet relations are clearly the most important concept of this segment of Kissinger's belief system. This is hardly surprising given the topic of the speech. However, the centrality of this concept is due to the fact that it is seen both as a key cause of other aspects such as the prospect of peace, the relations with allies, arms control treaties, and so forth, and as a complex consequence of the fear of nuclear holocaust, the balance of forces, competing values and ideologies, etc. Second, Kissinger's belief system exhibits a number of direct cycles of the type $a \rightarrow b \rightarrow a$. For example, US–Soviet relations are seen to be both a cause and as a consequence of the prospects of peace. Military and political power are seen to be mutual determinants of one another, and so forth.

Despite the relatively small number of causally-relevant concept-variables used by Kissinger, the detente speech reflects extraordinarily high levels of cognitive complexity. All the structural measures of this

Table 4.6. *Concepts in Kissinger's cognitive map*

No.	Concept	Subcategories	Concept-type	EC_i	C_i
1	Holocaust	Nuclear	Value	0.02	0.04
		Fear of	Value	0.04	0.08
2	Peace	World hopes for	Value	0.04	0.08
		Urgency of	Value		
		Search for	Policy		
3	US–USSR relations	Changes in	Event	0.24	0.26
		Constructive	Policy		
		Detente in	Policy		
4	Decisions (choices)	Deliberate	Policy	0.02	0.00
		Miscalculated	Policy		
5	War	Violence in	Policy	0.00	0.04
		Destructiveness of	Value		
6	Weapons	Nuclear	Policy	0.04	0.04
7	Values and ideology	Conflicting	Value	0.04	0.04
		Compatible	Value		
8	Histories of US, USSR	Differences in	Event	0.04	0.00
		Development of	Event		
9	Competition US–USSR	Political	Policy	0.02	0.00
		Military	Policy		
10	Allies and friends	Power of	Value	0.04	0.02
		Relations with	Policy		
11	Interests	National	Value	0.02	0.02
		Of allies	Value		
12	Risk	Intolerable	Value	0.04	0.02
13	Will	Imposition of	Policy	0.02	0.02
		Victory and	Value		
14	Foreign policy	US	Policy	0.06	0.06
		Conciliatory	Policy		
15	Intentions	Of USSR	Policy	0.02	0.00
16	Resistance	To pressure	Policy	0.02	0.00
17	Soviet foreign policy	Moderate	Policy	0.02	0.04
		Influence of	Policy		
18	Power†	Military	Value	0.02	0.02
19	Power†	Political	Value	0.02	0.04
20	Freedom		Value	0.00	0.02
21	Tyranny		Value	0.02	0.02
22	Change	Political	Event	0.00	0.02
		In other states	Event		
23	Life	Value of	Value	0.02	0.00
		Preservation of	Value		
24	Gains	Policy	Policy	0.02	0.04
		Mutual	Value		
25	Balance of Forces	Soviet perception of	Policy	0.04	0.00
		Parity in	Event		
26	Negotiation	East–West	Policy	0.02	0.00
27	Leadership in IR	USSR	Policy	0.02	0.00
		other states	Policy		
28	Economics	Problems in USSR	Policy	0.04	0.02

Table 4.6 (*cont.*)

		Prosperity in USSR	Policy		
		International	Policy		
29	Interdependence	Economic	Policy	0.04	0.04
		Perception of	Value		
30	International system	Transformation of	Policy	0.04	0.04
31	Technology	Science and	Policy	0.02	0.02
		Energy and	Policy		
32	International organization		Policy	0.00	0.02
33	Berlin	Problem of	Policy	0.00	0.02
34	Arms control	Progress in	Policy	0.00	0.02
35	Vietnam War	US involvement	Policy	0.00	0.02
36	Crisis	Management	Policy	0.00	0.02
		Deescalation of	Policy		
		Escalation of	Policy		

Index of Parsimony, IP = 0.237

Index of Explanatory Centrality, IEC = 0.265

$EC_i - C_i$ correlation = 0.855, p < 0.001

Cognitive complexity measures

Causal Connectedness, CC = 14.47

Cyclicality, CY = 0.387

Cognitive Imbalance, CI = 0.967

concept far exceed the range of values reported by Maoz and Shayer (1987) for Israeli prime ministers' argumentation in similar settings. Let us see how these measures are reflected in Kissinger's cognitive map. First, the network of causal relations among concepts is highly complex, and – what is more important – of a very special structure. The cognitive centrality of concept number 3 suggests that nearly all causal relationships go through it. This implies that the fairly "normal" number of causal relationships per concept in the first-order adjacency matrix (1.39) grows exponentially in the integration of all causal relations in the summary **CON** matrix. The causal connectedness score indicates that each concept is causally linked to over 14 other concepts, on the average.

Second, the complexity of this cognitive map is compounded by the presence of numerous cycles. Nearly 39 percent of the concepts in Kissinger's cognitive map are involved in cognitive cycles. In addition to the short (second-order) cycles discussed above, a significant number of longer cycles also exists. For example, consider the following cycle.

This cycle may be interpreted as follows: "The greater the fear from

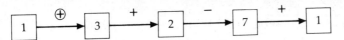

nuclear holocaust (1), the more constructive will US–Soviet relations be (3), the more constructive these relations, the greater the hope for peace (2), the greater the hopes for peace, the less conflicting the ideologies between the superpowers (7), and hence the less the fear from nuclear holocaust (1)." Although such an involved argument was never explicitly made by Kissinger in the speech, this causal path is a logical derivative of the explicit assertions that Kissinger did make. As in the case of the causal connectedness measure, the value of the cyclicality index is significantly above the upper bound of the range reported by Maoz and Shayer (1987) for this variable.

Third, the level of cognitive imbalance is strikingly high. Because of the high level of conceptual interdependence, the unfolding of the adjacency matrices and their eventual integration into the **CON** matrix transforms ambiguous causal relations (such as $\oplus$ and $\ominus$) into inconsistent causal paths. The substantive implication of this is that Kissinger's speech conveys a high awareness of the value tradeoffs entailed in US detente policy. That is, some important values are sacrificed for the sake of attaining other desirable goals. The avoidance of inconsistent causal paths in Kissinger's argumentation would render the interpretation of his belief system, as expressed by the detente speech, as far more simplistic and straightforward than it actually was. Kissinger would have appeared to be unequivocally more committed to detente than one would expect given the structural analysis of the speech.

4.8.5 Comparing operational codes and cognitive mapping approaches

Gallhofer, Saris, and Melman (1986) provide an initial comparison of different approaches to text analysis with a focus on the methodological aspect of these approaches, and with an emphasis on how each approach draws inferences from a given text. The following discussion emphasizes the *what* in the logical inference process, and is limited to the two approaches illustrated above. Briefly, operational code analysis and cognitive mapping approaches differ from one another on a number of counts. First, operational code analysis is primarily concerned with the *substantive contents* of an individual or

133

collective belief system. It asks essentially two questions. (*a*) What are the beliefs expressed by a person or a collective body with respect to a given range of problems? (Ideally, the range of problems should be as broad as possible if one is interested in inferring the general and basic beliefs of the organism under analysis.) (*b*) How can one relate these specific beliefs to a more general class of belief-types indicating personality structures that are generalizable across individuals and situations? These questions suggest that the interest of the operational code analyst lie in making inferences from a specific content of beliefs – that might differ drastically from case to case and from one individual to another – to a general typology of beliefs that seems to be characteristic of fundamental personality traits.

The version of cognitive mapping developed in this chapter focuses strictly on the inference of structural organization of belief systems in terms of cognitive complexity. While cognitive mapping approaches may afford answers to the same questions raised by operational code analysis, and are certainly capable of developing inferences from the substantive content of a belief system, this was not done here. Rather, the purpose was to derive aspects of belief structure in a manner that is not intuitively obvious and to infer from these aspects to levels of an important personality trait: cognitive complexity.

Second, the unit of analysis in both approaches is a statement (a sentence or phrase) rather than single words. Both approaches are concerned with beliefs as whole, rather than with specific components thereof.[12] The fundamental difference between these approaches lies in the relative precision of the inferences that can be drawn from each. Operational code analysis requires matching philosophical and instrumental beliefs with those that can be typically expected from different types of personality traits. For example, Walker (1983) attempted to infer Need for Power, Need for Achievement and Need for Affiliation from written statements by matching expressed beliefs with expected ones given each of these personality traits. Such inferences are subject to error as a person's views may exhibit less than perfect match with a given operational code type or a given personality trait. As the study of Kissinger suggests, the expressed beliefs in the detente speech can be seen as consistent with more than one of the types developed by George and Holsti. Walker's eventual determination of the operational code type of Henry Kissinger relied upon his modal belief based on a

---

[12] Other approaches attempting to systematically derive similar personality traits focus exclusively on the nature of words or expressions used by decision makers as indicators of such traits. See for example Hermann (1980).

frequency count of belief types. But such an inference is qualitative in nature. Belief Type **E** was only slightly more frequent than other belief types in the detente speech. This suggests that individuals may vary in terms of the degree they match a certain belief type even if the modal belief expressed by them is of the same type. On the other hand, the inferences drawn from the cognitive mapping measures developed here are quantitative with respect to each of the dimensions of cognitive complexity. This allows for a more reliable comparison among individuals, one which is less sensitive to: (*a*) the subjective interpretation of the researcher/coder, and (*b*) to degrees of fit between a set of expressed beliefs and an expected one given a personality trait.

Third, as Maoz and Shayer (1987) argued, analysts confront a host of problems when attempting to infer personality traits that operate on a subconscious level from written or oral addresses which are subject to conscious manipulation by the decision maker. Inferences based on the content of beliefs may be biased in that they will not be based on sincere beliefs, but rather on an image decision makers wish to convey to their audience or readership. The fact that the measures of cognitive complexity developed herein are based on an exploration of non-obvious logical implications of such beliefs may make the inferential process more reliable. As Maoz and Shayer showed, there is a significant difference between consciously manipulable beliefs and their complex logical implications even in the context of the same statement.

Finally, operational code classifications were developed specifically for a foreign policy context. The six-fold typology is based on notions which are typical to international politics (the sources of conflict: individuals, states, and the international system). This narrows the applicability of the approach to a specific set of issue areas. It would be extremely difficult to infer operational code types from statements on domestic politics, economics, and social issues. Cognitive mapping techniques are not prone to these limitations due to their focus on the structure of causal assertions regardless of the specific context in which they were made.

All this is not meant to suggest that one approach is superior to another. Rather, the two approaches seem to be complementary in that they serve different purposes. The present section explores some of the differences and similarities between them, but the comparison is far from comprehensive. The major point is that, depending on the goal of the researcher, one approach might be more suitable than another.

135

4.9 FORMAL STRUCTURES OF DECISION MAKING BODIES

Role-related variables serve to link individual perceptions of stress and ambiguity into collectively-shared perceptions of decisional stress and ambiguity.[13] The object of this section is to outline the process by which features of individual definitions of the situation are transformed into collective definitions. This will be done by analyzing some determinants of formal group structures.

Collective decision making bodies operating in a political context can be viewed as systems of individuals characterized by a formal hierarchy and by an informal structure. The formal hierarchy is defined by the distribution of roles in terms of rank, expertise, and responsibility. The informal aspects of the group structure can be seen in terms of the relations among individuals and their preferences. Since we have yet to discuss the process by which individual preferences are formed, the discussion at this point will be restricted to the formal aspects of group structure. In chapter 6 I will analyze the informal aspects of group structure and examine the effects of both types of group structure on collective decision making.

A useful analogy for explicating the nature of the problem involved in determining formal group structures is that of weighted voting bodies. Contrary to unweighted voting bodies in which every individual (or bloc of individuals) has the same number of votes, in weighted voting bodies the number of votes varies across individuals (or blocs). The logic underlying weighted voting bodies is that the formal voting resources of various individuals or blocs should be a function of some attributes of the system that are represented by the group. For example, proportional representation assemblies assign weights (proportion of seats) to parties in accordance with the electoral support such parties have in the population. City councils assign weights to borough representatives in proportion to the relative size of the population in each borough. The same logic underlies the apportionment of seats in the US House of Representatives. Weights are then designed to reflect some criteria of representation. They suggest that different individuals should have different impact on group decisions.

Political leaders participating in collective choice processes repre-

---

[13] This conception of "role-related variables" is drastically different from that offered by Walker (1987). Walker, following Holsti (1970), focuses on roles as substantive perceptions of a state's tasks and positions given a situation. What follows here is a discussion of the status, responsibilities, and functions of an individual in a governmental bureaucracy.

sent different organizations with stakes in, and resources necessary for, the implementation of national decisions. The formal structure of the decision making group reflects the importance, expertise, and resources of these organizations. How are these attributes of the various organizations reflected in a quantitative assessment of group structure?[14] To answer this question we must consider three variables that are seen as essential determinants of the relative authority of individuals in groups. These variables are hierarchical rank, expertise, and organizational resources. Hierarchical rank is the formal status of an individual within the political hierarchy. The study of organizational hierarchies normally employs pyramidal diagrams to create ordinary-level rank differentiation among officials. An example of such a diagram is given in figure 4.14.[15]

This diagram can be converted into a rank order of formal status, in which the highest-ranked official gets a score which is not larger than the number of participants in the group. If two individuals occupy the same rank in the hierarchy, they are given the same score. Note that this diagram depicts an ordinal scale. It does not tell us by how much the president's role is more important than that of the National Security Adviser in the conduct of foreign and security affairs. The rank structure of groups is fairly fixed within political systems. That is to say, such diagrams are fairly stable over time and across different administrations. Thus, we can depict the ordinal ranks of individuals by a set $\mathbf{H} = [h_1, h_2, \ldots, h_n]$ where each element h_i denotes the rank of individual i, and – given the ordinal nature of this set – we have $1 \leq h_i \leq n$ for all $i \in N$ (where N is the number of group participants).

Expertise is a context-dependent variable. It is defined as the degree of knowledge an individual has on the problem at hand. Actual ranking of individuals on this variable would vary over policy problems. For example, if the problem at hand is of a primarily military nature, individuals with a military profession or background will be assigned higher expertise ranks than those with little or no military expertise. Likewise, if the problem is seen to possess important financial aspects, members with business and financial responsibilities will be given relatively higher ranks than others whose background and responsibilities are not directly associated with such aspects.

[14] A distinction must be made between decisional resources and decisional power. Decisional resources are defined in terms of role, expertise, and responsibility. Decisional power – to be discussed in chapter 6 – depends to a large extent on individual preferences.

[15] See George (1980: 145–168) for a discussion of different models of presidential advisory systems in the post Second World War era.

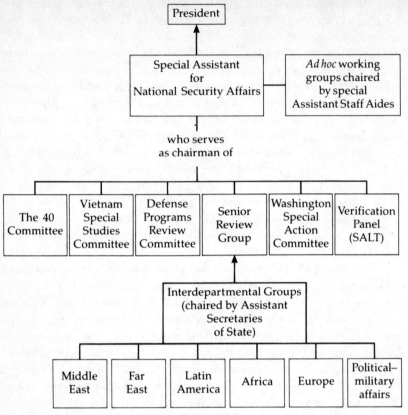

Source: George (1980:156). Printed with permission of author and publisher.

Rank order of formal hierarchy

Individual	Rank
President	1
National Security Adviser	2
Cabinet ministers in various policy groups	3
Assistant Secretaries of State	4
Others	5,6...

Figure 4.14 Foreign and security affairs hierarchy in the United States: the Nixon Administration

Decision problems with multiple dimensions pose a severe problem of determining expertise-related ranks. However, in such cases, the number of ties among individual participants will be larger than in decisions with few or single dimensions. The rank order of individual participants in terms of expertise is denoted by a set $E = [e_1, e_2, \ldots, e_n]$ where $1 \leq e_i \leq n$ is the expertise rank of individual $i \in N$.

138

a. General structure

	H	E	R
1	h_1	e_1	r_1
2	h_2	e_2	r_2
3	h_3	e_3	r_3
.	...	...	...
i	h_i	e_i	r_i
.	...	...	...
$n-1$	h_{n-1}	e_{n-1}	r_{n-1}
	h_n	e_n	r_n

b. Hypothetical example

	H	E	R
1	1	3	4
2	2	1	3
3	2	2	1
4	4	5	5
5	5	5	4

Figure 4.15 Rank-order matrix of individual scores on three dimensions of formal authority

The third variable that helps determine formal individual authority is the control over organizational resources. Two types of resources are seen as crucial in the context of political decision making: informational and implementative capacity. The director of the CIA, for example, has considerable informational resources but controls relatively few implementative resources. The treasury secretary possesses relatively few informational resources concerning foreign and security affairs, but has at his or her disposal considerable implementative capacity. In this case, ranks of organizational resources would vary according to the issue-area into which the decision problem falls. Multiple-issue cases may also present problems of determining organizational resource rankings of individuals. Assuming that a procedure is available for determining ranks for individual participants in terms of the organizational resources at their disposal,[16] we can denote the rankings of individuals on this dimension by the set

[16] Given the fact that we are interested only in ordinal ranks, and that ties between or among individuals are allowed, this need not pose a severe obstacle. Analysts must be warned, however, against retrospective rankings of individual participants on any of these dimensions. The best method one could use in attempting to rank individual

$\mathbf{R} = [r_1, r_2, \ldots, r_n]$ where r_i is the organizational resource ranking of individual $i \in N$, and $1 \le r_i \le n$, as before.

Taken together, the rankings of individuals on these variables can be presented by a matrix of order $n \times 3$. This matrix, denoted $\mathbf{T}$ has the ranking of the individuals in the group on all three dimensions of formal authority. Figure 4.15 depicts, first, a general $\mathbf{T}$ matrix of n individuals and, second, a hypothetical example of the authority ranking of five individuals on the three dimensions. Note that in the hypothetical example, the rankings of individuals on dimension $\mathbf{H}$ is a weak, that is, there is a tie between individuals 2 and 3. This implies that individuals 2 and 3 have the same hierarchical rank. On the other hand, the ranking of individuals on the other two dimensions is strict; each individual occupies a distinct rank, sharing it with no other individual. As stated above, both strict and weak rankings are perfectly reasonable and do not create any significant problems in the derivation of the formal authority index.

The next step in the process is to determine the relative importance of the three dimensions of formal authority. In general, the relative importance of these dimensions varies over political systems, as well as over governments within the same political system. For example, the hierarchical rank dimension will be of primary importance in traditional and totalitarian systems, whereas expertise and resource aspects of formal authority will be of higher (if not predominant) importance in bureaucratic and relatively open systems. Even within the same political system, the relative importance of these dimensions may change from one administration to another. For example, during the Rabin government in Israel (1974–1977), all three dimensions of formal authority had nearly the same relative importance. During the first Begin government (1977–1981), the relative importance of hierarchical rank increased slightly, whereas the resource dimension lost some of its importance. Expertise was still important as long as Dayan and Weizman were in the government, but its relative importance declined after they had resigned. During the second Begin Government (1981–1983), hierarchical rank became a predominantly strong determinant of formal authority, largely at the expense of the other two dimensions.

As was the case with the ranking of individuals on the various

particpants in terms of these three dimensions is to determine *a priori* a set of ranks on each of these dimensions with respect to a given set of issue-areas. For example, knowing the composition of a certain government, analysts can rank individuals on the three dimensions without reference to any given problem. These rankings can be applied to specific subgroups that are formed for the purpose of solving specific decisional problems.

a. General form

$$\mathbf{T} \times \mathbf{W^*} = \mathbf{Q}$$

	H	E	R		H	E	R		H	E	R
1	h_1	e_1	r_1	H	w_h	0	0	1	h_1w_1	e_1w_e	r_1w_r
.	..	..	..						..	..	..
i	h_i	e_i	r_i	E	0	w_e	0	i	h_iw_h	e_iw_e	r_iw_r
.	..	..	..						..	..	..
n	h_n	e_n	r_n	R	0	0	w_r	n	h_nw_h	e_nw_e	r_nw_r

b. Hypothetical example (Taken from figure 4.15)

$$\mathbf{T} \times \mathbf{W^*} = \mathbf{Q}$$

	H	E	R		.H	E			H	E	R
1	1	3	4	H	3	0	0	1	3	6	4
2	2	1	3					2	6	2	3
3	2	2	1	E	0	2	0	3	6	4	1
4	4	5	5					4	12	10	5
5	5	4	4	R	0	0	1	5	15	8	4

Figure 4.16 Integrated ranks of individuals on formal authority dimensions

dimensions of formal authority, determining the relative importance of these dimensions is a delicate task involving a fair degree of subjective assessment on the nature of policy making in different political contexts. Here we will assume that these relative importance scores are given and denote them by a set $\mathbf{W^*} = [w_j, w_e, w_r]$ where the subscripts stand for the three dimensions of formal authority. In order to combine the ranking of individuals on each of the three dimensions of formal authority with the relative importance weights of these dimensions, we construct a 3×3 diagonal matrix $\mathbf{W^*}$ (that is, a matrix with zeros in all of its non-diagonal entries and the relative importance scores in its main diagonal).

The combination of $\mathbf{T}$ and $\mathbf{W^*}$ is obtained by $\mathbf{Q} = \mathbf{TW^*}$, as shown in figure 4.16.

The bottom part of figure 4.16 represents a hypothetical example in which matrix $\mathbf{T}$ is as in the bottom part of figure 4.15. Note that the relative importance scores lead to different rank dispersions of individuals. Although the ranks in each of the columns in matrix $\mathbf{Q}$ are identical to those in matrix $\mathbf{T}$ (which is self-evident given that ordinal scales are invariant with respect to multiplication by a constant), the differences between ranks vary significantly across the two matrices.

The final stage in the procedure of determining relative authority scores in decision making bodies follows closely a method developed

a. General form

	1	2	...	i	...	
1	1	a_{12}	...	a_{1i}	...	a_{1n}
2	$1/a_{12}$	1	...	$1/a_{2i}$	...	$1/a_{2n}$
.	...	...	...	...	...	
i	$1/a_{1i}$	$1/a_{2i}$	...	1	...	$1/a_{ni}$
.	...	...	...	...	...	
n	$1/a_{1n}$	$1/a_{2n}$	...	$1/a_{in}$ ·	...	1

b. Hypothetical example (derived from figure 4.16)

		1	2	3	4	5
	1	1	0.57	0.57	$u^\dagger$	5.33
	2	1.75	1	1	u	8.5
A =	3	1.75	1	1	u	u
	4	0	0	0	1	0.57
	5	0.19	0.19	0	1.75	1

† u = undefined (zero denominator)

Figure 4.17 Authority ratio matrix

by Rapoport, Felsenthal, and Maoz (1988a) as a normative standard for seat-allocation in proportional representation systems. The first object of this method is to determine a matrix of preference ratios, **A**. (This label is predicated on preference ranking of parties by voters.) In order to determine this matrix, we define a variable d_{ij}^k as follows:

$$d_{ij}^k = \begin{cases} q_j^k - q_i^k + 1 & \text{if} \quad q_i^k \leq q_j^k \\ 0 & \text{if} \quad q_i^k > q_j^k \end{cases} \tag{4.26}$$

where q_i^k and q_j^k are the ranks of any two individuals i and j on dimension k. The authority ratio a_{ij} for individuals i and j is given by

$$a_{ij} = \sum_{k=1}^{3} \frac{d_{ij}^k}{d_{ji}^k} \tag{4.27}$$

Thus matrix **A** is a $n \times n$ reciprocal matrix (3×3 in our case) with entries a_{ij}, and the following properties: (*i*) it has non-negative entries in all of its cells, (*ii*) its main diagonal consists of ones, and (*iii*) $a_{ij} = 1/a_{ji}$ throughout. Figure 4.17 depicts a typical **A** matrix as well as one generated from matrix **Q** in figure 4.16. Note that several entries derived from figure 4.16 are undefined. This means that their denominator is zero. This is so because individuals 1, 2, and 3 strictly outrank individual 4 on all three dimensions of formal authority. This creates an apparent problem, but – as we shall soon discover – one that has a fairly simple solution. Matrix **A** serves as the basic data for the derivation of the formal authority structure of the group. Specifically, we wish to derive from this matrix a vector **F** of order $n \times 1$ whose entries represent the formal authority scores of the n individuals, and which has the following properties.

1 $\displaystyle\sum_{i=1}^{n} f_i = 1$

2 $\dfrac{f_i}{f_j} \approx a_{ij}, \quad i, j \in N$

Rapoport, Felsenthal, and Maoz (1988a) employ a scaling method due to Saaty (1977, 1980) known as the *eigenvalue procedure* which preforms – among other things – precisely this function.[17] Rapoport *et al.* show that their approach satisfies a number of desirable properties of social choice schemes. Of these, three are worth mentioning in our context.

First, the proposed solution weakly preserves the social preference order. In our context this implies that, given a matrix **T** (and regardless of the diagonal elements in matrix **W***), if individual i outranks individual j on more dimensions of formal authority than individual j outranks individual i, then $f_i \geq f_j$. That is to say, the formal authority score of individual i would be at least as high as that of individual j. The implication of this is that the final authority ranks of individuals will not be inverted by the method in a manner that is substantively unwarranted given their initial rankings.

Second, if a strict Pareto-superior individual exists, he or she is assigned all the weights of formal authority, and all other individuals are assigned no weights at all. Likewise, if a strict Pareto-inferior individual exists, he or she is assigned no score at all (or rather, a score of zero). In our context, a strict Pareto-superior individual is one who outranks all other individuals on all dimensions of formal authority. This occurs if there exists an individual i for whom $a_{ji} = 0$ for all $j \in N$. In other words, a Pareto-superior individual is one who possesses the highest hierarchical rank, the highest degree of expertise, and the highest control over organizational resources. It seems only logical in this event to assume that such an individual will have an absolute

---

[17] In addition to forming the desired vector of authority scores, the eigenvalue procedure provides a measure of consistency in the **A** matrix that allows assessment of the degree to which the results are interpretable. In our case, consistency is of secondary importance. See Rapoport *et al.* (1988a) for a discussion of these issues.

ability to determine the final decisional outcome of the group. A Pareto-inferior individual j is outranked by another individual, say i, on all three dimensions of formal authority, or if there exists at least one i for which $a_{ji} = 0$. A Pareto-inferior individual is, thus, a "dummy-participant," one whose preference and arguments will be always out-weighted by at least one other group participants who outranks the former on all three dimensions of formal authority.

In the example given in fig. 4.17 we do not have a strict Pareto-superior individual, but we do have two Pareto-inferior ones. Individual 4 is outranked by individuals 1, 2, and 3 on all the three dimensions of formal authority, and individual 5 is outranked by individual 3 on the same three dimensions. As I pointed out above, this feature of the example given in figure 4.17 creates some problems regarding the determination of the **F** vector. To resolve these problems, another property of the eigenvalue procedure must be invoked. This property is that if, for some reason, an individual who was initially a member of the group is either ejected from the final decision process, or volunta-rily absents himself or herself from the group deliberations, the weights of all other individuals will be unaffected. Formally,

$$\mathbf{F} = [f_1, f_2, \ldots, f_n \,|\, \mathbf{A}_n] \quad \text{and} \quad \mathbf{F}' = [f'_1, f'_2, \ldots, f'_{n-1} \,|\, \mathbf{A}'_{(n-1)}]$$

Then: $\dfrac{f_i}{f_j} = \dfrac{f'_i}{f'_j}$, $\quad \displaystyle\sum_{i=1}^{n} f_i = \sum_{i=1}^{n-1} f'_i = 1.$

In our case this implies that if individuals 4 and 5 who are Pareto-inferior are assigned exogenously $f_4 = 0$ and $f_5 = 0$, then the formal authority scores of individuals 1, 2, and 3 in figure 4.17 will be unaffected with respect to one another. Specifically, given the Pareto-inferior status of the former individuls, and given our assumption that they constitute "dummy participants", we can reduce matrix **A** in figure 4.17b to a 3×3 matrix consisting only of the three upper rows and the three leftmost columns, assigning to individuals 4 and 5 zero authority scores in vector **F**. This operation will leave the relative authority scores of the three individuals unaffected with respect to one another. In this numerical example, the eigenvalue procedure yields a vector of authority scores consisting of: $f_1 = 0.222$, $f_2 = 0.389$, $f = 0.389$, $f_4 = 0$, $f_5 = 0$.

Having devised a measure of formal authority in collective decision making bodies, we can now formalize group-level perceptions of stress and situational ambiguity as a function of individual-level perceptions of these inputs. Simply stated, a group-level perception of a given decisional input is defined as a weighted average of the individual

144

perceptions of that input, where the weights are the formal authority scores of the group participants. Formally, group-level decisional stress is given by

$$GS = \sum_{i=1}^{n} DS_i f_i \qquad (4.28)$$

and group-level perception of situational ambiguity is given by

$$GA = \sum_{i=1}^{n} SA_i f_i \qquad (4.29)$$

where DS_i is the degree of decisional stress experienced by individual i, SA_i is the degree of situational ambiguity experienced by i, f_i is the formal hierarchy score of that individual, and n is the number of group participants.

To exemplify the determination of formal authority and of the transformation of the individual-level perceptions of decisional stress and situational ambiguity into group-level perceptions, we consider again the Entebbe decision process (Maoz, 1981).

4.9.1 Formal group structure in the Rabin government

Maoz (1981: 702) pointed out that group decision processes during the Entebbe crisis took place in two settings: The first was the small ministerial team appointed by the government to cope with the crisis (consisting of Prime Minister Rabin, Defense Minister Peres, Foreign Minister Allon, Transportation Minister Ya'acoby, and Minister without Portfolio, Gallili). The second setting consisted of the entire cabinet. The following analysis is restricted to the three principal ministers, Rabin, Peres, and Allon, for two reasons. One is that we do not have sufficient data for determining the scores of the various decisional inputs for other individuals. Second, it could be easily shown that in terms of our measure of formal authority, each of the other individuals was Pareto-inferior to at least one of the principal decision makers.

Since the method used here differs from the one applied by Maoz (1981) to determine relative influence scores, the final authority scores would be inevitably different from those given by Maoz (1981: 703). Yet, the extent to which these two sets of results differ from one another would reflect the reliability of the two procedures and suggest the extent to which a set of results is sensitive to the method used to derive authority (or influence) scores. Figure 4.18 depicts the ranking of the three principal decision makers on the various dimensions of

	T			×		**W***			=		**Q**		
	H	E	R			H	E	R			H	E	R
Rabin	1	1	3		H	1	0	0		Rabin	1	1.2	3.6
Peres	2	2	1		E	0	1.2	0		Peres	2	2.4	1.2
Allon	2	2.4	2.4		R	0	0	1.2		Allon	2	2.4	2.4

Figure 4.18 Formal authority scores in the Rabin government

formal authority (matrix **T**), the relative weights of these dimensions (matrix **W***), and the weighted ranks of the decision makers by these weights (matrix **Q**).

The hierarchical ranking of the three decision makers in matrix **T** seems self-explanatory. However, some comments must be made regarding their ranking on the organizational resources dimensions. As a Defense Minister, Peres controlled more informational and implementative resources than both Rabin and Allon, not only during the consideration of the military rescue operation, but even prior to that. Since all the intelligence reports regarding the identity of the hijackers and the route of the hijacked plane passed through defense ministry channels, Peres was on top of every bit of information recieved prior to either of the other two decision makers. In the actual consideration of alternatives Peres had the implementative resources of the IDF. He also had, under his command, quite a few individuals who had had close personal ties to Idi Amin. Allon, as a Foreign Minister, controlled informational and implementative resources through Israeli diplomatic missions in the states who were included in the hijackers' demands (France, Germany, and Kenya). Thus his second highest rank on this dimension.

Another comment concerns the importance weighting of the three dimensions of formal authority. Rabin's government had a formal structure that was in some way atypical compared to other Israeli cabinets. This is reflected in the relative weights of the three dimensions. The technocratic nature of this government is reflected in the slightly higher weight given to the expertise and organizational resources dimensions compared to the formal rank dimension. Figure 4.19 shows the authority ratios matrix **A** and the resulting formal authority vector **F**.

The results of this figure closely resemble those obtained by Maoz (1981) in the original Entebbe study, suggesting that both a highly interpretive approach (used in the original study) and the more rigorous approach taken here yield similar results. However, more

	A				F	
	Rabin	Peres	Allon			
Rabin	1	1.24	1.91		Rabin	0.425
Peres	0.81	1	1.91		Peres	0.368
Allon	0.52	0.52	1		Allon	0.206

Group stress = GS = 0.075
Group Ambiguity = GA = 0.640
Diversity of Formal Group Structure = GD = 0.951

Comparison of Current Authority Scores with Maoz (1981)

	Rabin	Peres	Allon	Average Squared Deviation
Current	0.425	0.368	0.206	
				0.001
Maoz (1981)	0.410	0.340	0.250	

Figure 4.19 Formal authority weights in the Entebbe crisis

important is the fact that the **F** vector indicates a highly egalitarian distribution of formal authority in Rabin's government, hence the transformation of decisional stress and situational ambiguity to group-level perceptions regresses toward their mean values (in our case, that of Allon's perceptions).

4.10 SUMMARY AND CONCLUSION

This chapter has presented a formal analysis of the exogenous inputs affecting decision making processes at the individual level of analysis. It has also discussed how individual perceptions of situational factors are transformed into collective perceptions, taking into account the formal structure of the collective decision making body. The main motivation of this discussion was threefold. First, the need to integrate a diverse set of decisional inputs into composite concepts in order to reduce the number of exogenous variables commonly employed in decision making analyses. The main effort in this context has centered around the definition of decisional stress as a function of motivational factors (perceived threat and perceived opportunities) and of practical constraints (time pressure). Second, the need to formally define and measure decisional inputs which had been either treated in qualitative terms (e.g., formal authority which tapped

147

role-related inputs), or had been measured inadequately (e.g., the measurement of cognitive complexity in terms of belief content rather than in terms of belief structure). Third, this chapter represents a first cut into the development of a model linking individual-level perceptions of various inputs to the collective perception thereof.

Although the substantive basis for this formal analysis was laid out in chapter 3, this chapter has presented material which is quite novel and quite complex. The connection between the formal definitions of the various concepts and the structure and content of decision making is not readily apparent in the foregoing discussion. Nor should it be at this point because we have not yet explored the features of decision making processes. However, the analyses performed above serve several aims. First, I have attempted to show that there is a sound mathematical basis for the treatment of the inputs of decision making, and that such a treatment might provide important insights into pre-decisional processes such as diagnosis of decisional problems and definitions of the situation. Second, the logic underlying the establishment of these measures is extendible to the systematic measurement and analysis of various aspects of decision making processes at the individual choice level and at the collective decision level. This will be demonstrated in chapter 6 after we review the variants of decisional processes in chapter 5. Indeed, the methodology used to formalize the inputs of decision making will be used to formalize the content and structure of decision making processes.

5 MODELS OF THE DECISION PROCESS

5.1 INTRODUCTION

This chapter reviews the second generation of foreign policy research. It discusses the strategies that individuals and groups employ when dealing with problems in terms of the decisional stages outlined in chapter 2. The discussion will be both integrative and critical. I will attempt to group together rather diverse theoretical and empirical studies into general models of foreign policy decision making, and connect levels of analysis in the process. This will enable assessment of the progress made during the second generation of foreign policy research.

The shift from research focusing on identification of inputs and the construction of input-output frameworks toward theories of decision making processes is attributable to a profound dissatisfaction with the nature and quality of the scholarly product of the former research orientation. The key assumption of the second stage of decision making research was that the proliferation of decisional inputs and the apparent failure to integrate these inputs was due to a failure to explore how various inputs affected the strategies of selecting and appraising alternatives by decision makers. If decision making processes are described rigorously, one could construct more valid hypotheses regarding the effects of various inputs on the process, thereby narrowing down the rather long laundry-list of exogenous factors. Alternatively, one can group together seemingly distinct inputs in a coherent fashion insofar as such inputs are presumed to affect stages of the decision process. For example, note the subsequent devaluation of the surprise factor as a potent situational input to crisis decision making or the integration of threat perception and time pressure in terms of decisional stress (Hermann, 1972; Brecher, 1977; Holsti and George, 1975; Janis and Mann, 1977). The effects of various inputs, such as belief systems, stress, and ambiguity on foreign policy decisions can be understood only within the limitations they impose on the process of choice.

The focus on the features of decision making processes allows clarification of the linkages between distinct units of analysis. Foreign policy frameworks that fail to distinguish between individual choice behavior and collective decision making cannot assess reliably the relative potency of various inputs of foreign policy behavior even if they make room for notions concerning types of decision making structures. Open, developed, and large societies may still display considerable variation with respect to the ways decision making processes are organized. For example, the foreign policy structure that emerged during the Nixon–Kissinger administration was considerably more centralized than the one which characterized the Truman administration. Presumably, the relative potency of idiosyncratic factors on the policy outputs of the Nixon administration was more pronounced than the relative potency of idiosyncratic factors on the policy outputs of the Truman administration. Sweeping generalizations about the input-output relations in foreign policy settings prior to a more thorough understanding of the content and structure of decision processes may yield misleading results and erroneous inferences.

Finally, the epistemological rationale of the process specification stage had a policy-relevant facet as well. Political scientists can and should advise decision makers regarding the ways in which foreign policy making could be improved. The role of policy-relevant theory, as George and Smoke (1974: 618–619) put it, is one which "accepts the values of the constitutionally-authorized decision makers and offers contingent advice: 'if you want to accomplish x, do y in your policy.'" Such a theory includes "the important task of value-clarification . . . [it] should indeed urge that the objectives of current or contemplated policy be redefined to make them more consistent with . . . the more final goals of decision makers." In short, foreign policy analysts should help national leaders to make better decisions. But this task cannot be accomplished by an exposition of decisional input-output frameworks. Most of the important decision making inputs are politically non-manipulable. A decision making analyst has no control over the personality structure of decision makers or over their belief systems. Decisional stress arises from changes in the external environment over which neither the decision maker nor the decision theorist has a significant control.

Yet, decision theorists can aid decision makers to cope with foreign policy problems under conditions of acute stress, thereby modifying the disruptive effects of stress on choice behavior. They can warn decision makers against the risks entailed in routine and non-innovative handling of problems under seemingly non-stressful circumstances.

Decision theorists can advocate certain organizational structures of foreign policy making which would balance personality-related impediments to good policies.

However, to accomplish all these tasks, a better understanding of the ways in which national leaders cope with foreign policy problems is essential for the identification of biases, pitfalls, and fallacies that characterize decision making processes, and for the establishment of sound evaluative criteria of "good" decisions. To make policy prescriptions, decision theorists must be able to penetrate through the idiosyncratic considerations of foreign policy elites and uncover the mechanisms which guide their choices. These mechanisms ought to be placed within solid theoretical confines that can be assessed and analyzed empirically. In short, what is needed is a good theory of decision making whose central element is the process dynamics.

Given these considerations, the focus of second generation scholars was on the construction of conceptual models that provide theoretical approximations of the content and structure of decision processes at various levels of analysis. The wide variety of theoretical and empirical studies that developed during this stage can be grouped into four seemingly distinct models of the decision process. Each of these models addresses multiple levels of analysis including individual choice, organizational behavior, and collective decision making. This chapter will thoroughly review and evaluate each of these models.

5.2 THE ANALYTIC (RATIONAL) MODEL OF DECISION

The essential idea of this model is that human behavior is fundamentally logical, guided by reason and chracterized by an outstanding capacity to solve problems in a complex and rational fashion. Rationality is defined as *an ability to find the best (or most efficient) means under a given set of circumstances to accomplish a specified set of objectives*. This definition contains several implicit elements. First, rational decision makers must be able to comprehend the fundamental nature of the problem they confront and the characteristics of the environment in which this problem arises. Second, decision makers must be able to delineate a broad set of means that are potentially suitable for coping with the problem. A thorough understanding of the environmental context enables decision makers to determine the feasibility and relevance of various courses of action as potential solutions. Third, rational decision makers must be able to explicitly articulate their goals and values and establish priorities and preferences for these goals. They must analyze the relationships among various goals, to determine whether such goals are conflicting or complementary, and to evaluate all courses of action on the various goals. Fourth, decision makers must be able to make tradeoffs among conflicting goals, that is, to find optimal mixtures of goals that are achievable within the set of circumstances in which they operate. Fifth, rational decision makers must establish preferences to the various options in terms of the perceived ability of each option to maximize the set of relevant goals. Finally, decision makers must determine their preferences on the basis of the likelihood of realizing these goals given each of the options. Rational decision makers will choose that course of action which offers the greatest prospect of accomplishing the best mixture of goals. Thus the famous expected utility maximization principle.

Von Neuman and Morgenstern (1947), who laid down the foundations of expected utility theory, formulated a set of axioms which, if satisfied, lead to the expected utility maximization principles. The importance of these axioms lies in the kind of logic they impose on behavior, a logic that – as we shall soon see – does not always conform to reality, but which nonetheless imposes a set of constraints on decision making behavior.

1   The first axiom states that if there exists a set of outcomes [**O**], that is, states of affairs, and if x and y are two of these outcomes, then the uncertain occurrence of these outcomes is also a part of this set. To illustrate, consider a case where an unidentified airplane has entered a state's airspace. Suppose further that a decision maker thinks that this event can be broken down into the following possibilities: (a) this is a military plane belonging to our enemy, (b) this is a civilian airplane belonging to a friendly state which has deviated from its normal route', and (c) this is a civilian airplane belonging to our enemy which has entered our airspace by mistake. Given this set of outcomes, the first axiom states that assigning a certain probability distribution to the outcomes is perfectly logical. So that if outcomes a through c are part of the general set of outcomes **O**, then outcome a with a probability p, outcome b with a probability q, outcome c with a probability of $1 - (p + q)$ are also part of the general set **O**. This axiom is the *closure* property of rationality.

2   The *preference–indifference* axiom states that a decision maker must be able to establish a preference-or-indifference relation between any two outcomes with respect to some property. Stated differently, if a and b are two outcomes, and if the property on which they are

evaluated is the intelligence damage that can be caused due to detection of some secret military installations located in the area where the unidentified airplane is flying, then the decision maker must be able to determine whether outcome a is preferred to outcome b, outcome b is preferred to outcome a, or both outcomes are ranked the same with respect to that property. The second axiom is of paramount importance due to its implications regarding preference orderings of outcomes. These implications are as follows (Coombs, Dawes, and Tversky, 1970: 122–124).

a *Reflexivity* $x \geqslant x$ means that outcome x is at least as good as itself.

b *Connectivity* Either $x \geqslant y$ or $y \geqslant x$, or both. This means that there must exist a preference ordering between any two outcomes.

c *Transitivity* If $x > y$ and $y > z$, then $x > z$ this means that if one outcome is preferred to a second outcome, and the second outcome is preferred to the third one, then the first outcome must be preferred to the third.[1]

The implication of this axiom is that decision makers must be *consistent* in their preference ordering of outcomes, and that this consistency is a prime guidance for rational choice.

The last four axioms refer to the relationship between preference ordering of outcomes under conditions of certainty and the preference ordering of the same outcomes under conditions of risk or of uncertainty.

3 The *reducibility* axiom states that compound structuring of outcomes can be reduced to simpler outcomes. For example, suppose that in our unidentified airplane example the decision maker structures the problem in the form depicted in figure 5.1. The third axiom states that the gamble between these outcomes can be stated in a compound form and in a reduced form and that these two forms are logically equivalent. The compound form states that $(a, q; b)p; c)$ and the reduced form is $(a, pq; b); c$. The meaning of it is that in the reduced form, outcome a is obtained with probability of pq, outcome b is obtained with probability $p(1 - q)$ and outcome c is obtained with probability $1 - p$. Thus the complex gamble in figure 5.1 can be reduced to a simple gamble by integrating the probability terms. As Coombs *et al.* (1970: 124) put it, "axiom 3 asserts, in effect, that the preferences depend only on the final outcomes and their probabilities and not on the

---

[1] The transitivity of preferences principle looks like an outright trivia. However, Arrow (1963) has shown that this principle can be easily violated in a society of rational – and hence transitive – individuals. Moreover, Allais (1953) demonstrated empirically how people tend to violate this principle even if they are well familiar with it.

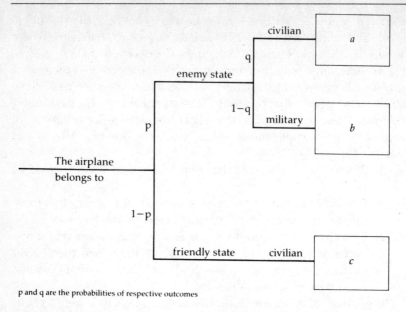

p and q are the probabilities of respective outcomes

Figure 5.1 A compound structure of the airplane problem

process by which they are obtained. Normatively, it makes perfect sense to suppose that the choices are invariant with respect to rearrangements of the gambling procedure, as long as the outcomes and their probabilities remain unchanged."

4   The *substitutability principle* states that if a decision maker is indifferent between two outcomes, then she will be indifferent between gambles in which these outcomes are interchanged. If one is indifferent between two job offers x and y, then one must be indifferent between getting job x with probability p (and job y with probability $1 - p$) and the case in which one gets job y with probability p (and job x with probability $1 - p$).

5   This axiom states that if a decision maker strictly prefers outcome x to outcome y, under conditions of risk or uncertainty, then she will: (*i*) strictly prefer a certainty of x over any probabilistic gamble involving x and y, and (*ii*) strictly prefer any gamble involving x and y over a certainty of outcome y. To illustrate this axiom consider the considerations underlying the Russian Roulette game. Suppose that the outcomes involved in this case are (1) staying alive, and (2) dying. Assuming that outcome (1) can be plausibly regarded as better than outcome (2), then if one faces the choice between playing and not playing Russian Roulette, which entails a probabilistic gamble of outcomes (1) and (2), one must choose not to enter this game.

154

Concomitantly if one is forced under gunpoint to play the game (in which case if she stays alive following the game, her life is spared), she must prefer playing the game than being killed not playing it.[2]

6   This axiom states that if one has a strict preference ordering of outcomes such that x is preferred to y and y is preferred to z, then there exists a probability that renders the decision maker indifferent between y and a gamble involving x and z. This is important for the derivation of continuous utility functions that are based on the notion of indifference between certain outcomes and probabilistic gambles. For example, assume that one prefers attending a class in which all students are certain to get A grades over a class in which all students are certain to get B grades, and prefers the B class over one in which all students are certain to get C grades. If that is the case, then a teacher can make every student indifferent between attending the B class and attending a class in which he or she could get A grade with probability p and C with probability $1 - p$. Of course, the value of p will differ from one student to another, but the point of axiom six is that a real valued p which is greater than zero but smaller than one, will exist for every rational student.

This allows the derivation of utility function for outcomes with unknown metrics, as follows:[3]

Axiom 6 states:

1   If $A > B > C$, then
2   there exists a probability p for which $B \sim (A, p; C)$.

Assume that for a certain person $p = 0.5$. Then according to the axiom, $B \sim (A, 0.5; C)$. Hence we can define U_B as follows:

$$U_B = 0.5U_A + 0.5U_C \qquad (5.1)$$

Now suppose that the grade of $A+$ is preferred to A such that $A \sim (A+, 0.75; B)$, then

$$U_A = 0.75U_{A+} + 0.25U_B \qquad (5.2)$$

Without loss of generality, we can set $U_{A+} = 1$ and $U_C = 0$. Then we have for equation (5.2)

---

[2] Yet can people who voluntarily enter the game be characterized as rational? The answer is decidedly positive and not inconsistent with axiom 5. If such an extreme form of gambling is seen to add excitement to life, then the gamble $(x, p; y)$ can be strictly preferred to either x or y. In this case, outcomes will be reformulated as follows (1) staying alive after playing the game, (2) staying alive without playing the game, and (3) dying in the course of the game. Thus $(O_1, p; O_2) > O_2$ (Coombs *et al.* 1970: 124–125).

[3] This little mathematical digression is optional and can be skipped without loss. It is useful, however, for the understanding of quantitative derivation of utilities.

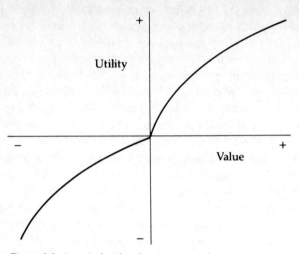

Figure 5.2 A typical utility function

$$U_A = 0.75 + 0.25U_B$$

Substituting for U_B in equation (5.1) yields

$$U_A = 0.75 + 0.25(0.5U_A + 0)$$
$$U_A = 0.75 + 0.125U_A$$
$$U_A = 0.875$$

Inserting this value in equation (5.1) yields $U_B = 0.438$

Thus, the utility function of this student with respect to ordinal grades is as follows:

$$U_{A+} = 1.0$$

$$U_A = 0.857$$

$$U_B = 0.438$$

$$U_C = 0$$

This is shown graphically in figure 5.2:

Taken together, these axioms lead to the important expected utility theorem which is the cornerstone of all rational choice models. This theorem is composed of two major points.

1 An outcome x is as least as good as outcome y if and only if the utility that a person assigns to x is at least as high as the utility assigned to outcome y. Stated formally: $x \geqslant y$ iff $U_x \geqslant U_y$.
2 The utility of a probabilistic gamble between two outcomes in which one is derived with probability p and the other with the

complementary probability is equal to the sum of these outcomes weighted by their respective probabilities. Stated formally: $EU(x, p; y) = pU_x + (1-p)U_y$.

This is the basic abstract logic that underlines rational decision making. Its major implication is that a rational decision maker will always select the alternative which entails – given one's utility function – the highest subjective expected utility (SEU).

It must be emphasized, however, that the maximization of subjective expected utility is the end result of a process – not its sole characteristic. In order to reach that result, one must satisfy several practical requirements, in addition to the logical axioms, without which the SEU principle may be inadmissible. It is this set of requirements which is the focus of the analytic model of foreign policy decision making.

5.2.1 Individual choice

5.2.1.1 *Diagnosis*

Formal theories of rational choice rarely treat systematically this stage of the decision process, which is usually referred to as "definition of the situation." However, less formally, the keyword describing analytic diagnosis is "comprehensive." A certain environmental cue in the external or internal environment of the decision-maker's state is apt to generate multiple – sometimes mutually exclusive – interpretations.[4] An analytic decision maker acknowledges this complexity and is aware of the difficulty of arriving at, and the risks entailed in, clear-cut interpretations. Hence, decision makers must develop several alternative interpretations of the decisional problem and of the conditions that led to its emergence. Each such definition of the situation must be contrasted against the information available to decision makers to determine its relative plausibility, thereby allowing them to narrow down the range of diagnoses. Consider medical diagnosis. Certain symptoms that are readily detectable by a physician may be consistent with more than one illness. A rational physician is consistently faced by uncertainty during diagnosis. This uncertainty forces the physician to suggest a plausible set of medical problems consistent with these symptoms, and then to run various tests to narrow down this set. These tests are done to uncover

---

[4] Recall that the need for decision arises where there exists a perceived discrepancy between an ideal or expected state of affairs and an observed one (Burnstein and Berbaum, 1983: 536).

unobservable symptoms and to relate all types of symptoms to each of the alternative diagnoses.

In foreign policy settings, diagnosis normally involves interpretations of the underlying intentions of other actors, specifically such intentions which may have been related to observable acts. These acts are seen as symptoms of a decision problem. Thus comprehensive diagnosis entails a dissemination of the potential causes of these symptoms. For example, the 1962 installation of Soviet nuclear missiles in Cuba necessitated diagnosis of the underlying Soviet intentions. The Executive Committee appointed by President Kennedy developed several competing interpretations of Soviet motives and analyzed the extent to which a given explanation was consistent with the known facts.

The first interpretation was that the Soviets placed the missiles in Cuba as a bargaining chip designed to insure subsequent withdrawal of American missiles from Turkey. This hypothesis was consistent with frequent Soviet statements regarding the threat posed by American missiles in Turkey to Soviet security. The geo-political similarity between Cuba and Turkey seemed compelling as supporting evidence. Yet, several facts worked against this explanation. First, the US had already publicly committed itself to the withdrawal of the Turkish missile bases. Second, the installation of Intermediate Range Ballistic Missiles (IRBMs) in addition to Medium Range Ballistic Missiles (MRBMs) suggested that the nature and scope of nuclear power in Cuba was disproportionate to that required for bargaining purposes. Moreover, the construction of expensive sites for these missiles in Cuba indicated that the Soviets intended them to stay rather than to be traded.

The last point undermined several other interpretations of Soviet motives. The scope and nature of the missiles in Cuba were inconsistent with hypotheses regarding an attempt to divert attention from the Berlin issue, or to use the missiles as a deterrent against another American attempt at overthrowing the Castro regime, or even as a typical tactic of cold war politics. Therefore, in spite of several weaknesses, the only viable explanation of Soviet motives was a strategic one. The placement of nuclear weapons in Cuba was a relatively cheap way of significantly increasing Soviet strategic power. Soviet apparent inferiority in Intercontinental Ballistic Missiles (ICBMs) and in Submarine-Launched Ballistic Missiles (SLBMs) posed a very difficult problem. It required a huge investment in development of such systems; a burden that the Soviet economy could not afford. Even if such a project proved economically feasible, its completion would have required a long time and the extent to which it would narrow the missile gap (given that US weapon acquisition and development plans were not paralyzed in the meantime) was a big question.

Thus, placing missiles in Cuba was believed to have doubled instantly Soviet strategic power at relatively low cost. At the very least it could serve as a temporary substitute for the missing Soviet ICBMs and SLBMs. As Schlesinger (1965: 796) suggests, this interpretation was not fool-proof. Yet, its relative plausibility was higher than that of other interpretations of Soviet motives (Allison, 1971: 40–56).

Comprehensive screening of the evidence in light of multiple diagnoses allows exploration of various facets of the decision problem while at the same time minimizes risks of simplification, premature closure, and erroneous conclusions. Such a process of diagnosis widens the search for policy options in response to the perceived challenge. One of the reasons for this is that since not all definitions of the situations are necessarily exclusive in the sense that acceptance of one explanation leads to outright rejection of other explanations, the search for policy options is expanded to such options which address multiple interpretations of the problem. The perception of multiple interpretations of the decision problem requires looking for responses that would prove adequate for more than one purpose. True, not all events that stimulate decision require multiple interpretations; yet the analytic model warns against simplistic diagnoses even when the problem at hand is perceived – on the face of it – as readily interpretable.

5.2.1.2 Search

Formal theories of rational decision making are preoccupied with the selection of optimal alternatives from a predetermined set of feasible courses of actions. The question of how one determines this set of available alternatives is largely unanswered. The general prescription of the analytic model is that decision makers explore all available courses of action that may eventually lead to a solution of the decision problem. Yet, how many alternatives should one explore? What are the criteria for including alternatives into the set which is evaluated? How does the cost of exploring additional alternatives affect the size of the feasible set of policies? Some of the criteria guiding analytic search processes can be indirectly inferred from available research.

Criteria determining the nature of explored options. The analytic model argues that a rational decision maker would employ two essential criteria to determine which options ought to be explored: *relevance* and

159

feasibility. The options considered by the decision maker should have a direct bearing on the issues at stake. Options which are remotely connected to the resolution of the problem would be ejected out of the plausible set of responses. The relevance criterion is admittedly ambivalent, and it may cause differences in subjective interpretation. For example, during the Cuban missile crisis, when the blockade option was suggested as a plausible response to the Soviet threat, opponents of this option required its rejection on the grounds of irrelevance. They argued that the imposition of the blockade would not bring about the removal of the missiles that had already been installed; all it could do, at best, was to prevent the Soviets from shipping more missiles into Cuba (Allison, 1971: 61). Likewise, one of the more persuasive arguments against a secret approach to Castro with the purpose of indicating him to demand that the Soviets withdraw the missiles from Cuba was that "the missiles belonged to the Soviet Union. Soviet troops transported, constructed, guarded and controlled the missiles. Their removal would thus depend on a Soviet decision" (Allison, 1971: 59).

During the May–June 1967 crisis, similar irrelevance claims were made by members of the General staff of the Israeli Defense Forces against the political leadership. The latter's tendency was to delay military action against Egypt pending the organization of an international flotilla by the US. The argument made by members of the General Staff was that the issue at stake was the failure of Israeli deterrence, not merely the blockade of the Tiran Straits. Israel could not re-establish its credibility by relying on other countries. It had to demonstrate directly to the Egyptians that violation of the status quo would be severely punished. Even the success of an international flotilla in bringing about the opening of the straits could not accomplish this goal (Stein and Tanter, 1980; Brecher, 1975: 397).

The feasibility criterion suggests that decision makers restrict themselves to consideration of those options which are within their immediate reach, or at least to such options that can be rendered feasible with minimal effort. Feasibility is not to be confused with effectiveness. When searching for policy options, the initial problem is not whether a given option has a high probability of accomplishing desirable goals or of preventing undesirable outcomes. Rather, feasibility-related considerations concern the availability of resources for its execution. The selection of a new car necessitates potential buyers to consider options within their budget limitations. In the Entebbe crisis, the General Staff of the IDF reviewed numerous types of rescue operations. Most of these plans, however, were eliminated on the

160

grounds of in feasibility. The airborne operation that was eventually carried out also had initial feasibility-related problems. For example, it was unclear whether the C-130 planes could cover the 400 miles distance to Uganda at low-level altitude to evade radar detection. Only when their ability to do so was firmly established did this option become a serious candidate for consideration (Maoz, 1981: 691).

Both criteria serve as systematic screening devices of options and are imposed to render the subsequent stages of the decision process highly efficient. Their importance rests on the premise that several practical restrictions must be placed on analytic search. These restrictions are necessary due to limitations on the cognitive capacity of humans and due to the situational bounds (time, resources) within which decision makers operate. However, it must be emphasized that, contrary to other models to be discussed below, these criteria do not create systematic biases in the sense that they impose illogical constraints on the search process.

Quantitative limitations. How many alternatives should rational individuals explore? After employing the relevance and feasibility criteria as qualitative screening devices, individuals may still be faced with an unmanageable number of plausible candidates for decision. The question then is whether they should invest their resources in a careful consideration of all the unelimated options? The clue to this dilemma lies in what rational choice models term as the "rational price of information" or "opportunity cost" (Raiffa, 1968: 27–33; Lave and March, 1975: 113–123). The exploration of additional alternatives is worthwhile as long as their subjective expected utility exceeds the costs in time and mental resources required for their dissemination. But how would one know *a priori* whether this is the case?

The simple answer is that there is no way one could know before the full implications of such alternatives have been analyzed. The available methodology for determining the rational value of information requires first computing its expected utility, and then subtracting its marginal cost. But then the value of information is a *post hoc* derivative.

Where do options come from? What are the sources from which one derives potential responses to the decisional problem? The analytic model of decision is ambiguous on this issue as well. Yet, given the previous discussion of the diagnosis stage it is obvious that the alternative definitions of the situation suggest potential courses of action which may be pursued in response to the implications they yield. Another potential source for option retrieval is the individual's past experience with similar choice problems, or one's ability to innovate.

Despite its apparent ambiguity on the foregoing issues, the analytic model contains a set of strict criteria for the structuring of the decision problem once alternatives have been identified. First, the survey of alternatives is done in a parallel manner. Each alternative is assigned a set of mutually exclusive and logically exhaustive outcomes. The structuring of the decision problem is completed when this process is done for all relevant and feasible alternatives. At this point, decision makers have a "model-design", or a "road-map" from which they can select a preferred course of action.

Before going into a discussion of the revision stage, several clarifications of the concepts employed thus far seem to be in order. First, I have used the terms alternatives and options interchangeably throughout this section. However, these terms are not synonymous. An alternative refers to a course of action which excludes other courses of actions. Going to a movie theater or staying at home to watch TV at a given evening are alternative courses of actions. Options, on the other hand, are non-exclusive courses of action. Several options can be pursued in parallel at any given point in time. For example, during the Cuban missile crisis the idea to present the issue of the Soviet missiles in the UN Security Council did not exclude other measures (Allison, 1971: 58–59). Likewise, the Blockade was deemed flexible in the sense that it allowed time for exploring other avenues towards the resolution of the crisis (Allison, 1971: 61). This distinction is important because it draws attention to the complexity of structuring decision problems. In outlining the various avenues toward the solution of the choice problem, the analytic decision maker must consider which of them are optional and which are alternative solutions. Formal models of rational choice require specification of alternatives because options are in some ways more difficult to cope with.

Another distinction which is important in this context is that between alternatives (or options) and outcomes. The former refer to events which are caused by and are under the control of the chooser. The latter refer to "states of the world," that is, to events which are beyond the immediate control of the decision maker. Some outcomes are completely independent of the selection of an alternative by the decision maker. For example, whether it would rain or not is unrelated to my decision to carry (or not to carry) an umbrella to work. Sometimes, however, outcomes may be partly conditioned by our decision though never completely so. An opponent's decision to attack us (or to hold back) might be dependent upon our previous decision to mobilize (or not to mobilize) reserves. Yet, as far as we are concerned, we have only partial control over an enemy's attack through our mobilization decision; an attack would also depend on what the opponent expects to gain or lose in each type of circumstances.

The analytic differentiation between alternatives and outcomes is tremendously important in the course of the search stage. A rational decision maker must be highly aware of the factual implications of each possible choice. The logical constraints of mutual exclusiveness and logical exhaustiveness on outcomes are a prerequisite for expected utility maximization. No such constraints are imposed, however, on the specification of actions under the decision maker's control, although in most cases the decision problems boil down eventually to choice among alternatives because the options pursued simultaneously exhaust themselves at some point.

5.2.1.3 Revision

The analytic revision process resembles the methodology of sampling. The problem confronting decision makers once the structure of the choice problem has been specified is how to employ the information at their disposal in order to make reliable judgments regarding the likelihood of occurrence of the various outcomes. Since most foreign policy decisions are made under conditions of uncertainty in which subjective likelihood estimates are necessary, the question is whether one could make optimal use of large amounts of information so that estimates would be as close to reality as possible. Furthermore, are there ways of updating or correcting estimates on the basis of additional information which arrives during the decision process?

Let us now consider the problem of sampling. A researcher who wishes to analyze some attributes or behavioral patterns of a given population (such as intended voting) most often conducts the research only on a small subset of this population due to practical constraints (time, money, ability to reach all members of the population, etc.). The selection of the appropriate sample is based upon two major considerations: the samples size and its representativeness. The selection of the sample size is based on the size of the population and on the degree of precision required from the sample. While the size of the population is a constant factor and must be treated as given, the degree of required precision varies with the specific needs of the researcher. In general, however, the higher the degree of precision required, the larger the sample relative to the population. Sampling theory provides straightforward algorithms for determination of the sample size.

Representation is more difficult to achieve on purely statistical grounds. Representativeness refers to the similarity between the sample and the entire population on a number of predetermined properties. Statistical theory states that if all possible random samples are drawn from a population, then they would, on average, provide an accurate and unbiased representation of that population. However, there is no guarantee that any one specific sample will also be representative. Thus, the researcher must make sure that there will be a good correspondence between the sample and the population on a number of properties that are considered crucial for the questions under investigation. One such approach to sampling is the stratified sampling technique. This technique involves specifying one or more variables that are seen as important determinants of the dependent variable and finding the distributions of these variables in the population. The population is broken down into strata consisting of the categories of these variables and the random sampling is done on each stratum. This ensures that the distribution of these variables in the sample would be proportional to their distribution in the population. For example, if one conducts an election poll, and has reason to believe that voting behavior is affected by level of education and by religious affiliation, then the distribution of education and religious groups in the sample must be identical to their distribution in the population. To accomplish this, the population is broken down into a joint education-religion distribution, and the researcher selects from each category a number of people proportional to the relative frequency of this category in the population.

Decision makers in foreign policy settings are confronted with an enormous amount of task-related information. Practical and cognitive constraints necessitate selection of only a small portion of the information for determining the likelihood of various outcomes. So they too are engaged in some sort of intuitive sampling, and the considerations underlying statistical sampling apply to rational revision as well. The analytic model argues that a rational decision maker will make reliable and unbiased estimates to the extent that: a) the relationship between the considered set of facts and the available one is such that sampling (or selection) errors would be minimized, and b) the body of considered facts would be representative of the entire body of facts. Analytic decision makers must be intuitive statisticians in their approach to judgment of uncertain events.

How could this be accomplished? The kind of information decision makers have in foreign poicy settings can be divided conceptually into two types: background information and current indicators. Background information consists of knowledge accumulated over time with respect to the general set of foreign policy issues a state normally confronts. It is analogous to information concerning the underlying attributes of a certain population in our sample example. Current indicators refer to the specific characteristics of the problem under consideration which may or may not be in line with the background information. Some researchers (e.g., Ben Zvi, 1976; Lanir, 1983) have made a similar distinction between strategic assumptions and tactical information in the context of national intelligence estimates.

Optimal revision is one in which likelihood estimates are based upon a balanced and systematic combination of both types of information. In order to make a reliable and unbiased estimate regarding the likelihood of a certain outcome, analytic decision makers must avoid several logical pitfalls. First, they must avoid exclusive reliance on one type of information at the expense of the other. They must avoid the temptation to disregard or discredit current indicators to the extent that they disconfirm or cast doubt upon prior assumptions. They must also avoid the polar tendency to ignore completely background information, assuming that the specific decision problem, as represented by current indicators, creates an entirely new situation.

Second, decision makers must be aware that most of the information in foreign policy settings is not unidirectional, and that information which is seemingly consistent with one hypothesis can be also consistent with another hypothesis. Taken together, these considerations suggest that the analytic decision maker should adopt the underlying logic of Bayesian analysis. In this type of analysis, likelihood estimates are based on a combination of: (a) the prior likelihood ratio which is generated from background information, and (b) the conditional probability ratio based on the perceived fit between a given set of current indicators and at least two alternative hypotheses. Each of these informational components receives an equal weight in the estimation process but the final outcome will depend upon their relative diagnosticity. If the prior probability ratio points strongly to one direction, current indicators must be highly discrepant (that is, strongly diagnostic of another hypothesis) for drastic revision of prior estimates. If, on the other hand, prior estimates reflect considerable uncertainty with regard to the relative likelihood of future outcomes, current indicators are highly instrumental in determining final esti-

165

mates even if their diagnosticity is relatively low. In the case of medical diagnosis, analytic revision consists of combining the medical history of the patient with the symptoms of the specific medical problem which makes diagnosis more reliable.

The revision stage includes updating likelihood estimates on the basis of incoming information during the decision process. Here, sensitivity to current indicators is of paramount importance. The logic of Bayesian analysis is particularly suitable to this kind of mental operation because it requires decision makers to constantly incorporate latter information into their prior estimates. The revision process during the Entebbe crisis (Maoz, 1981) illustrates how analytic decision makers go about intuitively estimating future events under conditions of uncertainty. One of the first things that Israeli decision makers had to figure out was the credibility of the hijackers' threat to execute hostages if their demands were not met. The key to such an estimate was the identity of the hijackers. It was established fairly early in the crisis that the Air France aircraft was hijacked by a mixed group of Palestinians from the Vadie Haddad organization and Germans from the Baader–Meinhoff group, and that the entire operation was directly controlled by Haddad. This fact led Israeli decision makers to look at past operations of this group such as the take-over of the American embassy in Khartoum in 1974, and combining it with current reports concerning the treatment of hostages by the hijackers allowed them to derive reliable estimates of the severity of the threat.

5.2.1.4 Evaluation

Analytic evaluation of alternatives involves several distinct steps. First the decision maker specifies all dimensions of value on which alternatives are to be evaluated. The goals that were perceived as potentially affected by the decision problem at the diagnosis stage are operationalized in terms of specific criteria which enable decision makers to establish preferences for various outcomes. Second, decision makers weigh these value dimensions in terms of perceived importance. This step is essential in cases where the accomplishment of one goal comes at the expense of other goals. This is an intrinsic characteristic of foreign policy problems, known as value tradeoffs. Trading among multiple and most incompatible goals requires specification of an "exchange rate" among non-equivalent goals such as national security and social welfare and finding optimal mixtures of goals within the array of available alternatives. The relative importance weights assigned to the various goals enable the decision maker to construct an integrated utility function. Third, decision makers scale the array of outcomes stemming from the various alternatives on each of these value dimensions separately. Each of the identified outcomes receives a separate (partial) utility score on each value dimension. Finally, partial utilities are weighted by the respective relative importance score of the value-dimensions to create an integrated utility. At this step, all the potential costs and benefits stemming from the occurrence of a certain outcome are incorporated into the overall utility evaluation.

These operations are both psychologically and methodologically difficult for a number of reasons. First, the number of value dimensions deemed relevant for the evaluation of policy problems may be exceedingly large. Some of those value-dimensions may not be applicable to all outcomes. For example, one of the arguments for the blockade during the Cuban missile crisis was that it provided the parties time for bargaining. However, the time for bargaining as an evaluative criterion was clearly irrelevant for the surgical air-strike or invasion alternatives. Second, in most foreign policy problems, establishing relative importance weights or exchange rates among value dimensions is an extremely complex and risky business. Consider the philosophical and ethical problems involved in determining the monetary value of human life, or in converting national security values into social welfare values. Third, it is extremely difficult to scale outcomes in terms of utility with non-quantitative values. If my favorite car color is red and I must choose between a beige and a purple car, which would I prefer? Given these problems, integration of partial utilities across value dimensions is extremely complex primarily because it involves complicated calculations.

5.2.1.5 Choice

The choice principle used by analytic decision makers is expected utility maximization. Each alternative is assigned an expected utility score by summing across all outcome utilities multiplied by their respective probabilities. The alternative with the highest expected utility is the one to be selected.

Some general principles of the analytic model ought to be stated before turning to a critique of its internal logic. First, the model emphasizes relativism. Diagnosis of the decision problem is done in terms of multiple interpretations. The plausibility of each is determined in relation to the other available interpretations. Search for policy alternatives is conducted in relation to other available alternatives. Likelihood estimates are based on the assessment of the relative fit between a given information datum and a given outcome, keeping in mind that the same datum may also fit other mutually-exclusive outcomes, albeit with a different probability. The utilitarian evaluation of alternatives is conducted by trading-off multiple value dimensions, whereby potential benefits on some of the goals shrink when potential costs on other goals are considered. Finally, the subjective expected utility maximization principle requires that the alternative which is perceived better when compared to other alternatives should be the one selected by the decision maker.

Second, the model emphasizes comprehensiveness. All the stages of the decision process require comprehensive treatment of data. Analytic diagnosis encompasses all plausible interpretations of the decision problem; search entails exploration of multiple alternatives; revision requires complex operations of information processing; evaluation requires appraising outcomes in terms of multiple values, and so on. At each given step in the process, decision makers must have a complete outline of the problem in order to perform the necessary tasks.

Third, the analytic model imposes a high degree of order and coherent structure on the process. Each of the stages is intimately related to previous ones and strongly affects the content and structure of later stages. The completion of all tasks at any given stage is a prerequisite for the fulfillment of subsequent tasks. The choice stage is a cumulative operation based on the entire structure of data which was collected and analyzed at earlier points in the process. This strict order is what assures that decisions would indeed be optimal.

Yet, by stating that analytic decision making breeds optimal decisions, I do not imply that the consequences of analytic choice would always be positive even within the confines of values the decision maker pursues. Such consequences are not due to the procedural deficiencies of analytic decision making. Rather, adverse results may stem from the uncertain context in which foreign policy decisions are made and from cognitive and situational limitations under which political leaders operate. First, making probabilistic estimates of future events is essentially an art which entails a considerable amount of guesswork. Decision makers do not possess a crystal ball and their estimates cannot be evaluated as right or wrong. Even low likelihood events are still possible, and their occurrence at certain points in time does not render previous estimates incorrect. A decision may be disastrous because some unwanted outcome occurred. Yet analytic decision makers wish to make sure that losses will be minimized as much as possible even in such cases. Limitations on the cognitive capacities of individuals and situational constraints may render the accomplishment of comprehensive decision making practically impossible. Decision makers may err not only in making wrong estimates but also in failing to devise appropriate policy alternatives, or in failing to analyze the available ones in terms of all relevant goals. Disastrous consequences may emerge when the outcomes that actually occur adversely affect unconsidered goals, or when such outcomes suggest that another, non-considered alternative may have been better than the one that was actually selected.

Nonetheless, all problems considered, analytic decision making insures that, on average, choices which were made according to these principles would yield better results than other decision making principles.

5.2.2 Group decision making

5.2.2.1 *Group-level choice problems*

The structure and sequence of analytic decision making at the group level closely resembles the steps of individual choice described above. In fact, at a very general level, foreign policy groups can be personalized, that is, treated as if they were a single individual engaged in a problem-solving process. The treatment of groups as unitary actors can be very useful in policy analyses or in theoretical examinations of international behavior (Allison, 1971: 35–38; Bueno de Mesquita, 1981: 25–29). This view rests on fairly solid empirical foundations as groups normally diagnose problems, jointly search after and explore policy options, argue and develop likelihood estimates for future events, and so forth (Burnstein and Berbaum, 1983).

However, such views are overly simplistic in that they tend to obscure the effects of interpersonal interaction on the structure and outcomes of collective choice. A basic characteristic of collective choice processes is that participants enter the process with pre-established policy preferences. These represent conclusions of the individual choice processes, not only with respect to the most preferred policy option but also with regard to the way other options are ranked. Individuals may differ in terms of the options that were identified and considered at earlier stages or in their utility functions. Thus, the preference orderings of policy options in the group will vary across individual participants. Options that were considered by one individual may not have been identified at all by others. Thus, the collective decision making problem concerns the aggregation or transformation of the different preference orderings of individuals into a single group-level preference ordering of the various policy options. Though some similarities exist, the internal logic of the group-level solution differs markedly from the simple expected utility maximization principle in the case of individual choice.

Group decision making is a bargaining process in which individual preferences are changed, modified, and aggregated in the course of the discussion and interpersonal interaction among participants. The mechanisms that transform the initial distribution of individual policy preferences consist of two factors: rules of interaction, and rules of preference-aggregation. The rules of interaction determine the structure of the discussion and argumentation among group members. The rules of preference aggregation determine the final scheme used to transform individual preferences into collective choices.

5.2.2.2 *Rules of group interaction*

Decision making groups can be seen as settings in which information and arguments are exchanged among members in the course of discussion. Studies of group decision making have found a significant group-induced shift in individual preferences. But why would rational individuals whose preferences are a logical conclusion of a comprehensive individual decision making process change their minds in group settings? The reason is that in the course of group discussion individuals are exposed to information and considerations that were not part of their original choice process, and this exposure alters the structure and content of their original decision. For example, individual estimates of future events may change drastically once new data is introduced by other participants. Options with which individuals were unfamiliar may be brought up, or additional evaluation criteria of options may persuade individuals to switch preferences. Group-induced shifts in individual preferences may be a result of persuasive argumentation and information exchange. But what are the factors that determine whether a given individual is likely to be persuaded by this argumentation to change preferences? Under what circumstances is an individual likely to be instrumental in persuading other members into changing their minds?

Four factors determine the relative influence of an individual on the group: the degree of conviction, the comprehensiveness of the individual's choice process, her expertise, and the pivotness of the individual's preference relative to other individuals. The degree of conviction is defined as the difference in SEU between the most preferred option and the next-to-best option. An individual who thinks that the policy option she prefers most is much better than any of the other options discussed by the group is considerably less likely to be influenced into shifting her preferences than an individual whose cross-option preference distance is relatively small. It would take a considerable effort to persuade the former into choice-shift, but only a small effort to convert the latter. Moreover, a strongly-convinced individual will work harder on influencing other individuals to adopt a particular policy because, from her perspective, all other policies are decidedly inferior.

The comprehensiveness of individual choice refers to the amount of information which was explicitly considered while generating one's preferences. A comprehensive individual choice process suggests that the decision maker was aware of all possible options, data, value-considerations and arguments for and against various policies. Thus she is unlikely to be surprised by novel arguments, additional information, or previously unconsidered options. Yet she is likely to be instrumental in conveying new information to members whose individual choice processes were less exhaustive. Most of the arguments made by other group members had been considered previously by that individual, yet the arguments made by such an individual are likely to be novel to other group members.

Expertise is the extent to which an individual is reputed to be familiar with, and experienced in, coping with problems similar to the one considered by the group. The notion of expertise refers to the prestige weight behind certain arguments. This prestige, however, does not derive from intangible attributes an individual is thought to possess, but rather from tangible skills such as knowledge and experience. Whether an argument in favor of a certain policy would be persuasive depends on who makes this argument.

The pivotness of a person's preferences taps the extent to which a person exhibits policy preferences that make her a likely candidate in a large number of coalitions, and that her addition to a certain coalition can render that coalition winning. The support such a person gives to a certain policy is deemed crucial by other groups members with similar policy preferences. People with policy preferences which are radically different from most other groups members are unlikely to be considered pivotal in that they can hardly be seen as potential candidates for coalition formation (Axelrod, 1970).

These points suggest that group-induced shifts in individual preferences are "eminently rational" (Burnstein et al., 1971; Vinokur and Burnstein, 1974). However, persuasive argumentation is but one characteristic of interpersonal interactions which emphasize substan-

171

tive shifts in individual utility functions, or some other alterations in the preference ordering of options. Another important mechanism of group interaction which does not necessarily involve reordering of individual preferences is the process of coalition formation and strategic choice.

Formally, a coalition is an agreement among two or more individuals on a joint course of action which maximizes the joint and separate utilities of its participants under a given set of circumstances. In the context of group choice, some coalitions are automatically formed once the individual preference orderings of options become known to all participants. The most natural coalitions in decision making groups consist of individuals with identical preference orderings. But the formation of such coalitions solves the group decision problem only when the group decides according to a simple majority rule and when there exists a coalition of individuals with identical preference orderings which constitutes such a majority.

Yet the fulfillment of both conditions is uncommon in foreign policy settings for a number of reasons. First, even in decision making groups whose decision rules are highly democratic under normal circumstances, such rules do not apply to crucial decision problems. For example, during the Entebbe crisis, the Israeli premier Rabin demanded that a decision on a military rescue operation must be accepted unanimously. Similarly, conviction of a person in first-degree murder must be unanimous. Moreover, in most governmental systems, simple majority-rule procedures are inapplicable constitutionally. Although the making of foreign policy decisions in the United States is a very complex process, and fairly democratic most of the time, the President is the final arbitrator of group differences and the final authority for foreign policy decisions.

Second, given the complexity of foreign policy issues and the diversity of interests represented by group participants, it is unlikely that a large enough coalition, composed of people with identical policy preferences, would form initially. The emergence of such a coalition may become more likely in the course of group discussion once the preferences of some individuals shift toward those of other individuals, but even this process is by no means guaranteed rationally. Clearly, such shifts are more difficult to accomplish than some more limited bargains among members.

Limited bargains among group members can take a variety of forms. First, a fairly natural limited coalition might be formed among members with an identical first preference. Although such members may disagree on the ranking of the other policy options, they form a natural block about their first choice. Second, a similar coalition can be formed among members whose least preferred policies are identical. These coalitions are formed for the sake of preventing or blocking undesired policies. These are "blocking coalitions." Blocking coalitions do not solve the group decision problem but they can restrict the number of candidate-policies to be considered by the group.

Perhaps the most interesting coalitions are those which involve members with similar – but not identical – preference orderings. Two or more individuals with different first but identical second preferences might agree to advocate their second best policy if they think that otherwise a third unpreferred policy is about to be adopted by the group. Such a coalition represents a mutual compromise on the best collectively-accepted policy.

Finally, a group member may be drawn into a coalition in return for some side-payments which increase the expected utility of the policy advocated by this coalition. Such a side-payment includes benefits which are not directly related to the issues under consideration. For example, a group member might be promised that in return for supporting a certain policy under consideration by the group at present, other members of the coalition will support him on some other policy issues in the future. This issue linkage process is a common bargaining device in coalition governments. Side-payments may also include material benefits to candidates such as promotions, privileged budgetary allocations in areas under the individual's responsibility and so forth. Of course, a member may be induced to join a coalition under threat of retaliation for failure to do so. Negative side-payments of this sort diminish the expected utilities of other alternatives relative to the expected utility of the one advocated by the coalition. Coalitions with side-payments involve substantive shifts in individual preferences, while coalitions among individuals with identical or similar preference orderings do not require preference change. In the latter coalition type, members make tactical compromises in order to accomplish the best under the circumstances or to prevent the worst from coming about. Such coalitions are eminently rational from the individual perspective in the sense that a rational decision maker must adapt optimally to the group-related constraints. Thus the shift occurs in tactics, not in substantive contents of the decision considerations. Side-payments, on the other hand, change the substance of the individual level rational calculus. Additional dimensions of benefits or costs are added to some options or subtracted from other options. The main postulates of the analytic model with regard to the form and content of group interaction are:

173

1   Group interaction consists of a free and unlimited flow of information and argumentation among members which leads to shifts in individual preference orderings of alternative policies either as the result of changes in the structure of the choice problem (e.g., when they become aware of the existence of previously unconsidered options), or of changes in the substantive contents of their considerations (e.g., revisions of likelihood estimates, changes in utility functions, etc.).

2   Group interaction leads to coalition formation processes. Several individuals agree on a jointly-accepted policy, which is either collectively (or both collectively and individually) the most preferred one, or is the best that can be accomplished given the different preference-orderings of options.

3   Both group-induced shifts in individual preferences and coalition-induced compromises are consistent with the axioms of rationality discussed above, and can be seen as a straightforward extension of individual level processes to the group level.

4   Thus, the procedural aspects of group decision making resemble – with the exception of the choice stage – those of individual choice. There is a comprehensive, multi-faceted diagnosis of the decision problem; comprehensive and parallel search for an exploration of options and outcomes; optimal revision and multi-attribute and integrative evaluation of options.

5.2.2.3   Rules of preference aggregation

These rules that can also be described as group decision rules are the conceptual equivalent of the principles that guide the selection of a preferred option by the individual at the choice stage. At the individual choice level we focused exclusively on the subjective expected utility maximization (SEU) principle. However, this rule is not transferable to the group level for the obvious reason that any given option may have multiple SEUs attached to it by various individuals. Decision making groups normally specify at the outset the procedures by which individual preferences are transformed into group decisions. The most conspicuous procedures of group decision are the majority rule and its variants, the consensus principle, and the tie-breaking rules. The majority rule states that the option with the largest number of supporters will become the group decision. Other options are ranked in terms of the numerical support for them by group members.

The variations on the majority rule range from simple majority to consensus. Simple majority (plurality) imposes no restrictions on the absolute number of supporters of the selected option beyond the requirement that this number be larger than the number of supporters for other policies. Another distinctive majority rule is that of absolute majority which requires that, in order to be selected, a policy must be supported by at least 51 percent of the group members. The consensus rule is an extreme form of the majority rule requiring across-the-board agreement on policy.

Tie-breaking rules – although normally not pre-established in a formal manner – are nonetheless necessary in order to resolve deadlocks. Tie-breaking may include either a random device for selecting among equally-favored policies which assures each an equal probability of being selected, or a predetermined decision that the status quo will be preserved if the group fails to agree on a new policy. For example, the national unity government in Israel during the 1984–1988 period which was split down the middle between Labor ministers and Likud ministers established a tie-breaking rule in the coalition agreement according to which in case of a deadlock the status quo would prevail. In another instance, during the 1976 Entebbe crisis, the Israeli Prime Minister, Rabin, argued that failure to reach a consensual decision on a military rescue operation implied that the previous government decision to negotiate with the hijackers would become the final policy.

Voting is the most conspicuous mechanism of preference aggregation in groups whose choice process is democratic in nature. When all has been said for or against the various policy options, and when the various coalitions have formed, the group votes for the eventual policy to be adopted. The most prevalent type of voting system is the *one-man, one-vote* rule in which a person singles out one preferred policy and votes for it.[5]

The literature on voting procedures is vast, and the topic is not of sufficient centrality to be explored here in much detail. However, three general findings of this literature are worth noting. First, the

---

[5] This policy may not be the most preferred one, as we have seen in the discussion on coalition formation. We must distinguish between two types of voting from the individual's perspective: sincere voting and strategic voting (Brams, 1976: 4–28). Sincere voting means choice that directly corresponds to the person's preferences. In the case of one-person-one-vote this means that all individuals cast a vote for their most preferred policy, irrespective of how other individuals are expected to vote, and hence of the anticipated decisional outcome. Strategic voting implies voting for the best option that could be accomplished given the anticipated votes of other individuals. In such cases individuals may vote for their second – or third–best policy if one has reason to believe that otherwise, worse policies may be selected by the group. (For discussions on the differences between sincere and sophisticated voting procedures and their implications see Farquharson, 1969; Riker and Ordeshook, 1973; Brams, 1976; Felsenthal and Maoz, 1988; Rapoport, Felsenthal, and Maoz, 1988c).

voting procedure affects the decisional outcome: a choice made by the group under one type of voting procedure would not necessarily be the same choice the group would make if it used another procedure. This finding does not assume that the group members change prefer- ences, nor is this finding dependent on whether decision makers vote sincerely or sophisticatedly. Second, no known voting procedure can be judged to be the single best in terms of its ability to select the collectively-best alternative. Third, none of the voting procedures known to us is immune to manipulation by some members of the decision making body in a manner that would advance their interests.[6]

These findings have important implications for collective decision making. First, they suggest that finding collectively-best option in group settings is not as straightforward as it is in the case of individual choice. The well known "paradox of voting" first found by the Marquis de Condorcet (1785) and formalized by Arrow (1963) states that no voting procedure based on the majority rule can convert transitive utility functions of several individuals into a transitive social utility function. This means that in some cases we cannot find an option that is the optimal group choice in a majority rule sense. This paradox suggests that "not only is there a qualitative difference between individual and social choice, but – on reflection – one should not expect otherwise" (Brams, 1976: 51).

Second, even if there exists a collectively-best alternative, there is no procedural guarantee that the choice rule would lead to its selection. Third, group interaction is a significant determinant of the ultimate outcome of the choice process not only in the sense of the processes of preference change or coalition formation among members, but also in the procedural sense. Decisions on procedures within groups can have as much impact on substantive group choices as debates over policy options.

The interdependence among group members and its behavioral implications create a much more diverse set of outcome-related predictions – some of them conspicuously counterintuitive – than individual level decision processes. Still, the analytic model's treatment of group decision making is relatively rigorous in the sense that it contains an explicit set of predictions regarding the behavioral characteristics and the substantive logic of the process whereby group decision are made.

[6] See Black (1958); Arrow (1963); Farquharson (1969); Riker and Ordeshook (1973); Gibbard (1973); Nurmi (1983); Dummett (1984); Felsenthal and Maoz (1988).

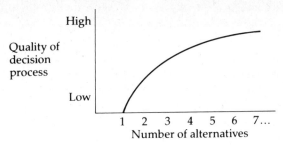

Figure 5.3 Number of alternatives explored and the quality of decision

5.2.3 General criticism of the analytic model

There are several problems with the analytic model in addition to those we have discussed thus far. First, there is a basic question concerning *degrees* of rationality. Is an individual who considers, on average, three alternatives per decision less analytic than an individual who considers four alternatives per decision, and if so by how much? Is the difference between choosing one out of three alternatives or choosing one out of four alternatives equivalent to the difference between a decision among four or a decision among five alternatives? Intuitively, it seems that the degree of analytic decision making should increase with the number of considered alternatives, with the amount of information reviewed during the revision stage, with the number of value dimensions on which alternatives are evaluated, and so forth. Yet, given cognitive and practical limitations, the more alternatives are explored, the fewer value-dimensions can be invoked for their utility-related evaluation. Concomitantly, the larger the number of possible outcomes, the more information is required for likelihood estimates, but, in fact, a smaller proportion of the available information can be actually reviewed. For example, consider one aspect of this relationship as shown in figure 5.3.

As this figure suggests, the more alternatives explored, the more analytic the decision process. But whereas the movement from a single-alternative choice process to a two-alternative choice process increases the degree of analytic decision making markedly, exploration of additional alternatives adds marginally less to the analytic quality of the decision making process. Simon (1957) notes that the marginal cost of comprehensive decision processes is such that, even if individuals were not impaired by cognitive constraints, it makes such processes less beneficial from a utilitarian point of view. The normative superiority of the analytic model may be challenged if considerably simpler decision models could produce only slightly inferior results at considerably lower investments of mental and material energies.

The second general criticism of the analytic decision making model concerns the ambiguous use of the concept of rationality. Luce and Raiffa (1957: 43) state that, at a very basic level, rationality is a tautological concept if it implies doing what is thought to be the best. This is a particularly telling point in the context of foreign policy analysis. Allison (1971: 13) suggests that it leads to backward inductive analyses of foreign policy behavior in which goals are inferred from consequent actions. If we assume that foreign policy decision makers behave according to the principles of rationality, one can explain virtually any kind of observed policy because one can always find a combination of goals that makes the observed policies logical behavioral consequences thereof. Such a perspective may render the analytic model irrefutable and hence worthless from a scientific point of view.

However, if one can postulate a set of behavioral properties that are consistent with the process of decision at each of its stages – not only with the expected utility decision rule – then the analytic model carries considerable explanatory value. The discussion of the procedural and substantive aspects of the process shows that analytic decision making is not merely a set of expected utility rules at the individual level or a set of preference-aggregation rules at the group level. Rather it is a much broader set of behavioral characteristics of which choice rules comprise but one aspect, and without which rational choice rules may be inapplicable.

5.3 THE CYBERNETIC MODEL OF DECISION

The term cybernetic decision making refers to a set of decision-related behaviors that appears in the literature under a variety of labels (bounded rationality, disjointed rationality, satisficing decision making, organizational processes and so forth). The point of departure of this model is a set of normative and empirical criticisms of the analytic model. These criticisms are:

1   The analytic model attributes to decision makers computational and information processing skills which they do not possess in reality. There is ample evidence that individuals cannot process and analyze more than seven (plus or minus two) informational items simultaneously (Miller, 1956). Contrary to the analytic model's emphasis on

comprehensive exploration of alternatives and other estimation or evaluation-related information, actual choice stages consist of very limited amounts of collected and analyzed information. The limitations are particularly important at the stage of evauation. Flesh and blood decision makers are incapable of, or severely limited in, their capacity to make complex value tradeoffs or to construct multi-attribute utility functions. Given the complexity of operations at the search and revision stages, decision makers can typically deal with no more than one value dimension at a time.

2   The parallel exploration and analysis of alternatives postulated by the analytic model is totally unrealistic. In reality, parallel exploration of options is unfeasible because options emerge sequentially. For example, the seller of a house is typically confronted with sequential price-offers, and not by an exhaustive bundle of offers from which she must select the best. Thus at each point in time the seller must decide whether to accept or turn down an offer. One can easily imagine situations where initially high offers are turned down by the seller only to discover subsequently that she must settle for lower offers because the initial buyers have found other houses. In complex choice situations, decision makers cannot create consistent utility functions for all possible outcomes even on a single-value basis. Nor can they consistently rank outcomes on an ordinal preference scale. Because the construction of utility functions and even of ordinal preference scale requires an exhaustive set (of at least $n(n-1)/2$) pairwise comparisons of outcomes, utility functions or preference scales are normally replaced by acceptability thresholds. Each outcome and each alternative are evaluated not according to interval or ordinal preferences, but rather in terms of whether they meet some pre-set level of aspiration. Levels of aspiration are not necessarily constant but rather vary as a function of the availability of alternatives at any given point in time.

This set of assumptions conveys a radically different conception of how decisions are made. The key terms of the cybernetic model of decision are *sequentiality, satisficing, incrementalism,* and *complexity reduction.* Each of these key words contrasts with the key words that characterize the analytic model: *parallelism, maximizing,* and *comprehensiveness.* The precise nature of these contrasts will be clarified by the following characterization of the cybernetic model for each of the stages of the decision making process.

5.3.1   Individual choice

5.3.1.1   *Diagnosis*

The idea that an external event provokes decision to the extent that it is discrepant from an ideal or expected state is a particularly telling point from the perspective of the cybernetic model. As long as developments in the external environment are perceived to take on routine forms, decision making becomes almost reflexive sub-conscious behavior. However, a discrepancy between observed and expected environmental cues becomes a real problem precisely because it evokes complexity of a type that decision makers wish to avoid. Yet, solving the problem by ignoring it altogether is impossible in high-stakes settings such as foreign or security affairs. Hence, individuals will seek to reduce the complexity associated with observed-expected discrepancies.

The general diagnostic rule for a cybernetic decision maker is: avoid multiple definitions of the situation. Multiple diagnoses induce num-erous uncertainties and thereby lead to complications at subsequent decisional stages that one wishes to reduce to a manageable minimum. Hence the cybernetic decision maker will search for the single most plausible definition of the situation, that is, for a characterization of the problem that seems to best tap its various features. But this prescription creates an apparent internal contradiction because the single-best diagnosis cannot be determined unless one is able to explore all available diagnoses and evaluate them in terms of relative plausibility. This, of course, is what the analytic model would argue should be done, therefore contradicting the complexity-reducing requirement.

Such an apparent contradiction is resolved by invoking a sequential diagnosis process, and by settling on a single, *reasonably satisfactory*, definition of the situation. The sequential diagnosis process consists of developing initially simple explanations of the problem and moving to more complex ones only if they fail to meet the "reasonably satisfic-ing" criterion. Axelrod (1973) asserts that this diagnosis process resembles a sequential flow-diagram used for computer programming and containing conditional feedback loops in cases where old diag-noses are deemed unsatisfactory.

In foreign policy settings, the sources of diagnosis are pre-existing analyses of contingencies that exist in bureaucratic systems. These analyses contain cue-identification and interpretation and cover a variety of anticipated events. Foreign policy decision makers have at their disposal readily available pre-established diagnoses to a variety of contingencies. The cybernetic diagnosis process thus reduces to a sequential semi-programmed review of diagnoses, the complexity of which depends to a large extent on the locus of a satisfactory interpretation in that sequence.

One of the most interesting examples of such processes is in a setting that, on the face of it, would seem least susceptible to cybernetic diagnosis: intelligence work. One of the reasons that is often cited in the literature for intelligence failures is the tendency to stick to preestablished diagnoses (Handel, 1976; Ben-Zvi, 1976; Betts, 1978). Apparently such diagnoses are perceived to be satisfactory explanations of cues that, in retrospect, are completely erroneous. For example, the massing of Egyptian and Syrian troops on Israel's borders in October 1973 was interpreted as routine maneuvers of those armies scheduled for this time of year. The assumption of Israel's intelligence was that: (a) Syria would not unilaterally attack Israel, but it may attack if Egypt joined; however, (b) Egypt would not attack Israel as long as its aerial capability was inferior to Israel's capability. Thus the new cues were interpreted in a manner that was consistent with those old assumptions. Since the military maneuvers had been expected, and seemed a reasonable explanation of the troop-movements, no competing interpretations were sought (Handel, 1976; Brecher, 1980; Lanir, 1983; Stein, 1985).

Whatever alterations in pre-established definitions of the situation do take place, these are marginal and are performed only to resolve discrepancies between the new environmental cues and the preexisting diagnoses. The main point is that decision makers normally end up with a single interpretation of the problem, that is the first satisfactory diagnosis they come by.

5.3.1.2 Search

One of the major difficulties associated with the derivation of relatively precise predictions from the cybernetic model stems from the fact that stages in this kind of decision process are hardly distinguishable from one another. This difficulty is particularly apparent at the search stage. While analytic search processes consist of a comprehensive structuring of the decision problem, and hence are conceptually equivalent to model-building in scientific research, cybernetic decision making typically merges the search for, and evaluation of, policy alternatives into a single step. Despite this difficulty, several distinct characteristics of cybernetic search processes can be spelled out.

First, cybernetic search for alternatives is sequential. Alternatives are explored and reviewed one at a time, rather than in a parallel manner. The sequential search for alternatives stems both from the need to simplify the complexity associated with simultaneous specification of multiple policies, as well as from the sequential emergence of alternatives over time.

Second – and here the distinction between the search and evaluation stages becomes somewhat blurred – the total number of explored alternatives for any given decision problem will be smaller than (or at most equal to) the number of alternatives explored by an analytic decision maker. Cybernetic decision makers explore only a subset of the set of feasible and relevant alternative whose size is a function of: (1) the availability of predetermined programs for coping with similar decisional problems, (2) the decision maker's level of aspiration, and (3) chance. Predetermined programs refer to contingency plans and Standard Operating Procedures (SOPs) that existing organizations have for dealing with routine problems and emergencies. When a decision problem is satisfactorily analyzed in terms of a pre-established diagnosis, there also exist several custom-made solutions that can be readily implemented. Decision makers explore these programs before they embark on additional search for alternatives. Hence, to the extent that such SOPs are available, the likelihood that additional alternatives will be explored tends to diminish.

The cybernetic search for alternatives continues until a satisficing policy is found. Whether or not an alternative is seen as satisfactory depends on the decision maker's level of aspiration, that is, on the extent to which acceptability thresholds are demanding. The higher the decision maker's initial level of aspiration, the more alternatives will be explored until a satisficing policy is found.

Chance is a peculiar type of determinant of the number of explored alternatives. Nonetheless, one can never tell when, in a sequential search process, a decision maker may hit upon an acceptable alternative. If one hits such an alternative early in the process, the number of explored alternatives will be small; if one fails to find a satisficing alternative, one may end up exploring a relatively large number of alternatives. Consider the following example. An urn contains n marbles out of which x marbles are red and $n-x$ marbles are black. The probability of drawing a red marble at any given draw is x/n. However, the number of draws without replacement until a red marble is found may vary between 1 and $n-x+1$. Thus, if a red marble represents an acceptable alternative, the number of explored alternatives will clearly depend on chance. Yet, the combination of the sequential search process with the level of aspiration criterion does not yield a totally indeterminate search because levels of aspiration change over time (Simon, 1957). If the seller sets a level of aspiration of 60,000 dollars for her house, but the offers she gets initially are substantially lower, she may reduce her level of aspiration gradually. This does not preclude her from accepting a high offer when one comes by. Yet it allows her to wait less time for an acceptable offer than would have been the case had she maintained constant the initial level of aspiration.

Cybernetic search for alternatives normally starts with simple alternatives and becomes progressively complex as a function of option availability, initial levels of aspirations and their adjustment over time, and, of course, as a function of chance. SOPs are sought initially because they require less effort in exploring policy implications; normally such implications are an integral part of the program. SOPs are seen as relatively less complex solutions because decision makers are familiar with them and because they contain less uncertainties than innovative policies. Only if available SOPs are deemed inadequate, do decision makers resort to search for new policies.

5.3.1.3   Revision

The magnitude of information explored and analyzed by cybernetic decision makers is a direct function of the search process. At each point in time, decision makers deal only with that information which seems relevant for the analysis of the single alternative under consideration. This sequential exploration of information considerably reduces the amount of information processed at any given point in time; yet cybernetic decision makers are still confronted by uncertainty-induced complexity. As Steinbruner (1974: 66) states,

> The cybernetic paradigm is based on the *assumption of uncertainty control*. According to this assumption, the decision maker – primarily and necessarily engaged in buffering himself against the overwhelming variety that inheres in his world – simply avoids outcome calculations . . . [C]ybernetic mechanisms which achieve uncertainty control do so by focusing the decision process on few incoming variables while eliminating entirely any serious calculation of probable outcomes. (italics in original)

Cybernetic decision makers are seen as signal detectors. The signals which they look for stem directly from their definition of the situation, and their estimation of future outcomes is based on the clarity of such signal-related information. Much like the dichotomous treatment of alternatives in terms of acceptability thresholds, information processing is done by screening out ambiguous and discrepant items in favor of clear and consistent ones. Uncertainty reduction occurs simply via the treatment of low-likelihood events as if they were entirely impossible, and high-likelihood events as being certainties. The implication of such revision processes is that likelihood estimates are rare and, by and large, dichotomous. Revision of probability estimates on the basis of incoming information tends to be conservative and incremental. The explored data represent a very small and generally biased sample of the available information, consisting primarily of data connected to few key variables deemed relevant for estimation. Contrary to the language of analytic estimators, cybernetic decision makers avoid the use of probabilistic expressions. Instead, the estimation process consists of deterministic treatment of future events.

The implication of such revision processes, it would seem, is that outcome estimates are frequently incorrect. The drive toward artificial reduction of environmental complexity and uncertainty through the focus on changes in few preselected variables must yield unrepresentative and inaccurate perceptions of reality and hence erroneous estimates. It may well be that when misestimation occurs it would be drastically off-target. But such disasters tend to be highly infrequent. If the preselected variables are important determinants of future developments – and given the fact that they constitute the net products of a vast amount of organizational knowledge and experience, they may well be good indicators – cybernetic estimations tend to be accurate most of the time. Moreover, the revision process carried out according to the sequential and fairly economical cybernetic process is considerably simpler and less demanding than the analytic probability calculation. In both types of revision processes complex outcomes are decomposed into sets of key operational indicators whose values are being traced and determined according to incoming information. Yet contrary to analytic integration of those indicators to produce final estimates, cybernetic decision makers base their estimates almost exclusively on the specific indices which are deemed immediately relevant for the prediction task.

Finally, the relationship between base-rate information and current indicators is biased toward the former. Base-rate information represents in terms of the cybernetic conception a body of knowledge that has been accumulated within organizations during a long period of time, and the fact that it remains unchanged reflects its reliability. It would be logically unsound to treat a single piece of discrepant current information as equal to base-rate information, even if it is highly diagnostic. If one must consider such information at all, it must be weighted as less important and indicative simply because it is unique.

This implies, of course, that current information will be of reduced value compared to prior information, thereby leading to generally conservative and slowly-changing estimates.

The major problem with these predictions regarding the cybernetic estimation processes is that they fail to account for drastic changes in decision makers' estimates as a result of single traumatic events. While it may be true that decision makers normally revise their estimates in a highly incremental and conservative fashion (Phillips and Edwards, 1966; Alker and Hermann, 1971), some environmental cues may result in substantial revisions of prior estimates. For example, the Soviet invasion of Afghanistan in December 1979 was, according to President Carter's statement, the single most influential event that completely transformed his views of Soviet intentions and of detente. Similarly, while the initial Egyptian troop movements on May 15–16, 1967 did not serve to change dramatically Israeli estimates regarding their intentions, the shipment of Egyptian troops from South Yemen to the Sinai peninsula had the effect of an electric shock on Israeli decision makers (Brecher, 1974: 371–377). The question is what are the limits of revision-related conservatism and what kind of cues force decision makers beyond those limits? Unfortunately, the cybernetic model contains no clear treatment of such topics, but it would seem that drastic revisions of estimates result from the complete elimination of previously held definitions of the situation, in favor of new ones.

5.3.1.4 Evaluation

As long as alternatives rise and fall sequentially until the first satisficing one is selected, evaluation processes play a minor role in the overall decision making. Yet, clearly not all decision problems render themselves to this strategy of selection. It is quite conceivable that cybernetic decision makers may be faced with multiple alternatives, each of which must be evaluated on multiple attributes, at a given point in time. The essence of free markets lies in the creation of competition among similar products and the minimization of monopolies over products, thereby creating a free-choice environment for prospective consumers. A person may try to sell his used car by advertising it in a newspaper and accepting the first "reasonable" offer, but one may also try to sell it by placing it at an auction, where one must consider simultaneous offers. From the car-buyers' perspective, going to a used-car lot forces one to consider simultaneously multiple offers.

Obviously such not unlikely situations create precisely the type of choice complexity that cybernetic decision makers wish to avoid, or at least to minimize. How would they go about evaluating multiple alternatives on several value-aspects without being overwhelmed by the complexity of the problem? Tverseky (1972) argued that the complexity of such situations can be and indeed tends to be substantially reduced by an evaluation procedure which uses both the sequential and satisficing rules in a highly simple fashion. The Elimination By Aspects (EBA) model provides a strikingly simple and robust procedure of evaluation that yields reasonable solutions to the most complex decision problems. To explicate this procedure, consider the person who wants to buy a new car. As anyone knows, the market is abundant with alternatives that differ from each other on a number of highly relevant attributes such as price, color, size, economy (gas-mileage), mechanical reliability, luxury features, and so forth. Suppose that our decision maker wishes to minimize the price paid for the car while maximizing its size, its fuel-economy, its mechanical reliability, and its built-in luxury features. Obviously these goals create complex tradeoffs between price and luxury items, between size and fuel-economy, and so forth. Yet analytic evaluation procedures that allow for optimal tradeoffs between incompatible goals are out of the question due to their enormous calculation-wise complexity. In order to avoid complex tradeoff calculations and to review as many alternatives as possible, the EBA model posits that our decision maker would proceed in the following manner. First, he will list all available alternatives. Second, he will select the most important (or restrictive) evaluation aspect and determine an acceptability threshold (or satisficing level) for that aspect. Suppose that such an aspect is the car's price, and the decision maker decides that he does not want to spend more than 15,000 dollars for the car. Third, by imposing this acceptability threshold he can at once reduce substantially the range of available alternatives: all of the cars that cost more than 15,000 dollars are eliminated from further consideration.

Yet the decision maker still faces multiple alternatives. To reduce the number of remaining alternatives, he invokes another evaluation aspect, again determining an acceptability threshold for that new aspect. Suppose that in our example that aspect is fuel economy, and our decision maker wants a car that would give him a rate of at least 17 miles per gallon. This results in the elimination of a new subset of alternatives. By this process of sequential introduction of evaluation aspects, our decision maker can progressively eliminate more and more alternatives that fail to meet the various acceptability thresholds. This elimination by aspects process is repeated until the decision maker is left with a single completely acceptable alternative. This alternative is satisfactory on each and every evaluation aspect evoked by the decision maker during the process, hence appearing to be the most reasonable choice.

This procedure is amazingly simple and robust because it allows the decision maker to review as many alternatives as he or she wishes, and to evaluate those alternatives on multiple goals without having to make even a single value tradeoff. It also overcomes many of the previously mentioned constraints on search and revision, while at the same time approximating the optimization requirement to a considerable degree. In some cases, however, this procedure may be insufficient. This happens either when decision makers run out of alternatives before they run out of evaluation criteria, or when the sequential EBA process fails to eliminate several alternatives. In such cases, it may be imperative to resort to analytic evaluation yet on a substantially reduced subset of alternatives and value-dimensions.

The sequence guiding the EBA process, and hence the nature of the satisficing alternative, will depend upon the rule by which evaluation criteria are employed. It is assumed that evaluation criteria are introduced by order of importance, where the most important aspect is employed first, and additional aspects are introduced in diminishing order of importance. This creates an interesting paradox in that relatively unimportant aspects tend to be the final determinants of actual choices. Thus two alternatives that are deemed satisfactory on all of the important evaluative aspects, will be divided into satisficing and unsatisficing ones on the basis of their performance on a relatively marginal evaluation aspect. Yet – and this is the potential suboptimality of the EBA approach – the alternative that was defined as unsatisfactory at the final elimination step, could have been much better than the satisfactory alternative on a previous and more important aspect. However, this kind of information is no longer of relevance to the decision maker.

Another rule for determining the precise sequence of aspects is by diminishing discriminatory power. One way to minimize the number of evaluations required to accomplish this goal is to start evaluation using highly discriminatory aspects. This allows the decision maker to eliminate a large number of alternatives at the outset, hence facilitating and minimizing subsequent evaluations.

5.3.1.5 *Choice*

The choice principle is a direct derivative of the EBA procedure and hence does not require much elaboration. Cybernetic decision makers either select the first alternative that is deemed satisficing, or use the EBA procedure to eliminate all nonsatisficing alternatives. Both methods lead to fairly simple choices which create very little post-decisional feelings of regret or of uncertainty.

5.3.2 Group decision making

Even if individual choice processes were cybernetic in nature, different sequences of search, different thresholds of acceptability, or different evaluation criteria may create a heterogeneous preference distribution at the group level. The need for complexity and uncertainty reduction which leads individuals to adopt the simple and semi-mechanical decision strategies posited by the cybernetic model is not sufficient to guarantee simple choices at the group level.

How does the cybernetic model treat this potential complexity in group settings? Burnstein and Berbaum (1983) offer a sequential model of group decision making which follows the basic logic of the cybernetic decision process at the individual level. This model consists of an iterative process in which the group explores one alternative at a time through the employment of the elimination by aspects procedure. Each option passes through a set of evaluative tests on a number of criteria suggested by members. If an alternative is judged to be unsatisfactory on one aspect, the group returns to the search stage, repeating the entire process until the first satisficing alternative is found. They point out that

> there is reasonably good evidence that groups design only *one completely developed custom-made solution*. Although the group selects among competing design proposals at each node or choice point, only one decision-tree is pursued to its conclusion and so only one complete solution emerges from the decision process . . . Hence, either because devising an original solution is exhausting or because their processing capacity is limited, the members of a problem solving group seem loath to develop more than one custom-designed solution.   (Burnstein and Berbaum, 1983: 542; italics in original)

This process of iterative exploration of alternatives follows closely the basic logic of organizational decision making as discussed by Cyret and March (1963), and by Janis and Mann (1977: 27–33). In contrast to analytic decision making at the group level, cybernetic processes are characterized by constrained argumentation, coalition formation processes, and limited information exchange. Group members are expected to limit their debates to dichotomous (acceptable/ unacceptable) evaluations of alternatives, or events. Information pertinent to the estimation of choice consequences will be differentiated in terms of certainty, that is, future events will be discussed in terms of whether they will occur or not. Probabilistic expressions are typically avoided. Finally, the exercise of formal or informal influence attempts by individual members is restricted to agenda manipulation both in terms of determining the sequence by which alternatives are reviewed and the sequence of the evaluation criteria.

5.3.3 Criticism of the cybernetic model

Perhaps the most important criticism of the cybernetic model is the point that this model reduces human thought processes to simple semi-mechanical rules, minimizes the ability of individuals and groups to adapt to, and comprehend, the complex features of their environment, and ignores their capacity for innovation. Moreover, the cybernetic model portrays individuals or groups as essentially responsive units which are limited in their capacity to drastically change their environment or to perceive and seize opportunities. Because they are guided by conservative predispositions, limited aspirations, and restricted capacity to plan ahead, decision makers seldom initiate significant policy changes. Foreign policy making is thus reduced to a process of incremental steps in which the best predictor of a nation's behavior at time t is its behavior at $t-1$. If that is the case, how does the cybernetic model account for the initiation of wars, for their termination, or for major realignments and systemic transformations in world politics? All these processes require some sort of deviation from marginality, a degree of foresight, and value-aspiration which are inconsistent with the cybernetic perspective.

Cybernetic decision making in foreign policy settings is said to be dominated by organizational problem solving strategies wherein diagnosis of problems and the search for, and evaluation of, policy options is heavily influenced by organizations with parochial interests and biased interpretations of overall national interests. As George (1968: 9) argues, such a model portrays the behavior and underlying considerations of such organizations in terms of "myopic, self-centered mediocrity," thereby downgrading the not infrequent cases in which such organizations display superior and innovative performance under difficult conditions.

Holsti (1976: 29–30) suggests several conditions where cybernetic decision processes do not seem to adequately reflect foreign policy making.

    1 "Nonroutine situations that require more than merely the

application of standard operating procedures and decision rules. For example, decisions to initiate or terminate major international undertakings including wars, interventions, alliances, aid programs, and the like."

2 "Decisions made at the pinnacle of the government hierarchy by leaders who are relatively free from organizational and other constraints – or who may at least define their roles in ways that enhance their latitude for choice."

3 "Long-range policy planning, a task that inherently involves considerable uncertainty, and in which conceptions of 'what is important,' 'what is likely,' 'what is desirable,' and 'what is related to what,' are likely to be at the core of the political process . . ."

4 "When the situation itself is highly ambiguous and is thus open to a variety of interpretations. Uncertainty may result from a scarcity of information; from information of low quality, or questionable authenticity; or from information that is contradictory or inconsistent with two or more significantly different interpretations, coupled with the absence of reliable means of choosing between them."

5 "Circumstances of information overload in which the decision makers are forced to use a variety of strategies (e.g., queuing, filtering, omission, reducing categories of discrimination, and the like) to cope with the problem . . ."

6 "Unanticipated events in which initial reactions are likely to reflect cognitive 'sets.'"

7 "Circumstances in which complex cognitive tasks associated with the decision making may be imparied or otherwise significantly affected by the various types of stresses that impinge upon top-ranking executives . . ."

Given this list, it may well be that Holsti implies that no major decision making process in foreign policy settings can be adequately explained by this model. Rosati (1980: 248–251) suggests that the organizational-bureaucratic model may well be limited to situations of routine problem solving that require little involvement and control by top-ranking political leaders and hence are characterized primarily by organizational maneuvering and routine handling.

5.4 THE COGNITIVE MODEL OF DECISION

The basic critique raised by cognitive theorists vis-à-vis the previous two models is that they distort the nature of actual decision processes due to their tendency to overlook or otherwise downgrade basic psychological variables that influence individual and group decision making. The problems attributed by cognitive theorists to the other two models are the following.

First, cognitive theorists share the argument made by cybernetic theorists that foreign policy decision makers lack the computational skills and the information processing capacity required for analytic decision making. However, the reasons for that are primarily psychological and only partly related to a limited cognitive capacity to process information and to make complex calculations. Some of the reasons leading individuals to employ various cognitive heuristics for simplification are motivational in nature. Moreover, the mechanisms by which this simplification of reality is accomplished have not been made entirely clear.

Second, the emotional aspects of the decision making process are ignored by both the analytic and the cybernetic models. The first model portrays decision making as a sterile and calculable process, devoid of pressures, feelings, tensions, and the like. The second model, on the other hand, describes decision making as a semi-mechanical process, much like a fairly simple computer program, driven by simple solution algorithms, again, leaving very little room for the idiosyncrasies of the individual, or to the dynamics of group interaction. Yet, problem solving, particularly in foreign policy settings, where national and personal stakes are normally very high, tends to be laden with emotions. Explanations of such processes must therefore take account of these motivational and emotive aspects.

Third, both models are very ambiguous on central issues in the decision making process. None of them really deals with the issues of where preferences come from, what are the sources of diagnoses, or what are the origins of options suggested by decision makers. (The cybernetic model identifies organizational SOPs as the main source for definitions of the situation and for option exploration, but as we have seen, SOPs are unlikely to cover novel situations, and are unlikely to be identified as adequate when major stakes are involved.) The reason for that apparent ambiguity is that the sources of interpretations of environmental cues and of option exploration are primarily psychological. They involve systems of beliefs held by individuals. The neglect of the relations between fundamental beliefs and choice processes resulted in the emphasis on the procedural aspects of individual and collective decision processes at the expense of generalizations concerning their substantive content.

Fourth, beliefs are not only important determinants of the substantive contents of choices made by high-level political leaders; they have a major impact on the procedural unfolding of individual and collective choices. For example, the quality of information explored and analyzed by decision makers is a function of the extent to which such information fits into pre-existing beliefs and expectations. Problems are analyzed by decision makers not only in the specific context they arise; they are treated in a broader context involving general concerns and aspirations which are not directly relevant to the immediate context.

5.4.1 Individual choice

5.4.1.1 *Diagnosis*

According to cognitive theorists, the diagnosis of decision problems entails affective as well as descriptive features (Janis and Mann, 1977: 45, 52–64). Decision makers evaluate and analyze environmental cues in connotative terms, that is, as promising and/or threatening situations. This kind of diagnosis is done by fitting some perceived features of the specific cues to normative beliefs derived from the decision makers' belief system. The beliefs that are invoked by the decision maker given a set of external cues determine to a large extent the nature and extent of threats and/or opportunities that will be perceived. These beliefs have therefore a major impact on the level of decisional stress experienced by decision makers.

We noted that analytic diagnosis entails parallel exploration of competing definitions of the situation and a competitive process of elimination whereby the implications of each definition of the situation are contrasted with the specific features of the problem. The cybernetic model posits a sequential diagnosis process whereby some key features of the problem are confronted with pre-set organizational contingency analysis involving institutional interpretations of similar cases. Diagnosis ends when a given interpretation of the problem is perceived as reasonably plausible. In both cases, however, decision makers are postulated to pursue a more or less critical review of the problems they confront, a review which is dominated neither by the specific features of the problem, nor by the test-criterion (be it the logical fit with a given set of interpretations or variables which are seen as critical in institutionalized interpretations).

The mechanisms that drive cognitive diagnosis are quite different, however. The most commonly used diagnosis strategy is that of *analogizing*. The implications of the problem at hand are defined in terms of the kind of past events it is perceived to resemble. For

192

example, President Truman, discussing the North Korean invasion of South Korea in 1950, wrote that this event invoked memories of the Japanese invasion of Manchuria in 1931 (Truman, 1964: 333). Yitzhak Rabin, the Israeli Prime Minister during the Entebbe crisis, recalls that the hijackers' decision to separate the non-Jewish hostages from the Jewish ones and to release the former invoked analogies of selection of Jews for execution by the Nazis (Maoz, 1981: 688).

Analogies serve to screen out competing definitions of the situation. Because the analogized past event dominates the diagnosis process, interpretations of the problem which suggest the inadequacy of an influential analogy are rejected (but the analogy is preserved). Moreover, once an analogy has been established, it defines to a large extent the connotative features of the current problem. It defines the perception of foreign actors' intentions as benevolent or malicious, it determines whether a given action is to be seen as threatening, neutral, or promising, and so forth.

Second, analogies serve as initial screening devices for option exploration, and – to a lesser extent – for evaluation processes. Past events invoked by decision makers suggest some behavioral "lessons." If the analogized event had been a disaster, options that had been employed in that case will be eliminated prior to any serious analysis. On the other hand, if the policies adopted by decision makers in the past had yielded adaptive outcomes, they become immediate candidates for further consideration. Jervis (1976: 271–279) and Janis and Mann (1977: 28–29) suggest that analogies invoked during the diagnosis stage have the effect of generating tendencies for premature closure or commitment for a certain course of action before it was adequately analyzed.

Several factors affect the kind of analogies that are typically invoked by decision makers for diagnosis of current decision stimuli.

1 *Recency*. Recent events are more likely to serve as analogies than remote ones. The cognitive limitations on recall and retrieval suggest that the human mind tends to move from the present to the past in a relatively ordered fashion. This implies that decision makers are strongly affected by memories that are relatively fresh in their minds. Only if such memories are deemed irrelevant to the problem at hand would the decision maker make a mental effort to go back into his/her memory in the process of searching for adequate analogies. Jervis (1976: 203) argues that "a person will perceive and interpret stimuli in terms of what is at the front of his mind." Although the notion of the evoked set discussed by Jervis refers to the analysis of novel problems

in terms of the immediate concerns of the decision maker, this discussion serves to illustrate the tendency to look at the stimuli as being immediately connected to the recent past.

2 *Salience*. Dramatic events that are judged to entail major historical or personal significance tend to be selected with a considerably higher frequency than routine events lacking such implications. Traumatic events of a personal or national nature tend to remain longer in a person's memory, and take precedence over more recent events of a routine nature. Dramatic events with a negative or positive connotation occupy a special place in memory. They tend to jump to the forefront of the recall process during diagnosis and would therefore become prime candidates for analogizing.

3 *Cognitive proximity*. Personal (or national) experience in a certain incident makes it a preferred candidate for analogizing relative to events of which the decision maker has only second-hand knowledge. The search for analogies proceeds from events in which the decision maker had some sort of personal involvement, through events which had affected his/her nation but in which he/she had not taken an active role, and only lastly to significant events that had not affected directly the decision maker or his/her nation (Jervis, 1976: 239–246).

4 *Similarity*. If decision makers are confronted by two or more analogies with significantly different implications for diagnosis, the analogy which seems to best resemble the case at hand would be selected eventually. Note that this factor serves as a decision rule affecting choice among competing interpretations of the current situation, and is generally taken to be a special case of cognitive diagnosis.

Both Jervis (1976: 266–270) and May (1973) argue that the most recent war seems to be an often-used analogy by decision makers in crisis situations.

Analogies have several effects on decision makers' definition of the situation. First, they serve to eliminate the necessity to base subsequent decisional stages on competing diagnoses, thereby reducing choice-complexity. Second, the lessons derived from these analogies invoke tendencies for premature elimination of some options and for premature closure on other options. Third, by generating an emotional disposition toward the current decision problem, analogies serve as a guide for reduction of cognitive conflict and tradeoff calculations.

All this implies that diagnosis processes are apt to be highly biased for several reasons. First, analogies are selected via criteria that are unrelated (or are even inversely related) to the relative frequency of such events. In fact, the criteria for analogy selection imply that the most frequently evoked analogies are low-probability events (that is, events whose historical occurrence is relatively infrequent). Hence, to the extent that history repeats itself, events that are more likely to serve as analogies are the ones that are least likely to repeat themselves.

Second, since the similarity criterion is inferior in terms of its influence on the analogizing process to other criteria, the fitting of current decision problems to past events may be biased by a small repertoire of analogies, given the elimination of more adequate analogies that fail to meet the recency, salience, or cognitive proximity criteria.

Third, the notion that success and failure repeat themselves in precisely the same form might be objectively false. In particular, the idea that policies that worked in the past would also work in the future, and that policies that failed in the past are also inadequate for future implementation create severe distortions in the subsequent stages of the decision process.

Finally, lessons from the past are largely based on events that happened. However, the normative or descriptive inferences from such events invariably include assumptions about what might have, but did not actually happen in the analogized event. For example, the lesson drawn by Western leaders from the Munich crisis is that appeasement encourages future aggression, and therefore the inferred lesson of the need to hang tough during times of crisis immediately seems to follow. Such inferred lessons are likely to be biased for several reasons. One is that it is impossible to postdict with any degree of reliability what would have happened if decision makers had behaved differently than they actually did in the past. Another source of bias is that the implied causality between the nature of the choices and the specific outcomes of the analogized events might itself be false. For example, if we assume that Chamberlain's concessions at the Munich Conference encouraged Hitler's subsequent aggression, we cannot immediately infer from that that a tough stand on Chamberlain's part would have averted it. The tendency to select options on the basis of how they performed in the past might therefore have severe shortcomings in terms of their general adequacy and – even more so – in terms of the adequacy in the specific case (Vertzberger, 1986).

5.4.1.2 Search

Two primary strategies influence the search for policy options according to cognitive theorists. The first is the learning mechanism by which lessons that are drawn from past analogies restrict the array of explored options to those that have some successful precedents in the past, or to those that are the opposite of seemingly unsuccessful precedents. The second mechanism is designed to check and minimize cognitive conflict during subsequent decisional stages. Since the learning strategy has been discussed above, I will focus on the emotional mechanism.

Janis and Mann (1977) argue that decision making processes are laden with emotions, and that one of the most important aspects of such emotions is the wish to avoid or minimize value-conflict. Value-conflict is defined as a state of incompatibility between two or more desirable (or undesirable) goals with respect to a given policy. A policy option is said to involve value-conflict if it maximizes one desirable value at the expense of another desirable value. Concomitantly, value-conflict occurs if an alternative that minimizes the prospect of an undesirable objective, maximizes – at the same time – the prospect of another undesirable objective. The classical guns–butter tradeoff is a good illustration of value-conflict.

Rational choice theorists solve this problem by finding optimal bundles of security and welfare for any given budget-constraint and any given set of utility functions for security and welfare. This is done by fitting a budget line on a set of indifference curves generated by joining the separate utility functions for the relevant values of security and welfare.[7] Cognitive theorists argue that individuals wish to avoid tradeoff calculations altogether even if this involves eventual selection of suboptimal policies. The need to reduce decisional complexity – an argument made by cybernetic theorists – is secondary to the need to reduce post-decisional stress. Thus, the need for elimination of value-conflict is primarily emotional rather than one that results from information overload.

This emotional conflict-avoiding tendency carries several implications for search processes. First, it suggests that the distinction between the search and evaluation stages is somewhat blurred. In fact, decision makers make a preliminary assessment of alternatives once they are discovered. This is done by exploring the extent of value-conflict such alternatives seem to entail. Alternatives that seem to invoke intense value-conflict are eliminated prior to any serious analysis.

Another implication of conflict-avoiding tendencies concerns conservatism in option exploration. Value conflict may arise not only from conflicting consequences of a given alternative, but also as a potential conflict between a new alternative and prior policies and commit-

7 See Lave and March (1975: ch. 5) for a non-technical illustration of this procedure.

ments (Janis and Mann, 1977). For example, Allison (1971: 193–196) reports that President Kennedy was predisposed to reject the "do nothing" alternative off-hand (and the diplomatic response as an exclusive reaction) during the Cuban missile crisis. Kennedy justified his strong disposition to decisive action on the ground that the placement of Soviet missiles in Cuba was a blunt violation of their previous promises to restrict their weapon shipments to Cuba to defensive systems. Moreover, Kennedy felt committed to strong reaction by his strong and unambiguous warnings of September 4 and 11, 1962 that the "gravest issues would arise" if the Soviets placed offensive weapons on Cuban soil. Inaction, or the restriction of the US response to the diplomatic level, were not fully explored during the crisis because they seemed to have contradicted decision makers' prior commitments. The upshot of this example is that the substantive aspects of cognitive search entail upgrading of, or focusing on, policies that do not depart radically from previous policies or previous commitments. This argument implies that consistency is preserved over time as well as among values at any single point in time.

Taken together, analogies and consistency-preserving mechanisms constrain the extent of search for options and render it conservative in terms of the substantive nature of the policies that tend to be moved to the following decisional step. Commitment to previous policies involves another potential violation of rational search: independence among alternatives. Anderson (1981) argues that foreign policy decision makers seldom explore distinct, mutually exclusive courses of action. Rather, they focus on complementary – and often redundant – options. This reduces search efficiency to a considerable degree. Supplementing measures that had been developed prior to the emergence of the specific problem with new measures designed to tailor previous policies to the problem at hand seems to be – in many cases – counterproductive and wasteful. It often comes at the expense of a critical appraisal of previous policies in light of new events.

5.4.1.3 *Revision*

In forming initial estimates of the likelihood of possible consequences of explored options, decision makers are strongly influenced by prior theories or "schemata" (Axelrod, 1973; Abelson, 1973) that they have on such events. The influence of prior theories comes largely at the expense of the careful consideration of current indicators of the nature of the problem at hand. One of the major sources of the strong influence of prior theories is the analogizing nature of the diagnosis process. Another source is the effect of beliefs, desires, and expectations on prediction.

Inferences based on analogies create an expectation that the consequences of various options will be in line with those of the analogized event. For example, Truman's view of the Korean invasion as analogous to the Japanese invasion of Manchuria led to the expectation that further Soviet aggression was highly likely if the US failed to respond decisively. He felt that the prospects of another world war would have increased if the US were to sit idly by. If the invoked analogy is that of an event in which the adopted policies had yielded adaptive outcomes, then the consideration of a similar policy alternative would yield excessively high likelihood estimates of positive outcomes, and excessively low likelihood estimates for unfavorable outcomes. Alternatively, if analogized events were shown to yield disastrous consequences, alternatives considered at present would differ dramatically from those employed in the past. In such cases, outcomes that had occurred in the past tend to be underestimated, and outcomes that had not occurred tend to be overestimated.

Similar influences are attributed by cognitive theorists to beliefs that are not based on any tangible past precedent. In many ways belief systems resemble political theories, that is, they can be seen as a set of interrelated laws connected by a general principle or a fundamental axiom. This set of laws allows for the derivation of empirical deductions or predictions about a wide variety of situations. To the extent that the perceived features of the decision problem are seen to fit a pre-existing belief set – and cognitive theorists argue that this is almost always the case – estimates of future outcomes will be heavily dependent on deductions derived from the belief system. Prior theories create expectations regarding the future with or without the direct intervention of the decision maker who subscribes to them. These expectations shape the nature of initial estimates and – even more so – the updating of initial estimates in light of new information.

Another widely discussed factor affecting the formation of initial estimates is the decision maker's desires. One of the main effects of desires on the formation of estimates is the well-known wishful thinking fallacy. In the context of foreign policy making, wishful thinking stems from two sources: commitments to prior policies and normative beliefs contained in prior theories. Commitment to prior policies leads to rigid perceptions and a desire to see them work despite the discrepancies between the current cues and prior expectations. The rigidity of such perceptions leads to estimates that tend to be in line with the original estimates that had formed the basis for the prior policies. Outcomes that seem discrepant with the prior policy's success tend to be underestimated, and those that are consistent with the desire to see such policies work tend to be overestimated.

Normative beliefs, that is, beliefs about how the political environment ought to function, generate similar patterns of wishful thinking. Because policies favored by a decision maker tend to be in line with such normative beliefs, there is a psychological commitment to events that are seen as positive from this perspective. This commitment strongly affects initial estimates.

The distinction between desires and expectations seems to be useful heuristically but is very elusive empirically. In most cases desires and expectations converge, hence their separate impact on the nature of likelihood estimates cannot be reliably assessed. However, in order to critically assess the separate impacts of desires and expectations on likelihood estimates we must analyze cases in which desires and expectations conflict with one another during a decision process. Jervis (1976: 356–381) argues that there is little experimental or historical evidence suggesting that wishful thinking affects decision making. Biases in cognitive revision are produced largely by expectations. Lebow (1981) corroborates this argument in his study of crisis decision making. On the other hand, Janis and Mann (1977) who emphasize the emotional effects of commitments on decision making argue that wishful thinking does have a marked effect on estimation processes.

What are the implications of cognitive processes for the quality of estimates? Cognitive estimation heuristics produce several significant biases in information processing and intuitive prediction. First, they lead to selective screening of information which is equivalent to systematic sampling error. Second, they result in conservative updating of prior estimates even in the face of highly discrepant information. Third, in order to overcome information overflow, these mechanisms yield a set of rules-of-thumb (or heuristics) that deepen bias by violating basic inferential logic.

Cognitive theorists argue that the portion of information that is actually reviewed by decision makers tends to reflect their expectations or beliefs rather than the actual distribution of data at their disposal. Given the biased nature of the data, the likelihood of erroneous estimates is considerably higher than the one expected by analytic theorists. In addition to the random error involved in sampling from vast amounts of informational items, there is a significant degree of systematic error caused by the distorting effects of beliefs and expectations.

Self-correcting mechanisms during the updating of initial estimates are largely ineffective and can even magnify initial biases. Because selective screening of information continuously influences revision, unsupporting evidence will be consistently overlooked, discounted, or explained away as actually consistent with initial estimates. Prior theories are strongly resistant to change; it normally takes a lot of unambiguously discrepant evidence to produce basic modifications (Nisbett and Ross, 1980). Decision makers are more likely to revise initial estimates if they receive discrepant information at once and in large chunks than if discrepant information filters in incrementally and in small doses (Jervis 1976: 308). Since the former case is unlikely to occur, cognitive revision tends to be highly conservative. Initial likelihood estimates change slowly and incrementally even in the face of strongly discrepant evidence contradictory to decision makers' prior beliefs (Phillips and Edwards, 1966; Alker and Hermann, 1971; Nisbett and Ross, 1980). Cognitive revision tends to be linear and slow relative to analytic revision based on Bayesian logic.

Biases in cognitive revision are also due to a set of heuristics which are commonly used by decision makers in intuitive judgmental and inferential tasks. Psychologists who studied the use of these heuristics argued that these heuristics serve to reduce task complexity and to facilitate prediction. However, their application often results in frequent systematic errors of judgment and predictions. Three of these heuristics are particularly telling.

1 *Availability.* People tend to associate the frequency or probability of events with the ease with which they are able to retrieve such events from memory. Events that are easily accessible in a person's memory tend to be overestimated (in terms of their relative frequency or probability), while events that are hard to recall tend to be underestimated. Since the availability of events in recall processes is not necessarily related to their relative frequency, the use of the availability heuristic may often result in judgmental and inferential biases (Tversky and Kahneman, 1973).[8]

2 *Representativeness.* Frequency or probability estimates of events are often based on the extent to which the features of the event to be predicted are representative of a class of known events. Events that share the same features with a known class of past events will be overestimated. Events that do not share such features tend to be underestimated. The bias here is often referred to as the "base rate"

---

[8] Note that availability seems to be a major determinant of diagnosis via analogies. Essentially, analogies that are most likely to be invoked are the ones that are most accessible in a person's memory, and the ones with relatively low actual frequency.

fallacy (Bar Hillel, 1982). It consists of basing estimates on the perceived fit between a datum and a general class while ignoring the frequency of such a class in the population. The diagnosticity of evidence is judged in terms of the *extent* of its representativeness, not in terms of the frequency of the class. Highly representative data of low frequency classes are disproportionately overestimated. Unrepresentative events of high frequency classes of events are disproportionately underestimated (Kahneman and Tversky, 1973).[9]

3 *Vividness*. Evidence regarding the expected occurrence of future events is often judged according to the vividness with which it is presented. Vivid data are viewed as highly diagnostic and lead to inflated estimates (Nisbett and Ross, 1980). The experimental evidence underlying the vividness heuristic is less conclusive than the experimental evidence suggesting biasing effects of the other two heuristics. Nonetheless, it is maintained that it is the manner in which evidence enters the system, rather than its diagnosticity, which affects cognitive revision of opinion in light of new information.

These cognitive mechanisms tend to lead to systematic biases and result in significant deviations from the Bayesian logic of revision attributed to analytic decision makers. However, there seems to be an internal contradiction in the postulates of the cognitive model regarding the precise nature of revision processes. On the one hand, prior theories and analogies are said to create expectations which both bias dynamic updating of initial estimates and result in conservative and incremental revision of prior beliefs. They are also highly instrumental in the generation of initial estimates, and only change marginally by additional information which is received and processed only after initial estimates had been formed. On the other hand, revision heuristics suggest a tendency to ignore or downgrade background information (or population base-rates) given highly vivid or representative evidence. This results in disproportionately rapid changes in initial estimates irrespective of the diagnosticity of the incoming data or of the amount of information upon which initial estimates are based. In fact, these heuristics may suggest that revision processes would be, in some cases, even more rapid than the one expected by Bayesian processes.

This contradiction is more apparent than real. Rapid revision through the application of the availability, representativeness, or vividness heuristics occurs only if evidence supports prior beliefs, not

---

[9] Jervis (1986) analyzed the extent to which historical evidence suggests the use of the representativeness heuristic. He concluded that outside the laboratory, there is not much evidence that political leaders rely on this heuristic.

if current data contradict prior expectations. Because overestimation is likely to occur only if current data are seen as representative of prior beliefs the revision heuristics are more likely to result in further deepening commitments to prior beliefs than in changing them. This suggests that, over time, decision makers will tend to become highly overconfident in their predictions and less sensitive to incompatible evidence.

Overconfidence refers to an excessive degree of trust in the accuracy of one's predictions. By an excessive degree of trust I mean that decision makers tend to believe. that their predictions are accurate irrespective of the amount of data upon which such predictions are based. Objective tests of the degree of overconfidence in probability estimates revealed that overconfidence tends to be particularly large near the fifty-fifty prediction range (that is, when decision makers are really unsure whether the predicted event would occur). Overconfidence in prediction creates additional resistance to change in estimates and in prior beliefs (Fischoff, Lichtenstein, and Phillips, 1982; Lichtenstein and Fischoff, 1977).

Finally, one of the most important features of cognitive decision making is the low tolerance of uncertainty exhibited by typical decision makers. Decision makers are cognitively ill-equipped to cope with uncertainty, they do not like to be confronted by situationally ambiguous data, and invest a lot of mental effort in reducing uncertainty. Kahnemann and Tversky (1979) suggested that violations of fundamental axioms of rational behavior in actual decision making are due to artificial reductions of uncertainty at extreme ranges of probability estimates. Specifically, low probabilities are treated as zero-probabilities, and high-probability events are treated as certainties. The implication of this is that in cases of high stress, decision makers will repress uncertainty by selective and biased inference from available information.

5.4.1.4 Evaluation

The need to reduce value-conflict and to avoid tradeoffs among conflicting goals is the main motivational factor driving cognitive evaluation of alternatives. This urge is exhibited by two complementary forms of evaluation processes: unidimensional (lexicographic) appraisal and artificial consistency-maintenance. Unidimensional appraisal of policy options, also known as lexicographic evaluation (Gallhofer, Saris, and Melman, 1986: 64), is a procedure for establishing value-consistency by limiting the evaluation of options to a single, most-important value dimension while disregarding all

202

secondary value-dimensions. Value-conflict is eliminated or mini-mized by denying its existence. This is so because different goals do not compete with one another in the evaluation process. If the price of a used car is seen as the most important evaluation criterion by a potential buyer, then she will rank all available cars from cheapest to the most expensive, while disregarding the fact that more expensive cars tend to be mechanically more reliable, more comfortable, have a higher performance, and so forth. Unidimensional appraisal of options does not only simplify the calculation involved in the evalu-ation process, but also reduces emotional difficulties associated with multi-attribute utility evaluation.

Artificial consistency maintenance differs from unidimensional appraisal in that it does not require the elimination of secondary value-dimensions, yet it seeks to preserve cognitive consistency given multiple evaluation-criteria. This is accomplished by a similar or identical ranking of outcomes over multiple value-dimensions. Deci-sion makers might base their evaluation of policy options on multiple criteria but artificially rank those options the same way over all criteria. Options that rank high on one attribute will rank the same way on all other attributes, and vice versa. The buyer of a used car will artificially rank cheap cars highly on mechanical reliability, road performance, fuel economy, comfort, and so on, even if this is not the case in reality. Jervis (1976: 128) labels this strategy irrational cognitive consistency, namely, a tendency to create dependence among seemingly distinct value-dimensions. For example, an academic job applicant who is seen as a competent researcher will also be seen as a gifted teacher.

Spill-over effects from one value dimension to another may bias evaluation in two important respects. First, decision makers will limit their evaluation of policy options to those value-dimensions that are most likely to guarantee consistent ranking of their outcomes, thereby minimizing value-conflict at the expense of thorough review of all actual values invoked by the decision problem. Second, spill-over effects distort the actual consequences of policies because one con-sequence is inferred from another. Accurate and objective appraisal of policy options is distorted by tradeoff-avoidance strategies (Snyder, 1978).

Yet, regardless of how much effort is invested in consistent ranking of options, the complete elimination of tradeoff calculations may be impossible in some cases. The purpose of cognitive evaluation is to find what game theorists term *dominant strategies*, that is, alternatives that are at least as good on most value dimensions and better on the remaining value dimensions than all the other alternatives. Lexicographic appraisal and artificial consistency maintenance over multiple value-dimensions are employed to maximize the likelihood of finding unequivocally best alternatives. Yet, while lexicographic appraisal or otherwise consistent ranking of options reduces conflict over multiple value-dimensions, the existence of a dominant strategy is not guaranteed. Multiple outcomes stemming from given options might conflict with one another. In other words, a dominant strategy is unequivocally best over both all relevant goals and over all of its possible consequences. For example, the ranking of all cars strictly in terms of price eliminates conflict over multiple goals. However, such a ranking might be insufficient for the elimination of tradeoff calculations if the decision maker thinks that any car has some probability of breaking down, therefore requiring repairs. In such an event, the cheapest car in terms of the purchase cost might be seen as expensive in terms of repair cost. Looking at the financial cost as the sole criterion for selecting a car will not eliminate value tradeoffs entirely.

In such cases, in comes a strategy labeled by Janis and Mann (1977) pre-decisional bolstering. This strategy consists of upgrading the benefits associated with an alternative which is seen as initially promising, while downgrading its associated shortcomings. Likewise, pre-decisional bolstering involves a tendency to downgrade the benefits associated with other alternatives while upgrading their associated costs. Additionally, bolstering may work on the revision of the probabilities associated with various outcomes. For example, our cognitive car buyer might discount or completely ignore the possibility that a cheap car might require considerable money for repairs. Cognitive theorists argue that decision makers have little tolerance for uncertainty. By gradually reducing the estimated probabilities of undesired outcomes to zero, negative outcomes tend to be dismissed, and cognitive consistency is established. Maoz's (1986) analysis of Israeli decisions prior to the Sabra and Shatila massacre indicates that the option of sending the Phalange Militia into the Palestinian refugee camps was specified in terms that precluded any possibility of adverse circumstances. Prime Minister Begin stated in his testimony before the Kahan inquiry commission that "it didn't even cross my mind that the Phalanges, if they entered the [refugee] camps to fight the terrorists, would commit acts of atrocity and massacre . . . We never even considered that any likelihood existed that they would massacre civilians" (Maoz, 1986: 154). The formulation of the decision problem as one under certainty prevented any form of tradeoff calculations from being introduced into the evaluation process.

5.4.1.5 Choice

Stein and Tanter (1980) who emphasize the impact of analogies on cognitive decision making label the choice principle "analogizing." This principle suggests that decision makers are most likely to employ that alternative which proved itself superior in terms of its consequences in past events. Maoz (1981; 1986) suggests that the typical decision rule employed by decision makers employing cognitive procedures is that of single-value maximization. This conclusion is also made by Gallhofer, Saris, and Melman (1986: 64–66). Given a lexicographic appraisal of policy options, a dominant strategy will be selected if one exists, or will be artificially established through pre-decisional bolstering.

Both the analogizing and the single-value maximization principles imply that cognitive decision makers will tend to make conservative choices. This implies that it might be difficult to distinguish between cognitive models and cybernetic ones strictly on the basis of the choice principle. In fact, these two models are substantively and procedurally similar (Maoz, 1981: 680–681; Steinbruner, 1974: 138–139).

An important ambiguity in the predictions of the cognitive model concerns the way decision makers are expected to choose in the absence of dominant strategies. If value-conflict cannot be entirely eliminated through consistent ranking of policy options over values and outcomes, how do decision makers go about selecting one? Cognitive theorists are not entirely clear on this issue. However, some tentative observations can be made on the basis of the conservative nature of cognitive choices. If value conflict has not been eliminated, and no dominant strategy has been established, decision makers are likely to employ a decision rule labeled the maximin principle. Briefly, the maximin principle suggests that decision makers single out an alternative whose worst outcome is preferred to the worst outcome stemming from any other alternative. The implication of the maximin rule is that the weighting of the consequences associated with the various outcomes is minimized or avoided altogether. Decision makers resort in such cases to a conservative worst-case analysis and select the "least of all evils" rather than the optimal or satisficing policy option.

The maximin principle seems consistent with the assumptions underlying cognitive decision models in that they imply both conservatism and a pessimistic outlook of the policy environment. Such a principle seems appealing in an imperfect world filled with uncertainty, especially when the decision problem involves high stakes. Moreover, a choice principle that minimizes the role of probability estimates helps reduce complexity in that it leads to prime reliance upon one's values rather than on guesses of others' behavior, and, as such, enhances one's confidence in the decision.

5.4.2 Group decision making

The essential problem in group decision making, viewed cognitively, consists of two aspects, only one of which has been systematically addressed by analytic and cybernetic models. First, predictions regarding collective decision processes address the manner by which individual preferences are aggregated and transformed into national choices. Second, the process of making collective choices entails potential conflict and rivalry within groups that require a certain degree of cohesion for effective long-term functioning. Contrary to the other two models, cognitive theorists assume that one of the functions of collective choice processes is to preserve long-term group cohesiveness in addition to efficiently solving the particular problem at hand.

The distinct contribution of the cognitive model to the understanding of group decision making lies in its emphasis on the effects of group structure and group-related considerations on individual preferences and on the nature of group choices. This emphasis stems from the awareness of the tradeoff between the need to reach collective choices given different individual preferences and the need to preserve group cohesiveness and to avoid or minimize risks to the group as a result of interindividual conflicts.

At the heart of the approach of cognitive theorists to this tradeoff is a set of assumptions about the special characteristics of policy groups. These assumptions shed new light on the dynamics of collective choices in foreign policy settings.

1 *Permanence*. Policy groups operate on a permanent, as opposed to an *ad hoc* basis. In contrast to *ad hoc* task-specific groups such as juries, foreign policy groups operate on a continuous basis, and their composition remains largely unchanged over time and across policy problems (and even across different issue-areas). This implies that group choices at one point in time will affect the subsequent effectiveness of the group at solving other problems at a later point in time. Another implication of the permanence characteristic is that individuals establish commitments to the group's well-being and tend to view the cohesiveness and the harmony of interpersonal relations within the group as values in their own right, above and beyond the

specific goals they pursue at any given decision. In contrast, individual commitments in groups that operate on an *ad hoc* basis are directed primarily to an effective solution of the problem at hand. The continuity and cohesiveness of the group play – almost by definition – a secondary role in their cognitive attachments.

2   *Multi-issue responsibility*. Policy groups have multi-issue responsibilities both in terms of their personal composition and in terms of the nature of their tasks. Cabinets, for example, are required to deal simultaneously with multiple issues almost all the time. Specific problems may require the setting up of *ad hoc* committees that are essentially single-task in terms of their mandate. But most crucial choices are dealt with in a multi-issue context. Cabinets are also composed of individuals representing a wide variety of organizations, each having its own areas of responsibility and its own interests. Even if a decision problem is highly specific, various perspectives are apt to arise due to the fact that the problem is analyzed in different light by each organization. Thus, there exist linkages between the specific issue-area of the decision problem and other seemingly extraneous issues that are not directly affected by it. This suggests that the treatment of specific policy problems is often clouded by seemingly irrelevant considerations. During the Cuban missile crisis, the Executive Committee faced pressures from the US ambassador to the United Nations, Adlai Stevenson, to release the aerial photographs of the Soviet missile sites in Cuba. Stevenson argued that world public opinion – including the public in NATO countries – expressed serious doubts regarding the validity of the US claim that the Soviets had placed nuclear missiles on the island. The Soviet delegation at the UN consistently denied American accusations, arguing that the whole affair was a pretext for an American invasion of Cuba. In principle, the argument made by Stevenson at the EXCOM meeting was very convincing. Yet, the fact that the CIA director and the joint chiefs of staff participated in the group deliberations required considering the potential damage to US intelligence operations caused by revealing aerial photographs (Abel, 1966; Sorensen, 1965).

3   *Hierarchical structure*. Policy groups have both formal and informal hierarchies. These structures have a profound impact on individuals' ability and willingness to present dissenting views, to reveal their true preferences, or to press their positions. Moreover, group hierarchies tend to affect changes in individual preferences in collective decision making settings.

4   *Accountability*. Policy groups are collectively accountable for their decisions with respect to subordinates, constituencies, and competing

elites. This imposes on individual members a sense of commitment to a consensual decision so that the group would appear as a unified entity *vis-à-vis* its constituency or competing elites. The leaking-out of intragroup divisions might weaken the group's bargaining position *vis-à-vis* other institutions when those decisions must be approved by external bodies. A divided cabinet faces considerable problems when attempting to pass a bill in the legislature. Knowledge of the scope and nature of intra-cabinet divisions provides opposition groups effective weapons with which to attack the government's policies. ("If you cannot agree amongst yourselves, how do you expect us to support you?") Seen in this light, the appearance of consensus may be valued by group members as a political necessity which takes precedence over insistence on dissenting views, hence resulting in preference change and reduced argumentation during the collective decision process. On several occasions during the Lebanon war, ministers in the Israeli cabinet were hushed down by their colleagues when expressing dissenting views. The argument made by Prime Minister Begin and Defense Minister Sharon was that such views provide the internal opposition with political weapons (Schiff and Yaari, 1984; Yaniv, 1987). The appearance of nations as unified political entities is sometimes seen as strengthening their position *vis-à-vis* the opponent, and the public voicing of criticism at times of crisis is seen as playing into the opponent's hands.

5 *Common history*. The fact that group members have been working with one another on a regular basis prior to the present decision has two important implications for their decision process. One is that members share a certain degree of common experience and common values which they wish to preserve. Another implication concerns a degree of commitment by members to the previous group policies. This suggests that – much like individual choices – group choices will reflect some conservative bias and attachment to group norms.

These characteristics of policy groups challenge the analytic model's image of group decision making as an open and dynamic process of argumentation, free and unconstrained exchange of information and opinions, bargaining, and coalition formation. The observation of cognitive theorists is that even in the most demanding tasks, group argumentation is often constrained and extremely limited. Individuals are often subject to group pressures for conformity. More significantly, individuals who are known to have different opinions from the one expressed by the leaders or other influential members fail to present them or to insist on their thorough consideration by the group.

The major explanation of cognitive collective choice processes is the *groupthink* model (Janis, 1982; Janis and Mann, 1977). This model is based on the assumption that the group is an autonomous entity which cannot be seen as a mere aggregation of individuals. Groups have a set of norms and a hierarchy that was established over a long period of social and political association. The preservation of these norms and the hierarchical structure become values in and of themselves. Individuals feel committed not only to their view of the desirable solution to the problem at hand, but also to the preservation of group norms. While other models designate a set of decision rules for aggregating individual preferences into collective choices, the groupthink model suggests that the solution of individual-group conflicts rests primarily with the individual members themselves.

The major aspect of the groupthink model is what Janis calls *concurrence-seeking behavior*, that is, a pattern of individual adjustment to what one perceives to be an emerging group consensus. Group-induced shifts in individual preferences are not a result of systematic brain-storming and persuasive argumentation in the course of a frank and open group discussion of all aspects of the policy problem. Rather, they are a consequence of setting-induced constraints on the exchange of argumentation and sincere expression of preferences. One of the explanations of group-induced shifts is what McGuire (1966) called the *value theory*. This theory asserts that deviations from the initial distribution of individual preferences depends on the particular attitude toward risk-taking that prevails in the group. Groups that share a common admiration toward risky behavior tend to produce considerably riskier policies than those expected given the initial distribution of individual preferences. If, however, group norms depict risk-taking as imprudent and adventuristic, resulting policies exhibit a marked degree of moderation compared to the initial distribution of preferences (Pruitt, 1971b). Value theory suggests that there exists a strong relationship between group norms and policy outcomes which is inconsistent with models suggesting a simple decision rule for the aggregation of individual preferences strictly through interindividual interaction. For such a process to occur, individual preferences ought to be revealed sincerely and fully in the course of group deliberations. Janis argued that, in many cases, individuals present views which they see as consistent with those of other members, especially with those of the group's leader. Moreover, sincere views – even if presented – are often self-suppressed or suppressed by the group. As a result, many of the alternatives that are considered by individual members prior to group deliberations are often not reviewed by the group or receive only superficial scrutiny before being rejected (Burnstein and Berbaum, 1983).

The hierarchical structure of policy groups often precludes full participation of junior or low-level members in the group discussion. Moreover, group leaders often manipulate the agenda in a manner that would eventually legitimize a policy that they favor at the expense of policies that might have otherwise been seriously considered and adopted. Agenda control is a powerful weapon in group discussions. Public choice theories of agenda manipulation and agenda control clearly suggest that the sequence by which options are analyzed and voted upon matters a great deal with regard to the final decisional outcome (Farquharson, 1969; Nurmi, 1983; Dummett, 1984). Individuals who – by virtue of their rank or expertise – can control that sequence may get their favored policy adopted by the group even if they cannot suppress the consideration of alternative policies. In fact, a large portion of group discussion can be characterized as strategic manipulation of agendas, rather than cognitive adjustment to group consensus (Riker, 1986). Nevertheless, it can still be seen as consistent with the essential ideas of the groupthink model. The precise ways in which agendas are set determine the kind of pressures operating on group members.

For example, in many cases during the Lebanon war, the Israeli government debated policy within the context of agendas set by Defense Minister Ariel Sharon. Sharon was well aware of a strong opposition within the government to a significant expansion of the Israeli invasion and to a direct confrontation with the Syrian army. This opposition messed up Sharon's war plans which necessitated the occupation of Beirut and a large-scale confrontation with the Syrians, designed to push them out of Lebanon. Despite this opposition, Sharon was able to bring the government to support both the expansion of the war and the confrontation with the Syrians. In most cases, these decisions were reached unanimously and only few counter-arguments were raised during the discussion. How was that accomplished? Sharon's secret can be traced to a process of agenda setting and manipulation of alternatives in the course of group discussion. His strategy was to present specific war-expansion plans in stark contrast to do-nothing alternatives. At each instance, the government was presented with a choice between a drastically escalatory policy and the preservation of an unsatisfactory status-quo. One such case was the decision to confront the Syrian army. The considerations underlying that policy, as presented by Sharon, were that the tactical situation that evolved in Lebanon was such that the forward units of the Israeli Defense Forces (IDF) were in a topographically inferior position to the Syrians. The Syrians could, if they decided to launch an attack, cause considerable damage to the IDF. The alternative to the initiation of a confrontation with the Syrians was to do nothing on that portion of the line, thus appearing as extremely risky and dangerous. The dichotomization of the choice problem created a strong bias toward Sharon's proposal which precluded any serious evaluation of the current situation and of other, less drastic measures (Yaniv, 1987; Schiff and Yaari, 1984).

This example suggests that concurrence-seeking behavior can be induced by agenda-setting. Ideas that were considered by individuals prior to group discussion may be excluded from the group deliberations because they appear out of context and irrelevant within the agenda discussed by the group. Individual members are therefore channeled into a context that constrains sincere expression of preferences. Agenda-setting may include value elimination. Paige (1968) reports that President Truman explicitly excluded the consideration of the domestic implications of US involvement in the Korean war from the agenda.

Group processes are thus characterized by constrained and limited argumentation and by high degrees of consensus stemming from tendencies for preference adjustment by individuals to what they perceive to be the leader's preferences or modal views. The cognitive model suggests that there is an inherent potential for cognitive conflict between individuals' commitments to certain policies and their commitments to the preservation of group cohesiveness and harmony, as well as their commitment to prior policies that the group represents *vis-à-vis* external actors. This conflict is often resolved by modifications in individuals' preferences in a manner that prevents such conflicts from explicitly spilling over to group deliberations due to insistence on their personal preferences. The consequence of groupthink processes is that the artificial consensus serves to diminish individual reservations toward policies with which they would have felt extremely uncomfortable otherwise. Group consensus generates perceptions of self-righteousness and of group invulnerability. Paige (1968), De Rivera (1968) and Janis (1982) report that members of the policy groups during the Korean War and the Bay of Pigs fiasco emerged out of the deliberations highly confident in their choices and strongly resistant to criticism and to opposing views. Halberstram's (1974) discussion of the US policy making process during the Vietnam war suggests similar patterns emanating from the continuous association of these members in the policy team.

Janis (1982; 1983) is careful to point out that the groupthink model is not always an accurate description of group decision processes. The American decision process during the Cuban missile crisis suggests important exceptions to the model. Moreover, Janis points out that groupthink is context-dependent, that is, it is likely to occur in groups with a long history of common association, under conditions of high stress, and in settings characterized by a rigid hierarchy.

5.4.3 Criticism of the cognitive model

The main theme of cognitive theorists is that defective decision making at the individual and group level are largely the product of cognitive and motivational constraints on units' capacity for vigilance and rational behavior. Cognitive theorists emphasize consistent patterns of deviation from rationality resulting – more often than not – in counterproductive and even disastrous policy outcomes. By implication, we are led to believe that awareness of these biases and cognitive pitfalls, and the introduction of corrective mechanisms, such as "devil's advocacy" or multiple advocacy, might significantly enhance decisional quality (Jervis, 1976: 409–424; George, 1972, 1980; Handel, 1976; Wohlstetter, 1962). Because the analytic model serves as the normative benchmark and the ideal-type to which decision makers should aspire, the identification of systematic deviations from it in real-life situations, enables cognitive theorists to evaluate normatively actual decisions, identify common sources of error, and make prescriptions about the appropriate corrective procedures (George, 1980; Kahneman and Tversky, 1982).

This is perhaps the main contribution of both the cognitive and cybernetic models to the study of decision making in foreign policy. The knowledge produced by these schools of thought is therefore not confined to pure and abstract research. In providing prescriptions concerning improvements in decisional procedures, scholars were loyal to the goal of policy-relevant research. Nonetheless, some of the most important weaknesses of the cognitive model of decision must be specified at this point.

First, the postulates of this model are stated at a very general level, hence making the task of deriving precise and refutable hypotheses extremely difficult. In many cases, the precise contents of strictly "cognitive" behaviors are undefined. For example, are unidimensional diagnoses that are not based on multiple analogies inconsistent with cognitive predictions? Likewise, since some degree of bias is likely to be found in any attempt to forecast future events on the basis of a fraction of the available evidence, any revision process can be made consistent with the cognitive postulates.

Second, cognitive theorists are very clear about how individuals and groups violate the principles of analytic decision making. Yet when it comes to causally explaining cognitive patterns of decision making, their predictions become very vague. For example Kahneman and Tversky (1979) and Tversky and Kahneman (1981, 1986) showed rigorously that the transitivity axiom of rationality is overwhelmingly violated in practice. They demonstrated a prevailing tendency for preference reversal which suggests that consistent utility functions cannot be established. However, they were considerably less successful in modeling alternative decision making patterns, which follow from this finding. The model they advanced, called *prospect theory*, does not suggest a clear pattern of alternative preferences.[10]

Third, the image that cognitive theorists portray is that of defective and biased coping with the most demanding problems. These explanations look very convincing when major policy blunders and fiascoes occur. Yet, however dramatic, such disastrous decisions are not necessarily the norm in international affairs. The reduction of individuals and collectives into units trapped by fears, desires, and other cognitive limitations fails to account for innovations in foreign policy making. The depiction of policy choices as conservative and conflict-reducing fails to explain major shifts in attitudes and policies and to account for highly vigilant decision processes under the most stressful conditions. Cognitive theorists create the erroneous impression that individuals and collectives are incapable of long-term planning of policy initiatives which contain major departures from previous commitments or beliefs. If the cognitive model were to characterize foreign policy processes, then some of the most important international events are unaccountable from a decision-theoretic perspective. For example, Handel's (1981) perceptive study of diplomatic surprises shows how, and under what conditions, leaders embark on policies signifying drastic shifts from prior policies, shifts which seem totally inconsistent with their prior beliefs and commitments. Although Handel readily admits that such shifts (e.g., the Ribbentrop–Molotov agreement, Nixon's opening to China, Sadat's peace initiative) constitute exceptions in the practice of diplomacy, these events are sufficiently significant to warrant a close questioning of the generality of cognitive explanations. This is not to suggest that the cognitive model

[10] A more detailed description of prospect theory is given in chapter 6.

fails to provide a good explanation of how foreign policy decisions are made. Rather, a narrow concentration on cognitive mechanisms and on the limitations they impose on foreign policy decision making may bias broader evaluations of decision making processes.

The principal question is under what conditions would cognitive processes be employed in a manner that significantly constrains the quality of decisions? It is not sufficient to postulate that the employment of conflict-reducing mechanisms and/or inferential heuristics invariably lead to suboptimal decisions. Rather, one must examine the limitations in contextual terms and show which of the biases are likely to influence choice quality in terms of specific circumstances. For example, Maoz and Shayer (1987) showed that political leaders tend to structure their post-decisional argumentation in more complex terms (including the specific acknowledgment of value tradeoffs) when the persuasion task is perceived as difficult and demanding than when this task calls for straightforward emotional argumentation. Specifically, they showed that peace-advocacy tends to be more complex than war-advocacy, even when individuals exhibit low levels of cognitive complexity on the average. Thus, while some decision makers may be particularly prone to the simplifying and biasing patterns of cognitive decision making in general, it is quite possible that their susceptibility to certain biases would vary with the nature of the specific decisional task, or with the circumstances under which it is made. The tendency to view cognitive processes in overly deterministic terms might therefore reduce the researcher's sensitivity to variations in choice behavior across decisional problems, and thus hinder the accuracy of the explanation.

5.5 THE BUREAUCRATIC POLITICS MODEL

This model was developed as an apparent alternative to the analytic model, or – more precisely – to what Allison (1971) termed as the *unitary rational actor* model of foreign policy. The bureaucratic politics model challenges both the unitary nature of decision making bodies and their ability to define and pursue a set of overarching goals and interests. The point of departure of this model is a set of assumptions relating the structure of states to the processes by which decisions are being made.

First, the image of states as unitary actors obscures the nature of organizational dynamics and of the political games that various organizations play with one another. The image of unitary actors is based on the premise that foreign policy problems diminish the differences between, and the parochial interests of, various organizations into mere insignificance. Foreign policy problems are assumed to be treated by states in terms of the threats or the opportunities they evoke with respect to a general set of goals which are common to all organizations within a state, and therefore the unitary rational actor model allows generalizations over those institutions. This assumption is seen as totally unrealistic by students of bureaucratic politics. In fact, very few policy challenges can unite the various individuals and organizations involved in policy making to such an extent that renders their different interests and perspectives secondary to a unified perception of ends and means. Moreover, since most foreign policy problems require routine procedures in the sense that they do not involve acute threats or opportunities to fundamental national values, organizational dynamics and interorganizational politics play a key role in the decision process.

Second, the precise contents of national interests are rarely agreed upon. Organizations involved in the formulation and execution of foreign policy may agree on generally phrased goals such as the need to maximize national security, national welfare, or the international reputation of the state. Yet, organizations often disagree on: (*i*) the operational implications of these goals, for example, on budgetary allocations for these purposes, and (*ii*) how tradeoffs among goals are to be resolved. This implies that it is unrealistic to expect that a single utility function would exist for any given nation, not even as a crude approximation.

Third, states cannot be pictured as rational actors because no consistent set of goals to be maximized can be reliably drawn. Rationality on a national scale cannot be defined without ignoring particularistic organizational interests which are independent and sometimes radically different from those of other organizations. The interests of the department of defense are not only the survival and prosperity of the nation as a whole, but also the survival and prosperity of the defense establishment. Sometimes these two sets of interests sharply contradict each other. Thus, attempts to form a consistent and fixed utility function on a national level are bound to be extremely imprecise. In addition, they are likely to misrepresent the nature of the policy process. The bureaucratic perspective does not question the cognitive capacity of individual decision makers to make complex calculations. But it does question the ability of groups to make coherent choices that are intended to maximize universally accepted national interests.

This is clearly a new line of attack on the analytic perspective of foreign policy decision making. But does it lead to a distinctly new explanation of how foreign policy decisions are really made? My argument is that the answer to this question is decidedly no. What is more, the bureaucratic politics model seems to be nothing more than an extension of the cybernetic model to the intraorganizational level and of the analytic model to the interorganizational level. In order to defend this argument, let us take a brief look at the contents of this model.

5.5.1 Individual choice

At the individual and organizational level, the bureaucratic model suggests that decision processes are strongly influenced by the bureaucratic role of the decision maker and by the standard operating procedures (SOPs) of the organization to which he or she belongs. The organizational and role-induced bias is reflected both in the conservative procedures employed and in the substantive content of the various decisional stages. But these grounds have already been covered by the cybernetic model which addresses not only role influences and organizational biases but also more profound biasing motives such as complexity-reducing constraints. The latter aspects operate on a more basic psychological level but have the same implications for organizational problem-solving. For example, the purpose of SOPs is to use the cumulative organizational experience and wisdom of the past to reduce the complexity of current problem solving. Thus SOPs can be treated as the organizational equivalent of the complexity-reducing mechanisms identified by the cybernetic model. The main contribution of the bureaucratic politics model to the understanding of individual choice processes in foreign policy settings is the insights it provides with respect to the effect of role on decision making dynamics in a highly structured institutional context. It is not in the fact that the model offers new propositions about the nature of these dynamics.

5.5.2 Group decision making

Foreign policy making according to the bureaucratic politics model is a process of "pulling and hauling." It is an arena wherein bureaucrats "play games" with one another through the formulation and dissolution of coalitions and the constant use of side-payments in order to advance their parochial interests, rather than to maximize a set of nonexistent national interests. The outcomes of such processes are almost always compromise solutions which reflect the relative power of the participants and the nature of the games being played by them. But what makes such processes irrational? They are inherently irrational if one assumes that an overarching national utility function exists. However, we have seen that Arrow's (1963) impossibility theorem (the paradox of voting) has long shown that the establishment of a transitive social utility function may not be possible even if all individuals have well-defined (i.e., transitive) utility functions. There is also nothing new in the idea that social choice may be suboptimal, certainly nothing that contradicts the propositions of rational social choice theories.

Thus, the criticism of the rational paradigm coming from the bureaucratic perspective seems quite misguided or misinformed. It is not and cannot be a critique of rationality because the problems attributed to rational models have long been recognized by rational choice theorists. In fact, one of the strengths of rational choice theory is that its rigorous axiomatic nature has enabled it to identify its own weaknesses both as a descriptive and as a normative model of human behavior.

Likewise, group decision processes seen from the perspective of the analytic model contain features which are nearly identical to those depicted by the bureaucratic politics model. In fact, there is nothing in the arguments of the bureaucratic politics model that either contradicts or otherwise differs from the analytic model's treatment of group choices. Hence, it is quite surprising that the bureaucratic politics approach is so often presented as a genuine alternative to the analytic model of decision. It is interesting to note in this context that Snyder and Diesing (1977: 408) found that these two models complement rather than contradict each other.[11]

5.6 EMPIRICAL EVIDENCE ON THE THREE MODELS

Much of the literature coming out of this stage of foreign policy analysis asserted that the various conceptual explanations of decision making processes complement one another. At an abstract level, these models can be seen as alternative paradigms of foreign policy making processes. In practice, individuals and groups tend to adopt a mixture of the procedural aspects of these models (Stein-

---

[11] In all fairness this is Snyder's view, but not Diesing's. Snyder argues that their case studies suggested that it was practically impossible to distinguish between analytic decision making and bureaucratic maneuver. His conclusion was that the latter model is merely a sophisticated formulation of the former in a political context.

217

bruner, 1974: 138–139; Horelick *et al.*, 1975; Stein and Tanter, 1980). Empirical tests of these models – some of which were conducted during the model specification stage and some of which were conducted during the subsequent synthesis stage – tend to strongly support this generalization. Allison (1971) showed that, depending on the underlying theoretical assumptions one starts with, the same decision process can be interpreted as consistent with any of those models. Specifically, the analysis of US and Soviet decisions during the Cuban missile crisis, were shown to approximate the predictions derived from the analytic, cybernetic, and bureaucratic models. Galhoffer and Saris (1979) and Galhoffer, Saris, and Melman (1986) showed that elements of analytic and cybernetic processes were operative during the Dutch decision process on the eve of the First World War.[12] Findings from studies on the Israeli decision making processes during the 1967 and the 1973 wars (Stein and Tanter, 1980; Brecher, 1980) and the 1976 Entebbe hostage crisis (Maoz, 1981) suggest the same conclusion, though one of the explanatory models tends to perform better than the others.

However, most of the empirical research on the plausibility of these models was conducted within a noncomparative single-model focus. Scholars attempted to demonstrate the practical prevalence of a certain model by basing their analysis of real-world choices strictly on the assumptions underlying that model. Studies by Levi and Tetlock (1980) and Maoz (1981) tend to support the analytic model. Bueno de Mesquita (1981a; 1983; 1985) applied expected utility theory to the analysis of conflict processes with a marked degree of success. The cybernetic model also seems to have received a significant degree of support. Anderson and McKewon (1987) showed that the expected utility model of war performs less well than a model that more closely approximates the satisficing, threshold-based cybernetic logic. Halperin's (1972; 1974) analysis of the ABM decision process demonstrates organizational and bureaucratic struggles which resulted in a forced and suboptimal compromise. Likewise, Neudstadt's (1970) study of the Skybolt affair, Steinbruner's (1974) study of the MLF decisions, and Shlaim and Tanter's (1978) study of the 1970 Israeli deep-penetration bombing decisions in Egypt all provide ample evidence for the prevalence of cybernetic and organizational dynamics in foreign policy choices. At a more aggregate level, Tanter (1974),

---

[12] However, in their aggregate study of 235 decisions in the 1900–1955 period, they found that an SEU maximization rule characterizes actual choices in only two cases. More than 70 percent of the decisions studied were reached through satisficing or lexicographic decision rules (Galhoffer, Saris, and Melman, 1986: 64–65).

analyzing the Berlin crises of 1948–49 and 1960–61, found mixed support for the incremental nature of crisis behavior which is consistent with organizational models. For example, Warsaw Pact's actions in these crises were better accounted for by incrementalism, whereas NATO's actions were more in line with an action-reaction process which seems consistent with rational models of crisis interaction (cf. Brams and Kilgour, 1987).

The evidence on various aspects of cognitive decision making is particularly rich. Shapiro and Bonham (1973), Bonham and Shapiro (1976), and Bonham, Shapiro, and Trumble (1979) used cognitive mapping approaches to analyze the ways in which State and Defense Department officials establish diagnoses of conflict situations in the Middle East. Their findings suggest strong influences of belief systems on interpretations of external events. Consistency preservation mechanisms tended to dominate definitions of the situation even in the face of sharply contradictory evidence. Snyder's (1978) analysis of Kennedy's decisions during the Cuban missile crisis demonstrated tendencies to choose options that minimized the necessity of making value tradeoffs. De Rivera (1968) found strong evidence of similar tendencies during the decisions of the Truman administration in the course of the Korean War. Jervis's (1976) anecdotal evidence and Lebow's (1981) comparative analysis of brinkmanship crises provided numerous illustrations of the prevalence of cognitive mechanisms in the various stages of foreign policy decisions.

The diversity of findings may suggest that none of the models constitutes the single best approximation to real-world decision processes. It also implies that the literature focusing on the contents and structure of foreign policy decision making came short of its stated aim to enhance our understanding of such processes. If at all, the major achievement of this stage was to increase the theoretical confusion it had attributed to the literature of the input-identification stage by providing an inconclusive account of the dynamics of individual choice and of group decision making. With this point in mind, let us review the contributions and shortcomings of the model-specification stage, taken as a whole.

5.7 THE STAGE OF MODEL-SPECIFICATION: AN APPRAISAL

Students of the process model-specification stage have developed a number of conceptual models which attempt to account for the procedural and substantive characteristics of decision making processes. Although the evidence for the prevalence of any of these models is far from conclusive, the literature that has emerged during this stage greatly enhanced our knowledge regarding the possible forms which foreign policy decision processes might take. In this sense, the research on decision processes imposed considerable structure and order on the field and clearly articulated the subtle aspects of foreign policy making. The picture emerging from these studies suggests that (*i*) there is a variety of explanations of the dynamics of decision making, (*ii*) there exists a clear differentiation among various levels of analysis, defining the contents and structure of decision processes at each level, and (*iii*) decision making processes are depicted as dynamic rather than simple input-output mechanisms. Finally, the research in this stage was particularly helpful in developing procedural standards of decision quality and in making important propositions regarding avenues of improvement in the organization of foreign policy systems (George, 1972, 1980; George *et al.*, 1975; Janis and Mann, 1977; Jervis, 1976).

Another feature of this stage was that much of the theoretical work was deductive, focusing on the construction of a body of logically consistent and substantively interrelated propositions about decision making. The rational choice model with its rigorous axiomatic foundation and its formal deductive structure served not only as a distinct model of decision making processes, but also as a model of model-building in decision making research. Since all other decision models were fundamentally based on a critique of the rational model, their explanations had to be developed in a manner that would allow meaningful comparisons to rational decision making. Although the resulting alternatives to the rational choice model were less than fully formal (and therefore entailed considerable difficulties in their empirical examination, as we are to discover soon), they cover the same grounds as the analytic model albeit from a different set of assumptions.

Considerable attention was paid to theories of decision making that had been developed in related fields such as economics, social and organizational psychology, cybernetics, and so forth. The incorporation of ideas from related fields into foreign policy research produced important insights into the strategic, psychological, and organizational aspects of foreign policy decision making.

Yet, some of the reasons for the unnerving ambivalence of the research findings and the resulting theoretical and empirical inconclusiveness of research on the dynamics of foreign policy decision making must be explored. First, and most important, there was a tendency toward excessive polemics. A good deal of the debates in this stage focused on attempts to discredit the assumptions underlying an opposing model and – at the same time – to justify one's own assumptions. This resulted in a strong tendency to treat each of the decision making models in rather deterministic terms, e.g., decision makers are either consistently rational, or they are not; organizational interests and SOPs either consistently influence group choices, or they do not. Such a tendency was due in large part to the exploratory nature of the research and to the wish to score a theoretical point in the debate rather than to portray deterministic conceptions of foreign policy. Yet, one of the unfortunate consequences of this tendency was that the relationship between situational and personality variables and the content and structure of decision making processes was rarely explored theoretically or analyzed empirically (Holsti and George, 1975; Holsti, 1979). In fact, the selection of case studies for empirical research suggests a tendency toward backward induction from decisional outcomes to explanation. Disastrous policy outcomes were explained primarily in cybernetic, cognitive, or bureaucratic terms, while successful outcomes are explained primarily in analytic terms.[13]

The literature on surprise attacks is a good case in point. Most studies of surprise attacks suggest that intelligence failures are almost never due to lack of information. Rather, they tend to stem from biased and defective processing and from misinterpretation of available information (Handel, 1976; Ben-Zvi, 1976; Shlaim, 1976; Lanir, 1983; Whaley, 1973; Wohlstetter, 1962). However, the study of so-called "surprises" is a study of disasters which implies that they could somehow be averted by more analytic estimation and evaluation procedures. Thus, most attempts to account for the occurrence of surprise attack focused on identification of the cognitive or organizational factors that were presumably responsible for intelligence failures. Likewise, attempts to explain successful coping with major policy problems focused on cases which turned out to be adaptive in the sense that major policy goals were ultimately accomplished. This suggests that scholars implicitly assumed the existence of a close association between the quality of decision making processes and successful outcomes. The consequence of this was the tendency to explain successful decisions in analytic terms and policy blunders in cybernetic or cognitive terms. However, the relationship between the

---

13 For example, it was claimed that the bureaucratic politics model was developed to explain the US involvement in the Vietnam war as a result of bureaucratic and organizational dynamics rather than as a consequence of conscious, deliberate, and calculated decisions of the President (Art, 1973; Caldwell, 1977: 94–96; Krasner, 1972).

substantive or procedural quality of decision processes and their outcomes cannot be assumed away, because we do not have as yet conclusive evidence about such a relationship in foreign policy decision making.[14]

The dichotomous and deterministic analysis of decision making models was unfortunate not only in that it discounted the possibility that these models may be complementary in a realistic context, but also in the sense that it prevented a more systematic specification of the differences and compatibilities among various models. The distinction among process models was not sufficiently formal in a manner that allows for discriminating empirical tests. Research in this stage has failed to identify areas of empirical compatibility among models, on the one hand, and areas of empirical discrimination, on the other. Consequently, determining whether a given decision making process was consistent with a given model boiled down to subjective judgment or to the researcher's favorite theoretical perspective. This explains why different researchers account for the same historical decision in terms of different models and why the empirical findings on any given model show a mixed record of support. It is interesting to note in this context that each of the three models applied by Allison (1971) to the Cuban missile crisis explains different aspects of the incident and that the facts accounted for by one model do not coincide with the facts accounted for by another model. The unitary rational actor model does not explain why, despite consistent evidence, information regarding the Soviet missiles in Cuba reached the president so late. Nor does this model account for the failure of the Soviets to invest more effort in concealing the construction of the missile sites on the Island. Both these facts are well explained by the cybernetic model in terms of the impact of SOPs on the organizational implementation of political decisions. However, the cybernetic model does not address directly US and Soviet choices during the crisis.

Finally, the diversity of methodological approaches used to investigate the empirical validity of various decision making models renders the task of evaluating the substantive findings extremely difficult. For example, it is impossible to assess whether a model that provides an

---

[14] There is, however, compelling psychological evidence that high-quality decision processes tend to yield adaptive outcomes. A number of studies that compared systematic decision and prediction models to "intuitive" or "common sense" models utilizing identical data showed consistently that the former models significantly outperform the latter. See Dawes's (1971; 1979) studies of graduate admission, Goldberg's (1970) study of clinical diagnoses, Ebert and Kruse's (1978) study of (financial) security analysts, as well as several studies in the Kahneman, Slovic, and Tversky (1982) volume. Of particular interest is Maoz's (1984a) study of intelligence forecasts. For a recent round of this debate see Herek, Janis, and Huth (1987).

adequate explanation of individual choices would also provide an adequate explanation of collective decision making. A clear differentiation between individual choice and group decision making was maintained in much of the theoretical research in this stage. The theoretical specification of the process models covered both levels of analysis. However, most of the empirical studies have rarely transcended a single level of analysis. Moreover, the relations between the procedural and substantive characteristics of individual choice processes and those of group decision making was not established in a clear manner. In this regard, the stage of model specification has compounded the confusion concerning the relations between individual choice processes and collective choice processes. The contributions of this stage to knowledge about foreign policy making notwithstanding, many of the problems attributed to the first stage of input-identification and framework construction were left unresolved.

6 A FORMAL CHARACTERIZATION OF DECISION PROCESSES

6.1 INTRODUCTION

In this chapter I develop a set of formal procedures for the empirical discrimination among the three decision process models discussed in chapter 5. These procedures consist of deductions derived from the analytic, cybernetic, and cognitive models with respect to individual choice and collective decision processes. The deductions are based on an integrative framework of foreign policy decision making developed by Stein and Tanter (1980) and extended by Maoz (1981; 1986).

In chapter 5, I pointed out that although it was readily admitted that the various choice models complement rather than contradict each other, no systematic effort was made either to integrate these models or to rigorously discriminate among them. The literature was characterized by a fundamental disagreement among scholars regarding which of the models best approximates real-world foreign policy decision processes. This was the point of departure of several studies belonging to the synthesis stage. In this chapter I will discuss one such study. In chapter 7, I will review the stage of synthesis in more detail.

The present chapter is designed as follows. First, I outline the Multiple Paths to Choice (hereafter, MPC) framework. Second, I discuss the formal aspects of individual choice processes that can be deduced from this framework. Third, I show how this framework – originally restricted to individual choice processes – can be extended to the analysis of collective decision processes. Finally, I discuss the implications of this framework for the analysis and evaluation of real-world decisions.

6.2 THE MULTIPLE PATHS TO CHOICE (MPC) FRAMEWORK

6.2.1 General description

Three general assumptions guided Stein and Tanter (1980) in developing this framework:

224

1   The complexity of foreign policy decision processes requires that they be decomposed into a set of interrelated stages.
2   Areas of empirical discrimination or compatibility among process models can be better identified if the models are analyzed in terms of specific propositions regarding their observable features at any given stage of the process. The more specific and precise the deductions derived from a given decision model, the more reliable is the analysis of actual decisions in terms of that model.
3   Decision making models represent abstract, ideal-type images of foreign policy decision processes. In reality, decision makers rarely employ the procedures posited by any of the models in a pure and unambiguous form. More likely, decision makers mix the procedural and substantive aspects of several models at different stages of the decision process. Stein and Tanter reasoned that the empirical validity of decision models varies not only across individuals and situations, but also over distinct stages of the very same decision process.

Thus, the question of which model best approximates actual decision making processes is fundamentally misconceived, and drastically misleading. It forces the researcher to think of foreign policy decision making as guided by a consistent, coherent, and integrated set of rules, and thereby leads to a tendency to ignore more subtle variations across decisional stages. Analysts are prone to search for "pure" paths to choice that are consistent only with one model, rather than to look for the more empirically plausible "mixed" paths to choice. The empirical acceptance or rejection of any given model on the basis of these implicit assumptions is premature and subject to systematic inferential error. Finally, conceiving of the decision process as a "pure" path impedes any serious effort to determine areas of empirical compatibility or empirical discrimination among the models.

Hence the real question seems to be which combination of paths best describes how a given decision was made? This question requires examinations of decision making processes in dynamic terms, that is, as a set of interrelated stages. What is to be explained is how decision makers move from one stage of the process to other stages, and what is the logic that guides this cross-stage flow of behavior. To illustrate this dynamic conception, consider figure 6.1.

All the horizontal arrows in figure 6.1 represent "pure" paths, that is, a process strictly consistent with a single decision model. All other arrows represent "mixed" paths, that is, processes consistent with more than one decision model. The idea behind the MPC approach is

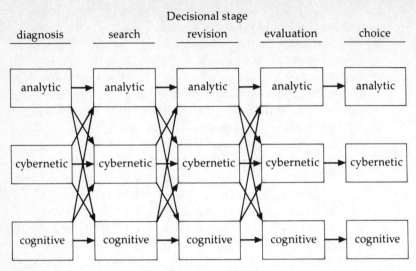

Sources: Stein and Tanter (1980:65); Maoz (1986:83).

Figure 6.1 Multiple paths to choice

that any combination of paths might provide a plausible description of real-world decision making processes. What needs to be explained, therefore, is not only the subset of pure paths of this framework, but also which particular model best describes a given decisional stage, and what *combination of paths* accounts for the entire process. Moreover, a central challenge in empirical decision analysis is to account for the transition from the procedures used by a decision maker at stage t (which might be consistent with those posited by one decision model) to a different set of procedures at stages $t+1$, $t+2$, and so forth. Table 6.1 summarizes the observable features of decisional stages as viewed from the perspective of each of the models discussed in chapter 5 (with the exception of the bureaucratic politics model).

Diagnosis. Two criteria serve to distinguish among process models at this stage: (1) the number of competing definitions of the situation being explored by an individual, and (2) the rules by which decision makers reduce competing interpretations of the decisional cue.

On average, one should expect a larger number of competing interpretations of the decisional cue by analytic procedures than by either cybernetic or cognitive procedures. The interpretations developed by analytic decision makers should be more diverse and contradictory than those explored by cybernetic or cognitive decision makers. Faced by competing interpretations, decision makers attempt to employ some criteria for eliminating some of the diagnoses. The elimination process is one whereby one contrasts the implications of the interpretation with the features of the environment in which the problem arises. Cybernetic decision makers reduce the number of competing interpretations of the decisional cue by selecting the first interpretation which seems to be acceptable or which fits the indicators derived from pre-established diagnoses. The prime criterion employed to eliminate competing diagnoses is the extent of fit between a given interpretation and the analogized events.

Search. Three features distinguish analytic search from other search procedures. First, the number of options explored and seriously considered by analytic decision makers is larger than that explored by cybernetic or cognitive decision makers. The explored options are not restricted to those implied by analogies, nor are they limited to courses of action entailed in pre-established SOPs. Second, analytic option exploration is parallel in nature. Options are explored and contrasted simultaneously. Third, decision makers assign to each of these options a set of mutually exclusive and logically exhaustive outcomes. Evidence contradicting these features raises serious doubts regarding the applicability of the analytic model to this stage.

Cybernetic search is characterized by sequentiality. A cybernetic decision maker explores only one option at a time. Moreover, a search process is said to fit the cybernetic model if no option which had been considered at time t was evoked at any subsequent point in time during the same decision process. The explanation of this criterion is very simple. If option a had been considered at time t and option b was considered at time $t + 1$, this implies that option a must have failed to satisfy the decision maker's level of aspiration. Thus it cannot be reconsidered at $t + 2$.

Substantively, the initially explored options are those included in organizational SOPs. Original or otherwise novel options are explored only if the standard pre-established solutions are deemed inappropriate or unsatisfactory. Finally, if the outcomes assigned to an option are non-exhaustive or non-exclusive, we may conclude that there exists evidence of cybernetic search.

Cognitive search is generally identified in substantive terms, that is, in terms of the options explored (or in terms of the nature of the outcomes assigned to the various options) rather than in terms of their quantity or the nature of the sequence by which options are invoked. Specifically, options invoked by cognitive decision makers are those that can be logically deduced from the analogies considered in the definition of the situation. Thus a criterion for refuting a hypothesis of

227

cognitive search is the exploration and consideration of options which are contradictory to, or otherwise incompatible with, the prescriptive implications of past analogies, for example, the consideration of options that were proven disastrous or counterproductive in the past, or the neglect of options that proved successful in the analogized events. Such behavior runs against the model's predictions regarding the effect of analogies on option exploration. Similar to the cybernetic prediction, cognitive search also implies that outcomes assigned to the various options are either non mutually exclusive, non logically exhaustive, or both. Also, both models posit that, on the average, the number of explored options is relatively small, though the precise meaning of "small" is unspecified. Evidence for either cybernetic and/or cognitive search consists of the exploration of a single policy alternative during a decision process.

Revision. Three criteria allow discrimination among models at this decisional stage: (a) the explicit use of "probabilistic" expressions, (b) the conformity to logical restrictions on such expressions, and (c) the conformity of the logic used for the updating of estimates to Bayesian rules. While it might be unreasonable to expect decision makers to make precise numerical estimates of events, analytic decision makers use "probabilistic" language when attempting to estimate the outcomes of various courses of action. Such expressions are taken to represent the subjective likelihood estimates of decision makers, as well as the degree of confidence they have in the occurrence of given outcomes. It follows that the use of deterministic expressions such as "it is *inconceivable* that event x will occur", or "event y is *bound* to happen", indicates cybernetic or cognitive revision. Because both cognitive and cybernetic decision makers attempt to reduce uncertainty-induced complexity, they tend to transform low-likelihood events into impossibilities and high-likelihood events into certainties (Kahneman and Tversky, 1979). Thus, probabilistic language is replaced by deterministic language.

Second, thinking probabilistically about future events requires conformity to a number of logical standards. These standards follow directly from the specification of decisional outcomes in mutually exclusive and logically exhaustive terms. For example, if each of two mutually exclusive outcomes is estimated as "highly likely", then we have a violation of the logic of probability because their sum exceeded unity (if highly likely is interpreted as a probability of more than 0.5). Likewise, if a decision maker identifies only two possible outcomes emanating from an option and assigns to both very low probabilities, then logical exhaustiveness is violated because the sum of the probabilities is smaller than unity. This implies that revision is non-analytic.

Finally, Bayesian logic is considered as the standard statistical basis of updating prior estimates in light of new information according to the analytic model. Bayesian analysis requires three basic operations: (a) the establishment of a prior probability ratio of expected outcomes in mutually exclusive and logically exhaustive terms; (b) determination of conditional probability ratios of newly observed events given the expected outcomes; (c) the updating of the initial probabilities by a multiplicative incorporation of prior and conditional estimates to produce a posterior probability ratio (which can be normalized to a posterior probability distribution over all expected outcomes). The intuitive approximation of revision processes to Bayesian logic requires the following observable features: (a) evidence that individuals incorporate incoming data into prior estimates, rather than relying strictly either on prior estimates or on the perceived diagnosticity of current indicators; (b) in assessing the diagnosticity of a given datum, decision makers are aware that it can be consistent with more than one hypothesis,[1] (c) there is a clear distinction between conditional probabilities $[P(D|H_i)]$ and posterior, or updated, probabilities $[P(H_i|D)]$. The two are not the same and confusing them constitutes a violation of Bayesian logic and hence of analytic revision.

Evaluation. The main criteria allowing discrimination among the models are: (a) comprehensive screening of outcomes over multiple value dimensions, (b) parallel appraisal of outcomes over multiple value dimensions, and (c) the awareness of existing value tradeoffs and an explicit effort of evaluating options without avoiding the tradeoffs involved in them.

The analytic model postulates that the violation of any one of these criteria constitutes evidence for non-analytic evaluation. Yet the nature of these violations indicates which of the explanations provided by the other two models seems more appropriate. First, the suppression of the number of value dimensions used for evaluating outcomes constitutes evidence for cognitive decision making. Normally, the value dimensions that are eliminated tend to conflict those that are included in the evaluation process. For example, during the Korean crisis of June 1950, President Truman eliminated the domestic

---

[1] Formally, this implies that the conditional probability of a datum given one hypothesis (denoted as $P(D|H_i)$) and the conditional probability of the same datum given a mutually exclusive hypothesis $P(D|H_j)$ where $(H_i) \cap (H_j) = \phi$) do not usually sum up to unity. [That is, $\sum_{k=1}^{n} P(D|H_k) \neq 1$.]

Table 6.1. *A summary description of decision making models*

Stage	Model		
	Analytic	Cybernetic	Cognitive
Diagnosis	*Multiple definitions of the situation*. Elimination of competing explanations based on fit between explanation and factual features of the situation.	*Sequential* development of explanations. Interpretation of problems and elimination of diagnoses based on pre-existing institutional indicators.	*Analogizing* diagnosis. Diagnosis accepted if seen to fit the main features of the analogized event.
Search	*Exhaustive and parallel*: across all relevant and feasible options.	*Sequential*: programmed consideration of a preselected number of options.	*Deductive*: through the general system of beliefs.
Revision	*Optimal*: unbiased sampling of information. Bayesian combination of prior information with current indicators.	*Incremental and conservative*: selection of informational items and their interpretation based on institutional indicators. Artificial conversion of uncertainty into certainty.	*Deductive and categorical*: unequal weights assigned to evidence supporting prior beliefs relative to discrepant information.
Evaluation	*Comprehensive*: cost-benefit analysis of outcomes over multiple value-dimensions; value integration producing consistent utility functions (or ranked preferences).	*Single-value analysis*: sequential elimination by aspects.	*Conflict-reducing*: lexicographic (unidimensional) analysis of costs and benefits, or consistent ranking of outcomes over multiple values.

Choice principle	*Maximization*: incorporation of utilities and probabilities for SEU maximization.	*Satisficing*: selection of first alternative to meet a set of acceptability thresholds.	*Single-value maximization*: or identification of dominant or maximin alternatives.
Main features of group decision process	*Weighted aggregation of preferences*: argumentation and coalition formation; exercise of formal and informal influence; extensive debate and screening of options.	*Sequential elimination by aspects*: limited argumentation; individual influence determined by formal authority and expressed in terms of agenda manipulation.	*Groupthink*: concurrence-seeking adjustment of preferences to perceived leader's preference or to group consensus; little or no argumentation.

Source: Stein and Tanter (1980: 65); Maoz (1986: 73).

support value from the decision process because it would have conflicted with the major value dimension used for the evaluation of appropriate US response to the invasion of South Korea (Paige, 1968: 141). The violation of this criterion leads directly to the violation of criterion (*c*) because the elimination of conflicting value dimensions tends to result in consistent ranking of outcomes over all the non-eliminated value dimensions, hence leading to elimination or suppression of value tradeoffs.

The violation of the parallel appraisal criterion constitutes definite evidence for cybernetic evaluation. Cybernetic evaluation consists of successive elimination of options due to sequential introduction of value dimensions. This implies that only one value dimension is used at a time, and that the number of options that are evaluated on a given value dimension is strictly larger than the number of options evaluated on a subsequent value dimension. This also results in the violation of the third (tradeoff) criterion.

Choice. As figure 6.1 indicates, the choice criterion is a direct consequence of the evaluation process. Since table 6.1 lays out clearly the choice principles predicted by the three models, no further description of this stage is necessary.

231

Option	Outcome	SE Value dimension				
		1	2	...	$m-1$	m
a_1	o_1	u_{11}	u_{12}	...	$u_{1(m-1)}$	u_{1m}
	o_2	u_{21}	u_{22}	...	$u_{2(m-1)}$	u_{2m}
a_2	o_3	u_{31}	u_{32}	...	$u_{3(m-1)}$	u_{3m}
	o_4	u_{41}	u_{42}	...	$u_{4(m-1)}$	u_{4m}
..	..	...	...	...	...	...
	..	...	...	...	...	...
	..	...	...	...	...	...
a_k	o_{n-1}	$u_{(n-1)1}$	$u_{(n-1)2}$	...	$u_{(n-1)(m-1)}$	$u_{(n-1)m}$
	o_n	u_{n1}	u_{n2}	...	$u_{n(m-1)}$	u_{nm}

a = option
o = outcome
u = utility

Figure 6.2 A general form search-evaluation matrix

6.3 THE FORMAL STRUCTURE OF THE EVALUATION STAGE

The evaluation stage allows for the application of the most powerful discrimination criteria among the three models because it incorporates many of the previously discussed procedural and substantive aspects of the models. To formally describe the content and structure of evaluation procedures, I invoke the search-evaluation matrix described in chapter 4. Figure 6.2 depicts a general form of a search-evaluation (SE) matrix.

When we reviewed the contents of analytic evaluation procedures it was noted that the keyword distinguishing between analytic and non-analytic evaluation processes was "comprehensive." Now we can define precisely what we mean by "comprehensive evaluation." From figure 6.2 it can be seen that for any given set of options $A = [1, \ldots, k]$, $(k \geq 2)$, any given set of outcomes, $O = [1, \ldots, n]$, $(n \geq k)$, and any given set of value-dimensions (goals, or normative criteria perceived as relevant for appraising options) $VD = [1, \ldots, m]$, $(m > 1)$, there exists a fully-filled matrix $SE = [1, \ldots, mn]$ whose entries u_{ij} indicates the utility (or ordinal ranking) of outcome i on value dimension j. By fully-filled I mean that none of the elements of SE is missing or otherwise undetermined.

In chapter 5, I noted that, at a very minimum, we must observe at least two options $(k \geq 2)$, and thus at least two outcomes $(n \geq 2)$ to conclude that a given empirically observed search process was analytic. If $n=k\geqslant 2$, then the decision was made under conditions of certainty (see chapter 3). If $n>k\geqslant 2$ then the decision was made under conditions of risk or of uncertainty. However, to satisfy the comprehensiveness criterion, we must impose a lower bound on the number of value dimensions used for option evaluation. Due to the complexity of problems in foreign policy settings, I assume that any given environmental cue invokes at least two relevant value dimensions that are deemed as appropriate for option appraisal. Thus, to satisfy the comprehensive criterion, the area of the **SE** matrix must be at least $m\times n\geqslant 2\times 2=4$.

Any observed search evaluation matrix which does not satisfy the minimum area requirement is sufficient evidence that the evaluation process is accounted for by a non-analytic model. Moreover, the actually filled area of the **SE** matrix can be used to indicate the *degree* of comprehensiveness in the evaluation process. Even if the minimum requirements on the size of the **SE** matrix are satisfied, decision makers may differ in the way they evaluate options. This should be reflected in the size of their search-evaluation matrices. Note that the dimensions of the **SE** matrix are defined by the number of options and outcomes identified by a decision maker (search extensiveness), as well as by the number of value dimensions invoked for their appraisal (evaluation extensiveness). Thus the area of the **SE** matrix is a good indicator of both distinct stages. This indicator serves therefore as a basis for a comparative analysis of the comprehensiveness of evaluation processes, allowing us both to distinguish among different models and to examine variations in comprehensiveness by decision makers who use the same model to evaluate options. To see why this is the case, consider a typical **SE** matrix which is consistent with cybernetic evaluation depicted in figure 6.3.

This matrix was constructed to conform with the logic of the elimination by aspects (EBA) procedure. Initially, a decision maker identifies a large number of options and outcomes, thus facing tremendous decisional complexity. The EBA model suggests that each value dimension introduced in the iterative evaluation sequence serves to eliminate some of the initially identified options from further consideration. Note that the total number of options (and thus the total number of outcomes) as well as the number of value dimensions used in the evaluation process might be quite substantial and might well meet the minimum criteria for evaluation comprehensiveness. Yet, this process is clearly non-analytic in nature for two reasons. First, the theoretical area of the **SE** matrix shown in figure 6.3 (given by TSE) is substantially

233

SE

Option	Outcome	Value dimension				
		1	2	$\ldots$	$m-1$	m
a_1	o_1	u_{11}				
	o_2	u_{21}				
a_2	o_3	u_{31}	u_{32}	Non Evaluated area		
	o_4	u_{41}	u_{42}			
	o_5	u_{51}	u_{52}			
.	..	Evaluated area	$\cdots$			
	..		$\ldots$			
	..	$\ldots$	$\ldots$			
.	..	$\ldots$	$\ldots$	$\cdots$		
	..	$\ldots$	$\ldots$	$\cdots$		
a_k	o_{n-1}	$u_{(n-1)1}$	$u_{(n-1)2}$	$\cdots$	$u_{(n-1)(m-1)}$	$u_{(n-1)m}$
	o_n	u_{n1}	u_{n2}	$\cdots$	$u_{n(m-1)}$	u_{nm}

Theoretical areas of SE: (TSE) = $m \times n$.

Filled Area of SE: FSE $= n+n-e_1+n-e_2+ \ldots +n-e_m = \sum_{j=1}^{m}(n-e_j) = nm - \sum_{j=1}^{m}e_j$

e_j = number of outcomes eliminated by the employment of value dimension j.

Figure 6.3 A typical cybernetic search-evaluation matrix

larger than the actually filled area of the matrix (*FSE*). Second, the typical cybernetic **SE** matrix is one in which value tradeoffs are deliberately avoided. If the search for, and evaluation of, policy options were analytic in a full sense, then the theoretically-defined area of the search-evaluation matrix must equal the actually-filled area. Denote the theoretical areas of the **SE** matrix by $TSE = mn$, and the actually-filled area by *FSE*. The extent of comprehensive evaluation at any given decision is, therefore, given by

$$CE = \frac{FSE}{TSE}, \quad 0 \leqslant CE \leqslant 1 \tag{6.1}$$

and $FSE = TSE$ if and only if $e_1 = e_2 = \ldots = 0$. This implies several things. An evaluation process is said to be analytic only if the actually observed **SE** matrix meets two necessary – but not sufficient – conditions:

    1 $n \geqslant k \geqslant 2$ and $m \geqslant 2$, where k is the number of options identified and evaluated by the decision maker, n is the number of outcomes explicitly assigned to these options, and m is the

number of value dimensions used to evaluate the explored options.

2 $CE = 1$, where $CE = \dfrac{FSE}{TSE}$ indicates the proportion of the search evaluation matrix which was actually analyzed by the decision maker.

Any observed evaluation process that fails to meet any one of these conditions cannot be defined as analytic.

Yet, sole reliance on the size and the filled area of the search evaluation matrix can be quite misleading. This becomes starkly evident when the formal aspects of cognitive evaluation processes are considered. As I pointed out in chapter 5, the deductions derived from the cognitive model with respect to the evaluation of policy options are very ambiguous. For one thing, there are several forms of evaluation that can be considered as cognitive in nature. Concomitantly, the formal aspects of the various forms of cognitive option appraisal are extremely imprecise. This is clearly shown in figure 6.4 which depicts three typical **SE** matrices that can be consistent with cognitive evaluation.

The first part of the figure represents unidimensional (lexicographic) evaluation. The **SE** matrix is given as an $n \times 1$ column vector, which clearly violates the first condition for analytic evaluation. (Note, however, that the second condition of $CE = 1$ is satisfied.) In this case we can clearly say that the evaluation process was non-analytic, and probably non-cybernetic in nature (because cybernetic evaluation will usually give us $CE < 1$). But, unfortunately, this is not the only form that cognitive evaluation processes can assume. The second part of figure 6.4 represents a multidimensional evaluation process in which low-probability outcomes (or undesirable ones) have been omitted, and hence the set of outcomes attached to some of the options is non-exhaustive. Without knowing anything about how a decision maker came up with this matrix (that is, what was left out and whether the actual contents of the matrix make any substantive sense), we might conclude that the evaluation process was analytic in nature because the **SE** matrix satisfies the two conditions for analytic evaluation. Finally, the third part of figure 6.4 represents a typical case of consistency preservation. The evaluation of options may be multidimensional in nature, but the selection of criteria used for their appraisal is such that it leads to consistent (or near-consistent) ranking of outcomes on all value dimensions. This is reflected in the near-identical ranking of outcomes over all value dimensions. Here too, basing our inferences strictly on the size and the filled area of the **SE**

a. Unidimensional (lexicographic) evaluation

SE

Option	Outcome	Value dimension
a_1	o_1	r_{11}
	o_2	r_{21}
a_2	o_3	r_{31}
	o_4	r_{41}
	o_5	r_{51}
.	...	...
.	...	...
a_k	o_{n-1}	$r_{(n-1)1}$
	o_n	r_{n1}

b. Reduced search

SE

Option	Outcome	Value dimension				
		1	2	3	...	m
a_1	o_2	r_{21}	r_{22}	r_{23}	...	r_{2m}
a_2	o_3	r_{31}	r_{32}	r_{33}	...	r_{3m}
	o_5	r_{51}	r_{52}	r_{53}	...	r_{5m}
.	..	...	...	...	...	...
	..	...	...	...	...	...
a_k	o_{n-1}	$r_{(n-1)1}$	$r_{(n-1)2}$	$r_{(n-1)3}$	...	$r_{(n-1)m}$
	o_n	r_{n1}	r_{n2}	r_{n3}	...	r_{nm}

c. Conflict reducing evaluation

SE

Option	Outcome	Value dimension				
		1	2	3	...	m
a_1	o_1	1	1	1	...	1
	o_2	3	3	3	...	3
a_2	o_3	2	2	2	...	2
	o_4	4	5	4	...	4
	o_5	5	4	5	...	5
.	..	...	...	...	...	...
	..	...	...	...	...	...
a	o_{n-1}	n	n	$n-1$	...	n
	o_n	$n-1$	$n-1$	n	...	$n-1$

r_{ij} = rank of outcome i on value dimension j.

Figure 6.4 Cognitive search-evaluation matrices

matrix would result in erroneous inference regarding the type of model characterizing this stage.

It seems, therefore, that any attempt to derive such conclusions must go beyond the structural aspects of option evaluation, which are represented by the size and filled area of the **SE** matrix and do not require any knowledge of its substantive contents. Such aspects give no clear indication of the thoroughness and difficulty of option evaluation in substantive terms. Most importantly, they do not reflect the tradeoff complexity of option evaluation, and thus of the emotional difficulty involved in making a particular decision. A more thorough assessment of the substantive problems involved in evaluating policy options requires exploration of the contents of the **SE** matrix; it necessitates inspection of the manner in which decision makers rank-order each of the outcomes on each of the value dimensions. The inspection of structural aspects of option evaluation relies upon the deductions of the analytic model as a baseline for making discriminatory inferences. Assessment of the substantive complexity of evaluation processes requires reliance on the deductions derived from the cognitive model as a discriminatory baseline.

As noted above, cognitive decision makers aim at minimizing or completely eliminating value conflict while evaluating multiple policy options. Decision makers are said to rank all outcomes consistently over different value dimensions. In the third part of figure 6.4 we see a typical pattern of near-consistent ranking of outcomes over multiple value dimensions. In contrast, analytic decision makers attempt to optimize over conflicting goals rather than disregard or artificially eliminate value conflict. In order to measure systematically the tradeoff complexity of a given **SE** matrix, no knowledge of the cardinal utilities assigned by decision makers to various outcomes is necessary. All we need to know is how these outcomes are ranked in terms of ordinal preferences over each of the value dimensions deemed relevant by a decision maker. The measurement of tradeoff complexity is important not only in the context of individual choice analysis, but – as will become evident – also as a measure of group polarization.

6.3.1 Tradeoff complexity

Given n outcomes ranked from 1 to n on m value dimensions, what is the maximum possible level of inconsistent ranking of the outcomes? (Inconsistency refers here to a comparison of the way outcomes are ranked across different value dimensions.) If $m = 2$, then the maximum level of inconsistent ranking of outcomes across the two value dimensions occurs when outcomes are ranked from 1, 2, . . ., n

on the first value dimension and the same outcomes are ranked as $n, n-1, \ldots, 1$ on the second. More generally, denote the ranking of outcome i $[i = 1, \ldots, n]$ on value dimension j $[j = 1, \ldots, m]$ by r^i_j. Denote the squared rank-distance between the rank of outcome i on value dimension 1 and the rank of the same outcome on value dimension 2 by $d^i_{12} = (r^i_1 - r^i_2)^2$. To examine the total disagreement between the ranking of n outcomes on one value dimension and the ranking of the same outcomes on another value dimension, we have

$$D = \sum_{i=1}^{n} d^i_{12} = \sum_{i=1}^{n} (r^i_1 - r^i_2)^2 \tag{6.2}$$

The maximum possible distance is given (as mentioned above) when $r^i_2 = n - r^i_1 + 1$ for all $i \in O$. Thus, in such a case, equation (6.2) can be expressed as

$$D_{max} = \sum_{i=1}^{n} [r^i_1 - (n - r^i_1 + 1)]^2 = \sum_{i=1}^{n} [2r^i_1 - (n+1)]^2$$

$$= \sum_{i=1}^{n} [4r^{i2}_1 - 4r^i_1(n+1) + (n+1)^2] \tag{6.3}$$

Using the rules of summation, we have

$$D_{max} = 4 \sum_{i=1}^{n} r^{i2}_1 - 4(n+1) \sum_{i=1}^{n} r^i_1 + n(n+1)^2 \tag{6.4}$$

Given that the sum of integers from 1 to n is

$$\sum_{i=1}^{n} i = \frac{n(n+1)}{2},$$

and the sum of the squared integers from 1 to n is

$$\sum_{i=1}^{n} i^2 = \frac{n(n+1)(2n+1)}{6},$$

we can substitute these expressions in equation (6.4), yielding

$$D_{max} = \frac{4n(n+1)(2n+1)}{6} - n(n+1)^2 = \frac{n(n^2-1)}{3} \tag{6.5}$$

Now we can generalize the computation of the maximum possible sum of squared distances among ranks for any given number of value dimensions. To do this, we must consider three separate cases, which vary in terms of the number of value dimensions included in a decision process. The first includes cases where the number of value dimensions is even, that is, when $m = 2, 4, 6, \ldots$ The second case is one

		SE				
	1	2	3	...	$m-1$	m
1	1	2	3	...	$m-1$	m
2	2	3	4	...	m	1
3	3	4	5	...	1	2
.	..	..	..	...	...	...
.	..	..	..	...	...	...
$m-1$	$m-1$	m	1	...	$m-3$	$m-2$
m	m	1	2	...	$m-2$	$m-1$

Figure 6.5 A cyclical preferences matrix

wherein the number of value dimensions used for appraising options is odd but not equal to the number of outcomes, that is, when $m = 1, 3, 5 \ldots$ and $m \neq n$. The third case is one where the number of value dimensions (which can be either odd or even) equals the number of outcomes ($m = n$).

When m is even, it is easy to verify that the maximum possible sum of square rank-distances occurs if precisely $m/2$ value dimensions are ranked identically, e.g., $r_j^1 = 1$, $r_j^2 = 2$, $r_j^3 = 3$, $\ldots$, $r_j^n = n$ for all $j = 1, 2, \ldots, m/2$, and all other value dimensions $q = m/2 + 1, m/2 + 2, \ldots, m$ are ranked identically and in precisely the opposite way, i.e., $r_q^1 = n$, $r_q^2 = n - 1, \ldots, r_q^i = 1$, for all $q = m/2 + 1, m/2 + 2, \ldots, m$. For this case, we can rewrite equation (6.2) as follows:

$$D_{max} = \sum_{i=1}^{n} \left[\frac{m}{2} r_1^i - \frac{m}{2}(n - r_1^i + 1) \right]^2 = \frac{nm^2(n^2 - 1)}{12} \tag{6.6}$$

The second case is one where $m = n$ (regardless of whether m and n are odd or even). In such a case, the search-evaluation matrix is square ($m \times m$), and the maximum possible rank differences occur when the SE matrix is of the general form shown in figure 6.5. In this case, it turns out that equation (6.6) provides D_{max} whether m is odd or even.

The third case concerns an odd number of value dimensions which does not equal the number of outcomes ($m \neq n$), and m is larger than n. For this case, the maximum possible sum of squared differences can be extrapolated from the previous two cases rather simply. The maximum sum of squared rank-distances in this case can be conceptualized as:

$$D_{max} = \sum_{i=1}^{n} \left[\frac{(m-1)r_1^i}{2} - \frac{(m+1)(n - r_1^i + 1)}{2} \right]^2 \tag{6.7}$$

239

$$\text{SE}$$

	1	2	3	$\displaystyle\sum_{j=1}^{2}\sum_{k=j}^{3}(r_j-r_k)^2$
1	1	2	3	$1+4+1=6$
2	2	3	1	$1+1+4=6$
3	3	1	2	$4+1+1=6$
				18

$$D_{max}=\frac{nm^2(n^2-1)}{12}$$

$$\text{SE}$$

	1	2	3	$\displaystyle\sum_{j=1}^{2}\sum_{k=j}^{3}(r_j-r_k)^2$
1	1	1	3	$0+4+4=8$
2	2	2	2	$0+0+0=0$
3	3	3	1	$0+4+4=8$
				16

$$D_{max}=\frac{(m^2-1)(n^2-1)}{12}$$

Figure 6.6 Maximum sum of squared rank differences when $m=n=3$

However, with $(m-1)/2$ value dimensions ranked identically, and $(m+1)/2$ value dimensions also ranked identically, we will have for each outcome i only $(m^2-1)/4$ valid (that is, nonzero) pairwise comparisons instead of the normal $m(m-1)/2$ number of valid pairwise comparisons. Thus equation (6.7) can be reduced to equation (6.5) multiplied by $(m^2-1)/4$. Simplifying this gives

$$D_{max}=\frac{(m^2-1)(n^2-1)n}{12} \tag{6.8}$$

To illustrate the difference between equations (6.6) and (6.8) when $m=n$ and both are odd, consider figure 6.6. When the maximum sum of squared differences is represented by matrix 6.6.1 the maximum sum of squared rank distances is 18, as computed through equation (6.8). However, when the same case (i.e., $m=n=3$) is represented by matrix 6.6.2, the maximum sum of squared differences, computed via equation (6.6), is only 16.

Table 6.2 provides a set of maximum sums of squared rank differences (D_{max}s) for various numbers of outcomes, n, and value dimensions m.

Table 6.2. *Maximum sums of squared rank-distances for* $m = [2, 9]$ *and* $n = [2, 10]$

Value dimensions (m)	Outcomes (n)	$D_{\max}$	Value dimensions (m)	Outcomes (n)	$D_{\max}$
2	2	2	6	2	18
	3	8		3	72
	4	20		4	180
	5	40		5	360
	6	70		6	630
	7	112		7	1008
	8	168		8	1512
	9	240		9	2160
	10	330		10	2970
3	2	4	7	2	24
	3	18		3	98
	4	45		4	245
	5	90		5	490
	6	158		6	858
	7	252		7	1372
	8	378		8	2058
	9	540		9	2940
	10	742		10	4042
4	2	8	8	2	32
	3	32		3	128
	4	80		4	320
	5	160		5	640
	6	280		6	1120
	7	448		7	1792
	8	672		8	2688
	9	960		9	3840
	10	1320		10	5280
5	2	12	9	2	40
	3	50		3	162
	4	125		4	405
	5	250		5	810
	6	438		6	1418
	7	700		7	2268
	8	1050		8	3402
	9	1500		9	4860
	10	2062		10	6682

Note: For even m or for $m = n$, $D_{\max} = \dfrac{m^2 n(n^2 - 1)}{12}$

For odd m and $m > n$, $D_{\max} = \dfrac{(m^2 - 1)(n^2 - 1)n}{12}$

241

The measure of tradeoff complexity uses the index of maximum sum of squared rank-distances in a decision layout with n outcomes and m value dimensions as the baseline for computation. Specifically, trade-off complexity represents a proportion of that maximum that is actually reflected in a given formulation of a decision problem. Formally,

1. For even m or for $m = n$:

$$TC = \frac{12 \sum\limits_{i=1}^{n} \sum\limits_{j=1}^{m-1} \sum\limits_{q=j+1}^{m} (r_j^i - r_q^i)^2}{nm^2(n^2 - 1)} \qquad (6.9)$$

2. For odd $m > n$:

$$TC = \frac{12 \sum\limits_{i=1}^{n} \sum\limits_{j=1}^{m-1} \sum\limits_{q=j+1}^{m} (r_j^i - r_q^i)^2}{(m^2 - 1)(n^2 - 1)n} \qquad (6.10)$$

where n = number of outcomes, m = number of value dimensions, and r_j^i, r_q^i = rank of outcome i on value dimension $j(q)$.

In general, the index of tradeoff complexity ranges from zero to one. It enables us not only to discriminate among different process models, but also to determine degrees of complexity within any given model. The general principle is that the higher the value of TC, the more analytic is the evaluation process. The value of TC will always be zero whenever options are evaluated on a single goal (value dimension) or when options are ranked consistently over multiple value dimensions. Thus this index allows detection of consistency preserving evaluation regardless of the number of outcomes or the number of value dimensions employed for option appraisal. In the case of the elimination by aspects (EBA) process, the tradeoff complexity index can be obtained by averaging – via a stepwise procedure – over separate TC scores obtained for s steps of elimination. This is formalized as follows: Suppose that a decision maker uses s evaluation criteria to eliminate all but one policy option. For each step, 1, 2, . . ., s, the tradeoff complexity score is computed over the filled (explored, area of the **SE** matrix. This can be conducted most conveniently in a backward fashion, starting with the sth step and going to the first. Thus, averaging over the s steps of elimination, we have

$$TC_{EBA} = \frac{1}{s} \sum\limits_{r=s}^{1} \left[\frac{12 \sum\limits_{i=1}^{n} \sum\limits_{j=1}^{m-1} \sum\limits_{q=j+1}^{m} (r_j^i - r_q^i)^2}{n_r m_r^2 (n_r^2 - 1)} \right] \qquad (6.11.1)$$

For even m_r or for $m_r > n_r$, at the rth elimination step, and

$$TC_{EBA} = \frac{1}{s} \sum_{r=s}^{1} \left[\frac{12 \sum_{i=1}^{n} \sum_{j=1}^{m-1} \sum_{q=j+1}^{m} (r_j^i - r_q^i)^2}{(m_r^2 - 1)(n_r^2 - 1) n_r} \right] \tag{6.11.2}$$

for odd m_r and $m_r n_r$ (where s is the number of elimination steps employed by the decision maker). Note that equations (6.11.1) and (6.11.2) are equivalent to equations (6.9) and (6.10), respectively, when $s = 1$ or when $m_1 = m_2 = \ldots = m_s$ and $n_1 = n_2 = \ldots . n_s$ (that is, when a single elimination step is being used). This implies that analytic evaluation is seen as a special case of the EBA procedure. This may sound quite counterintuitive but it actually is not. The analytic **SE** matrix is, as we have seen, a superstructure of the typical cybernetic **SE** matrix (figure 6.3), and both matrices may coincide in an extreme case.

The power of the tradeoff complexity index stems from two factors: its discriminative capacity, and the nature of information required for its computation. As we have just seen, this index allows accurate estimates of the complexity of the choice problem in terms of the way it was laid out by the decision maker. Thus it enables rigorous differentiation among the deductions of the three process models for the evaluation stage. It enables systematic comparisons of individuals who are engaged in the process of solving the same (or similar) problems in terms of how they interpret possible solutions. It shows how individual assessments of the problems differ in terms of the various outcomes perceived, or in terms of the criteria by which policy options should be evaluated. Moreover, this index is eminently applicable in empirical analyses of foreign policy decisions because it (as well as the CE index) does not rely on information that is difficult to obtain from available sources (such as cardinal utilities). Rather, it requires only information about ordinal preferences of a decision maker over the various outcomes he or she considered in a given situation.

Nonetheless, it must be emphasized that exclusive reliance on the index of tradeoff complexity in assessing which model was at work during evaluation processes can be quite misleading just as exclusive reliance on the CE index could be. Since the tradeoff complexity index is insensitive to any number of outcomes or value dimensions above two of each (i.e., $m \geq 2$, $n \geq 2$), it does not reflect the amount of mental effort required for evaluating a highly elaborate **SE** matrix in terms of its actually filled area. Therefore, the tradeoff complexity index must

243

be used in conjunction with both the FSE and CE indices to allow reliable inferences on the kind of model which best characterizes an empirical case of real-world evaluation.

6.3.1.1 *Tradeoff complexity in international crises*

To exemplify the way in which the various measures of evaluation processes can be applied to empirical data, I offer two illustrations of evaluation of policy options in historical cases. The first is taken from Maoz's (1981) study of the Entebbe crisis, and the second is taken from Stein and Tanter's (1980) study of the 1967 crisis in the Middle East leading to the Six Day War. In the Entebbe case, the search-evaluation matrices of the three principal decision makers had cardinal utility entries, but since the various measures of evaluation require only ordinal ranking of outcomes, the **SE** matrices will be transformed to ordinal preferences. Table 6.3 show these matrices along with the various quantitative properties of the evaluation process conducted by the three principal decision makers.

The data given in table 6.3 show that all three decision makers analyzed in the Entebbe study displayed a high level of comprehensiveness in their evaluation of the problem. This is evident both from the generally extensive area of the **SE** matrices, and from the fact that the CE measure for all three was at its maximal level of 1.0. This may lead us to conclude that all three decision makers were – procedurally speaking – highly analytic in their design and evaluation of the decision problem. Yet this conclusion would be highly premature (as was, in fact, the conclusion I derived from the data in the original study). A close inspection of the content of the matrices in terms of the way the decision makers ranked the outcomes over the various value dimensions reveals a strong conflict reducing tendency. This is well reflected in the low tradeoff complexity scores. These scores suggest a strong tendency to reduce value conflict by a similar ranking of outcomes over different value dimensions, and hence a relatively high dependence among the criteria used to analyze the problem.

Another useful aspect of the measure of tradeoff complexity that is revealed by the empirical illustration is our ability to differentiate among decision makers. Even though the procedural aspects of the evaluation process were identical for all three decision makers, as seen by the identical design of the **SE** matrix, substantive differences among them emerge when their tradeoff complexity scores are compared. Rabin and Peres, despite different ranking of outcomes, displayed nearly identical levels of tradeoff complexity, and these were slightly lower than those displayed by Allon. The implication of this is

Table 6.3. *Properties of evaluation processes in the Entebbe crisis*

a. Rabin

| Option | Outcome | Value dimension | | | | Squared rank differences |
		Hum.	Cred.	Dom.	Int.	
Mil. Res.	Success	3	1	1	1	12
	Failure	6	4	6	6	12
Negotiation	Success	1.5	3	3	2.5	6
	Failure	4.5	6	5	5	4.75
Amin	Success	1.5	2	2	2.5	2
	Failure	4.5	5	4	4	2.75
						39.50

$$CE_{Rabin} = \frac{24}{24} = 1.0; \quad TC_{Rabin} = \frac{39.50}{280} = 0.141$$

b. Peres

| Option | Outcome | Value dimension | | | | Squared rank differences |
		Hum.	Cred.	Dom.	Int.	
Mil. Res.	Success	3	1	1	1	12
	Failure	6	4.5	4	4	10.75
Negotiation	Success	1.5	3	2	3	6.75
	Failure	4.5	6	6	6	6.75
Amin	Success	1.5	2	3	2.5	2.50
	Failure	4.5	4.5	5	5	1
						39.75

$$CE_{Peres} = \frac{24}{24} = 1.0; \quad TC_{Peres} = \frac{39.75}{280} = 0.142$$

Key:
Mil. Res = Military rescue operation
Negotiation = Negotiation on release of Palestinian prisoners
Amin = Induce Amin to bring about release of hostages
Hum. = Human life
Cred. = Credibility of anti-terrorist policy
Dom. = Domestic support for the government
Int. = Israel's international standing

Table 6.3 (*cont.*)

c. Allon

| Option | Outcome | Value dimension | | | | Squared rank differences |
		Hum.	Cred.	Dom.	Int.	
Mil. Res.	Success	3	1	1	1	12
	Failure	6	5	5	6	4
Negotiation	Success	1.5	3	4	2	14.75
	Failure	4.5	6	6	5	6.75
Amin	Success	1.5	2	2	3	4.75
	Failure	4.5	4	3	4	4.75
						47.00

$$CE_{Allon} = \frac{24}{24} = 1.0; \quad TC_{Allon} = \frac{47.00}{280} = 0.168$$

that an identical procedural framing of a decision problem by different individuals should not be taken to reflect a similar substantive framing of the problem. The two dimensions are not necessarily related. Taken together, these two dimensions of the evaluation process may provide a more balanced assessment of the kind of model at work, and better discriminate among individuls. It is obvious that, contrary to the original conclusion that was based strictly on procedural aspects of evaluation processes, cognitive elements played a key role in the ordering of outcomes in terms of preferences. Conflict reducing tendencies are apparent despite the fact that all three decision makers in the Entebbe crisis did recognize and make value tradeoffs.

The Stein and Tanter (1980) study is less useful in terms of our ability to discriminate among individual evaluations of the decision problems involved. Nonetheless, it might be instructive to examine their **SE** matrices to see how they evolved over time and across decisions, and to examine the conclusions of these authors in terms of our measures. For the purpose of such an analysis, I will assume a unitary actor model which allows application of individual choice analysis in a decisional setting that was actually collective in nature. Table 6.4 depicts the four **SE** matrices representing the three major Israeli decisions during the 1967 crisis.

Let us now examine how the results of this analysis relate to the substantive interpretations of the four major Israeli decisions during the May–June 1967 crisis made by Stein and Tanter. (I restrict my

Table 6.4. *Evaluation processes in the Israeli cabinet (May 19–June 4, 1967)*

a. The May 19 mobilization decision

| Option | Outcome | Value dimension | | | | Squared rank differences |
		Mil. sec.	Econ. cost	Dom.	Int.	
Mobilization	Arab attack	3	3	—	—	0
	No attack	1	2	—	—	1
No mobil.	Arab attack	4	4	—	—	0
	No attack	2	1	—	—	1
						2

$$CE_1 = \frac{8}{16} = 0.5; \quad TC_1 = \frac{2}{20} = 0.10$$

b. The May 23 decision to delay attack

| Option | Outcome | Value dimension | | | | Squared rank differences |
		Mil. sec.	Econ. cost	Dom.	Int.	
Attack	US–Soviet int.	2	2.5	4	3	8.75
	US int.	1	2.5	3	1	12.75
	Soviet int.	6	4.5	6	5	6.75
	No int.	3	4.5	5	4	8.75
Delay	Arab attack	5	6	1	6	68.00
	No attack	4	1	2	2	19.00
						124.00

$$CE_2 = \frac{24}{24} = 1.0; \quad TC_2 = \frac{124}{280} = 0.443$$

c. The May 28 decision to delay attack

| Option | Outcome | Value dimension | | | | Squared rank differences |
		Mil. sec.	Econ. cost	Dom.	Int.	
Attack	US–Soviet int.	2	3.5	6	2	42.75
	US int.	1	3.5	5	1	46.75
	Soviet int.	4	5.5	8	4	42.75
	No. int.	3	5.5	7	3	46.75

Table 6.4 (*cont.*)

Delay	Flot.-Arab att.	7	7	1	7	108.00
	Flot.-No attack	5	1	2	5	51.00
	No Flot-attack	8	8	3	8	75.00
	No Flot.-No Att.	6	2	4	6	44.00
						457.00

$$CE_3 = \frac{32}{32} = 1.0; \quad TC_2 = \frac{457}{672} = 0.680$$

Note: The June 4 decision to attack has the same **SE** matrix as the May 28 decision to delay attack.
Source: Stein and Tanter (1980: 269–305).

comments to the interpretations of evaluation processes.) First, Stein and Tanter argue that the evaluation of the May 19, 1967 mobilization problem was cybernetic in nature, consisting of programmed analysis of the costs and benefits associated with the two available policy options (Mobilization or No Mobilization), and while avoiding value tradeoffs among the various values involved (Stein and Tanter, 1980: 140–156). My analysis of the procedural structure and the substantive content of this evaluation process lends clear support to this interpretation. Only half the area of the **SE** matrix in table 6.4a was actually considered. Moreover, the low tradeoff complexity score indicates a tendency for tradeoff avoidance. This account is incomplete, however, because the authors provide no evidence of sequential evaluation. Second, in the May 23 decision to delay military action, evaluation is interpreted as essentially analytic "within constraints" including trade-off calculations (pp. 165–175). Table 6.4b again supports this observation. The entire area of the **SE** matrix is filled, and the tradeoff complexity index is substantially higher than that of the May 19 evaluation process. The medium-level tradeoff complexity score indicates the effects of constraints on the analytic nature of evaluation.

Third, the May 28 decision to further delay attack (and allow for the formation of an international flotilla to open the Tiran Straits) is also judged to be essentially analytic both in terms of procedures and content (pp. 199–213). Again, table 6.4c provides support to this conclusion. Finally, the same interpretation is given by the authors to the June 4 decision to attack. However, they argue that the evaluation process was somewhat constrained in terms of tradeoff calculations. Specifically, "[t]his simplification of choice was not the doing of the decision makers: they did not have to simplify an unpleasant conflict of values since the, conflict of a week ago [May 28] had all but disappeared. Changes in the estimates of the costs and benefits converged to favor preemption, and members of the cabinet had very little integrating and trading-off to do" (Stein and Tanter, 1980: 248). The fact that the substantive content of the **SE** matrix of June 4 is identical to that of the May 28 **SE** matrix does not support this interpretation. In fact, the ranking of outcomes on the various value dimensions suggests a considerable tradeoff complexity. What made the preemption option more attractive on June 4 was not a change in value (or preference) estimates. Rather, it was the increase in the subjective probability of an Arab attack (from 0.61 on May 28 to 0.8 on June 4), and the probability of US support (from 0.15 on May 28 to 0.80 on June 4).

The formal characterization of evaluation processes provides important insights into more qualitative interpretations of the kind of model that accounts for them. The focus of this analysis on both the procedural and substantive aspects of evaluation adds considerable power to such interpretations. However, it is not always possible to get converging results from analyses that are based strictly on procedural aspects of evaluation processes and those that are based on the substantive content thereof. This creates some difficulties with respect to clear-cut interpretation of the results, as the analysts confronted by a procedurally analytic **SE** matrix may encounter low levels of tradeoff complexity when analyzing the substantive content of preferences. In such cases, judgment based on more qualitative data becomes indispensable. Yet, the fact that procedural and substantive aspects of evaluation processes do not always converge should not deter us from using both types of measures. On the contrary, they save us from unwarranted inferences and premature closure.

6.4   COPING WITH UNCERTAINTY: FORMAL ASPECTS OF INTUITIVE PREDICTION

This section examines the relationship between quantitative and qualitative expressions of uncertainty by decision makers and the extent to which subjective probability estimates can be reliably derived from documentary material. I discuss general rules for revising subjective estimates of uncertain future events in light of new information. These rules – which are generally associated with analytic revision processes – will be contrasted with systematic fallacies which are associated with cybernetic and cognitive revision.

6.4.1 The logic of "probabilistic" language

To understand the logic of coping with uncertainty, the distinction between decisions under risk and decisions under uncertainty (discussed in chapter 3) must be briefly recapitulated. Broadly speaking, decision under risk is one wherein at least one of the policy options considered by a decision maker can yield at least two outcomes over which there exists a known probability distribution. By a "known probability distribution," I mean that the decision maker is aware of the existence of an empirically established frequency distribution or a theoretically proven probability distribution which is associated with such outcomes. Probability distributions over outcomes associated with games of chance such as roulette are theoretically established by probability theory. Hence, they are "known" in the sense that they are deducible from a set of rules; they are also known through inductive generalizations based on large samples. Such probabilities are also called "objective" in that their values are independent of the judgment of the specific decision maker.

In contrast, conditions of uncertainty refer to cases where the probability distribution over multiple outcomes cannot be determined objectively, either because there exists no sampling distribution associated with this type of outcome, or no theoretical model referring to it. The precise nature of such a probability distribution is therefore a function of the decision maker's judgment. Probabilities assigned to a particular set of outcomes will represent subjective evaluations of the likelihood of their occurrence. Subjectivity, in such a context, takes on a different meaning. A subjective probability does not represent necessarily an estimate of the relative frequency of an event in a known population. Rather, it reflects the degree of confidence the decision maker places in the event's actual occurrence. It could be seen as equivalent to an amount of money that a decision maker is willing to place on a bet involving this event, relative to the total amount of bets placed by others. For example, saying that the probability of an outcome x is 0.3 is equivalent to saying "I am willing to bet one dollar against every two dollars and 33 cents that event x will occur." Likewise, saying that outcome y has a 0.8 probability is equivalent to betting one dollar for every quarter another person is willing to bet on the non-occurrence of this event. The idea here is simply that people may be willing to risk more money in betting on events they are confident will occur, and will require greater financial inducement to get into bets about events they are not very confident about.

Given this perspective of uncertainty, it is not surprising that foreign policy decision makers normally shy away from precise quantitative estimates associated with future events. However, the lack of precise quantitative estimates of the probabilities associated with decisional outcomes does not necessarily reflect a deviation from the tenets of analytic revision procedures. Decision makers may – and often do – use probabilistic language to express degrees of subjective confidence in the occurrence of the outcomes of policy options. However, to analyze the extent to which those probabilistic expressions of uncertainty conform to the mathematical and logical foundations of analytic revision, which are themselves based on the principles of probability theory, we must be able to systematically transform verbal expressions of uncertainty into numerical values.

A body of literature in social psychology deals with the implications of the usage of qualitative expressions of uncertainty in inferential and judgmental tasks.[2] One of the main issues this literature addresses concerns the extent to which people are consistent in their usage of "probabilistic" expressions over time and across events. The question is whether a qualitative probabilistic expression which is given in two different contexts (or in two distinct points in time) by the same person implies the same quantitative equivalent. The findings on this question are relatively unambiguous: people are generally consistent in the way they convert qualitative expressions of uncertainty to designate a certain level of confidence in the occurrence of an event in different circumstances and over time (Wallsten and Budescu, 1983; Budescu and Wallsten, 1985). Another important issue in this literature concerns interindividual differences in the usage and interpretation of quantitative probabilistic expressions. Do words like "unlikely," "better than even," "highly probable," imply the same quantitative equivalent to different people using them? Here the answer seems to be decidedly negative. Different individuals use the same expressions to denote different levels of uncertainty. These interindividual differences in the use of probabilistic language cannot be accounted for by intraindividual variations in the usage of such terms (Budescu and Wallsten, 1985).

However, our concern here is with general tendencies of translating qualitative expressions of uncertainty to quantitative ones, taking account of interindividual differences in such conversions. This can be done by using data on such conversions and looking at measures of central tendency and of dispersion for various probabilistic phrases. Several researchers have collected such data through questionnaires

[2] See Cohen (1972) and Wallsten and Budescu (1983) for reviews of this literature.

Table 6.5. *The Sherman Kent scale of probability phrase conversions*

Very good chance	Lower bound	Upper bound	Range	Midpoint
Highly unlikely	0.00	0.10	0.10	0.05
Little chance	0.02	0.20	0.18	0.10
Improbable	0.15	0.40	0.25	0.27
Unlikely	0.15	0.42	0.27	0.29
We doubt	0.20	0.45	0.25	0.33
Better than even	0.50	0.60	0.10	0.55
We believe	0.55	0.78	0.23	0.67
Likely	0.55	0.70	0.15	0.63
Probable	0.55	0.70	0.15	0.63
Very good chance	0.70	0.90	0.20	0.80
Highly likely	0.77	0.95	0.18	0.86
Almost certainly	0.90	1.00	0.10	0.95

Note: For the original version see Barclay *et al.* (1977: appendix B).

containing lists of probabilistic expressions which were submitted to experts and laypersons. Subjects were required to convert them into numerical probabilities (or ranges of probability). Table 6.5 presents the results of a study by Sherman Kent conducted in the CIA during the early sixties.

A more detailed study was conducted by Ruth Beyth-Marom (1982). She asked several high-ranking people in Israel's defense and intelligence establishment to complete a questionnaire containing several probabilistic phrases and replace them with precise probability scores. The assignment of numerical scores was done without any reference to a given context. Thus, Beyth-Marom labeled this an "in isolation" conversion. She then went on to examine the extent to which these assessments were consistent whether made in context (the context being intelligence reports containing probabilistic language) or in isolation. As noted above, she found considerable within-subject consistency but significant between-subject variability in terms of translation of verbal expressions of uncertainty to quantitative ones. The typical "in isolation" numerical values of probabilistic expressions are given in table 6.6.

Due to the recurrent finding of high levels of interpersonal differences in conversion of verbal expressions of uncertainty into numerical values, Beyth-Marom recommended a seven-point ordinal scale to be used by political and other organizations commonly engaged with such tasks to reduce misunderstanding of the degree of uncertainty implied in a given verbal expression. This scale is useful for our purposes as it allows some logical derivations concerning possible

Table 6.6. *The Beyth-Marom scale of probability conversions*

No.	Verbal expression	C_{25}–C_{75}		C_{10}–C_{90}		Midpoint
		Limits	Range	Limits	Range	
1	Not likely	0.05–0.15	0.10	0.02–0.18	0.16	0.10
2	Very low chance	0.10–0.18	0.08	0.04–0.23	0.19	0.14
3	Poor chance	0.11–0.25	0.14	0.04–0.33	0.29	0.18
4	Doubtful	0.16–0.33	0.17	0.11–0.39	0.28	0.25
5	Low chance	0.22–0.34	0.12	0.15–0.38	0.23	0.27
6	Small chance	0.22–0.36	0.14	0.17–0.42	0.25	0.29
7	Can't rule out entirely	0.24–0.49	0.25	0.12–0.58	0.36	0.35
8	Chances are not great	0.28–0.41	0.13	0.22–0.52	0.30	0.36
9	Not inevitable	0.35–0.56	0.21	0.26–0.59	0.33	0.42
10	Perhaps	0.36–0.53	0.17	0.28–0.58	0.30	0.43
11	One must consider	0.37–0.59	0.22	0.27–0.64	0.37	0.47
12	There is a chance	0.37–0.60	0.23	0.28–0.67	0.39	0.48
13	May	0.41–0.58	0.17	0.32–0.65	0.33	0.49
14	It could be	0.42–0.57	0.15	0.34–0.63	0.29	0.49
15	Possible	0.51–0.58	0.07	0.42–0.61	0.19	0.53
16	One can expect	0.51–0.63	0.12	0.42–0.69	0.17	0.56
17	Reasonable to assume	0.52–0.69	0.17	0.43–0.81	0.38	0.61
18	Likely	0.53–0.69	0.16	0.42–0.81	0.39	0.61
19	It seems	0.53–0.65	0.12	0.50–0.69	0.19	0.61
20	Non-negligible chance	0.53–0.67	0.14	0.36–0.77	0.41	0.61
21	It seems to me	0.54–0.67	0.13	0.50–0.73	0.23	0.62
22	One should assume	0.54–0.68	0.14	0.48–0.75	0.27	0.62
23	Reasonable chance	0.54–0.69	0.15	0.49–0.81	0.32	0.64
24	Meaningful chance	0.63–0.80	0.17	0.58–0.86	0.26	0.72
25	High chance	0.75–0.87	0.12	0.71–0.91	0.20	0.81
26	Close to certain	0.75–0.92	0.17	0.58–0.97	0.39	0.84
27	Most likely	0.78–0.92	0.14	0.72–0.97	0.25	0.85
28	Nearly certain	0.83–0.96	0.13	0.76–0.99	0.23	0.91
29	Very high chance	0.87–0.96	0.09	0.83–0.99	0.16	0.91
30	Certain	0.98–1.00	0.02	0.93–1.00	0.07	0.98

Note: C_{xx} = xxth percentile.
Source: Beyth-Marom (1982: 261).

violations of the principles of probability theory in actual revision processes. This scale is depicted in table 6.7. (The upper part of the figure is taken directly from Beyth-Marom's study whereas the lower part adds the expressions taken from the Sherman Kent scale.)

Either the numerical midpoints or the ordinal grouping of the verbal expressions of uncertainty allow a systematic assessment of how a given usage of probabilistic language can be interpreted in light of the three decision making models. We noted that using probabilistic language is not sufficient for inferring that an empirical revision

Table 6.7. *A suggested common scale for the numerical translation of verbal probability expressions*

Rank	1	2	3	4	5	6	7
Range	0.00–0.10	0.11–0.30	0.31–0.49	0.50	0.51–0.70	0.71–0.90	0.91–1.00
	Very small chance	Small chance	Perhaps	It could be	Likely	High chance	Very high chance
	Poor chance	Doubtful	May		Reasonable to assume	Close to certain	Most likely
			chance not great		One should assume		
					Reasonable chance		
					It seems to me		
					can expect		
					it seems		
	Highly unlikely	Improbable	We doubt		Better than even	Very good chance	Almost certainly
	Little chance	Unlikely			We believe	Very good chance	
					Likely		
					Probable		

Note: Words below the separating line are from the Sherman Kent scale.
Source: Beyth-Marom (1982: 267); Barclay *et al.* (1977).

process fits the analytic model. But the nonusage of probabilistic language in estimation of the potential consequences of a policy option (i.e., the usage of deterministic language) indicates a potential violation of analytic revision. Now we can go an extra step toward detection of which model best describes a given revision process. The following conditions must be met to satisfy the logical boundaries of probability expressions:

1 *Approximate logical certainty.* A decision maker is said to be logically exhaustive in the usage of probabilistic language if and only if, for every set of outcomes stemming from the same option, the sum of their verbal probabilities is not clearly unequal to unity. For example, consider a person who contemplates taking an umbrella to work and bases the decision on the chances of rain. The verbal estimation of the chances of rain by such a person would be considered analytic only if the verbal expressions assigned to the rain and no rain events fall in categories (or precise numerical ranges) that sum up to one. If this person says that there is a very small chance of rain, but then it may rain, the sum of these two probabilistic expressions attached to two mutually exclusive events is clearly below unity. We call such a tendency, following Tversky and Kahneman (1986), *subcertainty.* Likewise, if an intelligence analyst argues that there is a good chance of an enemy attack and a better than even chance of no attack, the sum of the ordinal (or cardinal) levels of uncertainty attached to these events exceeds unity. This is a *supercertainty* violation of probability. In both cases – that of subcertainty and that of supercertainty – it is safe to conclude that the logical principles of probability theory have been violated and thus the revision process is clearly non-analytic.

2 *Intrapersonal consistency.* If the way in which a person uses a probabilistic expression depends on the context in which the statement is made, then the revision process cannot be seen as analytic. This condition requires people to use the same (or similar) probabilistic expression to denote the same (or similar) degree of uncertainty regardless of context.

To examine some of the difficulties involved in determining whether a real-world revision process wherein probabilistic language is used meets these conditions, it is useful to consider some of the elements of a cognitive theory of decision which has evoked much controversy in the social sciences. This is *prospect theory* (Tversky and Kahneman, 1979, 1981, 1986). Prospect theory evolved out of a series of experimental findings which showed consistent behavioral violations of the fundamental axioms of rationality. Specifically, Tversky and Kahneman showed that people confronted with even the most trivial decision problems make different decisions if the same decision problem is framed in different terms, that they violate the transitivity principle and the dominance principle if the way in which the decision problem is presented disguises the existence of a dominant strategy, and so forth. Prospect theory attempts to account for these violations in two steps. The first step introduces a typical utility function which is concave for gains and convex for losses. The idea is that people are risk-averse for gains and risk-acceptant for losses, and that risk-acceptance for losses is higher than risk-aversity for gains. This utility function is designed to explain why a decision maker that prefers a certain gain over a probabilistic gain with a higher expected value would prefer a probabilistic loss over a certain loss with a higher expected value. To demonstrate this tendency, consider the following example given by Tversky and Kahneman (1986).

Subjects (N = 150) were given the following set of choices:

Decision (i) Choose between:

A. *A sure gain of 240 dollars* (84%)
B. *25% chance to gain 1,000 dollars and 75% to gain nothing* (16%)

Decision (ii) Choose between:

C. *A sure loss of 750 dollars* (13%)
D. *75% chance to lose 1,000 dollars and 25% to lose nothing* (87%)

where the parenthesized numbers indicate the percentage of subjects choosing each of the options. It is easy to see that the expected value of option A (240 dollars) is smaller than the expected value of option B (250 dollars). Yet, from the perspective of rational choice theory, there is nothing wrong in choosing A over B (as most subjects did) if a person is essentially risk-averse. However, the problem from the perspective of rational choice theory is that the same person may well prefer option D over option C although the expected value of option C (a sure loss of 750) is the same as the expected loss of 750 dollars in option D. Moreover, the portfolio selected by a majority of the subjects (options A and D whose joint expected value is − 502.5 dollars) is weakly dominated by those selected only by a small minority (options B and C whose joint expected value is − 500 dollars). By positing an atypical utility function of the sort discussed above, the authors attempted to account for the effect of framing on individual choices.

The second step of the theory concerns the way that people cope with different levels of uncertainty. Again, the starting point here is a violation of the dominance principle when the dominance relation is disguised in the framing of the decision problem. To illustrate this problem consider the following choice problem in which the dominance relation is highly transparent.

Consider the following two lotteries, described by the percentage of marbles of different colors in each box and the amount of money you win or lose depending on the color of a randomly-drawn marble. Which lottery do you prefer?

Option A:

90% white	6% red	1% green	1% blue	2% yellow
0 dollars	win 45 dollars	win 30 dollars	lose 15 dollars	lose 15 dollars

Option B:

90% white	6% red	1% green	1% blue	2% yellow
0 dollars	win 45 dollars	win 45 dollars	lose 10 dollars	lose 15 dollars

Option B weakly dominates option A in that the payoffs associated with any outcome stemming from the former option are at least as good, and sometimes better, than those associated with option A. Indeed, a vast majority of the subjects chose option B over A. Now, consider another framing of these options where the dominance relations are masked.

Which lottery do you prefer?

Option C:

90% white	6% red	1% green	2% yellow
0 dollars	win 45 dollars	win 30 dollars	lose 15 dollars

Option D:

90% white	7% red	1% green	2% yellow
0 dollars	win 45 dollars	lose 10 dollars	lose 15 dollars

Option D still dominates option C, but now 58% of the 124 subjects in the experiment chose the dominated option C. To explain this tendency, the researchers posited that people confronted by uncertain outcomes tend to assign subjective weights to the probabilities associated with them. The subjective weighting of probabilities is related to their actual values but gives rise to a function $\pi(p)$ which has the following properties (Tversky and Kahneman, 1986):

1. $\pi(0) = 0$, that is, impossible events are discarded.
2. The weighting scale is normalized such that $\pi(1) = 1$. (But the authors argue that "the function is not well behaved near the end points.")
3. For low probabilities, $\pi(p) > p$ but $\pi(p) + \pi(1-p) \leq 1$. This is the subcertainty property discussed above. This means that "low probabilities are overweighted, moderate and high probabilities are underweighted, and the latter effect is more pronounced than the former."

257

4   $\pi(pr)/\pi(p) < \pi(pqr)/\pi(pq)$ for all $0 < p, q, r < 1$. This property is called subproportionality. It means that "for every fixed probability ratio r, the ratio of decision weights is closer to unity when the probabilities are low than when they are high (e.g., $\pi(.1)/\pi(.2) > \pi(.4)/\pi(.8)$)."

Tversky and Kahneman show that this weighting function accounts for a number of violations of the rationality axioms that are observed experimentally. The problem with both the utility function and the subjective weighting function of uncertain events is that they were developed inductively, that is, both constitute generalizations based on observed data and designed to account for these data. Thus, it is extremely difficult to determine *a priori* whether decision makers use these functions in actual problem solving processes without knowing what choices they have actually made. This is even more so when they do not use numerical expressions of probability or utility. Prospect theory offers many insights into behavioral aspects of decision making, but it is difficult to test outside the laboratory. Its predictions can be tested only against actual decisions which seemingly violate (or conform to) the principles of rational behavior, not against procedural aspects of the stages of the decision process that take place prior to an actual choice. Prospect theory enables us to say which decisions would be made by people given a formulation of a decision problem, but it is not capable of predicting – and indeed not designed to predict – how a decision problem is framed. Our concern, however, is precisely with how decision makers frame the decision problem, and the framing process clearly determines the choice stage.

However, this should not cause despair. There are several cognitive principles that suggest a crude procedure for determining whether cognitive revision is taking place in an actual decision process. This procedure is focused not only on the use or nonuse of probabilistic language (or the minimal logical and consistency criteria of its usage), but also on the confidence accompanying a certain prediction.

If one is uncertain about the occurrence of a future event, yet must assign certain numeric or verbal expression describing this certainty, then one should express the confidence one has in that prediction in a manner that would be strongly related to the specific expression of uncertainty used. For example, if one thinks that an event is as likely to occur as another, mutually exclusive, event, then one should assign a confidence weight of about 0.5 (on an 0 to 1 scale) to the prediction. Likewise, if one thinks that an event is highly likely, one should assign a high confidence weight to this prediction. As cognitive theorists have argued, and as it emerges from experimental evidence (Einhorn and Hogarth, 1978; Lichtenstein, Fischoff, and Phillips, 1982), people are often overconfident in their predictions and judgments. As opposed to typical expressions of uncertainty (such as likely, improbable, better than even chance, and so forth), expressions of confidence consist of such phrases as, "I may be wrong, but," "I strongly believe that," "I would tentatively expect," etc. Such expressions commonly preface the usage of probabilistic (numeric or verbal) expressions in decision makers' statements.

It is important, however, not to confuse expressions of confidence with expressions of uncertainty. The typical distinction between the two is that expressions of confidence accompany the use of probabilistic expressions, they do not stand by themselves. Probabilistic expressions may well stand by themselves without accompanying expressions of confidence. As was the case in the transformation of verbal expressions of uncertainty to ordinal or cardinal values, expressions of confidence could be transformed in the same manner. An ordinal or cardinal scaling of expressions of confidence could be used in conjunction with the verbal-to-numeric scales of uncertainty expressions to determine whether the degree of confidence expressed by a decision maker is warranted given his level of uncertainty.[3] The deduction of cognitive models of decision with respects to revision process is therefore based on the experimental evidence on overconfidence. A cognitive revision process involving the explicit use of probabilistic language is often accompanied by expressions of confidence that are unwarranted by the degree of certainty entailed in the probabilistic expressions. The discrepancy between the degree of uncertainty and the degree of confidence may indicate overconfidence rather than underconfidence. It must be noted, however, that numerical scaling of expressions of uncertainty and expressions of confidence seems consistent with experimental studies conducted in a related context, but the extent to which it fits revision processes in foreign policy settings is presently unknown.

6.4.2 Updating probability estimates

A more rigorous set of principles for distinguishing among the predictions of the three process models at the stage of revision focuses

---

[3] A similar technique is often used to assess the extent to which people whose task includes probabilistic estimates of future events, such as weather forecasters, are calibrated with reality. This technique – called calibration analysis – matches subjective probability estimates with the observed frequency of events and examines systematic tendencies of over or underestimation. See Beyth-Marom (1982); Maoz (1984a). For a review of the literature on calibration, see Lichtenstein, Fischoff, and Phillips (1982).

on the process of revising or updating verbal or numerical estimates as a result of current indicators or other types of incoming data. Revision processes consist of two steps: the establishment of initial estimates for the various outcomes, and changing or preserving these initial estimates in a dynamic fashion as a result of additional information that enters the system. It is in the second step of the revision process that the differences among the three process models are most pronounced.

Assume a set O_a, $[o_1, o_2, \ldots, o_n]$ outcomes that are seen to be possible given the adoption of policy option a by the decision maker with a probability distribution denoted by P_a. (The probability of outcome i is given by p_i.) Assume further that the decision maker becomes aware of a new datum D_1 after she had established an initial probability distribution for these outcomes. The initial probability distribution is called the *prior* probability distribution. The problem is to derive a *posterior* probability distribution given the new datum. The optimal procedure of revision is based on a theorem proved in the eighteenth century by the Reverend Thomas Bayes, and known as the Bayes formula. The idea underlying Bayes's equation is very simple. A posterior probability distribution is based on the prior knowledge one has about the distribution of the set of outcomes (the prior probability distribution) and on the relative fit between the datum and each of the predicted events (the conditional probability ratio). This equation can be expressed as follows:

$$p(o_i \mid D_1) = \frac{p_i \times p(D_1 \mid o_i)}{\sum_{i=1}^{n} p_i \times p(D_1 \mid o_i)} \tag{6.12}$$

where $p(D_1 \mid o_i)$ is the probability of observing D_1 given that outcome o_i occurs.

The greatest pitfall in the application of intuitive usage of Bayesian revision is the failure to distinguish between posterior probability and conditional probability. People tend to equate the revised probability given the datum with the conditional probability of observing the datum given that an event is assumed to occur, or a statement is expected to be true, and so on. A conditional probability is defined as the probability of observing an event given that an event is expected to occur. Formally, it is given by

$$p(D_1 \mid o_i) = \frac{p(D_1 \cap o_i)}{p(D_1)} \tag{6.13}$$

Therefore it is, in general, not equal to the posterior probability of the hypothesis given the datum. (Posterior probabilities are equal to conditional probabilities only if the prior probability distribution is uniform, i.e., if $p(h_1) = p(h_2) = \ldots = p(h_n) = 1/n$.) The conditional probability of a datum given an outcome reflects the diagnosticity of that datum with respect to the outcome. But diagnosticity of data is relative. Moreover, the extent to which a datum is diagnostic with respect to one event is not necessarily related to the extent to which the very same datum is indicative of another event. In revising probability estimates given new information, the distinction between conditional probabilities and posterior (updated) probabilities is crucial. For example, analyses of medical diagnoses of breast cancer showed that physicians tend to confuse the results of tests (which are less than fully reliable) with the probability of observing a malignant tumor given the test, hence resulting in an alarmingly high number of unnecessary breast operations (Eddy, 1982).

A second violation of optimal revision is to infer the conditional probability of a datum given one event from the conditional probability of the same datum given another, mutually exclusive event. For a set of two outcomes, $[o_1, o_2]$ $(o_1 \cap o_2 = \varnothing)$ we have $p(D|o_1) + p(D|o_2) \neq 1$. Therefore, assuming that $p(D|o_2) = 1 - p(D|o_1)$ violates the Bayesian revision process. Thus, analytic revision is violated if the data indicates one of the following:

1   A decision maker confuses conditional probabilities with posterior probabilities.[4]
2   A decision maker creates dependency between conditional probabilities.[5]

Both tendencies indicate not only that the Bayesian rule for analytic decision has been violated but also provide positive evidence for cognitive revision.

The third aspect of revising prior probability estimates in light of new information concerns the rate of revision given the relative diagnosticity of new data. Bayesian rules require that the rate of change in probability estimates would be high or low depending on: (a) the prior probability distribution, and (b) the relative diagnosticity of the new information. However, some analysts who have used Bayesian methods in applied settings (e.g., CIA intelligence forecasts) have argued that Bayesian inference leads to revisions which are overly rapid. The idea is that the prior probability distribution is based on vast magnitudes of data, but a highly diagnostic current indicator

[4] This is essentially equivalent to the representativeness heuristic (Kahneman and Tversky, 1973) or the base-rate fallacy (Bar-Hillel, 1982).
[5] This is essentially what Jervis (1976) identifies as the cognitive tendency to assume that data which is consistent with one hypothesis is regarded as inconsistent with another, mutually-exclusive, hypothesis.

will cause unduly sharp revision of opinion (Heuer, 1978). This is so because the prior probability and the conditional probability (which denotes the relative diagnosticity of the current indicator) receive the same weight in the multiplicative integration of priors and conditional probabilities without taking into account the amount of data upon which they are based. The recommendation was that the prior and conditional probability will be weighted by the amount of data upon which they are based. However, the outcome of such a recommendation will be greater conservatism over time. Since information is processed sequentially, each new informational item will have a smaller impact on the extent to which prior estimates are changed than the previous item. Moreover, the more information used to determine the prior probability distribution, the lower the tendency to revise it regardless of the diagnosticity of the new data (Maoz, 1984a: 83–85). Another reason for rejecting such an argument is that the relative diagnosticity of the prior and conditional probabilities reflects already the amount of data on which they are based.

It stands to reason that weighting of prior and conditional probabilities is consistent with the logic of the cybernetic and cognitive models because it implies that revision of opinion in light of new information depends on the extent to which decision makers are committed to their prior beliefs. A strong commitment to a certain belief typically indicates a notion that this belief is based on a lot of prior knowledge, experience, and the like. It therefore takes a lot of discrepant information (i.e., many current indicators which are highly diagnostic) to revise them (Jervis, 1976; Nisbett and Ross, 1980). Hence, violation of analytic revision is observed whenever a decision maker:

3 Fails to incorporate prior beliefs with current indicators, or
4 Treats prior estimates as more important, potent, or otherwise diagnostic, than current indicators.

Finally, the major characteristic of revision processes in foreign policy settings is that most outcomes arising from the selection of policy options are highly complex events. Determining the probability of their occurrence usually involves some aggregation of various subcategories of events (Maoz, 1981). For example, during the Entebbe crisis, military planners decomposed the planned military operation into several phases in order to derive a reliable estimate of the probability of success. Changes in the probability of success of these components had major effects on the final estimate. To form an initial estimate of the probability of compound events in an analytic fashion, one must go through four steps: (1) decomposing compound events into component-events, (2) determining which of the component events are independent of one another and which are mutually or serially-dependent, (3) determining the compound probability of the dependent components via Bayesian analysis or hierarchical inference methods,[6] and (4) integrating all the probability estimates of the independent events (including the compound probabilities of the dependent events computed in (3) above) into an overall estimate using probability trees.

Intuitive probability estimates must, at the very least, satisfy the logical aspects of these operations. In other words, positive evidence for analytic revision consists of indications that complex events were decomposed, that a clear distinction was made between independent and dependent components, and that all component events were integrated into an overall probability estimate of the compound event. Usage of probabilistic language allows the analyst to use numerical equivalents of expressions of uncertainty to determine whether final estimates were consistent with such a process. If the available evidence on revision processes indicates failure to apply these minimal criteria, then one can reliably infer non-analytic revision. More importantly, evidence for cognitive revision is provided by an observed failure to distinguish between independent and dependent component events. Since the aggregation of independent events requires multiplication of their probabilities and dependence requires Bayesian analysis, a failure to differentiate between them results in biased estimates. Finally, updating probabilities of compound outcomes occurs if the probabilities of their components are revised. For example, during the Entebbe crisis, the probability of success of the military rescue operation was increased significantly as a result of changes in the probabilities of its component events (Maoz, 1981).

Discrimination among the predictions of the three models for the revision stage is not easy. Nonetheless, several criteria allow some degree of differentiation.

Analytic Revision. Evidence of analytic revision processes consists of the following items:

1 Decision makers use numerical probability estimates or probabilistic language in their estimation of the likelihood of future events.

2 The usage of numerical or verbal probability phrases by decision makers satisfies the approximate logical certainty criterion. The sum of such phrases over the estimates of all the outcomes stemming from the same policy option approaches

---

[6] See Barclay *et al.* (1977) for a description of hierarchical inference methods.

certainty. (Verbal to numerical transformations are required to determine whether this criterion has been satisfied in practice.)

3 The usage of probabilistic language (numeric or qualitative) should display cross-context consistency for any given individual using it. If the same phrase displays relatively different levels of uncertainty in different contexts or at different points in time, no reliable conversion of verbal to numeric values could be performed for that decision maker.

4 Expressions of confidence accompanying probabilistic phrases should match the level of uncertainty of these phrases.

5 The decision maker clearly distinguishes between conditional and posterior probabilities in updating prior estimates in light of new information.

6 There is a clear indication that conditional probabilities of a datum given two mutually-exclusive events are independent of one another (normally, they do not sum to unity).

7 Updating of prior probability estimates in light of new information indicates that the decision maker combined base rate information with current indicators.

8 The decision maker performing this combination does not weigh base-rate information or conditional probabilities by the amount of data upon which they are based. Conditional probabilities reflect only the relative diagnosticity of the datum and its probability. (For example, for any given $p(o_i \cap D)$, a decision maker would end up with a higher conditional probability $p(D|o_i)$ when the new information is of an unexpected nature, i.e., $p(D)$ is low, than when it is expected information, i.e., $p(D)$ is high.)

9 In estimating the likelihood of compound events, decision makers decompose them to component-events and determine which of the component-events are independent of one another and which are dependent. Analytic decision makers must analyze dependent events through hierarchical inference logic and aggregate probability estimates over independent events in a multiplicative fashion.

Cybernetic revision. Positive evidence for cybernetic revision processes is difficult to ascertain in a direct fashion. Normally, cybernetic processes are determined by default, that is, if we cannot find positive evidence of either analytic or cognitive revision. Nonetheless, the following provide some partial support for cybernetic revision.

1 Decision makers limit their search for information to that which is specified in existing SOPs.

2 At each point in time, estimation of outcomes is limited to those which stem from one and only one option. No attempt is made to relate information deemed relevant for the estimation of outcomes stemming from one alternative to the estimation of outcomes stemming from another alternative.

3 Revision of opinion in light of new information is conservative if the information pertains to the estimation of outcomes of SOP options, but is nonconservative if information pertains to newly-explored outcomes (those that are not covered by existing SOPs).[7]

Cognitive Revision

1 Cognitive decision makers avoid usage of probabilistic language. Outcomes are estimated in deterministic terms.

2 To the extent that decision makers use quantitative or qualitative expressions of uncertainty, they violate the approximate logical certainty condition. Specifically, the sum of probability estimates of all outcomes stemming from any one policy option is clearly not equal to one.

3 Decision makers using quantitative or qualitative expressions of uncertainty alter their usage of probability estimates across contexts.

4 There is evidence of overconfidence in probability estimates if numerical or qualitative expressions of uncertainty are used by the decision maker. Specifically, expressions of confidence in probabilistic forecasts are higher than associated expressions of uncertainty.

5 Decision makers confuse conditional probabilities with posterior probabilities, thereby ignoring base-rate information.

6 Decision makers treat conditional probabilities as mutually dependent: the conditional probability of observing a datum given one event is seen as the complement of the conditional probability of observing the datum given another, mutually-exclusive event.

7 Evidence indicates failure to combine base-rate information with current indicators in the process of updating probability

---

[7] When cybernetic decision makers are dissatisfied with existing SOPs (having analyzed them in the decision process) they may resort to search for new information in order to explore contingencies not dealt with by existing SOPs. In such cases, they may be more vigilant in their approach to information processing.

estimates given new data. Conditional probabilities of new data given existing hypotheses are reviewed selectively. Higher conditional probabilities are assigned to data consistent with prior expectations.[8] Alternatively, revision rates are slow and conservative despite discrepant current indicators.

8   In combining prior probabilities with conditional probabilities, decision makers weight them in terms of the amount of data upon which they are based, hence posterior probabilities are heavily affected by prior probabilities.

9   Decision makers do not decompose compound outcomes into component events, or, if they do, integrate component events into an overall probability assessment in a biased manner. Biases in integration are reflected in failure to distinguish between independent and dependent component events, in additive integration of independent component events into an overall probability estimate, or in selective integration of component events such that only some components are included in the final assessment.

6.5   ELEMENTS OF CHOICE

As seen in figure 6.1, the choice principle follows directly from the evaluation process. While in general this is satisfied in actual decision making processes, there are some difficulties involved in interpretation of the specific choice rule at work in a given decision. For example, an EBA process of evaluation might terminate when a decision maker runs out of evaluation criteria before she runs out of policy options. In such a case, she is forced to choose simultaneously among several options. Concomitantly, attempts to eliminate value conflict by artificial ranking of policy options on multiple value dimensions might be only partially successful. The decision maker might end up with some inconsistency in the ranking of options. In such cases, decision makers might resort to some variation of subjective expected utility maximization. Yet this maximization process cannot be regarded as analytic because prior biases prevent a fully analytic comparison of policy options. Some options have been eliminated during the evaluation stage and are not considered at the choice stage. Those options that are considered at the choice stage might have been evaluated in a biased manner. It is therefore instruc-

---

[8] This is reflected in high correlations between prior probabilities of events and the conditional probabilities of data given such events. Formally, we get high r scores between $p(o_i)$ and $p(d \mid o_i)$.

tive to consider the general form of choice principles from the perspectives of the three models.

6.5.1 Constructing integrated utilities

In assessing the characteristics of the three models in the evaluation stage we treated all the value dimensions (or criteria) used for option appraisal as if they were of equal importance. Usually, they are not. Typically, decision makers weight the various value dimensions in terms of perceived importance. The integration of utilities over multiple value dimensions requires therefore some form of incorporation of the importance weights assigned by the decision maker to the various value dimensions. The weighting of value dimensions in terms of perceived importance is essentially subjective. There is no *a priori* way of determining which value dimension will be considered most important in policy settings, and by how much it is more important than another value dimension. Derivation of relative importance scores for multiple value dimensions is done via content analysis of statements referring to various value dimensions. For example, Stein and Tanter (1980) and Maoz (1981) used frequency counts of statements pertaining to various value dimensions to reflect their relative importance. (See also Brecher, 1974a, 1974b, 1980.) Those who do not trust frequency-related weighting of value dimensions could rely on the cognitive centrality of concepts in cognitive maps to infer relative importance of value dimensions. Perhaps the most important determinant of the relative weights of various value dimensions by different individuals is the organizational role variable. Decision makers representing different bureaucratic organizations would tend to weight value dimensions relevant to their organizational concerns higher than other value dimensions. (Military considerations would be weighted higher by defense officials while economic considerations and criteria would be weighted higher by finance ministers.) Once relative importance weights were established (it is desirable to normalize these weights such that $0 \leqslant w_j \leqslant 1$, and $\sum_{j=1}^{m} w_j = 1$), the general principle used for creating an integrated utility for the various outcomes is given by

$$U_i = \sum_{j=1}^{m} u_{ij} w_j \tag{6.14}$$

In matrix form, we specify the weights of the various value dimensions by a $m \times 1$ vector $\mathbf{W}$ and integrate by

$$U = SE \times W \qquad (6.15)$$

with U being a $n \times 1$ vector of integrated utilities for the n outcomes. When utility scores for the various outcomes are unavailable, a crude procedure may be applied for creating approximate utility scores.[9]

Analyzing choices in terms of integrated utilities over multiple value dimensions helps to assess one of the crucial predictions of the analytic model: that decision makers make value tradeoffs when choosing among policy options with multiple objectives. Integration of value dimensions into an overall utility is necessary for expected utility maximization. Moreover, the weighting of values in terms of relative importance allows verification of cybernetic and cognitive choice principles. To determine whether a satisficing choice rule was applied by a decision maker, we must know the order by which alternatives were eliminated during the evaluation stage. As noted, the EBA sequence follows the relative importance weights (or ordinal importance ranking) of the evaluation criteria. The first elimination criterion would be the most important one, the second elimination criterion would be the second-ranked value dimension, and so on. In the case of cybernetic choice, value integration is partial. Only the uneliminated options would have an overall utility score; all other options are represented as missing data in the U vector.

To determine whether value tradeoffs were avoided (or eliminated due to application of consistency preservation devices), as cognitive models predict, importance weights for identified value dimensions are crucial to determine which specific choice rule was used. Lexicographic choice singles out the most important value dimension and selects the policy option that ranks highest on this dimension. Thus, we need to know which value dimension serves as the sole evaluation criterion and whether the option that ranks highest on this criterion was the one actually selected by the decision maker. Moreover, to the extent that such information is available, the ranking of other options should reflect their standing on the single value dimension applied for evaluation. Cognitive decision makers may resort to some semi-lexicographic rule (e.g., basing their choice only on a small subset of all relevant value dimensions). In such cases, the least important value dimension is eliminated and integrated utilities reflect the weighting of utilities over the subset of considered value dimensions. This

---

[9] Actually, there exist several procedures for transforming ranked preferences into utilities. (See, for example, Blechman, 1966; Wagner, 1974; Stein and Tanter, 1980; Maoz, 1986.) Since operations performed on such transformations are somewhat unreliable, they should be used only as validating devices of the more qualitative judgment concerning value integration.

procedure allows a clear comparison of the substantive predictions derived from a fully-integrated utility function (which is expected given analytic choice) and a partially-integrated utility function given semi-lexicographic choice.

6.5.2 Combining utilities and probabilities

Choice principles, whether analytic or not, require some combination of utilities and probabilities in risky or uncertain choice situations. The SEU of any given policy option cannot be determined unless such a combination is performed. Typically, this is the final – and most important – step in individual decision making under risk or uncertainty. Analytic models require a choice of policy options (or more generally, a preference ranking of all policy options) on the basis of the SEU principle which is given by

$$SEU_a = \sum_{i=1}^{na} U_i p_i \qquad (6.16)$$

where na is the number of outcomes stemming from option a, U_i is the integrated utility of outcome i, and p_i is the (updated) probability of this outcome. (See chapter 4 for illustrations.) Analytic choice requires that policy options be ranked according to their respective $SEUs$ and that a decision maker choose the option which has the highest SEU. Any observed choice of policy or any final ranking of policies that does not reflect this principle cannot be regarded as analytic.

Substantive differences between the preference ordering of options by analytic decision makers and the preference ordering of options by cognitive decision makers can be detected even if the most preferred option is the same. Given m relevant value dimensions, a decision maker using the semi-lexicographic decision rule integrates utilities for outcomes on the basis of only a subset (say $m-2$) of the value dimensions. Such a condensed utility might still entail some value tradeoffs across outcomes associated with any given alternative even if value conflict within outcomes (over conflicting value dimensions) does no longer exist due to the elimination of the two value dimensions. In such a case, a SEU analysis might be necessary. Once such an analysis is performed, the policy option with the highest SEU might well be the one that would have been selected if all value dimensions had been considered. Yet, choice is clearly non-analytic in nature. Looking only at the most preferred option or at the SEU principle leading to that result would not reveal that an admissible option was chosen by an inadmissible process which ignored certain value dimen-

Option	Outcome	Value dimension				Weight	Outcome	Utility
1	1	1.0	0.7	0.4	0.2	0.4	1.1	0.71
	2	0.3	0.4	0.5	0.8	0.3	1.2	0.42
2	1	0.4	0.9	0.1	0.5	0.2	2.1	0.50
	2	0.6	0.5	0.2	0.8	0.1	2.2	0.51
	3	0.2	0.6	1.0	0.1		2.3	0.46
3	1	0.5	1.0	0.0	0.9		3.1	0.59
	2	0.0	0.7	0.7	0.3		3.2	0.38

Probability vector

Outcome	Probability
1.1	0.3
1.2	0.7
2.1	0.4
2.2	0.4
2.3	0.2
3.1	0.1
3.2	0.9

Figure 6.7 Analytic versus non-analytic choice rules

sions in order to reduce value conflict. A *SEU* analysis on the entire **SE** matrix generates *SEU* scores for all options. This allows for a ranking of options in terms of their associated *SEU* scores from most to least preferred, assuming analytic choice. This ranking could then be compared to the ranking of options obtained through the semi-lexicographic rule. If the analytic and semi-lexicographic rules yield different results in terms of the resulting preference rankings, then we could estimate the extent to which choice processes using different rules give rise to different substantive preferences. To illustrate this point, consider figure 6.7.

If choice reflects a comprehensive integration of all outcomes across all value dimensions, then the integrated utility matrix is as given in figure 6.7. The combination of integrated utilities with the probabilities assigned to the various outcomes yields $SEU_1 = 0.507$; $SEU_2 = 0.498$; and $SEU_3 = 0.401$. The three policy options are ranked $A_1 > A_2 > A_3$. Now suppose that the actual evaluation procedure is the EBA. The decision rule applied is that the decision maker evaluates the options on the most important value dimension. Then, the option with the lowest expected utility on this dimension is eliminated and

Option	Outcome	Value dimension			Weight	Utility	
		1	2			Outcome	
1	1	1.0	0.7		0.57	1.1	0.87
	2	0.3	0.4		0.43	1.2	0.34
2	1	0.4	0.9			2.1	0.62
	2	0.6	0.5			2.2	0.56
	3	0.2	0.6			2.3	0.37
3	1	0.5	1.0			3.1	
	2	0.0	0.7			3.2	0.31

Probability vector

Outcome	Probability
1.1	0.3
1.2	0.7
2.1	0.4
2.2	0.4
2.3	0.2
3.1	0.1
3.2	0.9

Figure 6.8 Semi-lexicographic choice rules

the next value dimension is applied to the computation of the expected utilities, and so on. For that case, we find the expected utilities of the three options on the first value dimension by multiplying the utilities associated with the first value dimension by the probabilities of the outcomes. This yields $SEU_{11} = 0.51$; $SEU_{21} = 0.44$ and $SEU_{31} = 0.05$. Thus, option 3 is eliminated and expected utilities are computed for the two remaining options using the second value dimension as the evaluation criterion. This yields $SEU_{23} = 0.49$ and $SEU_{22} = 0.68$. Given this procedure we now have a preference ordering of $A_2 > A_1 > A_3$.

To illustrate how semi-lexicographic decision rules operate, assume that the decision maker ignores the two least important value dimensions. This requires normalization of the weights of the remaining two value dimensions such that they would sum to unity. This gives us $w_1 = 0.57$ and $w_2 = 0.43$. The integrated utility vector with two value dimensions is given in figure 6.8. And the expected utilities associated with this choice rule are $SEU_1 = 0.499$; $SEU_2 = 0.546$; and $SEU_3 = 0.350$, yielding a preference order of $A_2 > A_1 > A_3$. This preference order is the same as the one obtained by the EBA decision rule but different from the one obtained through the fully-integrated analytic process.[10]

This analysis suggests two general conclusions regarding choice rules. First, there is no quick and simple way to infer from an actual distribution of preferences the choice rule that determined them. While different choice rules frequently give rise to different preference orderings of policy options, this is not a general rule. It is quite possible that two different choice rules would yield the same substantive results. To connect a given choice procedure to a certain substantive decisional outcome it is necessary to work out different choice rules within a specified decisional frame and examine their substantive consequences. Second, focusing only on the selected policy option while ignoring those options that were not actually chosen might lead to biased conclusions with regard to the kind of rule that characterized the choice stage. The entire distribution of preferences over the considered policy options provides a more reliable basis for deciding which choice rule was applied.

The limitations of a quantitative formal analysis of individual choice in foreign policy settings must be recognized. Attempts to determine the kind of model which best describes any of the stages of individual choice processes in a precise and reliable fashion are hampered by the lack of reliable information about the thought processes of foreign policy decision makers. More often than not, indirect measurement of the principles applied by individuals is necessary, and the reliability of such measures is – at best – partial. Nonetheless, the procedures developed thus far are designed to allow a more rigorous basis for judgment of such issues. The criteria for discriminating among the process models are minimalistic both in terms of the amount of information they require and in terms of the demand for indirect inference they imply. But the exercise of judgment was not – nor could it be – completely eliminated in such analyses. With these limitations in mind, many problems could be resolved by utilizing more systematic criteria for discrimination, and many counterintuitive findings might emerge. This is the premise that guides the extension of the MPC framework to collective choice settings.

6.6 COLLECTIVE DECISION MAKING

Common to all three models of foreign policy decision making is the idea that final group choices do not necessarily reflect in any

---

[10] Note that if a strictly lexicographic (single-value maximization) decision rule were used, we would have obtained a preference order which is identical to the analytic one. But this is not a general principle. In most cases, lexicographic decision rules yield preferences which differ from the ones obtained through analytic decision rules.

direct manner the initial distribution of preferences over the individual participants. The history of these ideas is interesting in that it reflects how knowledge about collective choice processes has evolved over time.

Social psychologists have pointed out that groups resort to adoption of more risky alternatives than the ones that would have been predicted by the initial distribution of individual preferences. For example, in jury deliberations jurors tend to take an initial vote prior to the actual deliberations to determine the initial division of verdicts. This preliminary vote reflects an initial distribution of individual preferences within the group. However, it often turns out that the final verdict is significantly different from the one that would have been predicted from the initial votes of the jurors (Davis, 1973). More specifically, it was noted that groups tend to shift to the adoption of riskier options than those that most individuals would have adopted had they been forced to make the decision in isolation. This generalization was termed as the "risky shift" propensity of group choices (Pruitt, 1971a; Semmel and Minix, 1979).

However, subsequent research revealed that this generalization is misleading. It was found that in many cases when the initial distribution of preferences would lead one to expect the adoption of risky options, the outcome of group deliberations turned out to be considerably less risky than expected (Cartwright, 1971). This new evidence led to the conversion of the risky-shift generalization to the "group-induced shift" generalization. Briefly, this generalization suggests that the initial distribution of individual preferences in decision making bodies is generally a bad predictor of the outcomes of group deliberations. (This does not apply, of course, to decision making bodies that go directly to vote on the available alternatives without prior discussion.)

A variety of explanations has been offered by social psychologists to account for the group-induced shift phenomenon. Most of these explanations focused either on the structural attributes of the group, or on the dynamics of the deliberation process (Pruitt, 1971a, 1971b). Some of the structural attributes of groups that were hypothesized to affect such shifts include shared group values such as group risk-taking propensity (Cartwright, 1971). Dynamic process theories focused, among other things, on the nature and extent of information exchange and argumentation processes taking place in the course of group deliberations (Burnstein et al., 1971; Vinokur and Burnstein, 1974; Kaplan, 1977; Kaplan and Miller, 1977).

Most of these explanations have implicitly or explicitly assumed that the attributes of the group or the dynamics of the deliberation

273

processes tend to produce substantive shifts in individual preferences. However, it is possible that individuals change their vote as a result of strategic calculations that involve perceptions as to how other group members are likely to vote, and how unequivocal support of the best policy option would affect the final group decision. In such cases, we term the behavior of the individual as *strategic* (to distinguish it from *sincere* behavior), meaning that choice does not actually reflect one's true preferences. There is, of course, nothing irrational about strategic behavior provided that it is designed to maximize one's utility. Individuals who have reason to believe that if they vote for their most preferred policy option, then their least preferred option would be selected by the group, might actually do better to prevent this unfortunate outcome by voting for their second-best policy preference. Thus, the fact that group choices do not reflect the initial distribution of individual preferences does not provide a clear clue as to either the causes or the nature of the shift in individual preferences. Nor does this generalization indicate actual shifts in individual preferences.

To allow formal characterization of the processes that are posited to describe group decision making according to the three models, we must discuss two fundamental properties of decision making groups. The first property is that of group polarization. The second is the distribution of decisional power within groups. Group polarization is based strictly on the initial distribution of individual preferences over the available policy options. The concept of decisional power is based both on individual preferences and on their formal authority scores (discussed in chapter 4). These factors can be combined to account for the particular model which best characterizes a given collective decision process.

6.6.1 Group polarization

Group polarization refers to the degree of initial disagreement among group members regarding the appropriate way to resolve a particular problem. A polarized group is one whose members are in fundamental disagreement concerning the appropriate solution, a disagreement which is reflected in a radically diverse ranking of the available policy options by members. A homogenous group is one wherein the distribution of individual preferences over policy options is either identical or very similar. Obviously, the difficulty of the collective choice task increases proportionally to the degree of group polarization. In this section, I propose a formal definition and a precise

274

measure of group polarization which is based strictly on the ordinal ranking of m policy options by each of the n group members. Both the conceptualization and the resulting formal measure follow directly from the tradeoff complexity (TC) concept developed in section 6.3.1.

Briefly, assume n individuals participate in the group deliberations. Each individual has a complete (though not necessarily strict) preference ordering over m policy options. Each individual i can rank the options from 1 to m. Indifference between two policy options assigns both the midpoint score between the option ranked immediately above them, and the option ranked immediately below them.[11] This gives us a $m \times n$ group preference (**GP**) matrix which is a precise equivalent of the search-evaluation (**SE**) matrix discussed above. The rows of the **GP** matrix represent policy options, and its columns represent individuals. The measure of group polarization reflects the extent to which the preference ranking of the m options differs from one individual to another. Since it is meant to be a standard measure which is good for any number of individual participants and any number of policy options, it must be normalized by some baseline that would make it comparable across decisional groups and decisional settings. This baseline is seen as the maximum possible disagreement among the n group members regarding the ranking of the m policy options. Given the logical equivalence between the **GP** and the **SE** matrices, this maximum disagreement measure is the same as the $D_{\max}$ measure computed in equations (6.6) and (6.8) above.

Maximum levels of disagreement among group members can arise in either of two general cases. The first is one wherein the group is evenly split in terms of members' rankings of the available policy options, and in which one half of the group has a diametrically opposed ranking of options to that of the other half. The second case is one wherein the preference ordering of policy options by group members gives rise to a complete cyclical majority over all m policy options.[12] In both cases, group polarization is obtained by the same method used for computing $D_{\max}$ above. And the actual group polarization at any given case of deliberation is seen as the proportion of the actual sum of squared rank differences in the **GP** matrix to the

---

[11] If we have only partial information about the ranking of options by an individual, for example, we know only how she ranked a subset of the available options but not the entire set, then we can complete the order by making some fairly innocent assumptions. See for example, Rapoport, Felsenthal, and Maoz (1988b) for such a procedure.

[12] By *complete* cyclical majority I mean that all available policy options are part of a social preference cycle. For example, for a set of $A = [1, 2, 3, 4]$ options considered by a group, the cycle will be of the form $1 \geqslant 2 \geqslant 3 \geqslant 4 \geqslant 1$. This in contrast to an *incomplete* cycle of the form $1 \geqslant 2 \geqslant 3 \geqslant 4 \geqslant 2$.

maximally expected one. (See table 6.2 for details on maximum sums of squared rank differences.) However, to distinguish the context in which the index is being used, I will label the group polarization index as *GC* (Group Conflict) as opposed to the *TC* (tradeoff complexity) index which is used in assessing intraindividual tradeoff complexity.

It is easy to see why we use the same algorithm to measure two different concepts. These concepts are not at all different; they tap the same issue at different levels of analysis. The tradeoff complexity index reflects *intraindividual* conflict of interests (or motivations), and the group polarization index reflects *interindividual* conflict of interests. Moreover, both concepts reflect the level of difficulty entailed in resolving that particular problem, given (*a*) the way it was structured by an individual in terms of options, outcomes, and value dimensions, or (*b*) the way it is resolved by different individuals in their personal calculus and reflected in the preference ordering of options in the group. Axelrod (1970), in one of the most important works on the formal measurement of conflict of interests, has defined five criteria that have to be met by a measure of conflict of interests. These criteria are: symmetry, independence, continuity, boundedness, and additivity. He proved that there exists one and only one measure of conflict of interests that satisfies all five criteria (Axelrod, 1970: 32–46). The problem with Axelrod's approach is that it requires information of the cardinal utilities assigned by group members to the various policy options. This kind of information is normally hard to come by, but if it could be obtained, the measure of conflict of interests he proposed is valid. However, the measure of group polarization offered here is a precise equivalent of the measure proposed by Axelrod, when information about cardinal utilities is present, and is more general because it does not require such information to be applied. Let us see why that is the case. To do so, consider the version of the Prisoner's Dilemma given by Axelrod (1970: 59). This game is presented in table 6.8.

Since Axelrod proved that his measure satisfies the independence requirement, that is, the conflict of interest measure will be the same for any utility function having the same ratios between any pair of outcomes, it is convenient to compute it with the normalized utilities. Axelrod's procedure calls for the definition of a unit square (due to normalization of utilities on a zero-to-one range) and finding the proportion of this square which designates disagreement between players. Using our procedure, however, we know that for cardinal utilities normalized along the same 0, 1 range, the maximum possible difference for any given outcome between the utility assigned by player i and that assigned by player j is exactly one $(0-1)^2$. And since

Table 6.8. *Utilities and ordinal ranking of outcomes in a Prisoner's Dilemma game*

Player i's strategy	Player j's strategy	Player i's raw utility	Player j's raw utility	Player i's norm. utility	Player j's norm. utility	Player i's ord. rank	Player j's ord. rank
Cooperate	Cooperate	7	4	5/6	3/5	3	3
Cooperate	Defect	2	6	0	1	1	4
Defect	Cooperate	8	1	1	0	4	1
Defect	Defect	3	3	1/6	2/5	2	2

Note: Normalized utilities (ranging from zero to one) are obtained by the following formula:

$$U^*_k = \frac{U^i_k - U^i_{min}}{U^i_{max} - U^i_{min}}$$

where:
  U^*_k = the normalized utility assigned by player i to outcome k.
  U^i_k = the raw utility score assigned by the same player to the same outcome.
  U^i_{min} = the raw utility score assigned by player i to his/her worst outcome.
  U^i_{max} = the raw utility score assigned by player i to his/her best outcome.

the prisoner's dilemma game has only four possible outcomes, the maximum possible sum of squared utility differences is 4. All we have to do is to apply to equation (6.9) unnormalized utilities instead of ordinal ranks in the numerator of the algorithm. This yields a group polarization measure of 0.527 which is precisely what can be found by following Axelrod's procedure. When ordinal ranks are used instead of cardinal utilities, the group polarization measure yields a score of 18/20 = 0.9. The point is that the measure of disagreement developed here meets all the criteria suggested by Axelrod both for cases of available information on the cardinal utilities assigned by the group members to the various policy options, and for cases where only the ordinal ranking of policy options is known. It is also more general in that it taps conflict of interests at various levels of analysis.

It must be noted, however, that setting the maximum possible group polarization as the baseline for standardizing actual polarization makes an implicit assumption of equal weights to all group participants. Yet, we already know that in real-world foreign policy settings this is hardly the case. Nonetheless, this assumption seems defendable given the context in which this measure is being used. This measure is intended to reflect only the level of disagreement among members and the difficulty of reaching any decision independently of who prefers which policy option. (One of the criteria offered by Axelrod was that of invariance of the measure with respect to the labeling of the players. This is an important axiom which must be preserved.) The measure of group polarization must also be made independent of the kind of factors that might affect the actual decision making process in the group. (Primarily because group polarization itself is hypothesized to affect such processes.) In addition, this measure is based on an initial distribution of preferences. Whether or not this distribution actually changes in the course of group deliberations is an *a posteriori* fact that is not and should not be reflected in this measure. Formal and informal influences that are exerted by some group members on others by virtue of their rank, expertise, and organizational resources, must be seen as an issue that itself depends on the degree of initial polarization in the group. If the group is highly homogeneous in terms of its preference ordering of policy options, the exercise of influence and other kinds of pressures is not needed. The consensus is there and need not be induced or otherwise enforced. Information about authority structures in policy making groups forms the basis for the measure of individual power within groups which is the topic of the next section.

6.7 INDIVIDUAL POWER AND GROUP STRUCTURE

The premise of the following analysis is that individual power in collective choice settings is not reducible to individual control over resources or status, however relevant these resources or status may be for the decision problem at hand. This concept encompasses much more than the amount of decision-relevant resources controlled by an individual. In general, the conceptualization of individual power in decision making bodies refers to an *a priori* estimate of one's *ability to control decisional outcomes*. Decisional power refers to the ability of an individual to lead to decisions which are consistent with one's preferences. In order to transform this definition into an empirically-observable form, it is useful to consider some traditional measures of voting power in committees and legislatures composed of members with different voting resources (weights, number of votes, or formal authority scores). Two widely used measures of voting power are the Shapley-Shubik (1954) and Banzhaf (1965) indices that reflect an *a priori* potential of control over outcomes in decision making bodies. Since readers are not expected to be familiar with these measures, I will briefly discuss the basic assumptions underlying these measures and examine their plausibility with respect to foreign policy decision making.

First, it is assumed that the voting power of any given actor is measured with respect to one's ability to influence the passing or nonpassing of a certain bill, given a dichotomous agenda. The fundamental question these measures address is with what frequency an actor's support of a decision will be pivotal by making the coalition supporting that decision into a winning one. The indices of voting power analyze this issue by pitting all possible coalitions against a fixed quota required for the passing of a bill in a legislature. Although this quota need not necessarily be a simple majority (51%), most empirical applications of these indices assume a simple majority decision rule. This assumption is in fact equivalent to pitting one coalition against the complement subset of legislators (that is, against all members not in the coalition) in order to determine whether: (*a*) this coalition is or is not a winning one, and (*b*) the focal actor is or is not pivotal in the coalition, given that it is a winning one. Under the assumption of binary choices, this is a sensible strategy. However, in multiple-choice settings, the measurement procedure specified above is no longer plausible. To examine the influence of a voter over the outcomes of a multiple-choice agenda, one would have to measure voting power in terms of variable quotas because the choice principle is one of a relative majority. Thus, a given coalition in which voter i is a member will have to be pitted against various subsets of the complementary coalition.

Second, both measures of voting power assume that all coalitions are equiprobable. Although this assumption seems reasonable in certain contexts (even in political ones), it is difficult to justify in ideological decision bodies, and even more so in foreign policy settings. Obviously, a coalition which consists of actors with polarized preferences is considerably less likely to form than a coalition consisting of actors with similar preferences. Rapoport and Golan (1985) modified the Shapley-Shubik and Banzhaf indices in a manner that takes into account the ideological distances among parties as a determinant of the probability of coalition formation. Specifically, they argued that the probability of a given coalition is inversely proportional to the mean Euclidian distance between all of its members. (This idea is also applied to the Deegan-Packel (1982) power index which takes into account only minimally-winning coalitions.)

Third, the assumption of weak rank-preservation states that if the weight of actor i is higher than the weight of actor j (i.e., $w_i > w_j$), then the resulting power score of actor i will be at least as large as that of actor j (i.e., $k_i \geq k_j$). As Straffin (1982: 263) states, "having extra votes cannot hurt you." The problem with this condition is that it makes an *a priori* monotonicity assumption, hence yielding various paradoxes in actual application of these indices (e.g., the paradox of new members, see Brams and Affuso, 1976; 1985). In addition, this property follows from the notion of simple games in which members' preferences and ideological positions are not considered. However, it is clearly violated if the distribution of members' preferences over all possible $m>2$ alternatives is incorporated into the calculus of power. As Rapoport and Golan (1985) have shown for the generalized Shapley-Shubik and Banzhaf indices in their study of voting power in the Israeli Knesset, a number of significant rank-inversions occur once ideological affinities among parties become part and parcel of the power measure. Closely related to this is Kilgour's (1974) paradox of quarreling members, which suggests that two members of a weighted voting body can actually increase their power by never being members of the same coalition. This suggests not only that ideological positions can affect voting power, but also that power-related calculations can influence the adoption of optimal ideological positions. Straffin (1982: 280) showed that quarreling may well be used as a strategic vehicle for promoting one's power while simultaneously decreasing the power of an opponent. This suggests that individual power is based on both capabilities and preferences. Moreover, it seems that some other assumptions underlying traditional power indices, such as that of dichotomous choice agendas and fixed quotas, should also be relaxed (Nagel, 1975; Brams, Felsenthal, and Maoz, 1986). A formal characterization of these ideas is given below.

Classical power indices assume simple games. A simple game is characterized by two sets: N is the set of members of the voting body, and W is the set of winning coalitions of that body, that is, all subsets of N that can ensure the passing of a bill. W is assumed to satisfy three fundamental conditions:

1 $\emptyset \in W$ that is, the empty set cannot be a winning coalition.
2 $N \in W$, that is, the entire set of members can always ensure the passing of a bill, and hence is always an element of the winning coalition set.
3 If $S \in W$, and $S \subset T$, then $T \subset W$, that is, any superset of a winning coalition is also a winning coalition. (We shall see that this condition is violated in our definition of individual power.)

In some cases W may be restricted to the inclusion of only minimally winning coalitions, and is denoted as W'''. W''' is defined formally to consist of elements that satisfy the following property: if $S_1, S_2, \ldots, S_k$ are proper subsets of T, and $T \in W'''$, then

$S_1, S_2, \ldots, S_k \notin W'''$. In other words, the set of minimally winning coalitions includes only coalitions whose proper subsets are all losing coalitions. The Shapley-Shubik index differs from the Banzhaf index in that it assumes sequential voting and hence is defined as a vector whose elements represent the proportion of all possible permutations of voting orders in which actor i is pivotal. The Banzhaf index assumes simultaneous voting in which the power score for actor i is the proportion of all winning combinations (coalitions) for which i is pivotal, in that its presence is necessary to render these coalitions winning, regardless of the order of joining to the coalition. (The Banzhaf index must be normalized to allow comparison with the Shapley-Shubik index.) Both indices can be determined given the specification of the simple voting game $(q; N)$, where q is the quota necessary for the approval of a bill.

Contrary to these indices, I develop a measure of power that is predicated on a complex game. A complex game is defined by $(N; C; \mathbf{GP})$ where N is the set of actors in the voting body, C is the set of all possible coalitions derived from N, and $\mathbf{GP}$ is the distribution of the n actors' preferences over the available policy options. The difference between a complex game and a simple one is twofold. First, C consists of all possible coalitions in N, not only the (minimally) winning ones. This is due to the relaxation of the assumption of dichotomous choice agendas and the consequent assumption of fixed quotas. (In addition, one may relax the assumption of fixed quotas even for binary choice agendas if abstention is allowed.) Given variable quotas, it is impossible to define *a priori* the set of winning coalitions for the game. Second, the inclusion of the information on actors' preferences is necessary given the relaxation of assumptions concerning equiprobable coalitions. To assume that everything is possible in political games is not equivalent to assuming that everything has the same probability. A probabilistic representation of coalition formation relies, therefore, on the following set of alternative assumptions regarding the likelihood of any given coalition to form.

1   The likelihood of a coalition is a function of its cohesiveness. Cohesiveness is defined as the complement of the polarization of members within this coalition in terms of their policy preferences. Formally, let $\mathbf{GP}_s$ be the set of all policy preferences of the actors in coalition s, where each element gp_{sj}^i represents actor i's ranking of policy option j $(i \in s)$. Let P_s denote the probability of coalition s. P_s is obtained by:

$$p_s = 1 - GC_s \,|\, GP_s \qquad\qquad (6.17)$$

This implies that the higher the polarization of members in the coalition, the lower the likelihood of this coalition forming. An actor is less likely to join a coalition consisting of members with different policy preferences than one consisting of members with similar policy preferences. In a group composed of n members, there are r possible coalitions (where $r = \sum_{t=1}^{n} \binom{n}{t}$ is the number of all possible subsets of a set with n elements). Each of these possible coalitions has a certain GC score. This score determines how likely the coalition is to agree on a joint policy option. The more likely is a coalition to agree on such a policy, the higher the probability that this coalition will indeed form. The vector of probabilities of the various coalitions, $\mathbf{P}$ has the following properties: (1) $0 \leqslant p_s \leqslant 1$, and (2) $\sum_{s=1}^{r} p_s > 1$.[13]

2 *Only admissible coalitions will form* The classical measures of voting power address the issues of admissible and inadmissible coalitions indirectly by restricting coalitions that are relevant to power calculations to minimally winning ones. Non-minimally winning coalitions have been implicitly considered inadmissible insofar as the distribution of spoils among members is concerned (Riker, 1962). However, the notion of minimally winning coalitions is also predicated on the assumption of simple games with fixed quotas. To generalize this idea, I define an inadmissible coalition to be one whose value to at least one member is strictly smaller than the value of one of its proper subsets to that member. Formally, coalition T is inadmissible if: $V(T)_i < V(S)_i$ for at least one $i \in S \subset T$. Substantively, if actor i can do at least as well and sometimes better by being a member of a smaller coalition rather than a larger one, she will never join the latter. By "value of a coalition" I mean the amount of policy concessions an actor i can extract from other members of that coalition. An actor is in a position to extract concessions if she is pivotal for that coalition under some contingencies, that is, her presence in that coalition renders it winning against some other coalition(s), and her absence renders it losing. If an actor i can extract more concessions in coalition S than in coalition T where S

---

[13] This is so because coalitions are not mutually exclusive. For example, coalition [123] (read: coalition composed of voters 1, 2, and 3) contains in it six proper subsets [1], [2], [3], [12], [13], [23]. Note that any single member coalitions has p_s which is identical to any other single member coalition, and to that of any multi-member coalition composed of members with identical policy preferences. In addition, the probability of any single member coalition (or the probability of any multi-member coalition composed of people with identical policy preferences) is at least as high as any other multi-member coalition. This is so because every member is certain to be in a coalition with him or herself. By the same token, every member is certain to coalesce with like-minded members, those who share identical preferences.

Table 6.9. *Preferences ordering of options by four voters*

	GP Preferences of voter			
Option	(1)	(2)	(3)	(4)
a	1	3	2	3
b	2	2	1	1
c	3	1	3	2

is a proper subset of T, then i will not join the latter coalition, hence rendering it inadmissible.

Assume a set of four actors $N = [1, 2, 3, 4]$ with weights $W = [1, 1, 1, 1]$. Assume a **GP** matrix as shown in table 6.9. The set of all possible coalitions in N is $C = \{[1], [2], [3], [4], [12], [13], [14], [23], [24], [34], [123], [124], [134], [234]\}$, with the associated weights of $W_c = \{[1], [1], [1], [1], [2], [2], [2], [2], [2], [2], [3], [3], [3], [3]\}$. To compute the cohesiveness of various coalitions consider, for example, coalition [124]. For this coalition to form, its members must agree on a joint policy. This policy will have to be a function of individual members' policy positions. The probability that these three members would agree on a joint policy is a function of the initial distribution of members' preferences over the available policy options. It turns out that the conflict of interests within this group is $GC = 8/9$, and thus the probability of such a coalition forming is $P_{[124]} = 0.11$. Thus, the value of that coalition to its member is a product of the sum of individual members' weights and the probability of the coalition formation. Formally:

$$V_c = W_c P_c \tag{6.18}$$

Which in this case yields $V_{[124]} = 3 \times 0.11 = 0.33$. This suggests that coalition [124], although it has considerable voting resources and can easily win the decision against member [3], is in fact a very weak one simply because its members find it hard to agree on a joint policy position. Thus, coalition [124] is inadmissible because each of its individual members can get a higher value for him/herself by not joining it than by joining it. (The values of the three one-member proper subsets are, respectively, $V_{[1]} = V_{[2]} = V_{[4]} = 1$, and the values of the three two-member subsets of this coalition are, respectively, $V_{[12]} = 0$, $V_{[14]} = 0.5$, $V_{[24]} = 1.5$.) It is therefore easy to see that neither member gains anything from joining this coalition, so it is reasonable to expect that it would not form if the preferences of members remain unchanged. The admissibility assumption serves to reduce the number of coalitions that need to be considered in the calculation of the power index. It can be easily shown that an inadmissible coalition is wasteful in the sense that members of one of its proper subsets can defeat as many countercoalitions as the inadmissible one, so that having additional actors in a given coalition does not justify the extent of policy concessions that have to be made to form it.

Contrary to simple games in which power is measured in terms of the importance of actors in a coalition with respect to a specific quota, in our case, power is measured in terms of the ability of a coalition to defeat all other disjoint coalitions – with or without the participation of a given member. For example, in a simple game, coalition [124] is a winning one with respect to any $2.1<p<3$ quota, but will be rendered losing if one of the members defects. (According to the Shapley-Shubik index, each actor is pivotal in two out of the six permutations of this coalition in which he joins last; according to Banzhaf's index, each actor is pivotal in the *single* [124] combination.) In our case we examine the power of actors in that coalition in terms of whether their unilateral defection would render the remaining coalition losing against *both the complementary coalition and any of its proper subsets*. If policy preferences are not considered, none of the actors in the [124] coalition is pivotal because the defection of any single member would still leave the remaining two-member coalition in a winning position against [3].

However, once ideological affinities are introduced into the picture, the interpretation of members' power becomes quite different. Consider again coalition [124]. This coalition can compete only against member [3]. The probability of any single-member coalition forming is, by definition, always 1.0. Multiplying it by the capabaility (voting weight) of [3] we have $P_{[3]}W_{[3]} = 1$. Coalition [124] has – as seen above – a weighted capability of 0.33 hence losing to [3]. It does not make sense to a group member to join such a coalition because – if she had to compete with [3] by herself – she would have tied the contest with [3].

Consider now another (admissible) coalition [13]. The power of this coalition is $V_{[13]} = W_{[13]}P_{[13]} = 2 \times 0.75 = 1.5$. This coalition can face either another two member coalition [24] or two one-member coalitions [2], [4]. To examine the power of individual members in that coalition, we must assess the effect of their defection on the power of the remaining coalition. To do so, we compute the weighted resources of its one-member proper subsets. These scores are $V_{[1]} = V_{[3]} = 1$. Now, the defection of [1] would render the remaining one-member coalition [3] losing against the other two-member coalition [24] (with a weighted

284

score of 1.5) and tying against any of the one-member coalitions [2] and [4]. This implies that member [1] is half pivotal for each of the contests [13]–[24], [13]–[2], and [13]–[4]. The same applies to member [3]'s pivotness in coalition [13]. An individual is considered *strictly pivotal* in a coalition with respect to another coalition if and only if her presence in that coalition makes the value of the coalition strictly higher than that of the opposing one, and her absence from this coalition makes its value strictly smaller than the value of the opposing coalition. In such a case we assign to the individual a full unit score of pivotness. Likewise, an individual is weakly pivotal in either of the following cases:

1   His presence in a coalition renders the value of the coalition strictly larger than that of a given opposing coalition and his absence renders the value of the coalition equal to that of the opposing coalition.

2   His presence in a coalition renders the value of the coalition equal to that of a given opposing coalition and his absence from a coalition renders this coalition's value strictly smaller than the value of the opposing coalition.

In either of these cases, a weakly pivotal individual gets a half-unit pivotness score. With respect to single-member coalitions, the calculus of pivotness is done in the same manner. The calculation of individual power is done therefore by looking at all the admissible coalitions in which this individual is a member and contrasting them with all the possible disjoint coalitions. In each case, we compute the pivotness score of the individual. Proceeding in this manner, we can calculate the new measure of power and see how it relates to the Shapley-Shubik and Banzhaf indices. This is done in table 6.10. Table 6.10a consists of the basic data for the complex game. Table 6.10b is a $k \times k$ matrix of all admissible coalitions. (Note that the grand coalition [1234] is, by definition, inadmissible because: (*a*) one of its proper subsets always has a higher value, and (*b*) its complement coalition is the empty set.)

In calculating the power of actor *i*, we look at each row coalition in which *i* is a member and examine whether this coalition defeats, ties, or loses against all relevant column coalitions (i.e., those coalitions that are not marked by an asterisk). To determine whether, and against whom *i* is pivotal in that coalition, we subtract *i*'s weight from the coalition and examine what the remaining coalition does against all relevant column-coalitions. For example, consider coalition [13]. At the [13] row of the matrix, we see that this coalition defeats each of the actors [2] and [4] and ties the [24] coalition. Subtracting [1] from this

Table 6.10. *Individual power of group members (preferences are taken from table 6.9)*

a. Basic data

Measure	Coalition													
	[1]	[2]	[3]	[4]	[12]	[13]	[14]	[23]	[24]	[34]	[123]	[124]	[134]	[234]
W_c	[1]	[1]	[1]	[1]	[2]	[2]	[2]	[2]	[2]	[2]	[3]	[3]	[3]	[3]
P_c	[1.00]	[1.00]	[1.00]	[1.00]	[0.00]	[0.75]	[0.25]	[0.25]	[0.75]	[0.75]	[0.11]	[0.11]	[0.44]	[0.44]
V_c	[1.00]	[1.00]	[1.00]	[1.00]	[0.00]	[1.50]	[0.50]	[0.50]	[1.50]	[1.50]	[0.33]	[0.33]	[1.32]	[1.32]

$N = [1, 2, 3, 4]$
Admissible coalitions: [1], [2], [3], [4], [13], [24], [34]. All other coalitions are inadmissible.

b. Contents among coalitions

	[1]	[2]	[3]	[4]	[13]	[24]	[34]
[1]	*	=	=	=	*	<	<
[2]	=	*	=	=	<	*	<
[3]	=	=	*	=	*	<	*
[4]	=	=	=	*	<	*	*
[13]	*	>	*	>	*	=	*
[24]	>	*	>	*	=	*	*
[34]	>	>	*	*	*	*	*

* Irrelevant contest.
= Row coalition ties column coalition (the value of the row coalition is equal to that of the column coalition).
> Row coalition beats column coalition (the value of the row coalition is larger than that of the column coalition).
< Row coalition loses to column coalition (the value of the row coalition is smaller than that of the column coalition).

Table 6.11. *Unnormalized and normalized power scores for actors in table 6.10*

Actor	In coalition	Against coalition	Scores	Unnormalized total	Normalized total
[1]	[1]	[2], [3], [4]	0.5, 0.5, 0.5	1.5	
	[13]	[2], [4], [24]	0.5, 0.5, 0.5	1.5	
				3.0	0.214
[2]	[2]	[1], [3], [4]	0.5, 0.5, 0.5	1.5	
	[24]	[1], [3], [13]	0.5, 0.5, 0.5	1.5	
				3.0	0.214
[3]	[3]	[1], [2], [4]	0.5, 0.5, 0.5	1.5	
	[13]	[2], [4], [24]	0.5, 0.5, 0.5	1.5	
	[34]	[1], [2]	0.5, 0.5	1.0	
				4.0	0.286
[4]	[4]	[1], [2], [3]	0.5, 0.5, 0.5	1.5	
	[24]	[1], [3], [13]	0.5, 0.5, 0.5	1.5	
	[34]	[1], [2]	0.5, 0.5	1.0	
				4.0	0.286

coalition leaves us with the one-member coalition [3]. Since [3] only ties against [2] and [4], separately, but loses against coalition [24], we assign a score of 0.5 to [1] with respect to each of the competitions of [3] against [2], [4], and [24]. In the first two cases, [1]'s defection from the [13] coalition moves this coalition from a winning to a tying position against [2] and [4] separately, and from a tying to a losing position against coalition [24]. If the value of coalition [13] were higher than that of [24], then [1] would still receive half a score in each of the contests against [2] and [4] separately, but would receive a score of 1 against the [24] coalition, because its defection from the [13] coalition moves [3] from a winning to a losing position against [24].

This suggests that the preferences of actors have an important impact on their power. This point is illustrated in the next example, but before discussing it we must describe how unnormalized and normalized power indices are derived. The next table shows the scores of each actor over all admissible coalitions of which she is a member. The unnormalized power score for actor i, ψ'_i is simply the sum of decisive votes over all these coalitions. Finally, the normalized power score for actor i is given by:

$$\psi_i = \frac{\psi'_i}{\displaystyle\sum_{i=1}^{n} \psi'_i} \tag{6.19}$$

As we can see from table 6.11, actors [3] and [4] have the same resources as those of actors [1] and [2], yet the former have considerably more voting power than the latter. The reason for this is that the former are pivotal – due to their policy preferences – in a larger number of coalitions than the latter. Obviously, both the Shapley-Shubik and the Banzhaf indices produce a uniform distribution of power in this case. How, then would a shift of one of the actors' preferences affect the distribution of power in a decision making body? To answer this question, consider table 6.12 which uses the same **GP** matrix for actors [2], [3], and [4], but actor's [1] preference are now $b > a > c$ instead of $a > b > c$.

Note that the preferences of members [1] and [3] are identical. Therefore, the coalitions associated with these members are extremely powerful compared to those in which these members are not present. This increases their voting power compared to that of other members, because their defection renders such coalitions weak or even inadmissible. (In case of a coalition becoming inadmissible as a result of an actor's defection, all the subsets of the inadmissible coalition are contrasted against all disjoint subsets excluding the defecting member. For example, if actor [1] defects from coalition [123], the remaining coalition [23] is inadmissible. Thus, to determine whether [1] is pivotal to this coalition, members [2] and [3] are contrasted against member [4]. Since each of them individually ties member [4], but they all beat member [4] in coalition [123], [1] gets two half-scores for coalition [123].) Table 6.13 displays the power scores of the members as derived from the contests in Table 6.12.

Table 6.13 suggests that the change in member [1]'s preferences had a substantial effect on the distribution of individual power in the group, even though the formal resources at the members' disposal remained unchanged. The ability of members [1] and [3] to induce favorable outcomes by virtue of their preferences is dramatically higher than that of the other two group members. This is so despite the fact that both members [2] and [4] rank policy option a in last place. The problem with these two members is that, although they agree that policy a is the worst among the feasible options, they cannot agree which option is the best. In contrast, the Shapley-Shubik and Banzhaf indices would lead us to conclude that the distribution of

Table 6.12. *Individual power of group members*

a. Basic data

Measure	Coalition													
	[1]	[2]	[3]	[4]	[12]	[13]	[14]	[23]	[24]	[34]	[123]	[124]	[134]	[234]
W_c	[1]	[1]	[1]	[1]	[2]	[2]	[2]	[2]	[2]	[2]	[3]	[3]	[3]	[3]
P_c	[1.00]	[1.00]	[1.00]	[1.00]	[0.25]	[1.00]	[0.75]	[0.25]	[0.75]	[0.75]	[0.67]	[0.44]	[0.78]	[0.44]
V_c	[1.00]	[1.00]	[1.00]	[1.00]	[0.50]	[2.00]	[1.50]	[0.50]	[1.50]	[1.50]	[2.00]	[1.32]	[2.34]	[1.32]

$N=[1, 2, 3, 4]$
Admissible coalitions: [1], [2], [3], [4], [13], [24], [34], [123], [134]. All other coalitions are inadmissible.

b. Contents among coalitions

	[1]	[2]	[3]	[4]	[13]	[14]	[24]	[34]	[123]	[134]
[1]	*	=	=	=	*	*	∨	∨	*	∨
[2]	=	*	=	=	∨	∨	*	∨	*	∨
[3]	=	=	*	=	∨	∨	*	∨	*	*
[4]	=	=	=	*	*	∨	∨	∨	*	∨
[13]	*	∧	∧	*	*	∨	∨	*	*	*
[14]	*	∧	∧	∧	∧	*	*	*	*	*
[24]	∧	*	*	∧	∧	*	*	*	*	*
[34]	∧	∧	∧	∧	*	*	*	*	*	*
[123]	*	*	*	*	*	*	*	*	*	*
[134]	∧	∧	*	∧	*	*	*	*	*	*

Signs are the same as in table 6.10.

Table 6.13. *Unnormalized and normalized power scores for actors in table 6.12*

Actor	In coalition	Against coalition	Scores	Unnormalized total	Normalized total
[1]	[1]	[2], [3], [4]	0.5, 0.5, 0.5	1.5	
	[13]	[2], [4], [24]	0.5, 0.5, 1.0	2.0	
	[14]	[2], [3]	0.5, 0.5	1.0	
	[123]	[2]–[4], [3]–[4]	0.5, 0.5	1.0	
				5.5	0.306
[2]	[2]	[1], [3], [4]	0.5, 0.5, 0.5	1.5	
	[24]	[1], [3]	0.5, 0.5	1.0	
				2.5	0.139
[3]	[3]	[1], [2], [4]	0.5, 0.5, 0.5	1.5	
	[13]	[2], [4], [24]	0.5, 0.5, 1.0	2.0	
	[34]	[1], [2]	0.5, 0.5	1.0	
	[123]	[1]–[4], [2]–[4]	0.5, 0.5	1.0	
				5.5	0.306
[4]	[4]	[1], [2], [3]	0.5, 0.5, 0.5	1.5	
	[14]	[2], [3]	0.5, 0.5,	1.0	
	[24]	[1], [3]	0.5, 0.5	1.0	
	[34]	[1], [2]	0.5, 0.5	1.0	
				4.5	0.250

voting power matches the distribution of resources in this group, something which is quite implausible given the preferences of group participants.

The last issue to resolve here is twofold. First, since the measure of individual power developed above is based on *resources* and on *policy preferences*, how do we determine the resources available to members in policy groups? The second aspect concerns the derivation of propositions regarding the rational aspects of group decisions given that members are taken to pursue the best policy under the circumstances (where circumstances are defined in terms of the distribuion of preferences and resources). The measure of individual resources has already been developed in chapter 4. The weights of group members are simply their formal authority scores (composed of their hierarchical rank, expertise, and organizational resources). These formal authority scores and the group preference matrix allow computation of the distribution of individual power in group decisions. The major problem with the computation of the measure of individual power ψ is that it becomes extremely tedious as the number of individual participants in the group increases. This is so because the number of possible coalitions grows exponentially with the number of group members. Complexity increases also with the number of considered alternatives. However, this is a technical problem which can be easily solved with the aid of a computer.

The idea that group members are out to get what they believe to be the best possible policy implies that the notions underlying the measure of voting power might shed light on the group decision process from the perspective of the analytic model. Laying out all the possible coalitions in a group and eliminating the ones that are inadmissible provides the first step to the solution of the group decision problem. The elimination of inadmissible coalitions suggests that certain forms of collusion are impossible unless individuals change their preferences. Therefore, observing the actual formation of inadmissible coalitions without evidence indicating preference change suggests that a rational process cannot characterize what has actually happened in the empirical case under analysis. It is therefore safe to conclude that some other model must have been at work.

Yet, the absence of inadmissible coalitions in a particular group decision does not provide positive evidence for an analytic decision model. Such evidence can be found in analyzing the values of the admissible coalitions. If group members are assumed to maximize the chances of their preferred policy becoming the group choice, then they would join those coalitions that provide them the most power, that is, the best chance of accomplishing their goals at the expense of minimum policy concessions. In the case of the first example, all three-member coalitions are inadmissible, so they can be ignored at the first stage of the analysis. This leaves us with three admissible two-member coalitions [13], [24], [34]. Among those three, the [34] coalition is most likely to form for two reasons: it is a coalition between the two most powerful group members, and these members already agree on the best policy option. (Both of them rank policy b first.) The remaining two members cannot agree on a best policy. Yet, policy option b is seen by members [1] and [2] as the second-best policy, and since they cannot effectively block coalition [34] (to do that they must agree on voting either for policy a – which is seen by [3] as the worst – or for policy c – which is seen by [1] as the worst). Hence either one of them or both of them would end up supporting policy b, which would then become the group's choice.[14] Thus, the analytic model can predict what the group decision would actually be, given information on the distribution of individual preferences and on their formal authority scores. Given such a prediction, it is easy to differentiate between the prediction of the analytic model and alternative models in terms of the fit between the policy that was selected actually and the one predicted by the model. Any discrepancy between the expected decision and the actual one constitutes evidence for a non-analytic group process. In more general terms, the analytic model predicts that: (a) if there exists a policy option that constitutes the preferred (or acceptable) choice of the coalition with the highest value, and (b) no other counter coalition of equal value can block the former coalition, then the policy option advocated by the highest-value coalition should be the group choice.

The analysis of coalition formation in groups and the measure of individual power are predicated on the majority rule principle. Therefore it seems inapplicable to decision making bodies that are non-democratic in nature, or to ones where the formal responsibility for decision rests with a single individual (such as presidential systems). This impression is more apparent than real, however. Whether or not a group is democratic is not a key factor in either coalition analysis or in the computation of individual power. The extent to which a collective body is formally or informally democratic, and whether or not the authority for making a choice rests with a single individual should be reflected in the distribution of formal authority scores in the group. In any collective body, the formal or informal hierarchy is reflected – as we have seen in chapter 4 – in the weights of the three dimensions of formal authority, and in the distribution of individual positions on each of these dimensions. The distribution of the hierarchy dimension and its importance relative to other dimensions of the authority structure varies significantly across systems. Groups that are democratic in nature are represented by: (a) a fairly uniform distribution of hierarchical ranks, and/or (b) a relatively equal importance weight assigned to the hierarchical rank relative to the other dimensions of formal authority. The more hierarchical the authority structure of the group, the more skewed the distribution of hierarchical ranks and the higher its weight relative to that of other dimensions. The implication of this is that the authority structure of the collective decision body

---

[14] See Felsenthal, Rapoport, and Maoz (1988) for a model of tacit cooperation in committees which reaches similar results and, unlike other models of rational choice in committees, also receives a fair amount of experimental support.

would be reflected in the "voting weights" of the individual participants.

6.8 CHARACTERIZING GROUP CHOICES

The two predictions derived from the analysis of individual power in groups with respect to the characteristics of analytic collective decision processes i.e., that inadmissible coalitions would not form and that the policy choice of the group is the one which has a majority support in terms of the value of the coalition agreeing on it – not necessarily in terms of its numerical size – provide only a partial description of what the collective decision process looks like from the perspective of the analytic model. These predictions describe the substantive content of collective outcomes but they do not account for the procedural aspects of group choices. However, the procedural aspects are of critical importance in determining which coalitions are admissible and which policy option is actually chosen. Thus, it is important to examine the relationship between the procedural aspects of individual choice and those of group decisions.

An individual coping with a decisional problem on her own might consider a certain number of policy options, estimate their potential consequences, and evaluate them in terms of one or more value dimensions. She might then form a certain preference for these policy options. However, as a group member, an individual might not have an opportunity to allow her entire preference scale to be represented in the decision process. If one has considered three policy options before going into the group meeting, but the group deliberation is limited to discussion of only two of these options, then the third option (whatever its location on the individual's preference scale) becomes irrelevant. Alternatively, if an individual has preferences over three policy options before going into the group session, but the group considers four or five options, it is impossible to tell in advance what would be the individual's attitude to the new option(s). More typically, however, an individual is likely to be confronted with a situation wherein some – but not all – of the options she had considered prior to the group meeting are discussed by the group and some options she had not considered are also discussed by the group. This poses considerable difficulties in applying the coalition analysis developed in the previous section to analyze the procedural aspects of group decision processes. But this difficulty also suggests some ways of analyzing group choices from a procedural perspective. Specifically, if the set of policy options considered by the group is not identical

293

Table 6.14. *Preference ordering of options by four decision makers*

| | **GP** | | | |
| | Preferences of decision maker | | | |
Option	(1)	(2)	(3)	(4)
a	1	—	2	—
b	2	2	1	3
c	3	1	—	2
d	4	3	—	1

to the set of policy options considered by each of the individual participants, then the relationship between these two sets should tell us something about the procedures used by the group and about the model that seems to best describe these procedures.

Assume n individual participants in the group discussion. Each individual i has a preference ordering over k_i options. Since the number of options in the preference scale of individual i is not necessarily equal to the number of options in the preference scale of individual j (formally, $k_i \neq k_j$), we can form a more realistic group preference matrix which puts together the actual preference scales of the individual participants. An example is given in table 6.14.

As this figure shows, only individual [1] has complete preferences over all four policy options. Individuals [2] and [4] have preferences only over options b through d and individual [3] has preferences only over options a and b. While this tells us something about the comprehensiveness of the individual choice processes, we are not yet in a position to determine which model characterizes the group decision process, nor are we in a position to determine group conflict from this distribution of group preferences. To do these things we have to look at the subset of policy options that are actually discussed by the group. The size of this subset relative to the set of policy options that had been considered by the individual participants becomes, therefore, an important indicator of the level of comprehensiveness of group decision. In the example above, there are four policy options that had been considered by the individual participants (even if not all individuals had considered all four options). A fully comprehensive group process is one in which all four of these options are reviewed in the course of group discussions. If the group discusses fewer than four options, the group process is less than fully comprehensive, and the level of comprehensiveness declines with the ratio of the number of options considered by the group to the number of options considered by the individuals before the group discussion. (Even if in our example, individuals [1] and [2] had considered only options *a* and *b* and individuals [3] and [4] had considered only options *c* and *d*, a fully comprehensive group process should include all four options.)

The analytic model describes the group process as one of extensive argumentation and exchange of information. Thus, the higher the ratio between the number of policy options reviewed by the group and the theoretical set of options considered by the individual participants, the more analytic the group process. Formally, let **IP** be the set of all options considered by individual group participants. An option *k* is a member of **IP** if and only if at least one individual has a preference relation involving that option (i.e., either $k\ P^i\ j$, $j\ P^i\ k$ or $k\ I^i\ j$, where P^i denotes a strict preference for individual *i* and I^i indicates indifference). **IP** represents, therefore, all the policy options that must be discussed by the group if it is to be fully comprehensive in its approach to the decision problem.[15] Denote by **GO** the options actually discussed by the group during the deliberation process. An option *k* is an element of this set if and only if it has been raised as a possible solution to the decision problem at some point during group deliberations (whether or not it was seriously analyzed by the group). The comprehensiveness of group evaluation is therefore given by

$$GE = \frac{GO}{IP}, \quad 0 \leqslant GE \leqslant 1 \tag{6.20}$$

It is easy to see that the group comprehensiveness measure is a simple extension of the *CE* index from an individual choice level to collective settings with appropriate adjustments for setting-related differences. The adjustments are, of course, predicated on the need to consider the possibility that individual participants differ with respect to the number of options they had reviewed on their own. But the *GE* measure reflects only a relatively narrow procedural aspect of group deliberations. We must examine not only what proportion of the options that should have been reviewed by the group were actually

---

[15] One may object to such a criterion by arguing that if there exists an option that is ranked the lowest (either by all decision makers or by one decision maker and the others had not even considered it) it is pointless to have it actually discussed by the group. But this argument is somewhat weak in the sense that an individual who had considered such an option and had found it totally unsatisfactory has no way of knowing before the group discussion whether other individuals had considered it or whether they had ranked it the same way as she had. Given lack of knowledge about the status of this option, an individual might be planning how to confront support for such an option in the group discussion. Such an option becomes, therefore, part of the expectations of the decision maker regarding possible developments in group discussion, and therefore should be part of a fully comprehensive group evaluation process.

considered, but also *which* options were eliminated from the group deliberation process. Options that were not viewed favorably by most or all members "deserve" to be eliminated more than those which were viewed favorably by most or all individuals. In other words, a group commits a greater error in ignoring some options than in ignoring others. Thus, we have to resort to some normative criteria of social desirability developed in the theory of social choice.

In chapter 5, we noted that a social preference is a preference ordering, by a majority in the society, of the available alternatives in terms of their ability to defeat other alternatives in pairwise races. But perhaps the most important finding in social choice theory is that such a social preference cannot always be determined even if all individual members have transitive preference orderings over all social alternatives. The difficulty of deriving a social preference order is compounded if not all individuals have preferences over all social alternatives. In table 6.14, for example, only one individual has a complete preference ordering of all four policy options; it would therefore be impossible to conduct a meaningful set of pairwise contests among all four policy options.

One of the plausible alternative formulations of social preferences was developed by Jean de Borda in the late eighteenth century (Black, 1958). The well-known Borda count method assigns to each alternative a preference score on the basis of its location in the individual preference scale and sums over all individual preference scores to form a social preference score for each alternative. For k policy options, the highest ranked option in an individual preference order receives a score of $k-1$, the second-ranked option receives a score of $k-2$, and so on. (The least-preferred option gets a score of zero.) In table 6.9, for example, policy option a gets a score of 2 for individual [1], a score of zero for individuals [2] and [4], and a score of 1 for individual [3]. The social preference score for a is the sum of individual preferences scores, that is, 3. Option b gets a score of 1 from individuals [1] and [2], and a score of 2 from individuals [3] and [4]. Its social preference score is therefore 6. Option c gets scores of zero from individuls [1] and [3], a score of 2 from individual [2] and a score of 1 from individual [4]. The social preference order based on the Borda count is therefore $b > a \sim c$. (The pairwise social preference order in table 6.9 is the same.) In general, however, social preference scores do not yield the same preference order as pairwise preference scores, so it seems that which social preference order we get is a function of the procedure used to derive them. The case for a social preference based on preference scores is that the pairwise social preference procedure ignores rank differences in individual preferences. An individual who ranks option *a* first and option *b* sixth counts the same in the calculation of pairwise social preferences as one who ranks option *a* first and option *b* second. Yet, the first individual can be said to have a higher intensity of preference for option *a* over *b* than has the second individual for the same options. The fact that there are four other options separating *a* from *b* in the preference scale of the first individual suggests that this person finds *b* much less appealing than *a* compared to the relative appeal of these two options for the second person (Dummett, 1984: 55–56, 133–143).

However, the preference score procedure also assumes that all individuals have complete preference orders over all options. Thus, if this procedure is to be used to determine the social desirability of policy options that were omitted from group deliberations, it must be modified in a manner that takes into account how many individuals have expressed some sort of preference for each option in their individual choice processes (that is, how many group participants have considered a given option on their own prior to group deliberations), and how complete is each of the individual preference scales. To incorporate these things, let us first formalize the "pure" preference score procedure under the assumption that all individual participants have complete (but not necessarily strict) preferences over all available options, and then modify this procedure to allow for incomplete preferences.

Assume n individuals, each with a complete preference scale over k policy options. Denote the rank order of policy option j in individual i's preference scale by r_j^i. The preference score for policy option j derived from individual i's scale is therefore $ps_j^i = k - r_j^i$. The social preference score for policy option j is given by

$$PS_j = \sum_{i=1}^{n} ps_j^i \tag{6.21}$$

The social preference order of the k policy options is defined as a weak ranking of these options on the basis of their social preference scores such that the option(s) with the highest preference score is (are) ranked first, the option(s) with the lowest social preference score is (are) ranked last, and any two or more options with the same preference score are ranked the same. Now we can relax the assumption of complete preferences over all available policy options. Once this assumption no longer exists, we define for each individual i a different preference scale over k_i policy options ($1 \leq k_i \leq K$, where K is the total number of different policy options considered by any individual in the group.)[16] Now denote the number of individuals having expressed some sort of preference for policy option j as n_j. The modified preference score for option j by individual i (denoted by ps'^i_j) is therefore given by

$$ps'^i_j = \frac{k_i - r^i_j}{k_i - 1} \tag{6.22}$$

And the social preference score for policy option j is given by

$$PS'_j = \frac{\sum_{i=1}^{n} ps'^i_j}{n_j} \tag{6.23}$$

The rationale for such a modification is simple and could be best illustrated by the following example. Suppose there are $K = 11$ different policy options considered by (some or all of) ten group members. Suppose that all ten members have preferences over policy option a, eight members ranking it first and two ranking it last. The modified social preference score for option a is therefore $(8 \times [(11 - 1)/10] + 2 \times [(11 + 1)/10])/10 = 0.8$. Now assume another group considering the same number of options with eight members ranking option a first among only ten out of the eleven options and two not ranking it at all. In this case we have $8 \times [(10 - 1)/9]/8 = 1$. We clearly see that policy option a receives a higher preference score in the second case than in the first case. The reason is that had the last two individuals considered option a before going into the group discussion, they might have ranked it higher than last. Without knowing a *priori* how a would have been ranked, we may reasonably conclude that the potential preference score for this option is higher than that given to it in the first group. The procedure discussed above allows assessment of the initial support assigned by individuals to various options prior to group deliberations. The standard preference score procedure is modified in a manner that takes into account the possibility of incomplete preference orders of various individuals.

Now we can evaluate the substantive comprehensiveness of group deliberations. This measure reflects the extent to which the options that have been omitted from group deliberations were important or marginal in terms of the initial distribution of individual preferences. Simply stated, substantive group comprehensiveness is given by the ratio of the sum of preference scores for the options that were

[16] For example, if individual [1] considered and has preferences over policy options a and b, individual [2] has preferences over options c and d, and individual [3] has preferences over options a, c, and e, then $k_{[1]} = 2$, $k_{[2]} = 2$, $k_{[3]} = 3$, and $K = 5$.

considered during group deliberations to the sum of preference scores for all options in the **GP** matrix. Formally,

$$SGC = \frac{\sum_{j=1}^{n_1} PD_{jc}}{\sum_{j=1}^{N} PS_j} \qquad 0 \leqslant SGC \leqslant 1 \qquad (6.24)$$

where PS_{jc} denotes the preference score of considered option j. Obviously, the higher the substantive group comprehensiveness score, the more analytic the group process. It is important to note, however, that the elimination of an option which was ranked lowest by all group participants or an option that was ranked lowest by some individuals and was not ranked by the other individuals will have no effect on the SGC ratio. Thus this measure allows for rational deletion of options that have no chance of being selected without discounting the rationality of group deliberation. On the other hand, elimination of options that have high preference scores has a marked effect on the measure of SGC. Moreover, there is a close relationship between the procedural and substantive measures of group comprehensiveness. The fewer the options considered by the group, the lower would both measures be. But since the substantive group comprehensiveness index is sensitive both to the number of options omitted from group deliberations and to their individual rankings, this relationship may not be linear.

So far we have dealt only with continuous measures of group deliberations trying to assess the level of comprehensiveness of collective decision processes. While very useful in general, these measures do not provide clear thresholds for distinguishing between various models of collective choice. To allow for such discrimination, we must set some minimal standards for analytic group choice. First, the analytic model requires extensive discussion of most or all of the options that had been explored by individual participants. This implies three conditions:

1 At least two of the options that had been explored by individual decision makers must be discussed by the group.
2 If the group explores more than two options, the final decision among policy options must be simultaneous, rather than sequential.
3 None of the options that had been eliminated from the group discussion is one with the highest social preference score.

The first condition means that if there exists a genuine choice problem at the individual level (in the sense that some or all of the individual participants had considered more than one policy option on their own), then a genuine choice problem should also exist at the group level. A slightly more stringent version of this condition is that at least two of the options considered by the group should be action alternatives, that is, policies that require some active measures (as opposed to passive inaction policies). The rationale of such a requirement is that a group choice which contrasts a single action alternative with a single inaction alternative biases the choice in favor of the former. The brief discussion of the setup of the agenda in the Israeli cabinet during the Lebanon war illustrates this point. By framing the decision problem as a dichotomous choice between an action alternative designed to rectify an undesirable situation and an inaction alternative which left the undesirable status quo in place, the Israeli Defense Minister, Sharon, created a predisposition toward the former. This disposition may not have existed had the government considered other action alternatives.

The parallel decision condition requires the group to allow members' preferences to be expressed simultaneously with respect to all available policy options. Sequencing choices in the context of collective decisions creates opportunities for manipulation which would not have existed under simultaneous choice procedures. This condition is a straightforward extension of the analytic evaluation condition from the individual to the group level.

The third condition is a substantive rationality criterion. It suggests that if there exists an option that has the highest chance of being selected given the initial distribution of individual preferences, then it should not be eliminated from the group deliberations. This is not to suggest that such a policy option would or should be selected by the group, because if that were the case the deliberation process would be theoretically and practically meaningless. Rather, the third condition requires that it should be represented in the group deliberations. The elimination of such an option suggests some manipulation of the agenda or other aspects of the group discussion in a manner that is designed to reduce the chance of an option being actually selected by members who have a good reason to believe that if this option is brought up in the course of the group discussion, it would receive overwhelming support.[17]

[17] Social choice theorists (e.g., Arrow, 1963) argued for some other substantive criteria that must be satisfied by social choice rules. For example, the *Pareto* criterion asserts that if option a is preferred by all individuals to option b, then the latter should not be selected by the group. The *consistency* criterion asserts that if an option would have been the choice of all disjoint subsets of individuals, then it should emerge as the

These conditions are not to be seen as positive proof of analytic group decision processes. Rather, they serve as minima that must be satisfied in order to begin further exploration into the possibility of analytic group choice. The violation of either of these three conditions clearly suggests a non-analytic decision process at the group level. If these three criteria are satisfied, the group decision making process can be analyzed in terms of the other substantive criteria discussed above: that is, the admissibility of the actually-formed coalitions in the group and the choice of the policy option with the highest coalitional support. If it is possible to fill in the empty spaces in the group preferences matrix, the extent to which the substantive collective rationality criterion is met can be assessed. For a fully-filled matrix of preference orders (i.e., one in which each of the group participants has a complete preference ranking over all of the considered policy options), it is possible to measure the social preference score of each of the options and to see whether the option which was actually selected by the group is the one with the highest preference score (or whether it is the Condorcet alternative).

The violation of the second criterion (that of simultaneous decision) clearly suggests an elimination by aspects process by the group, thereby leading to the conclusion that the collective decision process is cybernetic in nature. Additional evidence giving rise to such a conclusion is that, since its introduction to the group discussion, the actually selected option defeats each and every other option that was introduced subsequently in a pairwise contest (although it might lose to an option that had been dropped prior to the introduction of the selected option, or one which was not brought up in the group discussion).

Note that both the evidence supporting an analytic choice process and a cybernetic one at the group level do not assume preference change within individuals. The analytic model specifies strategic behavior of group participants as evidenced by coalition formation processes. The cybernetic model focuses strictly on the sequencing (or queuing) of options. In contrast to these two models, the cognitive model (groupthink) stresses group-induced shifts in individual preferences in accordance with superior (or senior) participants' positions or with a seeming group consensus. The operational interpretation of such a process can assume two forms. The first is one wherein the first procedural rationality condition is violated, that is, only one option

social choice in the combined set (Young, 1974). I refrain from dealing with these substantive requirements because it was shown that they may be violated by even the most simple choice schemes in sophisticated choice settings (Felsenthal and Maoz, 1988).

301

receives serious consideration by the group (or the group contrasts a single action option with an inaction option). The fact that other options which had been considered in individual choice processes were not brought up at the group meeting suggests a relatively clear concurrence-seeking pattern of behavior. Second, the change in individual preferences is in the direction expected by the groupthink model. Specifically, a significant change in individual preferences constitutes supporting evidence for groupthink choice if individuals shift the option advocated by the group's leader (or the option that has a relative majority of first-place support) from some lower ranking to the top of their preference scale. By "significant" shifts I mean that the group preference matrix that is obtained at the end of group deliberations reflects: (a) a substantially lower level of group polarization than the initial matrix of group preferences, and (b) that the group polarization of all coalitions of which the group's leader is a member is substantially lower in the final **GP** matrix than it had been in the initial **GP** matrix. Formally, let **GP**$_b$ denote the initial group preference matrix (that is, the distribution of individual preferences prior to group deliberations), and let **GP**$_a$ represent the same matrix which is obtained following the group decision process (the subscripts b and a stand for before and after, respectively). A groupthink process requires the following evidence:

1   $GC_a < GC_b$, and
2   For each coalition which satisfies: (1) $w_i \geqslant w_j$ for all $j \neq i \in N$ and (2) $i \in C_s$, we have $P_{sa} \geqslant P_{sb}$.

The first condition follows directly from Janis's (1982) argument that groupthink processes yield a strong sense of group harmony in the post decisional stages. This implies that post decisional group conflict should be substantially smaller than predecisional conflict. The second condition asserts that decrease in group conflict is due to concurrence seeking adjustments in individual preferences. This implies that the likelihood of a coalition in which the group leader (the decision maker with the highest formal authority score) is a member would have a higher probability of forming given the post decisional group preferences matrix than it had given the initial group preference matrix. A corollary to this argument is that if one or more of the inadmissible coalitions before group deliberations had the group leader as a member, then it is quite possible that such coalitions would become admissible given an analysis of the post decisional group preferences matrix. This reaffirms our argument that the actual formation of inadmissible coalitions constitutes strong evidence of groupthink processes.

6.9 SUMMARY

This chapter has covered a large number of issues. Its aim was to develop a set of procedures allowing rigorous discrimination among the process models discussed in chapter 5. We started out with the basic outline of the Multiple Paths to Choice (MPC) framework and extended the logic of the framework to the collective choice level. The measures that were developed in this chapter allow, in some cases, a truly quantitative assessment of the predictions of the three models (e.g., the tradeoff complexity index). In other cases, these quantitative criteria serve as a basis for a more reliable qualitative judgment of the model that best characterizes a decisional stage. The treatment of issues in this chapter remains loyal to the distinction that was made in chapter 2 between substantive and procedural characteristics of decision processes, and the discussion of discrimination criteria relies on both the substantive and procedural elements of each of these models.

The primary aim of all the previous chapters was to set the stage for a general theory of foreign policy decision making. This is the topic of the next chapter.

7 A THEORY OF FOREIGN POLICY DECISION MAKING

Having reviewed the major concepts, theoretical approaches, and empirical findings of this field, we are now in a position to integrate them into a general theory which attempts to address three fundamental issues: (1) What are the factors that influence the procedures and substantive contents of individual decision making processes in foreign policy settings? (2) What is the relationship between individual preferences and collective choice processes in such settings? (3) What are the political and other characteristics of foreign policy groups and how do these characteristics influence the processes of collective choices on foreign affairs? The fundamental premise of this analysis is that the knowledge available to date on foreign policy decision making – both of the propositions that have received some empirical support and the propositions that have not yet been subjected to empirical tests – forms a sufficient basis for a general theory of foreign policy decision making.

The theory presented in this chapter is abstract, and the extent to which its propositions conform with reality is beyond the scope of the present study. Nonetheless, since none of the elements of the theory is novel (in the sense that they represent original ideas which are in some way different from those presented in previous research), it is possible to present some preliminary evidence for the plausibility of the various propositions by using studies of decision making that have been reviewed in previous chapters. The principal contribution of the present theory is its integrative nature. The novelty this theory brings to the study of foreign policy decision making is that seemingly isolated islands of theory and research can be meaningfully integrated into a comprehensive body of empirically testable propositions on the determinants, process, and outcomes of foreign policy decisions; that this body of propositions is logically sound; and that it has some preliminary empirical basis. I wish to argue that the theory developed below provides a substantive explanation of decision making which goes far beyond the sum of its various components. Advancement in our knowledge of how foreign policy decisions are made and implemented may come not only (or primarily) from further refinements in our partial models, or from competitive testing of seemingly contradictory models. Rather, the real breakthrough in foreign policy research will emerge from more general theories that encompass multiple models and approaches within an overarching logical structure.

This chapter is organized as follows. First, section 7.2 reviews some of the principal works associated with the synthesis stage. Sections 7.3, 7.4, and 7.5 describe the integrated decision making theory. Section 7.6 provides a logical and aesthetical evaluation of the theory (including some reference to previous research which indicates its empirical plausibility). Section 7.7 provides an overall assessment of decision making research in terms of criteria of internal and external validity. Finally, the assessment of foreign policy decision making research provides the basis for a formulation of problems concerning the relations between national choices and international consequences which lead directly into the second half of the book.

7.2 THE STAGE OF SYNTHESIS IN FOREIGN POLICY DECISION MAKING RESEARCH

Three fundamental features of previous research invoked among some scholars a profound dissatisfaction which led to a search for new ways of thinking about foreign policy choices. These features were: (*a*) the proliferation of inputs in the first developmental stage (see chapter 3), and the proliferation of process models in the second developmental stage (see chapter 5), (*b*) the lack of integration between inputs and processes, and (*c*) the apparent failure to connect decision theories with broader perspectives for analyzing world politics, e.g., bargaining theories and system theories. These epistemological and methodological stimuli represent the three major lines of research during this stage. The first line was already discussed in the previous chapter, namely, the effort to develop systematic procedures for discriminating among the various process models and to test these models in a competitive manner against empirical data. These studies represent critical-test approaches. The second line of research focused on attempts to theorize about and examine hypotheses linking inputs to processes and – to a lesser extent – to outcomes. Finally, there exists an initial effort to integrate decision-related perspectives with bargaining approaches and systems approaches under a single theoretical roof.

7.2.1 Discriminating frameworks

The Stein-Tanter and Maoz MPC frameworks were discussed at great length in chapter 6. However, additional efforts along these lines of inquiry are worth considering. Snyder and Diesing (1977) studied decision making and bargaining processes in international crises. Their main decision-related effort consisted of attempts to identify patterns of information processing and choice under crisis conditions. The main focus of their framework was on the procedural aspects of decision processes, in particular, on the number of policy options explored and analyzed by decisional units, and on the relationship between the size and structure of the decisional units and the type of procedures (i.e., number of explored options) used for choice. The obvious advantage of such a framework is its relative simplicity. The size of decisional units and the number of explored options are easily identifiable and quantifiable variables. Their empirical domain consisted of 16 international crises from the Fashoda crisis of 1898 to the Cuban missile crisis. Their findings are that decisional complexity increases with the size of the decisional unit and that a combination of analytic (rational) and bureaucratic procedures best characterizes decision processes under crisis conditions.[1] However, focusing interpretations of decision making processes strictly on the number of explored options can be extremely misleading. The number of explored options – while a valid indicator of decisional procedures – might not be sufficient for discriminating among process models, and the relationship between this variable and choice quality is not strictly linear.

Moreover, most of Snyder and Diesing's empirical analysis deals with collective choice processes. The distinction between individual choice and group decision making exists in this study only insofar as they divide their data into decisions that were made by single individuals or those that were made through group deliberation and through bureaucratic maneuvering. The failure to identify substantive

---

[1] It must be noted that the two authors disagree with one another with respect to the degree of overlap between what they describe as the bureaucratic model and what they describe as the analytic one. Snyder (1977: 407–408n), in a long footnote, argues that Diesing's conclusion on the very same page is erroneous. Snyder's interpretation of the data is that there exist no fundamental differences between the postulates of the two models, and that they are indistinguishable from an empirical point of view. This is contrary to Diesing's conclusion that bureaucratic politics rather than analytic models best describe crisis decision making. More importantly, Snyder argues that a loose version of the analytic (utility maximization) model fits the data quite well, contrary to Diesing's contention that "this model is quite besides the point of crisis bargaining."

aspects of decision processes and to explore the relationship between decisional procedures and substantive content limit the insights one could derive from their framework with respect to the identification of the modal patterns of decision making in crisis situations. Nonetheless, the primary contribution of Snyder and Diesing's (1977) research lies in the suggestion that crisis decision making may not be as suboptimal and as biased as previous scholars have suggested (e.g. Hermann, 1969a, 1972; Holsti, 1972a).

Gallhofer and Saris (1979; 1986) developed a discriminating scheme which they labeled the "empirical decision analysis" framework. The fundamental discriminatory principle used is the intuitive scale of measurement underlying decision makers' treatment of probabilities and values. They distinguished between procedures that use nominal scales, those that use ordinal or interval scores assigned to probabilities and values, and those that treat probabilities and values in ordinal or interval terms. The treatment of future events in nominal terms is roughly equivalent to our distinction between deterministic and probabilistic prediction patterns. The distinction between the assignment of intensities to values or the evaluation of outcomes in nominal terms is essentially similar to the ranking of outcomes on some criteria (either by explicitly assigning cardinal utilities or by ordinal ranking) as opposed to a threshold-related evaluation of outcomes, which is consistent with cybernetic evaluation patterns. By grouping these two aspects of decision making together, the authors defined a set of choice rules consistent with each of the four boxes in the 2×2 matrix.

First, in the box describing situations in which both probabilities and values are defined in cardinal terms, the SEU decision rule is said to apply, and the decision is described as essentially rational. Second, in the box with cardinal utilities and nominal probabilities, there are several possible decision rules: the *dominance* rule which asserts that the decision maker selects that policy option the outcomes of which are at least as good and at least one of which is strictly better than the outcomes associated with any of the other policy alternatives; the *lexicographic* rule which asserts that the decision maker selects the policy option which ranks highest on the most important value dimension; the *addition of utilities* asserts that in cases of multiple value dimensions, a decision maker would use a simple additive principle to generate an integrated utility scale.[2] Third, when the decision maker uses probabilistic language, but treats values in nominal terms, the

[2] This is actually equivalent to the treatment of all value dimensions as equally important in the determination of the integrated utility function.

decision rule employed is that of risk-avoidance. Specifically, the decision maker is said to select that policy option with the highest probability of a positive outcome or "which amounts to the same thing since probabilities are assumed to sum to one, of selecting the strategy with the lowest probability of negative outcomes" (Gallhofer, Saris, and Melman, 1986: 60). Finally, the rules associated with cases wherein decision makers treat future events in deterministic terms and evaluate options in nominal terms are basically variations on the satisficing theme of the cybernetic model: either selecting the policy which seems the first satisficing one or eliminating those policies whose outcomes are seen to be nonsatisficing.

The conceptual similarities between the EDA approach and the MPC framework are seemingly striking. Both procedures identify essentially the same universe of individual choice rules. Both deal explicitly with the ways in which decision makers might cope with uncertainty, distinguishing between deterministic and probabilistic approaches to estimation of future events. And both relate the processes of revision and evaluation directly the choice rule employed by the decision maker. However, this resemblance is more apparent than real. In an attempt to examine the extent to which these two procedures correspond, a verbatim transcript of the Dutch Foreign Minister's address before the council of ministers in October 1914 dealing with the question of Holland's neutrality during the First World War was analyzed using the two approaches. The results of this analysis suggest that there are marked differences in the way the two approaches interpret choice-related reasoning. For one thing, the EDA procedure includes in its definition of decisional outcomes items that are treated as values by the MPC framework. In the latter framework, outcomes are seen as events that are beyond the control of the decision maker and which, by themselves, entail no normative connotations. Values, on the other hand, are taken to be non-behavioral consequences that entail affective connotations (good, bad, desirable, undesirable) for the decision maker. Second, in the EDA framework, the distinction between nominal and cardinal treatment of probabilities and values is sufficient for suggesting the appropriate choice rule. The MPC framework, on the other hand, requires much more information before such a judgment can be made. While deterministic treatment of multiple outcomes associated with a given policy option makes SEU maximization inadmissible, it is not at all obvious that the opposite is also true. Treatment of outcomes in probabilistic terms does not imply SEU maximization, nor does the quantitative evaluation of policy options imply analytic choice. The premise underlying the MPC framework is that most decision making processes entail a variety of procedures, and that these procedures might be consistent with more than one process model. Consequently, the MPC procedure is likely to represent more mixed paths to choice and the EDA procedure is likely to base its final assessment of the kind of model at work on a more general description of the process.

Brecher's (1977a, 1979a, 1980) model of crisis decision making represents a more general discriminating scheme than those suggested by Snyder and Diesing or by Gallhofer and Saris. Brecher's research question concerns the effects of crisis-induced stress on decision making processes, but his unit of analysis was the decisional group rather than individuals. Brecher characterizes decisional groups along two essential dimensions: size and structure. (The structure of groups is divided into *ad hoc* and institutional.) The aspects of group choices examined are probe, information processing (scope and receptivity to change), consultation, and alternative search and evaluation procedures. Unfortunately, the criteria upon which the assessment of the type of decision model employed is based are specified in a general manner. No clear operational criteria are given. Nonetheless, this problem is not crucial in the research design due to the fact that crisis decision making is decomposed to distinct stages which are pretty much in line with the MPC framework. This study will be discussed in the following section.

7.2.2 Integrating inputs and processes

Holsti and George's (1975) article on the effects of stress on decision making ignited much of this research. For the first time in the study of foreign policy decision making an argument was made for thorough examination of the relationships between situational inputs and decision behavior, and in which decision behavior was taken to be context-dependent.[3] The suggestion that stress is related to decisional quality by an inverse-U shape function was also novel; in the past it had been assumed that stress is inversely related to decisional quality.

Brecher (1980) made the relationship between stress and decision behavior the key research question in the International Crisis Behavior (ICB) project. Stress is viewed as a combination of threat perception, time pressure, and perceived probability of war. His determination of

---

[3] Although aspects of this argument have been examined in the past, e.g., by Hermann (1969a), Holsti (1972b), and Janis (1982), Holsti and George argued for a two-step model of decision making that combines procedural and substantive elements which might vary according to varying levels of decisional stress. See also Holsti (1979).

stress in the various crises is not based on tangible criteria but rather on temporal intervals in each of these crises. Brecher's study of the Israeli decisions during the 1967 and 1973 crises is probably one of the very few attempts to integrate previous knowledge into an overall framework of crisis decision making. The study investigates a relatively large number of decisions during major security crises, thereby providing – perhaps for the first time – a body of carefully derived data suitable for a rigorous empirical assessment of the effects of situational inputs on decision processes.[4] Since the crises under investigation were decomposed to several stages, each of which was characterized by a different level of decisional stress, Brecher was able to look at the effects of stress on decision behavior. His findings provide the first – and most convincing – support for the hypothesis suggested by Holsti and George (1975) (and by Holsti, 1979) that the effects of decisional stress on choice behavior are curvilinear rather than inversely linear. The results of Brecher's extensive empirical analyses will be used to assess certain aspects of the theory developed below. The International Crisis Behavior Project (ICB) produced a large number of case-studies, all of which investigated crisis decision making using Brecher's framework (see Brecher, 1979b, for a sample) thereby providing a broad data-base for further investigations of foreign policy decisions under crisis conditions.[5]

Despite its unquestionably profound contributions to knowledge on foreign policy decision making, there are several problems with this line of research. First, the focus on crisis situations does not allow a complete exploration of ranges of decisional stress. Since Brecher's definition of crises identifies their starting point as a sharp rise in (subjective or collective) perceptions of threat to basic values, time pressure, and probability of military hostilities, the decision analysis begins at already abnormally high-stress levels. Routine problem-solving processes are not a part of the investigation. Even low-stress periods in times of crisis might be substantially higher than in non-crisis decision making. Second, Brecher's definition of crisis is defender-oriented. The focus is on responses of crisis targets to challenges posed by actions of other states to their security-related values. The considerations underlying initiators' decisions to launch a set of moves which – knowingly or unknowingly – precipitate an international crisis are, by and large, ignored (Maoz, 1982b). Yet,

---

[4] Contrary to previous investigations of similar issues (e.g., Hermann, 1969a, 1972, Holsti, 1972), Brecher's analysis is more comprehensive in the sense that it focuses on both pre and post-crisis periods as well as on several stages of the crisis period itself.
[5] For assessments of this project as well as other studies of crisis decision making see Tanter (1978) and Holsti (1979).

decisions to initiate crises might be in some important respects very different from decisions to respond to a perceived challenge. In particular, such decisions might be taken under conditions of low decisional stress. They may be made without awareness that certain moves would be perceived as extremely provocative by other actors. Empirical research on the causes and consequences of conflict initiation processes revealed significant differences between the behavior of initiators and the behavior of targets in conflicts (Bueno de Mesquita, 1981, 1985; Maoz, 1982a).

Third, the delineation of crisis periods in terms of different stress levels is somewhat arbitrary. Stress levels might vary within a given crisis period, and might differ substantially from one decision to another. Moreover, the generalization of stress over decision groups might overshadow individual differences in stress perception. For example, in April 1973 (a decision not studied by Brecher) the Egyptians massed troops along the Suez Canal. The Israeli government was extremely alarmed but the military intelligence played down the significance of the event arguing that the probability of an Egyptian attack was "extremely low." Nonetheless, Defense Minister Dayan ordered a partial mobilization, which proved to be costly and unnecessary (Handel, 1976; Shlaim, 1976; Herbig and Herbig, 1982; Stein, 1985). In October the same year, the Israeli government met again amid reports of Egyptian and Syrian troop movements and of large scale evacuation of families of Soviet personnel from Syria and Egypt. Again, assessments of intention varied from little or no concern, to mild and even grave fears of an attack. It is, therefore, unclear whether the generalization of low or rising stress levels describe equally well the perceptions of individual decision makers, although it might be a fair assessment of group-shared perceptions of stress. Fourth, the assessment of the findings relating stress to decision behavior is somewhat incomplete due to Brecher's strictly threat-based conception of stress.

George (1980) analyzed the relationship between institutional and group structures and the procedural quality of foreign policy choices. He examined a variety of formal group and consultative procedures and suggested that the quality of decision processes increases with the openness and flexibility of foreign policy groups. His analysis was fundamentally based on the ideas that effective information processing and critical option appraisal requires multiple and open channels of communication, and effective multiple advocacy (George, 1972).[6]

---

[6] In contrast to his original analysis of multiple advocacy, in this book, George develops a considerably more qualified argument regarding the usefulness of the approach.

311

George's work integrates a variety of analytical approaches in an attempt to analyze collective decision behavior in foreign policy settings. These approaches employ both cognitive psychological concepts and organizational theories. However, the emphasis is on formal structures of groups. Patterns of consultation and information exchange within collective interorganizational decision bodies are seen as a consequence of institutional designs. By implication, individual preferences – however they had emerged prior to actual group discussion – are seen as having secondary effects on final group outcomes. The emergence of coalitions within policy groups is implicitly taken to be a function of the distribution of formal group authority patterns, rather than of individual preferences.

It seems that George's approach is heavily influenced by the group-induced shift hypothesis as opposed to strategic adjustment or support for policy options. Another weakness in George's approach stems from the focus on procedural aspects of group decisions rather than on their substantive contents. George responds only partly to the two-stage approach he (and Holsti) had advocated in their seminal 1975 article. The empirical domain of George's analysis is also somewhat limited. His focus is on the American foreign policy system with its special constitutional and administrative structure which gives the president considerable power in designing and determining consultative and advisory bodies. Other political systems might display considerable differences in terms of the ability of any single individual to redesign decisional forums and patterns of advice. Thus, the external cross-national validity of this study has yet to be established.

7.2.3 Integrating decision making and bargaining approaches

The only study that has attempted such an integration is that of Snyder and Diesing (1977). These authors envisioned international crises as a "microcosm" of international politics in which all the relevant levels of analysis (individual, national, and systemic) have a significant bearing on behavior and outcomes. International crises are viewed as continuous and interdependent processes, and the primary perspective used to analyze them is that of bargaining approaches. Decision making and information processing approaches (as well as

Having multiple advocacy in group decisions might in some cases contribute to groupthink processes. Group members, knowing that a devil's advocate is present in the group, may not always insure that she would really count in the decision process. If that person does not receive active support from the group leader and her arguments are patiently tolerated by group members, the final sense of righteousness emerging from group discussion might actually be enhanced.

system structure) define the internal and external parameters of bargaining behavior, such as the power and resolve of the actors, their perceptions of each other's strategies and preferences, and the constraints on their crisis behavior patterns. Snyder and Diesing examine the effects of previous crises on the behavior of actors in subsequent crises. (See also Leng, 1983, 1988.) The treatment of each of these perspectives (bargaining, information processing, decision making, and system structures) in separate chapters is relatively thorough and provides important insights into crisis behavior and outcomes. Yet the promise of an overall synthesis of these approaches remains somewhat unfulfilled. Snyder and Diesing discuss only in general terms how these approaches merge to form an overall multilevel theory of international crisis behavior. The parts of this monumental work are relatively better designed than the whole.

This criticism should not be taken to detract from the significance of this work, however. This is probably one of the first attempts at an explicit cross-level-of-analysis integration in international politics, and – like any pioneering study – has its faults. Furthermore, the merging of theoretical perspectives is truly impressive in that it enables an initial assessment of the extent to which different traditions of research can be combined to produce an overall picture of complex and important processes in international politics.

7.3 FOREIGN POLICY DECISION MAKING: AN INTEGRATIVE FRAMEWORK

The theory of foreign policy decision making presented herein is composed of two causal blocs, each of which focuses on a different level of analysis. The first one describes the factors and processes of individual choice. The second describes group decision making. At each level, the theory is designed to explain two aspects of decision making processes: the specific path taken by an individual or group to selecting a certain policy option (the procedural aspects of the decision process) and the resulting preference ordering of policy options (the substantive outcome of the choice process).

Some introductory comments are in order. First, this is not an attempt to answer the question of which model best describes the structure and outcomes of foreign policy decisions. Rather, the question is which path – whether or not it can be directly related to a specific model – best describes a given decision process within a given context. (Context is defined in terms of a combination of situational, personality, and role variables at the individual choice level and in

313

terms of group structure and group characteristics at the collective choice level.) Second, studies of individual and collective choices in foreign policy settings seek to account for the courses of action or inaction which have been *actually* selected by an individual or group, while generally ignoring the ranking of policy options which do not constitute the top preference of the decision maker. This results in loss of a great deal of valuable information and might lead to biased conclusions. The focus on the most preferred policy option prevents reliable estimate of the relationship between individual choices and group decisions. It might also lead to erroneous inferences of preference change in collective settings when what might happen in fact is that individuals are led to support second-best options in order to prevent (or block) the adoption of least-preferred options by the group. In contrast, the present theory seeks to account for the final preference ranking of all the policy options that have been considered by an individual or group. This broad view of the dependent variables is important not only in the context of independent decision making (that is, in accounting for national choices) but also in the context of interdependent decision making (that is, in accounting for intersections of national choices in international processes).

7.3.1 General assumptions

Any theory has a set of fundamental assumptions that drive and give concrete shape to the causal process it outlines. The ability logically to evaluate theories is, therefore, based to a large extent on the clarity of these assumptions and on the way these assumptions give rise to various propositions. Assumptions, in and of themselves, are not directly testable. They could be evaluated in terms of whether they are plausible or implausible, useful or meaningless, whether the system of basic assumptions is complete, economical, or incomplete and redundant.[7] A key problem in scientific discourse is the existence of hidden, implicit assumptions in many social science theories, or even the failure to distinguish between untestable assumptions and testable propositions. This inhibits assessment of the logical consistency of a theory and precludes logical and aesthetical evaluation of the system of assumptions because one cannot tell which assumptions are crucial and which are marginal in the overall theoretical structure.

Contrary to the sweeping assumptions that characterize virtually all foreign policy process models (such as the assumption of rationality of

[7] For discussions of the structure of scientific theories see Hempel (1965); Kaplan (1964); Popper (1968); Lave and March (1975).

the analytic model or the assumption that individuals and organizations seek to reduce environmental complexity and uncertainty of the cybernetic model), the assumptions of the present theory are more limited in scope. These assumptions refer to three key issues: (a) the relationships between context, personality, and their effects on individual choice, (b) the relationships between individual preferences and group processes, and (c) the differences between individual and collective choice settings.

1 *Context–dependence*. Individuals are not consistently rational, nor are they consistently irrational. How an individual solves policy problems depends on the context in which the problem arises as it is reflected in the individual's perceptions. The same person would behave differently under different contextual conditions.

2 *Individual differences*. Different individuals may approach the same policy problems differently, they may analyze the problems from different perspectives, and may use different strategies to solve problems. Interindividual differences in decision making are due both to personality differences and to political and institutional factors. A corollary of this assumption is that unitary actor assumptions in foreign policy making are not very useful in explaining policy choices.

3 *Mixed paths to choice*. Individuals engaged in attempts to solve policy problems are more flexible in terms of the procedural and substantive strategies they use than is expected by any single decision process model. It is therefore quite reasonable to expect individuals to use different strategies (that is, strategies consistent with more than one process model) at different stages of the decision process. In fact, mixed paths to choice are more frequently utilized in real-world decision processes than pure paths to choice. A corollary of this assumption is that the characterization of foreign policy decision processes should be based on describing them as a series of interrelated procedures rather than as a coherent system of actions which can be clearly attributed to a specific process model.

4 *Preference ordering*. Any attempt to explain choice must account for the preference ordering of all the considered options by an individual (or group) rather than for the most preferred policy option. This is so because choice results in preference orderings rather than in selection of a single course of action (or inaction).

5 *Individual preferences and social choices*. It is impossible to understand group choices without knowing what the preferences of individual participants are and how they were established. It is also impossible to understand group choices strictly in terms of individual

315

preferences. Collective decision making is, therefore, a function of individual preferences, group structure, and interindividual interaction, whatever the formal decision rule is.

These assumptions are relatively straightforward and do not require justification in terms of plausibility. They are considerably less general than the assumptions underlying other decision process models and therefore more realistic. Most of these assumptions have also been discussed at length in previous chapters. The key question about these assumptions, however, is whether they form a coherent logical system which is both necessary and sufficient for the derivation of an *integrative* theory of foreign policy decision making. In addition, the way in which distinct assumptions are related to one another must also be addressed.

A theory of foreign policy that attempts to be general must encompass the relationship between inputs and processes and between processes and outcomes. Furthermore, any claim for generality requires that a theory address different levels of analysis and define the particular properties of each level and the flow of behavior across levels of analysis (or more specifically, the rules by which behavior is transformed across levels of analysis). The evaluation of the assumptions stated above must be based, therefore, on the extent to which they satisfy the claim for generality. The first two assumptions assert that there is a degree of variability in the use of choice procedures of: (a) the same individual over different situations, and (b) across different individuals (either in the same situation or over different ones). The same applies to the use of choice procedures by collective decision bodies. These assumptions establish an expectation of relationships between inputs and processes. Universal assumptions of rationality or irrationality demand no relationship between inputs and decisional procedures (although substantive variation in terms of the content of decisions might still be expected).

Assumpion 3 asserts variability in the choice procedures within a given decision process. It is designed to describe individual and collective choice processes in dynamic terms as required by the MPC framework. This assumption requires tracing the effects of various situational, personality, and role inputs on each of the stages of individual choice or group decision making, as well as the effects of the outcomes and procedures used at one decisional stage on a subsequent decisional stage. Assumptions 4 and 5 establish the links between individual choice and collective decision processes. Assumption 4 requires consideration of the entire preference ordering of policy options by an individual or group to allow examination of individual power and behavior within collective decision bodies and assessment of the relations between group choices and individual preferences. It is also necessary for the examination of relations between national decisions and international outcomes which is the keystone for assessment of the relations between procedures and outcomes in an interdependent international setting. Assumption 5 asserts that both lower level processes (i.e., individual choices) and the attributes of groups determine collective decision processes. This assumption leads to a set of principles allowing transformation of decisional outcomes across units of analysis.

Taken together, these assumptions set the stage for an integrative theory of foreign policy decision making which combines inputs with processes and processes with outcomes over two levels of analysis: individual choice and collective decision making. The actors playing in such games are taken to be top level political leaders and their immediate bureaucratic advisers (see chapter 2). Organizational dynamics are represented at both levels. At the individual choice level, organizational aspects are represented by role-related considerations in the substantive structuring of choice problems and in the evaluation of policy options. At the group level, organizational aspects are reflected in the formal structure of policy groups and in the determinants of this structure (see chapter 4).

7.4 INDIVIDUAL CHOICE PROCESSES

Three general factors affect the procedural and substantive aspects of individual choices in foreign policy settings: situational variables, personality traits, and organizational role. The theory specifies how these factors affect the structure and substance of preference generation processes by individual decision makers. I will first treat each of these factors separately, and then deal with various combinations of these factors in terms of their effects on individual choice. Before doing that, however, a brief delineation of the dependent variables is in order.

In general, individual choice analysis must attempt to explain two types of variables: the procedures used by a decision maker to generate preferences over policy options and the preference ordering of considered policy options. Contrary to other explanations which focus on the decision process as one seemingly coherent whole (described by one of the process models), the procedures used by a decision maker make up a "path to choice," that is, a series of procedures that is either "pure" (consistent with the predictions of *one* process model) or "mixed" (a combination of procedures consistent with *several* process models at different stages of the choice process). In terms of the procedural aspects of individual choice, the theory attempts to account for the dynamic flow of thought processes across decisional stages. The theory is set up such that the situational, personality, and role variables are related to each of the stages of the decision process. In addition, each stage in the process is said to be affected by the procedural and substantive aspects of previous stages.

The distinction between "pure" and "mixed" paths allows assessment of the overall fit between a given process model and the actual content of individual decision behavior. A certain path to choice is said to be pure or nearly pure if its elements conform or nearly conform to the procedures or substantive contents of a single model. Certain combinations of situational, personality and role variables are expected to yield nearly pure paths to choice, while other combinations are expected to yield mixed paths of a specified nature.

Decisional Stress and Choice Behavior. Decisional stress is defined in this study to be a combination of three factors: perceived threat, perceived opportunity, and time pressure. Threats and opportunities represent motivational antecedents of decision behavior while time pressure represents practical constraints. If the procedural quality of individual choice processes is taken to be synonymous with the predictions of the analytic model of decision,[8] then the main proposition concerning stress and decision behavior is as follows:

> *Proposition 1*
> *There exists a curvilinear, inverse U-shaped relationship between stress and procedural decision quality. The tendency toward analytic choice increases at medium stress levels, and diminishes when stress levels are either very high or very low.*

This relationship stems from both the elements of stress and the requirements imposed on decision makers by analytic choice procedures. Low stress can imply both low motivational drives and low practical constraints. Low motivational drives imply that the decision maker does not perceive the decisional problem of high (personal or

---

[8] A clear distinction must be made between *procedural* quality of decision behavior and its *substantive* quality. Procedural quality is defined as behavior which is seen as consistent with that prescribed by analytic choice procedures, and is *not* assumed to yield outcomes which are either expected, or adaptive from the point of view of the decision maker. Substantive decisional quality is the degree of fit between the actual decision and a theoretically-derived criterion of optimal choice in an interdependent context. At this point, the theory addresses only procedural decision quality, but not substantive decision quality.

national) importance, and low practical constraints imply considerable time for making a decision. Under such conditions, a decision maker is likely to resort to routine mechanisms for problem solving, and to considerable simplification of both the features of the problem (diagnosis) and the search for and evaluation of available solutions. The perception of the problem as non-pressing and relatively unimportant, yields a tendency for procrastination and nondecision. Thus, decision makers resort to readily available policy options without careful examination of the extent to which such procedures meet the requirements of the extant problem, or the suitability of these procedures for solving the problem at hand.

High stress occurs when there is either high threat to basic values or new opportunities that are likely to disappear if a decision is not made within a very short period. The motivational drive is extremely strong, and time pressure is acute. Since analytic procedures require careful and comprehensive consideration of much information, it is unlikely that such procedures would be met by decision makers. Emotional factors and practical constraints inhibit analytic procedures under high stress. Instead, decision makers tend to use cognitive shortcuts and conflict reducing principles to minimize emotional conflict while trying to solve the decision problem within a narrow time frame. Decision makers' belief systems and their personal experience serve as the basic anchor for the diagnosis of problems, for the search for policy options, for interpretation of incoming information, and for the appraisal of and choice among the available policy options.

Under medium levels of stress, threats and opportunities are seen as sufficiently important to warrant close and careful attention, yet not sufficiently crucial to invoke strong emotional pressures. There is sufficient time for option exploration and acquisition of information, yet a relatively definite time limit exists such that the problem cannot be put aside. Hence, decision makers tend toward analytic procedures. One particular feature of medium stress, the combination of significant threat perception and significant perceptions of opportunities, suggests that decision makers identify and accept value tradeoffs, which is one of the most important features of analytic models.

This discussion suggests not only a procedural relationship between stress and decision behavior but also a substantive relationship. The specific nature of the substantive effects of stress on decision behavior is given formally in propositions 2a and 2b.

Proposition 2a
Low levels of stress tend to be associated with cybernetic decision

behavior; medium levels of stress tend to be associated with analytic decision behavior; and high levels of stress tend to cause cognitive decision behavior.

Proposition 2b
As perceived decisional stress moves from very low levels to medium levels, decision behavior will exhibit increasingly mixed paths to choice. These paths will usually involve combinations of cybernetic and analytic procedures. As stress moves from medium to high levels, decision behavior will again display mixed paths involving analytic and cognitive procedures.

These propositions suggest that the fit between a given model and the overall path to choice taken by a decision maker varies with the level of perceived stress. Pure paths are associated with both extreme ends of the decisional stress continuum. Stress goes up from very low to medium levels when the importance of the values at stake increases, time for decision becomes limited and the adqeuacy of SOPs is therefore seen to decline. Although complexity-reducing mechanisms are still employed, decision makers tend to be more vigilant with respect to information processing and option appraisal. Thus, individuals are likely to mix cybernetic choice procedures (such as sequential diagnosis of problems or sequential search for policy options) with more analytic evaluation procedures. Early phases of the decision process are dominated by cybernetic procedures while the final stages (evaluation and choice) become more consistent with analytic principles.

As stress moves from medium to very high levels, increasing emotional pressure introduces cognitive elements into an otherwise analytic choice process. Discrepancies between expectations and actual events in the decision maker's environment create strong pressures for value-consistency. Prior beliefs and expectations become increasingly important determinants of choice behavior. Increasing cognitive biases in information processing, as well as conflict reducing strategies, enter the revision and evaluation stages. Processes that start out with careful definitions of the situation and comprehensive option exploration are rapidly converted into what Janis and Mann (1977) call "hot" cognitive processes at the revision, evaluation, and choice stages. Both the diagnosis of the problem and the exploration of options might serve to invoke a strong sense of stress (either by revealing the high likelihood of losing important values or assets, or the presence of strong opportunities with a strict and short deadline) of which one had been unaware. In fact, the perception of stress might well change considerably during a given decision process.

320

Purely analytic paths to choice are less likely to be observed in policy choices both because they impose considerable demands on decision behavior, and because the range of stress levels associated with such paths are less clear than with the other two decisional models. Nonetheless, increased tendency toward purely analytic paths to choice is apt to be observed when stress levels are neither extremely high nor extremely low. Situations containing both significant opportunities and significant threats are more likely to give rise to purely analytic approaches than situations that are seen as either strictly threatening or strictly promising.

Situational ambiguity and choice behavior. Situational ambiguity is defined as the degree of confidence decision makers have in their ability to understand the features of the choice problem and its future implications. More formally, this concept is represented by the variance of the probability distribution assigned by the decision maker to a (real or hypothetical) inaction policy. Perceived situational ambiguity is related to decisional stress: very high and very low levels of stress are associated with low ambiguity; medium levels of stress are associated with high levels of ambiguity.

> *Proposition 3*
> *The higher the level of perceived situational ambiguity, the higher the tendency toward analytic choice behavior.*

The ability of decision makers to impose clear and unequivocal interpretation on envirionmental conditions reduces their susceptibility to the requirements of analytic procedures. Low levels of ambiguity tend to be associated with the existence of preconceived procedures or beliefs that are seen to be consistent with the features of certain environmental cues. Situations are apt to be perceived as readily interpretable either when they conform with existing indicators in intelligence SOPs that the decision maker is aware of, or when these cues match existing schemas in the decision maker's belief system (Axelrod, 1973). If previously held beliefs form high levels of uncertainty (that is, when past interpretations of certain situations are themselves ambiguous, or when decision makers do not possess firmly-held beliefs with respect to a certain issue-area), drastic changes in the environment reduce the level of perceived situational ambiguity (e.g., the change in President Carter's view of the Soviet Union following the Afghanistan invasion). Readily interpretable situations in terms of indicators contained in existing SOPs give rise to cybernetic decision behavior because they immediately suggest existing contingency plans that fit into such interpretations. Decision makers are therefore apt to be engaged in sequential search for and evaluation of various courses of action with which their organization has had prior experience. Novel policy options are unlikely to be explored because existing solutions are seen as good enough for solving the "familiar" problem.

Environmental cues that are seen to match pre-existing beliefs about other actors or about a certain issue-area are likely to invoke cognitive choice procedures. Decision makers who find available analogies to current cues impose these analogies on their diagnosis of the problem. Hence, they continue to employ cognitive principles that follow from these analogies with respect to the search, revision, evaluation, and choice stages. A good match between expectations (or other forms of prior beliefs) and current cues tends to reinforce premature closure, leads to interpretation of new information in terms of evoked sets, and imposes strong emotional biases on the appraisal of policy options. It is important to note that low situational ambiguity does not distinguish well between subsequent cognitive or cybernetic decision behavior. All that is suggested is that low ambiguity is not associated with analytic choice procedures. It is reasonable therefore to suggest that low levels of perceived situational ambiguity would cause either pure cybernetic paths to choice, pure cognitive paths to choice, or mixed cybernetic-cognitive paths to choice.

Medium levels of situational ambiguity are likely to be associated with mixed paths to choice containing both cognitive/cybernetic and analytic procedures. As ambiguity increases, decision makers start with standard diagnoses that rely either on organizational SOPs or on prior beliefs. However, they tend to become skeptical about the appropriateness of existing diagnoses, or about the suitability of predesigned policies and look for additional policy options and information. While initial stages of the decision process might be characterized by cybernetic or cognitive elements, more advanced stages would be increasingly analytic in nature. Thus, under medium levels of perceived situational ambiguity, decision processes are typically characterized by mixed rather than pure paths to choice. These mixed paths involve elements that are consistent with all three models.

High levels of ambiguity arise when decision makers perceive a certain environmental configuration as novel, sharply departing from institutional or personal expectations. In such cases, decision makers search for diagnoses which are more directly related to the problem at hand than to pre-established diagnoses or analogized events. Existing standard operating procedures are seen as inadequate, and the personal repertoire of past events is unlikely to yield sufficiently representative analogies. Search for novel options is intensified. The need for new information designed to reduce ambiguity yields increasingly analytic procedures for information processing and revision. Search and processing of information is not biased by inferential heuristics or by prior expectations because there are no anchors that direct the search for and the weighting of incoming information. Option appraisal is comprehensive and value tradeoffs are acknowledged and incorporated into the final choice. Thus, highly ambiguous situations are likely to give rise to purely analytic choice behavior.

The two situational factors, decisional stress and perceived situational ambiguity, are seen in the theory as the key exogenous factors that influence the content and structure of individual choice behavior because their sources lie outside the behaving unit. Both factors are induced by events and developments in the decision maker's environment. Yet, how these events are perceived and how they are interpreted depends to a large extent on the decision maker's personal characteristics and organizational perspective.

Personality and choice behavior. The discussion of personality and choice behavior addresses interpersonal differences in terms of general tendencies toward any one of the three process models. This follows directly from the second assumption of the theory. The present discussion is limited to the assessment of the effects of the content and the structural characteristics of individual belief systems on general choice dispositions. Other personality traits that are relevant in decisional contexts will be mentioned only in passing. This is due to their assumed correlation with the substantive and structural characteristics of belief systems. The discussion of personality effects on choice behavior will ignore, for the moment, the interaction between personality traits and situational factors. Thus, the focus will be on general choice dispositions of individuals rather than on specific coping patterns.

> *Proposition 4*
> *Individual disposition toward analytic choice behavior increases with the level of cognitive complexity. Individuals with highly complex belief systems would, on the average, display more analytic choice procedures than individuals with low levels of cognitive complexity. Individuals who display medium levels of cognitive complexity will tend to mix analytic choice procedures with cognitive or cybernetic ones.*

Some analysts viewed cognitive complexity as the ability to differentiate and discriminate concepts, events, and beliefs in the person's environment (Hermann, 1974, 1976, 1980; O'Donnell, 1979). Others viewed it as consisting of both differentiative and integrative abilities (e.g., Tetlock, 1983; 1985). Maoz and Shayer (1987) defined cognitive complexity as the level of interdependence and indeterminacy in a personal belief system. Empirical research on the effects of cognitive complexity on choice related behavior revealed that there are significant differences between the structural and substantive aspects of this concept. Proposition 4 refers primarily to the effects of the structural aspects of cognitive complexity on individual choice behavior. The various dimensions of cognitive complexity specified by Maoz and Shayer (1987) reflect different aspects of the ways beliefs (especially those consisting of explicit causal assertions) are organized and related to one another in a given belief system.

Causal connectedness reflects the degree of interdependence among distinct beliefs. The belief system of cognitively complex people can be seen as an elaborate network of highly interrelated ideas. Cognitively simple individuals display a greater degree of independence among beliefs. Even if their belief systems are extremely elaborate in terms of the number of concepts or causal assertions included in them, they are characterized by several subsystems of beliefs that are not tied to one another. Each of these subsystems will have in it relatively few causal elements. *Cyclicality* reflects the conscious or subconscious notions of reciprocal effects of certain causal relations. This seems particularly important in political contexts as it suggests a degree of empathy and awareness of mutual dependence as an inherent feature of social interactions. *Cognitive imbalance* reflects a degree of indeterminacy in a belief system, as well as tolerance for uncertainty by the individual.

These dimensions are related to general choice propensities of individuals for the following reasons. First, individuals with highly complex belief structures tend to be tolerant of uncertainty and environmental complexity and are less disposed to reduce the complexity of the problem or the uncertainty surrounding other actors' behavior by artificial means. They are apt to examine multiple aspects of the problem in their diagnosis processes and devise multiple policy options for its solutions. Second, the structural interdependence among beliefs is likely to invoke multiple evaluation criteria and inhibit tendencies toward lexicographic or sequential choice. Third, high levels of cognitive imbalance suggest that individuals acknowledge a significant level of indeterminacy in their belief system and would therefore be tolerant of value tradeoffs inherent in existing policy options. To the extent that cognitive imbalance is associated with tolerance of uncertainty, it would predict complex and vigilant information processing strategies in line with those expected by the analytic model.

Low-complexity belief systems force an individual into employment of cognitive or organizational devices in order to reduce complexity, value conflict, and uncertainty that are inherent in most policy problems. Therefore, such individuals tend to employ procedures that are consistent with those expected by the cybernetic or cognitive models. Both highly complex individuals and highly simple individuals in terms of the structural organization of their belief systems are ones who are either consistently high or consistently low on all three dimensions of cognitive complexity. Their decisional procedures will therefore exhibit relatively pure paths (cognitive or cybernetic for low-complexity individuals and analytic for high-complexity individuals) to choice. Medium levels of cognitive complexity are reflected either by intermediate levels of complexity on all three dimensions or – more realistically – by high scores on some dimensions and low scores on other dimensions. Such individuals are likely to mix different procedures at different decisional stages. For example, individuals who are high on the causal connectedness dimension but are low on the cognitive imbalance dimension are likely to invoke multiple diagnoses of problems and multiple policy options, but are generally intolerant of uncertainty and use various cybernetic or congitive devices to reduce decisional complexity and uncertainty. Thus they start out with highly complex designs of decision problems but rapidly resort to sequential or lexicographic evaluations of these designs.

In addition to the effects of situational and personality variables on the procedural aspects of choice behavior, there exists ample evidence that the content of political belief systems are also related to substantive aspects of choice. Walker (1983, 1986) and Tetlock (1983, 1985) pointed out that the content and structure of beliefs are good predictors of the content of the policy options that are sought and advocated by decision makers in a variety of situations. The next proposition builds upon this body of research.

Proposition 5
The more classifiable the operational code of an individual, the less likely is one to display analytic choice behavior, and the more likely one is to display elements of cognitive or cybernetic choice behavior. On the other hand, individuals who fall into different operational code categories are more likely to display analytic choice behavior, and be less predictable in terms of the patterns of preferences over policy options.

325

Walker's operational code analyses provide a useful guide to the determination of the extent to which belief systems are classifiable in terms of substantive content. Walker (1986) developed a typology of operational codes and used it to code statements made by decision makers into this typology. He used the modal frequency in the coding results to determine the dominant operational code type of a given individual. However, the variance of such a distribution of belief types provides important information about a given personality. Specifically, judgment about a person is more reliable when this person tends consistently and predominantly to exhibit one type of operational code than when a person exhibits several different belief types, even though the latter person may exhibit one type of belief with a higher frequency than the other. The first person is more classifiable from the point of view of operational code analysis than the latter. The index of qualitative variation can therefore provide a useful measure of classifiability for distributions of belief types.

Thus, the extent to which a person is said to have a predictable belief system is related to the degree of procedural and substantive consistency in her decision behavior. A person whose belief system is highly classifiable tends to be strongly constrained in her choice behavior by rigid beliefs. These beliefs provide clear anchors for diagnosing decisional problems, a relatively limited pool of policy options that are repeatedly consulted in a wide variety of situations, strong expectations guiding search and processing of information, and fairly few evaluation criteria. Such a person seems to display behavioral patterns that are consistent with those described by Kissinger (1966) under the heading of "ideological leadership" or by Rokeach (1960) as a "close minded" personality. Substantively, such a person invokes few but recurrent analogies to characterize situations arising in the environment and applies a variety of consistency-preserving heuristics to eliminate value conflicts. The value dimensions such a person employs to appraise policy options are also highly predictable both in terms of their contents and in terms of their relative importance weights. It follows that a person who exhibits a highly classifiable belief system is prone to apply cognitive choice procedures and exhibit relatively stable decisional dispositions.

Decision makers exhibiting a diverse set of beliefs that are difficult to classify in terms of a clearly predominant operational code type seem to correspond to the "bureaucratic-pragmatic" leadership type discussed by Kissinger (1966) or to the "open-minded" personality described by Rokeach (1960). The boundaries of their belief systems tend to be vague and open to change and/or expansion, and their approach to problem-solving is pragmatic and *ad hoc*. Such people tend to be less constrained by their belief systems than people with rigid belief sets. Therefore it is reasonable to expect open-minded people to possess the cognitive flexibility that is required for analytic choice behavior. The substantive content of decisional behavior for those people is likely to change considerably over time and across decisional problems, and therefore they are likely to be influenced more by prevailing situational conditions than by their beliefs and expectations.

Organizational role and decision behavior. The three properties of organizational role discussed in chapter 4 were hierarchical rank, expertise, and control over organizational resources. The following propositions relate each of these properties to expected decisional behavior patterns. Next, I discuss some additional aspects of role such as length of tenure of a certain position, previous roles occupied by an individual, and role mobility. These aspects are also seen to affect individual choice behavior, albeit to a lesser extent than the rank, expertise, and resource aspects.

> *Proposition 6*
> *The higher a person's rank within an organization, the less likely one is to exhibit cybernetic choice patterns, and the more likely one is to exhibit either cognitive, analytic, or combined cognitive/analytic choice behavior.*

Increased organizational rank is associated with several variables that lessen organizational constraints on decision behavior, including: (1) accessibility to multiple sources of information which stem both from within the organization with which the person is affiliated and from outside the organization, (2) frequent contacts with people (and therefore with points of view) from other organizations, (3) demands and constraints which stem from interorganizational contacts (Stewart, 1972), and (4) cross-cutting pressures emanating from needs to manage and resolve intraorganizational problems and to relate organizational outputs and demands to those of other organizations. This imposes a need to adopt wider perspectives in problem solving processes than lower-level officials whose tasks, contacts and responsibilities are defined primarily within organizational channels. Thus, increased rank has substantive as well as symbolic and status aspects.

High-level officials operate within an environment that is already highly stressful, have an awareness of multiple demands and constraints on their organization, and with a sense of responsibility to issues and interests that exceed those with which their organization is concerned. As O'Donnell (1979), Rosati (1980), and Holsti (1976) pointed out, high-level officials are less likely to be influenced by organizational interests, information, and SOPs in their choice behavior than low-level bureaucrats. However, it is unclear which alternative model characterizes their choices. Holsti (1976: 30) argues that high-level decision makers are more likely to be influenced by their personal beliefs and value systems than by organizational routines. This implies that they are apt to engage in cognitive choice behavior. On the other hand, depending on the personality traits of the individual in question or on the specific situational configuration, some high-level officials might well engage in analytic choice procedures.

Lower-level officials are more involved with and close to organizational routines and procedures. They are more likely to identify themselves with the organizational well-being and see organizational interests as more compatible with their own. In most bureaucratic settings, low-level officials see their personal career as one which progresses within organizational channels and therefore tend to perceive their promotion or tenure prospects to be linked to the extent to which they perform organizational procedures. In addition, low-level officials have fewer contacts with other organizations and hence are more dependent on intraorganizational sources of information, and are less exposed to different points of view from those espoused within their organizations. This relative insulation and dependence on organizational considerations makes low-level officials more prone to engage in cybernetic choice behavior. Low level officials are likely to suppress personal values or beliefs in the face of existing organizational interpretations and SOPs.

> *Proposition 7*
> *The more expertise an individual possesses in the issue-area into which a given policy problem falls, the more likely is one to resort to analytic decision behavior. At the same time, the more expertise possessed by an individual on a certain issue, the higher the likelihood of judgmental overconfidence.*

This proposition seems somewhat self-contradictory. Yet, a second glance will reveal that this is not so. Expertise is a function of experience and education. Both factors contribute significantly to broad, comprehensive, and thorough understanding of the general issue-area into which the problem falls and serve as guards against simplistic solution strategies. On the other hand, expertise and knowledge are also likely to invoke overconfidence in one's judgments and

328

predictions. Experts might place too much value on their personal experience and downgrade different points of view. Past success in predicting foreign policy events (such as the behavior of other nations) is apt to be particularly damaging. Individuals might sidestep the boundaries of their knowledge when they had been successful in the past.

Since overconfidence in judgmental and inferential tasks is a key indicator of cognitive choice behavior, this proposition seems to entail an internal contradiction. The contradiction is only partial, however. High levels of expertise are likely to reduce the effects of organizational routines on the diagnosis of problems and on the search for and the appraisal of possible solutions. The suitability of institutional diagnoses and SOPs is apt to be challenged by such individuals if their judgment suggests that they might be inadequate for the extant problem. The ability to devise novel solutions to the problem and explore their implications is highly enhanced. Experts are likely to resort to comprehensive and careful diagnosis of policy problems, to search for multiple solutions, and to appraise each such solution in a comprehensive and complex manner. Yet, the revision process of such individuals is likely to be biased due to overconfidence. People who do not consider themselves experts on an issue-area are more likely to rely on existing institutional interpretations and SOPs, or on their prior beliefs in diagnosing problems or in exploring and evaluating policy options. However, their revision processes are likely to be more analytic in nature, and they are apt to be more cautious in the manner they process information and revise their estimates in light of new information.

Proposition 8
The higher the control over organizational resources an individual possesses, the more disposed he or she is toward analytic decision behavior.

The breadth of resources at a person's disposal affects mostly the scope of policy options considered during decision processes. A person whose organization controls a wide variety of resources is less likely to be constrained by feasibility-related constraints on policy options. People whose organizations have limited implementative resources are likely to restrict the range of considered policy options to the few that are seen as feasible given scarce resources. There are two kinds of pressures operating on representatives of organizations with limited informational and implementative resources. One is the wish to have their organization directly involved in policy formation and policy implementation. The other is that they feel that the resources available within their organization for dealing with these policy problems are extremely limited. The upshot is that representatives of organizations with limited informational and organizational resources are more influenced by single pre-established routines and limited sources of information and attempt to fit these routines and informational items to all kinds of situations and problems without examining their adequacy.

Proposition 9
The longer a person's tenure of a given position within an organization, the less disposed he or she is toward analytic choice behavior.

Length of tenure is likely to immerse a person's approach to policy problems in organizational perspectives. People with long tenure in a certain office are familiar with organizational routines and other SOPs, they are likely to have taken part in their development, and feel a strong sense of attachment to the organization's well-being. Therefore organizational perspectives are more likely to influence their substantive and procedural approach to policy problems than individuals with short tenure in office. In addition, length of tenure in a certain office is likely to raise propensity toward overconfidence in terms of prediction of future events and in terms of policy evaluation. Individuals with short tenure of a position are likely to invest in their approaches personal ideas and inclinations reflecting their prior knowledge and experience. They are less likely to feel bound by organizational routines, and less confident in their judgments and evaluations.

Proposition 10
The more diverse the role experience of an individual and the more extensive cross-organizational mobility one has had, the less inclined one is toward cybernetic decision behavior.

People whose career spanned extensive movement across different organizations within the foreign policy establishment have a wider perspective of foreign policy issues and feel less committed to organizational concerns and interests than those whose career was characterized by upward mobility within the same organization. The former type of people tend to adopt multiple perspectives for the diagnosis of foreign policy problems and feel less constrained by organizational channels of communication and by the SOPs of the current organizations they represent. Therefore, their inclination toward cybernetic choice procedures is significantly lower than the decision behavior of people who moved upward within a single organization.

Intraorganizational mobility has the same effect on choice behavior as that of long tenure in a given position. A decision maker with low mobility feels strongly attached and identifies personal or national interests with organizational interests. Familiarity with existing SOPs has a limiting effect on the search for novel policy options and on the extensiveness and care in information processing and option appraisal. However, the relationship between mobility-type and decision behavior is not as straightforward as it may seem. Interorganizational mobility reinforces comprehensive cross-organizational perspectives in decision making processes thereby serving to increase the tendency toward analytic choice behavior. Yet, experience in a certain role or upward mobility within an organization has the effect of providing a lot of experience with a certain set of issues which enhances the tendency toward substantively analytic consideration. In other words, there seems to be a tradeoff between cross-organizational mobility and expertise, and both are hypothesized to be positively related to analytic choice behavior.

> *Proposition 11a*
> *The substantive aspects of decision behavior reflect the concerns, interests, and viewpoints of the organization a person is affiliated with. The extent to which these organizational concerns, interests, and viewpoints are reflected in any given individual choice process is a function of all the variables discussed above (i.e., tenure in formal rank, expertise, control over resources, length of tenure, and type of mobility).*

The point made by proposition 11a is that, whether or not the procedural aspects of choice behavior conform to those postulated by the cybernetic model, the substantive aspects of decision making will exhibit certain organizational influences. Specifically, organizational interpretations of decisional cues are apt to come up at some point during diagnosis processes. Whether or not they survive closer scrutiny against available facts or analogies drawn from other sources depends on the role, expertise, and experience of the decision maker. A secretary of defense is more likely to invoke security-related interpretations of decisional cues than a secretary of the treasury.

The options sought and explored by a person affiliated with one organization differ in content from those sought and considered by a person with a different organizational affiliation. These differences are likely to reflect feasibility-related considerations or SOPs that are specific to the resources available to different organizations. Information processing by different people will be a function of the sources of data coming from their respective organizations. Decision makers

331

usually downgrade the accuracy and reliability of data sources from other organizations to the extent they contradict the information made available to them through the organization with which they are affiliated. The criteria used to evaluate options also reflect organizational concerns. The areas of responsibility of a given organization are reflected in the value dimensions used by a given individual. This is not to imply that issues beyond those directly relevant to a certain organization are not considered by a decision maker. It is not implausible that a secretary of defense will evaluate options in terms of the domestic support for the administration, or in terms of the economic costs associated with them. Rather, secretaries of defense are more likely to include security criteria in their evaluation processes, even if the decision problem does not directly invoke security issues, and treasury secretaries are likely to include economic criteria in their evaluation of policy options, even if the problems examined do not have significant economic implications. This is a crude formulation of the "where you sit is where you stand" proposition of the bureaucratic politics model. A more specific and falsifiable proposition based on this idea is the following:

> *Proposition 11b*
> *Decision makers representing different organizations tend to place a heavy weight on value dimensions which represent their organization's responsibilities relative to the weights they place on value dimensions that represent the areas of resonsibility of other organizations. Moreover, the extent of organizational effects on decision behavior is reflected in the relative weighting of different value dimensions.*

This proposition holds regardless of the procedural aspects of the evaluation process exhibited by a person. If a person employs analytic evaluation criteria, then the value dimensions representing one's organizational concerns are more heavily weighted than those value dimensions that represent other organizations' concerns. Thus, security issues will be more heavily weighted by a secretary of defense than economic issues and the relative weighting of security criteria is likely to be less important compared to that of economic criteria by a secretary of the treasury. Moreover, the more attached a person is to one's organization (in terms of length of tenure and upward mobility) the heavier is the weighting of organizational evaluation critiera relative to other criteria. If a person applies an EBA procedure to the evaluation of policy options, the order of elimination criteria applied reflects organizational interests, such that the options eliminated first tend to be those that are seen negatively by the decision maker's organization or those on which the organization has little influence. Lexicographic or semi-lexicographic evaluation will be limited to the appraisal of policy options on value dimensions that reflect organizational concerns.

Decisional inputs and individual choice processes: a synthesis

Not all the inputs discussed above occupy the same role in the theory and not all of them are of equal importance. Some inputs seem to generate choice propensities which contradict the choice propensities postulated by others. It is therefore important to consider the joint effects of the three groups of variables on individual choice behavior.

The simplest formulation of the integrative theory of foreign policy decision making is given by the following general equation:

$$Decision\ behavior = SIT.\ VARS + PERS.\ VARS + ROLE\ VARS \tag{7.1}$$

where decision behavior can be any set of characteristics (combination of specific paths) of a given decision process, such as evaluation comprehensiveness, tradeoff complexity, choice rule used, and so forth. Situational, personality, and role variables are any combination of factors discussed in the various propositions. The functional form represented in equation (7.1) combines the propositions discussed above into an overall explanation of decision behavior. But the explanation represented by this equation encompasses more than what is provided in the various propositions. These propositions reflect only the main effects of various inputs on decision behavior. The interaction effects represented by the multiplicative portion of equation (7.1) have been left unspecified. The main aim of this section is to discuss how various combinations of input variables explain given combinations of decisional paths employed by an individual.

First, it is important to note that the applicability of the variables differs in terms of how the equation is actually used in an empirical investigation of decision making. Situational variables can be used to explain how the same individual's choice behavior varies over time or across policy problems. Personality and role variables can be used to explain how different individuals will cope with policy problems under similar or identical situational conditions. This equation is designed to reflect simultaneous effects of situational, personality, and role factors on the choice behavior of individual decision makers.

The absence of interaction terms means that each of this set of factors stands on its own as an explanation of individual choice behavior. Maoz and Shayer (1987) found no interaction effect between

333

personality traits and situational factors (measured in terms of political circumstances) on the complexity of political argumentation in public settings. The same idea is reflected in proposition 12a which deals with the relationship between situational factors, personality factors, and choice behavior.

> *Proposition 12a*
> *The procedural quality of a cognitively-simple individual is lower than that of a cognitively-complex individual for any comparable level of decisional stress. However, it is not generally true that highly complex individuals are more predisposed toward analytic choice behavior than cognitively-simple ones across different levels of decisional stress. Cognitively-simple individuals might be more inclined toward analytic choice behavior under medium stress than cognitively-complex individuals would be inclined toward analytic decision making under very low or very high levels of stress.*

This proposition suggests that, when taking into account the personality types of the decision makers under examination, there will be two parallel inverse U-shaped functions relating decisional stress to decision behavior. The lower function will display the relationship between stress and decision behavior for cognitively-simple individuals and the upper function will display the same relationship for cognitively complex individuals. For any given level of decisional stress, cognitively-complex individuals display greater propensity toward analytic choice behavior than cognitively-simple individuals. Yet, cognitively-simple individuals are not less inclined toward analytic choice behavior regardless of the level of stress they confront. Ignoring the level of cognitive complexity of the individuals under examination, might distort the relationship between stress and choice behavior. The same applies to the operational code aspect of personality (Endler and Edwards, 1982: 40–43; Mangusson, 1982: 248–249).

> *Proposition 12b*
> *Individuals with highly classifiable operational codes are less disposed toward analytic choice behavior than individuals with diverse operational codes under identical conditions of stress. However, individuals with highly classifiable operational code types are more disposed toward analytic choice behavior under medium stress than individuals with diverse operational code types who operate under conditions of very low or very high stress.*

These two propositions suggest that personality traits serve as an intervening factor between the exogenous situational factors and the

334

observed path to choice taken by an individual. Although propositions 12a and 12b discuss only the joint effects of decisional stress and personality type on individual choice behavior, the same applies to the joint effects of situational ambiguity and personality type on individual choice behavior. Moreover, the joint effects of situational factors and role factors on choice behavior is of a similar form, as suggested by proposition 13.

Proposition 13
Individuals occupying different roles (in terms of rank, expertise, and control over organizational resources) and having different career patterns (in terms of length of tenure in a given position, diversity of organizational roles occupied in the past, and type of organizational mobility) display different inclinations toward analytic decision behavior under comparable levels of stress and high situational ambiguity. However, individuals with role characteristics that are related to cybernetic decision behavior might display higher inclinations toward analytic choice when operating under medium stress and high ambiguity than individuals with role characteristics that are related to either cognitive or analytic choice who operate under conditions of very low or very high stress and low ambiguity.

Taken together, the message conveyed by propositions 12a, 12b, and 13 is that perceptions of situational conditions such as the threats and opportunities and time constraints invoked by an environmental cue are mediated by the personal characteristics of the individual in question and the organizational context in which one operates. Ignoring these latter factors is likely to yield biased interpretations of the effects of situational conditions on decision behavior. This point could be illustrated by two studies which examined the effects of stress on foreign policy decision making. Gallhofer, Saris, and Melman (1986: 65) report that, "results of a [previous] study (Saris and Gallhofer, 1984), where the effects of situational, personal, and functional characteristics of the decision makers on their formulation of the problem were investigated and proved to be almost absent, . . . suggest that decision makers use these rules quite arbitrarily." Yet, a close inspection of that study reveals that these effects were not examined in the manner suggested here, but rather in terms of strictly independent bivariate relationships. This, in addition to the fact that the EDA approach discussed above is too general to allow a clear differentiation among paths to choice, suggests that these findings should be viewed with some caution. Brecher's (1980) and Dowty's (1984) studies of crisision decision making allow preliminary assessment of the

Table 7.1. *Decision stress and choice behavior, Israel 1967 and 1973 and the United States, 1970 and 1973*

1. Brecher's (1980: 361–397) study

Stress level	Decision process			Total
	Cybernetic	Analytic	Cognitive†	
Low	4	0	1	5
	80%	0%	20%	100%
Medium‡	5	23	12	40
	12%	58%	30%	100%
High	2	6	4	12
	17%	50%	33%	100%
Total	11	29	17	57
	19%	51%	30%	100%

2. Dowty's (1984: 356–361, 366–369) study

Stress level	Decision process			Total
	Cybernetic	Analytic	Cognitive†	
Low	7	3	4	14
	50%	21%	29%	100%
Medium‡	0	12	1	13
	0%	92%	8%	100%
High	3	8	9	20
	15%	40%	45%	100%
Total	10	23	14	47
	21%	48%	31%	100%

† I interpret Brecher's and Dowty's terminology as follows: routine decision processes are taken to be equivalent to cybernetic decision behavior; rational decision processes are equivalent to analytic decision behavior; affective decision processes are equivalent to cognitive decision behavior.

‡ Medium stress in this table incorporates three distinct stress levels that were analyzed by Brecher: the rising stress phase, the higher stress phase, and the moderate-declining stress phase. This is done to simplify the presentation of the results but has no substantive effects of my interpretation of Brecher's findings. In Dowty's study, low stress was seen as the pre-crisis stage, medium stress was the post-crisis stage, and high stress was the crisis stage.

independent effects of stress (viewed as a combination of threat, time pressure, and subjectively perceived probabilitiy of military hostilities) on choice behavior. An aggregation of Brecher's and Dowty's data by stress and decisional quality is given in table 7.1.

The statistical association between decisional stress and choice behavior as expected by the theory is given by $\nabla=0.189$ for Brecher's data and $\nabla=0.401$ for Dowty's data. This means that the expected relationship given the model reduces the error by about 19 percent for Brecher's study and by over 40 percent for Dowty's study.[9] Although this association between stress and decision behavior is statistically significant, it is very low for Brecher's study and medium for Dowty's. The explanation of this is that these analyses are done at the group level, and that the definitions of decisional stress are based on threats and time pressure but not on perceptions of opportunity. (The same applies to Saris and Gallhofer's analysis.) More importantly, however, Brecher's and Dowty's analyses do not enable us to control for the personality traits of the various decision makers involved in these crises, nor do they allow examination of organizational influences on the decision making processes. A more precise measure of association, based on Chi-square, which was developed by Maoz and Abdolali (1989), suggests a higher level of statistical association between the inverse U-curve hypothesis and decision behavior ($m_b=0.457$ for the Brecher study and $m_b=0.838$ for the Dowty study).[10]

Dynamic aspects of choice behavior. The model represented by equation

[9] The del (∇) measure of association is due to Hildebrand *et al.* (1977). It is a proportionate reduction in error measure based on a prespecified model. The error cells in table 7.1 are as follows: in the low stress row – analytic and cognitive columns; in the medium stress row – cybernetic and cognitive columns; and in the high stress row – cybernetic and analytic columns.

[10] This measure requires *a priori* specification of *consistent* and *inconsistent* cells in the contingency table. A *consistent* cell is one in which the proportion between the expected and observed frequencies is as posited by a given directional hypothesis. (Expected frequencies are computed as in the calculation of χ^2.) For example, if at low levels of stress we expect that decision behavior will be predominantly cybernetic, then the expected frequency in the Low-Cybernetic cell should be lower than the observed frequency (that is, we should observe more cybernetic decisions than expected by chance alone). Likewise, the expected frequencies in the Low-Analytic and Low-Cognitive cells should be at least as high or higher than the observed frequencies in those cells. If the relationship between an observed and exected frequency in a given cell is inconsistent in such a way with a given hypothesis, we call it a *consistent* cell; otherwise, this cell is said to be *inconsistent*. The m_b measure is therefore obtained by:

$$m_b = \frac{\sum_{j=1}^{m} \frac{(0_{cj}-e_{cj})^2}{e_{cj}} - \sum_{r=1}^{n} \frac{(0_{ir}-e_{ir})^2}{e_{ir}}}{\chi^2}$$

where c is a difference between observed and expected frequency which is consistent with a directional hypothesis and i is a difference between expected and observed frequencies which is inconsistent with a direction hypothesis, and m and n represent, respectively, the number of consistent and inconsistent categories. This measure varies from -1 to $+1$, and as it approaches $+1$, the data is said to be increasingly in line with the directional hypothesis. (Negative vaues of m_b suggest that the opposite hypothesis is supported.

(7.1) is static in nature. Its focus is on a general characterization of individual choice behavior in terms of one of the three models. As such, it does not meet the *multiple paths to choice* assumption, nor does it capture the flow of thought patterns across distinct stages of the decision process. In order to specify the individual choice part of the theory in more dynamic terms, the dependent variable – decision behavior – must be decomposed into different decisional aspects (or stages), and equation (7.1) would be substituted by a system of equations, as follows:

$Diagnosis = SIT. VARS + PERS. VARS + ROLE VARS$ (7.2.1)

$Revision = DIAGNOSIS + SIT. VARS + PERS. VARS + ROLE VARS$ (7.2.2)

$Search–Evaluation = REVISION + SIT. VARS + PERS. VARS + ROLE VARS$ (7.2.3)

$Choice = SEARCH – EVALUATION + SIT. VARS + PERS. VARS + ROLE VARS$ (7.2.4)

Where the diagnosis, revision, and choice variables are nominal-level variables denoting the type of model which best accounts for this stage, and the search-evaluation variable can be conceptualized either as a nominal variable whose levels represent a type of model or a certain interval characteristic associated with it such as evaluation-comprehensiveness (CE) or tradeoff-complexity (TC). (See chapter 6 for a discussion of the discrimination criteria for the various models at each of the decisional stages.) The point is that the kind of procedural and substantive strategies employed by a decision maker at each decisional stage are determined by: (*a*) situational variables (decisional stress and perceived situational ambiguity), (*b*) the personal character-istics of the decision maker (cognitive complexity and operational code type), (*c*) the organizational role of the decision maker, and (*d*) the procedural and substantive strategies used at an earlier stage. The effects of the last factor can be described by the following proposition:

> *Proposition* 14
> *The procedural and substantive strategies employed by a decision maker at a certain stage will affect the use of decisional strategies at a later stage. The use of procedures derived from one model at one stage creates a disposition toward the procedures derived from the same model at later stages.*

Proposition 14 implies a strong tendency toward pure paths to choice. This seems inconsistent with the mixed-paths-to-choice assumption. The reason for this proposition is that the procedural and substantive contents of behavior at one decisional stage strongly define the boundaries of admissible behavior at a subsequent stage. If

338

decision makers employ multiple definitions of the situation, a wide variety of policy options seem to be required for the search process. When decision makers explore multiple courses of action that are deemed feasible and relevant as solutions to the decisional problem, hence designing a complex choice dilemma, they will be forced to explore multiple data in order to be able to assess the probability distributions over outcomes. By definition, complex decisional setups require complex evaluation, and complex evaluation tends to produce optimizing choice behavior. A decision maker who starts out with a pre-designed institutional diagnosis of the problem will tend to rely on institutional solutions which entail both revision and evaluation criteria. Finally, a decision making process that starts out with analogy-based diagnosis of the problem will tend toward cognitive behavior all the way toward the final choice stage.

Yet real-life decision making is more likely to be characterized by mixed rather than pure paths to choice because the effects of situational, personality, and role variables modify the effects of the decisional procedures employed at previous stages. When the situational factors under which the decision is made reinforce a pure behavioral pattern, previous behavior will serve to reinforce subsequent behavior. This occurs in decisions under extreme (very low or very high) stress or extreme (very low or very high) perceived situational ambiguity. When the situational conditions under which the decision maker operates are not extreme, the effects of prior decisional behavior on subsequent behavior will be of a less restrictive nature. The same applies to personality and role-related effects on the flow of behavior over decisional stages.

Equations (7.2.1–7.2.4) do not specify compound cross stage effects. Decision behavior at one decisional stage is said to be affected only by the behavior exhibited during the stage immediately preceding it but not by behavior during stages prior to that. Diagnosis processes directly affect revision processes but not search-evaluation processes; and revision processes directly affect search-evaluation processes but not choice processes. Decisional inputs (situational, personality, and role variables), on the other hand, affect behavior at each decisional stage. Underlying this specification is the idea that each stage involves some degree of qualitatively different mental and logical operations. Thus, second-order carry-over effects are less likely to occur than first-order effects. On the other hand, decisional inputs are instrumental in defining the bounds of decision-related capacity irrespective of stage. Moreover, the relative potency of various decisional inputs may vary across decisional stages. For example, the rigidity or flexibility of belief systems is likely to be particularly instrumental in determining the nature of revision processes and the level of tradeoff-complexity in evaluation. Stress and ambiguity are apt to be particularly instrumental in shaping the content and structure of diagnosis and the comprehensiveness of evaluation. Role variables are of particular importance in determining the content of evaluation processes, and so forth.

7.5 COLLECTIVE DECISION MAKING

In chapter 4, I argued that the formal structure of policy groups provides for a transformation procedure of individual perceptions into a group-level perception of the nature of the decisional cue and its implications. Group structure serves as an important determinant of the procedures and substance of collective choice processes. However, a fundamental proposition linking individual choices to group decision making must be stated at the outset.

> *Proposition* 15
> *There is no direct relationship between the procedures and substance of the decision processes of individual group participants and the procedures and substance of collective decision processes.*

This is the benchmark proposition about collective choice. If there were a direct relationship between the two levels of analysis, there would be no need to analyze collective processes, let alone collective decision processes. All that would be needed is some aggregation rule that specifies how a group choice emerges from individual preferences. It is this proposition that has given rise to several traditions of research within and across social science disciplines, such as the literature on group behavior in social psychology and the public choice literature. The group-induced shift phenomenon inspired a great deal of research in social psychology. Likewise, the paradox of voting inspired a great amount of work in economics and political science. Proposition 15 suggests that any attempt to understand how individual preferences are transformed into collective decisions must focus on the structure of the collectivity and on the processes operating in group settings. The following propositions focus on: (*a*) the characteristics of groups as a function of individual preferences, (*b*) the formal structures of policy groups in terms of the role attributes of individual participants, and (*c*) the combination of preference and structure characteristics of policy groups.

Individual preferences and group conflict. Gaenseln (1980) points out a tension between political science notions of group consensus and psychological notions of such a consensus in terms of how it affects the performance of task-oriented groups. Political scientists who are concerned with order and governability view group consensus in a positive light in that it enhances efficient performance of collective decision bodies, reduces tensions, and facilitiates task accomplishment. Consensus can be accomplished both by individual subscription to a commonly-shared set of norms and decisional procedures (such as majority rule) or to some imposed order (either through constitutions or dictatorial imposition of values by a leader on subordinates). The lack of such consensus creates political stalemates which hinder effective governmental performance. Coalition governments which require minimum common denominators for policy implementation find it harder to launch major policy initiatives and therefore tend to be conservative and employ marginal policy changes. Concerned about their ability to survive internal friction and political competition, such groups tend toward compromise solutions which maximize their internal cohesion but which do not, in general, reach to the heart of the problem. Strong leaderships, on the other hand, feel less constrained in terms of their need to satisfy competing claims of constituencies and legitimacy groups. Hence they are capable of more innovative decision behavior and effective problem-solving. Handel (1981) argues that leaders with considerable personal or constitutional powers, are more inclined toward major diplomatic and foreign policy shifts than leaders who operate under considerable constitutional or political constraints.

The psychological attitude toward consensus is drastically different. Groups characterized by high value-homogeneity and preference-similarity are prone to bias and suboptimal decisions. Such groups tend to ignore or downgrade tensions and inconsistencies in their shared value-system, suppress opposing views and contraditory information, and view consensus within the group as a sign of righteousness which inhibits self-criticism (Janis, 1982). Value-conflict within groups tends to lead to careful scrutiny of the problem and its implications, to careful analysis of multiple solutions and to optimal decisions. Coalition building and political maneuvering within policy groups contributes to, rather than impedes, effective problem solving.

The problem is that both bodies of literature might be right because they address different things. Psychologists are concerned primarily with the ways groups go about making decisions and whether these decisions are good or bad from a normative point of view. Political scientists are concerned with the ability of governments to carry out policies. The issue of governability is one of implementation. Whether right or wrong, a governmental decision can be feasible or unfeasible. Sometimes the decision that does most good to most of the people cannot be made because the few that stand to lose are sufficiently powerful to effectively block it. Knowing that, members of a collective body might opt for feasible rather than optimal decisions, and these can be accomplished only through suboptimal structures and decision making processes in which reasonable views are often disregarded or suppressed. The theory of foreign policy decision making makes a clear distinction between the processes and outcomes of group decisions.

> *Proposition 16*
> *The more diverse the initial distribution of individual preferences –*
> *and hence the higher the degree of group polarization – the more*
> *analytic is the group decision process. Therefore the more likely is the*
> *group to select the optimal policy option if one exists.*

Group polarization reflects the degree of initial disagreement among group members regarding the appropriate way to resolve a particular policy problem. When the group is highly polarized, members engage in extensive discussion of policy options and their implications. Since group members cannot agree *a priori* which policy best solves a given problem, they engage in intense discussions with the aim of persuading other group members to shift their preferences. Such discussions force members to make explicit and comprehensive justifications of their preferences. Members attempt to expose the considerations underlying their policy recommendations in an extensive fashion because they feel such an exposition is the best way of influencing preference change in other members.[11]

As the degree of initial group polarization declines, individuals sense a greater degree of consensus within the group and feel more constrained in presenting arguments which go against the majority preferences. Pressure toward conformity with the emerging group consensus increases and voluntary or group-induced suppression of dissident views becomes stronger. The main effort in such cases is to

---

[11] Such expositions of individual considerations are not necessarily sincere. Individuals may well attempt to present such considerations in a manner they perceive to be most effective in persuading others. This may not be the same as presenting the true considerations that generated a commitment to a certain policy option. For example, the personal benefits that a decision maker associates with a certain policy will usually not be part of the decision maker's argumentation in group settings. Maoz and Shayer (1987) pointed out that conscious manipulation of arguments is only part of the structuring of arguments in policy settings. There are a lot of non-manipulable aspects of policy argumentation which reflect true beliefs and considerations.

make the initial consensus complete by influencing individuals who hold minority views into preference shifts. In addition, the premises and underlying considerations behind the policy option advocated by the emerging majority are left largely unchallenged. The strong initial support for a certain policy option is also enhanced by the fact that members holding other views might themselves be split in terms of the policy options they advocate. In such cases group discussion tends to assume a binary choice structure wherein the majority view is contrasted sequentially versus other advocated policies. This might increase biases in group decision because a contrast between the policy advocated by the majority (policy option a) and one of the policy options (b) advocated by one of the minority subgroups might increase the support for the majority view. Members of another minority group would rather see a selected than b (although they actually think that c is better than both). However, once they support a against b, the group might stop and ignore c. On the other hand, when neither of these alternatives seems to have excessive initial support, it is quite likely that all three would be raised and thoroughly discussed by the group.

Proposition 17
As the degree of initial group polarization increases, members are more likely to reveal their entire preference ordering of policy options. Hence, the likelihood of analytic group choice increases.

The extensiveness of group discussion and the parallel (as opposed to sequential) comparison of policy options by group members is, in general, greatly enhanced if group members reveal more than their most preferred policy options. However, for members to assess what kind of coalitions and strategies of argumentation and collusion are feasible, they must know the preference ordering of policy options by other members. A highly polarized group is faced by a serious problem of preference aggregation, hence members are likely to probe one another into revealing more than their first choices. This introduces additional options into the group discussion and enhances parallel consideration of multiple solutions. The ability of individuals to manipulate the agenda in a manner that avoids consideration of some policy option is reduced. Finally, pressures toward conformity are less pronounced if members feel they have other strategies of supporting second-best options rather than adjusting their preferences so as not to disrupt group harmony. Revealed preference orders by group members has some important substantive implications. A group may be extremely divided in terms of members' first-place support for the various policy options, but members might agree on

Table 7.2. *Preference ordering of four options by a five-member group*

a. Base data

Option	Preferences of individual				
	[1]	[2]	[3]	[4]	[5]
a	1	3	4	3	1
b	2	2	2	2	3
c	3	1	3	4	2
d	4	4	1	1	4

b. Preference scores of the four options

Individual	Option			
	a	*b*	*c*	*d*
[1]	3	2	1	0
[2]	1	2	3	0
[3]	0	2	1	3
[4]	1	2	0	3
[5]	3	1	2	0
Total	8	9	7	6

Note: See chapter 6 for a discussion of preference scores and the optimality of collective choices.

the second-best option. The second best-option might be the collectively best policy for that group. However, if individuals do not reveal their entire preference order, it is unlikely that this would be realized by the group. To illustrate this point, consider table 7.2.

In this example, option *b* is the collectively-best choice. It receives the highest social preference score (and is also the Condorcet winner), though it is not ranked first by any of the individuals. The group is strongly-divided in terms of first-place support between options *a* and *d* (both having two strong supporters), but members are unlikely to realize that they could conveniently agree on policy *b* unless they reveal their entire preference orderings.

Formal group structure and collective decisions. Despite its focus on the American political system, George's (1980) analysis provides important insights into the possible effects of organizational structures and policy making, building both on organizational theory and on political psychology. Although the focus of this work is on normative aspects of collective decision making (i.e., how to enhance the quality of such processes), the discussion of institutional setups that maximize argumentation and effective use of information lead to the following proposition.

> *Proposition* 18
> *The more diverse the formal authority structure of a decision making group, the more likely it is to engage in analytic choice behavior.*

Diversity of formal authority in groups implies both a lack of a rigid hierarchy of roles and a heterogeneous composition of the group in terms of levels and areas of expertise and organizational affiliation. Diverse groups are likely to exhibit analytic decision behavior because of the substantive effects of organizational role on individual choice behavior. Since people's choices reflect to some extent organizational interests and concerns, the same policy problem is apt to be analyzed from different angles by people affiliated with different organizations. It is also plausible to expect that these perspectives will produce different policy conclusions. Hence, interorganizational policy groups exhibit a greater diversity of preferences than groups that are composed along well-defined organizational lines. If group discussion is allowed to flow freely, and if individual participants do not feel pressured to conform to the mainstream view, these different perspectives enhance comprehensive argumentation. Wide-ranging organizational representation in policy making groups also reflects multiple expert opinions and informational sources. However, if the policy group has a rigid rank hierarchy, decision behavior will be constrained even if the composition of the group is highly diverse in terms of organizational representation. Spatial diversity creates a potential for extensive and unbiased screening and evaluation of multiple policy options. Whether or not this potential is realized in group deliberations is a function of the flexibility in its vertical hierarchy.

Policy groups that are either narrowly-composed in terms of role diversity or are characterized by a rigid formal hierarchy exhibit strong tendencies toward cybernetic or cognitive decision behavior. The tendency toward cybernetic decision processes is particularly strong in groups that are organizationally homogeneous even if the formal rank hierarchy is fairly egalitarian and flexible. The individual perspectives will not be all that different and participants are likely to exhibit a great degree of shared norms and concerns. Thus, the likelihood of initial disagreement in such groups would be sharply reduced. Groups characterized by a rigid rank hierarchy are likely to exhibit groupthink patterns even if they are organizationally diverse.

Potential disagreements among members are suppressed, and the group exhibits strong concurrence-seeking patterns of behavior (Janis, 1982). The rigidity of rank hierarchies is reflected by a high weight assigned to the hierarchical rank dimension of the formal authority index compared to the weights assigned to the expertise and control over organizational resources of that index. Organizational diversity is reflected by the extent to which the group is composed of different organizational representatives as well as by the presence of people representing different branches within a given organization.

The relationship between group structure and decision behavior as specified in proposition 18 seems to contradict a recurrent finding in organizational psychology that the optimal size of problem solving groups is between five and seven members. It was found repeatedly that groups of fewer than five members and of more than seven members usually do worse than the average individual participants in terms of efficient problem solving (Jewel and Reitz, 1981). Thus, psychological theory suggests that there exists an inverse U-shaped relationship between the group size and group performance. The requirement for widespread representation in policy groups seem to suggest that the propensity toward analytic decision making might increase with group size.

This contradiction is more apparent than real, however, for three important reasons. First, there is no definite relationship between group diversity and group size. Except in extremely small groups (with two or three members such as "kitchen cabinets") interorganizational diversity can be accomplished even in medium-size groups. Second, the indicators of efficient problem-solving used in psychological analyses may not be the same as the indicators of efficient problem solving in political context. In particular, the existence of a "correct" solution is not all that obvious in political decision making, and the political problem is how to aggregate preferences in an optimal way, not only how to find the right solution. Third, optimal group size cannot always be controlled in political settings. Constitutional authority for making crucial policy decisions may rest with one person and the size of policy groups arises only in the context of consultative bodies. In other cases, constitutional authority for making policy decisions is vested in a large collective body such as a cabinet.

However, it is useful to consider in this context two studies that have examined the relationship between the size of decision making groups and crisis decision making. First, Snyder and Diesing (1977: 375–376) found a strong positive relationship between group size and the procedural quality of decisions. Second, Brecher (1980) discusses

Table 7.3. *Size of policy groups and decision behavior, Israel 1967 and 1973*

Group size	Decision behavior			Total
	Cybernetic	Analytic	Cognitive	
small	4	2	2	8
medium	2	7	2	11
large	5	20	13	38
Total	11	27	19	57

Notes:
1 Error cells according to the inverse U-shape hypothesis of group-size and decision behavior are: for small groups – Analytic decision; for medium groups – Cybernetic and Cognitive decisions; for large groups – Analytic decisions. The inverse U-shape hypothesis performs by $\nabla = 0.126$ better than chance (which indicates low support to this hypothesis in Brecher's data).
2 Error cells according to the direct size-performance relation hypothesis are: for small and medium-size groups – the same as in note 1 above, and for large groups – Cybernetic and Cognitive decisions. The direct positive relationship hypothesis relates to the data by $\nabla = 0.189$, which is a significant improvement over the previous hypothesis, although the relationship between group size and decision performance is still low.
Source: Brecher (1980: 361–397).

the size and institutional composition of decisional forums as a function of changing stress perceptions. Thus, it is possible to construct from Brecher's data a table relating size of groups to their decision behavior. This is given in table 7.3.

The Chi-square score for this table is 6.89 which, with four degrees of freedom is not statistically significant at the .05 level. Since these data do not deal directly with the interorganizational character of policy groups, the tests conducted for table 7.3 do not provide unequivocal support for either of the two hypotheses.[12]

The relations between decision behavior and implementation. As noted above, the debate over the effect of group polarization on decision quality revolves about relations between decision behavior and implementation of national decisions. This issue is addressed by proposition 19.

---

[12] From Brecher's (1980) data it is possible to test a slightly modified version of these hypotheses. Brecher distinguished between institutional and *ad hoc* decisional forums. When these two types are related to type of decision behavior used, the association is $\nabla = -0.118$, which means that the predicted association between type of forum and decision behavior does worse than chance. This supports my contention that interorganizational diversity is independent of the size of the group or its institutional character. Dowty's (1984) data do not permit such an analysis.

Proposition 19
The more analytic the group decision process, the lower the likelihood of post-decisional consensus. The lower the degree of post-decisional consensus, the lower the fit between the decision and its implementation.

Probably the most important contribution of the bureaucratic politics literature to the study of foreign policy making is the proposition that political decisions might be implemented in ways that are sometimes very different from those intended. In other cases, political decisions may not be implemented at all (Neudstadt 1964; Allison, 1971; Allison and Halperin, 1972). This gap between decision and implementation is due to both motivated and unmotivated misinterpretations by bureaucracies of "the spirit of decision". Motivated misinterpretation occurs when an organization which is responsible for the implementation of a policy decision disagrees with it, feels threatened or otherwise harmed by it, and so on. Misinterpretation consists of attempts to stall or circumvent the damaging effects of a decision by changing the ways in which it is carried out. This may include playing dumb and arguing that the implementative implications of the decision were misunderstood, or by arguing that organizational constraints (resources, external factors, *force major*) inhibited proper implementation.

Unmotivated misinterpretation occurs when organizational SOPs for carrying out a policy are applied without regard to how they change the "spirit" of the decision. In the Cuban missile crisis, the Navy's SOPs for blockading Cuba required a wide perimeter in order to reduce the vulnerability of the ships to the weapons located on the island. However, the blockade decision was designed, among other things, to provide the Soviet leadership sufficient time for decision before a clash between Soviet and American vessels took place on the open sea. This required tightening the blockade around Cuba (Allison, 1971). The bureaucratic politics model asserts that there is no automatic guarantee that organizations implement decisions the way policy groups intended them to.

Proposition 19 specifies the conditions under which motivated misimplementation is likely to occur. When the degree of consensus in a decision making body is low, organizational representatives who are put in charge of implementing a policy option may not be pleased with the decision and may try to circumvent it by failing to implement it or by minimizing damage through misimplementation. Janis (1982) points out that groupthink patterns are apt to result in highly consensual decisions and invoke a strong sense of harmony among group members. This sense of harmony is often accomplished through post-decisional bolstering which reduces motivated misimplementation. Unmotivated slippages in implementating policies are due essentially to a failure of the political decision makers to closely supervise the organizations which are supposed to implement policies. As was argued by organizational theorists (e.g., Cyret and March, 1963; Halperin, 1974), unmotivated misimplementation occurs irrespective of the kind of decision process that produced a certain policy. In fact, unmotivated slippages in implementation are less likely to arise if the decision making process relied heavily on SOPs because the decision itself is already bound by organizational routines.

The seeming conflict between psychological and political perspectives of consensus in decision making is resolved by this proposition in the sense that consensus is damaging with respect to the decision process, whereas dissent is damaging with respect to implementation. Decision making processes that are simplistic and non-analytic in nature create artificial perceptions of consensus, thereby reducing motivated slippage between decision and implementation. Analytic decision processes reduce pre-decisional or post-decisional bolstering effects, thereby increasing the likelihood of motivated misimplementation.

Individual power and collective decision behavior. The starting point of the measurement of individual power was the assumption that neither formal authority ranks of individual participants in policy groups nor their preferences are good predictors of the extent to which individuals can get their advocated policies adopted by the group as a whole. The combination of formal authority and individual preferences provides a possible set of ideas linking individual choices to group decisions. This link is specified in propositions 20a–c.

> *Proposition 20a*
> *If the group decision process is analytic in nature, the higher the power of an individual group member (defined as the potential for controlling decisional outcomes) the more likely is the final group ordering of policy options to resemble the individual's ordering of policy options.*

> *Proposition 20b*
> *The greater the ability of a group member to control the agenda during group deliberations, the higher the likelihood that the final preference ordering of policy options by the group would resemble his own. Likewise, if there are other indications of a cybernetic-type EBA*

349

process at the group level, members with higher degrees of control over informational or implementative resources are more likely to have the group adopt their favored policies.

Proposition 20c
In settings characterized by a rigid role hierarchy that are likely to exhibit groupthink patterns of decision, the higher the formal rank of an individual, the more likely is the final preference ordering of policy options by the group to resemble one's preference ordering.

In settings characterized by extensive and parallel screening of options, and by the free flow of information and argumentation, both the formal authority of individuals and their policy preferences determine the degree of actual influence they have on the group. Proposition 20a suggests that analytic decision behavior in group settings yields decisional outcomes that conform to the substantive predictions of that model: (1) inadmissible coalitions do not form, and (2) the group orders its preferences in a manner consistent with the preferences of the coalition with the most power. The measure of individual power should therefore be related to the group decision such that individuals who are highly pivotal are more likely to control decisional outcomes than those who are less pivotal. It is important to note in this context that an individual's power is a function of both formal authority and preference structure. Thus, a corollary to proposition 20a is that the index of individual power discussed in chapter 6 should have a higher predictive potential than any of its two components separately.

But individual power can be fully expressed only if individuals have an opportunity to reveal their entire preference ordering of policy options and if coalition formation is an important characteristic of the deliberation process. When group deliberations restrict the revealing of preferences or the flow of argumentation and interindividual collusion, the components of individual power have a higher predictive potential than the composite influence score. Proposition 20b deals with agenda manipulation and EBA processes at the group level. Sequencing of policy options during the deliberation process gives greater power to those who control the order of presentation. Whether or not other individuals actually change their preferences is of secondary importance in sequential choice settings.

The key to understanding substantive group choices is how options or evaluation criteria are sequenced. Thus, individual control over decisional outcomes is a function of one's ability to control the agenda. In EBA processes, the sequencing of evaluation criteria determines which policy options would be selected. Individuals who control information or implementative resources are likely to be instrumental in determining the evaluation sequence. Because options are evaluated in terms of feasibility before they are evaluated on other normative criteria, feasibility-related considerations come prior to value judgments of the consequences. In addition, assessment of the probability distribution associated with the outcomes of policy options is likely to precede normative evaluation. Because the tendency in cybernetic decision processes is to reduce complexity and uncertainty, informational resources are crucial in structuring choice problems. The tendency to eliminate low-likelihood outcomes from the evaluation process gives individuals who control informational resources great influence in determining which of the outcomes associated with the policy options will be included in their appraisal. Individual preferences play a minor role in sequential choice processes for two reasons. First, they are unlikely to be revealed completely because of the binary nature of choices. Second, individuals have little opportunity for forming coalitions because they may not know others' preferences and because they cannot control the sequence by which policy options are introduced.

Settings that are vulnerable to groupthink patterns, in terms of the situational conditions and in terms of the formal structure of the group, increase the influence of individuals with higher formal ranks. Specifically, if groupthink processes are characterized by adjustment of preferences with what is seen as the leaders' preferences, then leaders' preferences become a major determinant of decisional outcomes. The point of proposition 20c is that low-rank officials are engaged in a process whereby they try to guess the leader's preferences and adjust their preferences accordingly. This is done either by withholding judgment until the leader has expressed her preferences or by extrapolating the leader's preferences from her known positions on related issues. If members are unsure of the leader's preferences, they substitute the emerging group consensus for the leader's preferences and adjust their views accordingly. In groupthink decisions, individual preferences are a bad predictor of the final decisional outcomes (except those of the highest-ranking officials) because they are assumed to change in the course of group deliberation. Thus the measure of individual power is likely to lose much of its predictive potential as well. The slack is taken up by the hierarchical rank dimension of the formal authority index.

These propositions depict the ability of individuals to influence group decisions as dependent upon the structure of group deliberations. Which attributes of individual members will be instrumental in accounting for their personal influence depend on the kind of pro-

351

cedures adopted by the group for aggregating individual preferences into group outcomes. But in addition to these ideas, there are some characteristics of individual preferences that account for group members' behavior regardless of the type of model that describes group decisions. The most prominent among these characteristics is put forth in proposition 21.

> *Proposition* 21
> *The higher the degree of conviction of an individual, the higher the influence of that individual on group decision processes.*

By degree of conviction I refer to the extent to which an individual believes that her most preferred option is superior to another option. Operationally, this is defined by the difference between the subjective expected utility assigned by an individual to her highest ranked option and the subjective expected utility assigned by this individual to any other policy option on the floor.[13] Although cardinal values for individuals' SEUs are difficult to obtain in empirical research on foreign policy decision making, the preference score method discussed in chapter 6 may provide a crude approximation. Yet, independently of measurement problems, the issue addressed by proposition 21 concerns which individuals are more likely to shift their preferences in the course of group deliberation and which individuals are likely to induce others into substantive preference shifts. Irrespective of how an individual decided on a certain policy option, if she is strongly convinced that this is the best course of action (or inaction) under the circumstances, she would be less inclined to change preferences than another individual who is less convinced that the option he advocates is the best. Consequently, the highly-convinced individual is more committed to influencing others and less receptive to influence attempts made by other group members. This relationship between individual conviction and individual influence holds irrespective of the pattern of group decision making because one is more reluctant to change preferences regardless of how decision processes are structured.

Situational variables and collective decision making. I have left the discussion of the impact of situational variables to the end because the values

---

[13] Formally, denote the subjective expected utility (SEU) of the most preferred option by SEU_1 and the SEU of another option on the floor by SEU_a. The degree of conviction by individual i is given by $IC_i = SEU_1^i - SEU_a^i$. It is, in general, incorrect to define individual conviction in terms of the difference in SEUs between the highest and the second-highest ranked option because the second-highest option might not be discussed by the group. Another important comment is that the concept of SEU could be made independent of the kind of process that led to an individual preference ordering. See the section on individual choice rules in chapter 6.

these variables assume in group settings can be understood only in terms of how individual-level perceptions are transformed into group-level perceptions through the formal group structure. As seen in chapter 4, the rule for transforming individual-level perceptions of stress and ambiguity is a weighted aggregation of these perceptions where the weights are the formal authority ranks of individuals. The ability of an individual to convey a sense of the threat, opportunity, and uncertainty that are invoked by an environmental cue depends on the status of that individual in the group. Propositions 22a–c deal with the impact of the group-level perceptions of stress and ambiguity on the structure and substance of collective choice.

> *Proposition 22a*
> *There is a curvilinear inverse U-shape relationship between group-shared stress and the procedural quality of group decision behavior. Under low-levels of group-shared stress, policy groups are likely to exhibit cybernetic paths to choice. As stress rises from low to medium levels, policy groups are likely to mix cybernetic and analytic decision procedures. At medium stress levels, groups are likely to exhibit purely analytic paths to choice. As stress goes from medium to high levels, policy groups are likely to mix analytic with groupthink choice patterns. Finally, at high levels of stress, policy groups are likely to resort to groupthink patterns.*

> *Proposition 22b*
> *The higher the level of group-shared perceptions of situational ambiguity, the more likely is the group to resort to analytic decision behavior. Under very low levels of group-shared ambiguity, groups are likely to use either cybernetic choice procedures, cognitive choice procedures, or a mixture of both. As situational ambiguity rises, increased elements of analytic choice processes are introduced into the process.*

> *Proposition 22c*
> *If key political leaders perceive a given environmental cue to involve low stress and ambiguity, they will delegate decisional authority to the relevant organizations without becoming fully involved in the decision making process. In such cases, policy groups are primarily intraorganizational with highly homogeneous structures. At medium stress levels and high ambiguity situations, policy groups consist of elected public officials as well as professional bureaucrats and are very diverse in terms of personal and organizational composition. In high-stress, low-ambiguity situations, political leaders tend to resort*

353

to institutional cabinet-type bodies with high representation of political appointees and elected officials. Professional bureaucrats play only a marginal consultative role in the group decision making process.

The hypothesized effects of stress and ambiguity on collective decision behavior are the same as those discussed at the individual choice level. The difference resides merely in the fact that individual perceptions of stress and ambiguity can be transformed into collective perceptions through a weighted aggregation procedure which takes into account who perceives what in the group. To illustrate this, consider Robert McNamara's assessment of the threat posed by the Soviet missiles in Cuba during the famous crisis. McNamara's low threat perception was challenged by Paul Nitze who pointed out the reduction in warning time and the effects the placement of Soviet missiles in Cuba had on the overall strategic balance (Allison, 1971). The aggregate perception of threat in the Executive Committee can be assessed neither as extremely low as that of McNamara nor as extremely high as that of Nitze. Once the transformation of individual perceptions of stress and ambiguity into a group-shared set of perceptions is specified, the identical effects of situational factors on individual choice and on collective decision making follow logically.

Proposition 22c is inspired by Brecher's work on crisis decision making. Briefly, Brecher (1980: 397–402) found that crisis-induced stress affects the structure and composition of decisional forums. Specifically, he argued that as stress increases, the scope of consultation by high-level decision makers increases steadily, but reaches its peak at medium stress levels. Moreover, reliance on large institutional decisional forums increases with stress but reaches its maximum level at medium stress levels.[14] The aim of proposition 22c is to expand on Brecher's important findings in a manner that pays specific attention to the relationships between individuals and collectivities in foreign policy settings, and while taking account of crisis as well as non-crisis decisions. Decisional forums in foreign policy settings can be both institutional, such as cabinets, and *ad hoc* task-specific teams. In institutional settings, key decision makers have somewhat limited control over the structuring of the group. Participation in institutional decision making bodies is normally predefined along organizational and political lines. While specific professional civil servants can be

---

[14] I interpret somewhat freely Brecher's delineation of stress levels in crisis. What I call medium stress levels is what Brecher refers to as declining stress stage, that is, a downswing in stress levels following peak crisis periods.

invited from time to time to provide expert assessments, they do not have a formal say in actual decisions. In *ad hoc* settings, the deliberative boundaries between politicians and appointed civil-servants are less obvious, and group leaders have more flexibility in determining who will participate and what will be the precise role of various participants.

Proposition 22c suggests that stress and ambiguity have an added indirect effect on decision behavior through their impact on the composition of decisional bodies. The initial perceptions of stress and ambiguity by key political leaders affects the composition of decisional forums they summon to cope with the problem. When problems seem relatively insignificant and non-pressing, political leaders delegate decisional authority to subordinates and display little or no involvement in much of the decision making process.[15] At extremely high-stress (and low-ambiguity) levels decision makers resort to institutional decisional forums because of the need for broad legitimization of decisions which are seen as crucial. The emphasis on consultation with fellow politicians takes precedence over the mixed consultation with different levels of foreign policy bureaucracies. Politically, decisions at such levels of stress require strong control and agreement among those who are constitutionally in charge of a nation's foreign policy. Practically, multiple level consultation is seen as extremely cumbersome. Political leaders are supposed to represent the collective wisdom and expertise of their respective organizations. They are assumed to be well-informed by subordinates of their organizations' view of the problem and the availability of resources for their solutions. Time constraints require swift and efficient problem solving procedures which do not facilitate extensive consultation.

Under medium stress and high situational ambiguity, broad consultation and mixed political-bureaucratic involvement in the decision process is both necessary and feasible. Thus, the role-diversity of decisional and consultative forums reaches its peak, as Brecher pointed out.

The determinants of collective decision processes: a synthesis

The main theme of this section is that collective choices are conceptually identical to individual choice processes in two fundamental ways. First, they consist of the same flow of decisional stages; they are characterized by the same models in terms that are essentially

---

[15] Note that this kind of policy problem could not be tapped by Brecher's analysis because of its focus on crisis decision making which, by definition, involves a somewhat increased threat perception.

identical to the treatment of individual choice procedures and substantive contents; and they produce the same outputs: preference orderings of policy options. Second, and most importantly, collective choice processes are determined by a conceptually identical set of exogenous and endogenous factors: situational, personality, and role.

The hypotheses linking group structure to decision behavior are conceptually similar to the hypotheses linking role variables to individual choice behavior. But what about the personality variables? Can groups be said to have collective "personalities"? Doesn't the notion of "collective personality" contradict the corollary of assumption 2 of the theory which states that unitary actor assumptions are not very useful in explaining policy choices? What does a "collective personality" mean? Simply stated, a collective personality is represented by the concept of group polarization which is a function of individual preferences. The conceptual equivalents of cognitive complexity and operational code types in group settings are seen here as residing in the ways individual members rank order policy options and in the implications of this preference ordering for choice processes. Groups can have a simple or complex preference structure the same way an individual can have a simple or elaborate belief system (or a highly classifiable or unclassifiable operational code type). It is not by mere coincidence that group polarization is measured in the same way as intraindividual conflict: both are conceptually similar.

Neither individual beliefs nor collective preferences constitute a coherent, consistent, and well-classifiable system. Rather, the complexity and classifiability of individual belief systems and group preference structures span a continuum ranging from complete uniformity and consistency to complete conflict and indeterminacy. The precise location of an individual or collective body on this continuum has predictable and theoretically meaningful effects on decision behavior. Seen in this light, propositions 16 and 17 which establish the causal effects of group polarization on collective decision behavior become the group-level equivalents of propositions 4 and 5 which establish the causal effects of personality structures on individual decision behavior.

But having argued that collective decision behavior is conceptually identical in terms of structure, content, and causally-relevant antecedents to individual decision behavior does not have to imply that unitary actor assumptions in foreign policy making are theoretically acceptable or empirically plausible. Quite the opposite. One of the main features of the theory discussed herein is that of decision dynamics. Decision dynamics were discussed in the section dealing with individual choice processes as a process by which an individual moves across distinct decisional stages in the process of solving a policy problem. The dynamic element in the individual choice part of the theory was represented by cross-stage effects on decision behavior. The same cross-stage effects – although not discussed in detail – take place in collective decision processes. Now I wish to introduce a third kind of dynamic into the theory: that of cross-level effects. This is simply a set of rules that transforms individual preferences into collective decisions. The theory addresses the transformation process in two distinct forms: one consists of rules for transforming situational variables into group-level perceptions. The second consists of the effects of individual preferences and group structure (and the interaction of both) on group choices. A unitary actor assumption sidesteps these dynamics, downgrades their importance, or outright ignores them. For example, Bueno de Mesquita (1981) was aware of the potential individual-group dynamics and the problems they raise. He clearly pointed out the difficulty of aggregating individual preferences into national utility functions. Nonetheless, he solved this problem by assuming it away. The "strong leader" assumption of this theory argues essentially that it is not implausible to avoid this difficulty in analyses of peace and war decisions.

In the present theory, the linkage between individual preferences and group decision dynamics allows identification of the conceptual similarities and differences between these two levels without resorting to the unitary – certainly not to the rational – actor assumption. The processes at these two levels of analysis are conceptually identical; they are not empirically identical. Conceptually, individual-level perceptions of stress and ambiguity are identical to group-shared perceptions of stress and ambiguity. However, the actual scores of these variables are not identical across levels of analysis. The same applies to the other factors. Moreover, group-level choices are not expressed as a simple aggregation of individual choices. Proposition 15 specifies that there is no direct link between individual choice processes and collective decision processes. Given the conceptual similarities and structural differences between these two levels of analysis, it is possible to delineate an overall synthesis of collective choice processes and combine the two levels in the final formulation of the theory.

The theory of collective choice processes in foreign policy settings is specified in much the same way as was done for individual choice. The static formulation is presented in equation (7.3).

Decision behavior=SIT. VARS+GROUP POL.+GROUP STRUCTURE (7.3) where:

>   *Decision behavior*=any combination of paths from diagnosis to
>   choice. (Implementation processes will be given separate
>   attention below.)
>
>   *SIT. VARS*=Group-shared stress, group-shared perception of
>   situational ambiguity.
>
>   *GROUP POL.*=Group polarization as measured by the degree
>   of disagreement in the initial distribution of individual pref-
>   erences.
>
>   *GROUP STRUCTURE*=Can be represented by either formal
>   authority structures as measured by the formal authority
>   index developed in chapter 4, or by the power index devel-
>   oped in chapter 6.[16]

The propositions developed in the section on collective decision
making above specify the effects of the various factors on collective
decision behavior. The dynamic cross-stage characterization of collective decision processes are given in equations (7.4.1–7.4.4).

Group Diagnosis=SIT. VARS+GROUP POL.+GROUP STRUC. (7.4.1)

Group Revision=DIAGNOSIS+SIT. VARS+GROUP POL.+
GROUP STRUC. (7.4.2)

Group S-E=REVISION+SIT. VARS+GROUP POL.+GROUP
STRUC. (7.4.3)

Group Choice=GROUP S-E+SIT. VARS+GROUP POL.+
GROUP STRUC. (7.4.4)

These equations establish the similarity between individual choice
dynamics and collective choice dynamics in terms of the content and
structure of decision processes. Groups, like individuals, can apply
mixed as well as pure paths to choice. The conditions under which a
given set of procedures will best characterize a given stage of the
process are assumed to be a collective equivalent of the conditions
postulated for individual choice processes. Moreover, the dynamic
effects of the procedures and substantive aspects employed by the
group at one stage on the content and structure of another stage are
also similar to the ones postulated at the individual choice level.
Another element of the theory of collective decision making in foreign
policy settings deals with the relations between individual power and
group outcomes. This is given by equation (7.5).

---

[16] This ambiguity is due to two factors. First, as posited in propositions 20a–20c, the
explanatory and predictive potency of power indices and formal authority structures
is not a constant, but rather varies with decisional patterns. Second, the power index
is itself a combination of formal authority structures ("voting weights") and group
polarization. Thus, the specific effects of group structure on collective decision
behavior are not entirely clear and require further empirical exploration.

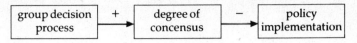

Figure 7.1 Decision process and policy implementation

Ind.−Group Ag. = *Ind. Power* + *Ind. Conviction* + *Decision Process* (7.5)

where:

Ind.−Group Ag. = index of agreement between the preference ordering of policy options by an individual prior to a group discussion and the final preference ordering of options by the group.[17]

Ind. power = as measured by the index developed in chapter 6. (When controlling for the type of group processes, individual power might be replaced by its formal authority element to test propositions 20b and 20c.)

Ind. Conviction=the extent to which an individual prefers the option which is ranked highest on one's preference scale to other policy options considered by the group.

Decision Process=the predominant group decision patterns.

This part of the theory examines the ability of individuals to influence group choices, an aspect which is typically excluded from decision making analyses. This relationship is an important aspect of any theory of foreign policy and international politics which concerns itself with the extent to which individuals matter in international affairs. For any single individual to have an impact on the courses and consequences of international processes, a person must have the capacity to affect a nation's foreign policy. As a national decision maker, a person must have the conviction necessary for making policy that counts rather than being driven by external events or by colleagues and advisers. Moreover, one must be able to utilize the policy making system, rather than be manipulated by it. The idea developed here is that the role, preference structure, and personal conviction of an individual, as well as the decision system in which one operates determine the extent to which an individual makes a difference in the policy making process.

The final element of the theory of collective decision making focuses on the relations between decision and implementation. This aspect is exclusive to group-level analyses of foreign policy decisions because, in most cases, individuals who make decisions on foreign policy issues are not the ones who implement them. Proposition 19 establishes the

---

[17] Individual–group agreement can be measured via the rank-order correlation between the individual and group preference ordering of policy options.

relations between group processes and policy implementation. This is captured by figure 7.1.

The idea expressed by this figure is that group level analyses of foreign policy should focus on two types of outputs: decisional outputs and actual policies. Decisional outputs – expressed in terms of a group-level preference ordering of policy options – denote a mental commitment to a certain course of action (or inaction). Actual policies are observable actions. The two are not always the same, and assuming they are is bound to lead in some cases to erroneous inferences (Jervis, 1976).

7.6 A LOGICAL AND AESTHETICAL ASSESSMENT OF THE FOREIGN POLICY DECISION THEORY

The basic premise of the theory is that research on foreign policy decision making over the last three decades has produced a body of theory and evidence which is – relatively speaking – fairly cumulative, and internally valid. Yet, it was only in the last decade that foreign policy decision making approaches started to put bits and pieces of theory and evidence together in a meaningful way. The present study seeks to continue this trend toward synthesis by outlining a general theoretical framework that is fairly comprehensive and empirically testable.

Theories are typically evaluated in terms of three sets of criteria: logical consistency, empirical validity, and aesthetical value. Logical consistency concerns the extent to which the assumptions of the theory fit together and complement one another, and the extent to which the propositions advanced by the theory follow from its basic premises. A theory is a system of interrelated premises which allows derivation of testable propositions about observable features of the world. Theories – for the most part – cannot be evaluated in terms of whether the premises are true or false, because premises often take on non-testable forms. Yet, premises can be evaluated in two ways: (a) the extent to which they form a coherent explanatory system, that is to say, whether they comprise an interrelated set of statements which is not contradictory in nature, and (b) whether they are capable of producing a system of logically coherent and empirically falsifiable propositions. The propositions of a theory are evaluated in terms of their relation to the assumptions of the theory and in terms of their internal consistency.

Contrary to the evaluation of assumptions, propositions can and should be assessed in terms of falsifiability. The falsifiability criterion establishes the conditions under which a set of propositions would be proven empirically incorrect. A desirable method of logical evaluation of a system of propositions is setting up a null (or naive) model which constitutes an empirical benchmark against which this system of propositions is tested. In practice, however, this method is difficult to apply. For example, we have seen in chapter 6 that prospect theory challenges the essential deductions derived from the rational theory of decision. Yet, it is not entirely clear how this theory provides an axiomatically equivalent body of logically deduced propositions that are testable. The principal difficulty is that the propositions of prospect theory are based on a seemingly arbitrary utility function and on an even more arbitrary weighting function of probabilities. Since theories attempt, almost by definition, to impose some sense of conceptual and logical order on reality, naive models are normally based on some sense of disorder. In decision making research, naive models tend to postulate a considerable degree of erratic and inconsistent behavior. The principal difficulty of logical evaluation of the propositions derived from a theory is to establish the conditions under which the theory itself is threatened by problems inherent to some (but not all) of its propositions (Waltz, 1979).

Aesthetical criteria of theory evaluation are, more often than not, ignored or discounted as legitimate ways of assessing theories in the social sciences because most social scientific theories are already laden with logical and empirical problems. Aesthetical evaluations focus upon three desirable properties: simplicity, fertility, and beauty. *Simplicity* refers to the extent to which the processes contained in a given explanation are straightforward and understandable. For any two logically consistent theories of about equal empirical validity, the simplicity criterion suggests that the one which sets up a process that is more simple, straightforward, and understandable than the other, is to be aesthetically preferred. This is so assuming, of course, that further logical and empirical tests are incapable of ranking these theories on purely non-aesthetical grounds.

Fertility is defined by Lave and March (1975: 64) as the number of propositions per assumption. This criterion is better known as the *parsimony* criterion. The fertility criterion allows evaluating theories in terms of how general they are, but the trick is to be general without having to make many extra assumptions. If the system of assumptions can be made simple and yet allow for many logically derived and empirically falsifiable propositions, a theory is said to have a strong aesthetical appeal. Of the various aspects of *beauty* discussed by Lave and March, the *surprise* criterion is probably the

361

most relevant here. A theory is said to be "surprising" if it is capable of deducing counterintuitive propositions. To be sure, this is a highly subjective criterion: what is obvious to one person might be counterintuitive to another. Yet, the surprise contained in a theory should be judged primarily in terms of the explanation the theory conveys, rather than in terms of external factors. Taken together, the aesthetical criteria provide a middle-of-the-road approach to theory evaluation in cases wherein logical or empirical assessments turn out to be inconclusive.

7.6.1 An assessment of the assumptions and propositions

Evaluation of the assumptions. Popper (1968: 312–335) provides an interesting comparison between dialectics and philosophy of science in terms of how these approaches treat the evolution of knowledge. It is instructive to examine the analogy in this context since the theory developed above claims to be a systematic synthesis of previous theory and research on foreign policy. A crude description of the dialectic method as a theory of knowledge and evolution of thought focuses on the dialectic triad of thesis, antithesis, and synthesis. A thesis can be a statement about the world or various segments thereof. A thesis often produces an antithesis, that is, an opposing view of the domain of facts the thesis purports to explain. The struggle between the thesis and the antithesis continues until

> some solution is reached which, in a certain sense, goes beyond both thesis and antithesis by recognizing their respective values and trying to preserve the merits and to avoid the limitations of both. This solution . . . is called the *synthesis*. Once attained, the synthesis in its turn may become the first step in a new dialectic triad, and it will do so if the particular synthesis reached turns out to be one-sided or otherwise unsatisfactory . . . which means that the synthesis can then be described as a new thesis which has produced a new antithesis. This dialectic triad will thus proceed on a higher level and it may reach a third level when a second synthesis has been attained. (Popper, 1968: 314; italics in original)

The question is whether the theory presented above indeed satisfies the conditions of a synthesis in terms of the assumptions it makes and the propositions deduced from it. To deal with this issue properly, the thesis and antithesis of foreign policy decision making theories must be identified. Whichever foreign policy decision theory gets to be called a thesis or antithesis is really immaterial. What matters, however, is that the debate among proponents of seemingly competing decision process models, as described in chapter 5, has been and still is a major feature of contemporary research on foreign policy making. The sweeping generalizations about human capacity to deal with complex issues that underlie all of these models, and the general and unconditional outline of each model as the single-best approximation to actual choice behavior provide a good basis for what some may call a struggle between competing paradigms or between theses and antitheses.

The rationale of the foreign policy decision theory as a seeming synthesis was the need for reformulation of the basic question. Seen in this light, the issue raised by the present theory is which factors affect the tendency of individuals and groups to use the procedures and substantive characteristics postulated by a given model. The fundamental aspect of the present theory is that each of the process models has some claim for empirical validity, and that none of them is fundamentally false, nor is any of them constantly true. The *context–dependence* and *individual differences* assumptions address both thesis and antithesis by accepting both as partial and incomplete descriptions of reality. The synthesis seeks to establish a new focus of research wherein process models, which had been conceived of as independent variables used to explain foreign policy choices, are treated as dependent or outcome variables explained by situational, personality, and organizational variables. These two assumptions modify, rather than change, the sweeping premises underlying the various process models by putting them into some empirically testable context through the propositions linking inputs to processes.

The claim for a synthesis status of the present theory is further illustrated by the *mixed paths to choice* assumption. Researchers who had advocated different explanatory models of foreign policy decision making claimed that the various decision models seem to be compatible in many important respects. This assumption allows actual examination of the differences and compatibilities among various process models. The claim that real-world decisions entail a mix of the procedures posited by the various models is strongly supported by empirical research. For example, out of the 57 decisions examined by Brecher (1980), 35 (or over 61 percent) involved mixed paths to choice. Other analyses which have decomposed decision processes into distinct stages (e.g., Stein and Tanter, 1980; Maoz, 1981) have also suggested that procedures posited by different process models were utilized by the decision makers. The principal merit of this assumption is that it enhances the internal validity of empirical accounts of foreign policy decisions that rely on secondary data sources.

The final two assumptions are necessary for linking individual choices to collective decision processes. The preference ordering assumption raises the possibility that individual decision makers would behave strategically in collective settings. Rather than changing their preferences, they might support second-best strategies in order to prevent adoption of options that they disapprove of even more. Focusing only on selected options artificially rules out strategic choice because it is impossible to interpret the support of non-favored options by an individual as anything else than a substantive preference change. In such cases, group-induced effects on individual preferences is seen as the only plausible explanation even if this is not necessarily the case. The last assumption about individual preferences and social choices emphasizes the effects of the unique attributes of each level of analysis on the process and outcome of national choices. It allows a meaningful explanation of the flow of decision behavior from individual to collective levels. The point made by this assumption is that no single level is capable of producing a complete explanation of national choices, and the trick is to examine how individual and groups interact in the policy making process.

The claim for the label of synthesis seems to be appropriate for these assumptions. They clearly build upon the strengths of previous conceptual and theoretical frameworks in the field while recognizing the biases, partiality, and other limitations of those approaches. They form a coherent view of decision processes in which the flow of behavior is from the bottom up, that is, from individual preference to national preference generation process through a dynamic pattern wherein the specific properties of one level interact with those of the higher level of aggregation. But in addition to recognizing what these assumptions encompass, we must specify what these assumptions seem to ignore. First, these assumptions are – and should be properly viewed as – partial in the sense that they focus strictly on intra-governmental politics. The effects of extra-governmental actors such as public opinion, news media, interest groups, political parties, legislatures, and judiciaries are not part of the account of foreign policy decision processes. This is not to suggest that these are unimportant actors in the foreign policy game. On the contrary, each of these actors may be extremely influential in foreign policy decisions. These assumptions also do not detail the impact of extra-national actors and of the international system on national decisions. Clearly, one cannot properly understand foreign policy decisions without explaining how they are influenced by the behavior of other nations or by the structures and processes in the international system.

There are three good explanations for this deficiency. First, to satisfy simultaneously the simplicity and fertility criteria, some things must be left out even in a theory that claims to be integrative in nature. This theory focuses only on decision making processes. Its emphasis is therefore only on the factors and actors that seem to be relevant for and active in such processes in a direct way. Incorporating internal non-governmental actors or systemic forces would complicate an already complex explanation to a degree that is practically and theoretically unmanageable. Second, both non-governmental actors within states and external actors or systemic processes *are* part of the theory insofar as they comprise value dimensions by which policy options are appraised by individuals and groups. The elements of situational inputs (stress and ambiguity) are determined by perceptions of external or internal factors. Threats can be perceived in terms of the nation's security or prestige *vis-à-vis* other actors, in terms of the public support for the head of state, or in terms of the government's image with the public. Both internal and external issue-areas are normally part and parcel of the policy appraisal process. Brecher (1980), Stein and Tanter (1980), Dowty (1984), and Maoz (1981, 1986) showed that both internal and external factors were used by decision makers to evaluate policy options in crisis conditions. The political structures of groups is strongly affected by both the nature of the policy problem it is trying to resolve and by the broader structure of the political system. The balance of forces in societies tends to be, more or less, reflected by the structure and composition of policy groups. Finally, providing systemic factors a proper role in theories of foreign policy requires going beyond such theories. Thus, I defer discussion of this issue to a later section.

Evaluation of the propositions. One of the most important features of the present theory is that the flexibility of its assumptions does not impose strict logical constraints on the propositions to the same extent that more restricted decision making models do. Therefore, the power of a logical analysis of the propositions is somewhat low. Moreover, since the theory postulates a relatively large number of variables which affect individual and collective choice processes, it is difficult to examine to what extent these factors – and only these factors – determine the domain of variables the theory seeks to explain in a manner that follows directly from relatively few assumptions.

An aesthetical evaluation of the theory reveals the tradeoff between simplicity and fertility.[18] Compared to the relatively few and relatively

---

[18] This is somewhat equivalent to Jervis's (1980: 86–88) discussion of the tradeoff between richness and rigor in foreign policy research.

simple assumptions, the theory of foreign policy decision making produced a fairly large number of propositions. The list of propositions contained in this chapter is by no means exhaustive: each proposition is – in and of itself – fairly general and can be broken down to more precise hypotheses. Each proposition is in principle falsifiable. However, the processes that the system of propositions depicts are far from simple. These are certainly more complex than the processes postulated by simple hypotheses which link specific inputs to processes or hypotheses which depict partial dynamics of individual and collective decision behavior. Yet, I believe that this is more than a reasonable price to be paid for generalizable and integrative approaches to choice. The conceptual similarity between the dynamics of individual choice and collective decisions helps simplify things quite a bit, without losing track of the level-specific attributes.

An additional question is whether the breakdown of decision processes into distinct stages contributes to the explanation of the relations between inputs and processes. Brecher's monumental work on Israel's decision processes during the 1967 and 1973 crises suggests that it does. Recall that we found a low curvilinear association between stress and (group) decision processes in Brecher's data (table 7.1). However, the analysis was based on a non-decomposed decision process, as well as on crude determination of stress levels. In table 7.4, I show how a more refined decomposition of choice processes and of stress levels can be used to improve the same analysis. Brecher decomposed decision processes into four distinct stages: probe – which is equivalent to diagnosis in our terminology; receptivity to information – which is equivalent to revision in our theory; search for alternatives; and evaluation of alternatives. He also provided a general assessment of the decision process which was used to construct table 7.1. Rather than using Brecher's general assessment of the type of decision process, I examine decision processes as consisting of both pure and mixed paths to choice. I also break down stress levels in line with Brecher's more refined distinctions. The results of this analysis are given in table 7.4.

Table 7.4 suggests moderately strong support for the propositions relating stress to foreign policy decision behavior. Compared to the low association between these variables given in table 7.1.1, the current analysis reduces the remaining error-variance by 58 and 73 percent for the ∇ and m_b, respectively.[19] Thus the complexity of the

[19] This result is given by

$$PIP = \frac{0.657 - 0.189}{1 - 0.189} = 0.577$$

for the ∇ measure, where PIP is proportional improvement in prediction. A similar measurement applies for the m_b statistic.

Table 7.4. *Stress and decision behavior in the 1967 and 1973 crises: an analysis of mixed paths to choice*

Stress level	Path to choice†						Total‡
	Cy	Cyb-An.	Cyb-Cog-An	An.	An-Cog	Cog.	
Low	2	1	1	0	0	1	5
Low-Med*	0	2	1	3	3	0	9
Medium*	0	1	2	3	4	0	10
Med-high*	1	3	0	7	10	0	21
High*	0	0	0	1	7	4	12
Total	3	7	4	14	24	5	57

* The asterisk next to the various stress levels indicate the following interpretation of stress based on Brecher's levels. Low stress is equivalent to the "lowest" stress level in Brecher's data. Low-medium stress is the rising stress level. Medium stress is equivalent to the higher stress stage. High stress is equivalent to the highest stress phase. High-medium stress is equivalent to the moderate, declining stress phase.

† A "pure" path to choice (e.g., analytic, cybernetic, or cognitive) is one in which at least three out of the four components (including evaluation) are consistent with a given model. (It must be noted that in the diagnosis and revision stages it is impossible to distinguish between the cybernetic and cognitive models in Brecher's data.) A "mixed' path is defined in terms of its elements. The sequence of paths is ignored, i.e., an analytic-cybernetic path is equivalent to a cybernetic-analytic path.

‡ Error cells in the table are: An., An-Cog, and Cog. for low stress; An-Cog and Cog. for low-medium stress; Cy., Cy-An, and Cog. for medium stress; Cy., Cy-Cog-An, and Cog. for high-medium stress; and Cy, Cy-An, and An. for high stress. The association between stress and decision behavior in this table is $\nabla = 0.657$, which is a substantial proportionate reduction in error. Using the Chi-square-based measure of proportionate reduction in error we obtain $m_b = 0.853$.

MPC approach foreign is more than compensated by a greater accuracy and internal validity.

Some of the propositions developed above seem to be counterintuitive. For example, the relationship between decision and implementation which is explained by the degree of post-decisional consensus is not obvious from the perspective of previous bureaucratic politics models. Likewise, the ability of cognitively-simple individuals to reach relatively high levels of decisional quality under medium stress is also not self-evident. Yet, the element of surprise in the present theory is, in general, not very substantial. This is so because the theory builds on previous knowledge to a greater extent than it provides original ideas. Surprise in a synthesis is an admirable – but hardly practical – goal.

The falsifiability of the propositions advanced by the theory does not imply that they are easy to test in empirical research. The principal difficulty of testing these propositions resides in the scarcity of high-quality data to be used in research of this type. The problems involved in empirical research on political decision making are discussed below.

7.6.2 Some difficulties in empirical research on political decision making

Some of the more important obstacles in empirical analysis of decision making theories are worth noting at this point. First and foremost, models of individual choice behavior represent attempts to understand the content and structure of *thought processes*. Actual observation of such processes is extremely difficult in any kind of setting; it is a virtual impossibility in foreign policy settings. Empirical research on individual choice behavior in foreign policy settings is normally done on the basis of actual observation of behavior (verbal or physical), which is taken to be a – more or less valid – indicator of underlying thought processes. The primary source of documentation used for the inference of individual decision behavior in foreign policy setting is various statements made by a decision maker. These statements may be retrospective, such as autobiographical reconstructions of a given decision process, or argumentative, such as statements made by the decision maker at the time one was actually engaged in trying to resolve the problem (e.g., letters and authentic diary entries, or statements made by a decision maker during group discussions). Each of these sources is biased in some way, and therefore raises serious issues of validity.

The primary problem of inferring thought processes from written or verbal reconstructions is that such reconstructions: (*a*) entail some degree of *post hoc* rationalization of what had actually happened, and (*b*) entail some degree of instrumentalism which had been absent when the focal person made the decision.[20] Empirical examinations of individual choice behavior are therefore somewhat limited in their ability to truly represent thought processes, and this difficulty should be always kept in mind.

Second, the quality of the sources is dubious most of the time. The ability of a researcher to obtain primary sources declines proportionally to the recency of the decision. Primary sources on fairly recent

---

[20] By "instrumentation" I refer to a goal-directed reconstruction of thought processes, where goals can range anywhere from persuasion of other decision makers or constituencies in the course of collective decision processes, to facilitating the

historical decisions are less available than primary sources on more historically remote decisions. Yet, researchers of foreign policy behavior have been generally more interested in studying contemporary decisions than in studying past decisions. This trend has forced most students to rely on secondary accounts of decision processes, the validity of which is relatively low (Maoz, 1986).

A variety of procedures and methodological devices has been employed to minimize biases in inference of thought processes from observed behavior or other forms of reconstruction. Usage of multiple sources, reliability tests, and other kinds of sophisticated measures have been developed and applied over the years to address these problems, but none of them provides an absolute safeguard against incorrect inference. Experimental research paradigms have their merits in that they allow examinations of causal relations under controlled conditions. Yet, it is difficult to replicate the conditions that operate in foreign policy settings in the laboratory. Moreover, the typical subjects that are being analyzed in experiments might be different in some crucial respects (such as experience in politics) from real-life foreign policy elites. This does not suggest that controlled experimentation lacks any significance. On the contrary. Findings stemming out of experimental studies of decision making shed a lot of light on political decision making. Yet their limitations with respect to external validity should be recognized (Jervis, 1986; Maoz, 1984a).

The problem of high-quality data is somewhat less acute in examinations of collective decision processes. Minutes of government meetings or other primary sources are – in principle – available. In some cases they might be even accessible to a scholar. Nonetheless, there is a question to what extent arguments made by individuals in group settings represent their authentic views. If it could be reliably established that individuals voice their sincere beliefs and considerations in the course of group deliberations, then one could infer the content of individual decision processes from these arguments. (This is what Gallhofer and Saris, 1986, have done although they admitted that they were unsure of the extent to which arguments made by individuals reflected their sincere beliefs.) But if that is the case, then one may encounter major methodological problems in analyzing certain aspects of collective decision making, most importantly, groupthink patterns. There is a built-in assumption in such models that individuals generally suppress their true beliefs and present arguments that are consistent with what appears to be the group consensus.

To what extent is any model of individual or collective choice truly

formation of a certain image for historical judgment of the decision made in the past. See Holsti (1976) and Maoz and Shayer (1987) for a discussion of these problems.

testable given the nature of the data available for, and the methodological problems entailed in, empirical analysis? Is a theory which is designed to be both comprehensive and scientific not self-defeating in the sense that it can be empirically tested only on data whose quality is generally low?

These questions merit some response. First, the value of any theory is independent of the data used to test its propositions. Even the most valid and reliable data cannot substantiate the empirical validity of a theory. Empirical tests do not provide positive proof for the validity of a theory. All that can be accomplished via an empirical investigation is some tentative confirmation or disconfirmation of a body of propositions deduced from a theory. The primary test of a theory is of a non-empirical nature: it is the test of logic and in-principle falsifiability (Popper, 1968). The lack of high quality data is therefore an important impediment of empirical testing but it – in and of itself – does not disqualify a theory. A theory should be made testable in principle even if practical testing is difficult. Lack of good data is a problem which is not exclusive to theories of foreign policy decision making, and certainly not exclusive to the present theory. The fact that we might never be able to examine thought processes should therefore not prevent us from theorizing about them.

Second, the record of academic research on decision making in general and on foreign policy decision processes in particular strongly suggests that these problems are not insurmountable. High quality research, whether qualitative or quantitative, suggests an awareness of these problems and extremely promising methods for minimizing their impact on the substantive findings. My ability to demonstrate the theoretical points made in this and earlier chapters is due to existing empirical investigations such as those of Dowty (1984), Stein and Tanter (1980), Brecher (1980), and Wagner (1974), all of which devoted a great deal of attention to empirical detail.

Finally, the key to a reasonable solution to these problems lies in Tetlock and McGuire's (1986) suggestion for incorporation of multilevel and multi-method approaches to the analysis of foreign policy problems in which different methods and data sources are used to examine a given set of propositions. If laboratory experiments, qualitative or quantitative case-studies, and aggregate data analyses yield convergent findings, the specific limitations of any given empirical approach are greatly reduced.[21] In science, in general, and in the social

---

[21] Or course, the real problem arises when different approaches using different sources of data disagree in terms of their empirical findings. The simple answer is that in such cases, theories would be viewed with some degree of skepticism.

and behavioral sciences, in particular, empirical tests are always tentative, and finding a fool-proof method of examining a theory is still beyond our grasp. This should not discourage us from looking for solutions to the empirical problems, and certainly not preclude us from theorizing.

7.7 THE MERITS AND LIMITATIONS OF DECISION-RELATED APPROACHES TO WORLD POLITICS

Having completed the review of more than four decades' worth of foreign policy decision making theory and research, and having attempted to develop a general integrative theory based on much of this literature, we can now take stock of what has been accomplished by this research and examine avenues for future research. In this and previous chapters, I have attempted to trace, in relatively broad brushstrokes the historical and topical evolution of foreign policy decision making research, and its contribution to knowledge on international politics. The focus of the review and integration was on the substantive content of the knowledge accumulation process. However, as a prelude to prescriptions of future avenues of research, we must consider both the structural progress in research on foreign policy decision making over time, as well as the content of this research program (Lakatos, 1970).

7.7.1 Contributions of decision making research

The shifts in the theoretical and empirical concerns that marked the termination of one developmental stage of foreign policy decision research and the onset of another did not occur as a result of a feeling that the major tasks in the former stage had been completed. Rather, these shifts were a result of a growing conviction that research in the previous stage has exhausted itself and that real progress in the field was possible only through an attack on the theoretical issues from a different angle. The contribution to knowledge that each developmental stage has made is essentially independent of the kind of knowledge produced by a previous stage. Each stage was characterized by a fair amount of cumulative research, but there was little cross-stage accumulation.

Despite the seeming disorder in the structure of knowledge accumulation process, the distinct contributions of the various traditions of research seem to add up rather well into an integrated picture of the

371

field, one which enabled the construction of the foreign policy decision theory in the present chapter. The work done during the input identification stage gave us a notion of the key exogenous inputs to foreign policy decision making. Situational variables, personality variables, and role variables seem to be the most potent ones because they cut across decision domains, issue-areas, and units of analysis. An initial – but far from complete – understanding of how these variables affect individual and collective choice behavior was made possible both through bivariate associations between these variables and distinct aspects of decision processes, and through initial attempts to construct conceptual frameworks of foreign policy processes. However, the drawbacks of this tradition were lack of a clear delineation of decision processes, a failure to specify how and to what extent different exogenous variables relate to one another, and how they can be conceptualized, measured, or assessed across different levels of analysis.

The work done during the second developmental stage, provided us with a reasonably good handle on the kind of processes that may take place at both the individual and group level from the moment a decision problem is identified to the time a decision is implemented. Research on process models revealed a number of possible strategies that characterize problem solving approaches by individuals, organizations, or interorganizational bodies in foreign policy. But the mapping out of those processes and the delineation of their essential characteristics represents a tremendous contribution. The problem of this research tradition was that it was overly polemic. Scholars attempted to identify *the* model that "best" approximates real-world decision processes, thereby downgrading or outrightly dismissing the possibility that the fit between a conceptual model and real-life decision making processes is context-dependent. Consequently, very little effort was invested in developing propositions regarding the kind of situational, personality, or role and organizational variables that give rise to each of the models in real-life situations. Moreover, the overly general specifications of the analytic, cybernetic, and cognitive models precluded serious attempts to identify areas of empirical discrimination or empirical compatibility among them. This made the task of judging which model best fits reality an extremely difficult one. Finally, the model specification stage treated individual choice and collective decision processes as two different and seemingly unrelated levels of analysis. Very little effort was put into investigations of the transition processes connecting these levels.

The preliminary impression from the research of the synthesis stage is that we have a beginning of a systematic and fairly formal effort to address many of the open and unexplored issues in foreign policy decision making theory. This effort consists of meaningful integration of seemingly distinct exogenous variables into composite decision-relevant inputs (the combination of threat, opportunity, and time pressure into decisional stress, and the combination of formal and informal aspects of group structure into individual power indices are good examples); the development of formal discriminating frameworks among decision process models which acknowledge the possibility that they can be used almost simultanteously in real-life situations; and a beginning of formal specifications of the relations between inputs and processes and between processes and outcomes. Finally, there is an initial effort to systematically link decision theoretic approaches to other, more general, approaches to world politics such as bargaining and systems approaches.

The theory presented herein is predicated on a fundamental conviction that there is a grain of truth in much of the research conducted on decision making thus far. Combining different traditions and approaches in an integrative framework is both possible, given the state of our knowledge, and sensible in that it has the potential of producing an overall explanation which is more precise and complete than any explanation which focuses on further refinements of partial theories. This theory is one of the few efforts I am aware of to explicitly connect different levels of analysis in foreign policy decision making research. It develops propositions regarding the content and structure of choice behavior at each level as well as the flow of choice behavior across levels. The present theory depicts foreign policy decision processes as dynamic in nature by looking at behavioral changes across distinct decisional stages and across levels of analysis. By doing that, it offers what I believe is a more realistic view of how individuals and groups go about solving policy problems in real-life situations.

Yet, the present theory is not without its faults. There are things it deliberately leaves out, as we have seen above, and there are severe problems of empirical analysis and data availability which make the testing of the theory practically difficult. Moreover, one may argue – not without basis – that the theory is far from parsimonious, it is overly complex and inclusive to an extent that makes its value questionable. These are serious issues and I have attempted to address them in the previous section. But, it seems to me that these are not the most fundamental problems of either the decision making theory developed here or the research and theory upon which it is based. The real issue concerns the extent to which *any* decision theoretic framework can enhance our understanding of more general issues in world politics.

7.7.2 Limitations of decision making research: independent versus interdependent choice

I have noted that decision-related approaches are viewed as "reductionist" (Waltz, 1979), "microlevel" (Dougherty and Pfaltzgraff, 1971) or "middle-range" theories of world politics. Given the single-state, single-case nature of much of the research in the field and the tendency to treat decisions in discrete and independent terms, such views are not unfair. But it was not supposed to be this way according to the founding fathers of the approach. The original idea was that world politics can be understood in terms of a *continuous and interdependent interflow of decisions and actions among states and/or other actors in the international system* (Snyder, Bruck, and Sapin, 1962). The main problem of decision making research has been its inability to even approach the point where it could be used as a vantage point for understanding long-term multiple-actor processes. Instead of examining how decision making processes can shed light on broader aspects of world politics, researchers have focused on the analysis of discrete decisions.

The consequences have been twofold. First, a number of theorists have severely downgraded the significance of this approach in explanations of international politics, arguing that prolonged international processes are shaped by structural conditions over which decision makers have little or no control. Decision-related approaches can provide only *ad hoc* explanations for the outbreaks of wars, the signing of treaties, and so forth, but they cannot account for macrochanges in the international system over prolonged periods of time (Waltz, 1979; Bull, 1977; Choucri and North, 1975).

Second, the overly restrictive application of decision-related approaches to world politics had some unfortunate effects on the ability of scholars to examine key issues in the approach itself: most importantly, the relationship between the quality of the decision process and the quality of its consequences. In order to make decision making approaches more central to the study of world politics, as well as to deal with some of the most important topics in the approach itself, a major reorientation in the approach must take place. This reorientation requires a theoretical shift from independent to interdependent decision making. To justify this claim, the fundamental problems of decision making research – which are also the fundamental problems of the theory presented above – must be discussed in some detail.

First, decision making was seen as a process by which a nation independently – rather than interdependently – attempts to solve problems involving its relations with external actors. The focus has been on the perceptions and coping strategies of individual leaders or collective decision making bodies. Perceptions of other actors' strategies and preferences were examined through the independent perceptual lens of the individual or group under study. The problem is that the most significant aspect of world politics is its interdependent character, that is, the fact that no actor can single-handedly determine the consequences of its own decisions. What a nation can or does accomplish in world politics is a consequence of other actors' behavior as much as it is a result of the nation's choices. Understanding the factors that affect national choices is very important, but it is not enough if what we really want to know is what these choices actually accomplish in an interdependent environment. To do that we have to look at the system of interactions that results from interdependent choices of many actors. Single-nation analyses do not provide much insight into the real interdependent character of international interactions.

The other half of the problem concerns the inability to analyze relationships between choice and consequences in foreign policy settings. Most researchers have approached the question of choice quality from a procedural perspective: a good choice is one that was made as a result of a systematic and analytic decision process. The reason that researchers resorted to this definition was that they lacked normative standards which allowed evaluating decisions in terms of their consequences (Holsti and George, 1975; Janis and Mann, 1977; Brecher, 1979a). The – hidden or explicit – assumption was that there is a strong positive relation between good decision making and adaptive outcomes, and the policy-relevant implication is that you can improve your lot in world politics by improving the procedural quality of your decision making (Jervis, 1976; Janis, 1982; George, 1980). While there is some evidence supporting this contention (Herek, Janis, and Huth, 1987), there is increasing evidence, coming from rational choice models of world politics, that the relationship between rational choice and adaptive consequences is all but straightforward. In some situations, behavior that would be regarded as suboptimal in terms of decisional procedures, such as deliberate foreclosing of options, might produce more adaptive results that sensible analytic decisions (e.g., Schelling, 1984, 1978; Maoz and Felsenthal, 1987). Thus the question of which decision behavior is more desirable in that it is likely to produce adaptive outcomes is an empirical one and cannot be assumed away. However, to investigate the relationship between decision making and decisional outcomes, we must resort to interdependent decisional settings. The failure of decision making research

375

to address systematically interdependent decision processes imposes considerable limitations on the insights provided by this research.

Second, much of the research on foreign policy decision making treated decisions as discrete events rather than continuous ones. This approach was very convenient in empirical analyses that went beyond the single case-study (e.g., Dowty, 1984; Brecher, 1974, 1980; Stein and Tanter, 1980). Discrete decisions are discrete observations and therefore some general hypotheses can be tested on multiple cases. Decision analysis of single nations can be made systematic and rigorous. Without degrading the significance of this research, the fundamental problem is that the decisions that were studied in these cases were not discrete: the seemingly different decisions were temporally related. A decision at stage 1 was partly responsible for an outcome which served as the stimulus for the decision made by the nation under investigation at stage 2. Due to the interdependent nature of decisional outcomes, the relationship between the first and second decision is not a direct one – it is mediated by the decisions and actions of other actors – but it cannot be altogether ignored. The tendency to downplay the continuous and interdependent nature of national choices reduces the ability of foreign policy decision making research to transcend its micro-level status.

Scholars working in the field were bothered by the fact that the separation between micro perspectives of world politics – decision-related approaches being a prominent member of this population – and macroperspectives of world politics is both artificial in nature and theoretically damaging. In a sense, it could be argued that we constructed a division of labor in world politics which is analogous to that which characterizes sister-disciplines such as economics. But this is where the analogy ends. In economic theory, macroeconomics and microeconomics are two sides of the same coin. Macroeconomics accepts the fundamental premises, concepts, and findings of microeconomics. For example, monetary models of national markets and international trade accept at their very basis the fundamental laws of diminishing marginal returns, supply and demand, and consumer choice, all of which have been developed by microeconomists looking at the behavior of individuals, households, and firms. Virtually all economic theories accept the principle of utility maximization as the fundamental axiom of economic behavior. The division of economics into micro and macro theories is just a convenient way of dividing labor in order to create a better product in an efficient manner (the product being a better understanding of economic behavior and processes).[22]

---

[22] This differs from Waltz's (1979: 109–110) interpretation of the relations between micro and macroeconomics and micro and macro approaches to world politics.

In the study of world politics, however, this division of the field into micro and macro perspectives is extremely damaging in that it creates a struggle between two camps, each of which is claiming, if not monopoly over theory, at least supremacy. Arguing that one should be careful in extrapolating findings from one level of analysis to another, Singer (1961) does not imply that theories of international politics should be unit-bound. Yet, the fact of the matter is that not only theories of international politics *are* unit-bound, but also that there exists a trench-warfare among unit-bound perspectives for the title of Theory with a capital T. The decades-old debate about whether the system characteristics shape the behavior of the units (i.e., states) or whether the behavior of the units is essentially autonomous with respect to the system (although it is certainly influenced by perceptions of external factors, state behavior is fundamentally determined by domestic factors) and therefore shapes the attributes of the system, is still underway without apparent end in sight. The depiction of international politics as a Greek tragedy where the fate of actors is predetermined by forces beyond their control and whatever they do has little or no impact on aggregate international outcomes is, I think, not only empirically unfounded but morally unacceptable. This view negates the role of individuals and groups in shaping reality and implies that most observable and significant international phenomena can be best described as "no-choice" situations.

Decision theoretic approaches to international politics represent a potential for a sensible alternative to such grim perspectives of international politics. Their fundamental assumption is that changes in systemic conditions are – intended or unintended – consequences of motivated (though not necessarily rational) action. The flow of behavior in international politics, viewed from a decision theoretic perspective, is from the bottom up; that is, from individual preferences to international processes. Unfortunately, the significance of this perspective has yet to be fully assessed, and the potential contribution has yet to be converted into an actual one. Both the review of the literature on foreign policy decision making and the resulting integrative theory have focused on the processes leading to the formation of national preferences and to consequent foreign policy behavior. The realization of the potential of decision-based perspectives of world politics requires going beyond decision theoretic approaches. The first step must involve an incorporation of decision theories with bargaining theories. This will be the focus on the second part of the book.

8 THE ANALYSIS OF
INTERNATIONAL OUTCOMES

8.1 INTRODUCTION

There is a fundamental difference between bargaining and negotiation. Bargaining denotes a process of *interdependent decision making* wherein each party acts to get the most for itself out of a situation in which the final outcome depends both on its choices and on the choices of other actors. Negotiation refers to a *joint decision making* process wherein the parties involved seek to coordinate their choices in order to assure a collectively desirable outcome (Zartman, 1977; Bartos, 1977). Negotiation, therefore, should be seen as a proper subset of bargaining processes: all negotiations entail bargaining, but not all bargaining processes entail negotiation. Another distinction between bargaining and negotiation is that the former process involves some degree of direct or indirect communication between the parties, while the latter process need not involve communication at all. In the first seven chapters, the analysis focused on independent decision making, in which nations try to resolve problems arising in their internal or external environment using their domestic resources. In the second part we analyze the relations between the ways nations go about solving these problems and what they actually get in an interdependent and interactive setting.

This chapter discusses how static theories of bargaining can aid our understanding of the emergence of international outcomes, how such outcomes are affected by intranational choice processes, and how they are affected by the interdependent structure of the environment. A primary aim of this analysis is to establish a method of assessing the substantive quality of national choices in an interdependent context. This will enable us to analyze the relationship between national choices and international consequences. It will provide a tool for assessing the extent to which the reliance on different decision making models at the national level is related to the kind of outcomes a nation secures for itself at the international level. The structure of this chapter is as follows. I start with a brief review of game-theoretic models of bargaining in section 8.2. I review some psychological models of bargaining in section 8.3. A synthesis of these two approaches is provided in section 8.4. Section 8.5 develops a scheme for assessing the relationship between national choices and international outcomes. Section 8.6 provides a brief assessment of the model.

8.2 GAME-THEORETIC MODELS OF BARGAINING

Game theory is a theory of rational decision making under conditions of interdependence. It was invented by John von Neuman, a mathematician, and Oskar Morgenstern, an economist, and was first laid out in a comprehensive fashion in 1944 (von Neuman and Morgenstern, 1944). Since then, it has created a body of followers which is probably second to none in the social sciences. It would be preposterous to review all nuances of the theory and its applications in this chapter. Instead, I will discuss only a few ideas that have a direct bearing on analyses of the relations between national choices and international outcomes.[1]

A "game" is a model of a given situation which is characterized by four features: players, alternatives, preferences, and rules of play. Players are the participants in the situation whose behavior is to be explained by the theory. Game theory is divided, broadly speaking, into *two–person* game models and *n–person* game models (where $n>2$). Single-person games are termed as games against nature and fall properly into decision-analytic models of rational behavior. The alternatives denote the courses of action or inaction open to players, and they can range anywhere from two to infinity. The number of alternatives available to players defines the possible set of outcomes in a game. An outcome is an intersection of choices by all players. It denotes a situation which might arise if each player selects a specified alternative. The number of outcomes in a given game is a product of the number of players and the number of alternatives available to each. Formally:

$$O = \prod_{i=1}^{n} a_i = a_1 \times a_2 \times \ldots \times a_n$$

where n is the number of players and a_i is the number of alternatives available to player i. The simplest game in terms of the number of outcomes is the 2×2 game which consists of two players with two

---

[1] Good reviews of game theory are found in Luce and Raiffa (1957), Shubik (1982), Davis (1983), Zagare (1984b), Ordeshook (1986).

alternatives available to each (Rapoport, 1966). Outcomes are objective situations which are formed by intersections of choices. Preferences are subjective evaluations of such situations by each of the players. Game theory can deal with two types of preferences: ordinal and cardinal. Ordinal games contain information about how players rank-order the various outcomes but provide no indication regarding the intensity of these preferences. Cardinal games contain actual utilities assigned by players to the various outcomes. Cardinal games provide more flexibility in analysis of situations in that they contain more information about players' preferences than ordinal games, but the same principles apply whether one has information about ordinal or cardinal preferences.[2]

The rules of play specify the sequence, order, and number of allowable moves for each of the actors, as well as the permissible behaviors of players other than independent selection of alternatives (such as communication, coalition formation, the giving and accepting of side-payments, and so forth). The theory distinguishes between simultaneous-choice and sequential choice games. In simultaneous-choice games, all players select an alternative at the same time. Sequential games specify an order of choices by the players (usually with players who move later possessing knowledge about the choices of previous players). Another distinction is between single-shot games and iterative ones. Iterative games are those in which participants play the same game over several times (with or without sequential choice). The rules of play also stipulate whether players are allowed to communicate with one another, to collude with one another, and so forth.

Another important division of game theory is to the type of motives which characterize the players' preference structures. There are three classes of games: pure-conflict games, mixed-motive games, and cooperative games. Pure conflict games are those in which players' preferences are diametrically opposed. Zero-sum games represent an extreme example of such problems. In pure-conflict games, there is at least one "winner" and at least one "loser" in each outcome (though there may be more of each). Zero sum games are those in which the sum of the winners' gains and the losers' loss always equals zero. In such games, winning and beating the opponent amount to the same

---

[2] Brams (1985a) showed that, with a few reasonable assumptions, ordinal games can be subjected to rigorous analyses typically associated only with cardinal preference games. This is done by normalizing ordinal preferences such that the highest-ranked outcome is assigned a utility of one, the lowest-ranked outcome is assigned a utility of zero, and all other outcomes are assigned unknown values ranging from zero to one and preserving their order.

thing. Rapoport (1960) referred to such games as "fights" in which the objective is to eliminate the opponent. Chess, poker, and single-winner elections are examples of zero-sum games. Mixed-motive games are those in which there exists (*a*) at least one outcome wherein *all* players either win together or lose together (although the amounts "won" or "lost" may vary over players), and (*b*) at least one outcome in which at least one player wins and at least another player loses. Players are confronted by conflicting objectives. Each player wants to assure for itself the maximum gain and/or the minimum loss, but all players want to jointly avoid the outcomes that represent collective losses or to accomplish the outcomes that represent collective gains. There are both conflictive and cooperative tendencies that simultaneously drive players' behavior. Arms races, nuclear deterrence, and excess vote-sharing in proportional representation systems are typical examples of such games. Cooperative games are those in which all outcomes represent situations in which all players either win together or lose together, though the amount of gains and losses might vary from one player to another and from one outcome to another. There is some conflict in such games as one player's best outcome might not be the best outcome for another player, but the principal drive of players in such games is the wish to maximize joint gains or to minimize joint losses. This wish very often coincides with players' self-interests.

The object of game theory is to explain, predict, or prescribe how players would choose (or ought to choose) among their available alternatives, what outcomes would (or should) arise given these choices, and what would (or should) be the payoffs of the various players if their choices follow a rational logic. Game-theoretic models of bargaining have a dual status: they can be seen as descriptive models that attempt to account for actual behavior in interdependent settings, or as normative models that prescribe optimal behavior. The ambivalence of functions of game-theoretic approaches is a source of a great deal of controversy. Some researchers argue that game-theoretic applications should be limited to the normative level because the assumptions underlying the theory are consistently violated by people. (This is, for example, the position of social psychologists such as Tversky and Kahneman, 1986.) Others see fundamental problems even with the normative facet of the theory. (See for example Elster, 1979; Schelling, 1984.) Despite this controversy, there have been extensive applications of game-theoretic models to international politics. Some of these analyses have made profound contributions to the understanding of issues such as deterrence, arms races, crisis behavior, and so forth. The present discussion focuses on some elementary concepts and ideas discussed by the theory, as well as some of the principal problems associated with it.

Game theory provides probably the best formal distinction between bargaining and negotiation. All games (except games against nature) depict bargaining situations, but only some games depict situations that are negotiable. Consider the question of when two rational actors would enter negotiations. Raiffa's (1982: 44–50) analysis serves as a good starting point. Raiffa argues that a rational player attempts to resolve a conflict of interests through negotiations when his most preferred outcomes can be obtained only through an agreement with other players, and that this range of outcomes is strictly preferred to what the player can get on its own. This preference structure need not cover all outcomes: there might exist outcomes that can be accomplished through an agreement which are strictly less preferred to the outcome of no agreement. However, negotiation is seen as a rational alternative only if players are convinced that there exist possible agreements that make each of them strictly better off than what they could obtain on their own. What each player can get on its own (that is, through unilateral action) is seen as the absolute minimum that a player would be willing to pay for an agreement. This minimum is called the "reservation price." All cooperative outcomes that give a player a higher payoff are acceptable agreements from this player's perspective – though some agreements are preferred to others. All cooperative outcomes that provide the player a smaller payoff than its reservation price constitute unacceptable agreements because the player can do better by resolving the conflict of interest through unilateral action.

The central problem in negotiations is to find an agreement that constitutes the best distribution of goods under contention.[3] But before this issue can be resolved, the feasibility of any kind of agreement must be established. A conflict of interests is said to be negotiable if there exists a "zone of agreement", that is, an array of outcomes in which the payoffs of all parties involved are strictly higher than their reservation prices. The difference between negotiable and non-negotiable problems can be nicely illustrated by figure 8.1.

The first part of this figure depicts a situation wherein there exists a zone of agreement within which all outcomes are preferred by both parties to what they can get in the absence of an agreement (that is, to their reservation prices). In the second part of the figure, the reserva-

---

[3] By "best" I mean that such a distribution of goods must reflect some normative criteria of optimality and efficiency at both the individual and collective levels.

1. Negotiable problems

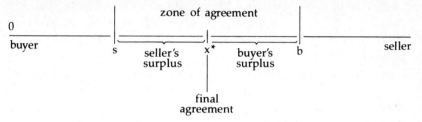

2. Non-negotiable problems

Source: Raiffa (1982: 46).

Figure 8.1 Negotiable and non-negotiable games

tion prices of the parties are so far apart that no agreement which is acceptable to one party is also acceptable to the other in the sense that it provides the latter a higher payoff than its reservation price. Although this presentation of the problem of "negotiability" makes perfect sense intuitively, it is unclear how reservation prices are established. Nor is it clear how the parties ought to agree to settle their differences. To clarify these issues, consider the two games in figure 8.2.

Game 1 represents a typical zero-sum case in which players' choices

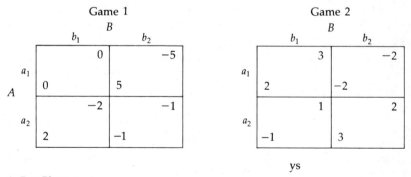

A, B = Players
a_1, a_2 = Strategies available to player A; b_1, b_2 = Strategies available to player B. Number in lower-left corner of each cell represents player A's payoff; number in upper-right corner represents player B's payoff.

Figure 8.2 Negotiable and non-negotiable games

383

depend on the choices of other players. Neither player has an unequivocally-best strategy independent of the other player's choice. However, in this game there exists no possible agreement which is seen by both players as preferable to what they can accomplish through a unilateral resolution of the conflict of interests.[4] Von Neuman and Morgenstern (1944) proved that all zero-sum games have a unique solution in either pure or mixed strategies. This is one of the fundamental results of game theory, which suggests that a certain class of games is completely solvable. It also implies that, for this class of games, players can do at least as well or better by unilateral action than by trying to coordinate their moves through some agreement. This result is extremely robust in that it is relatively insensitive to alterations in the rules of play.[5] This implies that players' reservation prices do not overlap and joint decision making for the sake of finding a mutually-acceptable solution is meaningless. Allowing players to communicate or to reach binding agreement would not alter the outcome of the game.

Game 2 is a typical mixed-motive game (known as the Battle of the Sexes). In this game, both players wish to avoid the -1, -1 and the -2, -2 outcomes, because each of these two outcomes is strictly less-preferred to any of the other two outcomes. This is the cooperative motivation underlying players' calculations. Yet, the players are in disagreement regarding which of the other two outcomes is the best. Player A prefers the lower-right outcome to the upper-left outcome, while B prefers the upper-left outcome to the lower-right outcome. A mixed strategy solution (wherein each player uses each of its strategies with a probability of 0.5) will give them an expected value of 0.5, each. This is the most that player can hope to get given resolution of the conflict of interests through unilateral action. Yet, even the least-preferred cooperative outcome provides each player a higher payoff. The issue is, therefore, how should players coordinate their behavior in a manner that assures each the highest feasible payoff. Nash (1950) proposed a well-known solution to this problem.

[4] This game has a mixed-strategy equilibrium solution wherein player A uses strategy a_1 with a probability of three-eighths and strategy a_2 with probability of five-eighths, and player B uses strategy b_1 with probability of three-quarters and strategy b_2 with probability of one-quarter. In this case A can expect to get a value of 1.25 and B can expect to get a value of -1.25. See Rapoport (1966), and Davis (1983) for non-technical explanations of mixed-strategy solutions of zero-sum games.

[5] By relatively I mean that the content of the solution may vary when the rules of play are changed. If this game is played sequentially and A moves first, the outcome of the game will be 0, 0 (the upper-left cell), regardless of the number of iterations. However, the existence and the uniqueness of a solution is insensitive to any alterations in the rules of play.

The solution consists of taking what each actor can accomplish through unilateral action as the baseline of negotiations. This value (0.5, 0.5 for players A and B, respectively) is taken to be the intersection of players' reservation prices, and thus an agreement should give each at least as high a payoff as one's reservation price.

In Nash's solution concept, the intersection of players' reservation prices serves as the baseline from which the "fair" bargaining solution is calculated. The -1, -1 and -2, -2 outcomes are ignored because they are inefficient: each player by acting rationally can assure itself an expected payoff of at least a 0.5 units of utility whatever the other player chooses to do. However, it would be senseless for the parties not to strike a deal whereby they would be able to maximize their payoffs. The problem is that the row player wishes that this agreement would be one wherein column always selects b_2 (and row always selects a_2, which gives row its maximal payoff), whereas the column player wishes that row would always select a_1 (and thus column would always select b_1 which would give column its maximal payoff). Nash's argument was that if the intersection of the players' reservation prices is taken as the baseline of the cooperative solution of the bargaining problem, then the "fair" agreement is the point on the efficient set (that is, the line connecting the end points of the zone of agreement, points 2, 3 and 3, 2) which minimizes the distance between the "no agreement" point (point 0.5, 0.5) and the efficient set. In this particular game, the agreement should be at the 2.5, 2.5 point, which means that the players should agree to coordinate their choices such that they choose a_1, b_1 half of the time and a_2, b_2 half of the time.[6] The solution of the bargaining problem should satisfy some minimal criteria. First, it should be individually-rational. This means that the agreement should provide each player with a payoff which is at least as high as what this player could have received had it acted without an agreement. Second, the solution should be collectively rational, that is, it should entail a distribution of payoffs that is collectively undominated. In other words, an agreement is said to be collectively rational if there exists no other agreement that provides all the players with a higher payoff.

Different solutions of the bargaining problem vary in terms of their conceptions of "fairness", that is, in their notions of what properties of the players an agreement should reflect. Nash's approach assumes that an agreement should reflect the relative stakes that the parties

---

[6] Nash's solution of the bargaining problem is not the only one around. See Rapoport, (1966: 104–122) for a discussion of various solutions to the bargaining problem in 2×2 games.

Game 3

B

		b_1	b_2
a_1		3	−2
A		2	−2
a_2		0	2
		−1	3

A's mixed strategy is $p(a_1) = \frac{1}{2}$, $p(a_2) = \frac{1}{2}$. The value of the game to player A is $V_a = 0.5$.

B's mixed strategy is $q(b_1) = \frac{4}{7}$, $q(b_2) = \frac{3}{7}$. The value of the game to player B is $V_b = 0.86$.

Nash's bargaining solution for this game is $2.36, 2.64$ for A and B, respectively. This means that both players should select outcome a_1, b_1 about 36 percent of the time and a_2, b_2 about 64 percent of the time.

Figure 8.3 An asymmetrical negotiation process

have in the negotiations. This is reflected in the location of the "no-agreement" point in the utility space formed by intersecting players preferences. To induce a player that stands to gain very little by cooperation into an agreement, one has to make more concessions than to induce a player that stands to gain a lot from an agreement. In figure 8.3, the column player has less of a stake in an agreement than in the game of figure 8.2. In this case, player B benefits considerably more from the agreement than player A simply because he or she has less of a stake in a negotiated settlement than its opponent.

Thus, negotiation is seen as the rational solution of a conflict of interests only if it provides the players with a settlement which makes each and every one of them better off with an agreement than without it. Whether or not a bargaining problem is also a negotiable one is determined by what players can do on their own. What the players get out of the agreement is also strongly affected what they expect to get out of their interdependent interaction in the absence of coordination. Yet, to provide a more general account of game-theoretic solutions to problems of interdependent decision making, it is important to explicate how game theory prescribes behavior in such contexts.

8.2.1 Stability analysis and decision analysis in interdependent choice settings

Apart from the lack of universal acceptance of the rationality assumption, one of the reasons that gives game theory a rather limited appeal to social scientists is that it does not always prescribe determinant principles of behavior. More often than not, game theory is ambivalent in terms of its prescriptions regarding the meaning of optimal choice. A major cause of this ambiguity is the existence of multiple criteria for evaluating choices. This section discusses some of these criteria.

First, it is important to explain why many scholars see game theory as a superior approach to rational decision theory under conditions of interdependence. The key argument is that the combination of utilities and probabilities embodied in the SEU is meaningless under conditions of interdependence. To develop a probability estimate regarding an event, a player must be able to assume some sort of regularity underlying the behavior of the other player. However, under conditions of interdependence, the only generalization one can reliably make regarding the behavior of other players is that their behavior depends on one's own behavior. Since the focal player who tries to estimate the probabilities associated with various outcomes has yet to decide how to behave, it is virtually impossible to establish probability estimates of other players' behavior with any degree of reliability. Players who go about the solution of interdependent choice problems in expected utility maximization terms may well end up running around in logical circles of the "he thinks that I think that he thinks . . ." sort. The fundamental rationale of game theory is therefore that the SEU maximization principle is not suitable to choice under conditions of interdependence because of the difficulty to establish and to interpret probabilities. Game theory is therefore a theory of rational choice without probabilities.

Seen in such light, it seems obvious why game theorists opt for solutions that are designed to make one's choice independent of the choices of other players. In other words, the key to choice under interdependence is to eliminate interdependence. The *maximin* principle in pure or mixed strategies in constant-sum games is a good illustration of such an approach. A player's optimal choice in zero-sum games is to select an alternative (or a certain mixture of alternatives) that would yield a minimum payoff no matter the other players choose to do. This allows for precise (and therefore falsifiable) predictions of the outcomes of zero-sum interactions. The maximin principle in zero-sum games is both a prescriptive and descriptive rule: it tells us both what are the optimal choices of the actors and what would be the stable outcome of the game. *In zero-sum games, stability analysis coincides with decision analysis as well as with the normative property of rationality which states that rational behavior yields optimal outcomes.* However, this property of the theory disappears in non-zero-sum games. In such games, the conflict between decision analysis and stability analysis is almost pathological. On top of this, there is a conflict between rational behavior and optimal outcomes. To examine these problems, let us consider the nature of decision analytic solutions when SEU principles are inapplicable.

The first – and seemingly most simple – solution is the *dominance* principle. This principle asserts that a player should use a dominant strategy if such a strategy exists. By implication, a player should assume that another player who is known to have a dominant strategy would use it with certainty. Briefly, a dominant strategy is one which provides a player with a strictly higher payoff than any other strategy in at least one outcome and with at least equal payoffs as any other strategy in all the remaining outcomes. A player having a dominant strategy and using it can do at least as well in some outcomes and better in other outcomes than by not using it, whatever other players choose to do. Players using dominant strategies simultaneously maximize their payoffs and make their choice independent of the choices of other players.[7] Dominance coincides with the SEU principle because a dominant strategy yields a higher SEU than any other strategy regardless of the probabilities associated with the various outcomes. A corollary of the dominant strategy principle is that a player should not use a dominated strategy, nor should one assume that other players would use dominated strategies. Although a player may not have a unique dominant strategy, the principle can serve to eliminate inferior strategies from further consideration, thereby simplifying one's choice problem. If one or more of the strategies is strictly (or weakly) inferior to one or more of the other strategies available to a player, the former one(s) should not be used. Reduction of games by elimination of dominated strategies helps both in simplifying analyses and in increasing the determinacy of the solution. To exemplify these properties of the dominance principle, consider the two games in figure 8.4.

---

[7] A distinction must be made between *strict dominance* and *weak dominance*. The definition of dominance given above is that of the weak variant. Strict dominance implies that a strategy provides a player a higher payoff in each and every outcome of the game than any other strategy.

Game 4

B

		b_1	b_2	b_3
	a_1	8 / 8	9 / 5	7 / 1
A	a_2	5 / 9	6 / 6 *	4 / 2
	a_3	1 / 7	2 / 4	3 / 3 *

Outcomes are ordinal preference only, running from 9 = best to 1 = worst.
*Nash Equilibrium.
Source: Maoz (1989).

Game 5

Admissible voting strategies

No. of players	Pref. order	1	2	3	4	5	6	7	8	9	10	11	12	13	14	15	16	Dominant (ultimately admissible strategy)
8	$a>c>b$	a	a	a	a	a	a	a	a	c	c	c	c	c	c	c	c	a 3rd reduction
10	$b>c>a$	b	b	b	b	c	c	c	c	b	b	b	b	c	c	c	c	b 1st reduction
6	$c>a>b$	c	c	a	a	c	c	a	a	c	c	a	a	c	c	a	a	a 2nd reduction
3	$c>b>a$	c	b	c	b	c	b	c	b	c	b	c	b	c	b	c	b	c 1st reduction
Outcome		b	b	a	a	c	c	a	a	c	c	c	b	c	c	c	c	Winner is a

Source: Maoz and Felsenthal (1987).

Figure 8.4 Simplified and "solvable" games using the dominance principle

In game 4, strategies a_1 and b_1 are dominated by strategies a_2 and b_2, respectively. Neither player would use its dominated strategy and hence the game is reduced to a 2×2 game consisting of strategies a_2, a_3 and b_2, b_3 for players A and B, respectively. The dominance principle serves to simplify the analysis, but it does not solve the decision problem entirely because neither player's decision can be made independent of the other player's decision. As evident from the figure, this game has two equilibrium outcomes, a_2, b_2 and a_3, b_3. The fact that the first equilibrium is the best outcome for both players does not assure that it would be selected: we cannot predict with absolute confidence that a strategic interaction characterized by this preference

389

structure would result in the superior outcome a_2, b_2. In fact, as we shall soon see, it is quite plausible to predict that the outcome of the game will be a_3, b_3.

In the second *n–person* game (game 5), the dominance principle serves to define a determinate outcome, that is, a unique strategy combination that is the predicted outcome of the game. The right-hand column of game 5 shows that the 10 players with preference *bca* (read *b* is preferred to *c* and *c* is preferred to *a*, transitivity implies that *b* is preferred to *a*) have a (weak) dominant strategy *b* and the 3 players with preference *cba* have a dominant strategy *c*. Assuming that these two blocs of players would not employ their dominated strategies, the 6 *cab* players now have a *unique admissible* strategy *a* and the 8 *acb* players have a unique admissible strategy *a*. The outcome of this game is therefore column 3 which yields outcome 3.[8] The problem with the dominance principle in this particular game is that the unique outcome it determines is socially inferior to outcome *a*. (It can be easily verified that *a* is the Condorcet alternative.)

These two games already hint to the clash of principles in game theory. However, to further explicate the nature of these problems, we must discuss choice principles in games wherein the dominance principle is not sufficient for providing the players a clear behavioral prescription. Consider again game 4. In this game each player's best choice depends on what a player expects from its opponent. If player *A* thinks that *B* intends to use b_2, then it should choose a_2 (because a payoff of 6 is preferred to a payoff of 4 which it would get if it chooses a_3). However, if *A* expects *B* to select b_3, it has no choice but to select a_3. The fact that there exists a collectively-superior equilibrium in a_2, b_2 does not help the players to make up their minds in situations wherein communications and binding agreements are impossible. This is so because they cannot select an equilibrium; they can only select strategies. Whether or not a certain equilibrium outcome is realized is a function of the choices of *both* players. Game theorists are at loss in such situations when they must advise decision makers what to choose because the game does not provide for an unequivocally best choice.

Another decision principle that becomes a serious candidate in such cases is the maximin rule. In game 4, the maximin principle requires both players to select the strategy that results in the highest payoff

[8] The solution of such games is due to Farquharson (1969). Maoz and Felsenthal (1987) explain how such games are solved. A *unique admissible* strategy is defined as a strategy which is weakly dominant given that the dominated strategies of other players have been eliminated from further consideration.

Game 6

B

	b_1	b_2
a_1	10 * 10	4 −3
a_2	−3 4	5 * 5

A

A's mixed strategy is $p(a_1) = \frac{1}{14}$, $p(a_2) = \frac{13}{14}$. The value of the game to player A is $V_a = 4.44$.

B's mixed strategy is $q(b_1) = \frac{1}{14}$, $q(b_2) = \frac{13}{14}$. The value of the game to player B is $V_b = 4.44$.

* Nash equilibrium

Figure 8.5 A two-person game where mixed strategies dominate maximin choices

among the worst outcomes associated with the various strategies. This implies that players A and B should select strategies a_3 and b_3, respectively. But the resulting outcome of such a choice is both individually and collectively inferior to the choice of a_2, b_2. The virtue of the maximin principle in mixed-motive games is that it provides a clear choice principle that guarantees the player at least some minimal payoff whatever other players choose to do. This rule may be inferior in some cases to another decision rule which also rests on an independent choice incentive: mixed strategy selection. To illustrate this point, consider game 6 in figure 8.5.

It is evident that in this game a player can mix strategy choices and be assured of an expected value of 4.44 which is higher than the guaranteed minimum of 4 that a player gets under the maximin rule. But mixed strategy selection is both difficult to implement in real-life situations – especially if the decision maker does not expect repeated play of the game.

This discussion suggests that game theory cannot always provide decision makers with simple algorithms of decision. On the one hand, game theorists reject the use of SEU analysis in interdependent choice situations because the derivation of reliable probability estimates of the opponent's strategy choice is practically impossible. On the other hand, game theory offers only partial substitutes for SEU analysis in the form of dominant strategies, maximin or mixed strategy choices. All of these principles are inflicted by major problems. Perhaps the most fundamental problem with these seemingly optimal choice

Game 7

B

		b_1		b_2	
a_1		4			3
	3		1.5		
a_2		1			2
	4		1.5 *		

*Nash Equilibrium.
Sources: Maoz and Felsenthal (1987: fn. 3); Fraser and Kilgour (1986: 84, Game No. 332). Fraser and Kilgour provide a complete listing of all 2×2 games with weak ordinal preferences.

Figure 8.6 Clash of principles: dominance versus Pareto-efficiency

principles is that they clash with two other principles of optimality: Pareto-efficiency, and stability.

Pareto-efficiency defines a set of outcomes that is collectively preferred by all players to outcomes not in this set. A Pareto-efficient outcome is better for at least one player and not worse for all other players compared with outcomes that are not Pareto-efficient. When comparing any outcome which is an element of a Pareto-efficient set with any outcome which is not an element of the set, at least one player in strictly better-off and no other player is strictly worse-off in the former outcome than in the latter one. Pareto-efficiency is a normative criterion of what is *collectively* optimal. It differentiates between outcomes that are good for everyone taking part in a strategic interaction and those that are good for no-one. In game 6 only outcome a_1, b_1 is Pareto-efficient; it is individually and collectively preferred to any other outcomes of the game. Yet, as we have seen, it is by no means assured. The principles which guide rational players choosing in interdependent settings (dominance, maximin, mixed strategies) are problematic in that quite often they yield Pareto-deficient solutions. The notorious Prisoner's Dilemma game is perhaps the most acute example of this problem. Since both players have dominant strategies, they end up with an outcome of mutual non-cooperation which is both individually and collectively inferior to the cooperative outcome. A more severe example of the clash between the decision principle of dominance and the normative Pareto-efficiency principle is seen in figure 8.6.

The clash of principles in game 7 is more severe than in the Prisoner's Dilemma (PD) because: (*i*) it yields the worst outcome (as opposed to the second-worst outcome for the player with a dominant strategy, and (*ii*) the actor with the dominant strategy is harmed more than the actor without a dominant strategy: the latter acts simply on the assumption that the actor with the dominant strategy would use it. Thus, choice principles that are generally sound may yield suboptimal outcomes.

In contrast to decision analysis in interdependent settings, stability analysis seeks to locate equilibrium outcomes in games. As Fraser and Kilgour (1986: 9) put it:

> Under the first interpretation [decision analysis in our terminology], the only meaningful (normative or descriptive) question is ' 'which strategy [should be selected]?'' whereas under the second [stability] one the question "which (if any) change of policy?" is paramount. Maximin analysis provides a criterion for strategy selection whereas stability analysis tries to identify those outcomes which a player (or players) would not voluntarily leave.

The most widely used stability criterion is the Nash-equilibrium concept (Nash, 1950). Briefly, an outcome is a Nash-equilibrium if no player can improve his or her payoff by a unilateral shift of strategy from that coutcome. The Nash-equilibrium concept is myopic in that it requires players to examine what would be accomplished by them immediately following their departure from a given outcome. If the immediate shift of strategy does not yield a strictly more preferred outcome, they are assumed not to depart from the outcome. Nash-equilibria are also conservative in that they expect a player to depart from an outcome if and only if some gain can be made doing so. However, a player is not expected to depart from an outcome if this move – though not beneficial in an immediate sense – would not be harmful. For example, in game 7, Player A is assumed not to be inclined to change strategy from a_2 to a_1 because such a move would not be beneficial (but would also not be harmful because outcome a_1, b_2 is neither better nor worse than outcome a_2, b_2).[9]

Stability analysis is extremely useful in defining outcomes that can be seen as "prominent solutions" (Schelling, 1960). For example, in game 6, the upper-left outcome (a_2, b_2) is a case in point. It also has a strong substantive appeal in that it requires players to think in terms of whether they can improve on a certain outcome once they have reached it. However, as was the case with the elimination of dominated strategies in game 3, stability analysis does not always yield

---

[9] Other stability criteria which are based on the fundamental notion described by Fraser and Kilgour but which are less myopic or conservative than the Nash-equilibrium are discussed by these authors (Fraser and Kilgour, 1986: 14–21).

Game 8: *Prisoner's Dilemma*

		B	
		b_1	b_2
A	a_1	3 3	4 1
	a_2	1 4	2 * 2

Game 9: *Chicken*

		B	
		b_1	b_2
A	a_1	3 3	4 * 2
	a_2	2 * 4	1 1

***Nash-Equilibrium.**
Outcomes are ranked from best = 4, to worst = 1.

Figure 8.7 Prisoner's Dilemma and Chicken

unique outcomes. Moreover, in many cases it yields no results in that a game may have no stable outcome. In games 2, 3, 4, 5, and 6, there are multiple Nash-equilibria. If a Nash-equilibrium is designed to identify prominent solutions, then it does a less-than-complete job. But this is not the most severe problem about stability analysis, for stability analysis may often clash with both decision analysis and normative evaluation principles such as Pareto-efficiency. To illustrate this problem, consider figure 8.7 which depicts two notorious games: the Prisoner's Dilemma (PD) and the game of Chicken.

In the PD, stability analysis coincides with decision analysis (as was the case in game 7). The selection of dominant strategies leads to a Nash-equilibrium. But both stability analysis and decision analysis clash with the Pareto-principle in that the outcome of the game (which happens to be the only stable solution) is Pareto-inferior to another outcome (a_1, b_1). In the game of Chicken, stability analysis is both indeterminate (the game has two Nash-equilibria in outcomes a_1, b_2 and a_2, b_1) and clashes with both decision analysis and the Pareto-criterion (the two latter principles coincide with one another). Since neither actor has a dominant strategy in Chicken, the next-best decision rule might well be the maximin principle. If both use the maximin principle, the game will end at outcome a_1, b_1 which also happens to a Pareto-efficient outcome. The problem here is that this outcome is extremely unstable: if one player suspects that the other intends to use its maximin strategy, it is well advised to use its non-maximin strategy leading to one of the two Nash-equilibria. However, if both players work from this set of assumptions, they might both use their defection strategies a_2, b_2 and end up getting their worst outcomes.

The game of Chicken is heuristically important in another respect. Implicit in our discussion of game-theoretic models was an assumption of complete information. That is, all players in a game are assumed to be fully-informed regarding all of the dimensions of the game: the identity and number of all other players, the strategies available to all other players and their preference ordering of the various outcomes (or even of the cardinal utilities assigned by players to the various outcomes), and the rules of play. The realism of such an assumption in applied settings (especially in international politics) is questionable. However, the lesson of Chicken is that even if players were rational and endowed with full information, this is not enough to get them out of trouble. Knowing your opponent's preferences is not tantamount to making a decision which does not involve guessing. And it is this kind of guess-work which might cause a lot of problem in interdependent decision making. In fact, this game demonstrates that mutual ignorance might be an asset rather than a liability in some strategic interactions. If each player knows the other player's strategies (and hence the array of possible outcomes associated with the game of Chicken) but none of the players knows the other's preference ordering of outcomes, then the *only* reasonable thing to do is use the maximin strategy. This results in the mutually-cooperative outcome a_1, b_1.[10]

8.2.2 Current trends in game theory

The clash of principles in game-theoretic models of social behavior is probably one of the most important stimulants of research

---

[10] Shubik (1982: 274) presents a more interesting illustration of such a point in the context of cooperative games. Rapoport, Guyer, and Gordon (1976: 431) argue that in Chicken, "[m]utatis mutandis, it is frequently to the advantage of a player to make himself incommunicado. For instance, someone who cannot possibly receive a message need not fear that his child will be kidnapped and is, in fact, immune to all forms of blackmail – provided, of course, that the kidnappers or the blackmailers *know* that he cannot be reached."

in the social sciences, both in terms of research which confines itself to game-theoretic paradigms and in terms of research which starts out with these game-theoretic problems and then uses other paradigms to explore processes of interdependent problem-solving. There exists a very high correlation between the number of studies of certain games and the extent of clash among principles contained in them: the more problematic a game is in terms of the existence of contradictions among principles, the more extensively has it been studied. The power of game theory is not necessarily in that it provides clear or simple choice algorithms in interdependent settings. Rather, game theory is one of the few theories of social behavior which recognizes its own problems and attempts to systematically address them.[11]

There are three general approaches in game theory which attempt to resolve the clash of principles as well as to specify games in a manner that would lend realism to the assumptions. One approach focuses primarily on the development of alternative solution concepts. The principal focus of this approach is on alternative principles of equilibrium that reduce the frequency and severity of clashes between stability analysis and the Pareto-criterion. The second approach focuses primarily on modification of the rules of play. This approach examines how change in rules affect behavior and whether these behavioral changes resolve the paradoxes inherent in other rules of play. The third approach focuses on identifying exogenous variables (such as specific attributes that some or all players are seen to possess) and examining the effects of such variables on the behavior of players and on the outcomes of their strategic interactions.

One of the most interesting attempts to develop alternative solutions that resolve the clash of criteria is the Brams-Wittman concept on *non-myopic equilibrium* (Brams and Wittman, 1981). A non-myopic equilibrium is an outcome from which no actor has a long-range incentive to depart, because once it departs the game might end in a worse outcome in the long run (that is, after a long sequence of moves and countermoves by the players). This kind of analysis is not predicated on change in the rules of play but rather on the ability of players to use non-myopic reasoning processes that overcome the Curnot-rationality assumption underlying Nash's equilibrium concept. Players are said to think several steps ahead and envision the strategic interaction *as* if it were a series of moves and countermoves

[11] By "recognizing its own problems" I mean that game theorists are aware of the possible contradictions among the assumptions underlying the theory, and attempt to reconcile them. This is not to suggest, however, that game theorists are equally willing to accept criticisms of the realism of rationality assumptions.

which, at some point, might stabilize. Brams and Wittman showed that the PD has a non-myopic cooperative equilibrium, hence suggesting that cooperation that is irrational in the short run is eminently rational in the long run. Related to this is the *n-horizon* stability concept developed by Kilgour (1985) which asserts that stability analysis and decision analysis might coincide if players look several steps into the future. These approaches are mere extensions of the Nash logic of stability which also implies a reasoning process wherein players consider what they might do if a certain outcome arises and they are given a choice between staying in that outcome (i.e., not changing their strategy) and changing the outcome (by a unilateral strategy shift). The idea behind these alternative equilibria concepts is that players who are capable of looking forward only one step at a time might be rational but not very bright (because the data for making predictions several steps into the future is in the game).[12]

The major trends in modifications of the rules of play are two fold: one focuses on the relaxation of the simultaneity rule; the other relaxes the single-play rule. Under the first modification, players are assumed to move sequentially with each player knowing the "history" of the game thus far (i.e., what each of the other players had done in the previous moves). It was shown that some cases of discrepancy between decision analysis and stability analysis (or more importantly between decision and stability analysis, on the one hand, and Pareto-efficiency, on the other) are resolved. (See Wagner, 1983, and Maoz and Felsenthal, 1987, for examples.) The discrepancy between decision and stability analysis and Pareto-efficiency in game 7 is easily resolved if player A is allowed to move first; the potential clash of criteria in game 6 is also resolved under sequential play no matter which player moves first. The rationale for the relaxation of the simultaneity assumption is that in applied settings, simultaneous choice is not very realistic.

In the second modification, players are assumed to play the same game over and over again (whether choice is simultaneous or sequential at any given iteration). There is a distinction between finite and infinite repeated plays. This distinction is crucial because it has a major effect on the results of the analysis. For example, in the finitely iterated PD, if players know the number of iterations, they would reason back from the final iteration to the first and would defect throughout. On the other hand, if the number of iterations is either very large or

---

[12] The practicality of this reasoning processes decreases exponentially with the increase of two parameters: the number of outcomes and the length of the horizon. Kilgour (1985) showed that most 2×2 games stabilize after a horizon of six (that is, after six "periods" of moves and countermoves). The implication is that if players can reason ahead six steps, games tend to stabilize.

		B			
		CR	TiFTa	TaFTi	DR
	Cooperate	3 3	3 3	4 1	4 1
A	Defect	1 4	2 2	1 4	2 * 2

CR = Cooperate Regardless (of what the row player did in the first move).

TiFTa = Tit-For-Tat (emulate your opponent's previous move: cooperate if your opponent cooperated and defect otherwise).

TaFTi = Tat-For-Tit (do the opposite of what your opponent did on the previous move: defect if your opponent cooperated and cooperate otherwise).

DR = Defect Regardless (of what the row player did in the first move).

*Nash Equilibrium.

Figure 8.8 First-order metagame matrix of PD

unknown, the proportion of cooperative outcomes increases significantly.[13] Metagame theory (Howard, 1971) combines both repeated play and sequentiality in order to identify new equilibria solutions to various games. This theory is based on a reasoning process (not necessarily on a redefinition of the rules of play) wherein a player has to define all possible responses to previous moves of the opponent and uses decision analysis and stability analysis to predict outcomes. For example, a first-order metagame matrix of the PD is given in figure 8.8.

The first-order metagame matrix conveys no news. Player B still has a dominant defection strategy, player A, knowing that, can still do no better than defect also, and the outcome is still the Pareto-inferior mutual-defection cell. However, if actors think in terms of a second-order metagame matrix, an entirely new situation arises.

The second-order metagame matrix in figure 8.9 reveals three equilibrium outcomes, two of them are cooperative. Moreover, A's second-order metastrategy $D_1 C_2 D_3 D_4$ dominates all other metastrategies, hence it is the best that this player can do. Knowing that, B's best strategy is to play Tit-For-Tat and the cooperative Pareto-efficient outcome is obtained. The metagame extension seems like a major complication of a relatively simple decision problem. Given that A

[13] Rapoport and Chamma (1965), and Rapoport, Guyer, and Gordon (1976) report experimental results of the PD as well as other 2×2 games that are affected by the number of interactions.

		B						
		CR		TiFTa		TaFTi		DR	
	$C_1C_2C_3C_4$	3	3	3	3	1	4	1	4
	$C_1C_2C_3D_4$	3	3	3	3	1	4	2	2
	$C_1C_2D_3C_4$	3	3	3	3	4	1	1	4
	$C_1D_2C_3C_4$	3	3	2	2	1	4	1	4
	$C_1C_2D_3D_4$	3	3	3 $*$	3	4	1	2	2
	$C_1D_2C_3D_4$	3	3	2	2	1	4	2	2
	$C_1D_2D_3C_4$	3	3	2	2	4	1	1	4
A	$C_1D_2D_3D_4$	3	3	2	2	4	1	2	2
	$D_1C_2C_3C_4$	4	1	3	3	1	4	1	4
	$D_1C_2C_3D_4$	4	1	3	3	1	4	2	2
	$D_1C_2D_3C_4$	4	1	3	3	4	1	1	4
	$D_1D_2C_3C_4$	4	1	2	2	1	4	1	4
	$D_1C_2D_3D_4$	4	1	3 $*$	3	4	1	2	2
	$D_1D_2C_3D_4$	4	1	2	2	1	4	2	2
	$D_1D_2D_3C_4$	4	1	2	2	4	1	1	4
	$D_1D_2D_3D_4$	4	1	2	2	4	1	2 $*$	2

Player B's (column) strategies are defined in figure 8.8.

Player A's meta-strategies are defined for each column of B, such that S_i = Row strategy given that column uses strategy i. For example $C_1D_2C_3D_4$ means: Cooperate if B cooperates regardless; Defect if B uses Tit-For-Tat; Cooperate if B uses Tat-For-Tit; and Defect if B defects regardless

*Nash Equilibrium.

Figure 8.9 Second-order metagame matrix of PD

developed second-order metastrategies, why can player A not develop a third-order set of metastrategies, and so on? The answer is that the development of higher order metastrategies would not reveal any new equilibria. Hence, the cost of complicating the simple game is more than compensated by the emergence of a set of cooperative, Pareto-efficient metastrategies. As Brams (1976: 90–91) points out, there are several problems with this approach. For one thing, this approach provides less of a solution to a pathological paradox of game theory and more of a reformulation of the problem based on an implicit assumption of preplay communication among players which forms a basis for expectations about their future behavior. Moreover,

> [M]ost actors, at least in international politics, do not operate from a metagame perspective. Whether they lack information about an opponent, the ability to forecast his behavior, or simply mistrust him,

> their focus is not on metastrategies but on strategies, which is, after
> all, what they choose in the end. (Brams, 1976: 91)

Another approach attempts to assign certain attributes to the players which are exogenous to the game itself in the sense that they are not reflected in the game matrix. This line of inquiry seeks to assess the impact of these attributes on the behavior of the players and on the outcomes of their strategic interaction. Most prominent among these are various forms of "power" assigned to players. Early formulations of cooperative solutions (such as Nash, 1951) used the concept of threat power to define the locus of the optional solution on the Pareto-frontier. More recently, however, Brams (1985b) and Brams and Hessel (1983, 1984) introduced different notions of moving, staying, and threat power to sequential games. Briefly, moving power represents the ability of a player to continuously move in a game (by shifting its strategy) when the other player must stop. Staying power refers to the ability of a player to hold off making a strategy choice until the other player has made its choice (even when both are at an outcome that harms the former). Threat power (divided into compellent and deterrent types) refers to the ability of a player to harm other players by shifting to a "mutually disadvantageous outcome in the single play of the game to deter untoward actions in the future of this or other games" (Brams, 1985b: 213). The effect of these kinds of powers on the outcomes of 2×2 ordinal games is that while they tend to benefit the player who possesses them this is by no means a general result. There are quite a few games in which such powers make no difference in terms of the outcome, and other cases in which such powers can actually harm the player that attempts to exercise them.

8.2.3 Applications of game theory to international politics

Game-theoretic applications to international polictical issues have assumed predominantly two forms: games were used as heuristic models of some key problems in international politics, and as a descriptive theory of national behavior in interdependent settings. The use of game theory as a normative tool for the evaluation of actual behavior is quite rare.

Games as heuristic models. One of the most appealing features of game theory is that it allows representation of extremely complex phenomena in terms of straightforward and manageable games. Seen in such a light, game theory is a heuristically powerful tool for illustrating some of the problematique inherent in international relations. Historically, one of the first applications of this type was Schelling's (1960, 1966) analysis of nuclear deterrence as a game of Chicken. Curiously, Schelling's starting point was a call for a "reorientation" of game theory in a manner that would allow for introducing elements of commitment and resolve in strategic interactions, so as to make game models of international processes more realistic. Schelling's primary aim was to highlight one of the key problems of nuclear deterrence – the tradeoff between the magnitude of the threat involving global annihilation and its credibility.[14] This line of thinking opened up a whole new approach to nuclear deterrence and had a noticable effect on American nuclear policy.[15] Closely related to game-theoretic modeling of deterrence is the attempt to illustrate problems of arms races and arms control using the Prisoner's Dilemma (Brams, 1985a; Majeski, 1984; Schelling, 1975; Russett, 1983), or variations thereof such as a combined Prisoner's Dilemma–Stag-Hunt game (Maoz, 1989).

The assumptions underlying game theory and the assumptions underlying the realist paradigm to world politics seem to be closely related. In fact, most of the traditional applications of game theory as heuristic models of international phenomena have – implicitly or explicitly – adopted the realist perspective of international politics. This implies a view of states as the key actors in the system, the conception of states as unitary-rational actors, the conception of a fundamental state of anarchy which makes non-cooperative games especially suitable for modeling such an environment, self-centered egoism as the fundamental motivation of players, and so forth (Wagner, 1986). This relationship between realist and game-theoretic assumptions, renders broader issues of international politics, particularly questions of system structure and system stability, usefully illuminated by game-theoretic models. Kaplan (1957) relied heavily on game theory to discuss the relationships between structure and process in the international system. Riker (1962) used the size principle and the theory of n-person games to show internal inconsistencies in Kaplan's "rules-of-the-game" in balance of power systems. More recently, Wagner (1986) and Niou and Ordeshook (1986) used n-person game theory to examine conditions of stability and instability

---

[14] For a more formal formulation of the problem and a new set of solutions see Brams (1985a) and Brams and Kilgour (1987).

[15] See Jervis (1979, 1984); George and Smoke (1974); and Morgan (1977) for reviews of deterrence theories. The line of thinking on deterrence based primarily on game theory has been labeled the "abstract-deductivist" model to distinguish it from the more empirical and inductive writings on the topic which rely largely on political psychology (Jervis, Lebow, and Stein, 1985).

in balance of power systems. Jervis (1978) used game theory to convert Rousseau's Stag-Hunt metaphor into a model of the security dilemma. Maoz and Felsenthal (1987) used a variety of two and n-person asymmetric games to illustrate pathological problems of international cooperation and to suggest some ways of resolving them. Maoz (1989) applied a variety of game-theoretic models to explore paradoxes of war.[16]

It is surprising to see that scholars who have recently attacked the realist paradigm by questioning its assumptions have also used game theory to illustrate issues in political economy and cooperation under conditions which are less than anarchic. Most notable in this respect are works by Keohane (1984), Lipson (1986), and Snidal (1985) which have focused on problems of coordination in international economic regimes. The attempts to expand the use of game-theoretic models beyond the traditional issues (such as strategy, conflict, and arms races which highlight the non-cooperative features of international politics) to a new set of substantive issues which encompass more cooperative and organized aspects of the field suggests increased fascination with the possibilities of the theory.

Whether or not game-theoretic models of international politics do justice to the phenomena under investigation in reducing them to simple game-structures is still a matter of debate in the discipline. However, the use of game theory as a heuristic tool has rather limited objectives. Its primary intention is to shed a new light on some aspects of international politics which might not be obvious from different and more complex angles of attack; it is not necessarily to explain and predict the evolutions in the game of nations. Most applications of this sort were based on few typical games such as the PD, Chicken, and the Stag-Hunt. These were seen to illuminate pathological properties of the system; there was no concrete effort to determine dynamic changes in the environment in terms of variations in game structures. The static aspects of theory are useful for two reasons. First, by definition, pathological problems of international politics are those that exhibit little variation over time. For example, the free rider problem in alliances, or the security dilemma are ills of international politics that are unlikely to change. The same applies to the arguably stable structure of nuclear deterrence. To model stability, a theory that requires considerable variation in the variables it employs is not very

---

[16] One of the most important bodies of work in this area has been that of Axelrod (1980a; 1980b, 1981; 1984; 1986) on the iterated Prisoner's Dilemma and on the Norms game. I defer discussion of this body of work to chapter 9 because it involves dynamic rather than static models of international politics.

useful. The focus on stable situations in games and the substantive properties of such situations is what makes game-theoretic models particularly appealing from this perspective.

Second, whether defined in static terms or in dynamic ones, game theory is not always a helpful model of change in international politics, for it lacks a theory of preference change. Substantive processes of change in international politics, on the other hand, almost invariably entail major shifts in the calculations of players which result in different preference ranking of outcomes over time. For example, Gilpin (1981) asserts that a major change in the system occurs when: (*a*) a sufficient number of key actors becomes dissatisfied with the prevailing systemic equilibrium, and (*b*) these actors perceive the benefits of changing this equilibrium to outweigh the costs associated with doing that. In game-theoretic terms this implies that at least one actor in a game feels that shifting its strategy (associated with a certain equilibrium) would result in immediate gains. This implies that a situation that was in equilibrium is no longer in equilibrium. It is difficult to explain such a change through an analysis which is endogenous to game theory without allowing some form of dynamic preference change.

Descriptive applications of game theory. The use of game theory as a descriptive scheme is less widespread than its use as a heuristic device. The most common application of game-theoretic models as a descriptive tool involved interstate interactions in two – not unrelated – types of settings: international crises and international negotiations. Researchers attempt to identify the players and their alternatives and to define games in terms of the preference ordering of outcomes by the players. Actual behavior is matched with expected behavior from a game-theoretic perspective and, when they differ, explanations are developed to account for these discrepancies.

Brams (1985a) analyzed superpower behavior in the Cuban missile crisis of 1962 and the nuclear alert decision of October 1973. Using the theory of moves, Brams explained how the crises have stabilized. Related analyses of crisis behavior using the non-myopic equilibrium concept, as well as various concepts of power were done by Zagare (1982, 1983, 1985), and by Brams and Hessel (1984). Zagare also applied game theory to the analysis of international negotiation processes, specifically, the Vietnam negotiations (Zagare, 1977) and the 1954 Geneva Conference (Zagare, 1979). Maoz and Yaniv (1989) analyzed Israeli–Syrian interactions over the 1948–1984 period as a supergame of compound escalation wherein each stage leads to a greater degree of hostility than the previous one. Maoz and Felsenthal

(1987) applied game-theoretic analysis to the Sadat peace initiative of 1977 and to the Israeli decision to withdraw from Lebanon in 1985.

The most ambitious effort to use game theory in an empirical study is that of Snyder and Diesing (1977). They attempted to demonstrate bargaining processes during international crises as outcomes of simple 2×2 games where actors have a simple binary choice of strategy: defection versus cooperation. However, their interpretations of solution concepts of central games such as the PD is at odds with the theory. For example, they argue that the dilemma of the PD game disappears in sequential play of the game (Snyder and Diesing, 1977: 44). This is far from either the theoretical or empirical truth. (See Zagare, 1984b: 54–55 for a theoretical refutation of this claim; Rapoport and Chamma, 1965; and Rapoport, Guyer and Gordon, 1976 for experimental evidence.) Moreover, they use game theory to explain crisis bargaining in an *ad hoc* way. It is not clear which solution concepts are used, and whether the rules of the game are fixed or changing. At some points they assume sequential play while at others they use simultaneous play, and so forth. Much of their substantive explanation of crisis outcomes involves concepts such as resolve and bargaining power which are external to the game itself, hence making the role of game theory in the overall explanation unclear.

But this problem is not unique to Snyder and Diesing. Most empirical applications of game theory to international politics have not been very rigorous, to say the least. There seems to be a strange wedding between game theory and single case studies in which different cases are examined as different games and according to different solution concepts. This is very surprising because, as a highly rigorous and precise tool, game theory offers an opportunity for rigorous statistical tests of actual behavior of states in interdependent choice situations. Unfortunately, I know of no empirical investigation in international politics which tested game-theoretic predictions on aggregate empirical data. There are two general reasons for this deficiency: one stems from the clash of principles in game theory, the other stems from the difficulty of assigning either cardinal utilities or even ordinal preferences to actors' perceptions of outcomes. Empirical applications of game theory require that there exist a general solution concept that would encompass all kinds of games under all kinds of rules of play. However, as Shubik (1982: 332–334) puts it,

> [T]he search of a singular unifying solution theory to apply to all games is akin to the search for the philosopher's stone. Not only is it intuitively unlikely that our solution concept will be reasonable in all instances; even if it were, it would still be unlikely that the solution

theory would yield a unique solution point that would satisfy all properties deemed desirable for a solution . . . [I]t has been shown that in general, for virtually any property, such as optimality, uniqueness, or stability, a game can be constructed with non-cooperative equilibria that lack the property. The existence of counter-examples does not, however, vitiate the usefulness of the non-cooperative-equilibrium solution or its modifications.

The difficulty of assigning preferences to actors over a multitude of possible situations is perhaps the main deterrent of statistical analyses of game theoretic models in international politics. Even attempts to define ordinal preferences over given outcomes are prone to considerable disagreements in the literature.[17] Since case studies allow for an in-depth examination of actors' preferences they can be seen as more amenable to game-theoretic analyses than aggregate behavioral data.

The use of game theory in this chapter will assume an entirely new form. Game theory serves neither a descriptive function, nor a heuristic one. Rather, it serves as a systematic standard which facilitates comparison between the actual outcomes of interdependent national decisions, on the one hand, and the expected or theoretically-optimal outcomes, on the other. Game theory is used as a framework through which national decisions can be evaluated in terms of the kind of outcomes they yielded relative to the outcomes decision makers expected, or relative to the outcomes that would obtain if decision makers made the best decision under the circumstances.

8.3 PSYCHOLOGICAL THEORIES OF BARGAINING

Psychological approaches do not maintain the distinction between bargaining and negotiation. One of the most general reviews of psychological studies on the subject uses these terms synonymously (Rubin and Brown, 1975: 2). The mixture of these two terms creates some confusion in that there is no clear difference in psychological writings on the topic between situations in which parties "are at least temporarily joined together in a special kind of voluntary relationship" (Rubin and Brown, 1975: 7) and those in which parties must simply choose among alternative courses of

---

[17] See for example the debate between Brams (1975; 1985a) and Snyder and Diesing (1977) on the preferences of the superpowers in the Cuban missile crisis, between Zagare (1979; 1982) and Thakur (1982) on the Geneva Peace Conference, and between Brams (1985a) and Zagare (1985; 1987) on the structure of the game of nuclear deterrence.

action knowing that the outcomes of their choices depend on the choices of other actors.

8.3.1 Psychological factors affecting bargaining outcomes

The major dependent variable in psychological analyses of bargaining and negotiations is the outcome of the social exchange, the existence and nature of an agreement between the parties. What accounts for the vast diversity of studies is the range of independent variables used to explain bargaining outcomes. Again, due to the large amount of work done by social psychologists, I will restrict the discussion only to few ideas and empirical findings that seem relevant to the subsequent attempt to formulate a model linking national choices to international outcomes in interdependent settings.[18]

Broadly speaking, psychological studies of bargaining focus on two classes of independent variables: situational factors and the personal attributes of the parties involved in the process. Situational factors include physical aspects of the bargaining site, the presence or absence of audiences, the characteristics of the bargaining problem (including the nature of the issues involved, the number of issues, the amount of time available to the actors, and so forth). The attributes of the parties range from personality traits of individuals to the degree of inter-dependence among actors and the degree of dependence of the bargainers on their constitutents of superiors.[19] More recent works focus on the impact of norms (of reciprocity and equity) on bargaining behavior. Norms are distinct from either the characteristics of the situation and independent from the attributes of the bargainers, and are seen primarily as superimposed rules which act as guides or constraints on the bargainers (Strauss 1978; Axelrod, 1986).

Attributes of the bargainers. Several factors fall into this category: bargainers' personalities, their interpersonal (or, more relevant to our subject matter, their international) orientations, and their basic moti-

---

[18] There exist four good sources that summarize and review psychological research on bargaining and negotiation. Rubin and Brown (1975) and Pruitt (1981) are excellent reviews of psychological research. Strauss (1978) reviews sociological aspects of negotiation. Raiffa's (1982) general review of negotiation contains many examples (some of them taken from international politics). The classical text on international negotiation is Ikle (1964). A nice integration of theoretical and practical aspects of negotiations is given by Zartman and Berman (1982).

[19] Walton and McKerzie's (1965) study of labor negotiation contain one of the first and probably one of the best treatments of the bargaining process as a combination of distributive interaction wherein each side tries to maximize its share of the pie, and integrative bargaining wherein each actor is seen as a mediator between its constituency (labor negotiators) or its superiors (management as representative of the board of directors or shareholders) and the opponent.

vations. The finding in psychological studies of bargaining and negotiation is that personality traits (most of these that were discussed in
previous chapters) account for different bargaining styles. The agreement on the nature of these relationships is less general, however
(Pruitt, 1981: 45–46). Nonetheless there seems to be some consensus
that dogmatism, authoritarianism, and cognitive simplicity seem to be
associated with non-cooperative behavior (or low rates of concessions
over time) whereas high level of open-mindedness and cognitive
complexity are associated with more cooperative bargaining styles
(Druckman, 1968; Hermann and Kogan, 1977).

Game theory was used as the primary instrument for assessing the
effects of motivational orientations on bargaining behavior. The
measure of behavior was the proportion of cooperative outcomes in
games such as the PD or Chicken. Experimenters manipulated the
motivational orientations of the subjects, distinguishing among three
general types of motivation: cooperative, competitive, and individualistic (or egoistic). Cooperative motivation refers to behavior designed
to maximize joint gains. Competitive behavior is designed to maximize relative personal gains (the objective is to get *more* than the
opponent, irrespective of the total gains to oneself: this implies a
tendency to behave as if all games were zero sum). Individualistic
motivation is one which aspires at maximization of self-gains irrespective of the gains (or losses) or other actors. (This is what we normally
associate with the term *rationality*.) Not surprisingly, cooperative
Motivational Orientation (MO) produced a higher frequency of cooperation than either an individualistic MO or a competitive one.[20]

These findings seem to be consistent with findings reported in
earlier chapters on personality effects on decisional and behavioral
styles (e.g., Hermann's findings on personality correlates of foreign
policy behavior; Walker's, 1983 and Starr's, 1984 findings on Kissinger's bargaining style; Tetlock's, 1985b findings on the effects of
integrative complexity on US–Soviet interactions, and so forth). From
a psychological perspective, bargaining behavior is seen as a straightforward extension of decision behavior to interdependent settings. It
is important to note, however, that the outcomes of the interdependent exchange depend not on the mental makeup of the
individual bargainers but on the combination of the bargainers'
make-up, that is, who is playing against whom. Yet, there is little
empirical research on the question of whether one MO dominates
another when people with different MOs are locked into a bargaining

---

[20] See Rubin and Brown (1975: 200–203) and Pruitt (1981: 112–113) for a summary of
relevant research findings.

relationship. Nor have there been empirical studies of whether bargainers adapt or modify their behavior in a manner that takes account of the type of opponent (that is, do people with cooperative MOs remain cooperative even if they play against a person who is known to have a competitive MO).

The literature on the personal and motivational attributes of the bargainers draws attention to levels of empathy induced by certain personality traits or motivational orientations. Empathy refers to an ability to understand the opponent's values and perceptions of the bargaining problem and is taken to contribute significantly to the level of successful (but not necessarily cooperative) behavior. Players will get their way more often when they perceive correctly their opponent's behavior and values than when they make little effort to understand those things.

Situational determinants of bargaining behavior. Rubin and Brown (1975) provide a sensible typology of situational factors that affect bargaining behavior and outcomes. The structural context of bargaining refers to what we called the "rules of the game" in the discussion of game-theoretic approaches. Social psychological approaches examine the effect of non-participants on the behavior of bargainers, the accountability of the bargainers to superiors or constituents, and so forth. The pressures induced by the physical and social context of the bargaining process, such as stress, time pressure, or support have all been assesssed, without conclusive findings as to whether, and in what ways they affect bargaining behavior (Rubin and Brown, 1975; Pruitt, 1981).

Interdependence and bargaining outcomes. In game theory, interdependence is reflected in terms of the distribution of players' preferences over the various outcomes which defines the extent to which one actor's best choice depends on the choices of other actors. Psychological studies consider interdependence to be a function of the motivational or personal orientations of bargainers or of the distribution of power among them. Seen in these terms, interdependence denotes the extent to which the personalities and/or the resources available to bargainers allow for a certain cooperative outcome. In general, experimental studies show that bargaining combinations of parties with equal power and cooperative MOs or Interpersonal Orientations (IOs) are likely to result in efficient solutions of the joint decision problems, again, a hardly surprising result.

Norms. Norms, conventions, and ethics are only briefly addressed by psychologists in a direct way. For most part, they are treated as variables that mediate between bargainers' characteristics or the

408

situational factors and the outcome variables (concession making, agreement indices, and so forth). Rubin and Brown (1975: 41–80) discuss the effects of the social components of the bargaining process such as the presence of audiences, the availability of third parties, and so forth. The effects of these variables on bargaining outcomes are mediated by norms that they invoke during the exchange process. Likewise, motivational orientations are seen to create norms in the sense that actors have not only a sense of what is "proper" behavior, but also what is expected from the opponent in terms of reciprocity, equity, and so forth.[21]

8.3.2 Applications of psychological approaches to international bargaining

Several interesting attempts have been made to deal with the effects of psychological factors on international negotiations processes. Jervis (1970) discussed problems of signaling in international politics. Cohen (1983) provides an interesting historical analysis on "rules of the game" largely based on Jervis's study. Lockhart (1979) and Leng (1980) discuss the effects of influence strategies (especially the use of threats) in crisis bargaining. The most insightful part of Snyder and Diesing's (1977) analysis of crisis bargaining is their analysis of resolve and bargaining power as well as of information processing in bargaining processes. Pillar's (1983) study of war termination provides both applications of rational choice strategies (Zeuthen's [1932] and Cross's [1969] economic models) as well as psychological aspects. There are several studies of mediation in international politics which draw upon psychological factors. Touval's (1982) study of mediation efforts in the Arab–Israeli conflict, and Rubin's (1981) edited volume on Kissinger's mediation of the disengagement agreements in the Middle East provide good examples.

The major contribution of psychological studies of international bargaining is that they enable us to assess the effects of individual dispositions and perceptions on bargaining outcomes. Their main drawback is that they lack a good explanation of the dynamic unfolding of negotiations. By and large, these studies manipulate one or more independent variables to explain variations in the final outcome of the social exchange. However, the process invoked by the independent variables is either inferred indirectly or altogether ignored. The discussion of influence strategies (such as the use of threats or positive inducements) and their effects on bargaining outcomes is a good

[21] See Axelrod (1986) for a discussion of the processes by which norms emerge.

illustration of this point. The question examined in this context, is which influence strategies are best in the sense that they elicit concessions from the opponent. However, when and how various influence strategies are effective or ineffective during a negotiation process is a question that is typically not analyzed. Pruitt's (1981) focus on demand levels and concession rates seems to offer only a partial remedy to the problem.

Psychological approaches offer a tremendously diverse checklist of factors that are instrumental for understanding bargaining behavior and bargaining outcomes. There is no good general theory that either details the relative potency of various factors or that integrates some or all of these factors into a more general image of the bargaining structure. Compared to the parsimonious image of bargaining (and negotiation) conveyed by game theory, psychological approaches present a far more complex and elaborate image of these processes. Due to the diversity of these approaches, it should come as no surprise that the applications of these approaches to international politics are all over the place in terms of findings, methodologies, and substantive conclusions. With one notable exception – the study of mediation processes (Young, 1967; Rubin, 1981; Touval, 1982) – there is very little agreement in the applied literature on: (a) what are the key factors that affect the outcomes of international negotiations, (b) what kind of influence strategies are most effective and under what conditions, and (c) how psychological theories aid negotiators in their tasks.[22]

The major problem of psychological approaches to bargaining is that they attempt to impose notions of linear relations between factors that reside at one level of analysis (for example, the personality traits of negotiators) and the bargaining outcomes which are a product of a different level of analysis (a social exchange or "strategic" level). Yet the discussion of decision making theories clearly suggests that any simple transformation of individual (or national) choices to bargaining (or international) outcomes should be viewed with a great deal of empirical skepticism. What is being controlled in a well-structured experimental setting, is not usually controlled in real-life situations, and the trick is to discover what happens in a system wherein nations interact with one another under conditions of interdependence. The manner in which national preferences produce and relate to inter-

---

[22] Zartman and Berman's (1982) study offers an interesting combination of theory and practice in international negotiations. They have brought together views of theoreticians and practitioners in international negotiations and have shown that there exists a wide gap between what negotiators need and what theorists of negotiation can provide.

410

national outcomes is, therefore, the focus of the remainder of this chapter.

8.4 NATIONAL CHOICES AND INTERNATIONAL OUTCOMES

The key question of a theory that seeks to connect national choices to international outcomes concerns the extent to which individual and collective choices affect the outcomes of international interactions in interdependent settings. Specifically, the issue is whether procedural decision quality defined in terms of the degree of analytic decision making within national settings tends to yield substantive international outcomes which are seen as optimal (or at least as acceptable) by individuals and collectivities. The answer to this question must be empirical; theoretically, there is no reason to expect such a relationship. As the review of the clash of principles in game theory reveals, there is no guarantee that rational choices would produce Pareto-efficient outcomes. However, on the theoretical level, there are different types of bad outcomes. There are bad outcomes that arise due to a given strategic configuration defined by players' preferences and by the rules of the game. (The Prisoner's Dilemma is a case in point.) In such cases, individual rationality is not of much help. On the other hand, the strategic configuration might afford opportunities for optimal outcomes, but players fail to capitalize on such opportunities due to cognitive or other imperfections in their decision making process. The aim of this section is to distinguish between what is theoretically accomplishable within a given strategic configuration and what is empirically observed, given players' choices. In addition, I attempt to identify sources of discrepancy between optimal outcomes and actual ones.

The decision analytic part of the theory of international processes allows a more or less reliable formulation of a national preference ranking of an array of international outcomes. Every national decision can be characterized by two underlying features: a rationale and an outcome-related expectation. The rationale is simply the justification of the decision in terms of the preference ranking of outcomes. The expectation refers to the predicted consequences of various courses of actions. None of these elements alone is sufficient for accounting for the decision. Only one type of preference ranking of outcomes can explain a decision without incorporating expectations: this is when a nation possesses a dominant strategy. In the absence of a unique dominant strategy, expectations about the behavior of other actors are

411

required to account for a national decision. Even when a nation possesses a dominant strategy, the payoff it actually obtains depends on what other actors do. Thus, outcome-related expectations involve estimating the behavior of other actors. This implies, of course, estimating the array of policy options available to other actors and the preference ranking of the resulting outcomes of the strategic configuration by those actors.

Because rationales are subjective in nature, it is difficult to evaluate whether or not they are theoretically sound. Decision analysis helps reveal how national preferences were generated and whether they were established through analytic or other processes. But at the international level it is immaterial how national preferences were established: they are given in the game of nations. The Soviet leaders may think that only crazy people would prefer an exacerbation of the arms race through the SDI but they have to accept this preference distribution of the American administration as given and deal with it as best they can.

On the other hand, the extent to which outcome-related expectations are realistic can be evaluated theoretically. This operation involves three issues. First, does a player accurately perceive the array of alternatives available to other actors? Second, does he or she accurately perceive the distribution of preferences of other players over the array of outcomes formed by the intersections of available alternatives? Third, does he or she make correct inferences from this distribution with respect to the expected behavior of other actors? The central issue in a theory that attempts to relate national decisions to international outcomes is whether nations are actually playing the game they think they are playing.

In order to establish a theoretically meaningful relationship between national choices and international outcomes it is important to distinguish between subjective and objective games. A subjective game is a strategic configuration defined in terms of players, alternatives, and preferences as seen from the vantage point of each of the players involved. By definition, there can be no misperception involved in the way given players define their own alternatives or in their preference ranking of the outcomes they perceive as feasible. But a player can misperceive: (a) the number and identity of other players, (b) the alternatives available to the other players, and (c) the preference ranking of the various outcomes by the other players.

An objective game is defined as an intersection of players' self-perceptions. Specifically, it consists of all players that see themselves

412

as participants in a strategic configuration, of the alternatives each of these players has and of the preferences each player defines over the array of possible outcomes he or she perceives. Objective games can be completely defined or partially defined. A completely defined objective game is one wherein all of the players have complete preference orderings over all of the outcomes. A game is completely defined if and only if none of the actors misperceives the number and identity of all other actors and the array of alternatives available to each. A partially-defined objective game is one wherein at least one of the actors misperceives either the number and identity of other actors, their available alternatives, or both. In such cases, not all actors will have complete preference orderings over the objective array of outcomes. Partially-defined objective games can exist even if all players make accurate perceptions about the preference distributions of all other players over those outcomes they identified. Because some outcomes will be empty in the sense that actors did not take them into account and hence have not expressed explicit preferences toward these outcomes, the structure of such games is not complete. We will see below how decision theory helps in completing the structure of partially-defined games, but for the time being, I illustrate the concepts of objective and subjective games.

8.4.1 Objective and subjective games: the 1973 Middle East crisis

The situation in the Middle East on October 5, 1973 will be used as a case study for this purpose.[23] The players in this game were Israel and the Egyptian–Syrian coalition. Each player had two alternatives: the Egyptian–Syrian alternatives were to attack Israel or not to attack and the Israeli alternatives were to mobilize reserves or not to mobilize. (I am assuming that each actor accurately perceived the alternatives available to the other, though not necessarily the other's preference ordering of the outcomes.) This forms a 2×2 game with the outcomes being: (1) AM – Egyptian–Syrian attack and Israeli mobilization, (2) $A\overline{M}$ – Egyptian–Syrian attack and no Israeli mobilization, (3) $\overline{A}M$ – no Egyptian–Syrian attack and Israeli mobilization, and (4) $\overline{A}\,\overline{M}$ – no Egptian–Syrian attack and no Israeli mobilization (status quo). To determine players' preferences over the various outcomes, it is necessary to determine the dimensions of value on which these outcomes

---

[23] The following analysis relies heavily on Brecher (1980); Sadat (1978); Heikal (1975); and Stein (1985). This analysis should be taken as illustrative in nature. It is not implied that an actual decision analysis underlies the preference structure of the actors in this game.

Table 8.1. *Egyptian search-evaluation matrix on October 5, 1973*

Outcome	Value dimension					Squared sum of ranks
	Diplomacy	Military	Casualties	Inter-Arab	Morale	
AM	4	3	1	2.5	3	24.0
$\overline{AM}$	3	4	2	4	4	16.0
$\overline{A}M$	2	2	3.5	2.5	2	8.5
$\overline{AM}$	1	1	3.5	1	1	18.0
Total						76.5

Notes:
The characteristics of the Egyptian evaluation of outcomes are:

$$CE = 20, \; FSE = \frac{20}{20} = 1.0, \; TC = \frac{76.5}{125} = 0.612.$$

Outcomes are ranked from best = 4 to worst = 1. Indifferences between outcomes are assigned the midpoint between the two ranks.
Integrated ranking of outcomes is given by: $A\overline{M} > AM > \overline{A}M > \overline{AM}$.
Source: Compiled by the author.

were appraised.[24] The Egyptian assessment of the decision problem was based on the following dimensions: (1) the need to create strong incentives for superpower involvement designed to bring about Israeli concessions and forward movement toward a settlement of the Arab–Israeli conflict (this dimension will be labeled Diplomacy), (2) military success defined in terms of limited territorial gains in the Sinai (Military), (3) minimization of casualties (Casualties), (4) the inter-Arab status of Egypt (Inter-Arab), (5) domestic support for the Sadat regime defined in terms of Egyptian prestige (that is, public morale which was at an all-time low since the Egyptian defeat in 1967, hence Morale). The Egyptian search-evaluation matrix is depicted in table 8.1.

It can be readily seen from this table that the Egyptian choice problem was a tough one, even before taking into account the expected Israeli behavior. Nonetheless, the fact that the diplomatic and military dimensions were seen by Sadat as far more important than the casuality dimension resulted in an evaluation in which the

[24] For the sake of simplicity, I am making a unitary actor assumption. This allows me to specify a coherent set of preferences over these outcomes. This assumption is unrealistic, however, because the historical evidence strongly suggests different individual preferences over these outcomes in both Israel and Egypt. Nonetheless, the following discussion represents the end results of group deliberations in these states. In Israel, Dayan's evaluation of the situation was finally accepted as the most valid one, and in Egypt, Sadat's analysis was superimposed on the reluctant military command.

Israel

	M	$\overline{M}$
A	3 * 3	1 4
$\overline{A}$	2 2	4 1

Egypt

*Nash Equilibrium.
Outcomes are ranked from best = 4 to worst = 1.
Source: Compiled by the author.

Figure 8.10 The Egyptian view of the 1973 crisis game

attack option emerged as a dominant strategy.[25] This suggests that the Egyptian–Syrian decision was seemingly independent of the Israeli mobilization decision: the Egyptians and Syrians thought that they were better-off attacking than not attacking whatever the Israelis were expected to do. However, whether the Egyptians and Syrians got the best or second-best outcome depended on what the Israelis were expected to do. The expectations of the Egyptian–Syrian bloc were based on their view of the Israeli preferences. Sadat believed that Israel was determined to perpetuate the status quo which allowed it to control the Sinai and strengthens its hold over the other occupied territories. The Israeli rejection of his 1971 offer for a limited agreement served as the primary evidence of this view. Sadat believed that Israel preferred to maintain the status quo without having to mobilize reserves (the $\overline{AM}$ outcome) over escalation of the situation (the $\overline{A}M$

[25] A word should be said on the ranking of outcomes on the military, inter-Arab, and morale dimensions. After long planning, the military objective set by the Egyptians and Syrians was of a highly limited nature. It was to recover a small portion of the territories occupied by Israel in 1967; not all of these territories. In terms of the Egyptian side of this alliance, this meant occupying a narrow strip of land East of the Suez canal. (The most ambitious goal was occupying the western portion of the Sinai desert up to the Mitla and Gidi passes.) The best outcome from an inter-Arab perspective would have been a successful surprise attack. This would have re-established Egyptian leading role in inter-Arab affairs. From this perspective, Arab support of Egypt would have been the same whether its attack were less than fully successful (in the event of Israeli mobilization) or whether there was a war scare in the Middle East as a result of Israeli mobilization without an Egyptian attack. However, the continuation of the status quo $(\overline{AM})$ was seen by Sadat as leading to a gradual erosion in Egyptian inter-Arab standing. The domestic dimension follows the same logic, except that an Israeli mobilization without an Arab attack was interpreted as a sign of weakness of a regime that kept promising a recovery of lost national honor. See Heikal (1975), Sadat (1978), and Stein (1985) for extensive accounts of the Egyptian calculus. Unfortunately, there are only indirect accounts of the Syrian calculus (Maoz and Yaniv, 1989; Yaniv, 1985).

415

outcome), but preferred to mobilize if it expected an attack (the AM outcome) over being caught unprepared (the $A\overline{M}$ outcome). This suggests that Sadat viewed Israeli preferences as $\overline{AM} > AM > \overline{A}\overline{M} > A\overline{M}$. The game viewed from Cairo is thus given in figure 8.10.

This game suggests that from Sadat's vantage point, a surprise attack was the preferred but not the expected outcome. In fact, Sadat's estimate of the Egyptian casualities during that war was vastly higher than the actual figures. This is not to suggest that Egypt did not invest in deception; only that Sadat was not optimistic about actually surprising Israel. The existence of a dominant strategy suggests that Egypt would have attacked whether or not the Israelis mobilized reserves.

Let us turn now to the Israeli calculus. First, it is important to note that by October 4 (with incoming reports about a large-scale evacuation of Soviet families from Egypt and Syria), the Israeli cabinet correctly perceived the alternatives available to the Egyptians and Syrians as those of attack and no attack.[26] Thus, the array of possible outcomes from the Israeli perspective was the same as the one viewed by the Egyptians. The dimensions of value that were brought up in the October 4 cabinet meeting to evaluate the various outcomes were: (1) the military security dimension, defined in terms of two different, but complementary values: military effectiveness (either effective deterrence of an attack or its successful repellence) and minimization of casualties, (2) diplomatic support defined primarily in terms of US–Israeli relations, (3) economic costs (of mobilization or of war), and (implicitly) (4) domestic support for the government. The ranking of the four outcomes on these value dimensions is given in table 8.2.

Two things emerge from this table. First, the Israeli decision process seems to have involved little tradeoff complexity. Second, and more importantly, it is obvious that Sadat's perception of Israeli preference structure was very accurate. Whether or not Sadat went into the various elements of the Israeli calculus is not of major significance, the results were a correct assessment of Israeli preferences.[27] Sadat's subjective assessment of the game conformed to the objective assessment of this game. But what about the Israeli assessment of Egyptian–Syrian preferences? The Israeli intelligence assessment of Syrian and Egyptian intentions was based on two basic premises, both of which involved an inferential leap from capabilities to intentions: (a) Syria would not attack Israel without Egypt's active participation, (b) Egypt

---

[26] This was the core of the discussion in the October 4 cabinet meeting in Israel although there was some discussion on a limited Syrian retaliation following the shooting down of 13 Syrian Mig-21s over Lebanon in September.

[27] This is contrary to what Stein (1985: 38–59) sees as misperceptions on Sadat's part.

Table 8.2. *Israeli search-evaluation matrix on October 5, 1973*

| | Value dimension | | | | Squared sum |
Outcome	Military	Diplomacy	Economic	Domestic	of ranks
AM	2	2	2	3	4
$A\overline{M}$	1	3	1	1	12
$\overline{A}M$	3	1	3	2	11
$\overline{AM}$	4	4	4	4	0
Total					27

Notes:
The characteristics of the Israeli evaluation of outcomes are:

$$CE = 16, \ FSE = \frac{16}{16} = 1.0, \ TC = \frac{27}{80} = 0.337.$$

Outcomes are ranked from best = 4 to worst = 1. Indifferences between outcomes are assigned the midpoint between the two ranks.
Integrated ranking of outcomes is given by: $\overline{AM} > AM > \overline{A}M > A\overline{M}$.
Source: Compiled by the author.

would not risk an attack on Israel as long as it lacked sufficient air power to counter Israeli aerial superiority. Without going into the implications of these assumptions, it seems fairly obvious that the Israeli perception of Egypt's (and therefore of Syria's) preferences was: $A\overline{M} > \overline{A}M > \overline{AM} > AM$. Thus, the game the Israelis thought they were playing is given in figure 8.11.

The Israeli misperception of Egyptian preferences suggests that it failed to realize that Egypt had a dominant attack strategy. But this misperception does not explain the Israeli failure to mobilze reserves,

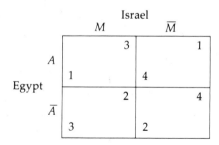

Outcomes are ranked from best = 4 to worst = 1.
Source: Compiled by the author.

Figure 8.11 The Israeli view of the 1973 crisis game

417

for in the subjective Israeli game there was no pure-strategy equilibrium outcome. The explanation of the Israeli decision not to mobilize reserves on October 4 is based largely on the estimate of a very low probability of an Arab attack. In terms of a game-theoretic analysis, this suggests that the military intelligence which was largely responsible for this characterization of the Egyptian–Syrian preferences made an incorrect inference from this preference order. Specifically, the military intelligence assumed that the Egyptian decisions had been predicated on the maximin rule. This assumption allowed a very self-confident chief of military intelligence to express a nearly unequivocal commitment to the low probability estimate of A. The Israeli decision not to mobilize reserves given the game they thought they were playing may have been imprudent for another reason. Note that the Israeli maximin strategy would have been to mobilize reserves. If the Israelis were to make their choice independent of those of the Egyptian and Syrian choices they should have mobilized. However, since it was believed that the Egyptians followed their own maximin strategy, the no mobilization decision seemed sensible. The Egyptians who have correctly perceived the Israeli preference ordering of outcomes (and also assumed that Israel would do the best in the circumstances) actually benefited from the Israeli blunder, getting their best outcome.

Discrepancies between subjective games and objective ones are what we typically describe as misperceptions. Misperceptions can take on many forms in international politics. In this case the misperception was that of failing to understand the opponent's preference structure. The result of this misperception was that Israel got its worst payoff and Egypt, unexpectedly, got its most preferred outcome.

8.4.2 Defining objective games and their solutions[28]

The analysis of the outbreak of the 1973 war serves to illustrate some features of the process by which national decisions are converted into international outcomes. It also suggests ways of assessing the substantive quality of foreign policy decisions. The first step in the aggregation of national choices into international outcomes is to determine the general structure of the objective game. This is done by: (a) identifying the relevant players, and (b) identifying the alternatives available to each of them. This requires identification of the policy

---

[28] For a related treatment of the issues discussed henceforth see Fraser and Hipel (1984). This work describes a new branch of game theory called "hypergame analysis" which enables systematic modeling of misperceptions in game-theoretic form.

options that were considered by each of the national bodies that made relevant decisions on the issue under inquiry. The analysis of the policy options considered by each state is done without regard to the extent to which national decision makers took into account the policy options available to other states. The combination of players and their policy options allows us to construct an empty game matrix and define the number of possible outcomes in the objective game.

Next, we attempt to fill out as many outcomes as possible in the game matrix by examining the rank-ordering of outcomes by each of the participating states, as reflected in its decision process. This entails looking at the criteria by which outcomes were evaluated by each of the national players, ranking the perceived outcomes on each criterion independently of the ranking of outcomes on other criteria, and then aggregating over the various criteria to produce an integrated preference ranking of outcomes. This preference ranking is inserted into the objective game matrix to represent the national preferences over the perceived outcomes. Having done this for all actors involved, we determine the extent to which the objective game is defined. The degree of completeness (DC) of an objective game with O outcomes is simply the number of outcomes that have explicit payoff rankings for all players over the area of the game matrix.

$$DC = \frac{o_f}{O}$$

where o_f is the number of fully-defined outcomes and O is the total number of feasible outcomes in the game (the total area of the game).

The third step depends on whether or not the objective game is fully-defined. In fully-defined games (such as the Egyptian–Israeli game of October 1973), the third step requires defining a solution. In partially-defined games, this step is divided into two phases. The first phase requires extrapolation of preference ranks for each state on the outcomes for which the state had no preferences because they were not considered by its decision makers. This is a tricky operation because the reliability of such an extrapolation is quite questionable. However, given the information we have about the criteria used by each state to evaluate outcomes and the principle by which integrated preferences were produced for those outcomes that were identified by national decision making bodies, it is reasonable to ask how decision makers would have ranked all the outcomes if they had perceived them. If we restrict ourselves only to ordinal rankings, rather than attempting to define cardinal utilities, this extrapolation becomes less far-fetched than it appears at first glance.

The extrapolation of preferences for non-considered outcomes is done as follows:

1 Insert all outcomes of the objective game into the rows of the national search evaluation (SE) matrices.

2 Given the ranking of actually perceived outcomes on each of the considered value dimensions, produce a new preference ranking of outcomes which includes both the actually considered outcomes and the non-considered ones on each value dimension.

3 Use the original aggregation rule to create new integrated preference rankings.

4 Insert the new preference rankings of all states into the objective game matrix.

Now we have fully-defined objective games whether or not these games have been actually defined (since all states involved had actually ranked the various outcomes) or whether they were completed by extrapolation. While the difference between fully-defined objective games and partially-defined ones is important for purposes of evaluation of the substantive outcomes of national decisions, we will ignore these differences for the time being. The solution concepts used here are predicated on some assumptions concerning the rules by which objective games are played. The rules of play assumed to characterize objective games are: (1) simultaneous choice, (2) full information, (3) no communication, no cooperation, and no enforceable agreements, and (4) single play. Taken together, these assumptions imply that games are solved through decision principles that stipulate what each player can optimally do and what each player can realistically expect independently of what other actors are doing, and assuming that other actors follow the same logic. This rules out solutions that involve extraneous alternatives such as jointly coordinated behavior through communication or enforceable agreements, the issue of threats or side-payments, various possibilities that are formed by sequential or iterative play of the game, and so forth.

It is by no means implied that in real-life situations nations behave as if they indeed follow these assumptions. For one thing, the notion of objective games is a theoretical construct. Nations do not play objective games, they play subjective ones. The extent to which a game that a state thinks it is playing conforms to an actual objective situation is an empirical question. My hunch is that – by and large – subjective games differ from objective ones to a significant degree, and I will attempt to formalize possible conceptual differences between subjective and objective games. At this juncture, the object of finding a solution to an objective game is to provide a normative anchor which allows evaluation of the actual outcome of the interdependent inter-section of national decisions. This solution is to be seen as *what we would expect, had national decisions been indeed the best that players could make under an objective set of circumstances, where this objective set of circumstances is represented by the structure of the objective game.* This outcome is labeled the *theoretical outcome* of the game. The theoretical outcome will then be compared to the actual outcome of the game and will be used to evaluate the substantive quality of national choices.[29]

The principles used to derive unique solutions of objective games are the following:

1 Identify the dominant strategies (if any) of all the players in the game. If a player has a unique dominant strategy, elimi-nate all outcomes associated with the dominated strategies of that player from further consideration. If a player does not have a dominant strategy, check if one of the strategies of this player is dominated by one of the other strategies. Eliminate all the outcomes associated with dominated strategies from further consideration.

2 For players without a dominant strategy, check if there exists a unique admissible strategy, that is, a dominant strategy assuming that those players with unique dominant strategies would use them. If a player does not have a unique admissible strategy, check if one or more of its strategies becomes inadmissible given the elimination of the dominated strategies of the other players. Once this has been done, reduce the game further by elimimating all inadmissible strategies of players without unique dominant strategies.

3 Continue the reduction of the game by repeating step number 2 until either of the following results obtains. (1) You are left with a single outcome. If that is the case, then this outcome is the theoretical outcome of the game and the optimal decisions of the players consist of the strategies which give rise to this outcome. (2) If you are left with more than one outcome, determine the maximin strategies of all players without a dominant or unique admissible strategy. The outcome associ-ated with these strategies is the unique solution of the game.[30]

4 In games where no players can eliminate dominated strate-

---

[29] The theoretical outcome of games is what Rapoport, Guyer, and Gordon (1976: 17–19) call the *natural outcome* in ordinal 2×2 games. I use a different label because this concept is extended in the present analysis to include games with a larger array of outcomes.

[30] It should be noted that these steps follow Farquharson's (1969) model of sophisti-cated voting, with the modification of usage of maximin principles in indeterminate games. This modification is required for creating determinancy in situations wherein the original Farquharson model does not produce a unique outcome.

gies, simply find the unique outcome associated with the maximin strategies of all players.

Note that this procedure does not necessarily produce solutions which are either equilibrium outcomes or Pareto-efficient ones. In addition, it rules out solutions associated with mixed strategies. However, for the purpose of aggregating national decisions to international outcomes we are not interested in any of these criteria. Rather, the central concern here is to identify what could theoretically be expected had actors operated under ideal circumstances that involve full information and rationality. Because the notion of a theoretical outcome is designed to serve as a benchmark for the evaluation of the actual choices made by national players, we cannot develop criteria that are ambiguous in the sense that they do not yield unique outcomes, nor can we incorporate multiple criteria that might clash with one another in actual applications.

Seen in this light, the unique theoretical outcome of objective games represents a theoretically derived state of affairs that has the following properties. (*a*) It is independent of how states actually made their decisions. Such an outcome can be derived whether the decision making process of some players was analytic in nature and that of others was cybernetic or cognitive. The theoretical outcome of an objective game represents a *minimum substantive rationality* condition which is independent of the degree of procedural quality of empirical decision processes.[31] (*b*) If a game has a unique Nash-equilibrium in pure strategies, the theoretical outcome will *always* coincide with the equilibrium outcome. However, the theoretical outcome may not coincide with an equilibrium outcome if a game has more than one Nash-equilibrium. (For example, the theoretical outcome of the PD coincides with the unique non-cooperative Nash-equilibrium. However, in Chicken, the theoretical outcome is not one of the Nash-equilibria, rather, it is the mutual cooperative outcome.) (*c*) The theoretical outcomes of objective games are not necessarily the maximum actors can get. In fact, in some games, the payoff derived by some of the players might be their worst. For example, the theoretical outcome of game 4 above is outcome a_3, b_3 which is a Pareto-inferior Nash-equilibrium (and is obtained because both players are assumed to use their maximin strategies). In game 5, the theoretical outcome of the game is outcome number 3 in which the 10 players with preference order $b > c > a$ and the 3 players with preference order $c > b > a$ get their worst outcome. Likewise, in game 7, the

---

[31] The word *minimum* is designed to take care of the fact that this outcome might be neither a Nash-equilibrium, nor a Pareto-efficient outcome.

theoretical outcome a_2, b_2 is one in which player A gets its worst payoff.

Before we go any further in the analysis, some possible objections to this definition of theoretical outcomes must be addressed. Probably the most powerful objection is that this kind of outcome has built-in paradoxical features. If such an outcome is predicated on a set of assumptions which stipulates seemingly optimal choices under seemingly ideal conditions (such as full information) and yet might entail the worst possible payoff to some or all of the players, then it is theoretically and empirically possible that players who make seemingly suboptimal choices under less-than ideal conditions might wind up with better payoffs. Another objection is that in games with multiple Nash-equilibria, the theoretical outcome tends to be the one which is Pareto-inferior. Finally, the objection to Curnot-rationality raised with respect to Nash-equilibria applies here as well. While these objections raise important issues, a solution concept which is both general (that is, applies to both zero-sum and non-constant sum games and to cooperative and non-cooperative ones), unique, and involves only pure-strategy choices must pay a theoretical price. The price is giving up the stability constraint and the Pareto-efficiency criterion. Paradoxical features are already part and parcel of more traditional game-theoretic ideas and one cannot single out a solution concept which has no pretension of resolving paradoxes that are not resolved by other solution concepts as well.

The focus of this approach on a decision perspective is due to the professed aim of creating a benchmark for the evaluation of actual national choices in terms of the outcomes they yield. The fact that actual outcomes may afford players with higher payoffs than theoretical outcomes is explored in greater detail below.

8.4.3 Defining and characterizing subjective games

The notion of subjective games is predicated on the way each actor perceives and evaluates its environment. A subjective game consists of national perceptions of: (*a*) the other players which are relevant for the analysis of a given strategic configuration, (*b*) the alternatives available to oneself as well as the alternatives available to other players, (*c*) the preference ordering of the outcomes that result from intersecting the alternatives of all relevant players by the focal player, (*d*) the attribution of preference orderings of outcomes to other players, (*e*) the attribution of choice principles to other players, and (*f*) the selection of a strategy. In a nutshell, this definition is, in fact, a

423

recapitulation of the decisional stages discussed in the first part of the book, modified to allow for choice under conditions of inter-dependence. In this context it is appropriate to discuss national choices in unitary-actor terms because all the elements of subjective games represent results of group decision processes. As we have seen in the case study of the 1973 crisis, to derive subjective games it is necessary to enter the national decision making processes. Because game theory has no way of telling us how the preferences of players are generated, the decision analytic focus in the first part of the book is indispensable for understanding how national choices are aggregated into international outcomes.

The characterization and evaluation of subjective games involves a systematic comparison to objective ones. To perform such a comparison, we must consider two dimensions along which subjective games may differ from objective ones. The first dimension concerns the structure of the games, the second refers to their content. The structure of objective and subjective games is defined operationally as the number of possible outcomes they contain. (Recall that the number of possible outcomes is a product of the number of alternatives available to each of the players.) The content of games is given by the distribution of preferences over these outcomes. In the comparison between subjective and objective games, the content dimension is restricted to the distribution of preferences over the joint subset of outcomes of the objective and subjective games.

Structural comparison of subjective and objective games. The structural comparison of objective and subjective games is done by specifying the two matrices *without* filling their cells with preferences. There are several types of structural relationships between objective and subjective games. These are depicted in figure 8.12.

The first case depicts a situation wherein the structure of the subjective game matrix is identical to the objective game matrix. This implies that a decision making unit has correctly identified the number and identity of all other players, and has attributed to each and every other player precisely the same alternatives that the other player had attributed to itself. This does not imply that the subjective game is completely identical to the objective one: a state can still misperceive the preference ranking of outcomes by other players. In the 1973 case, Israeli decision makers perceived correctly the identity of other players and the alternatives available to them, but they misperceived the preference ordering of outcomes of their opponents.[32]

---

[32] When game theorists discuss games of incomplete information they normally refer to games of this type, i.e., cases wherein each player knows the number, and identity of

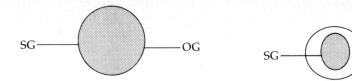

1. Correct identification

2. Under-identification

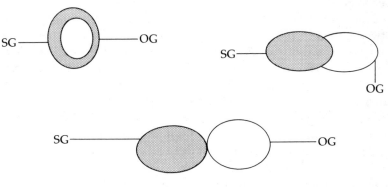

3. Over identification

4. Partial identification

5. Non-identification

Figure 8.12 A structural comparison of objective (OG) and subjective (SG) games

Case number two describes under-identification of an objective game. This refers to a subjective national analysis of a strategic configuration which is more simplistic than reality. Under-identification may be due to one or both of the following errors. First, a player underestimates the number of relevant players in the particular game. For example, the American view of the arms race between the superpowers might be a vast oversimplification of the actual problem insofar as Soviet armament policies are seen in strictly bilateral terms. It is quite possible that the Chinese are an important actor in the game of armament: that both the Soviets and Chinese see the game as a three-person game (Hsiung, 1985). Second, under-identification may result from attributing to one or some of the players fewer alternatives

the alternatives available to all other players, but has no way of knowing for sure their distribution of preferences over the correctly identified outcomes. Hypergame analysis (Fraser and Hippel, 1984: 53–74), is probably the first attempt at modeling structural misperception.

425

than they actually have. Young's (1968) analysis of crisis management illustrates this point. He argued that actors in international crises attempt to impose on the opponent a choice between giving in and disastrous escalation. Each actor wishes to provide the other with "the last clear chance" (Schelling, 1966) to avoid escalation. In such cases it is possible to underestimate the opponent's flexibility of action. The opponent might find a way out of the dilemma by developing an intermediate alternative which places the ball back into the initiator's court. This is what Young called "the initiative that forces the opponent to initiate." The American airlift to Berlin in 1948–1949 is used to illustrate this case. The Soviets thought that the US response to the blockade of West Berlin would involve an uncomfortable choice between accepting the Soviet *fait accompli* or initiating a major war. However, the range of actual alternatives available to the US was wider than that perceived by the Soviet leadership. In either case (underestimation of the number of players or underestimation of the number of alternatives available to the correctly identified players), the subjective game matrix is a proper subset of the objective game matrix: All of the outcomes in the subjective game are also outcomes in the objective game, but not all outcomes in the objective game are outcomes in the subjective game.

Over-identification refers both to perceiving other states to be actively involved in certain strategic configurations when they are actually not (the conviction of US decision makers that the Soviet Union and Communist China were behind the North Korean attack on the South in 1950 might be a case in point), and to the attribution of more alternatives to other states than they actually have. Jervis (1976) argued that decision makers tend to think that their opponents have more options than they themselves do. If that is the case, then over-identified subjective games should be fairly common in international politics. Over-identified subjective games are a superset of the objective games: they include all the outcomes of the objective game but also some outcomes which are not part of reality.

Type 4 is a case of a partially correct identification. Decision makers perceive correctly some of the outcomes of the objective game, miss some outcomes of the objective game, and identify some outcomes that are not part of the objective game. This type is represented by a partial overlap between the two games as well as by some non-overlap. Finally, a generally uncommon type of misperception is the one described by the fifth type of relationship (actually, a non-relationship) as non-identification. In this case, none of the outcomes identified by decision makers in their assessment of the situation is part of the objective game. This happens when decision makers completely err in identifying the alternatives available to other players.

Set notation will be used to assess the type and degree of structural misperception. Denote the set of outcomes of the subjective game as **SG** and the set of outcomes of the objective game by **OG**. Next, denote all outcomes that are elements in **SG** but not of **OG** as $\mathbf{SG} \cap \overline{\mathbf{OG}}$ and the number of these outcomes by the letter a. The set of outcomes that are elements of both the subjective game and the objective game is denoted by $\mathbf{SG} \cap \mathbf{OG}$ and the number of these outcomes is given by the letter b. Finally, the set of outcomes that is part of the objective game but not of the subjective one is given by $\overline{\mathbf{SG}} \cap \mathbf{OG}$ and the number of such outcomes is given by c. The proposed measure of structural identification is given by[33]

$$SI = \frac{(a+1)b}{a+b+c} - abc$$

The properties of this measure are as follows:

1. $SI = 0$ iff $b = 0$. This means that, irrespective of the extent to which a subjective assessment of reality is structurally complex, if such an assessment has nothing in common with objective reality, the measure of structural identification yields a value of zero. (This is the case of non-identification.)

2. $0 < SI < 1$ iff $a = 0$ and b, $c > 1$. This describes a case of under-identification of the objective game. In this case, the structural identification index approaches unity as the number of outcomes that are common to both games approaches the number of outcomes of the objective game (that is, as b increases and c decreases).

3. $SI = 1$ iff $a = c = 0$ and $b > 1$. This is the case of correct identification. All the outcomes of the objective game, and only those outcomes, are also the outcomes of the subjective game.

4. $SI > 1$ iff $c = 0$ and a, $b > 1$. This is the case of over-identification where the objective game is a proper subset of the subjective game. Again, this index will approach one as b increases and a decreases.

5. $SI < 0$ iff a, b, $c \neq 0$. Partial identification is always given by a negative number. The primary reason for that is to distinguish this case of structural misperception from all the other cases. Again, the degree of misperception of this sort will decline (that is, SI will approach zero as a declines and b increases) but

[33] I wish to thank Gary King for his help on the development of this index.

the relative size of these sets will determine whether decreasing misperception (denoted by the increase of b) tends toward under-identification, over-identification, or correct identification.

The deviation of the structural identification index from unity in either direction represents therefore a discrepancy between subjective perceptions of reality by national decision makers and the "true" or inter-subjective features of a strategic configuration. The type of deviation represents the nature of structural misperception. The absolute difference between SI and one represents the magnitude of structural misperception. The direction of this deviation represents the type of relationship between subjective and objective games.

Content-based comparison between subjective and objective games. A state can correctly identify the structural aspects of the objective game and still have a completely distorted view of reality. This happens when decision makers misjudge the preference ordering of outcomes by other players. Content-based comparisons between subjective and objective games are done in terms of the degree of fit between the preferences that one player attributes to other players and the preferences that other players attribute to themselves. Since one cannot ascertain with a sufficient degree of reliability how decision makers assess the preferences of other players over outcomes that were not identified, the content-based comparison of attributed and actual preferences must be done only on the set of outcomes which are elements of both the subjective game and the objective one (i.e., on the outcomes of the set $\mathbf{SG} \cap \mathbf{OG}$).

This restriction creates some difficulties as not all outcomes of the objective game matrix will be used in such a comparison. However, these difficulties arise only when structural misperception is either of the under-identification variety or of the partial identification one. Under non-identification, a content-based comparison of subjective and objective games is meaningless. There is nothing to compare because these games have nothing in common. In cases of perfect identification, such a comparison is both natural and fully reliable because we will have good information about the attribution of preferences to other players over all outcomes of the objective game. Finally, in cases of over-identification, a simple procedure allows reliable transformation of the preferences attributed to other players in a manner that restricts the comparison only to the subset of outcomes in the subjective game that also constitutes the outcomes of the objective game. In general, a content-based comparison of subjective and objective games requires the following steps.

1 Determine the subjective and objective games. Create a subgame for relevant comparison consisting of the outcomes that are common to both games.

2 Create a matrix of order $o \times (2n-2)$ where rows represent the o outcomes of the subgame and columns represent, respectively, the preferences attributed by player i to player j and the preferences that player j attributes to itself. In games with n players each comparison will be done over $n-1$ pairs of preference sets (excluding the preferences a player attributes to itself).

3 For each pair of preference sets i, j compute the discrepancy between attributed preferences and actual ones using the following measure:

$$PSD_{ij} = 1 - \frac{3 \sum_{k=1}^{o} (r_i^k - r_j^k)^2}{o(o^2 - 1)}$$

PSD_{ij} is a measure of pairwise substantive discrepancy between the preferences attributed by player i to player j, o is the total number of outcomes which are elements of **DG ∩ OG** (this is the number b in the structural comparison of games) and r_i^k, r_j^k are, respectively, the rank that player i attributes to player's j evaluation of outcome k and the actual rank that player j assigns to that outcome. (These ranks are normalized such that $1 \leq r_i^k, r_j^k \leq o$, with indifferences indicated by the midpoint of adjacent ranks.) The measure of pairwise substantive discrepancy varies between zero (when the preferences attributed by player i to player j over the o commonly identified outcomes are the same as those that player j attributes to itself) and one (when the ranking attributed by player i to player j is the precise opposite of the ranking assigned by j to the various outcomes).[34]

4 Compute the total substantive discrepancy between the subjective game of player i and the objective one by

$$TSD_i = \sum_{j \neq i} PSD_{ij}$$

It is possible – but not recommended – to measure average substantive discrepancy by dividing the total substantive discrepancy index by $n-1$. Average substantive discrepancy might provide a useful stan-

---

[34] Note that this measure is the complement of the measure of tradeoff complexity with $m = 2$ value dimensions and n outcomes. See chapter 6 for details on the derivation of this index.

dard for comparative analysis of perceptions of strategic configurations while controlling for the number of players involved. The problem with this measure is that it is precisely the increase in the number of players that makes substantive misperceptions of preferences more likely, and this is somewhat obscured by averaging out.[35]

So far it was assumed that the array of outcomes in the subjective game is the same as that of the objective game. Substantive discrepancy was therefore measured over a perfectly identified set of outcomes (which can only be true in cases of correct structural identification). In other cases, attributed preferences have to be adjusted so that they would refer only to those outcomes of the objective game that were correctly identified. This is done by looking at the preferences that each actor assigns to the others on those outcomes that were correctly identified and normalizing them by assigning the highest-ranked outcome of the correctly identified subset a rank of o, the lowest-ranked outcome a rank of 1, and all other outcomes intermediate ranks in between while preserving their order. For example, consider a case of structural over-identification in a two-person game. Player i attributed to player j four alternatives and to himself only two whereas player j attributes two alternatives to each. (I am assuming that the four outcomes that were identified jointly by these two players are a result of correct identification of two alternatives for each of the two players.) From the perspective of player i, the subjective game is over-identified. As a result, i attributes to j a preference ordering over eight outcomes whereas j defines its preferences over only four outcomes. To conduct a substantive discrepancy analysis, we must normalize the preferences attributed by player i to player j over the four commonly identified outcomes. Suppose that i's perception of j's preferences over the eight outcomes is 1, 2, 3, . . ., 8 over outcomes 1 to 8, respectively. Suppose that the commonly identified outcomes are only 3, 4 and 7, 8. Normalization is done simply by changing the ranks of these outcomes in i's subjective subgame from 3, 4, 7, 8 to 1, 2, 3, 4, respectively.

Note that the kind of information required for the comparisons between subjective games and objective ones is quite minimal. The feasibility of structural and content comparisons is greatly enhanced by the fact that they rely strictly on nominal-level identification and on ordinal-level ranking of outcomes. Information on cardinal utilities would be useful and applicable to the framework discussed above but is not necessary. Hence, the empirical potential of this approach is

[35] It should be noted that total substantive discrepancy varies between zero and $n-1$ whereas average substantive discrepancy varies between zero and one.

considerable. However, the empirical feasibility of such an approach does not imply that it is useful. The question remains what could be done with this line of inquiry that cannot possibly be done through less rigorous lines of inquiry or through using game-theoretic analysis of international outcomes under the assumptions of correct perception of outcomes and full information about actors' preferences. To respond to such a challenge, let us examine the Agadir crisis of 1911 as a case study of misperceptions and their consequences.

8.4.4 Structural and substantive misperceptions in the 1911 Agadir crisis

The Agadir (or second Moroccan) crisis was in some ways a replay of the first Moroccan crisis involving French and German maneuvers for control over an unstable Morocco. The French tried to establish their hold over Morocco while Germany attempted to frustrate these efforts, and – at a later point – to extract territorial concessions in the Congo in exchange for recognition of the French role in Morocco. The crisis also involved Great Britain and Austria-Hungary, the allies of the two primary antagonists. The crisis broke out when, following internal unrest in the Moroccan capital Fez, the French sent troops under the pretext of protecting the life of French citizens. The Germans, who interpreted this move correctly as a French attempt to finalize the colonization of Morocco, sent their gunboat *Panther* to Fez as a signal of commitment to the independence of Morocco. The British intervention on the side of France brought the crisis to the threshold of war. The Austro-Hungarian Kaiser indicated to the Germans that he did not consider the alliance with Germany to cover German imperialistic interests in Africa, suggesting that Austria-Hungary would not support Germany in the event of war. After a summer of intense bargaining, the crisis was finally resolved through an agreement that gave France complete control over Morocco, and the Germans some territorial concessions in the French Congo with access to the sea.[36] This crisis was divided into three essential phases: the opening phase (during the period of April–May 1911) which involved the dispatch of French troops to Fez and the visit of the *Panther*, the bargaining phase (of June–July 1911) during which the French–German talks were stalemated and the British stepped in, and the resolution phase (August 1911) during which the agreement

---

[36] For detailed historical accounts of this crisis, see Barlow (1940) and Williamson (1969). Snyder and Diesing's (1977) analysis of the bargaining tactics of the parties during this crisis serves as a primary source for the following analysis.

431

Actor	Alternative							
France	Stand firm				Concede			
Germany	Stand firm		Concede		Stand firm		Concede	
Great Britain	SF	NSF	SF	NSF	SF	NSF	SF	NSF
Austria-Hungary	SG NSG	SG NSG	SG NSG	SG NSG	SG NSG	SG NSG	SG NSG	SG NSG
Outcome	1 2	3 4	5 6	7 8	9 10	11 12	13 14	15 16

Great Britain's alternatives are denoted by: SF = Support France, and NSF = Don't support France.
The Austro-Hungarian alternatives are: SG = Support Germany, and NSG = Don't support Germany.

Figure 8.13 Outcome matrix of the 1911 Agadir crisis

was finalized. The analysis of the objective game is restricted to the first stage of the crisis.

The objective game. The game consists of four players: France, Germany, Great Britain, and Austria-Hungary. Each player had two alternatives. France's and Germany's alternatives were to stand firm (insist on their respective demands) or concede (accept some or all of the opponent's demands). Britain's and Austria-Hungary's alternatives were to support their respective allies or refrain from doing so. The game matrix consists therefore of 16 possible outcomes. It is depicted in figure 8.13. The content of these outcomes and the payoffs for each of the players are given in table 8.3.

The theoretical outcome of this game is column six which represents a German defeat. This outcome is obtained because Great Britain had a dominant strategy of supporting France. France, assuming British suppport, had a unique admissible strategy of standing firm. Austria-Hungary's unique admissible strategy, given British support of France and France's unique admissible strategy of standing firm, was not to support Germany. Finally, Germany's choice between a war against France and Great Britain and without Austro-Hungarian aid and concession was to select the latter strategy. This interpretation of the outcome differs from Snyder and Diesing's (1977: 90–92) view of the outcome as a compromise (represented by outcome number 14 in figure 8.13), the agreement between France and Germany is not seen as a compromise. For one thing, the agreement gave France complete control over Morocco. Moreover, Germany's gains in the French Congo were minor. They were given to them more as a face-saving charity than as a reflection of the German bargaining power. The

432

Table 8.3. *Outcomes and payoffs in the 1911 Agadir crisis (Objective Game)*

Outcome number	Substantive meaning	Payoffs for			
		Fr	Ger	GB	AH
1	General war	5	4	4	1
2	War without AH	8	1	8	6
3	War without GB	7	8	3	5
4	Bilateral war Fr–Ger	3	6	6	8
5	Ger and AH humiliation	15	3	15	3
6	Ger humiliation	16	2	16	4
7	Fr victory; weakening of Fr–GB alliance	11	7	9	7
8	Fr victory; weakening of Ger–AH alliance	12	5	11	2
9	Ger victory	2	14	7	14
10	Ger victory; weakening of Ger–AH alliance	6	13	5	9
11	Ger victory; weakening of Fr–GB alliance	1	16	1	16
12	Ger victory; weakening of both alliances	4	15	2	10
13	Compromise	13	10	13	12
14	Compromise; weakening of Ger–AH alliance	14	9	14	11
15	Compromise; weakening of Fr–GB alliance	9	12	10	15
16	Compromise; weakening of both alliances	10	11	12	13

Outcomes are numbered as in figure 8.13.
Fr = France; Ger = Germany; GB = Great Britain; AH = Austria–Hungary.
Ranking of outcomes is from 16 = best to 1 = worst.

current interpretation of the crisis outcome in the objective game yields a theoretical outcome which coincides with the actual outcome of the crisis.[37]

The subjective games of the four participants suggest that none of the actors made noticeable structural misperceptions. Each state understood who was involved and what were the alternatives available to the various actors. France was aware that its actions in Morocco would stir German outrage. These actions had the same effect on the Germans in 1905. The French also knew that Germany's active challenge would put Great Britain and Austria-Hungary on the horns of a dilemma concerning military and diplomatic support for their

[37] Snyder and Diesing's interpretation of the Agadir crisis of 1911 as a two-person PD suggests that they have a problem of interpreting the lack of fit between the theoretical outcome of their game and the actual outcome of the crisis. In our case, there exists a similar problem if the game is viewed as a two-person French–German crisis. Such a game (consisting of the payoffs of the two states in columns 4, 8, 12, and 16) yields a French defeat, which is obviously different from what had actually happened. However, the British payoff structure is a key to the theoretical outcome of the crisis, as Snyder and Diesing themselves (1977: 544) indicate.

Table 8.4. *The Agadir crisis from the French perspective*

| Outcome number | Perceived versus actual preferences | | | | | | |
	Fr–Fr	Fr–Ger	Ger–Ger	Fr–GB	GB–GB	Fr–AH	AH–AH
1	5	5	4	4	4	2	1
2	8	2	1	8	8	6	6
3	7	8	8	3	3	5	5
4	3	7	6	6	6	3	8
5	15	3	3	15	15	7	3
6	16	1	2	16	16	4	4
7	11	6	7	9	9	8	7
8	12	4	5	11	11	1	2
9	2	14	14	7	7	13	14
10	6	13	13	5	5	10	9
11	1	16	16	1	1	16	16
12	4	15	15	2	2	9	10
13	13	10	10	13	13	12	12
14	14	9	9	14	14	11	11
15	9	12	12	10	10	15	15
16	10	11	11	12	12	14	13

Fr = France; Ger = Germany; GB = Great Britain; AH = Austria–Hungary.
Fr–XX = France's perception of nation's XX preferences (XX = Germany, Great Britain, Austria–Hungary.)
XX–XXX = actual preferences of nation XX.
Ranking of outcomes is from 16 = best to 1 = worst.

$$PSD_{f-ger} = \frac{6}{1360} = 0.004; \quad PSD_{f-gb} = 0; \quad PSD_{f-ah} = \frac{48}{1360} = 0.035.$$

$TCD_f = 0.039.$

allies. The same applied to the other actors' perceptions of the situation. Thus the comparison between the subjective games and the objective one suggests a case of correct structural identification of the problem. Where some (but not all of) these states erred was in the attribution of preferences to the other states over the available outcomes. I will restrict the presentation of subjective games to those of France, Germany, and Great Britain. The Austro-Hungarian decision makers seem to have perceived correctly the actual preferences of the players, hence their view of the crisis conforms to that given in the objective game. Let us look first at the crisis from the French perspective. This is given in table 8.4.

France's decision makers made some, but fairly minor, misperceptions in terms of the preferences they attributed to the other players. These misperceptions, however, caused the French to develop a very pessimistic outlook of the crisis. Germany was seen to have a dominant strategy of standing firm, which the Germans did not actually have. The key to this conclusion was the French view that the Germans preferred war to yielding even if Great Britain supported France and Austria-Hungary withheld its support from its ally. Moreover, French decision makers, correctly perceiving British position in the crisis, expected that the Austrians would indeed withhold their support from the Germans, even though Austria-Hungary's preferences were perceived less accurately than those of Germany. The outcome the French expected was a war between themselves and the British, on the one hand, and an isolated Germany, on the other. Indeed, war preparations were considerable in France, and the probability of war was judged to be high.

From the British perspective, the situation was fairly similar. The British interpreted German preferences to be more competitive than they actually were, though their perception of the French and Austrian preferences were basically accurate. Thus, there is no need to present the British subjective game matrix separately. The expected outcome – seen from the west side of the channel – was a war in which they would have to fight alongside the French against the Germans. Both British and French misperceptions yielded behavior that did not, in fact, differ from their optimal behavior. Yet, due to their misperception of the German preferences, both the British and the French's expected outcome was 2 rather than outcome 7. The same applies to the Austro-Hungarian decision to withhold support from Germany.[38] The difference between the theoretical outcome and the actual outcome of the crisis resides in Germany's reduction of its demands during the course of the crisis. Indeed, with the wisdom of hindsight, it could be plausibly argued that Germany would have been better off had it stayed out of the Moroccan mess. To explain German behavior, we must examine the subjective German crisis game. This is done in table 8.5.

The German assessment of the preferences and expected behavior of the other players differed quite significantly from the objective game. The major error of preference attribution was the failure of Germany to see the dominant strategy of Great Britain and the attribution of a dominant strategy to the Austro-Hungarians. From the German perspective, the Austrians were seen to have a dominant strategy of supporting their allies. Neither the British nor the French were

---

[38] Maoz (1984a) used the 1911 Agadir crisis as a false-alarm case in which the outcome of the crisis turned out to be more peaceful than was the expectation of the various decision makers involved.

Table 8.5. *The Agadir crisis from the German perspective*

Outcome number	Perceived versus actual preferences						
	Ger–Ger	Ger–Fr	Fr–Fr	Ger–GB	GB–GB	Ger–AH	AH–AH
1	4	4	5	1	4	2	1
2	1	8	8	3	8	1	6
3	8	7	7	6	3	5	5
4	6	2	3	4	6	4	8
5	3	15	15	15	15	6	3
6	2	16	16	16	16	3	4
7	7	10	11	9	9	8	7
8	5	9	12	10	11	7	2
9	14	3	2	2	7	10	14
10	13	5	6	7	5	9	9
11	16	1	1	5	1	16	16
12	15	6	4	8	2	11	10
13	10	14	13	13	13	13	12
14	9	13	14	14	14	12	11
15	12	12	9	11	10	15	15
16	11	11	10	12	12	14	13

Fr = France; Ger = Germany; GB = Great Britain; AH = Austria–Hungary.
Ger–XX = Germany's perception of nation's XX preferences (XX = France, Great Britain, Austria–Hungary.)
XX–XXX = actual preferences of nation XX.
Ranking of outcomes is from 16 = best to 1 = worst.

$$PSD_{f-ger} = \frac{30}{1360} = 0.022; \quad PSD_{ger-gb} = \frac{134}{1360} = 0.10; \quad PSD_{ger-ah} = \frac{98}{1360} = 0.07.$$

$$TCD_{ger} = 0.193.$$

perceived as having a dominant strategy. Given the perceived dominant strategy of the Austrians, German decision makers thought that Germany had a unique admissible strategy of standing firm, and the British were seen to have a unique admissible strategy of witholding their support from the French. The French had, according to this view, a unique admissible strategy of standing firm. Thus, the expected outcome from the German perspective was a war between Germany and France with the British cheering on the sidelines. Once the British government indicated quite bluntly that Great Britain intended to stand by its ally, and the Austro-Hungarian government expressed its intention to stay out of the confrontation, the Germans quickly revised their estimates and entered into an agreement that was just short of a total humiliation.

The Agadir crisis demonstrates certain interesting aspects concerning the manner by which national choice processes are transformed into actual international outcomes. The first, and most important, point is that when the outcomes of national choices depend on the choices of other states, the ability of decision makers to make correct judgments about the alternatives available to other states and their preferences over the possible outcomes is perhaps the most significant factor determining whether the expectations underlying a certain decision will be realized. Misperceptions of available alternatives and of opponents' and allies' preferences may result in adoption of policies that are counterproductive to their initiator. This is hardly a surprising conclusion. What is less obvious, however, is that misperception is not always damaging. In some cases, misperception of preferences might be minimal in the sense that an actor might still be able to make correct behavioral predictions even if it failed to accurately perceive other players' preferences. Both France and Great Britain misperceived to some degree the preferences of Germany and Austro-Hungary. This misperception caused them to overestimate the likelihood of war, but it did not result in their selection of suboptimal strategies. In fact, both states benefited from the more serious German misperceptions.

Ironically, Austria-Hungary which accurately perceived the structure of the strategic problem and made the "right" decision did not benefit a great deal from the outcome. Rather, the outcome of the game introduced some strain into the Austrian–German alliance. But could the Hapsburgs have done better by choosing to support Germany? The answer is, probably not. Because the outcome of the objective game (which was also the historical outcome of the crisis) is a Nash-equilibrium, a unilateral choice shift by the Austrians would have simply harmed them as no other player would have altered its strategy choice. Given the structure of the Austro-Hungarian choice problem, the decision makers indeed did the "best under the circumstances," and therefore got no more and no less than what they had expected to get. Granted, what they expected to get was not very much; they would have preferred to support Germany if they had thought that it would get its way. Yet they were aware that by doing that they would only increase the risks of war over an issue to which they attached little importance.

Another important point about the implications of misperceptions for the outcomes of interdependent choice processes is that the complexity of international processes – particularly those involving multiple actors – is such that almost everybody is bound to make errors of judgment and attribution at some point or another. Because of the intrinsic interdependence of choice problems, the misperceptions of one player affect not only what it derives for itself, but also what other players get, even if their choices are also based on some degree of misperception. The implication is that it is the *relative* rather than the *absolute* degree of misperception that affects the degree of correspondence between the expected outcome of a decision and the actual outcomes. Actors whose misperceptions are less severe than those of other actors might end up benefiting from the errors of their opponent even if their choices were less than optimal.

Finally, it must be emphasized that misperceptions – however important – are not an exclusive determinant of deficient decisional outcomes. In both cases examined in this section it seemed that actors that made serious errors of judgment of other actors' preferences could have secured better outcomes for themselves had they made better behavioral inferences on the basis of the information they had (i.e., on the basis of their subjective views of the game). The problem was that errors of judgment were confounded with errors of inference, and that it was the latter type of error which was primarily responsible for the disastrous outcomes. Had Israel acted on the basis of a maximin strategy on October 4, 1973, it would have been considerably less vulnerable to the Egyptian–Syrian attack, although it was doubtful that it could have prevented it. In many cases, actors' misperceptions may not be as severe as to lead them to assume that their opponents have a dominant strategy which is different from their actual dominant (or unique admissible) strategies. Actors might err in assuming that they can capitalize on what is seen to be the use of a maximin strategy by their opponents. However, such an assumption may be self-defeating in two respects.

First, since the business of attributing preferences and intentions to other actors is fraught with possibilities of error, one must be sensitive to the possibility (indeed, probability) of miscalculation. Although the use of a maximin strategy might be excessively conservative in some cases, and might lead to significant problems in others (Maoz, 1989), its virtue is that it secures a minimum payoff whatever the opponent does. Hence this principle might serve as a guard against misperception: when the analysis of the situation does not indicate a clear behavioral propensity of the opponent, prudent choice might well be one which follows the maximin principle. Second, because one does not know for sure whether the kind of game one thinks it is playing will be repeated, and – in fact – one doesn't really know whether it is actually playing the game one thinks it is playing, maximin principles might serve as a device for learning with minimum cost. Especially in international politics where an error might terminate the game altogether (think for example what happens in a nuclear Chicken game if each actor attempts to capitalize on the expectation of prudent behavior of the opponent), improving upon the maximin outcome as a result of information acquired from previous plays might not be as costly as recovering from a nuclear or conventional winter.

8.5 NATIONAL CHOICES AND INTERNATIONAL CONSEQUENCES: A MODEL

In this section I attempt to incorporate the ideas and concepts discussed above into a more coherent model of choice and consequences in settings characterized by intrinisic interdependence. The model of national choices and international outcomes addresses three funamental questions: (1) How do international outcomes emerge from a set of seemingly distinct national decisions? (2) How can these outcomes be used to evaluate the substantive quality of national choice processes? (3) What are the relationships between the content and structure of decision making processes within states and the outcomes of interdependent interstate interactions?

It should be clear by now that an international outcome is seen as an intersection of national decisions under conditions of interdependence. I am using the term *interdependence* objectively, that is, as an intrinsic attribute of international politics which exists whether or not individual actors perceive their choices to be affected by the choices of other states. The common conception of an international outcome is that of an event or an intersection of choices. It describes what the actors in a given strategic configuration have actually done. (Recall that this is not necessarily equivalent to what actors have decided to do, due to the problem of mis-implementation of national decisions.) In contrast to actual international outcomes, the model allows specification of *theoretical* outcomes that serve as a basis for the evaluation of national decisions. A theoretical outcome is simply the outcome of an objective game which is derived according to the procedure discussed above. It is the intersection of the choices that actors involved in a certain strategic configuration *should have made had they been rational and had they acted under conditions of full information, non-cooperation, simultaneous choice, and single-play of the objective game.*

Before we go on, two points about the nature of theoretical outcomes should be recapitulated. First, theoretical outcomes of objective games represent a state of the world that specifies what each of the involved actors could get had each acted to secure at least an acceptable minimum under the objective circumstances. Thus, actual outcomes may deviate from theoretical outcomes in either direction. An actual outcome may provide some (or all) of the actors involved a higher or lower payoff than the one they would have obtained in the theoretical outcome.

Second, theoretical outcomes represent single-shot consequences of decisions. If players are assumed to maximize an expected payoff which is the sum of payoffs they obtain over a long series of play of the same game, the theoretical outcome might be different from the one derived in this chapter. An actor might be better-off by behaving in a seemingly suboptimal manner at stage t of the process to maximize its long term payoff.[39] Moreover, even from a traditional game-theoretic perspective, theoretical outcomes may be unstable in the sense that they may not coincide with an equilibrium outcome of the game.

Yet, this notion of theoretical outcomes seems reasonable because there is no way of establishing *a priori* whether actors act to maximize long-term objectives as opposed to short-term ones. Nor is there any theoretical basis for the assumption that either subjective or objective games are the same over time, even if the actors involved in a strategic configuration remain fixed. Even if the assumptions underlying the derivation of objective outcomes are taken to be implausible, I would argue that any alternative perspective of international interactions under conditions of interdependence which emphasizes the dynamic and long-term aspects of international processes must rely on *this* set of assumptions as a baseline. A model which assumes that actors are using well-defined long-term strategies of international interactions must use the short-term conception of international outcomes as a naive model against which strategic interactions – if they exist – are to be compared and tested. Such a strategic conception of international processes, if empirically valid, should explain international processes at least as well as an *ad hoc* conception which relies on the assumptions of short-term calculations and variations in the structure and content of strategic configurations over time.

8.5.1 Aggregating national choices to international outcomes[40]

The model of interdependent choice attempts to account for the discrepancies between theoretical or expected outcomes and actual ones. It also uses the concept of theoretical international

---

[39] See Elster (1979) and Schelling (1984) for discussions of precommitments that illustrate this line of thinking about relationships between short-term and long-term rationality. Brams and Wittman's (1981) non-myopic stability concept is also a case in point.

[40] Some of the ideas in the following sections draw on Arthur Stein's (1982) analysis of the effects of misperceptions on international outcomes.

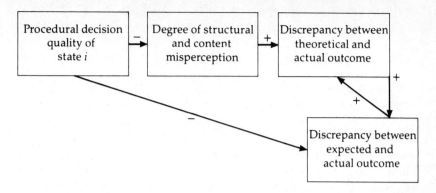

Figure 8.14 A model of national choices and international outcomes

outcomes as a benchmark for evaluating the substantive quality of national decisions. There are two levels at which one could evaluate national decisions in terms of their consequences (as opposed to procedural evaluations of foreign policy decisions, the focus of which is on the manner by which individuals and collectivities analyzed and solved problems). The first level provides an answer to the question: was a given decision made by a state the best it could have made under a given set of circumstances? The second level provides an answer to the question: was the actual outcome of a given national decision the same, better, or worse than the one expected by the people who made the decision? For the first question, a comparison between the subjective game and the objective game relates actual to optimal choices. Consequently, a substantive evaluation of foreign policy decisions becomes possible under this framework. The second question relates expected outcomes of national choices to the actual outcomes.

The essential ideas regarding the relationship between national choice processes and international consequences is depicted schematically in figure 8.14.

The most basic propositions of this model are as follows.

Proposition 1
The more analytic the decision process within states, the lower the level of structural and substantive misperception of the objective game.

Proposition 2
The more analytic the national decision making process, the better the fit between expected outcomes of a decision and actual outcomes. Stated differently, the more analytic the national decision process of a state, the more likely is the actual outcome of an interdependent interaction pleasantly to surprise decision makers than unpleasantly to surprise them.

> *Proposition 3*
> *The lower the level of structural or substantive misperception of the objective game, the lower the discrepancy between actual and theoretical outcomes.*

These propositions seem neither surprising nor terribly novel. They conform to the assumptions of most foreign policy decision theorists about the relationship between national choices and international consequences.[41] Yet, the model offers, for the first time, a systematic framework for an empirical assessment of these propositions. The analysis of subjective and objective games allows systematic measurement of types and magnitudes of misperceptions. It also offers a measure of discrepancy between: (a) theoretical outcomes and actual ones, and (b) expected outcomes and actual ones. Measures of substantive discrepancies between actual outcomes, on the one hand, and expected or theoretical outcomes, on the other hand, are developed below.

The actual outcome of a given international exchange is given empirically. To measure whether and to what extent this outcome differs from the theoretical outcome of the objective game, the payoffs of a state which are associated with each of these outcomes must be identified. Let r_t^i denote the preference rank assigned by state i to the theoretical outcome t, let r_a^i denote the preference rank assigned by state i to the actual outcome of the game, and let r_{min}^i, r_{max}^i denote, respectively, the preference rank assigned by state i to the least preferred outcome ($r_{min}^i \geqslant 1$) and the preference rank assigned by state i to the most preferred outcome ($r_{max}^i \leqslant o$, where o is the total number of outcomes of the objective game). The discrepancy between actual and theoretical outcomes of national decisions is given by

$$TD = \frac{r_a^i - r_t^i}{r_{max}^i - r_{min}^i}$$

where TD stands for theoretical outcome discrepancy. This measure varies from minus one to plus one. A negative score indicates a deficient decision, that is, a case where the actual outcome of a state's decision is worse than the theoretical outcome. A positive score indicates that the actual outcome of the game was better from the state's perspective than the theoretical one. As the TD score approaches zero the discrepancy between the actual outcome and the theoretical one is said to decline.

The expected outcome of a national decision is defined to be the

---

[41] See, for example, Brecher *et al.* (1969: 81); Jervis (1976); Janis and Mann (1977); George (1980); Herek, Janis, and Huth (1987).

442

outcome of the subjective game of that particular state. The preference rank assigned by state i to that outcome is r_e^i, and the discrepancy between expected and actual outcome is given by

$$ED = \frac{r_a^i - r_e^i}{r_{max}^i - r_{min}^i}$$

where ED denotes expected outcome discrepancy, and its mathematical properties are similar to the theoretical outcome discrepancy measure.

Propositions 1–3 suggest that the more analytic the state's decision process (here decision process is taken to be identical with collective choices within states), the more accurate will be the state's perception of the strategic configuration. This will be expressed in terms of low discrepancies between the structure and content of the state's subjective game and the objective one. In such cases, decision makers are apt to draw the "right" conclusion from their assessment of the situation, and their decisions are likely to reflect the best they could do under the circumstances. If the decision rules used by decision makers resemble the ones that lead to the derivation of the theoretical outcome of the objective game, then the preference rank assigned by decision makers to the actual outcome of the game can – by definition – be no lower than the preference ranking of the theoretical outcome or the expected one. Being "pleasantly surprised" in an interdependent choice situation implies that the actual outcome of the objective game is preferred to either the expected outcome, the theoretical outcome, or both.

In 1973, we had two national decision processes: the Egyptian decision process leading to the initiation of the 1973 war, and the Israeli decision process leading to the non-mobilization decision. A brief look at the tradeoff-complexity scores of the two decision processes suggests that the Egyptian decision process seemed far more complex (perhaps more analytic) than the Israeli one, Consequently, the Egyptian subjective game coincided with the objective game whereas the Israeli subjective game reflected a significant degree of substantive misperception. (The level of perceived substantive discrepancy for Israel is $PSD_{is-eg} = 0.333$.) The result was that Egypt was "pleasantly surprised" by the actual outcome of the game ($TD_{eg} = ED = (4 - 3)/3 = 0.333$). Israel's surprise, on the other hand, was far from pleasant ($TD_{is} = (1 - 3)/3 = -0.667$ and $ED_{is} = (1 - 4)/3 = -1$). The actual outcome of the game was worse than what Israel could have obtained had it acted in an optimal way and from what it had expected to derive from the game.

The Agadir crisis provides another illustration. France which had a

443

relatively low degree of total misperception obtained an actual outcome which was the same as the theoretical outcome of the objective game ($TD_{fr} = 0$) but was considerably higher than what it had expected ($ED_{fr} = (9 - 1)/15 = 0.533$). On the other hand, Germany had paid a heavy price for its misperception for in the course of the crisis it was forced to drastically alter its assessment of the problem and change its strategy. Consequently, the actual outcome of the crisis was valued by Germany less than the outcome it had expected to obtain at the beginning ($ED_{ger} = (9 - 15)/15 = -0.4$). This leads directly to the fourth proposition of the model.

> *Proposition 4*
> *The higher the degree of structural and substantive misperception of an actor relative to the misperceptions made by other actors, the more likely is this actor to obtain an actual outcome which is worse than the theoretical outcome of the objective game and than the expected outcome of the subjective game. Likewise, an actor whose relative degree of structural and substantive misperception is lower than those of other actors is more likely to obtain an actual outcome which is better than the theoretical or expected outcome*

It follows that the model of national choices and international outcomes provides an opportunity to conduct an assessment of the effects of misperceptions on decisional outcomes in relative rather than in absolute terms. This is hardly possible from a purely decision theoretic perspective. The idea behind proposition 4 is that misperception, like power, is both continuous and relative. The extent to which decision makers accomplish what they expected to or what they could have accomplished depends, therefore, on the extent to which their view of the environment in which they work is more or less accurate than the views of other actors. Contrary to decision-theoretic conceptions, the present model suggests that small errors of judgment and inference are not necessarily detrimental. The effects of such errors on decisional outcomes depend on whether these errors are more or less severe than similar errors made by other nations.

Propositions 1–4 must be qualified, however. Misperception does not always matter. The reason that we explored different types of misperception is that these types seem to have different effects on decisional outcomes. The following propositions specify expected relations between types of misperceptions and decisional outcomes. Propositions 5 and 6 deal with structural misperceptions and propositions 7 and 8 discuss the effects of substantive misperceptions on decisional outcomes.

Proposition 5
The relationship between structural misperceptions of objective games
and decisional outcomes is non-monotonic across types of structural
misperceptions and monotonic within types of structural mispercep-
tions. Each type of structural misperception is apt to have a different
effect on the nature of decisional outcomes. However, a high level of
structural misperception of a certain type would result in a more
severe discrepancy between expected or theoretical outcomes and
actual ones than a lesser misperception of the same type.

Proposition 5 suggests a severity ranking of structural misperceptions. The case of complete non-identification of the objective game is
obviously the most severe because it renders any analysis of substantive misperception practically impossible. Partial identification of
objective games results in more severe discrepancies between
expected or theoretical outcomes and actual ones than either over or
under-identification. Under-identification of objective games results
in more severe discrepancies between expected or theoretical outcomes and actual ones than over-identification of objective games.
Correct identification of objective games is most likely to be associated
with a good fit between the expected outcome and the theoretical
outcome and between the expected outcome of the subjective game
and the actual outcome.

Within each type of structural misperception there is a monotonic
association between the magnitude of misperception and the discrepancy between theoretical or expected outcomes and the actual ones.
For each type of structural misperception, as the *SI* score approaches
unity (correct identification), the discrepancy between theoretical or
expected outcomes and actual ones declines.

The logic underlying proposition 5 is fairly simple. Different types of
structural misperception are due to different types of deficiencies in
the national decision making process. There is a fundamental difference between seeing in a strategic configuration more (actors or
alternatives) than it actually entails and seeing only part of the
strategic configuration. The former tendency is a result of an excessively vigilant decision process, and is typically associated with a
relatively minor degree of substantive misperception of other states'
preferences. The latter tendency stems from over-simplification of the
decision problem which is typically associated with other errors of
attribution and inference: these will be expressed in terms of significantly high levels of substantive misperceptions. From this point it
follows that there should exist a relationship between the degree of
structural misperception and the degree of substantive misperception.

Proposition 6

a. *Under-identification and partial identification of the objective game are likely to be associated with attribution of a dominant strategy to other players who do not actually have one, or a tendency to attribute unique admissible strategies to players who do not have a dominant strategy.*

b. *Over-identification of objective games is likely to be associated with failure to identify actual dominant strategies of other players, rather than with attribution of dominant strategies to players who do not have one.*

c. *The lower the degree of structural misperception of objective games, the lower the degree of substantive misperception.*

Proposition 6 follows from the decision-theoretic analysis of the previous chapters rather than from the analysis of interdependent international outcomes in the present one. The more comprehensive the decision process within states, the more accurate is the analysis of the situation. Diagnosis and revision processes are key elements in national decisions. Both decisional stages entail assessing the identity of the actors involved in a situation, the alternatives available to those actors, and their "intentions" (in terms of game theory this is equivalent to attributing preferences to other actors over the array of perceived outcomes and inferring the expected choices of other actors among the alternatives available to them). If diagnosis and revision processes are comprehensive and unbiased, it is to be expected that both the structure and the content of the objective game would be correctly identified.[42]

Deviation from optimal diagnosis and from optimal revision normally entail some simplification of the objective situation. Prevailing definitions of the situation and information processing tend to yield under-identified objective games or partially identified ones rather than over-identified objective games. Hence, the degree of substantive misperception is likely to be high because actors see only a portion of the array of possible outcomes. Moreover, the uses of SOPs or analogies in processes of diagnosis reduce the number of alternatives

---

[42] Recall that analytic dianosis entails development and analysis of multiple definitions of the situation. This requires that individuals and collectivities analyze situations in terms of multiple actors, multiple alternatives available to each actor, and, perhaps, alternative preference structures of other actors over the array of identified outcomes. Likewise, analytic revision requires analysis of incoming information in terms of its degree of diagnosticity with respect to more than one hypothesis. This implies that revision of probability estimates in light of new information must be based on the attribution of more than one alternative or possibly more than one payoff structure to an opponent.

attributed to decision makers of other states as well as the likelihood that the preferences attributed by decision makers to other states are the same as the ones those states attribute to themselves. Because structural misperception is likely to yield substantive misperception, the process suggested by the propositions made thus far is as follows:

$$SI_i = f(PDQ_i)$$
$$TCD_i = f(PDQ_i,\ SI_i)$$
$$TD_i = f(PDQ_i,\ SI_i,\ TCD_i)$$
$$ED_i = f(PDQ_i,\ SI_i,\ TCD_i,\ TD_i)$$

where

PDQ = Procedural decision quality defined in terms of the specific path characterizing a national decision process.

SI = Structural identification of the objective game.

TCD = Total content discrepancy defined as the total sum of squared rank-differences between the preferences that an actor i attributes to another actor j over all outcomes of the objective game and the preferences attributed by actor j to itself.

TD = Theoretical discrepancy defined in terms of the relative difference in preferences between the actual international outcome and the theoretical outcome of the objective game.

ED = Expected outcome discrepancy defined as the relative difference in preferences between the actual international outcome and the outcome expected by national decision makers on the basis of the subjective national game.

In words, the more analytic the decision process within a given state, the lower the likelihood of substantive or structural misperception of the objective game and – controlling for the decision quality of other states – the higher the fit between the actual outcome and the theoretical one, as well as between the actual outcome and the expected one. But all these propositions discuss quantitative degrees of misperception. The distinction between types of misperception is limited to the structural comparison between the subjective and objective games. There may be different types of substantive misperceptions with special effects on the discrepancy between theoretical or expected outcomes and actual ones. These qualitative misperceptions are clouded by the quantitative assessment of substantive misperceptions. For example, the French misperception of German preferences in the Agadir crisis is more severe than is suggested by the quantitative score of the pairwise substantive misperception score in table 8.4. France attributed to Germany a dominant "Stand Firm" strategy when Germany's actual preferences did not support such an inference.

Table 8.6. *Macro-comparison of attributed and actual preferences*

Attributed decision rule To player j, ADR_{ij}	Decision rule of player j, ADR_{jj}					
	Dom_x	Dom_y	UAS_x	UAS_y	$Other_x$	$Other_y$
Dom_x	0	2	1	2	1	2
Dom_y	2	0	2	1	2	1
UAS_x	1	2	0	2	1	2
UAS_y	2	1	2	0	2	1
$Other_x$ (maximin)	1	2	1	2	0	2
$Other_y$ (maximin)	2	1	2	1	2	0

Dom = Dominant strategy; UAS = Unique (ultimately) Admissible Strategy; $Other$ = Other choice rule (normally, maximin).
x, y = any strategy choice attributed by player i to player j, or actually employed by player j. An entry having x in its row and x in its column means that actor i attributed to j a strategy which was actually selected by actor j. The same applies to an entry having y in its row and y in its column. On the other hand, an entry having x in its row and y in its column (or y in its row and x in its column) implies that the strategy attributed by player i to player j was different from the strategy that player j actually employed.
Numbers in cells represent types of substantive misperceptions with 0 = little or no misperception, 1 = misperception of decision rule but not of actual strategy choice, and 2 = misperception of strategy choice (with or without misperception of decision rule).

The quantitative index of substantive misperception is based on an outcome-by-outcome comparison of the preferences attributed by one actor to another actor and the preferences attributed by the other actor to itself. However, a macrolevel comparison of attributed and actual preferences is more likely to highlight the kind of general inferences that an actor might erroneously make due to either structural or substantive misperceptions. This kind of macro-comparison stems from the procedures developed in this chapter to find unique solutions to objective games, and combines structural and substantive misperceptions with errors in inferring decision rules of other players.

A case of correct perception entails a correct identification both of the structure of the objective game, of a high fit between the preferences attributed to other players over the various outcomes, and of correct attribution of strategy choices to other actors. If an actor can accomplish all these things in his or her internal decision process, then the actual outcome of the game for that actor cannot be worse (and might actually be better) than either the theoretical or expected outcome of the game. But this is unlikely to happen in most interdependent decision making cases in international politics. What might be more common is that actors do quite well (in the sense that the actual outcomes of their decisions would be at least as good or better than the expected or theoretical outcomes) even if their choices are based on some degree of misperception. Here we are interested in understanding those situations where errors do not matter a great deal as opposed to situations in which perceptual or attributional errors entail adverse consequences for decision makers.

Table 8.6 describes these situations. The diagonal entries in this matrix refer to cases where a state i attributes to state j a decision rule and a substantive strategy selection which are the same as those actually used by state j. Obviously, all cases of perfectly correct (structural and substantive) perception fall into this category. But this category might also contain cases involving minor misperceptions. For example, a state can make some substantive misperceptions of another state's preferences but still infer correctly how a state would select its strategy and what that strategy would be. A more serious type of misperception entails attributing to another actor a decision rule which is different from the one that he or she has actually employed. Such a misperception might have only marginal consequences for the focal state if the substantive strategy that state i attributes to state j is the same as that actually employed by j. (These cases are denoted by a score of 1 in table 8.6.) Finally, structural and substantive misperceptions of the objective game might have serious consequences if a state i attributes to state j both a decision rule and a substantive strategy which are different from the ones actually employed by state j. This is nicely illustrated by the Israeli calculus during the 1973 crisis and by the German calculus during the 1911 Agadir crisis. In both cases, these actors attributed to other actors choice rules and substantive strategies which were different from the ones actually employed by the latter. In both cases, these attribution errors stemmed directly from substantive misperceptions. And in both cases, these macro-misperceptions resulted in suboptimal choices and led to undesirable outcomes. These problems form the core of the next two propositions.

Proposition 7
The higher the degree of micro-level structural and substantive misperceptions, the higher the likelihood that a state would base its own behavior on flawed assumptions about how other actors choose and the strategies they would select. Thus, the higher the likelihood that the actual outcome of the game would differ from the expected outcome. Moreover, if such a state does not possess a dominant strategy, the actual outcome of the game will differ also from the theoretical outcome.

Proposition 8
A decision made by a state would still be theoretically optimal (that is,
it would coincide with the strategy choice of a state leading to the
theoretical outcome of the objective game) if a state has a dominant
strategy and uses it. In such a case, the extent to which a subjective
game misrepresents the objective game will have no bearing on the
theoretical outcome as it relates to that particular state. On the other
hand, there might be severe discrepancies between the actual outcome
of the game and the outcome this state thinks will occur (the expected
outcome).

Proposition 7 establishes the connection between microlevel and macrolevel misperceptions in interdependent settings. Because macrolevel misperceptions represent inferences about the behavior of the other actors on the basis of the structure and content of the subjective game, the higher the discrepancy between the subjective game and the objective game, the higher the likelihood that a state would act on the basis of flawed inferences. However, the extent to which these flawed inferences matter in the final analysis depends on the extent to which a national decision relies upon the choices attributed to other actors. If a state lacks a dominant strategy, then microlevel misperceptions would lead to flawed macrolevel inferences, and macrolevel inferences would lead to suboptimal choices, and to surprising consequences.[43] Yet, the possession of a dominant strategy by a state offsets the adverse impact of misperceptions and unwarranted inferences on its behavior. The reason is that a dominant strategy is independent of the behavior attributed to other actors, even if these attributed behaviors were wrong. A state using its dominant strategy can be seen to have done the best under the circumstances even if it misperceived the circumstances.

Proposition 9
Two primary factors affect the degree to which states misperceive the
objective strategic configuration and the extent to which behavior based

---

[43] Again, it must be pointed out that this conclusion should be viewed in relative rather than in absolute terms. Whether the actual outcome of the objective game is inferior (from the state's perspective) to the theoretical or expected one depends not only on the degree of micro-misperceptions and macro-inferences of the individual state, but also on the degree of misperception and inaccurate inference made by other states. It is quite possible that the degree of misperception or incorrect behavioral inferences made by one state is lower than that of other actors. In such cases, the former can actually benefit from the mistakes of others even if it made some mistakes of its own. For example, Sadat who perceived correctly the structure and content of the objective game, erred in attributing to Israel a maximin strategy of mobilization. However, the Israelis who attributed to Egypt a maximin strategy of no attack, made the wrong decision. Thus Sadat was pleasantly surprised by the actual outcome of the game and for the Israelis this outcome constituted a disaster.

on such misperceptions is suboptimal: one is the procedural quality of the national decision process (over which decision makers have at least partial control), and the other is the objective complexity of the situation (over which national decision makers have little or no immediate control). The more deficient is the national decision process and the more complex the strategic environment in which the state operates, the more likely are misperceptions to arise and adversely affect the outcomes of national choices.

This is a key proposition of the theory of international processes. It specifies one of the main conclusions of the critical assessment of foreign policy decision theories in chapter 7. Decision making matters a great deal in international politics in that it determines to a large extent whether states make the right choices. But it is insufficient – by itself – to account for the outcomes of these choices, nor is it sufficient to serve as an evaluation criterion of their substantive quality. States might be able to follow analytic choice procedures quite closely, but their ability to fill these procedures with realistic content depends on the complexity of the environment they are facing. Operationally, the complexity of the strategic environment is a function of the nature of the objective game, that is, of the number of players involved and of the available alternatives to each. Stated more generally, the more complex the objective game, the higher the likelihood of misperceptions, and the higher the likelihood of substantive decisional deficiencies independently of the procedural quality of national decision making processes.[44]

The reason for that is quite simple. The number of calculations and estimates of other players' alternatives and preferences that a state has to make in settings characterized by intrinsic interdependence increases exponentially with the number of outcomes of the objective game. The ability of national decision makers to come up with an accurate depiction of the situation (that is, to construct a subjective game which resembles in content and structure the objective one) declines substantially with the increase of strategic complexity. This suggests that the situational determinants of foreign policy decision processes (e.g., stress and situational ambiguity) which were discussed in essentially subjective terms in previous chapters, may themselves be seen as consequences of a strategic configuration. The bottom line of the model is this:

[44] This sounds as if we are back to the old debate on system structure and international stability (e.g., Waltz, 1964; 1979; Deutsch and Singer, 1964; Rosecrance, 1966; Wallace, 1973; Singer, Bremer, and Stuckey, 1972; Bueno de Mesquita, 1981b). The key issue in this debate is whether bipolarity which reduces environmental uncertainty breeds more international stability than multipolarity or vice versa. I will come back to this issue in chapter 10.

Proposition 10

The aggregation of national choices into international·outcomes is neither simple nor as straightforward as it appears to be. Whether one uses a systemic perspective or a decision making perspective to analyze international politics, an analysis which focuses on the features of the environment without also focusing on the features of actors' decision processes is bound to be misleading. The same applies to an approach focusing strictly on decision making processes. Both approaches yield simplistic views of interdependent international outcomes in that they suggest an ability to make linear extrapolations from national decisions to international outcomes, or – worse – from international outcomes to the decisions that presumably formed them. The theme of this model is that such connections between national choices and international outcomes are all but linear. And the key to uncovering these connections is to be found in a careful analysis which combines the decision-related calculus of individual states with the objective features of the strategic environment in which states operate.

Some, but by no means all, of the possible connections between national choices and international outcomes have been specified in the model. In addition, rigorous procedures for examining these connections empirically have been set up and illustrated through historical cases. The last task is to discuss how the model of national choices and international outcomes creates, for the first time, an opportunity to assess the relationship between procedural decision quality, seen in terms of the components of the decision-theoretic model developed in the first part of the book, and substantive decision quality whose elements were introduced in the present chapter.

8.5.2 Evaluating national choices

The substantive evaluation of national choices addresses two questions: (1) what is the relationship between procedural decision quality and substantive decision quality? (2) which procedural errors in decisions cause which kinds of deficient substantive outcomes? To address these questions we must delineate a criterion by which a national decision is to be evaluated. This criterion is simply the theoretical outcome of the objective game. The relevant comparison is between the actual decision made by a state and the decision it should have made had it selected its optimal strategy in the objective game. A state is said to have made the "right" decision if it selected the same strategy as the one associated with the theoretical outcome of the objective game. I will label this strategy as the theoretical choice of the state. On the other hand, a state is said to have made a "wrong" decision if its actual decision differed from the theoretical one.

Although this is both a feasible and sensible procedure given the model of international outcomes developed herein, and might even yield some interesting insights into the relations between choice quality and outcome quality, there are several complicating factors suggested by the model. Answering the first question without paying close attention to the second question might lead to incorrect inferences. Specifically, a simple count of national choices in terms of whether or not they deviated from the theoretical choices might lead us into inferential traps that could be avoided with the aid of a more careful analysis of the causes of discrepancy between actual choices and theoretical ones. For example, a purely cognitive path to choice taken by decision makers of a given state might lead them to conclude that they have a dominant strategy. By definition, the selection of a dominant strategy would coincide with the theoretical choice of that state. This is so because the solution of the objective game does not depend on the manner by which states have established preferences over outcomes, it depends only on the substantive nature of these preferences and on their distribution over the various outcomes. In this case, suboptimal decision processes can be said to have yielded a "correct" decision. On the other hand, national decision makers can employ extremely sophisticated decisional procedures and still come up with the "wrong" decision due to some misperceptions of the objective situation which can be seen as perfectly understandable in the context of a highly complex objective game.

The substantive evaluation of national choices must be done therefore in two phases. The first focuses on identification of the extent to which a national decision was the optimal one in the sense that it coincided with the theoretical choice in the objective game. The second examines whether this fit (or non-fit) between the theoretical choice and the actual one stems from some imperfection in the decision process itself or from the peculiarities of the strategic environment. A substantively good decision process is not only one which yields the "right" choice in theoretical terms, but rather one in which the "right" choice emerges from a more or less accurate understanding of the structure and content of the strategic environment. Sadat's decision to attack Israel in 1973 would have been the "right" choice even if he had grossly misperceived Israeli preferences. This is so because Sadat possessed a dominant strategy. Likewise, the Israeli decision not to mobilize was the wrong one not only because the

Israeli decision makers misperceived Egypt's preference structure, but also because they acted contrary to what they should have done given that Egypt was perceived not to possess an unequivocally-best strategy.

The extent to which the logic that seems to give rise to a certain national decision is justified given the structure and content of the objective strategic environment is the key element in a substantive evaluation of national decisions. In evaluating the path used by national decision makers to select a certain strategy and the reasoning underlying their ultimate selection of a policy option must be seen in the context of how difficult it is to make any kind of decision within a given strategic environment. It is more difficult to make any kind of decision in a strategic configuration that offers no straightforward basis for an optimal decision than in a strategic configuration which is sufficiently clear to make a reasonable choice. For example, when no actor in the objective game has a dominant strategy, it is extremely difficult to infer how other states would behave. Thus, the likelihood of correctly inferring other actors' behavior in such situations and making the "right" choice is considerably lower than in situations wherein others have dominant choices. In the second case, a failure of a state to make the "right" choice is more severe than a failure to make the "right" decision in the first case. Likewise, when the preference structure of the focal state is such that it actually has an unequivocally-best strategy irrespective of the strategies of other actors and fails to realize this, then its error is much more severe than in a case where its strategy choice depends on the choices attributed to other states and it fails to make the "right" decision. Thus, the substantive evaluation of national decisions should be based on the conceptual scheme given in table 8.7.

The assessment of national choices on the basis of the table is done as follows. First, the objective difficulty of the decision problem is defined in terms of the degree of independence of the objective choice rule from the decisions of other actors involved in the process. Complete independence of the choice rule (e.g., the existence of a dominant strategy) is the least difficult of the three objective choice rules. Next comes the maximin strategy in which independence is partial in the sense than an actor who cannot determine which choices will be made by other actors attempts to select a strategy that will be minimally acceptable independently of what other actors might do. Finally, the UAS rule is seen as the most dependent on the choices attributed to other actors.

Second, the relationship between the type of decision making process used by a state and the substantive level of decisional quality

Table 8.7. *Decision processes, the rationale of choice and the consequences of national decisions*

Actual decision process			Theoretical decision		Substantive evaluation	
Decisional path	Decision rationale	Strategy choice	Decision rule	Strategy choice	Difficulty of choice	Choice quality
Cybernetic	Dominant	x	Dominant	x	Independent	High
Cyb-Cog	Strategy	x	Dominant	y	Independent	Low
Cyb-An-Cog		x	UAS	x	Dependent	Medium
Cyb-An		x	UAS	y	Dependent	Low
Analytic		x	Maximin	x	Dependent	Medium
An-Cog		x	Maximin	y	Dependent	Low
Cog						
	UAS	x	Dominant	x	Independent	Medium
		x	Dominant	y	Independent	Low
		x	UAS	x	Dependent	High
		x	UAS	y	Dependent	Low
		x	Maximin	x	Dependent	Medium
		x	Maximin	y	Dependent	Low
	Maximin	x	Dominant	x	Independent	Medium
		x	Dominant	y	Independent	Low
		x	UAS	x	Dependent	Medium
		x	UAS	y	Dependent	Low
		x	Maximin	x	Dependent	High
		x	Maximin	y	Dependent	Low
	Inferential	x	Dominant	x	Independent	Medium
	Rules	x	Dominant	y	Independent	Low
		x	UAS	x	Dependent	Medium
		x	UAS	y	Dependent	Low
		x	Maximin	x	Dependent	High
		x	Maximin	y	Dependent	Low

Dom = Dominant strategy; *UAS* = Unique (ultimately) Admissible Strategy.
Inferential choice rules entail some form of assessment of other actors' strategies which is not a dominant or uniquely admissible, and a decision based on that assessment. This was, for example, the decision rule used by Israel in 1973, namely the selection of a best strategy assuming that Egypt and Syria would use their maximin strategy.
Objective decisional quality is based on table 8.6.

are related to one another, controlling for decisional difficulty. This implies that for each level of objective difficulty (i.e., complete independence, partial independence, and dependence) we would test the association between procedural decision quality and substantive choice quality. The real test of the hypothesis that the type and

455

procedural quality of national decision processes affect the substantive quality of the outcomes is that the relationship between decision process and substantive outcomes should be roughly the same across levels of objective difficulty.

> *Proposition 11*
> *At low levels of objective decisional difficulty, procedural decision quality is unrelated to the type of substantive choice quality. The fit between actual choice and the theoretical choice will be good irrespective of the procedural quality of the national decision making process. At medium levels of objective decisional difficulty, the relationship between procedural decision quality and theoretical choice is low or moderate, at best. Only at high levels of objective decisional difficulty will there be a strong positive association between the procedural quality on national decision processes and the fit between actual and theoretical outcomes.*

Proposition 11 suggests that the objective difficulty which a state confronts at a given decision process has an independent main effect on the fit between what was actually selected by the state and what this state should have done. Contrary to the conventional decision-theoretic wisdom, the present model argues that while national decision makers can do quite well with simplistic and somewhat biased decisional procedures when confronted by fairly simple foreign policy problems, the same cannot be said about the ability of simple decisional procedures to produce adaptive outcomes when choice problems become objectively complex. In the latter case, which involves multiple actors and a high degree of interdependence, the extent to which national decision processes approximate the analytic model strongly affects the extent to which a state can indeed get the maximum given the objective circumstances.

8.5.3 National choices and the collective adaptability of international outcomes

It is appropriate to ask at this point whether there is a relationship between some aggregate level of procedural decision quality over all the actors involved in an international process and the *collective* adaptability of the actual international outcome. Stated differently, if all national decision processes approximate the analytic model of decision, would the international outcome be Pareto-efficient? Likewise, if all actors involved in a strategic interaction exhibit deficiencies in their national decision processes, are we likely to observe Pareto-deficient international outcomes?

The simple – if noncommital – answer is that the relationship between the aggregated cross-national level of procedural decision quality and the Pareto-efficiency status of international outcomes depends on the structure and content of the objective game. Specifically, if the theoretical outcome of the objective game is Pareto-efficient, then the more analytic the national decision processes of the participants, the more likely is the actual international outcome to coincide with the theoretical outcome of the objective game, and, hence, the more likely is the international outcome to be Pareto-efficient. However, if the theoretical outcome of the objective game is itself Pareto-deficient, the model of national choices and international outcomes offers a major surprise to decision analysts: It is quite possible that the *less analytic* are national decision processes, the *more likely* is the actual international outcome to be Pareto-efficient. This follows from the clash of principles in game theory, especially from the ones that refer to discrepancies between solution concepts and the Pareto-efficiency criterion. In games that are paradoxical in the sense that their solution lead to Pareto-deficient outcomes, rational behavior (which in the present model is seen to be short-sighted) would yield actual outcomes which coincide with the paradoxical theoretical outcomes. Seeing the trap does not mean that rational actors can avoid it. In fact, the less likely are actors to identify the structure and content of the objective game, the more likely is their behavior to differ from what should be their "optimal" choices, therefore, the less likely is the actual outcome to coincide with the Pareto-deficient one.

This conclusion follows from the argument I have made above about the general relationship between national choices and international consequences. The rationale of the analysis of bargaining processes, or – more broadly – the analysis of interdependent decision making is not a straightforward extension of the analysis of independent national decision processes. Skipping from the national level-of-analysis to the international one requires new concepts and different perspectives. And, indeed, as Schelling (1978: 14) argued, sometimes the results are surprising. They might be surprising both in the non-linear relationship between individual (national) choices and their consequences, as well as between collective (interdependent) international choices and the outcomes of strategic interactions.

8.6   NATIONAL CHOICES AND INTERNATIONAL OUTCOMES: AN ASSESSMENT OF THE MODEL

The approach developed in this chapter attempts to relate foreign policy decision processes that rely primarily on decision analytic models under conditions of risk or uncertainty, to international outcomes, the analysis of which is based on theories of rational choice under conditions of interdependence. This approach has two primary functions: descriptive and evaluative. The descriptive function concerns the attempt to understand relationships between the choices of individual nations and international outcomes. The evaluative component concerns an attempt to assess the extent to which certain decision making procedures affect the quality of the outcomes obtained by nations. This approach differs considerably from the strictly decision-theoretic approaches and from the strict interactive approaches, both of which serve as the components of the framework of interdependent decision making. It was shown that neither of these distinct elements is, in and of itself, sufficient to account for the transformation of national decisions into international outcomes. Decision-theoretic approaches fail to provide a satisfactory explanation to the fact that actual international outcomes tend to differ – sometimes quite dramatically – from the outcomes that are expected by decision makers, even if the decision process which has led to those choices was quite sophisticated and analytic. Bargaining theories fail to explain why actors behave differently from what is to be expected according to game-theoretic prescriptions.

In this sense, the model produced a synthesis of decision theories and theories of strategic interaction which is not only more than, but also different from, the sum of its components. Both the independent incentives and calculations of individual states and the interdependent characteristics of a system of interstate interactions led to propositions which are sometimes surprising, and sometimes different from those stemming from decision theories and bargaining theories. This is, as I pointed out in chapter 7, a key test of the value of a synthesis.

Another important feature of the synthesis of decision and bargaining theories is that it leads to a set of empirically testable and refutable propositions concerning the relationships between choice and consequences in international politics. In addition, this model provides an original opportunity to assess the relationships between the procedures used by national decision makers to resolve problems and the substantive quality (or adaptability) of the outcomes of their choices. Moreover, the model yields a whole new set of propositions which attempts to explain why, in some cases, we should *not* expect good decision processes to cause successful outcomes.

How does this model compare with other efforts to understand similar issues in international politics? The breadth and complexity of the propositions developed by the present model suggests that a comparison to either systemic theories or microtheories of international politics is unfair: neither of these theories directly addresses international outcomes in a similar manner. Decision or other micro-approaches to international politics suggest that there is a linear relationship between choices (or other kinds of domestic attributes) of states and the outcomes of their behavior. We have seen that this is at odds with the arguments made by the model. Systemic theories claim that national behavior is predominantly the outcome of systemic factors which are pretty much beyond the control of the individual states. National decision makers are seen to make straightforward choices from a largely predetermined menu of policies whose contents are externally-defined. Each type of theory pays appropriate lip-service to the other one, but the key difference lies in the relative potency of external (systemic, structural) versus internal (state attributes, decision processes) factors in explaining international outcomes. Whether or not the proposition of the present model are more accurate empirically than either microlevel propositions or macrolevel ones remains to be seen. The empirical analysis of this model is beyond the scope of the present book. What is obvious is that a linear combination of micro and macrolevel theories would not yield a set of propositions which is remotely similar to the ones discussed in the present chapter, no matter how one defines the relative potency of internal or external determinants of international outcomes.

The only comparable effort to synthesize decision theory and bargaining theory is that of Snyder and Diesing (1977). As we have noted in previous chapters, this is not a real synthesis because their analysis does not make it clear how decision theories and bargaining theories add up into a new product. Yet, their discussion of distinct elements of such a synthesis is, nonetheless, highly original, and the idea of incorporating both into a more general theory of international crises is most important. The present model certainly builds on these ideas to a significant extent, but the focus is on the relationships among the decision and bargaining components rather than on each of the components taken separately.

There are, however, several problems with the new perspective offered in this chapter. One is that it addresses only one of the main criticisms leveled at the decision making approach in chapter 7 but not the other. The model of national decisions and international outcomes relates decision theories to international outcomes by exploring the impications of interdependent international interactions for foreign policy choices. However, international outcomes are treated in the present model as discrete events that emerge out of the choices of states acting under conditions of interdependence. Because this model relies heavily on static aspects of decision and bargaining theories, it fails to account for the dynamic evolution of international processes. This is a serious, but only temporary liability of the present model. We will extend it in the next chapter to deal with the dynamic unfolding of international processes over time.

The assumptions used to derive theoretical outcomes in the model may create problems when it comes to the interpretation of actual behavior that differs significantly from the behavior expected by theory. This may be particularly crucial in cases where subjective games nearly or completely coincide, but the actual behavior of actors is different from the expected one. In such cases, decision makers cannot be said to misinterpret the objective strategic environment, and what they are doing differs from what they are expected to do because they might be playing under an actual set of rules of play that is different from that postulated by the model. In such cases it would be both misleading and unfair to evaluate national decisions which assumed one set of rules by a standard (the notion of theoretical choice) whose basis is a totally different set of rules of play. For example, if actors think that they play the same game over and over, one cannot try to evaluate their behavior using a standard which assumes that the game is played only once.

The adequacy of the evaluation criterion developed in this chapter is indeed based on a certain arbitrary set of assumptions about the rules of play in the objective game. But the extent to which these assumptions represent reality seems to be unrelated to the validity of this standard. Because the theoretical outcome of objective games (and the theoretical choices of the players which are associated with such outcomes) represents a minimum solution (based essentially on a conservative maximin principle), actors whose behavior is based on a set of less restrictive assumptions, should actually do better than what the theoretical outcome has in store for them. If national decision makers base their behavior on sequential and/or iterated games, they should get at least as good, and sometimes better, outcomes than the theoretical ones. The fact that in reality nations do considerably worse than those minimum standards, suggests one of two things: first, that the assumptions underlying the derivation of theoretical outcomes of objective games are not all that unrealistic; or, second, that national leaders can make even more severe misperceptions than the cases examined in this chapter suggest they are capable of. Most importantly, they can misperceive the rules of play as well as the structure and content of the objective game. Even if national decision makers behave according to long-range plans, it still makes sense to evaluate their short run performance. I cannot see an alternative to the assessment of decision processes that are specifically designed to resolve particular, and very specific problems (e.g., trade agreements, weapon deals, or the resolution of international crises) in terms of the immediate outcomes of those decisions.

Even so, neither the explanation nor the evaluation of national behavior can be restricted to immediate consequences of certain decisions. This follows directly from the main argument of the present chapter. If there is no simple linear relationship between high-quality choice processes and the immediate consequences of national decisions which is independent of the structure of the strategic environment, then there is no reason to expect a linear relationship between international outcomes over time. It is quite possible that a state that does extremely well in terms of the outcomes it obtains at one stage of the process will do terribly in the long run.

Finally, the relationship between national choices and international outcomes as depicted by the model seems to be overly narrow in that it relies exclusively on the internal characteristics of the game and discounts the role of factors that are not being modeled by objective or subjective games but which nonetheless have important effect on the outcomes of international interactions. For example, the role of resolve, various types of power (such as moving, staying, or threat power) are not seen as part of the process by which national decisions are aggregated into international outcomes. Nor does the present model acknowledge the possibility that players can – through tacit or explicit communication – accomplish outcomes which are both jointly and individually superior to the theoretical outcomes of the game. This hampers the predictive power of the model which assumes that actors in international politics aspire to a unilateral resolution of problems, whether they arise in internal settings or in external, interdependent ones. All these problems suggest that perhaps the prediction of theoretical international outcomes should have been based on less conservative assumptions, for example, allowing for cooperative as well as for non-cooperative solutions.

While these are all valid points, they create two major obstacles for the analysis of international outcomes. First, an expansion of the set of assumptions used to derive theoretical outcomes of objective games to allow communication and cooperative solutions will lead to violation of the uniqueness property of the current solution because most cooperative games have more than one viable solution. Second, such an expansion would all but strip the model of its evaluative power

461

because outcomes that are based on either assumptions of cooperative play or on assumptions of non-cooperative play imply that virtually any outcome of the game is a "theoretically correct" outcome. Moreover, the characterization of the theoretical solution as representing the minimum one can accomplish by unilateral choice applies here as well. Coordination (where it is rational) would suggest that the actors involved managed to do better than the minimum, and there is nothing wrong with that from the perspective of the model.

9 THE EVOLUTION OF INTERNATIONAL PROCESSES

9.1 INTRODUCTION

The primary objective of theories in international politics is to account for the *evolution* of some aspects of the relations among states over time. So far, our discussion of international outcomes has ignored completely the time dimension. The focus of this chapter is on how international processes evolve over time. The discussion of international outcomes in the previous chapter serves as the basis for reviewing two general approaches to the evolution of international processes: the *ad hoc* approach and the strategic approach. The essence of the *ad hoc* approach is that national decision makers are generally myopic in their approach to internal problem solving. Their reactions to environmental changes are determined primarily by the outcomes of their previous decisions and by their perceptions of the immediate situation they are facing. The strategic approach, on the other hand, asserts that decision makers are pursuing long-range and well-defined strategies, and that their behavior at any given point in time is a result of general strategies. Each of these approaches provides a seemingly different image of international processes. I attempt to explore the implications of these images for the study of international politics, in general, and international processes, in particular.

This chapter lays the final, and most central, brick in the theory of international processes. The focus of the discussion in previous chapters has been on the immediate conditions that account for national decisions or on the immediate factors affecting the processes by which national choices are transformed into international outcomes. The present chapter examines how situational, organizational, and even psychological factors that affect national decision processes are themselves determined by the structure of the environment in which decision makers operate. On a more general level, I develop propositions about the adoption of, and revisions in, long-term strategies used by states.

Decision making models (as well as some bargaining models) suggest that there is a feedback loop going from the consequences of prior decisions to the structure and content of subsequent decision processes. However, the nature of this feedback loop is rarely discussed. Thus, several questions are addressed here. (1) How are the procedures used by individual decision makers or by policy groups affected by the interdependent outcomes of previous decisions? (2) Which particular aspects to international outcomes affect the various elements of subsequent decision processes and why? (3) What kind of motivational and situational issues are invoked by certain outcomes? (4) If decision makers learn from their past experiences, what kinds of experiences invoke which learning patterns?

While the *ad hoc* approach to international processes differs quite substantially from the strategic approach, the logic of feedback processes is – by and large – the same whether an international process is characterized as a series of actions and reactions of states to one another or as a clash among long-term and carefully crafted strategies. Thus, one cannot develop a strategic conception of international politics without incorporating some essential ideas of the *ad hoc* approach of international processes. The opposite is not necessarily true, however. It is possible to analyze international processes in strictly *ad hoc* terms without resorting to a strategic analysis. Nonetheless, any empirical analysis of international processes in *ad hoc*, context-specific terms would be incomplete if it does not use the strategic approach as an alternative model against which it is to be tested.

What follows is a general characterization of the two macro-perspectives of international processes and their illustration through historical examples.

9.2 STEP-BY-STEP INTERNATIONAL PROCESSES

> There exists no regular staff procedure for arriving at decisions; instead, *ad hoc* groups are formed as the need arises. No staff agency to monitor the carrying out of decisions is available. There is no focal point for long-range planning on an inter-agency basis. Without a central administrative focus, foreign policy turns into a series of unrelated decisions – crisis-oriented, *ad hoc* and after-the-fact. We become the prisoners of events.
>
> (Kissinger, 1979: 339; italics in original)

This title reflects the essence of the *ad hoc* approach to international processes. The fundamental assumptions of this approach are the following.

464

1 Although national decision makers have general values and objectives which determine their view of politics and of policy making, their approach to most policy problems is characterized by attempts to solve specific problems rather than by implementations of comprehensive strategies derived from general world views.

2 Consequently, political leaders evaluate their policies in terms of their short-term ramifications rather than in terms of their long-term results.

3 Likewise, national choices are based on short-term stimuli rather than on persistent concerns, and are affected by the immediate expectations of national decision makers bout their environment (including the intentions and values of other actors).

4 Hence, variations in the content and structure of individual and collective choice processes over time are affected by the nature of the actual international outcome of the prior decision rather than by cumulative consequences of several past decisions.

A word about the reasoning underlying these assumptions is in order. First, one must consider the kind of setting we are discussing. Political leaders operate within an agenda in which multiple problems of an extremely diverse nature have to be dealt with almost simultaneously. They have to resolve, on a daily basis, multiple problems on a wide spectrum of issue-domains. The daily schedule of senior government officials is hectic and can be organized only partly by secretaries and chiefs of staff. Much of what decision makers do is determined by external or internal events rather than by their personal choices. Even during a "normal" day in which a decision maker can keep all his or her appointments or in which all scheduled meetings take place, a person switches from one issue to another at a rate of about one per hour. Even if one wanted to, long-term strategy planning is virtually impossible in this kind of pace. This is especially true during crises when there is very little time for reflection and long-term calculation of general strategies, or when people are overwhelmed by events and information, and are constantly trying to keep pace with what is happening.

In such settings, decision makers do not plan or act strategically; they do not look ahead several steps into the future, nor do they attempt to carefully detect patterns in opponents' and allies' past behavior. This is not to suggest that general values and attitudes do not go into the decision making process, and that – while solving specific problems – individuals and groups do not examine the possible effects of various solutions on general goals and values. Rather, their considerations do not sum up to the establishment and implementation of long-range strategies.

The essential ideas of the *ad hoc* appropach to international processes can be summarized in the following points.

1 The primary stimulus for national choices is the discrepancy between expected and actual international outcomes.

2 The nature of this discrepancy determines to a large extent the content and structure of subsequent individual and collective decisions. The higher the discrepancy between expected international outcomes and actual ones, the higher the likelihood that subsequent decision processes will differ in content and structure from previous ones. Hence, the higher the likelihood that states will alter their choices over time.

3 Variations in international outcomes over time are due to changes in national decisions. Changes in national decisions are due to discrepancies between expected international outcomes and actual ones. Discrepancies between expected and actual outcomes are due partly to deficiencies in prior national choice processes, and partly to the structural difficulty of making good choices in a complex strategic configuration.

4 International processes can therefore be understood as a causal chain consisting of several elements (or models), each of which defines a set of relationships among several factors, as follows: (*a*) A relationship between situational, personality, and organizational factors and individual decision processes of key political leaders of states (or other actors). This is the individual choice aspect of international processes. (*b*) A relationship between individual preferences, group structure, and the content of national decisions. This is the national choice aspect of international processes. (*c*) A relationship between the content and structure of national decision making processes and the nature of the international outcomes that follow from intersecting national choices. (*d*) A relationship between international outcomes and subsequent individual and collective choice processes within the participating states.

5 The main theme of this approach is that the evolution of international processes and the variations in international outcomes over time cannot be understood unless the content of that causal chain running from individual preferences to international outcomes is spelled out. Specifically, analyses of international processes must focus on a two-way interaction

466

between preferences (individual and national) and international outcomes. Individual and national preferences affect international outcomes as much as international outcomes shape and affect individual and national preferences.

In order to discuss in detail the nature of this causal chain, I recapitulate the essential ideas advanced in previous chapters regarding the determinants and processes of national decision making and the aggregation of national choices into international outcomes. (*a*) Individual preferences are shaped by situation, personality, and organizational (role) factors; (*b*) Individual preferences, along with the formal and informal structure of groups, shape the content, structure, and resulting preferences of nations; (*c*) National preferences, along with the characteristics of interdependent international settings affect the nature of international outcomes, and therefore the relations between national choices and international consequences. Specifically, they determine the degree to which national expectations regarding the outcomes of decisions converge with the actual outcomes of those decisions. The starting point of the *ad hoc* approach to the analysis of international processes is precisely that discrepancy between expected and actual international outcomes. The following issues are addressed:

1 How do the magnitude and the direction of discrepancy between the expected and actual international outcomes affect the content and structure of national decisions?
2 What kind of expected-actual discrepancies cause which kind of changes in individual and collective choice processes?

Whether or not one accepts the notion of theoretical international outcomes as established in chapter 8 is not really essential for the present analysis. Theoretical international outcomes are useful primarily for the substantive evaluation of national decisions. They are not needed for the determination of the relationships between prior consequences and subsequent choice behavior. On the other hand, both expected and actual international outcomes have rather concrete meanings. Expected outcomes are what decision makers think that will take place as a result of the way they choose and other actors respond to that choice. Actual outcomes denote situations that have actually arisen out of an intersection of national choices.

As noted in the decision making theory (chapter 7), a stimulus for decision rises when an expected international outcome differs from the actual outcome. The magnitude and type of difference between expected and actual outcomes determines the nature and magnitude of the subsequent decision problem. In fact, the nature of discrepancy between the expected outcome and the actual one forms the basis for the diagnosis stage of the subsequent national decision. It defines for individual decision makers (and policy groups) the perceived scores of the situational variables. Let us see how these issues are related to the concepts of decisional stress and ambiguity developed in previous chapters.

There are two types of discrepancies between expected and actual outcomes. The first includes situations wherein actual international outcomes are worse (that is, valued less) than expected ones. The other consists of situations in which actual international outcomes are better (valued more) than expected ones. Both discrepancies constitute surprises for decision makers albeit of different sorts. The first case is what I called a "negative surprise." Israel's shock as a result of the 1973 Egyptian–Syrian attack was of this sort. (So was Germany's surprise in the course of the 1911 Agadir crisis.) The second case was labeled a "positive surprise." This was exemplified by the success of the strategic surprise in the 1973 War for the Egyptians and Syrians. The measure of expectation-based discrepancies incorporates both the magnitude and the direction of discrepancies between expected and actual international outcomes.

9.2.1 Outcome-discrepancies, attribution processes, and subsequent decisions[1]

Differences between expected and observed outcomes affect subsequent national decision processes through changes in the values of the situational variables, decisional stress and perceived situational ambiguity. Both decisional stress and situational ambiguity are determined on the basis of current environmental cues, hence perceptions of such cues are affected by the manner decision makers interpret such discrepancies. Let us examine some common principles used by individuals to interpret discrepancies between expected and actual outcomes and assess their implications for subsequent decisions processes.

---

[1] There is a vast body of theory and empirical research on the determinants and behavioral consequences of causal attribution processes. The following section does some injustice to this rich and important body of knowledge by focusing on one of its more salient findings. For the main findings and theories of causal attribution in psychology see Kelley (1973); Kelley and Michela (1980); Weiner (1986); Antaki (1982); Tetlock and Levi (1982); Duval and Duval (1983). Larson (1986) criticizes game theory for its apparent failure to account for behavior (especially reciprocity) due to the fact that it ignores, among other things, the motives attributed by one actor to its opponents. For an interesting application of attribution theory to political interpretations see Heradsveit and Bonham (1986).

Rational attribution. The common question one asks when a given situation differs significantly from an expected one is: "what happened"? This requires examining whether, and to what extent, this difference was a result of the focal actor's behavior and/or the behavior of other actors. Rational attribution processes entail examination of the self-made and environmental causes of outcomes irrespective of whether the discrepancy between the expected outcome and the actual outcome has been of the positive surprise type or of the negative surprise one.[2] Such an analysis is case-specific because it is impossible to determine *a priori* what combination of factors accounts for a given discrepancy between expected and actual outcomes. Rational attribution processes entail, therefore, a conscious effort to explore one's own decisional mistakes whether the actual outcome was worse or better than the expected one. The rational process of attributing causes to outcome discrepancies should be invariant with respect to the type of discrepancy between expected and actual outcomes.

If follows, of course, that the diagnosis process of the subsequent decision should be more than, or at least as analytic as, the diagnosis process of the previous decision irrespective of the type of discrepancy. Moreover, the higher the absolute value of the discrepancy between expected and actual outcomes, the more detail and effort should go into diagnosing the new decision problem. Subsequent improvement in diagnostic accuracy is due to the fact that each international outcome provides decision makers with better information about the preferences and intentions of other actors. Decision makers who make a conscious effort to learn from the environment utilize the environmental feedback (international outcomes) well. Because the procedural quality of diagnosis processes affects the procedural quality of subsequent stages, rational attribution processes result in progressively improved decision making behavior over time, irrespective of the type of discrepancy between expected and actual outcomes.

Irrational attribution. Irrational attribution processes are characterized by a significant relation between the kind of attribution that takes place and the kind of discrepancy between expected and actual outcomes. Specifically, studies of attribution processes suggest that people tend to attribute successes to their own behavior and failures to the situation or to factors that are beyond their immediate control. When diagnosing discrepancies between expected and actual outcomes, positive surprises are apt to be interpreted as confirmations of

---

[2] When the expected and actual outcomes coincide, the attribution process entailed in the previous decision is confirmed because all actors behave as the focal actor expected them to.

the calculus underlying previous decisions, and therefore would yield little or no re-analysis of the problem. This happens even if the positive surprise was due to the fact that other actors made more severe decisional errors than the focal actor, but the focal actor's decision process was not error-free. On the other hand, negative surprises tend to be interpreted in terms of failure to estimate correctly other actor's intentions and preferences rather than other types of deficiencies in one's own decision process. Thus, in such cases, some changes in the diagnosis stage would take place, but this stage tends to consist mostly of reassessments of other actors' intentions and preferences.

The outcome of the 1973 case examined in chapter 8 was that an inquiry commission was appointed by the Israeli government following the Yom Kippur war to investigate the causes of the surprise. This commission (known as the Agranat commission, after its chairman, the Supreme Justice at that time) based most of its report on the errors in assessments of Egyptian and Syrian intentions by Israeli military intelligence. It did not discuss at all the logic by which the government had decided not to mobilize reserves, which – as we have seen – was as much responsible for the actual outcome as was the mis-estimation of the Egyptian–Syrian preference structure. The government was all but absolved from responsibility for the actual outcome. Likewise, the Kahan inquiry commission which was appointed to examine the process that led to the Sabra and Shatilla massacre (Maoz, 1986) focused its attention on the failures of the government and the civilian and military intelligence to correctly assess the intention of the Christian militia, the Phalanges, to avenge the assassination of their leader Bashir Jemayel. No mention was made in the report of the failure to explore additional options, the fact that the information leading to the decision to enter the refugee camps was itself misconstrued by the minister of defense, Sharon, and so forth.[3]

Irrational attribution processes seem to entail interesting paradoxes. Negative surprises may well cause increased vigilance in subsequent individual and collective choice processes, whereas positive surprises may cause increased bias and decreased tendencies toward analytic decision making. This is so to the extent that successes that are not entirely attributable to one's decision (or prediction) are interpreted as

[3] Sharon and Begin claimed in their testimony before the commission that they had had information about the presence of 2,000 armed Palestinian guerrillas in these camps. This prompted the decision to send the Phalanges into the camps. However, neither the chief of military intelligence nor the head of Mossad made any mention of this information. It became obvious following the massacre that this information was very far from the truth. Moreover, the inquiry commission never bothered to ask what was the logic of sending no more than 150 Phalange militias into camps in which there were 2,000 armed guerrillas. See Maoz (1986) and Dupuy and Martell (1986: 181–186).

a direct outgrowth of a basically "correct" decision process. Such interpretations lead to subsequent overconfidence in prior estimates of other actors' preferences and intentions, and thereby increase the likelihood of subsequent misperceptions. For example, there is little doubt that the seeming "success" the Israeli military intelligence to predict that the Egyptians and Syrians would not attack Israel in the spring of 1973 contributed to the overconfidence underlying the same predictions in October of the same year, and to the acceptance of the intelligence estimates by other decision makers (Handel, 1976; Lanir, 1983; Stein, 1985).

On the other hand, negative surprises lead to reassessment of prior estimates of other actors' intentions and preferences, in the process of a new definition of the situation. This might result in a more accurate assessment of the objective reality and in a more sensible response. Brecher's (1980) study of the Israeli decision making process in 1967 and 1973 suggests that the initial failure to treat seriously the crises that had evolved, and the adverse consequences of the initial Israeli reactions to these crises, led to more care in the subsequent diagnosis processes and thereby contributed to more analytic decision processes later on. (See also Stein and Tanter, 1980.)

9.2.2 Effects of outcome-discrepancies on situational variables

The effects of attribution processes on the values of decisional stress and perceived situational ambiguity vary along two dimensions: whether the attribution process is rational or not, and according to the previous values of these variables.

Effects of outcome-discrepancies under rational attribution processes. Under rational attribution, the change in prior perceptions of stress and ambiguity depends on the degree of discrepancy between expected consequences and actual ones, but not on the type of discrepancy. Whether or not an actual outcome is valued less than an expected one, decision makers examine how the combination of national decisions made up the international outcome. The results of this analysis determine whether the degree of decisional stress would increase or decrease. In such cases, the larger the discrepancy between expected outcomes and actual ones, the more extensive is the change in the values of perceived stress and ambiguity. The nature of the prior values of these variables would determine the direction of change. Figure 9.1 displays the effect of expected-actual outcome discrepances on decisional stress and perceived ambiguity.

471

a. *Outcome discrepancy and decisional stress*

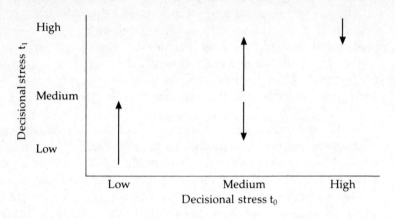

b. *Outcome discrepancy and perceived situational ambiguity*

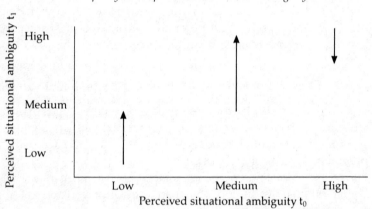

Figure 9.1 The effects of outcome discrepancy on decisional stress and perceived situational ambiguity (assuming rational attribution)

1. *Low prior levels of stress and ambiguity.* Low prior levels of perceived stress and situational ambiguity are converted into higher levels when discrepancies between expected and actual outcomes arise. This occurs irrespective of whether the expected outcome was valued more than the actual outcome or vice versa. Negative surprises produce an increase in stress and ambiguity perceptions because of the reduced confidence one is willing to place in prior estimates of other actors' intentions or preferences. Increased stress is also due to the rise in threat perceptions as a result of the negative valuation of the actual

472

outcome compared to the expected one. Positive surprises cause higher levels of decisional stress due to an increased sense of opportunity. Positive surprises might signify to decision makers that other actors were not as bright as they had originally thought and that it is possible to capitalize on other actors' mistakes.[4]

2.   *Medium levels of prior stress and ambiguity.* At medium levels of previous stress, negative surprises generally invoke higher decisional stress, whereas positive surprises generally invoke lower decisional stress. Negative surprises increase threat perceptions whereas positive surprises increase opportunity perceptions. Increased perceptions of opportunity cancel out previous perceptions of threat, hence, the final level of stress is apt to decline. Negative surprises lead to the magnification of previous threat perceptions and therefore to increased stress. On the other hand, perceived situational ambiguity increases whatever surprise takes place because previous expectations were not met, thus lowering the degree of confidence decision makers are willing to place on previous predictions.

3.   *High levels of prior stress and ambiguity.* When decision makers have experienced high prior levels of decisional stress and perceived situational ambiguity, discrepancies between expected and actual outcomes lead to slight reductions in the values of these variables. This is due to the increased level of experience gained from the new information entailed in the actual international outcome. This reduction may not be significant to the point that it lowers stress to levels that are typically associated with analytic decision making.

Effects of outcome-discrepancies under irrational attribution processes. When the attribution process is of the irrational type, changes in the values of decisional stress and situational ambiguity depend on the nature of the discrepancy between expectations and actual outcomes. Specifically, negative surprises generally result in higher levels of stress than previous ones whereas positive surprises generally result in lower levels of perceived stress. Likewise, perceived situational ambiguity increases with the magnitude of negative surprise, and diminishes with the magnitude of positive surprises. This is given in figure 9.2.

1.   *Low prior levels of decisional stress and ambiguity.* For low prior levels

---

[4] For example, if an actor made a prior decision anticipating that other actors would use their maximin alternative, and assuming no substantive misperception, then if the actual international outcome was better than the expected one, an actor could conclude that one or more of the other actors had chosen according to a different rule. Once this rule is discovered, an actor might conclude that new, hitherto unforeseen, opportunities exist. A higher perception of opportunity might contribute to increased decisional stress as much as a higher perception of increased threat in the case of negative surprises.

a. *Outcome discrepancy and decisional stress*

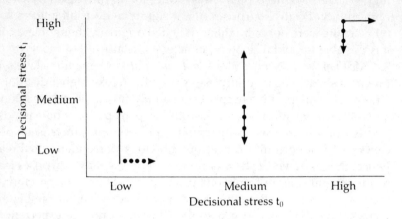

b. *Outcome discrepancy and perceived situational ambiguity*

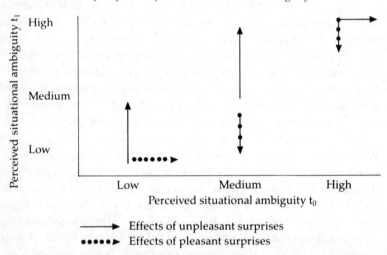

→ Effects of unpleasant surprises
•••••► Effects of pleasant surprises

Figure 9.2 The effects of outcome discrepancy on decisional stress and perceived situational ambiguity (assuming irrational attribution

of stress and ambiguity, positive surprises have little or no effect on subsequent levels of these variables, thus decisional procedures are unlikely to change from one point in time to another. On the other hand, negative surprises are likely to increase subsequent levels of stress and ambiguity, moving them from low to medium. This renders subsequent decision processes increasingly analytic.

2. *Medium prior levels of decisional stress and ambiguity.* At this level, whether the surprise experienced by decision makers is of the positive or of the negative type, the procedural quality of the subsequent decision process is likely to decline. However, the nature of the decline in the amount and significance of analytic components depends on the nature of the outcome discrepancy. Positive surprises lead to reduction both in the level of decisional stress, due to reduced threat perceptions, and in the level of situational ambiguity due to increased confidence in prior estimates. This has the effect of reducing the significance of the decision, and of introducing a substantial element of predictability into the subsequent diagnosis process. The consequence is greater reliance on SOPs and other elements of cybernetic decision making. Negative surprises move stress levels upward, thereby introducing substantial cognitive components into the decision process. However, the parallel increase in the level of situational ambiguity tends to modify the increased tendency toward cognitive decision processes.

3. *High prior levels of decisional stress and ambiguity.* If prior levels of stress were high, positive surprises might reduce stress thereby resulting in higher levels of procedural decision quality. Primarily through the reduction in the level of threat or opportunity perceptions, stress levels may decline from high to medium. This tends to result in more vigilant approaches to the new decisional problem and to increased reliance on analytic procedures. Negative surprises have either no effect on subsequent levels of decision quality or tend to reinforce the reliance on biasing cognitive dynamics as decision makers explain the actual outcome in terms of the opponents' behavior. On the other hand, high prior levels of situational ambiguity either increase or remain unchanged as a result of a negative surprise, thereby contributing to the quality of subsequent decision processes.

The key distinction between the effects of outcome-discrepancies on subsequent decision procedures under rational attribution processes and irrational ones is therefore the following: Under the former types of processes, there is no difference between positive and negative surprises. Under the latter type of process, the effects of positive surprises are markedly different from the effects of negative surprises. The surprising part of the analysis is that – given the effects of stress and ambiguity on individual choice and collective decision making processes – *irrational attribution might produce increased vigilance in subsequent decisions under certain circumstances. On the other hand, rational attribution processes might reduce the procedural quality of subsequent decisions.* Another implication of this analysis is that it is not always possible to distinguish between the effects of rational attribution processes on decision and the effects of irrational attribution processes on decision behavior. A comparison of figures 9.1 and 9.2 reveals that, under low and medium levels of stress and ambiguity, negative surprises have the same effect on subsequent decisional stress and situational ambiguity whether or not the attribution process is rational. Under high levels of prior decisional stress and ambiguity, positive surprises cause reduction in subsequent levels of stress and ambiguity.

However, given independent information on the nature of explanation developed by individual decision makers when expected international outcomes differ from actual ones, it is possible to infer the nature of the attribution process and to predict the effect of outcome discrepancies on the situational variables. More importantly, the propensity of an individual toward rational attribution can be seen as a function of one's personality in the same way that traits such as cognitive compelxity are seen to affect individual dispositions toward analytic decision making. Interindividual differences in drawing lessons from (positive or negative) surprises might be accounted for – at least in part – by personality types. Cognitively complex individuals will have, on the average, a higher disposition toward rational attribution than cognitively simple ones.

One of the important empirical implications of the preceding analysis is that we must attempt to understand cross-time variations in the scores assigned by individuals to the situational variables in terms of three factors: (a) the values of these variables in prior decision processes, (b) the magnitude of the discrepancy between expected international outcomes and actual ones, and its direction (i.e., positive as opposed to negative surprises), and (c) the type of the attribution process employed by the individual to explain this discrepancy. The significance of attribution processes in decision making is that they tend to reflect very well one's cognitive complexity. Specifically, they enable us to assess the manner by which unexpected events are interpreted by a decision maker, and how this interpretation affects the procedures and outcomes of subsequent choice processes.

9.2.3 Relations between national decisions over time

Now we can make some observations on how states change the processes and substantive outcomes of their choices over time. This seems to follow fairly clearly from the nature of the decision theory presented in chapter 7. The principal point of the *ad hoc* approach is that changes in national decisions over time are due primarily to two types of factors: changes in the procedures employed by individuals and collectivities to solve problems arising in their environment, and changes in the substantive preferences of individuals or groups. These two factors are, obviously, interrelated. When an individual or group uses a decisional procedure which differs from one that had been used previously, it is likely that the substantive content of the decision process, and the individual preferences over outcomes would change from one point in time to another.[5] The ideas of the *ad hoc* approach with respect to the relations between national decisions over time can be summarized by the following empirical propositions:

1 The higher the discrepancy between expected international outcomes and actual ones at time t, the more likely are the structure and content of individual choice processes at $t+1$ to differ from those at the previous period.

2 The higher the discrepancy between expected international outcomes and actual ones at time t, the more likely are the substantive individual preferences at time $t+1$ to differ from those at previous periods.

3 Variations in the structure, substance, and outcomes (preference ordering of policy options) of individual choice processes over time are a function of the effects of outcome discrepancies on situational variables. Changes in the values of the situational variables determine the nature of changes in choice processes and outcomes.

4 The higher the discrepancy between expected international outcomes and actual ones, the more likely is the structure, substance, and outcome of collective choice processes at time $t+1$ to differ from the previous national choice process.

5 Hence, the higher the discrepancy between the expected international outcome and the actual one, the more likely is the behavior of states at time t to differ from their prior behavior.

Discrepancies between expected and actual outcomes may have three types of effects on the determinants of group decision making.

---

[5] It is, however, possible for preference change to occur even when there are no changes in the procedures employed by individuals and collectivities to analyze problems. One of the important deficiencies in decision theory is the lack of research on the bases of individual preferences or on the personality and cultural determinants of risk-dispositions. The possibility that substantive value-changes might occur independently of problem-solving procedures is mentioned frequently in the decision theoretic literature but is rarely researched. The following ideas should be seen, therefore, as highly tentative.

First, they may affect the substantive content of the group preference matrix (that is, the distribution of individual preferences over policy options due to changes in the structure and content of individual choice processes). Second, they may affect the group structure, its pattern of authority and the identity of individual participants. Third, they might affect the individual influences on group outcomes. Let us discuss briefly each of these changes.

Effects of outcome discrepancies on the initial distribution of individual preferences. Given that outcome discrepancies are expected to cause changes in individual preferences, the group preference matrix at time $t + 1$ will be, by definition, different from the group preference matrix at time t. This occurs even when group participants are the same in both cases. Two tentative propositions can be logically derived from the reasoning of the *ad hoc* approach. First, negative surprises are likely to generate group preference matrices that are more complete than the previous ones. This is so because individuals faced by negative surprises are likely to explore more options than they had in the past. Hence, it follows that the comprehensiveness of group discussion would increase as a result of negative surprises.[6] On the other hand, positive surprises are more likely to produce little or no change in the structure of group preference matrices, and even to reduce the level of comprehensiveness of group discussion. This is so to the extent that individuals become convinced that their prior decisions had been effective in producing the desired consequences and therefore limit their focus to the previously used options. The same applies to small outcome discrepancies or to matches between expected international outcomes and actual ones.

Secondly, discrepancies between expected and actual international outcomes affect the substance of group preference matrices and hence the level of group polarization. Specifically, negative surprises increase group polarization whereas matches between expected and actual international outcomes or positive surprises produce reductions in the level of group polarization. This proposition is based on the assumption that there are interindividual differences in terms of: (*a*) attribution processes used to account for these discrepancies, and, consequently, (*b*) the decisional paths used. In general, it is implausible to assume that an actual international outcome which differs from the expected one at the group level will also constitute a (positive or negative) surprise for all individual participants. Since there is no

[6] The comprehensiveness of group discussion is measured by the ratio of all policy options considered by the group to the options that had been considered in all separate individual choice processes. (See chapter 6.)

reason to expect that all individual expectations would converge at the group level, what might constitute a surprise for one person would not necessarily constitute a surprise to another person. Thus, the extent and nature of preference change at the individual level varies according to individual expectations regarding the outcome. At the group level, however, those who were most surprised by an international outcome are most likely to shift preferences.

Since national decisions are based on the preferences of either a numerical majority or a powerful minority of group participants, surprises of a negative nature are likely to lead at least some people who held the majority view to shift preferences away from the majority. These people are (a) more likely to be surprised than group participants holding the minority view, and therefore (b) might change their choice procedures. This would reduce the size of the previous majority (or the weighted impact of the influential minority), thereby resulting in greater group polarization. On the other hand, matches between expected and actual outcomes or positive surprises might result in little or no preference change among individuals who had belonged to the majority subgroup, but cause preference change among individuals who held minority views. These preference changes are generally toward the majority view and therefore group polarization is apt to diminish. The process and substance of collective choices is thus affected by outcome discrepancies through changes in the level of group polarization.

Effects of outcome discrepancies on formal group structure. Decision theory contains few analyses of changes in group composition and group structure following discrepancies between expected and actual international outcomes. This makes it very difficult to develop precise propositions concerning the nature of changes in formal group structures following various types of outcome discrepancies. It is, however, relatively safe to make the following suggestion. Negative surprises cause changes in group composition: the higher the degree of negative discrepancy between expected and actual international outcomes, the less resemblance between the composition of the group at $t + 1$ and the composition of the previous policy making group. Negative surprises of high magnitudes spell disaster; disasters lead to head-rolling, government, or even regime changes.[7] Groups that emerge following negative surprises differ from prior groups both in terms of the identity of the participants – which suggests another possible expla-

---

[7] Stein and Russett (1980) pointed out that defeats in wars are likely to result in either government or regime changes, whereas victories in war are most likely to result in the persistence of the incumbent government and the regime.

nation of preference change – and in terms of their formal hierarchies. Generally speaking, formal authority patterns in groups that are formed following negative surprises tend to differ from those of prior groups in the opposite direction. If the authority structure in prior groups is relatively decentralized and egalitarian, a negative surprise of high magnitudes tends to cause movement toward more rigid hierarchical structures. On the other hand, a highly rigid hierarchy which produces a very negative surprise tends to be followed by a more egalitarian and diversified authority pattern. Matches between expected and actual outcomes as well as positive surprises are apt to reinforce existing authority structures.

Effects of outcome discrepancies on individual influence. Generally, negative surprises tend to reduce the influence of individuals who had supported the previous decision and increase the influence of individuals who were opposed to the previously selected policy option. Positive surprises tend to increase the power of individuals who had supported prior choices and reduce the opposition's power.

The impact of outcome discrepancies on the structural characteristics of policy groups reflects the political nature of decision processes. Collective choice processes in foreign policy settings are political games in which the status, prestige, and careers of the participants depend to a large extent on the positions they take on various issues and the outcomes of the decisions on those issues. People who had made the "correct" prediction or the "correct" policy prescription stand to gain in terms of personal influence on the group. Their views count more in subsequent decision processes. Those who had made the "wrong" prescriptions lose influence in subsequent decision processes.[8] This is so independently of whether the expected outcome coincided with the actual one, or of the nature of the outcome discrepancy. If a person sided with the majority view and the international outcome was inferior to the expected decisional outcome, that person stands to lose personal influence (if not to be ejected from the group altogether). If the actual international outcome coincides with the expected international outcome, or if the actual international outcome constitutes a positive surprise, a person who prescribed the prior policy option or who predicted the actual outcome

[8] By "correct" judgments or policy prescriptions I do not mean to imply a relation to theoretical outcomes. Rather, a person may be seen to have made a correct prediction to the extent that the international outcome predicted by him or her coincided with the actual one. Likewise, a "correct" policy prescription is one that is seen to have maximized the group's preferences given an actual international outcome. It is obvious, of course, that a correct prediction tends to be associated with a correct prescription, and a negative discrepancy between the expected international outcome and the actual one tends to be associated with an incorrect policy prescription.

stands to gain influence. Outcome discrepancies affect coalition formation and breakdown through the changes in individual preferences, the identity of group participants, and the changes in the personal influence on group members. Negative surprises of high magnitudes lead to the breakdown of previously winning coalitions and to the strengthening of opposing ones, whereas continuously positive surprises or matches between expected and actual international outcomes are likely to be associated with the defection of members from the minority coalition to the majority one.

An illustration of these ideas seems in order at this point. In the 1985 arms deal between the United States and Iran, two coalitions existed in the Reagan administration. The first was composed of the National Security advisors, Robert McFarlane and John Poindexter (his successor), members of their staff, and the CIA director, William Casey. This coalition supported the deal arguing that it would be instrumental in improving US–Iran relations as well as enable the release of the American hostages in Lebanon. The other coalition was led by the secretaries of state, George Schultz, and defense, Caspar Weinberger. This coalition not only objected to the deal on the ground that it would contradict the administration's commitment not to yield to terrorism, but also because they could not see the improvement in US–Iran relations coming out of this deal. As soon as the details of the deal were leaked to the press by the Iranis, and even before it became evident that money from the deal had been diverted to the Contras in Nicaragua, a major shift in the balance of forces took place in the administration. With Schultz given actual control of the signing of deals of this sort in the future, it became evident that the outcome of the deal meant more than new faces in the National Security Council. Many of the subsequent changes in US policy toward negotiations with Iran resulted from the new balance of power within the administration.

The major implications of the analysis of the nature of the feedback loop leading from international outcomes to subsequent national choices are that discrepancies between expected and actual outcomes cause major changes in: (a) the content and structure of individual choice processes, (b) the formal structure of, and individual influence on, foreign policy groups, and consequently, (c) the nature of national choices. This suggests that consistency in national decisions on foreign affairs is more likely to be an exception rather than a rule. Moreover, a state is expected to exhibit a consistent pattern of behavior over time to the extent that this behavior is rewarded in the sense that the expectations of its decision makers are – more or less – fulfilled.

9.2.4 How do international processes evolve over time according to the *ad hoc* approach?

Is there a pattern to the fluctuations of international outcomes over time? Do international outcomes stabilize at some point in a manner that could be conceptualized as something akin to an equilibrium in game-theoretic terms? To answer all these questions, it is necessary to think of the problem in terms of the possible relationships among three types of international outcomes: theoretical outcomes, actual outcomes, and sets of expected outcomes (wherein elements are the expected outcomes of each of the participating states).

The simplest situation to analyze is one in which all types of outcomes converge. This reflects cases wherein all participants in an international game satisfy three conditions. (*a*) They behave precisely as they should have (that is, all states make theoretically "correct" choices). (*b*) Such behavior is not incidental but based on correct assessments of the strategic environment by all states and on correct behavioral inferences. (*c*) Each state expects all other states to behave in precisely the same manner as they actually do. This case will be labeled as the *full convergence* situation. Other situations include cases of *partial convergence*.[9] Finally, the pathological – but probably most common – case from the perspective of the *ad hoc* approach is one of *full discrepancy*, that is, when all three types of international out comes are different. In this case, all or some of the states, (*a*) misperceive the strategic international environment they are facing, (*b*) do not behave as is expected from them, assuming rational choice, and (*c*) make incorrect predictions concerning the expected behavior of other states.

I introduce first the general propositions of the *ad hoc* approach with respect to the evolution of international processes, and then discuss in some detail each of the situations of full convergence, partial con-

---

[9] There are various combinations of partial convergence. *Expected-actual convergence* denotes convergence between expected and actual outcomes but discrepancies between these two types of outcomes and theoretical international outcomes. *Expected-theoretical convergence*: cases in which theoretical and expected international outcomes coincide, but the actual international outcome is different from both. *Theoretical-actual convergence*: situations in which the actual behavior of all states coincides with what was theoretically expected but the expectations of (all or some) states about each other's behavior differ from their actual behavior. There are also various forms of partial convergence between expected international outcomes of some states and actual and/or theoretical outcomes, that is, situations wherein only some of the states make correct predictions about the actual international outcome but others make incorrect predictions.

vergence, and full discrepancy. The main propositions of the *ad hoc* approach regarding the evolution of international processes are the following:[10]

1 The higher the convergence among the three types of international outcomes (with one exception to be discussed below), the more stable international outcomes would be over time.

2 Partial convergence between expected international outcomes and actual ones is likely to yield even lower levels of convergence in the subsequent time period than any other type of partial convergence or full discrepancy. International outcomes characterized by expected-actual outcome discrepancies (even if expected outcomes and theoretical outcomes coincide or if actual outcomes and theoretical outcomes coincide) are likely to cause increasingly smaller levels of convergence over time. Such cases are pathological in that they fail to produce long-term stability in international behavior compared to any other type of international outcomes.

3 From the perspective of international outcome analysis, there is no conceptual or practical difference between positive surprises and negative ones: both types of surprises are expected to generate identical patterns of subsequent international outcomes.

4 Cases of full discrepancy result in two long-term patterns of international outcome flow over time. The first pattern is one of increased long-term convergence, and, eventually, of long-term stability. This pattern is observed to the extent that subsequent international outcomes are not characterized by partial convergence of the type described in proposition 2 above. The second pattern is one wherein one observes a greater degree of convergence in the immediately following international outcomes, but no long-term stability. This pattern is observed to the extent that the international outcomes that occur immediately following full-discrepancy international outcomes are characterized by partial convergence of the type described by

---

[10] These propositions are predicated on the assumption that at least some of the structural aspects of objective international games remain unchanged over time. I am referring, in particular, to the identity of the players and to the rules of play. While the number and content of the alternatives available to each of the players might change over time, this change is normally slow and could be accommodated by the propositions of the model. Although the plausibility of this assumption in empirical settings is questionable, it is necessary for the development of general propositions about the evolution of international processes from the perspective of the *ad hoc* approach.

proposition 2 above. If the international outcome that immediately follows a full-discrepancy outcome is characterized by a discrepancy between the expected international outcome (from the perspective of at least one of the states involved) and the actual one, then proposition 2 takes over and long-term stability is not expected.

Before these propositions are explicated, a definition of stability is in order. The term "long-term stability" is different from the concept of equilibrium in game theory. Outcome stability does not involve either explicit or implicit assumptions of incentive structures underlying changes in behavior which exist in virtually all game-theoretic notions of stability analysis. By *behavioral stability* I refer to replication of actual international outcomes over a large number of consecutive international games which results from the existence of a set of stable (correct or incorrect) expectations of the actors toward one another. Stated more generally, an international process is seen to have behaviorally-stabilized if the following conditions hold:

1 The structural and substantive characteristics of objective games remain unchanged over a large number of iterations.

2 Structural and substantive misperceptions either decline and approach zero,[11] or they remain stable over a large number of iterations. In other words, the structure and content of subjective games approach those of the objective games over time. Alternatively, the differences between the structure and content of the subjective games and those of the objective games becomes constant. Hence, actors' behavior stabilizes either because their problems become fixed due to correct perceptions, or because there are no changes in the level and content of their misperceptions about one another.

3 The convergence between expected and actual international outcomes is increasingly high over time. (This is so whether or not misperceptions diminish or become fixed over time.)

4 All states behave the same over time.

These conditions contain both structural aspects (such as the char-

---

[11] That is, as the structural identification indices (SI) of successive games approach one, and as the total substantive discrepancy indices (TSD_i) approach zero for all states.

$$B$$

*Nash Equilibrium.
Outcomes are ranked from best = 4 to worst = 1.
The focal state is A. The preference order of B is as seen from A's perspective.

Figure 9.3 A hypothetical subjective game (the game as viewed by each of the states)

acteristics of games and the nature of individual states' expectations) and behavioral ones. Thus, the definition of stability requires more than lack of change of actual behavior; it demands that the foundations of stable behavior be also stable (correct or incorrect) expectations of actors toward one another. The idea here is that there might exist situations of stable behavior which are the result of fundamental misperceptions of one state toward the other, and in which the stable behavior of the opponent serves only to reinforce the flawed perceptions.

For example, suppose that two states interact with one another, and each sees the international environment to be characterized by the subjective game shown in figure 9.3. In this case, if A's decision makers base their choice on the assumption that their opponent has a dominant alternative of b_2, then they would choose a_2. However, a_2 is not their maximin alternative, though it is a reasonable choice given the subjective game. Now, if both A and B think that they are faced with a game of this sort, the expected and actual outcomes of the game will coincide. As a result, each actor's perception of the opponent's preference structure would be also reinforced. Thus, behavioral stability is likely to follow: actors would see an identical game over time and would not alter their behavior. However, from a theoretical point of view, the outcome of the game should be (a_1, b_1). This is so because the objective game is actually as shown in figure 9.4.

Obviously, in such a game, the outcome is the Pareto-optimal a_1, b_1 outcome. Thus, the actual stability in both behavior and expectation

485

B

	b_1		b_2
a_1		4		1
A	4		2	
a_2		2		3
	1		3	

Outcomes are ranked from best = 4 to worst = 1.
The theoretical outcome of this game is a_1, b_1 (which is a Nash as well as a non-myopic equilibrium), and is obtained as a result of the fact that it coincides with both states choosing their maximin alternatives.

Figure 9.4 A hypothetical objective game

that is observed as a result of the subjective game is based on perceptual flaws that are enhanced as a result of actual behavior.

Let us now examine the propositions of the *ad hoc* approach. The general issues addressed by these propositions are these: What kind of lessons can be drawn by states (which are assumed to act in a myopic fashion) from international outcomes, and how do these lessons affect their behavior? Does behavioral stability emerge in a world made up of such actors? If so, under what conditions? What kind of stability is to be expected? In order to get any sort of stability (behavioral or game-theoretic), the first requirement is that of stable expectations. An actor must know not only who are its counterparts, but also to have some data about their alternatives and about their preferences over these alternatives. This is required in order to make inferences regarding the future behavior of other players. If the expectations of one actor regarding the identity of other actors, their alternatives, and their preference structures change from one point in time to another, the actor's behavior is also likely to change, and thus stability will not be obtained. From this, proposition 1 (p. 483) immediately follows.

In situations of full convergence, actors' expectations *vis-à-vis* one another will be most stable. Since expected outcomes coincide with actual outcomes for all states, little revision in the definitions of the situation will take place within states. Hence, states are unlikely to revise their estimates of other actors' preferences over the various alternatives: the international outcome seems to have confirmed the initial preferences attributed by each nation to all other participants in the game. Since both actual and expected outcomes coincide with the theoretical outcome of the game, states are seen to have already done the best under the circumstances. They cannot improve their lot by changing their behavior. Therefore, as long as other exogenous factors (such as leadership change, regime or government change, the emergence of new alternatives as a result of technological innovation, etc.) have not affected preference change within states, all actors in the international game are going to replicate their previous behavior. More generally, the more stability exists in the expectations of one state *vis-à-vis* another, and the more optimal is the choice process within each of the states, the more behavioral stability is expected. This applies also to cases where actors have profound misperceptions of each other's preferences, as long as these misperceptions are not accompanied by other decisional deficiencies such as incorrect inferences with respect to choice. In such cases, the actual international outcome might differ from the theoretical outcome, but the convergence between actual international outcomes and expected ones produces stability in national definitions of the situation even if all these definitions are fundamentally flawed. Stability in the definitions of the situation is likely to produce ultimate behavioral stability. The games in figures 9.3 and 9.4 illustrate this situation very well.

Proposition 2 is the most interesting and the most counter-intuitive argument of the *ad hoc* perspective of international process. It refers to cases wherein some of the actors experience some sort of discrepancy between the actual international outcome and the expected one. Those actors re-assess the situation they are facing. One of the consequences of this re-assessment is that the surprised actors revise their estimates of other actors' alternatives and/or preferences. Either as a result of changes in the alternatives and preferences that the surprised decision makers attribute to other states, or as a result of changes in decisional procedures (due to alteration of stress and ambiguity levels), the national preferences of surprised actors might change. The upshot of this is that the objective game which is played at stage $t+1$ is different from the objective games at time t. It also follows that those actors that did not face a discrepancy between expected and actual outcomes at time t will think that the game at $t+1$ is the same as the game at stage t. This may occur regardless of the level of structural or substantive misperceptions of actors at stage t. Hence, the actual international outcome at $t+1$ is unlikely to be the same as that at stage t. Moreover, since some of the actors think that the game had not changed – when in fact it did – these actors are likely to face a discrepancy between expected and actual international outcomes at $t+1$, and will revise their estimates of the structure and content of the game at $t+1$. Thus the game at stage $t + 2$ will again be different from the previous game, and behavioral stability will not be observed.

Proposition 2 is therefore the heart and soul of the *ad hoc* approach. Its bottom line is this: *variations in international outcomes over time are due to the fact that both the games that decision makers think that they are playing in the international system (the subjective games) and the games that they are actually supposed to play (the objective games) differ from one point in time to another. The factors affecting the nature of these changes are to be seen not in some objective features of the international environment, but rather in individual and collective decision processes.*

Proposition 3 is a corollary of proposition 2. It suggests that behavioral stability might be beyond reach in cases of outcome-discrepancy whether or not actors experience negative surprises or positive ones. There are two primary reasons for this argument. First, a positive surprise for one actor at time t might lead to a negative surprise for that actor at $t + 1$. Such an actor might have actually benefited from the errors of other actors. Thus, other actors are likely to be negatively surprised and revise their subjective game including changing their preferences. On the other hand, the actor that experienced a positive surprise might either revise his or her assessment of other actors' preferences (given rational attribution) or maintain them (given irrational attribution). Consequently, this actor is likely to misperceive the content and structure of the objective game at $t + 1$ and draw the wrong behavioral conclusions. If that is the case, then this actor would experience a negative surprise at stage $t + 1$ and would revise its assessment of the problem and, possibly, its preferences at stage $t + 2$, and so forth.

The second reason for the similar effects of positive and negative surprises on behavioral stability is that actors might differ in the type of their attribution processes. If collective diagnosis processes in different states vary in terms of the attribution logic which characterizes them, then even if all actors experience positive surprises or if all actors experience negative surprises, behavioral stability may not be obtained. Take for example a case where two states are playing a game of Chicken, but each state thinks that it is actually playing a game of "called bluff" (Snyder and Diesing, 1977: 46). This situation is depicted by the two parts of figure 9.5.

In this case, the actual international outcome is a positive surprise to both actors. Both choose to cooperate because they think that the opponent has a dominant defection alternative (b_2 in figure 9.5a), and expect that the outcome will be a_1, b_2. The mutually-cooperative outcome is therefore valued by both actors more than the one they had

a. *The subjective game*

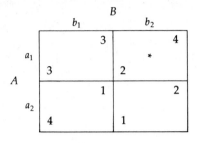

b. *The objective game*

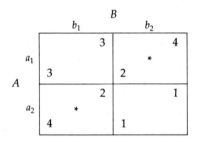

*Nash Equilibrium.
Outcomes are ranked from best = 4 to worst = 1.
The focal state is A. The preference order of B is as seen from A's perspective.
The theoretical outcome of the objective game is a_1, b_1 (which is also a non-myopic
equilibrium), and is obtained as a result of the fact that it coincides with both
states using their maximin alternatives. This is also the actual outcome given
that both states use their maximin alternatives in the subjective game.

Figure 9.5 Joint positive surprise and its effects on behavioral stability

expected to get. If both use a rational attribution process to explain the
discrepancy between the expected outcome and the actual one, they
would conclude that the other actor cannot have a dominant defection
alternative, and its preferences are such that either b_1 is a dominant
alternative or a maximin alternative. If they conclude that b_1 is a
dominant alternative, then they will both defect in the next iteration
and will experience a maximum negative surprise at stage $t+1$. This
will cause them to revise their estimates again and to change their
choice at $t+2$, and so on. If they conclude that the cooperative
alternative is the maximin of the opponent, they can attribute to the
opponent a preference structure that would render the subjective

489

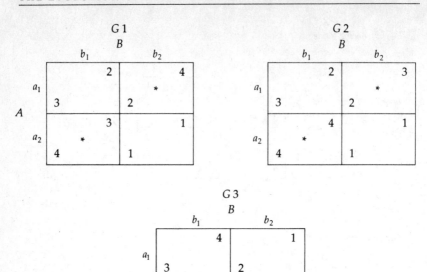

*Nash Equilibrium.
Outcomes are ranked from best = 4 to worst = 1.
The focal state is A. The preference order of B is as seen from A's perspective.

Figure 9.6 New subjective games arising of rational attribution processes as a result of joint positive surprise

game at $t+1$ either a Chicken (which means that the subjective and objective games at stage $t+1$ coincide) or one of the games shown in figure 9.6.

In games 1 and 2, the sensible choice of an actor is to shift to the a_2 alternative because it would lead the outcome to the Pareto-superior cell of a_2, b_1. In either of these cases, an actor who is fairly confident about the extent to which its perception of the opponent is realistic, can shift its choice to the non-cooperative alternative. If that is the case, then both actors would experience a negative surprise at the next stage. Only if both actors think that the objective game is Chicken, or if both think that the objective game is G3, their sensible choice is to cooperate, and that might help stabilize their expectations and lead to behavioral stability in the future.

Given that states may differ in terms of their attribution processes, it is not inconceivable for one of the states to conclude that the positive surprise was due to the opponent's flawed behavior rather than to its own misperception of the opponent's preferences. As a result, this state may fail to revise its subjective game at stage $t + 1$, while the other would. If the result of the revision process of the second state is one of the games wherein defection is a rational choice, it would lead to an actual international outcome which constitutes a negative surprise to the state which failed to revise its assessment of the opponent's preferences. At the same time, the state that had revised its subjective game in a manner that is still substantively different from the objective game will experience no surprise. For the latter state, the expected and actual outcomes at stage $t + 1$ coincide.

Proposition 4 specifies the circumstances under which an international process that started out with a case of full discrepancy might either stabilize or remain constantly unstable. If an international process goes through outcomes that surprise a lot of actors who participate in it, it is unlikely to stabilize. However, during the process wherein each actor attempts to guess the preference structure of the opponent through trial and (sometimes costly) error, the expectations of states toward one another might stabilize in a manner described in proposition 1. If that happens, behavioral stability is expected to follow. The point of proposition 4 is that the *ad hoc* approach associates stable behavior with stable expectations. These expectations can be conceived as lack of change in the content and structures of subjective games over time. On the other hand, fluctuations in international outcomes over time are due to changes in the content and structure of the subjective as well as the objective games: outcomes vary over time because the actors change their assessment of the environment as well as their own preferences over time.

The fact that the *ad hoc* perspective envisions both stability and constant fluctuations in international processes seems a bit paradoxical. The approach seems to suggest that everything is possible in long-term international interactions. This might raise serious doubts about our ability to falsify its propositions. This is particularly relevant to proposition 4 which could be interpreted as arguing that international processes might either stabilize or they might not. The problem is not a severe one, however. Because proposition 4 is based on the previous three propositions, it merely suggests the possible paths that might be observed in different international processes. Its message is that the *ad hoc* approach does not envision international processes as being necessarily a collection of different (objective and subjective) games which are related to one another by changes in the structure and substance of national choice processes. Although this might be the norm, in some cases it is reasonable to expect that stability would set into the relations among states. The main ideas of this approach focus on the factors leading to variations in behavioral stability as seen in terms of the relations of international processes over time.

Taken together, the various levels in which the *ad hoc* approach is specified characterize long-term international processes as a causal path leading from individual choice processes to international outcomes, and from international outcomes to subsequent individual and national choices. Both stability and change in long-term, multiple-actor international processes can be understood in terms of this causal path.

9.2.5 Israeli–Syrian crises, 1948–1985: an empirical illustration of the *ad hoc* approach[12]

The conflict between Israel and Syria is one of the most intense and violent in the Middle East. It is also a classical case of an enduring international rivalry, or what some scholars have described as a protracted conflict. In an effort to understand the evolution of this conflict over time, Maoz and Yaniv (1989) identified 23 crises involving these states over the 1948–1985 period. They attempted to characterize each of these crises as a 2×2 game by identifying the preference ordering of outcomes by the two states and examining the extent to which the actual behavior of each state conformed with the theoretical outcome of the game. Table 9.1 provides a summary of these crises.

Before interpreting the results of this table, it is important to explain what the preference structures represent in terms of the research design used by these authors. The principal aim of this study was to determine the *objective*, that is, observable pattern of evolution of the Israeli–Syrian conflict over time. Thus the authors examined each of the states separately, and – on the basis of historical and biographical accounts of these cases – determined a generalized preference ordering of outcomes. However, they did not examine the process that led to the establishment of these preferences. Rather, they assumed that the historical sources reveal how national elites, seen as unitary actors, rank ordered these four outcomes. This is equivalent to the process of identifying objective games discussed in chapter 8. Having identified each game, the authors examined the extent to

492

which the actual international outcome coincided with the theoretical outcome.

Since no data on the content of subjective games is given, the attempt to illustrate the *ad hoc* approach in this case involves some amount of indirect inference about when misperception might have mattered in inducing changes in game structures over time. A really outstanding feature of this table is that a vast majority of the actual outcomes coincided with the theoretical outcome. This might suggest a fundamentally correct understanding of the opponent's preferences over time, even when the preferences themselves change. Yet, this impression can be very misleading. In most of these cases there was no need to have a correct assessment of the opponent's preferences in order to behave in a way that is seen as theoretically correct. Note that the PD game is the most frequent model of the Israeli–Syrian crises. Called Bluff and Chicken come, respectively, a close second and third. In the PD cases, there need not be a correct perception to get a match between theoretical and actual outcomes: it is enough to assume that each actor realized that it had a dominant alternative and used it.

In the Called Bluff cases, the match between the theoretical and actual outcomes is again due to the fact that the actor with the dominant alternative used it and the actor without a dominant alternative used its maximin rule. Again, to get such a fit between theoretical and actual outcomes, neither actor's choice necessarily required correct assessment of the opponent's preferences. Suffice it to suggest that an actor would follow a certain choice rule which is not unreasonable given the inability to know for sure what the opponent's preferences might be. This idea is easily extendable to the cases described by the game of Chicken. In such cases, the mutual cooperation outcome might emerge whether or not actors have correct information about their opponent's preferences, or whether actors actually incorporate such information into their decision processes. In fact, I suggested above that in these cases, good information might be a liability rather than an asset. In the Israeli–Syrian conflict, one could reasonably suggest that the compromises in the cases characterized by a Chicken preference structure resulted from the fact that both states acted on worst case assumptions. Information about the opponent's preference structure might not have been incorporated at all into the decision process. Thus, the good fit between theoretical outcomes of the game and the actual ones cannot be taken as evidence of either correct perception or of analytic decision processes.

One may, however, infer from this fit that actors have behaved

Table 9.1. *Israeli–Syrian crises, 1948–1985 – a game-theoretic characterization*

Historical phase	Game no.	Date	Name of incident	Pref. order		Game type	Theoretical outcome	Actual outcome
				Israel	**Syria**			
DMZ and Hulla (1949–1955)	1	4–7, 1948	Armistice agreement	*TRSP*	**TRSP**	Chicken	Comp.	Comp.
	2	3, 1951	Hulla (Indicent 1)	*TRPS*	**TRPS**	PD	Deadlock	Deadlock
	3	4, 1951	Hulla (Incident 2)	*TRPS*	**TRPS**	PD	Deadlock	Deadlock
	4	4, 1951–8, 1955	Hulla (Incident 3)	*TRPS*	**TRSP**	Called bluff	Israeli victory	Israeli victory
Lake Kineret clashes (1955–1956)	5	9–11, 1955	Fishing rights	*TRPS*	**TRPS**	PD	Deadlock	Deadlock
	6	12, 1955–10, 1956	Kinneret raid	*TRPS*	**TRSP**	Called bluff	Israeli victory	Israeli victory
Dormant conflict (1956–1960)	7	11, 1956	Sinai campaign	*RPTS*	RTPS	*	Syrian attack	Comp.
	8	1, 1957–1, 1960	Post-Sinai period	*TRSP*	**TRSP**	Chicken	Comp.	Comp.

Period	No.	Date	Crisis	Game			
Israeli diversion project (1960–1963)	9	2, 1960	Diversion incident	*TRPS* **TRPS**	PD	Deadlock	Deadlock
	10	2, 1960	Tawriq Raid	*TRPS* **TRSP**	Called bluff	Israeli victory	Israeli victory
	11	3, 1962–12, 1963	Nuqeib Raid and aftermath	*TRPS* **TRSP**	Called bluff	Israeli victory	Israeli victory
Syrian diversion and Six Day War (1963–1968)	12	1, 1964–3, 1967	Syrian diversion project	*TRPS* **TRPS**	PD	Deadlock	Deadlock
	13	4, 1967	Air battle incident	*TRPS* **TRPS**	PD	Deadlock	Deadlock
	14	5–6, 1967	Six Day War	*PRTS* **TRSP**	Inverse bully	Comp.	Israeli attack
Attrition and frustration (1969–1973)	15	3, 1969–8, 1970	War of attrition	*TRPS* **TRPS**	PD	Deadlock	Deadlock
	16	9, 1970–9, 1973	Black Sept. and aftermath	*TRPS* **TRSP**	Called bluff	Israeli victory	Israeli victory
	17	10, 1973–4, 1974	Yom Kippur War	*RPST* **TPSR**	Modified deadlock	Deadlock	Syrian attack

Table 9.1. (*cont.*)

Historical phase	Game no.	Date	Name of incident	Pref. order Israel	Pref. order Syria	Game type	Theoretical outcome	Actual outcome
Disengagement agreement	18	5, 1974–1987	Disengagement agreement	*TRSP*	**TRSP**	Chicken	Comp.	Comp.
Lebanon Conflict (1976–1987)	19	6, 1976–4, 1981	Syrian entry into Lebanon	*TRSP*	**TRSP**	Chicken	Comp.	Comp.
	20	5, 1981–5, 1982	Mount Sanin incident	*TRSP*	**TRPS**	Called bluff	Syrian victory	Syrian victory
	21	6, 1982	Lebanon war	*TPRS*	**TRSP**	Bully	Israeli attack	Israeli attack
	22	8, 1982–2, 1985	Aftermath of Lebanon war	*TRPS*	**TRPS**	PD	Deadlock	Deadlock
	23	3, 1985–6, 1987	Israeli withdrawal	*RTPS*	**TRPS**	# 48**	Deadlock	Comp.

T = Temptation (unilateral escalation) payoff; R = Reward (mutual cooperation) payoff; S = Sucker's (unilateral cooperation) payoff; P = Punishment (mutual escalation) payoff.

A Historical phase is a general division of the period into specific subperiods which characterize stages in the Israeli–Syrian conflict.

Payoff structures list the preference ordering of each actor over the four outcomes with the most preferred outcome on the left and the least preferred outcome on the right. Thus, preference order TRSP implies that an actor prefers the unilateral escalation outcome over the mutual cooperation outcome, the mutual cooperation outcome over the unilateral cooperation outcome, and the unilateral cooperation outcome over the mutual escalation outcome. The general game structure is given by

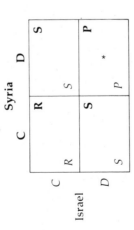

*Nash Equilibrium.

A number instead of a label to a given game represents the number of this game in the Rapoport and Guyer (1966) taxonomy of 2 × 2 games. See also Rapoport, Guyer, and Gordon (1976).

**Game no. 23 is derived from Maoz and Felsenthal (1987). It does not appear in the Maoz–Yaniv article.

Source: Maoz and Yaniv, 1989.

myopically. Specifically, this study provides rather strong evidence for some aspects of the *ad hoc* approach. First, the fact that actors used their dominant alternative when they had one and the maximin alternative when they had none may imply that the elites of the two states acted on a premise that the game they were playing would not be repeated. Moreover, the fact that they shifted from a defection alternative when they had a PD preference structure to a cooperative alternative when they had a Chicken preference structure adds some credence to this suggestion. For example, the Syrian shift from a series of defections in games 1, 2, and 3 to a cooperative alternative in game 4 was repeated in games 5 and 6, and again in games 9, 10, and 11, as well as in games 12 and 13. This suggests that a change in an actor's preferences which implies a necessity of change of choice rule (and sometimes a choice shift) is indeed observed in this conflict. This is obviously consistent with the *ad hoc* approach.

Second, the change in the nature of the games and the fact that no single game type dominates this kind of international interaction suggests a substantial degree of preference change over time. We shall see that evidence of preference change is an important, though not definitive, indication of an *ad hoc* perspective. The incidence of preference change was not a typical characteristic of one actor; it characterized the sequence of games of both actors over time.

Can we draw any inferences from the variation in the content of the Israeli–Syrian games (and their outcomes) over time with respect to the expected relations between international outcomes according to the *ad hoc* approach? It is very difficult to draw such inferences in the absence of information about subjective games. Because we cannot tell whether the actual outcomes of the games differed from the ones decision makers had expected, it is hard to say whether preference changes were indeed the results of outcome-discrepancies. However, research done by Russell Leng (1988, 1983) can help us shed light on the notion that previous game outcomes affect subsequent outcomes.

Leng discussed a model of learning which he labeled *the experiential Realpolitik* model. According to this model, state behavior in subsequent crises is a function of the outcome of the previous crisis and the bargaining strategy it had used in that crisis. Specifically, the lessons that states draw from a given crisis are a function of what they get in that crisis. If the outcome of the crisis is successful, a state would replicate its behavior in the previous crisis. If it experienced a diplomatic defeat, it normally infers that its bargaining tactic was overly accommodative; hence increasing its level of hostility and demonstrated resolve in the subsequent crisis. This is a fairly simple model of cross-crisis learning, but it has an interesting implication. Crises involving the same actors are more likely to escalate to war the more they recur. As long as one crisis breeds a winner and loser, the loser will increase its level of hostility in the subsequent crisis. If the subsequent crisis ends in an asymmetrical outcome (with a winner and loser, whoever these are), the loser will again increase the level of hostility, and so forth until the war breaks out. Leng's analysis of recurring crises provided strong empirical support to this implication. In a subsequent research, Leng (1988) formulated this reasoning process as a game-theoretic model involving preference change.

The analysis of Israeli–Syrian interactions supports that notion as well. In three out of the four wars that these analyses encompass, there is a distinct pattern of escalation wherein the preferences of actors become more and more polarized. For example, using the index of group polarization to measure the conflict of interests inherent in a certain game, the typical games in this conflict get the polarization score of 0.9 for the PD, 0.7 for Called Bluff, and 0.4 for Chicken. The movement from Chicken to Called Bluff to PD signifies escalation both in terms of actual choices and in terms of polarization of preferences. Such patterns are seen prior to the Six Day Way, to the Yom Kippur war, and to the Lebanon war. Some learning is taking place, and it is not unreasonable to suggest that it follows Leng's relatively simple experiential *Realpolitik* model.

But now does this model converge with the predictions of the *ad hoc* approach? The answer is somewhat speculative in the absence of reliable information regarding the nature of subjective games. Leng's model seems to be consistent with an irrational attribution process wherein success reinforces prior behavior (because it is attributed to the actor) and failure causes change in prior behavior in that it leads to revision in an actor's definition of the situation. Finally, the lack of an overall pattern of repeat behavior suggests that the consistent instability in game content and game outcomes is due to partial convergence between expected and actual outcomes which results in frequent preference changes and choice shifts.

9.3 THE STRATEGIC PERSPECTIVE OF INTERNATIONAL PROCESSES

The image of international politics as portrayed by the *ad hoc* approach may seem excessively narrow in that it assumes that statesmen lack an ability to maintain stable preferences and images of friends and foes. It may also seem excessively complex in terms of its ideas regarding the unfolding of international outcomes over time. International processes may display more stability and continuity than is depicted by the *ad hoc* approach, and therefore a different way of looking at such processes requires going beyond a narrow decision-outcome-decision-outcome notion. It requires exploring the underlying principles of action in an interdependent international environment. These principles cannot be found in an approach whose focus is on first-order relationships between international outcomes and national choices. General principles of this type can be uncovered only through a macro approach to interdependent behavior whose focus is on national strategies which describe patterns of outcomes over time. Accordingly, the fundamental assumptions of the strategic approach to international processes are the following:

1 States have some basic values that they see as their national goals irrespective of the type of government in power or the individuals who hold leadership roles. These values are generally stable over time with respect to most issues that are likely to arise in international politics.[13]

2 As a result of the stability of national preferences, international processes are best conceived as an iterative play of the same game over a relatively long period of time. Alternatively, if games do change over time in terms of their structure or content, these changes are rare and far apart.

3 Because, in most cases, nations face a relatively stable international environment consisting of the same friends and the same foes, they are capable of developing long-range (but not necessarily optimal) strategies of international conduct. These strategies consist of a set of behavioral rules which may (or may not) be contingent on a set of prespecified conditions. Such rules cover nearly all possible situations that might arise in a given international game, and they vary from one state (or one game) to another along some known dimensions.

4 States base their behavior on the knowledge they have of the opponents' preferences and strategies. However, the information states have about these things is assumed to vary over

---

[13] It is quite conceivable, however, that the values a state applies to determine its choices differ across issue-areas. For example, the US applies one set of moral standards to its dealing with the Soviet Union and quite another set of values to its dealing with pro-Western authoritarian regimes such as Saudi Arabia, Chile, and the like. This assumption asserts simply that national preferences exhibit considerable cross-time stability with respect to any given issue-area or actor.

time and across space. Specifically, states are capable of adjusting their perceptions of other actors' preferences and strategies, and these adjustments might affect the strategies they use, but not their preferences.

5 States are aware of the uncertainty which prevails in international politics in the sense that one is not quite sure which game one is playing. Hence, variations in national strategies, and in international outcomes are a result of search and detection processes used by states to ascertain the preferences and strategies of other actors.

The principal idea of the strategic approach to international processes is that national decision makers – be they rational or not – follow a set of goals that is stable over time. This, and the fact that they think other actors also follow a generally stable, if different, set of goals, leads national decision makers to see a stable international environment, or, in the terminology of the previous chapter, the same subjective game over time. In such cases, states develop long-term and fairly comprehensive plans for dealing with this environment and stick to them as long as this perception of stability is preserved. Strategies used by states change if and when decision makers have a good reason to believe that some fundamental features of the environment have changed, making the previous strategy no longer adequate for dealing with the "new situation." Most general ideas about international politics – certainly all systemic theories – rely implicitly or explicitly on this general notion of the evolution of international processes over time.

Before going into the details of this approach, let me make some remarks about the role of rationality in this image. All the ingredients of rationality seem to be present in the assumptions of the strategic approach, yet I have deliberately indicated that the strategies adopted by states may not be the optimal ones. There is no necessary connection between the assumptions implying long-term stability of national preferences, national perceptions of the environment, and rational strategies. A state can develop a suboptimal strategy for a wide variety of reasons, some of which have to do with its approach to risks, that is, its willingness to rely on its perceptions of the environment. A suboptimal strategy may be selected because a state might think that some or all of its opponents are either not entirely rational (that is, do not have a consistent preference structure) or that the leaders of other states are not in complete control over their subordinates. In such cases, a strategy must be geared to meet consistent inconsistencies in other actors' behavior.

The notion of strategic behavior is well developed in game theory,

501

and some of the key ideas of a supergame approach have been discussed briefly in chapter 8. Here, however, a more detailed connection between the evolution, change, and stabilization of strategies in international interactions is required. In addition, it is important to examine how an analysis of international processes in terms of a clash of strategies can be developed in the absence of strict rationality.

To begin with, from the strategic perspective what needs to be explained is not the relationship between changes in the content and outcomes of games, but rather variations in the outcomes of the same game over time. It is useful to start the discussion of the strategic approach with a review of Axelrod's (1984) work on the PD. Axelrod reasoned that one could assess the effectiveness of strategies in the PD in terms of how well they performed when pitted against one another in a round-robin tournament. He asked a number of game theorists from various disciplines to submit proposed strategies for an iterated version of the PD. Once these strategies were given, Axelrod converted them into computer programs and pitted each strategy against all other strategies, recording the score that each strategy obtained in the tournament. The results of this tournament were surprising: the strategy that emerged as the winner was TIT-FOR-TAT, the simplest strategy that participated in the tournament. As may be recalled from chapter 8, TIT-FOR-TAT is a strategy that cooperates on the first iteration and then does whatever the other strategy did in the previous move (Axelrod, 1980a).

Next, Axelrod provided the game theorists with a detailed report of the tournament, of the way the results were calculated, and of the strategic problems associated with some of the strategies that had been submitted for the first round. These experts were then invited to revise, change, or keep their original strategy given these results. The results of the second tournament were very similar to the first. TIT-FOR-TAT won the second tournament as well; more complex strategies did not do significantly better or worse than simple strategies, and the only property that seemed to have correlated with the tournament score of a program was whether or not it was "nice". (A "nice" strategy, as defined by Axelrod, is one which is never the first to defect.)

On the basis of these computer tournaments, Axelrod began to ponder how cooperation emerges and what factors might affect survival and effective performance in an environment of egoists operating under conditions of anarchy. This led to some important theoretical insights about the properties of successful cooperative strategies. Axelrod (1981, 1984: 206–215) proved a number of propositions about the properties of successful and stable strategies in the iterated PD. For example, if the value of each outcome in an iterated PD is smaller than the value of the same outcome in a previous iteration, there is no strategy that is independently best. In other words, which strategy is optimal depends on the environment in which one lives, in terms of the strategies used by other players. In addition, he demonstrated that in a large population of "meanies," an invasion by a surprisingly small population of players using nice strategies such as TIT-FOR-TAT can be extremely successful, whereas no population of TIT-FOR-TAT players can be invaded by exploitative strategies.[14]

Although these results are restricted to a single – albeit important – game, they do suggest some ideas concerning a more general approach to the analysis of long term international processes. Some of these ideas are discussed below.

9.3.1 Classification of strategies

As pointed out in chapter 8, some of the assumptions made by much of game theory are unrealistic. Even if one is willing to accept the rationality assumption, the notion of full information is questionable in most real-world settings. To begin a more general delineation of strategies and their various types, it is instructive to examine a hypothetical "state of nature." Suppose that two states first come to some sort of contact with one another, without having known anything about each other. In such a case it is very difficult to establish expectations about the other state's preferences, let alone to predict which strategy it is going to use. If the stakes involved in the state of nature are relatively important (for example, the two states face an environment of limited resources, and thus there exists a potential conflict of interests over the division of these resources), decision makers will attempt to develop a strategy that would enable them to best detect what the other state wants and how it plans to get it. But detection of the opponent's strategy might be risky: by the time a state discovers what the other one is planning, it might suffer great losses. Thus, detection of the opponent's plans, however important, should not overshadow the importance of preserving or accomplishing one's values.

Let us consider two general types of strategies that a state might employ under such a state of nature. One is a *safety* strategy, that is, a strategy that is relatively invulnerable, or otherwise insensitive, to

---

[14] But Hirshleifer and Martinez-Coll (1988) and Carrol (1985) showed that this proof is limited to very narrow circumstances.

either the preference structure of the opponent or to its strategy. This is, by the way, what Axelrod (1984) calls a "collectively" stable strategy. I prefer the "safety" label because such a strategy is not necessarily optimal even if the opponent's preferences are correctly perceived. What may make such as a strategy attractive is that it assures a certain minimum payoff whoever the opponent might be and whatever strategy it might be using. The other strategy is a *detection* strategy. The primary aim of the strategy is to force the opponent to reveal both its payoff structure and the strategy it is using.

Safety strategies are easy to develop, and they are easy to recognize given knowledge of an actor's preferences. For example, permanent choice of a maximin strategy is probably the best representative of the notion of safety. In the PD this is what Axelrod calls ALL D, but such a strategy is more general in that it encompasses all games. TIT-FOR-TAT is also a sort of a general "safety" strategy. It is more sensitive than ALL D to the possibility of encountering a conditionally cooperative opponent (i.e., one that might cooperate if its opponent cooperates), but it does not make a deliberate effort to find out what kind of opponent it is playing.

Detection strategies are more complex and more difficult to detect. One example of a clever detection strategy in the iterated PD tournament is the strategy known as DOWNING (after its inventor). DOWNING starts by defecting on the first two iterations and uses Bayesian rules to update the probabilities of cooperation given its own actions. In short, it attempts to guess the general attributes of the opponent's strategy and then fits the best strategy to counter it (Axelrod, 1984: 34–35). Another, less typical, example of a detection strategy is TESTER (Axelrod, 1984: 44–45). This rule starts by defecting on the first move and then examines the opponent's response. If the opponent responds by defecting, it cooperates on the next move and plays TIT-FOR-TAT thereafter. If the opponent seems soft in that it does not respond by defection, TESTER cooperates on the next two moves and defects every other move thereafter. What connects both these strategies is that they attempt to guess what kind of opponent they are playing and then adjust their subsequent strategy to the opponent's strategy.

Detection strategies consist of two initial components: a detection algorithm, and an adjustment rule. The detection algorithm is a set of rules which stipulates how this strategy ought to behave in the first part of the game, and what kind of clues to look for in the opponent's responses. The adjustment rule stipulates what one is to do given a conclusion derived from the detection algorithm. Detection strategies might also have an error-checking mechanism which is designed to give the decision maker a signal that the adjustment rule is not producing the expected results. Once the mechanism gives an error signal, the strategy reverts to the initial detection algorithm.

There may be four reasons for an error signal: (1) the detection rule failed to detect the opponent's preferences, (2) the detection rule detected the opponent's preferences but failed to detect the kind of strategy it had been using, (3) the detection algorithm did a good job but the opponent, at some point, changed preferences, and (4) the opponent changed strategy without changing preferences. A good detection algorithm has in it a logic that may enable it to detect both a general type of preference structure and general properties of strategic behavior. For example, a simple inferential procedure will be to repeat a given strategy several times. If the opponent does not alter its strategy, one can conclude that the outcome obtained in the previous few moves cannot be the least-preferred by the opponent; if it were, the opponent would not have repeated its behavior. Next, the detection strategy shifts its choice, reverting to a new alternative and repeating it several times. If the opponent changes his choice, then we can make another inference, that the previous alternative used by the opponent cannot be dominant, or else it would not have shifted its choice. Proceeding in this manner, additional possible preference structures are ruled out by a process of elimination.

The problem of detection algorithms is that they have a high initial cost. An actor must be willing to pay some price for attempting to detect the opponent's payoff structure and strategies. Sometimes an actor may have to get its worst outcome in order to guess which opponent it is facing. In addition, since the adjustment rule fits an optimal strategy to the one attributed to the opponent, one must be willing to pay for errors in the detection process, or for re-adjustment to new preferences or new strategies used by an opponent.[15] The startup costs and the correction costs involved in the implementation of a detection strategy may force actors to revert to relatively simple

---

[15] The beauty of the TIT-FOR-TAT rule is that it really does not matter who the opponent is. Its behavioral principle is such that no detection is required, but rules that have detection algorithms will: (a) easily recognize TIT-FOR-TAT, and (b) once they do, they will cooperate with it. One must be reminded, however, that our knowledge of the properties of the TIT-FOR-TAT rule is rather limited. First, it is restricted to PD settings. Second, it is restricted to some assumptions about motivations of players, or about the rules of the tournament. See Behr (1980); Dacey and Pendegraft (1986, 1987) for analyses suggesting the limitations of the TIT-FOR-TAT rule under different conditions.

and straightforward safety strategies, and stick to them as long as they possibly can (which is usually as long as a given preference structure holds).

The distinction between safety strategies and detection strategies is somewhat crude and superficial. There are strategies that are neither safety devices, nor do they contain devices for detecting the opponent's preferences and strategies and adjusting to them. These strategies are called *idiosyncratic* because they reflect some fundamental attribute of the actor using them. In Axelrod's tournament, idiosyncratic strategies are TIT-FOR-TWO-TATS, JOSS, and some other rules. The attributes of these rules are that they are relatively insensitive to the opponent they are playing against, while – at the same time – they do not make an effort to develop a highly deterministic behavioral pattern. The actual behavioral pattern in these cases is guided by some fundamental dispositions of their users. TIT-FOR-TWO-TATS, for example, is willing to be somewhat lenient with respect to the opponent's defection. It is willing to accept the possibility of error and to forgive non-systematic defection. JOSS, on the other hand, plays TIT-FOR-TAT 90 per cent of the time and defects ten percent of the time. Given the single game setting of the Axelrod tournament, it seems obvious that the number of categories into which strategies could be classified is nearly as large as the infinite number of possible strategies one could devise to play an iterated PD. For this reason, it is useful to stick with the simple dichotomy of safety and detection strategies.

It might be useful to consider how our classification scheme compares with other schemes used in the literature. Axelrod (1984) distinguished between nice strategies and ones that are not nice. In our scheme, safety strategies might be either nice or not nice. Detection strategies are, by definition, not nice strategies: Once they detect their opponent's strategy, they might be the first to defect. Another distinction is between simple and complex strategies (where complexity might be operationalized in terms of the number of programming steps required to model a given strategy). Here the relationship is also obvious: safety strategies tend to be simple ones whereas detection strategies are generally complex. The reason I did not resort to these or other dimensions to classify strategies is that these dimensions have a built-in evaluative connotation. They represent classification in terms of the properties of strategies. In our case, however, we need a description of strategies in terms of what they imply for the analysis of international processes.

9.3.2 Rules governing strategy selection and strategy change

The first issue to examine when applying a strategic perspective to international politics concerns the determinants of the type of strategies selected by states. This issue has either a very simple or very complex answer. The simple answer is that the most important determinant of the type of strategy selected by a state is the nature of its preferences. The more complex answer is that strategy selection and strategy change are determined by a number of exogenous factors. The effects of preferences on strategy selection is relatively easy to explain. Certain preference structures will, by definition, yield safety strategies, whereas other preference structures create strong incentives for detection strategies. Specifically, a highly deterministic preference structure[16] renders one's best choice of a long term strategy clearly independent of the other actors' preferences or of their choices of long-term strategies. (For that matter, it also makes little or no difference to an actor whether its opponents use long-term strategies or basically act in an *ad hoc* fashion.) However, when an actor's best strategy is not independent of the strategies used by other actors, a detection strategy might become appealing.

Obviously, this is an overly simplistic argument. For one thing, one does not know where the line between deterministic and inter-dependent preference structures is to be drawn. Is a PD preference structure deterministic or not? Even if we were able to draw such a line (for example, in terms of the existence of a dominant strategy), we still would need to say something about the relative propensity of actors without a clear-cut safety strategy to actually find one. Let us therefore move to the more complex analysis of the determinants of strategy selection in international politics. Before I do this, two points must be reiterated: First, I do not assume rationality of states in the sense that they always select an optimal long-term strategy given their preferences. Second, how decisions to select national strategies had been made is of little or no importance as long as we can determine which strategies were actually selected.

Whether a state selects a safety strategy or a detection strategy depends on the attitude of its decision makers toward risk. This attitude, contrary to game-theoretic notions, is not necessarily reflected in the national preference structure. Nor is the attitude toward risk assumed to be independent of the stakes involved in the

---

[16] For example, this might be a deadlock-type preferences – to use Snyder and Diesing's (1977) terminology – or what Schelling (1984: 246–247) calls a yes! configuration (it could as easily be described as a no! configuration) in the context of arms control.

game or of the assumptions one is making about the opponent (particularly about the opponent's propensity to risky choices).[17] In our case, initial selection of strategy is seen as a function of risk propensity in that the more risk averse a national decision making body is, the more inclined it would be to adopt safety strategies. Risk-neutral or risk-acceptant actors will be more inclined toward detection strategies. But the precise nature of the detection strategy would depend on the magnitude of risk acceptance.

The stakes involved in the game will also have an effect on strategy selection. The higher the stakes, the more risk averse an actor would be, hence the more likely is that actor to select a safety strategy over a detection strategy. Finally, assumptions about the risk propensity of other actors will determine whether a detection strategy is at all useful. Not knowing exactly what are the opponent's preference does not imply that one does not know some general things about the opponent, such as whether in general the opponent is risk averse or risk acceptant. For example, in US scholarship about the Soviet Union, the consensus seems to be that the Soviets are generally risk averse in their approach to foreign policy. (While it may well be that the assumption made by the US foreign policy bureaucracy about the Soviet risk-taking propensity are quite the opposite.)[18] To the extent that US policy toward the Soviet Union is a carefully crafted strategy, it might be based on the notion of Soviet attitudes toward risks. In general, the rule is that an actor will adopt a strategy which addresses in some way

[17] The strict game-theoretic view is that all these things are reflected in the actors' preference structure, and that risk-propensities vary across players but not within players and over situations. I differ from this view for two reasons. First, preferences are defined over a discrete set of outcomes, not over long-term strategies *given* a set of outcomes. Since Axelrod has shown that there is no single best strategy independent of the environment, one must make assumptions about the environment when selecting such a strategy; these assumptions will affect the strategy choice, and hence actors who differ with respect to risk-propensity would differ in the kind of long-term strategies they select, even when they have the same preferences. This is very much evident from the fact that the game theorists who submitted strategies to the PD tournament differed a great deal in terms of the strategies they thought would be the most effective. Second, preferences for game outcomes are taken out of a more general context in which the game is played. Such preferences represent only the ordering of outcomes that are part of the game but not how these outcomes are ordered relative to outcomes that are not in the game. (This is the famous axiom concerning "independence of irrelevant alternatives." See Arrow, 1963 for details, and Rapoport, 1966 for critical comments.) Given the more general context, it is possible that actors would vary their risk-propensity as a result of changes in stakes over games.

[18] For a perceptive study of Soviet risk-taking in the 1948 and 1961 Berlin crises and a very useful discussion of conventional wisdom on this topic see Adomeit (1982), especially pp. 51–66. Adomeit argues that Soviet crisis behavior is of a highly calculated strategic nature, displaying essentially a risk-averse pattern (pp. 328–345). See also Kaplan (1981: 667–686).

the risk-disposition that an opponent is assumed to have. If the opponent is seen as risk-acceptant, a safety strategy would seem appropriate. If the opponent's attitude toward risk is seen to be cautious, an actor might be inclined to adopt a detection strategy.

The complexity of the game (as defined in chapter 8 in terms of the number of actors and the strategies available to each) is also a potentially important determinant of strategy selection. The more complex the game, the more likely actors are to resort to safety strategies. Complexity renders detection strategies risky and costly. Hence, safety strategies become more appealing from both rational and cognitive perspectives. For example, in the n-person PD, TIT-FOR-TAT is ineffective because one defector leads to its eventual extinction (Hirshleifer and Martinez-Coll, 1988).

What about the factors that affect strategy change? Before we deal with such factors, it must be noted that the strategic perspective deals with two types of strategy change: exogenously induced change and endogenously induced change. Exogenously induced change refers to strategy change that results from changes in national preferences. This approach assumes that national preferences do not change very often, but they are not entirely fixed either. National preferences might change as a result of regime or other structural change in states, or as a result of factors that have little or nothing to do with the strategic interaction which is being analyzed. The preferences of a state in a strategic interaction might be altered by a shift in the relations between itself and a third party which has not been a major actor in that interaction. One example might be the possible change in the relations between the United States and the Soviet Union as a result of Nixon's opening to China.

Endogenously induced change is a result of learning. Typically, such change is a part of the detection strategy. It occurs either when the detection process results in some conclusion regarding the preferences and strategy of the other player (thereby activating the adjustment rule which identifies the most effective strategy to be used against the opponent's strategy), or when the feedback mechanism indicates that the selected strategy performs below par (in which case, one reverts to the detection algorithm).[19]

---

[19] Note that endogenously induced strategy shifts are unlikely under a safety strategy. If an actor uses a safety strategy, the only factors that can affect strategy shifts are exogenous (to the game, not to the actor). On the other hand, strategy changes for actors who rely on detection strategies can be caused by either exogenous or endogenous factors.

9.3.3 Strategies in international processes

Given the assumptions of the approach and the types of strategies discussed above, the evolution of international processes can be seen in the following terms. First, an analytic or empirical starting point is required. A starting point can be conceived of as a historical (or hypothetical) instance when governments define their preferences over the outcomes they see and make an "initial" strategy selection. Here the strategic theorist may wish to explain why the strategy selection was the one attributed to each state. If this is of interest, decision theory is instrumental. Initial strategy selection is a major foreign policy decision, and must be explained even if historically we cannot identify an occasion where such a decision was made. Take, for example, an attempt to analyze the Cold War a clash of strategies. The strategic perspective requires identification of a point where the Soviet Union has selected a strategy of dealing with the United States, and a point where the United States decided which strategy to use *vis-à-vis* the Soviets. Whether or not we can actually identify a historical decision point (such as the Truman Doctrine, NSC-68, etc.) is not really important. However, if we want to account for the selection of one strategy over whatever other strategies might have been considered (or not considered), we cannot avoid dealing with decision making.

Second, the type of strategies that actors have chosen determines the next step. Here we are examining how these strategies were applied and what kind of behavioral patterns they imply. The key question is why and under what conditions stability is obtained. In most cases where a strategic analysis seems suitable, some time passes before states change their strategies. This time is the "normal science" stage of the perspective because it allows examining historical developments in terms of prior strategies. It is here where we can test whether the strategy we attribute to a state is indeed consistent with its actual behavior. The evidence we would be looking for concerns: (*a*) indications of stability of preferences (preference change would be a bad sign for the strategic perspective), and (*b*) the extent to which actual behavior was consistent with what the strategy prescribes. At this stage decision theory will not be of much interest because the application of a strategy is a fairly straightforward process. (One may still want to rely on some decision theoretic material to show how a detection strategy works, or how it makes inferences about the opponents' preferences and strategies from their actual behavior.)

To come back to the Cold War example, suppose that the Soviet leadership decided on a certain confrontational strategy toward the end of the Second World War. (This would be interpreted as a safety strategy in our terminology.) Suppose that the US strategy has been initially a detection strategy which begins by cooperation and then looks at the Soviet response to determine their intentions. After a number of "lessons" from Soviet behavior in Iran, Greece, Turkey, and Czechoslovakia, the US has finally made a strong commitment to a "containment" strategy. The next step would be to derive the implications of these strategies for the behavior of the actors in the Berlin and Korea crises and match these expectations with actual behavior. However, one might also be interested in how the Soviet preferences and strategy were interpreted by the Truman administration when the adjustment (or containment) rule was applied. In this case, decision theory is instrumental in explaining the link between detection of the opponent's strategy and adjustment of one's own strategy.

The third step of the approach is to determine when and how strategies change and whether or when other actors become aware of the changes. One may want to identify historical or hypothetical turning points in the strategies of the actors (the Cuban missile crisis is an oft-mentioned case in analyses of Soviet–American relations). An explanation of strategy change normally involves decision theory as it brings us back to step one.

In this manner the cycle continues. Instead of examining each international outcome and explaining how it has arisen, the strategic approach urges us to look for turning points (initial strategy selection, strategy change) and predict regularities in terms of the consequences of these turning points. Some of the implications of the strategic approach with respect to the analysis of international politics are summarized by the following points.

1. In analyzing international politics in general, and international processes, in particular, we should attempt to understand not only the preferences of states over outcomes, but also the kind of strategies that they use in order to deal with each other. Understanding national preferences is important, especially since these are relatively stable over time. But in most cases it is impossible to infer strategies from preferences. Most preference structures might be compatible with a large number of possible strategies which are more or less dependent on the strategies used by other players.

2. An international process involving states whose decision makers select safety strategies will be characterized by a high degree of behavioral stability (as defined in the context of the *ad hoc* approach).

This suggests that factors affecting the selection of such strategies by all actors (such as risk aversiveness) will be instrumental in generating stability.

3.   An international process involving some risk-averse and some risk-acceptant actors will be characterized by low degrees of behavioral stability at the beginning but will tend to stabilize very rapidly. Initial instability in such cases is due to the variation in game outcomes resulting form the activation of detection algorithms by the latter type of actors. Such algorithms involve rapid choice shifts which are designed to test the opponent's responsiveness. However, since safety strategies are easy to recognize, stability sets in fairly early in the process as the detection strategy reverts to the adjustment rule and follows a stable strategy of its own.[20]

4.   The larger the number of actors who resort to detection strategies in a given international process, the less behavioral stability is to be expected. This is so because all actors will attempt to outguess and outmaneuver their opponents, hence strategy shifts will occur even without preference changes. To the extent that such strategies contain an error-checking mechanism, these would be activated rather frequently, forcing frequent strategy changes.[21]

5.   The existence of stability in interstate interaction has no *a priori* normative value either in terms of the collective rationality of the recurring outcome or in terms of the payoffs for individual players. International processes may stabilize on a collectively and individually inferior outcome, or on a collectively superior one. Whether stability is individually or collectively (that is, internationally) desirable depends on the specific details of the game being played and the actual strategy selections of actors.

The employment of long-term strategies does not imply that international processes would be characterized by behavioral stability. This is so despite the fact that this perspective seems to entail more stable elements than the *ad hoc* approach, such as stable preferences and

[20] Stability is not necesarily expressed in terms of lack of variations in game outcomes over time. Use of a strategy which is optimal against a given safety strategy might entail choice shifts at some points in time. Yet, such variations are predictable, once the features of the optimal strategy are known. Also, in many cases, a stable safety strategy by one actor might induce a stable strategy by other actors who had been using a detection strategy. This is the case when various detection strategies confront a TIT-FOR-TAT rule in the iterated PD.

[21] Resort to detection strategies suggests some degree of sophistication on the part of the actors. It is possible that, while attempting to detect the strategies of their opponents, actors will simultaneously engage in a process of deception which is designed to misrepresent one's preferences and/or strategy. (See Brams, 1977 for a discussion of deception in simple 2×2 games.) The use of deception is likely to

stable expectations. As was the case of the *ad hoc* approach that does not envision international interactions to be erratic and unpredictable, the strategic perspective does not depict international politics as being fully deterministic.

The process of strategy selection and the nature of strategy change has not been discussed for two reasons. First, the theoretical basis of this approach is very limited. We know quite a lot of things about strategic play of the iterated PD. But there exists no general formulation of a strategic approach to iterated games. (By *general* I mean that such a perspective should encompass all types of games.) Second, without a solid theoretical foundation, the number of possibilities one must consider when dealing with all possible strategies is infinite. A more fully-developed theory would provide for a more manageable set of viable strategies or some rules for strategy identification and analysis.

The features of a formal theory of strategic interaction are therefore: (*a*) the set of assumptions that describe the elements of the strategic perspective, i.e., constant preferences, constant strategies, and so forth, (*b*) a set of exogenous variables which affects the selection and change of strategies, and (*c*) a set of derived propositions dealing with the conditions under which stability would arise in long-term international interactions. Although the strategic perspective downplays the significance of decision theoretic approaches in explaining behavior under "normal" conditions, i.e., when actors behave according to pre-established strategies, it does resort to decision analysis in "turning point" decisions. The propositions of the approach are not very specific, but they do suggest some interesting implications. In order to explore some of the implications of this approach more fully, let us examine the *ad hoc* perspective and the strategic one as complementary ways of analyzing international processes.

9.4 A COMPARATIVE ANALYSIS OF *AD HOC* AND STRATEGIC PERSPECTIVES OF INTERNATIONAL PROCESSES

The first question that requires discussion concerns the extent to which these two approaches are empirically distinguishable. It is clear that the answer to this question cannot be found in the existence of behavioral stability or lack thereof. Behavioral stability is not a unique feature of a strategic approach, nor is constant behavioral

increase instability because error-checking mechanisms are going to be activated very frequently. The concept and process of deception in international politics is fascinating, but unfortunately beyond the scope of the present analysis.

Table 9.2. *Areas of convergence and divergence between the* ad hoc *and strategic approaches*

Variable	Predictions of the		Comments
	Ad hoc approach	Strategic approach	
Preferences of focal actor	Subject to frequent change	Stable for the most part	Stability of preferences depends on the type of attribution process under the *ad hoc* approach
Perceptions of other actors' preferences	Unstable for the most part	Stable for the most part	Partial convergence
Behavior of actor	Unstable for the most part	Stable or unstable	Depends on the degree of stability implied by the strategy
Behavioral stability	Infrequent	Frequent	Partial convergence

instability a unique characteristic of the *ad hoc* approach. In order to get a better sense of the areas where these two approaches converge or diverge, table 9.2 might be of some help.

One of the clues that could be helpful in attempting to determine which perspective is at work in a given international process is the extent to which actors' preferences are stable over time. Frequent preference changes suggest that actors' behavior cannot be explained in terms of a strategic perspective. However, the opposite is not necessarily true. If actors' preferences seem to be constant over time (or change very slowly), the *ad hoc* approach may still provide an adequate explanation of the evolution of international processes.

Suppose we are looking at two players involved in a game of chess. Our aim is to determine: (*a*) whether the players are using strategies or whether they respond to the configuration of the game as it evolves without long-term plans about how to win, and (*b*) if they use strategies, which ones they employ and why. In this situation, players' preferences are, by definition, constant. Therefore the structure of the objective game is fixed. Substantive misperceptions of preferences are also eliminated. Thus, instability of preferences seems to rule out the possibility of a strategic interpretation. Stability of preferences, on the other hand, is not sufficient for establishing the validity of a strategic interpretation.

According to the *ad hoc* perspective, the preferences an actor attributes to other actors are stable when expected international outcomes converge with actual outcomes (or when an actor experiences a positive surprise). In such cases, stable perceptions are consistent with the *ad hoc* approach. However, in most cases, the *ad hoc* approach envisions frequent changes in the preferences that an actor attributes to opponents. Under the strategic approach, both stable and unstable perceptions of others are possible. When an actor uses a safety strategy, peceptions of others' preferences do not play a prominent role in strategy implementation. Empirical evidence suggesting that decision makers tend to discount or ignore information concerning other actors' preferences – whatever this information might be – can be taken as indirect evidence of the use of a safety strategy. When an actor uses a detection strategy, it is not implausible to observe rapid changes in its percpetions of other actors' preferences and/or strategies. Typically, however, the strategic perspective is more consistent with the notion that actors view their environment as relatively stable.

Stable behavior of actors over time does suggest the existence of a strategy. This is so whether or not documentary evidence indicates that decision makers think in strategic terms. Because the strategic approach does not require that actors use optimal strategies, stable behavior seems to indicate that actors' behavior is guided by some sort of general rule (even if this rule seems to be clearly suboptimal). However, unstable behavior cannot be taken as clear-cut evidence of either approach. Changes in an actor's behavior can be due to a detection algorithm, or to an adjustment rule which requires frequent behavioral shifts (as we have seen with the DOWNING and TESTER rules). Under the *ad hoc* approach, behavioral shifts are the norm.

Behavioral Stability refers to persistently stable behavior of all actors in a given strategic configuration over a relatively long period of time. This indicator is probably the least reliable in terms of its ability to discriminate between the two approaches. Although the frequency of behavioral stability might provide us a clue as to what to look for in terms of these two approaches, it is not an exclusive feature of each of them.

The bottom line of this analysis is simple. Strict reliance on any one of these variables is likely to lead to erroneous inferences regarding the kind of approach that characterizes the historical evolution of an

515

international process. However, taken together, these variables might present a better sense of the kind of forces that were instrumental in guiding the course of history. The difficulty of identifying positive evidence for these two perspectives stems from the fact that they are very broad in terms of what they contain. Their predictions are not very specific, and – for the most part – not very helpful in providing clear criteria of discrimination.

This is particularly the case with the strategic approach that seems, on the surface, to be the most practical one. Specifically, it allows for both short-sighted (or short-memory) and long-term strategies; it allows for both safety and detection strategies. More importantly, it does not impose a rationality assumption on strategy selection, thereby preventing the restriction of the range of strategies to ones that are not dominated. But this difficulty does not render this perspective useless. On the contrary, this perspective becomes particularly useful when the *ad hoc* perspective seems to perform rather poorly in accounting for variations in international outcomes over time. For example, consider a case wherein actors' perceptions of the objective game are essentially accurate, the evidence indicates that most or all decision makers followed analytic procedures, and yet actors' actual choices differed from the theoretical ones. In such cases, the *ad hoc* perspective fails to explain the international outcome. If such failures recur frequently in the course of an international process, it is time to look for long-term strategies. The task might be difficult because the menu is very large, but a pattern might suggest itself eventually.

The task of identifying which of the two perspectives best accounts for an international process becomes even more difficult if one considers the not implausible case that some of the actors are using strategies and some approach their strategic environment with a rather *ad hoc* perspective. Consider Kissinger's (1966) classification of leadership types. Kissinger's bureaucratic-pragmatic leadership type adopts essentially an *ad hoc* problem-solving approach in foreign policy. On the other hand, ideological leadership types are inclined to apply rigid doctrines in their international dealings. If Western leaders are predominantly of the first type, and communist leaders are predominantly of the second type, then a valid analysis of international processes involving East and West must include both perspectives.

The two perspectives are not contradictory: they should be treated as complementary models of international politics rather than alternative ones. How, then, can we apply these two perspectives to the analysis of international processes if it is so difficult to determine which actor uses what approach? The answer is that we cannot determine this until we have unfolded the entire international process. Stated differently, from an empirical perspective, one would have to amass a great deal of data to determine whether or not actors have used strategies, and if they did, which strategies were used, why they were selected and how they were modified over time. These data are a whole series of international outcomes, and this means a long stretch of history.

I have noted that stable preference structures do not rule out *ad hoc* approaches. But we can go further than that. In some cases, both approaches have identical predictions regarding the evolution of international processes. These concern some of the conditions under which behavioral stability is expected to arise. For example, when the *ad hoc* approach envisions stable expectations of actors toward one another (whether or not these expectations are based on correct perceptions of others' preferences), it expects to find considerable behavioral stability. In this case, the myopic logic which guides actors' decisions converges with the notion of safety strategy in the strategic approach. The predictions of actual behavior of actors as well as the predictions about behavioral stability of both approaches are similar.

A word of caution is in order here. Because it is difficult to distinguish between these approaches in an empirical context, there is a natural tendency to jump to conclusions on the basis of a very small number of observations. This temptation is all the more understandable when analysts act under a policy relevance ressure. The general tendency in such situations is to assume stable preferences and carefully calculated strategies of opponents (Jervis, 1976: 319–342).[22] Likewise, short-term evidence of stability of preferences or stable behavior will be seen as consistent only with a strategic approach, whereas variation in actual behavior and revealed preferences will be seen as consistent with an *ad hoc* approach. Both kinds of inferences can be equally misleading when based on less than comprehensive evidence.

Failure to account for an actor's behavior in short-term logic may be taken as a sign of strategy implementation. This is especially true when dealing with influence relationships such as in most bargaining processes in international politics. Again, in a game of chess, an actor might feel that her opponent is actually applying a carefully crafted strategy when he does not fall for baits or other short-term temptations she has offered him. When we see that actors do not take

---

[22] This is another aspect of attribution bias, typically called the observer–participant difference. Observers of others' behavior tend to attribute this behavior to dispositional causes. The behaving agents tend to attribute the same behavior to situational factors.

advantage of existing situational opportunities, or do not respond to immediate threats, we had better begin looking for a strategy. The analyst's task is to figure out the details of such a strategy. Unfortunately, there is no theory that can guide such a search, and it is beyond the scope of the present book to develop one. The point to be made is that the strategic approach might be empirically valid in the sense that states use these strategies, and political leaders tend to think that their opponents use such strategies even if they, themselves, do not. For these reasons, development of more precise theoretical formulations of this approach is an important area of future research.

However, given the difficulties to determine which approach provides the best account of a given international process, one might rightly ask what added value do we get from dealing with these approaches. Isn't it much simpler to assume that one approach or the other is more valid and to go on from there either to empirical research or straight to the policy setting? Why are these approaches important to the understanding of international processes? The importance of these two approaches is both theoretical and practical. Failure to realize the significance of these approaches in analysis of international proceses can cause a great deal of theoretical confusion, and – what is not less important – policy disasters. To illustrate these points, consider the Hitler crises from 1933 to 1939.

9.4.1 The Hitler crises, 1933–1939: an empirical illustration of an international process[23]

The main aim of this section is to demonstrate some of the implications of the mode of analysis discussed above for the study of international processes. It is also intended to demonstrate the practical and theoretical role that the two approaches play in such a mode of investigation. The following analysis is not to be taken as an attempt to test the two approaches against empirical data, but rather as a crude interpretation of one of the most dramatic periods in human history.

Like many other significant periods in international politics, historians disagree over the interpretation of the chain of events that led to the Second World War. Here, however, the problem is not lack of reliable information. Most of the primary sources relevant for an

---

[23] The analysis below is based on the following sources: Churchill (1948), Bullock (1952), Shirer (1960), Taylor (1963), Weinberg (1970, 1980), and Martel (1986). The more analytical discussion of Hitler's bargaining style is based on Handel (1981). One of the crises discussed here was analyzed by Snyder and Diesing (1977: 111–113) as a game of chicken. While I agree with their interpretation of the preference structure of the parties, I differ with respect to the interpretation of the outcome of the Munich crisis.

analysis of this international process are available. The disagreement is over interpretation of the available information, or, more precisely, over the interpretation of the nature of the international process. Two schools of thought are identifiable in this debate: The first, represented primarily by A. J. P. Taylor (Taylor, 1963), claims that Hitler was an opportunist who capitalized on the confusion and indecision in the Western camp. Things got out of hand not due to some master strategy employed by a crazy politician, but rather because bit-by-bit Hitler was able to accomplish one foreign policy aim after another, and that his success drove him and Germany as a whole over their heads. The argument is that Hitler did not plan, nor had he been interested in the kind of war that ensued.

On the other side we have a group of historians (e.g., the views in Martel, 1986) who maintain that Hitler had a master plan, and that he followed it to the last point during this period. The failure of the western democracies was phenomenal: despite all the signs they did not realize the nature of this strategy until it was too late. Despite numerous opportunities to stand up to Hitler when Germany was militarily weak and politically unstable, the leaders of the two major powers, Great Britain and France, pursued a policy of appeasement which assumed either that Hitler was like a spoiled child who wants a nice toy, and once getting it, will be satisfied and stop crying, or that Hitler made valid claims against the West, and that one must give in to those claims to satisfy the Germans. Each German claim was thus treated on its own merit, and those who claimed that all these things fell into a pattern leading to war were ignored or ridiculed (Churchill, 1948).

The first argument represents a pure *ad hoc* approach, while the second argument represents an interpretation of this period in terms of the strategic perspective. From the first line of reasoning it is obvious that Hitler was assumed to have altered his preferences and behavior on the basis of the outcomes of prior international outcomes. Specifically, he embarked on initiatives and was constantly surprised by the failure of the two Western powers (and to some extent the Soviet Union) to respond decisively to these initiatives. These surprises were all of the positive type, causing increased rigidity of beliefs that he could demand more and get it, failing to realize that the crises he had initiated gradually served to change the preferences of Great Britain and France into more competitive ones. By the time that the Danzig crisis transpired, Hitler was confident that the French and British would eventually give in. Alternatively, he believed that at least the British would – after appropriate lip service to Poland – come to realize that there was no point in fighting Germany. On the other hand, it is obvious that the policy of the two major powers was of an *ad hoc* nature, dealing with one problem at a time, with considerable misperception of the opponent's preferences. At each of these crises, the notion was that of managing the immediate problem rather than checking a master strategist.

The second perspective views this process as a clash of strategies: one was highly sophisticated and exploitative, and the other was simply a misguided strategy of appeasement. But both were based on stable preferences and on stable perceptions of the opponent's preferences and strategy. According to this view, Hitler's strategy was a fairly clever detection principle: he kept probing for resistance by posing demands and backing them with military moves. Given a sign of weakness and willingness to negotiate, he raised his demands to such extremes that when he made a slight concession, the opponent saw it as a major victory. On the other hand, when he detected strong opposition to his demands, he normally backed down. This pattern repeated itself several times over the 1933–1939 period, and accounted for the ability of Germany to get much of what it had lost in the Versailles Treaty and more (e.g., Austria and Czechoslovakia) without having to fire a single shot.

The best description of the Western strategy, according to the traditional perspective, is TIT-FOR-n-TATS (where n is assumed to be very large). This strategy implies that the West was willing to swallow a lot of frogs before it was ready to resist Hitler by force. The notion was that if Hitler would be given what was seen as essential German claims, he would not go further, thereby risking what Germany had already gained. To further document this debate and derive the empirical implications of these approaches, consider table 9.3 which outlines the essential strategic features of the Hitler crises.

Clearly, the table represents an oversimplified image of the process. Most of these crises are best represented by n-person rather than by two-person games. Moreover, one may question the interpretation of the preferences assigned to the players. Nonetheless, the description of the objective games in this table serves to illustrate the ideas of the strategic and *ad hoc* approaches. Let us examine the features of this process. The first observation is that the game of Chicken dominates this process. The preferences of the parties have been stable throughout the period. This suggests that a strategic interpretation of the process cannot be ruled out, but this is not clear positive evidence for such an interpretation. Where we have some indirect evidence for a strategic interpretation is in the discrepancies between theoretical and actual outcomes which is another obvious characteristic of this process. The third feature is that in the last game (game 10), the preference structure of both parties changed. The result was that both reacted in a manner that is consistent with the theoretical outcome of the game. Let us examine what these features suggest about the evolution of this international process. The discussion is divided into two parts.

9.4.1.1 An ad hoc interpretation of the Hitler crises

If Hitler were to operate in an *ad hoc* fashion, going from crisis to crisis and drawing lessons from the outcomes of previous crises, then his behavior can be explained only in terms of fundamental misperception of the British and French preferences; otherwise it is difficult to explain why he repeatedly defected in the Chicken game against the Western powers (but not in the games involving the Italians and Soviets). Especially in the first three and a half years of his regime (1933–1936), a war with the two Western powers was seen as a disaster even by Hitler.[24] This assessment is reinforced by the fact that Hitler displayed a great deal of restraint during the Dollfuss crisis (the assassination of the Austrian chancellor during a *coup* attempt by the Austrian Nazis), disassociating himself from the *coup* and assuring the alarmed Mussolini that he had no intention of annexing Austria.

The misperception of the Western preference structure that allows placement of the consistent defection of Hitler within the context of an *ad hoc* interpretation such as Taylor's (1963) can only involve an attribution of a dominant cooperation strategy to Great Britain and France. There exists sufficient evidence to suggest that Hitler's assessment was that the two Western powers would not react forcefully to his initiatives. This suggests that Hitler's behavior can be seen as a strictly *ad hoc* set of tactics. This interpretation suggests that Hitler's subjective game throughout most of the period is represented by figure 9.7.

This subjective game could have characterized Hitler's initial perception of the British and French preferences but not those of the Italians and Soviets. If that were the case, then the outcome of the disarmament decision coincided with his expectations, thereby reinforcing this perception of the dominant cooperative alternative of the two powers. The decision to invade the Rhineland which everybody – including Hitler himself – agreed was a highly risky venture,

---

24 Shirer (1960: 293) quotes Paul Schmidt, Hitler's interpreter, who heard Hitler describing the Rhineland crisis: "The forty-eight hours after the march into the Rhineland . . . were the most nerve-racking in my life. If the French had then marched into the Rhineland, we would have had to withdraw with our tails between our legs, for the military resources at our disposal would have been wholly inadequate for even a moderate resistance."

Table 9.3. *The Hitler crises, 1933–1939*

Historical phase	Game no.	Date	Name of incident	Pref. order *Germany*	**West**	Game type	Theoretical outcome	Actual outcome
Probing stage 1933–1937	1	10/14/1933	Withdrawal from disarmament talks and League of Nations	*TRSP*	**TRSP**	Chicken	Comp.	German defection
	2	7/25/1934	Dollfuss affair	*TRSP*	**TRSP‡**	Called bluff	German defeat	German defeat
	3	3/16/1935	Rearmament decision	*TRSP*	**TRSP**	Chicken	Comp.	German victory
	4	3/5/1936	Occupation of Rhineland	*TRSP*	**TRSP**	Chicken	·	German victory
	5	10/21/1936	German–Italo Axis	*TRSP*	**TRSP‡**	Chicken	Comp.	Comp.
Escalation stage 1938–1939	6	2–3/1938	Anschluss	*TRSP*	**TRSP**	Chicken	Comp.	German victory
	7	3–9/1938	Czechoslovakia I	*TRSP*	**TRSP**	Chicken	Comp.	German victory
	8	3/1939	Czechoslovakia II	*TRSP*	**TRSP**	Chicken	Comp.	German victory
War	9	7–8/1939	Ribbentrop–Molotov ag.	*TRSP*	**TRSP†**	Chicken	Comp.	Comp.
	10	3–9/1939	Danzig crisis	*TRPS*	**TRPS**	PD	War	War

T = Temptation (unilateral escalation) payoff; R = Reward (mutual cooperation) payoff; S = Sucker's (unilateral cooperation) payoff; P = Punishment (mutual escalation) payoff.

A historical phase is a general division of the period into specific subperiods which characterize stages in the German–Western conflict.

Payoff structures list the preference ordering of each actor over the four outcomes with the most preferred outcome on the left and the least preferred outcome on the right. Thus, preference order TRSP implies that an actor prefers the unilateral escalation outcome over the mutual cooperation outcome, the mutual cooperation outcome over the unilateral cooperation outcome, and the unilateral cooperation outcome over the mutual escalation outcome. The general game structure is given as

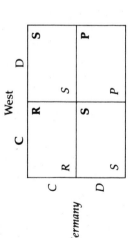

‡ In general, German counterparts in the games are Great Britain and France (games 1, 3, 4, 6–8, 10). A double-dagger indicates that the other actor in the game is Italy (games 2, 5). A dagger indicates that Germany's counterpart was the Soviet Union (game 9).

West

	C	D
C	4 / 3	3 / 2
D	2 / 4 *	1 / 1

Germany

*Nash Equilibrium.
Preferences are ranged from 4 = best to 1 = worst.
This is game #4 in the Rapoport and Guyer (1966) typology.

Figure 9.7 An *ad hoc* interpretation of Hitler's subjective game

must have been made with the outcome of the rearmament crisis in mind. The outcome of the Rhineland crisis clearly influenced Hitler's behavior in the Anschluss and Munich crises, and so forth.

From this perspective, the declaration of war by the British and French following the invasion of Poland must have surprised Hitler. In other words, Hitler's perception of the opponents' preferences could not have changed given that six months earlier neither power moved a finger to save Czechoslovakia. Even if Hitler did expect the Western powers to declare war, he assumed that they would not pursue it with much vigor. Again, there is some evidence to that effect, but there is no clear indication that Hitler was really surprised by the French and British decisions.[25] However, at this point, the assessment of the French and British preference was of little significance to Hitler, for his own preferences entailed a dominant defection strategy. This preference change came about as a result of the Ribbentrop–Molotov agreement. Hence, despite last-minute alarm in Germany as a result of information that Mussolini intended to back down and disassociate himself from the alliance with Hitler, the latter was willing to go on with the planned invasion of Poland.

Can we interpret the behavior of Hitler's opponents as *ad hoc* reactions to Hitler's initiatives? From this perspective, it is not difficult to interpret the behavior of the Italians and the Soviets. These two actors behaved as they were expected to according to the *ad hoc* perspective whether or not the preferences they had attributed to Hitler

[25] On August 25, 1939, the Germans learned of the signing of the Anglo–Polish defense pact. This indicated clearly that Great Britain intended to go to war over the Polish issue.

were accurate. The behavior of the two Western powers, France and Great Britain, is more difficult to place in an *ad hoc* context without speculating on their perceptions of Hitler's preference structure. The *ad hoc* interpretation of the French and British behavior would focus on the learning process over crises. Leng's (1983) experiential *Realpolitik* learning model does not work very well in this case, for its prediction would be that the losers of a crisis escalate their behavior at a later crisis against the same opponent.[26]

The French and British preferences exhibit remarkable stability over time despite several negative surprises. So does their behavior. One possible interpretation of this pattern is that both powers were affected to some extent by Hitler's hostile maneuvers but they were even more affected by Hitler's cooperative gestures which followed each of the crises. A good example is the British reaction to the rearmament decision. In his Reichstag speech of May 21, 1935 which followed the announcement of rearmament, Hitler made a list of specific "peace" proposals. One of them was to limit the German navy to 35 per cent the size of the British navy. The British reaction was very enthusiastic, virtually ignoring the fact that the rearmament decision constituted a blunt violation of the Versailles treaty (Shirer, 1960: 284–290). Moreover, the 35 per cent proposal actually implied legitimization of a considerable increase in the size of the German army. The failure of the British and French to revise their estimates of Hitler's preferences are due to the fact that their prior expectations led them to ignore the hostile acts and to believe the conciliatory statements following these events. The tendency to treat the various crises one at a time, caused the French and British governments to fail to see a pattern and make *ad hoc* decisions based on the maximin principle.

9.4.1.2   *A strategic interpretation of the Hitler crises*

The problem with attributing to Hitler an *ad hoc* approach is threefold. First, it is unclear what made Hitler such an optimist when it came to an assessment of the French and British preferences and behavior, and a pessimist when it came to Italy. Hitler's caution with regard to Italy was evident not only from the Dollfuss crisis but also

---

[26] Leng (1988) argued that winners of prior crises do not alter their preferences and behavior but losers transform their preferences and their behavior to a more hostile mode. This version of the model does not fit the current interpretation of the Western powers' behavior, but it does account for the pattern of preference change in the Syrian–Israeli crises.

from the Anschluss crisis of 1938.[27] The same applies to Hitler's assessment of the Soviet Union. Second, there is strong evidence to suggest that Hitler was willing to go ahead with several of his initiatives despite signs of resistance from the Western powers. For example, the operational plans drawn for the German army in Czechoslovakia and the deployment of troops during the Munich crisis were very real and cannot be depicted as bargaining leverage. The invasion of Austria was also done without real prior consultation with the Italians. Third, the pattern of bargaining exhibited by Hitler in four cases (the rearmament decision, the Anschluss crisis, Munich, and Czechoslovakia, 1939) was too systematic to be depicted as a short-term outlook (Handel, 1981). If Hitler's preferences up to the Ribbentrop–Molotov agreement are indeed of a Chicken type, and if indeed a war with the West was seen as the least preferred outcome, then it is very difficult to interpret Hitler's bargaining behavior as strategy-free.[28]

Two strategies are commonly attributed to Hitler in the literature. The first is an ALL-D type of strategy. The other is a more cautious type of strategy in which an actor attempts to exploit an opponent as long as one possibly can, and then cooperates when one is sure that if one does not cooperate, the opponent will also defect. The ALL-D strategy does not seem particularly convincing in this case. My hypothesis is that Hitler's strategy (to the extent that one existed) was a fairly sophisticated detection strategy wherein you start by defection, and keep on defecting as long as you can. However, after each successful defection, you pacify your opponent with a cooperative gesture. This strategy is pursued as long as your opponent cooperates. If the opponent defects, you revert to cooperation. This seems to fit Hitler's behavior over virtually all of the crises mentioned above.

Starting with the German withdrawal from the disarmament talks and the League of Nations, each defection was matched by a cooperative gesture. With respect to the crises which have directly involved the two Western powers, Great Britain and France, this pattern is not obvious because what is observed is only a sequence of German

[27] According to Shirer (1960: 343–344) Hitler was more concerned about the Italian reaction to the Anschluss than about the French and British who were supposed to be the guarantors of the Versailles Treaty. See also Weinberg (1980: 298–299).

[28] The brinkmanship style of personal bargaining exhibited by Hitler on several occasions during the period is a vivid illustration of the rationality of the irrational (Schelling, 1966). Handel (1981) remarks that Hitler used personal intimidation of opposing heads of states quite often and repeatedly hinted that he was about to lose control over his behavior. One may attribute this bargaining style to his true mental state, but it is not inconceivable that it was merely an image-making exercise in the course of bargaining.

defections and *fait accompli*s. However, taking into account the cooperative game played with the Italians (which included most directly the Italo–German pact of 1937, but also the joint support to the Spanish Fascists throughout the Spanish Civil War, and the diplomatic support of the Italian invasion of Ethiopia in 1935), this strategy seems to account very well for the German behavior throughout the period.

What about the two last games in this process: the Danzig crisis and the Ribbentrop–Molotov agreement? From the reaction of the major powers to the occupation of Czechoslovakia and the threats they made with respect to Poland, Hitler's assessment was that his strategy has exhausted itself. Given his hostility toward the Soviet Union, this is the only explanation of the German eagerness to sign an agreement with Stalin (Shirer, 1960: 520–551; Weinberg, 1980: 573–611).

Turning to the behavior of the two Western powers, the strategic interpretation focuses on appeasement as a safety strategy. Here there is little problem in refuting an *ad hoc* interpretation. The failure of the French and British to revise their assessments of Hitler's preferences and to shift their behavior until very late in the process suggests that the *ad hoc* approach has little to offer. The two states had committed themselves to the notion of appeasement, expected it to work, and believed it would work despite ample evidence to the contrary. The famous interpretation of the Munich agreement by Chamberlain as a major diplomatic achievement that would guarantee peace in Europe is clear evidence that such a strategy motivated both Western powers and guided their behavior throughout the period.

Three points can be derived from this analysis. First, that a theoretical interpretation of the debate among historians in terms of one of these two perspectives may help shed light on complex and long-term international processes. Second, that one can establish criteria for distinguishing among the two perspectives empirically. Although this was not done in this chapter, such an attempt seems logically and operationally feasible. Third, for this international process, it seems that Hitler's behavior cannot be clearly depicted either in terms of the *ad hoc* approach or in terms of the strategic one; both perspectives make very similar predictions about Hitler's behavior and these predictions largely conform to the actual behavior of Germany. In such cases, opening the black box through systematic decision research might be helpful. For the Western powers, the *ad hoc* approach does not seem to provide an adequate explanation of their behavior, but the strategic perspective does. Admittedly, the strategy of appeasement appears not to have been a very rational one, but it is consistent with the historical facts. Again, the choice of the two Western governments to stick to this strategy despite ample indications that it does not work is a puzzle that can be resolved through decision research.

9.5 INTEGRATING *AD HOC* AND STRATEGIC PERSPECTIVES OF INTERNATIONAL PROCESSES

My disposition toward various perspectives or models should be known by now: I do not believe in theoretical determinism, not when it comes to social sciences. This implies that while I presented the two essential perspectives of international processes as dichotomous in nature, the purpose was not to suggest that they are always distinct. In fact, the more we understand the content, the logical structure, and the empirical implications of the two perspectives, the more we realize how difficult it is to distinguish between them and how many substantive compatibilities exist. But, in many ways these two approaches differ. They differ in their assumptions, especially those that concern the ability of foreign policy decision makers to reason far into the future and to consistently follow their plans. They also differ in the extent of emphasis they place on choice dynamics. Both perspectives view national choices as indispensable elements in the explanation of international processes, but the *ad hoc* approach is immersed in microlevel choices, whereas the strategic approach emphasizes macrolevel planning and implementation. Obviously, there exist many cases where these approaches differ in terms of their implications.

This reminds us very much of the state-of-the-art in the decision making field during the process model specification stage (see chapter 5). Given this similarity, the answer to the question: "how do we integrate these approaches" becomes more manageable. The general direction of integrating these perspectives is similar to the strategy that was followed in chapters 6 and 7 with regard to the decision making approach. The following steps are suggested:

1   Define the major assumptions of the two perspectives. This was done in the present chapter, but one may want to add, omit, or revise these assumptions, as more research is done on these two perspectives.

2   Identify the major stages that characterize international processes. This has not been done, but one may want to consider how we can identify the beginning of an international process, the end of an international process, what intermediate stages exist in international processes, the criteria by which an actor qualifies as a participant in

528

such processes, and so forth.[29] Some of the examples discussed here might provide a basis for such a determination of stages, but there is no solid theoretical foundation for stage-characterizations of long-term and multi-actor processes.

3   Develop detailed predictions of the two perspectives with regard to the various stages of the process. For example, what does each perspective predict about the process by which actors form expectations toward one another when the process has just begun?[30] What are the factors that cause perceptual and preference changes at more advanced stages of international processes? (These were discussed here in terms of attribution processes operating with respect to *ad hoc* approaches and in terms of strategy change with respect to the strategic approach.) How and under what conditions do preferences, expectations, perceptions, and behavior stabilize? (These were the general propositions I have discussed for each of these perspectives.)

4   On the basis of these predictions, determine what are the areas in which the predictions of the two perspectives converge and what predictions allow empirical discrimination among them. Develop a set of discriminating criteria for each of the major stages of international processes. (This was not done here. More empirical research is required to establish a general framework for discriminating among these perspectives, as in the MPC framework discussed in chapter 6.)

5   Determine the theoretical antecedents of these two approaches. The key questions in the analysis of international processes are the following: who (what kind of leader, what are the characteristics of the state or of its political and social organizations) is more likely to resort to a strategic approach in foreign policy, and under what circumstances is an actor prone to shift from one perspective to another.[31]

The last item on this list requires some elaboration. The assumptions that guide the general theory of foreign policy decision making are applicable to the level of international processes as well. Specifically, *it is incorrect to determine which approach provides the "best" approximation to the behavior of states in an interdependent setting. Both the* ad hoc *and the*

---

[29] An interesting mathematical model describing the evolution of an enduring dyadic rivalry was developed by Yaniv and Katz (1980). This model describes stages in the evolution of such a rivalry.

[30] One approach to this kind of issue in the context of arms race processes is discussed in Maoz (1989: ch. 2). This approach is based on a cognitive perspective dealing with the inferential bases of expectations in international politics.

[31] In many ways the *ad hoc* approach is a special case of the strategic approach. It is a special and very complex strategy which involves both detection mechanisms (entailed in the process of attribution), adjustment rules (subsequent decision processes), and error-checking devices (discrepancy principles). Seen in this light, shifting from a strategic perspective to an *ad hoc* perspective is conceptually equivalent to a strategy shift.

strategic approach are context-dependent. Some states might be more inclined to use strategies than other. The same state might approach different international processes from a different perspective.

This is the principal aim of the theory of international processes: to describe, explain, and predict how actors shift from one strategy to another, from one international outcome to another, or from a strategy to a purely *ad hoc* perspective. For example, Handel (1981) argued that leaders are more likely to initiate a major diplomatic surprise if they have an authoritarian personality and work in an authoritarian state. In our context it is not implausible to argue that a strategic perspective is more likely to be used by: (*i*) People with rigid personality structures, authoritarian, cognitively-simple, and the like who work in (*ii*) political systems where these features are allowed to be expressed during the political process, i.e., hierarchical, totalitarian or otherwise strongly centralized regimes. Strategic behavior is more likely to be observed by those that seek to change the status quo than by those who wish to preserve it. Actors might resort to strategy when they begin a major foreign policy initiative and stick to it as long as it is seen to serve its purpose, but abandon a long-term, stable preference perspective altogether when the original strategy does not seem to work.[32]

But these are some very general theoretical ideas. They are neither formally developed, nor are they based upon solid empirical work. The aim of this chapter was to outline some general principles of the theory of international processes, not to solve all of the problems. With respect to the determinants of strategic or *ad hoc* evolutions of international processes and their consequences this implies that a more rigorous explanation is required. From this explanation a better understanding of international politics will emerge. How the contents of this study affect the ways we look at international politics is the subject of the last chapter.

---

[32] Some of my work on international conflicts and international crises suggests that initiators of international disputes behave quite differently than targets. Specifically, initiators seem to be more equipped to control the sequence of events during the conflict, exhibit higher levels of resolve, and prevail even when they are militarily inferior to the target (Maoz, 1982a, 1983). In a theoretical discussion of this phenomenon (Maoz, 1982b), I identified three types of international crises: calculated crises, unintended crises, and crises with domestic precipitation. My discussion of the deliberate calculus of initiation touches upon determinants of strategic action. The general idea there is that such initiatives are typically planned well in advance, when decision makers operate under little time pressure and where their motivation to change the status quo is high. See also Bueno de Mesquita (1981a).

10 INDIVIDUAL PREFERENCES, NATIONAL CHOICES, AND INTERNATIONAL SYSTEMS

10.1 INTRODUCTION

The theory of international processes connects individual preferences, choices, and actions to international politics. It consists of four layers. The first layer explains how individuals form preferences over policy options. The second layer links individual preferences to national choices via collective decision making. The third layer connects the ways nations make choices and the outcomes they get in an interdependent international setting. The fourth layer describes aspects of the evolution of international processes over time.

From the definition of international processes as a chain of temporally related and spatially interdependent intersections of national decisions, it is obvious that the theoretical framework developed herein is of the "bottom-up" type. That is to say, it is a theory in which the whole – the international process – evolves as an aggregation of elements. The theory specifies a causal chain starting with individual traits and perceptions and ending with levels of long-term stability in international interactions. To be sure, the aggregation process is quite complex, for it involves several processes by which inputs are transformed into outputs at each level of analysis.[1] The principal theme of this theory is that complex structures and processes in international politics do not have a life of their own which is independent of and – to a large extent – determines the behavior of the units. Rather, what we observe at the systemic level is a consequence of the interaction among its units, each of which has its own logic of operation and each of which has its own behavioral principles. This is the notion of micro-motives and macrobehavior as coined by Schelling (1978). The link-

---

[1] The terms *inputs* and *outputs* vary over levels of analysis. At the level of individual choice, inputs are decisional stimuli and outputs are individual preferences over policy options. At the level of collective decision making, inputs are individual preferences and outputs are national choices. At the international level, inputs are national choices and outputs are international outcomes. At the level of international processes, inputs are international outcomes and outputs are long-term behavioral patterns (defined in terms of levels of behavioral stability).

ages between micromotives and macrobehavior stand in sharp contrast to the notion that the whole in international politics is responsible to the behavior of its units, that structures in international politics determine the behavior of the actors. This view is represented by a variety of structuralist approaches including Marxist approaches and system theories.

The present chapter explores the relations between the theory of international processes and things which are excluded. I examine how this theory relates to more parsimonious and holistic approaches to the field that have a fundamental "top-down" point of view. In particular, I examine the extent to which a bottom-up approach is necessarily reductionist as Waltz (1979, 1986) seems to suggest. I also examine how meaningful is an integration of a theory of international processes with systemic theories.

This chapter is designed as follows. First, a brief summary of the main aspects of the theory is given. Second, I discuss the major implications of the theory of international processes with respect to how we study and practice international politics. Third, I provide a brief evaluation of the theory as a whole. Fourth, the theory of international processes is related to systemic theories of international politics. Finally, I suggest some areas of future research using the theory developed in this book.

10.2 SUMMARY OF THE THEORY OF NATIONAL CHOICES AND INTERNATIONAL PROCESSES

Individuals respond to stimuli in their environment when these stimuli are seen to create a pressure for decision. These stimuli create motivation of decision making in that they invoke threat or opportunity perceptions. These stimuli also define the practical parameters of the decision problem by limiting the time available for decision. The kind of paths that are selected by decision makers to convert perception of problems into practical solutions depend on three types of factors: situational factors (e.g., decisional stress), personality factors (cognitive complexity), and political or organizational factors (role variables). These variables define the combination of paths an individual uses to choose from among alternative courses of action or inaction one which is designed to solve the perceived problem. The outcome of individual decision processes is not only a choice of a policy option, but a preference ranking of the various policy options which had been considered along the way.

Individual enter group discussion with those pre-estblished preferences. The distribution of individual preferences over the various policy options defines the extent to which the group is initially polarized in terms of its policy positions. The level of group polarization as well as the formal structure of the policy group affect the process and substance of governmental decision making processes as well as the kind of influence individual decision makers exert on it. These factors help shape the national preference ordering of policy options and, of course, national choices.

National choices are made in an interdependent setting wherein outcomes are never under the complete control of those who make the decisions. In most cases, what one state gets out of its decision is a function of other states' choices. The relationship between national choices and international outcomes depends both on the kind of processes which had given birth to the decisions within states and on the nature of the setting in which states operate. The theory of international processes distinguishes between objective games and subjective ones. The former are intersections of players' self-perceptions (in particular, states' perceptions of their preferences as those emerge as outcomes of group decision processes). Subjective games are perceptions of the environment by individual actors (including both self-perceptions and perceptions of other players' alternatives and preferences). The distinction between objective and subjective games serves two purposes: First, it is a basis for a framework which allows assessment of the extent of interdependence in a state's environment and the objective difficulty of making "correct" national choices. Second, it forms a framework for an outcome-based evaluation of national decisions. The relations between national choices and international outcomes are defined in terms of discrepancies between actual outcomes and (*a*) theoretical outcomes which denote the kind of international outcome that would have obtained if all states chose the way they should have according to theory, or (*b*) expected outcomes which are those decision makers envision given their choice. The theory suggests that the quality of the national decision making process affects, but does not determine, the nature and extent of discrepancy between actual and theoretical outcomes and between actual and expected outcomes. This discrepancy is also determined by the choices of other states and by the degree of interdependence inherent in a given strategic configuration.

The discrepancies between expected and actual outcomes form one of the bases for the analysis of long-term international processes. The theory of international processes considers two different – but not mutually exclusive – perspectives. The *ad hoc* perspective views long-term international processes as evolving out of short-range national decision making processes of individuals and groups who are trying to solve specific problems arising in their environment. Changes in national decisions define variations in international outcomes over time. These changes are triggered by discrepancies between expected and actual international outcomes which alter definitions of the situation of individual decision makers, and/or affect the structure and composition of policy groups. International processes stabilize when national perceptions of the environment stabilize, whether or not these perceptions are accurate.

The strategic perspective considers the evolution of international processes as a clash of long-range, carefully calculated and executed national strategies. According to this perspective, states have long-standing world views (including stable perceptions of the environment) and comprehensive plans for accomplishing their goals. These assumptions require exploration of the factors which affect the choice of grand strategies and the attachment to them once they are underway. These factors include the risk dispositions of national leaders, the nature of national preferences, the stakes of the game and its objective complexity. Strategy change occurs due to exogenous factors such as preference change as a result of regime changes or of changes in a state's relations with third parties. However, strategy change might also be due to learning of and adaptation to the preferences and strategies used by other actors in the game. The *ad hoc* and strategic perspective can be used simultaneously to explain the evolution of historical processes whose interpretation is problematic given available approaches.

10.3 THEORETICAL AND PRACTICAL IMPLICATIONS OF THE THEORY OF INTERNATIONAL PROCESSES

What are the contributions of the present theory to the substantive understanding of international problems, and in what ways does this theory help practitioners make the world a better place to live in? Do the time and other resources we have to spend on the study of international politics from the perspective of this theoretical approach constitute a solid investment in the sense of providing otherwise unattainable insights and guides to action?

The answer to this question is divided into two parts. The first focuses on the intellectual contribution of the theory, that is, on the extent to which it enhances our understanding and knowledge of world politics. The second emphasizes the practical implications, if any, that can be derived from it. These questions assume that theories are instrumental, that is, they serve a purpose that is both intellectual (knowing more about the political world around us) and practical (using this knowledge to improve on things, to advance our goals, and so forth). There is also a hidden assumption that, as far as knowledge is concerned, more is better. A better understanding of world politics would not harm and might even benefit us. While these assumptions are questionable, I will accept them for the time being in order to outline the implications of the theory.

10.3.1   Theoretical implications

I think that the merit of the theory developed in this study is not necessarily its novelty, for it is not all that novel in terms of most of its ingredients. Rather, the first and most important contribution of the theory is that it offers an integrated set of propositions about how foreign policy decisions are made, how they are converted into international outcomes, and how international processes evolve over time. This new perspective allows for a meaningful analysis of the relations between individuals and collectives, between national units and international outcomes, and between international outcomes and other international outcomes over time. As such, the present theory constitutes an attempt to bridge between microtheories of foreign policy and more macrolevel analyses of long-term and multi-actor processes. It is a first attempt to cross this kind of bridge in international politics. Whether or not this integration is successful in empirical terms is a question that will have to be dealt with in future studies that attempt to apply this theory. Here, however, the potential must be recognized.

This potential is twofold. One aspect is that the present theory offers a new way to organize historical material into a set of meaningful frameworks. Trying to link international outcomes over time is something that historians, political scientists, and journalists are engaged in all the time. But in most cases this is done intuitively and haphazardly. The value of the theory is that it offers a systematic way of doing it. For example, students of the origins of the Second World War have related the treaties of Versailles and Locarno to the emergence of Nazism in Germany, to Hitler's foreign policy, and to the reaction of the Western powers to these policies. Another linkage in the historical literature is that between the outcomes of the first few crises that Hitler initiated during the years 1934–1936 and his behavior in the subsequent crises. As we have seen, the theory of international processes does not provide a precise and unequivocal interpretation of this sequence. It does, however, provide some useful guidelines to organize the historical material. It also suggests ways in which one could convert notions of historical connection between events into testable hypotheses.

Second, the theory of international processes is a framework within which hypotheses about historical processes, or aspects thereof, can be tested empirically. Because the theory is specified in stages, each of which contains a set of empirically testable propositions, it is possible to examine which parts of it withstand empirical tests, and which parts of it need correction or modification. The theory is useful not only as an integrated body of propositions about international processes; each of its various parts contain aspects that are theoretically useful in and of themselves, that is, independently of the usefulness of the other layers of the theory. This is obviously true for the decision making part of the theory which offers new insights into the foreign policy process. But it is also true about the study of international outcomes which provides interesting insights into the relations between choice and consequences in international politics. And, to a lesser extent, the same holds for the analysis of international processes from the *ad hoc* or strategic perspectives. Even if one does not wish to accept the connections between the various layers of the theory as I have specified them, one might find some value in the elements. The testability of each of the elements of the theory makes them useful to various researchers who work on more limited topics such as specific individual choices, collective decision processes, bargaining processes, long-term interactions among states that could be analyzed from a strategic perspective, and so forth.

The third theoretical contribution of the theory is that it offers a relatively comprehensive alternative to systemic theories of international politics. It helps alleviate the microlevel status of foreign policy approaches. At the same time, it relieves analysts of the need to make simplistic assumptions about the nature of the behaving units in world politics. It also rejects the polar tendency to make simple-minded extrapolations from choices to consequences. Most importantly, it suggests that the level of analysis problem which Singer (1961) saw as one of the most important difficulties in international relations research does not reduce to a need to choose one level of analysis and ignore others. On the contrary, the theory suggests that one could move quite comfortably across levels of analysis in theorizing about international politics.

The fourth contribution of the theory is that it is a dynamic account of a dynamic international environment, one which allows for both

536

stability and instability in international interactions. Many theories of conflict and collaboration are either static snapshots of certain episodes or ones that focus primarily on the macro studies of certain processes.[2] The theory of international processes specifies both microlevel and macrolevel dynamics. The microlevel dynamics are obvious in the *ad hoc* perspective. They concern the effects of outcome discrepancies on subsequent choices. In the strategic perspective, microlevel dynamics concern cases of strategy selection and strategy change when one or more international actors use a detection strategy. The macrolevel aspects in the *ad hoc* and strategic approaches concern the propositions dealing with the determinants of stability and instability in international interactions.

10.3.2 Practical implications

How can the theory of international processes be useful in aiding the process of policy making? Before dealing with the policy relevance potential of this theory an important caveat is in order. As I have argued elsewhere (Maoz, 1982a: 208–212), jumping into the policy relevance business before the empirical status of the theory has been established is extremely risky. This is especially the case in the social sciences. Therefore, the practical implications discussed below should not be seen as policy recommendations. In order to make such recommendations, a theory would have to be considerably more specific than the one developed in this book. The practical implications concern primarily ways in which policy makers can use the ideas, logic, and methods of this theory to make better choices. The theory may make the world a better place to live in not in the sense of suggesting how it could be designed to provide for some desirable values, but rather in the sense that it may help some important people

[2] The work of Choucri and North (1975) on the relationship between lateral pressures and war and the work of Organski and Kugler (1980) on power transition constitute good examples of such macro accounts of international processes. In both cases, the theories are specified as a set of factors that eventually lead to a certain outcome. Choucri and North's study explores a set of complex relationships between industrialization, arms races, alliances, and war. The study on power transition contains a model of differential rates of growth in national capabilities. Both models are dynamic in that they account for the evolution of international politics over time. However, they are not designed to account for dependencies among their observations. In other words, the statistical tests they employ assume that observations are independent of each other (or when they are not, methods are employed to deal with the violation of the no auto-correlation assumption). However, they have no explanation as to why observations ordered over time might be related to one another. Choucri and North themselves assert that the processes that they have outlined are not the ones that have accompanied the nations into combat, but must be seen as the background underlying the crisis decisions of July-August, 1914.

to avoid some costly mistakes that carry severe international ramifications.

Theory can help policy makers in two ways. First, it generates empirical knowledge that can be applied in the policy making process. A theory that specifies which elements of deterrence are the most effective (or to paraphrase Huth and Russett, 1984, "what makes deterrence work") can tell decision makers how to design effective deterrence policies. Such theories can make the world a better place to live in to the extent that deterrence prevents war, and to the extent that the prevention of war is indeed a desirable value. In order for such a theory to be politically useful, it must have a solid body of empirical evidence to back its propositions. This is obviously beyond the scope of the present study. The other way in which theory can aid policy is that it may help decision makers think or analyze problems in a manner that is superior to that which they would have used without it. I pointed out in chapter 7 that the work of Alexander George on presidential decision making is precisely of this type. It is designed to identify traps and pitfalls in policy making and policy implementation that could be avoided with a little care and attention. In this sense, the policy relevance of theories is a set of analytical tools that does not provide decision makers with actual solutions to problems but helps them to find ways to reach such solutions.

The policy relevance of the theory stems directly from its bottom up approach to international politics. Most – if not all – of the factors that it views as determinants of foreign policy decision making and international processes are politically manipulable. To the extent that certain aspects of individual decision making or group structures are seen to be associated with defective choices, theory can aid in improving decisional strategies or in institutional reforms precisely as George, Jervis, and others have recommended. In this sense, I do not have many new insights to offer. Most ideas on how to improve decision making in national settings have been made already by others, and I generally agree with these recommendations.[3] What is new about the present study is that for the first time we can assess the

---

[3] As I pointed out elsewhere (Maoz, 1984a: 82) there is a difficulty inherent in implementing many of the policy recommendations that have been made by decision theorists. Since these recommendations are based on fundamental defects in the cognitive posture of individuals or in the structure of political groups, they are difficult to uproot. George (1980) has recognized this problem with respect to the multiple advocacy idea. Although multiple advocacy had been institutionalized in several policy making organizations (and in several states) it was shown that in many cases it was not effective in generating genuine policy debates. Rather, decision makers often used devil's advocates to argue that their decisions were based on consideration of opposing points of view.

links between the procedural and the substantive quality of national choices. The substantive standards of decisional quality which are based on international outcomes allow assessment of the extent to which decisional procedures affect the outcomes of interdependent choices. The quality criteria developed in chapter 8 allow assessment of the extent to which various aspects of the decision making process are responsible for counterproductive international outcomes. As we have seen in this chapter, the relationship between procedures and outcomes is not necessarily linear. This point was reinforced in the discussion of the effects of outcome discrepancies on national choices. To the extent that empirical evidence supports the propositions regarding the relations between choice and consequences, it may become possible to improve policy recommendations on these issues in two ways. First, research on the basis of the present theory may reveal new areas of improvement in the policy process. Second, such research may make policy recommendations more persuasive to decision makers in the sense that it shows specific linkages between defective procedures and bad outcomes.

The policy relevance of models that identify systematic deviations from optimal decision behavior is very obvious. The identification of deviations suggests potentially correcting principles. (See for example, George, 1980; Nisbett and Ross, 1980; and Kahneman and Tversky, 1982.) The problem is that if the deviations are fundamental in the sense that they are part and parcel of the cognitive makeup of people (such as the principles of cognitive dissonance theory, or the theories focusing on inferential heuristics) they cannot be easily corrected even if decision makers are aware of their tendency to fall into inferential traps and are sincerely interested in avoiding them. The most effective correcting mechanisms of defective procedures that are observed at one level of analysis are those that are applied at higher levels of analysis. The best way to ensure that an individual does not resort to consistency maintenance principles is to make him or her a group member, because the group is less likely to repress competing goals than individuals.

At national levels, defective aspects of collective decision processes are likely to be identified as a result of negative surprises, that is, cases wherein the actual international outcomes are valued less than the expected ones. This is not to suggest that I recommend occasional national disasters. Rather, it is to point out the difficulty of implementing institutional reforms designed to yield a more sound foreign policy (George et al., 1975). For example, there have been numerous studies that attempted to assess conditions that contribute to the effectiveness of nuclear and conventional deterrence. However, effective deterrence can be defined only in negative terms, i.e., a policy which did not fail in the sense of a violation of the status quo by the deterred party. Most studies of this topic determined the conditions of effective deterrence to be the opposite of those that have been associated with failures of deterrence.[4] Thus, to know what makes deterrence work, we must first know what makes it fail. The same applies to changing decisional processes through institutional reforms. The single best predictor of substantial institutional reforms in foreign policy are policy disasters. The lack of disasters does not suggest that decision making structures work.

The part of the theory dealing with the strategic perspective of international processes provides ideas about how to think and plan in crucial areas of international affairs such as bargaining and diplomacy. For example, it pays to invest not only in exploring the preferences of friends and foes but also in whether or not they act, and think strategically. When an opponent is seen to act in an *ad hoc* fashion, development of a detection strategy is useless. The best one can do under such circumstances is to resort to a safety strategy. On the other hand, assuming that an opponent employs a strategy when it actually behaves in an *ad hoc* fashion might lead to erroneous inferences even when the preferences of the opponent are correctly determined. One might spend considerable time and resources trying to detect a strategy when none exists. The theory might enable national institutions charged with the assessment of the intentions of friends and foes to develop analytic and interpretative procedures which operate under different assumptions not only about preferences, but also about the particular perspective employed by states. The sensitivity of various policies to different assumptions about preferences and general (strategic or *ad hoc*) orientations might be an important aspect of sound policy planning.

10.4 EVALUATION OF THE THEORY OF INTERNATIONAL PROCESSES

This section discusses three central criticisms of the theory: (*a*) The theory is extremely complex, hence raising questions of practical ability to test it. (*b*) The theory is elaborate on issues that are considered marginal by many scholars, (e.g., individual and collective choice) but it leaves out factors that many consider to be the key

---

[4] See Jervis, Lebow, and Stein (1985); Huth and Russett (1984); Maersheimer (1983); and George and Smoke (1975).

ingredients of any theory of international politics e.g., national power, the structure of the international system, alliances, and so forth. (c) The theory is indeterminate and even vague on the issues that, even in terms of its own logic, are the most important aspects of international politics, that is, on the evolution of international processes.

10.4.1 Complexity

The issue of complexity of a given theory is composed of four interrelated questions.

1 Does the focal theory provide a better explanation of the dependent variables than alternative theories that are more simple, that is, contain fewer variables, more straightforward linkages, and so forth. In our case, this question concerns the extent to which the synthesis of decision making models, on the one hand, and bargaining models, on the other hand, provide better explanations than simple choice models or event-interactions analyses.

2 Is the extra accuracy of the focal theory worth the added complexity? Provided that the theory of international processes allows for extra, does this extra accuracy justify the price of increased complexity?

3 If the world is complex, the role of theory is to simplify it. But if theory is complex, why is it needed?

4 Complexity creates practical problems. A complex theory is not useful because its empirical testing is difficult, and its applicability in real-world settings is questionable.

In terms of the issues addressed by the theory of international processes, several alternative theories come to mind. Each of these theories is more limited in scope than the theory of international processes, but it is also considerably simpler. Any of the decision making models discussed in the first part of the book provides a simple explanation of national choices. Consider for example the relative performance of the analytic model and the MPC framework on Brecher's (1980) data as shown in chapter 7 (tables 7.1 and 7.4). In table 7.1, the analytic model accounts for 29 of the 57 decisions studied by Brecher (50.8 percent) whereas the MPC framework accounts for 31 decisions (54.4 percent). In the refined version of this table (table 7.4) the purely analytic model accounts for 14 decisions (24.6 percent) and the MPC framework accounts for 38 decisions (66.7 percent). At least in the simple version of the MPC framework which considers only pure paths to choice, the complex model does only marginally better than the simple analytic model.

A similar case can be made with respect to the part of the theory that focuses on the evolution of international processes. Here a variety of very simple models that address identical issues suggest themselves. Action-reaction models of the sort applied to the analysis of the 1914 case (Holsti *et al.*, 1968, 1969) have a strong appeal to those who are committed to a decision making perspective because they focus on the linkages between perception and action in international politics.[5] More relevant to the problem of international processes is the work that follows the tradition set by Lewis F. Richardson (1960) in the context of arms races. Richardson's model consists of a set of equations, each of which describes how a state's defense expenditures are affected by the defense expenditures of its opponent in the previous period and by internal factors of national fatigue. This model has been applied to other international interactions quite successfully (Zinnes, 1976). It is obviously more simple than the elaborate explanations offered by the present theory regarding the evolution of international processes.

The response to this criticism is twofold. First, the fact that a given model makes predictions which are almost as good as those of the present theory does not make that model more useful just because it is simpler. There are other criteria by which the aesthetical properties of a theory can be judged. Generalizability (or what Lave and March, 1975 call fertility) is another one. When the analytic model is extended to the international level, its predictions cease to be simple or specific. This is evident from the discussion of the clash of criteria in game theory and from the discussion of the strategic perspective in chapter 9. Other models of international interaction such as the Richardson model have their own problems. For example, Zinnes (1980) pointed out that when the Richardson process model is applied to arms races and to international interactions, what seems to be its most plausible aspect, the action-reaction component, receives little or no empirical support. According to this finding, arms races as well as other competitive international interactions are driven purely by domestic inertia (Organski and Kugler, 1980). This is hardly a compelling explanation of international politics. Moreover, each of the relatively simple terms in the simple models of international processes disguises a host of extremely complex dynamics. For example, Ward (1984) showed that threat perception variables and types of weapon systems describe the effects of the opponent on the level of armament of states.

[5] But see Jervis's (1969) criticism of this kind of research.

By the same token, budgetary dynamics within states may account for the seemingly inertial effects of prior levels of defense expenditures on current levels. Thus, even the simple models become complex when their contents are inspected closely.

Second, if there were general agreement on any single decision, bargaining, or interaction model in international politics, there would have been no need for other models, especially not for complex models. The sad fact is that there is no agreement regarding any single decision model, bargaining model, or interaction model. Under these circumstances, complexity may not be a very useful criterion for judging new theories. For example, I pointed out in previous chapters that many decision theorists have viewed the various models as complementary rather than contradictory. The present theory puts real empirical meaning into this idea. By showing how different decisional strategies complement one another and how they could be detected in empirical settings, the theory adds substantive insight into the manner we conceive of foreign policy decision making. This is a good return for whatever added complexity the new theory requires. The question is whether the theory will generate more consensus than any one of the models that serve as elements in the synthesized framework.

Because this theory deals with several levels of analysis, it is very complex. Unlike simpler theories of decision making or international interactions, the present theory makes only minimal assumptions on levels of analysis that are not addressed by it. In other theories, there are heroic inferential leaps when it comes to dealing with levels of analysis that have not been directly discussed. For example, the unitary actor assumption which prevails in most of the *Realpolitik* literature has raised a lot of objections. Other frameworks that focus primarily on decision related approaches are seen as reductionist. A theory that seeks both generality and accuracy must pay a price. This is usually the price of extra complexity.

This theory requires a lot of data of a very complex nature to be tested empirically. This is due not only to the fact that it utilizes a lot of variables in its explanations, but primarily to its integration across levels-of-analysis. The difficulty to test the theory empirically also stems from the fact that its most general predictions concern long-term international interactions. This is a fundamental problem when the theory is considered as a whole. However, the problem is less acute with regard to certain layers of the theory. Research on individual and collective choice utilizing the theory of foreign policy decision making can be conducted in a fairly rigorous manner. Research on long-term patterns of international interaction can be conducted following the examples discussed in chapter 9 (although this kind of research needs considerable improvements). More importantly, however, one of the main difficulties in empirical research is not necessarily that of collecting adequate data, but conceptualizing and measuring the key variables and setting up a sensible research design. In this respect the chapters dealing with the measurement of the key concepts of the theory would be useful to those who wish to test it.

10.4.2 Imbalance in terms of theoretical emphases

Here too, three issues can be raised.

1 To what extent do the weights given by the theory to certain issues adequately reflect the significance of these issues in international politics? Does the strong emphasis on individual and group choice reflect the importance of these issues in international politics?

2 Some of the most persistent and most important concepts commonly invoked in theories of international politics have been left out of the present theory. Concepts such as the national interest, national power, international systems, international anarchy, order, norms, regimes have no apparent place in a theory that attempts to link various levels of analysis.

3 If the theory claims to be integrative, and given that it is already extremely complex, why not go all the way? In other words, why not include systemic factors as Snyder and Diesing (1977) have done?

A theory must be assessed in terms of its own internal logic. The emphasis given to certain issues and the fact that the theory ignores other issues reflects the ideas of the theory itself, not of other theories. Factors such as national interest, the structure of the international system, national power, regimes and norms, while useful in other contexts of international politics, do not serve a major purpose in the present theory. One could argue that all these things are reflected in the perceptions of individual decision makers and as such are part of the theory. That is possibly true, but it does not dispel the lack of emphasis on these concepts. The answer to these arguments is that one would have to assess the overall usefulness of the theory compared to theories which emphasize the concepts of the national interest, national power, etc.

The discussion of decision making theories suggests that the notion of national interest, national power, and the like have no meaning which is independent of their perception by key decision makers. Whether or not a certain policy reflects a national interest depends on the extent to which it is seen as such by the participants in the decision making processes. A given policy can be said to reflect national interest to the extent that it holds a *normative* superiority over other policies in terms of the preferences of the society or its representatives. This can be judged only if the preferences of the key decision makers are known and if the focal policy is a Condorcet or Borda alternative. As I have argued in the discussion and conceptualization of individual power in decisional settings, the concept of power as the potential to control outcomes in an interdependent setting consists both of preferences and of capabilities. This can be easily extended to an international setting. A state's power is also composed of its capabilities and its preferences. Whether decision makers think that they have power and whether or not the state actually controls considerable capabilities may have only partial effect on the state's ability to assure favorable outcomes and to avoid undesirable ones. Notions that other scholars see as crucial for an analysis of international politics are meaningful only to the extent that they play a role either in the perceptions of decision makers or as variables in the theory.

Theories must be evaluated not in terms of what they include or exclude but rather in terms of their logical structure, substantive and aesthetical value, and empirical performance. If the present theory is deemed satisfactory in these terms, when compared to other theories which emphasize alternative concepts, then their absence from the former is not a liability. If it is not satisfactory in terms of these criteria, then adding alternative concepts will not help. Because the internal logic of the theory will be transformed altogether if these concepts are added, one might do better by abandoning the present theory and relying on alternative theories of national interest or national power and the like.

The inclusion of system level factors in the theory of international processes was avoided not only because of the wish to limit it and to stop short of an overall synthesis of micro and macro theories of international politics. Rather, it is due to the view of system level factors as relying on an entirely different logic. Thus, concepts such as norms, anarchy, system structure, and international regimes are predicated on a top down perspective. Since I will have more to say on this in the next section, I will not elaborate here. In general, however, the reply to the criticism of microlevel biases is that at some point one has to make a choice as to what kind of factors and processes are crucial to the analysis of international politics. This choice invariably exposes one to accusations of bias and selective emphasis on some factors at the expense of other factors. The question is whether a given selection makes substantive sense and whether it results in an insightful and empirically valid set of explanations.

10.4.3 Imbalance in terms of levels of specificity

Here the theory is not criticized in terms of what it includes or excludes but rather in terms of what it seeks to explain and how it does it. The issues that require consideration are the following.

1. There is a basic imbalance in the propositions that are derived from the theory. On the one hand, the theory is very specific on the content and structure of decision making processes. On the other hand, its propositions regarding the evolution of international processes are very general and even ambiguous.

2. The value of the process analysis is questionable. The criteria for distinguishing between the *ad hoc* and the strategic perspectives are vague; the precise nature of strategies is unclear; and the classification of strategies into the safety and detection categories is too crude to be of any real empirical value.

3. There is a considerable overlap between the predictions of these two approaches. This overlap renders the distinction between the *ad hoc* approach and the strategic perspective almost meaningless.

The imbalance in the weighting of decision making and bargaining in this theory is again to be seen in the context of the internal logic of a "bottom up" perspective rather than in terms of the generality of the predictions derived from the theory. Since the key players of this theory are people rather than unitary state actors, explanation of their behavior is the focus of the theory. Everything else – national choices, international outcomes, and the long-term evolution of international processes – follows from this behavior. Moreover, whether one relies on an *ad hoc* or strategic perspective, individual preferences and individual choices play key roles in shaping international processes. The key theme of this book is the same as the point of Bueno de Mesquita and Singer (1973: 238), that we cannot truly understand any international behavior or process unless we specify the role of individual decision makers in the process. Even if we accept the asumptions of the strategic perspective that posit considerable stability in national preference, the choice of strategies and their shifts over time must be explained in terms of the decisions that triggered them.

The value of the process analysis and its contribution to the argument is not totally dependent on the specificity and precision of this part of the theory. However, a theory is valuable not only in the sense that it solves a given problem or provides a fool-proof explanation of some domain. If that were the case, I wonder whether any theory developed in the social sciences would be judged valuable from this perspective. Rather, one of the values of a theory is that it opens new avenues of inquiry by suggesting a way of conceptualizing and thinking about various phenomena. The contribution of theories such as Axelrod's (1984) work on cooperation is not that it had solved the problem of why cooperation emerges in a society of egoists, but because it helped us to think in terms of strategic perspectives and in terms of properties of various strategies. The lack of specific criteria for distinguishing between the *ad hoc* and strategic perspectives should not be taken as permanent and inherent weakness of the theory. The way is open for better or more rigorous classifications. Independent of the progress made in this area, there is still an inherent value in thinking about international processes in terms of either a clash of actors who operate under a short-term *ad hoc* logic, or as a clash of actors using carefully-crafted strategies (or as combinations of both).

I will discuss some ideas for future research on these issues in the last section, but before doing that, the relations between the theory of international processes and systemic theories must be discussed.

10.5 INTERNATIONAL SYSTEMS AND INTERNATIONAL PROCESSES

Systems theory represents a real alternative to the theory presented here in several respects. First it is a "top down" approach, in which the attributes of the whole determine the behavior of the elements. Second, it is a parsimonious theory which addresses some of the key issues of stability and instability in international politics. Third, it is holistic as opposed to the unit-bound theory of international politics. The only other study that has attempted an integration of various levels of analysis (Snyder and Diesing, 1977) devotes a chapter to the analysis of system-level effects on behavior during international crises. In this section I address the relations between the theory of international processes and some of the key ideas of systemic theories of international politics.

The notion of a top down perspective of international politics is that the attributes of the international system determine the behavior of the units; that, in some sense, state behavior is determined by factors that are beyond its immediate control. There are two versions of this notion: a weak one and a strict one. The weak version of the top down logic is best represented by the "menu for choice" idea discussed by Russett and Starr (1984). The structure of the international system and its key attributes determine for states the parameters within which they can act. Specifically, the menu metaphor is that states are confronted by a menu of things they can do in international politics. This menu is fixed and any single state has little or no control over its content. What states choose is determined by their tastes, appetite, budget, etc. This means that how states select is determined mainly by internal factors and processes. Another way of conceiving of the weak version is that system level factors operate as mediating variables between the motivations and drives of states and their actual behavior. This variant was used by Bueno de Mesquita (1981a) to operationalize the assumption that decision makers are affected by environmental uncertainty and this uncertainty intervenes between their expected utility calculations and actual choice. It was also used by Maoz (1982a) in the analysis of the factors that affect dispute initiation, where the effects of motivational factors and opportunities on dispute initiation were seen to change at different levels of systemic stability.[6]

The strict version is represented by the notion that systemic structure and prevailing conditions not only determine the menu but also define actual choices. To extend this metaphor one step further, a giant waiter comes to you and politely but firmly recommends the house's specialty. Whatever your taste, appetite, or budget, your choice is very predictable. This version is represented by structural realists such as Waltz (1979), Kaplan (1957), and Deutsch and Singer (1964). It must be noted that strictness is a matter of degree. I know of no systemic theorist who explicitly states that units have no freedom of choice. Strict versions, however, envision national latitude of decision as being extremely limited. The notion that system structure is *the* independent variable in international politics follows from the explicit downgrading of unit-level approaches viewing them as reductionist, the black-boxing of states, and the avoidance of anything that has to do with national preferences in systemic analyses.

In what follows, I explore the relations between the bottom up

---

[6] Gilpin's (1981) discussion of the economic, technological, and domestic political determinants of system change qualifies him as an advocate of the weak version, although his study is considered to be in the tradition of structural realism. See Ashley (1984); Gilpin (1984).

approach of international processes and systemic theories. Specifically, I shall argue that systemic variables can be useful in understanding international processes only to the extent that the weak version of the approach is accepted. The strict version has no real value in international political analysis: it is useless theoretically, it is empirically meaningless, and it is normatively objectionable.

In order to substantiate this argument, it is instructive to start with a brief overview of the key themes of system theories. Before doing that, however, it must be noted that – much like the state-of-the-art in decision making research – there is no such thing as *a system theory*. Rather, there are many such theories and the diversity in terms of the twists and turns in their content and empirical predictions is very substantial. The same applies to the definition of the concept of international system. However, most system theories of international politics share several things in common. I will therefore try to characterize system theories in terms of their common features and then discuss some of the variants.

A system is defined as a collection of elements that are in constant interaction with one another under a set of rules and regulations. One may add to this definition – for reasons that will become apparent below – that these elements are activated by a common input and that the purpose of their interaction is to produce a certain output.[7] To demonstrate the elements of this definition it is instructive to focus on a mechanical system such as an automobile. A car has a variety of parts and elements, but the best way to understand it is as a whole concept in which the various elements (engine, electrical system, the gears, the steering system, etc.) operate in tandem, according to a certain set of principles, to produce movement. The human body can be considered as another system that contains a command and control center (a brain) and a variety of subsystems such as the blood system, the respiratory system, the muscle system, etc. These systems are typically activated by some external input or trigger. The car is activated by gasoline and the driver's actions. The human system is activated by perceptions of the brain of external stimuli through the senses; but it can also be activated by internal needs such as hunger, thirst, sexual urges, and the like. Systems produce a common output. That is their purpose. Cars produce movement, human beings produce a variety of things that change their environment, and also reproduce themselves.

In some cases, an attempt to understand an organism or a thing in

---

[7] For definitions of international systems that focus on the first part see Kaplan (1957); Waltz (1979); Russett and Starr (1984: 77). Easton (1965) incorporates the second element into his definitions of a political system.

less than holistic terms is self-defeating, for the enumeration of elements and their interrelations will have no superior meaning. The advantage of the systemic conceptualization is that one can comprehend complex relationships as a system, thereby overcoming the need to know how the various parts make up a coherent whole. The pet notion of system theorists that the whole is more than a mere collection of its parts is a good representative of this idea. The logic of system analysis is very appealing when one works in a complex domain, for it allows leaping above the relationships among the elements to a coherent and economical description of the realm under study. In politics this implies that, instead of studying the relationships among individuals and other individuals and between individual and collectivities or between institutions and other institutions, one is engaged in a process of outlining a big picture. Thus, the political system is one that describes the authoritative allocation of values for society, and the international system is a collection of states that interact with one another under conditions of anarchy and produce stability and change.

The big picture appeal of systems analysis in international politics derives from the fact that the complexity of this domain is reduced not only to a level that is cognitively manageable, but also to a point where large-scale theorizing is easy and extremely persuasive in the abstract, no matter how little evidence exists to back these ideas up. Waltz's (1979) theory of international politics starts by distinguishing between unit-level theories (that are seen as reductionist) and system theories. Waltz's distinction rests primarily on the level of the theory's generality, and in this sense system theory clearly emerges as superior to unit-level theories.[8]

A couple of simple assumptions are common to most, if not all, systemic theories of international politics. These concern the nature of the principal units in international politics (states), their principal motivation (survival), their characteristic principle of action (unitary actors making rational choices), the fundamental conditions of the environment (anarchy). These assumptions set the stage for systemic theories of international politics. The key dependent variable is the same as in the theory of international processes: the level of stability in international interactions. The operational meaning of this variable varies: sometimes this means the level of conflict in the system, sometimes it means the frequency and magnitude of change in the

---

[8] In all fairness, Waltz does not argue that unit-level theories are useless in international political analysis, only that one cannot add them up to a general theory of international politics. Such a theory must be systemic.

attributes of the system such as the number of key actors, the identity of the major blocs (major powers, alliances) and their number, the distribution of capabilities over the various blocs, and so forth.

This variable is accounted for by a process produced by these assumptions. What follows is a very general (and even superficial) account of this process, based only on the common themes of very different theories. The key assumption of this process is that of the condition of anarchy which requires that states rely for their survival only on their own resources. States seek to optimize (rather than maximize) their capabilities so as to increase their chances of survival in an anarchical international system.[9] The distribution of capabilities represents the scale on which states measure their chances of survival in international politics. A state that finds itself low on this scale, feels a strong threat to its survival. This is so because other states might seek to eliminate it in order to increase their own chances of survival by swallowing the former's resources (Wagner, 1986; Riker, 1962). In order to meet this threat, states resort to the other option whereby they can increase their capabilities (and therefore their chance of survival): making or joining international alliances. For a small loss of autonomy, a state gets a large addition to its capabilities. The capabilities of other members of the alliance now become effectively that of the focal state.

The process of alignment and realignment produces a structure, typically operationalized in terms of the number of blocs in the system. The other element in the theory is the content of "rules of the game" which define the parameters of international interactions. Most of the work on international systems focused on identification of these rules and on exploring their effects on behavior in international politics. Only recently (Axelrod, 1986) have political scientists begun to investigate the processes by which norms and other kinds of rules are formed. Taken together, structure and rules of interaction define the outcomes in the international system: the level of stability, the frequency and magnitude of alignments and realignments, the change or preservation of the basic attributes of the system given changes in the units, and so forth.

But here is where the commonalities end and where the big debates

[9] Since states are rational actors, they are assumed to be on their production possibility curve in terms of internal capabilities. In other words, states are assumed to utilize their resources efficiently at any given point in time. Of course, economic developments and technological breakthroughs can move the production possibility curve of any given state upward (Gilpin, 1981), thereby changing its position in the system. But the implication of this is that – for the most part – states cannot do much internally to increase their chances of survival because, as rational actors, they already do whatever they can in terms of domestic politics to serve that purpose.

start. As noted above, there are differences in terms of the extent to which structure and rules determine outcomes. There are differences in terms of the extent to which certain structures are associated with certain rules. For example, Kaplan associates a pentagonal structure with six behavioral rules to produce the balance of power system. Riker (1962) and Waltz (1979) argue that these rules are (*a*) internally inconsistent, and (*b*) not deducible from the pentagonal structure. Niou and Ordeshook (1986) and Wagner (1986) show that there is no inconsistency in these rules and so does Simowitz (1982). Another, and more significant, source of disagreement concerns the relationships between independent and dependent variables that can be deduced from these assumptions. This debate starts with the controversy between Waltz (1964) and Deutsch and Singer (1964) regarding the stability of a bipolar system compared to a multipolar one, and goes through a series of empirical investigations relating polarity to stability in international politics (Singer, Bremer, and Stuckey, 1972; Wallace, 1973; Bueno de Mesquita, 1975, 1978; Li and Thompson, 1977; Levy, 1983). The results of these analyses are largely mixed and inconclusive.

Having described the commonalities and differences among various theories of international systems in terms of what they include, it is necessary to describe them in terms of what they ignore. Here the best term that describes system theories is sterility. Virtually all the versions of system theories are sterile in the sense that they ignore not only national structures such as regime types, ideology, leaders and decision processes, but even things that are inherently part of big picture analyses of international politics, namely, national preferences. To be more precise, states are attributed a set of fixed and common preferences and these preferences are typically seen to have some sort of power equivalent (Niou and Ordeshook, 1987: 390–392). While theorists such as Waltz criticize unit-level theories of international politics as reductionist, the implicit or explicit reduction of national preferences to a capability-based scale is even more so.[10]

The notion that everybody can form coalitions with everybody else in the international system is the cornerstone of balance of power theories of world politics. Imposition of restrictions on the coalition formation process in terms of variables that are extraneous to those of the model (such as ideology) is seen to be a factor that accounts for the breakdown in the system due to violation of its basic logic. The breakdown of the classical balance of power system at the turn of the

[10] This is what Vasquez (1983) characterizes as the tendency of the realist paradigm to attribute to states a fixed hierarchy of goals.

twentieth century is attributed to the freezing of the alliances and the fact that ideological and other restrictions entered into the picture that was supposed to rest strictly on the six rules of interaction posited by Kaplan.

Some recent formal investigations of the conditions under which stability is produced in balance of power systems specified some necessary and sufficient conditions of equilibrium of two types: stability in terms of the number of states and stability of the distribution of resources (Wagner, 1986; Niou and Ordeshook, 1986). This was done without incorporating any notion of preferences into the analysis. Indeed, the non-ideologically restricted formation of international coalitions is the cornerstone of the balance of power system. The problem is that some of the implicit assumptions of these analyses are totally implausible. For example, Niou and Ordeshook (1987, 1986) and Wagner (1986) assume that the pool of capabilities in the system is fixed, and that the entire resources of the loser of a war are transferred to the winner. This implies that war is costless. In other words, the winner's human and material casualties as well as those of the loser do not count in the computation of resources.

Another key issue that is ignored by system theories is manipulability of rules by individual states (or what in our terminology is labeled strategies). Even if it is plausible to assume that states have fixed preferences and are aware of the constraints imposed by the structure of the system and the rules of interaction, manipulation of rules is impossible. For example, a state cannot work within the rules of the system to transform it. If one of the key rules of balance of power is that all members must oppose an actor who aspires to a position of dominance in the system, then a state cannot use this rule to its advantage (that is, to become dominant).[11] Much criticism from many directions has been leveled at system theories of international politics. The plausibility of the most fundamental assumptions has been repeatedly questioned. It was argued that states are not the only key actors in the contemporary international system: international, subnational, and transnational actors play an increasingly important role (Keohane and Nye, 1977; Mansbach and Vasquez, 1981). It was argued

---

[11] Suppose that we have a system composed of five actors a through e, and that the distribution of capabilities in the system is as follows:

$$a>b>c>d>e \tag{1}$$
$$a<[bcde] \tag{2}$$
$$b>[cde] \tag{3}$$

In this case, b can invoke the dominance principle to form a coalition against a, which – once defeated and reduced in power (even if its formal status as a full-fledged member is restored) – cannot, together with $[cde]$ defeat the victorious b.

553

that the unitary-rational actor assumption no longer holds true for states, and that one cannot generalize over different political structures to derive a coherent set of preferences over all issue-areas (Keohane, 1983). The fundamental condition of anarchy was also challenged. This challenge has been twofold. One follows from the regimes literature that identifies norms and institutions which constrain egoistic behavior of states even in the absence of binding laws and enforcing authority. Second, the lack of hegemony in international politics is not all-encompassing: in certain time periods and in certain issue-areas there were hegemons that were able to make and enforce rules in international politics. This was certainly true about the US hegemony in international economy during the 1944–1972 era (Keohane, 1984).

Another type of criticism concerns the disagreement among various systemic theories. Ashley (1984) criticizes the work of Gilpin and Waltz for its apparent departure from the spirit of classical realism. Waltz (1979) criticizes the work of Singer and his associates on the grounds of its inductivism. Waltz also criticizes Kaplan's work for being internally inconsistent.

How does the theory of international processes compare with system theories? Is there anything that the two share in common? Can any theory of international politics claim a general status if it lacks any elements of system-level factors? The first thing that must be noted is that both theories attempt to characterize international processes. However, they differ in terms of the definition of the dependent variable. System theories define international processes in terms of stability or change in the fundamental characterstics of the system (its structure and rules). The theory of international processes defines international processes in terms of intersections of national choices. It also attempts to account for stability and change in international interactions. However, stability is defined here in terms of what system theories take to be the starting point of its analysis, namely, invariance of national preferences, expectations and strategies over time.

Obviously, both theories differ in terms of the direction of the causal process they postulate. System theories emphasize factors that are outside the national boundaries and are largely non-manipulable by any given national actor. These factors are seen to be either key determinants of how the national units act, or the only determinants of national actions. In the second case, information about the structure of the international system and about the rules of interaction allows predicting the most important kinds of national actions, which states

554

would go to war, when, and against whom; what kind of alliances would form, when, and under what conditions would they change. No information regarding national decision making processes or national strategies is required for those predictions. On the other hand, the theory of international processes does not require big-picture data concerning distribution of capabilities, and rules of the game to predict the level of stability in a given process.

The theories differ in terms of the level of generality at which their propositions are specified. Systemic theories provide big-picture predictions. Most important investigations of international politics in terms of system level variables focus on the most powerful states in the world, namely, on the major powers. A system level analysis of the Peru–Ecuador dispute makes very little sense, but a system analysis of the Franco–Prussian dispute sounds more sensible. Second, most of the propositions of system level theories concern large-scale trends in international politics, such as what alliances form, when and why general wars break out, and so forth. System theories do not pretend to account for routine, day-to-day choices of states. But they do suggest that even when one uses a unit-level approach to account for day-to-day choices of states, one must include in the explanation system level variables. This is certainly true for unit-level explanations of major national choices (Choucri and North, 1975; Waltz, 1979; Snyder and Diesing, 1977). On the other hand, when attempting a general explanation of a large-scale trend in international politics such as the processes leading to the two world wars, it is not necessarily clear that system theorists would urge examination of unit-level factors. It is quite conceivable that a systemic explanation could be done without actually demonstrating how the perceptions, decisions, and maneuvers of the people and groups involved in this process made a difference. For example, the explanation of the origins of the First World War in terms of the tightening of the alliance system at the turn of the century does not require an assessment of the role of the Kaiser or the Tsar in the process, nor does such an explanation leave much room for factors such as the rigidity of the mobilization processes of the main participants in the crisis (Levy, 1986).

Obviously, many people call for a synthesis between system level and unit-level explanations of international politics, in accounting for international wars (Levy, 1985; 1986), or in explaining trends in the global economy (Keohane, 1984). The question is whether this is at all possible and whether it is practical. The extent to which such an operation is possible depends on which version of the top down approach is accepted. Under the strict version in which system structure determines national choices, one wonders whether an integration between system level and unit-level theories is not a contradiction in terms. Under weaker versions of the top down approach, such a synthesis appears possible in principle but is an extremely difficult operation in practice. One key difficulty is the assumption of fixed national preferences which renders any attempt to penetrate the black box of states substantively meaningless. Since states are assumed to be unitary rational actors, and since their preference structures are deterministic, there is very little room for maneuver in terms of theorizing about how the personalities of their leaders, the structure of the government, the decisional processes used, and the implementation of national decisions affect their national choices. There is also very little room for explanations which suggest that states occasionally force choices which are out of the boundaries of the system-defined menu. For example, how does a system theory account for a Hitler; how does a theory of Hitler incorporate system level factors of the distribution of capabilities when attempting to account for his rearmament decision or the decision to invade the Rhineland knowing that Germany might be humiliated if the French decided to react forcefully?

System theories could have been extremely powerful if they had been able to make predictions on the conditions that produce stability or instability in international politics without including national preferences. However, many of the key issues in systemic theories turn out moot when national preferences are incorporated into the analysis and when some variability in these preferences is assumed. Bueno de Mesquita (1981b) showed that once some simple assumptions about national preferences and risk-disposition are satisfied, there is no logical basis for any sort of proposition linking structure to stability in international politics. Likewise, Morrow (1988) showed that it is meaningless to talk about any kind of effects produced by a structure without incorporating some variability in national preferences. It is true that one can get a lot of explanatory mileage using a fixed preference assumption, but then one must invoke strategies and account for their selection in decision-theoretic terms. Unless one wants to assume that the choice of strategy is also fixed (this cannot be so because it contradicts the rationality assumption; recall Axelrod's [1984] proof that there is no best strategy independent of the strategies against which it plays), fixed preferences or fixed strategies do not go with a synthesis of system level and unit-level approaches.

However, once the assumption of fixed preferences is relaxed, systemic factors lose much of their power. Consider, for example,

Bueno de Mesquita's theory of international conflict which rests on some assumptions that are identical to most systemic theories yet is clearly a unit-level theory. In the original version of the theory (Bueno de Mesquita, 1981a), it was assumed that a state defines its preferences over the outcomes associated with war–no-war alternatives in terms of political benefits or losses and in terms of the probabilities associated with these outcomes. But the end result of the expected utility analysis is based on two sets of calculations: the bilateral calculations, and what the author calls a "multilateral lottery." The latter represents an assessment of the focal actor about how other actors might react to a bilateral conflict (join the initiator of the conflict, join the target of the conflict, or remain neutral). System level factors enter this theory twice: once as an element in the expected utility equation, and once as an external element which determines the decision rule used by a state following this calculation. As such, it seems that systemic factors play an important role in the success of the expected utility theory to account for the initiation and outcomes of international conflicts. This is not so. First, Wagner (1984) and Maoz (1984b) showed that there is a strong correlation between the overall expected utility for initiation and the relative capabilities of the actors. If that is the case, then the "multilateral lottery" plays a minor role in national decisions to initiate conflict. Second, in subsequent work, Bueno de Mesquita (1985) realized that the exogenous definition of national risk dispositions is not consistent with expected utility theory. Hence, he developed an endogenous definition of risk-dispositions. This definition enabled him to include in the model situations wherein actors misperceive each other's risk attitudes and hence their expected utilities. In this version which responds to several criticisms leveled at the original version of the theory, the impact of system level calculations on decisions to initiate and escalate international conflicts is reduced considerably.

There are at least five reasons why I think that the strict version of systemic theories cannot be a meaningful theory of international politics. These are: (1) the inability to account for turning points in history; (2) failure to account for the rise and fall of actors in international politics; (3) failure to account for the instruments of change; (4) the fundamental contradiction that exists between the assumption of fixed national attributes and preferences and variability of system structure; (5) consistent historical evidence shows that individual leaders have manipulated or defied rules, and – in too many cases – with great success.

System theories have consistently failed to account for the most important aspect of the domain which they attempt to explain: abrupt and fundamental change. When accounting for changes over time, system theories invoke notions of gradual erosion in the factors that hold the system at a state of equilibrium (i.e., distribution of capabilities and rules). For example, the rigidity of alliances is an explanation of the demise of the balance of power system. However, it is unclear why some systems transform themselves peacefully into new ones (e.g., the contemporary change in the structure of the international system from a tight bipolar one to a multipolar one) while others collapse via major earthquakes. System theories that have been developed to account for these changes are no longer of the strict top down type. For example, both Choucri and North (1975) and Gilpin (1981) suggest that system transformation must be based on some national choice. This is particularly apparent in Gilpin's work which assumes that such changes will occur only to the extent that key actors decide that they are better off with a new structure than with an old one. This requires a bottom up perspective, because one must explain the change in the commitment of some states from one that wishes to preserve the systemic structure to one that wishes to transform it. A fundamental difficulty with the latter approach is that it portrays the process of system change as conscious and intentional. However, cases such as the outbreak of the First World War suggest that no key leader had any intention of transforming the system (Tuchman, 1962; Lebow, 1981). Whether or not system transformation is a result of an intentional process, it is obvious that explanations of abrupt changes must focus on national decisions.

Strict top down perspectives systematically failed to explain how actors rise and fall and when they become important and unimportant in the system. Apart from the fairly trivial proposition that a general war alters the system in the sense that it reduces defeated actors from the status of major powers to the status of minor powers and elevates others to the status of major powers, strict top down perspectives have little to offer (Levy, 1985; Mansbach and Vasquez, 1981). They cannot account for the voluntary entry and exit of actors from the game of nations. Up to the late nineteenth century, states such as China and Japan just did not want to become a part of the international political system and voluntarily closed themselves to the rest of the world. In some ways, the isolationist policy of the United States with regard to Europe and the Far East up to the turn of the century is inexplicable from a systemic perspective. Can we say that up to 1894 Japan did not attempt to maximize its chances of survival, and after that year it did? What does system theory offer regarding the American re-adoption of an isolationist stance following the First World War. The international system might have been very different had the United States been willing to take the political responsibilities of a major power. How does system theory account for the decay of empires into oblivion through a gradual process? Turkey, Spain, and Holland are three examples.[12]

War is seen by system theorists as the single most important instrument of system transformation (Levy, 1985; Gilpin, 1981; Waltz, 1979). However, strict top down approaches cannot explain why one war causes system transformation while another does not. The Napoleonic wars were no less destructive or general than the First or Second World Wars in terms of the military technology and the size of the interstate system of the respective time periods. The Napoleonic wars did not alter the structure of the international system: the balance of power system which prevailed in eighteenth century Europe was reinstated by the winners and prevailed in the post-Napoleonic era. However, this was not the case following each of the world wars. Without looking at the bargaining processes and the decisions made in each of the peace conferences that followed each of these wars, it is impossible to explain how wars have served to transform or preserve the structure of the international system. During the nineteenth century, there were several, fairly large-scale wars between or among major powers (the Crimean War, the Seven-Week War, the Franco-Prussian War, etc.). None of these wars transformed the system. Why? System theory would explain this in terms of the rules of the game in balance of power systems that allow restoring losers to their prior status. However, it is not clear, according to this logic, why the winners of the First World War decided to break down the Austro-Hungarian empire and to impose on Germany vicious terms of surrender which reduced it to the status of a minor power.

If the fundamental assumption of system theories is that state behavior is determined by the same motives and logic irrespective of the number of poles, the distribution of capabilities, and the rules of the game, then it is unclear why there is any variability in system structure. Moreover, one cannot explain in systemic terms why systems transform themselves. This is a fundamental contradiction in a strict top down approach. States are assumed to be rational actors seeking to survive in an anarchical system. Moreover, strict top down

---

[12] For an interesting discussion of this problem and an interpretation of recent and contemporary history in terms of a framework whose focus is on the rise of actors and issues in world politics see Mansbach and Vasquez (1981).

perspectives suggest that internal charcteristics of states do not matter much in international politics. If this is the case, then states should do whatever it takes to reach to an equilibrium that maximizes their survival. If this equilibrium implies that no state should be eliminated or added to the system, then there is no reason for system change, because if there were, the assumptions of the model would be violated.

If a balance of power system requires an unequal number of actors (at least three) then the addition of a state to the system can cause its breakdown. Allowing a new major power to emerge endangers the equilibrium. Thus, existing states should oppose this. If they do not, then either the rationality assumption is violated, or the motivation is not survival. More generally, once a system structure is defined in terms of a distribution of capabilities and a set of rules, each state must follow an optimal policy which will establish an equilibrium. Once in an equilibrium, change should not occur. If change does occur, one must account for it in non-systemic terms, because the assumptions of a theory that claims that structure is the single best determinant of behavior are violated, and the theory is no longer useful.

If the rules of the system are binding in the sense that states must follow them or they would harm themselves, then there is a heavy penalty on violation of rules. For example, if you are in a certain camp with a bipolar system and you defect, you will be punished (unless you join the other camp). Likewise, a tight bipolar system cannot allow minor states to derive simultaneous benefits from both major powers. However, there is a lot of historical evidence suggesting that leaders have constantly manipulated, defied, or otherwise, disobeyed the rules of the game of the system, and have been able to get away with it. The non-aligned movement is a superb example of this idea. Yugoslavia divorced the Soviet Union in the late forties but did not join the Western camp. It received Western aid through the Marshall Plan but did not make any significant political overture toward the West. It has yet to be punished for violating or manipulating a tight bipolar structure to its own advantage. The same goes for India which has consistently played the two superpowers against each other in South-east Asia. Up to the early sixties, India relied on a variety of sources from which to acquire weapons; some of the weapons were purchased from the Soviets, and some were purchased from the West. Following its defeat in the Sino–Indian war, both the United States and the Soviets increased their arms supply to India (Maoz, 1989: ch. 2).

The policy of President Sadat of Egypt is perhaps the hallmark of manipulation of system structure and system rules. As we pointed out

INTERNATIONAL SYSTEMS AND INTERNATIONAL PROCESSES

in chapter 8, Sadat realized that detente has established a new code of conduct in local conflicts among the superpowers. These norms were designed to cause mutual restraint and reduce the chances of unwanted escalation. This, in Sadat's view, would have perpetuated the Israeli grip over the occupied territories. The decision to initiate war in this case is a prime example of how a tail wags the dog and why system theory is at a loss to explain how rules are manipulated and defied. Sadat planned to use the spirit of restraint to force the major powers to violate their norm of restraint in order to eventually invest in solving Egypt's problems with Israel. The implication is that if system level rules are being manipulated and defied, then they are not very useful in determining by themselves the behavior of actors.

It must be noted that Waltz's (1979, 1986) theory is very sensitive to the unintended consequences of intentional national behavior in an anarchic environment. System structure acts to produce outcomes that are independent of the wishes of its units. This property of the international system is probably one of the key rationales for the top down study of international politics. In a way, it is the same rationale suggested by Schelling's (1978) micromotives and macrobehavior approach. While the existence of a structure which circumvents national intentions is an important aspect of any theory of inter- national politics, it is not a unique top down property, not if structure can be interpreted in the way we have done in chapters 8 and 9 as an intersection (objective or subjective) of players, their policy alter- natives, and their preferences over the resulting outcomes. Once conceived in top down terms, the paradoxical implications of systemic structure for national behavior make unintended consequences una- voidable because structure is almost impossible to change. In bottom up terms, the unintended consequences of intentional behavior can either be amended through learning, or they can be manipulated through strategy.

But having criticized the strict version of systemic theories that claim that structure is the single best predictor of national behavior and of system level processes, it is time to examine how the weaker version, that combines structural and unit-level explanations, converges with the theory of international processes. Four points might be useful here.

1 *Systemic factors form the context of international processes.* They deter- mine when international processes begin and end, which actors participate in the process, when they enter and exit, and why. I started the analysis of the Hitler crises in 1933 with the coming to power of the

Nazi party in Germany. However, a more detailed investigation of this process should have started with the end of the First World War. The answer as to why this is the "right" place to start the analysis of this international process, and which actors ought to be included in such an analysis can be found in the structure of the international system at that time. The definition of an international process is not sufficiently specific to determine the starting and ending points of such processes or the identity of the participants. Such decisions require some judgment that relies on system level factors.

The analysis of international processes relies to some extent on assumptions concerning actors that are not part of the process. These actors play an important role in the perceptions of the participants in the sequence of international interactions that is to be explained, but they cannot be considered active participants. For example, in the analysis of the Israeli–Syrian interactions, Maoz and Yaniv (1989) assumed that they could isolate the interactions of these two states from the interactions of each with other states in the Middle East or with the superpowers. In their case, this was a working assumption which was defended in terms of practical considerations, but not in theoretical terms. Indeed, given the structure of the Middle East subsystem, such an assumption is questionable on empirical grounds. On the other hand, the analysis of the Hitler crises suggested that one could reliably ignore the role of the United States as a participant in the process. The same applies to Japan's role despite its alliance with Germany and Italy. The structure of the international system determines to a large extent which actor can be assumed irrelevant for an analysis, and which actor is relevant in the background although it is not directly involved in the sequence of interactions to be explained.

2 *Systemic factors affect basic national dispositions to strategic behavior.* Systemic factors may affect: (*a*) the extent to which actors are disposed to adopt a strategic or *ad hoc* perspective, and (*b*) if they use strategies, which ones are actually employed. The notion of structural uncertainty that runs as a common theme in the writings of many systems theorists (e.g., Waltz, 1964; Deutsch and Singer, 1964; Rosecrance, 1963, 1966; Singer, Bremer and Stuckey, 1972; Bueno de Mesquita, 1981a), is particularly relevant here. When structural uncertainty is high, that is, actors are not sure where all other actors stand in terms of their commitments and loyalties, the tendency to resort to strategic perspectives and to utilize safety strategies might increase. When structural certainty is high, actors may be more amenable to detection strategies or to *ad hoc* adjustments (Bueno de Mesquita, 1981a; Maoz, 1982a).

When actors are seen to employ long-term strategies, or when actors who employ *ad hoc* perspectives stabilize their expectations, the importance of decision processes diminishes anyway, and a convergence between unit-level notions and system level notions of stability might be expected. In such cases, a systemic perspective is to be preferred due to its more parsimonious nature. However, in accounting for major systemic transformations in history, an international process perspective is indispensable.

3 *Systemic factors affect fundamental perceptions of decision makers.* If people such as Metternich, Bismark, Lloyd George, Clemanceau, Hitler, Stalin, Chamberlain, and Kissinger acted and thought in terms of a global distribution of capabilities and in terms of norms that are derived from this distribution, we must ascertain this through the analysis of how these factors affected their choices.

System level factors are expressed in the theory of international processes in several ways. First, the characteristic of the international system which is emphasized in the theory of international processes is that of *interdependence* rather than anarchy. States act in an environment where they are not in control of the outcomes of their choices. This is so irrespective of the distribution of power in the system and of the degree of order and the power of international norms. It is this fundamental interdependence which drives the analysis of international outcomes and the evolution of international processes. Second, system level factors define to a large extent what I called the "rules of play" (chapter 8). The function of rules of play in the theory of international process is that they define the theoretical international outcomes. Both the actual and expected international outcomes are determined by decision makers' choices.

Third, the dynamics of international processes converge to a large extent with systemic factors. Three types of dynamics are involved: intentional, unintentional, and incidental. Intentional dynamics refer to description of international processes in terms of a clash of strategies which had been selected in a conscious and intentional fashion. Unintentional dynamics refer to the description of the evolution of international processes in *ad hoc* terms. Incidental dynamics concern outcomes that are exogenous to both systems theory and to the theory of international processes that cause preference and/or strategy change.

Fourth, the theory of international processes can be useful in accounting for the role of individual decision makers in system tranformations. Because the transformation of an international system can be due as much to the decisions of some individuals as to long-term dynamics and power transitions, it is important to investigate this aspect of systems change as well. Lebow (1981) whose focus was on the role of individual decision makers in international crises pointed out that systemic theories have little to offer in accounting for why some crises escalate into full-blown wars while others do not. If this is indeed the case, bottom up approaches can be very instrumental in accounting for system transforming wars.

The major conclusion of this discussion is simple. Top down and bottom up approaches of international politics are not necessarily contradictory. However, this is not to suggest that an integration of the two is feasible or desirable. And even if such an integration is feasible and desirable, it is not easy. A strict systemic perspective which denies a key role to unit-level factors in the analysis of international history is useless for the analysis of international politics. A weaker version of systems theory that acknowledges the roles of individual preferences and national choices in the shaping of international processes might in many ways help improve on the theory of international processes as much as the theory of international processes might help improve on the theory of systemic stability and change.

10.6 FUTURE RESEARCH ON INTERNATIONAL PROCESSES

The theory of international processes presented in this study should be seen only as a beginning rather than an end. The questions this theory raises and leaves open are more numerous and – in some ways – far more important than those it attempts to answer. Instead of enumerating the questions that need to be answered in future investigations, let me point out three general areas that future research using the ideas of this study and its approach might focus upon: theoretical development of process analysis; empirical investigation of the propositions derived from the theory; and investigation of the relations between the bottom up unit-level perspective of the theory and systemic approaches.

The strategic perspective of international processes provides an important opportunity to study how states develop, implement, and change long-term strategies in international politics; which strategies work under what circumstances, and which strategies fail and why. In particular, better classifications of strategies in foreign policy are required, and a better understanding of the components of various strategies would be an important theoretical contribution.

The most obvious future research direction is that of empirical

564

analysis of the propositions of the theory of international processes. This requires a considerable effort in data collection on a large number of decisions made by several states over a relatively long period of time. The cases that were mentioned briefly in this book: the Egyptian–Israeli peace process; the Syrian–Israeli interactions, the Hitler crises, are all candidates for such analyses. So is the issue of the origins and course of the cold war. The empirical analysis of this theory will enable one to shed light both on the relations between choices and consequences in international politics and on the evolution of international processes.

A more detailed investigation that might include both theoretical and empirical analyses might establish the relations between the bottom up perspective presented in the book, and systemic theories which have been studied only in the last chapter. The synthesis of systemic approaches with bargaining approaches which was attempted by Snyder and Diesing (1977) did not go very far, and the present study did not even try one. One of the fundamental problems of the study of international politics is still open and awaiting serious consideration.

REFERENCES

Abel, E. (1966); *The Missile Crisis*. Philadelphia: J.B. Lippincott.

Abel, T. (1941); "The Element of Decision in the Pattern of War," *American Sociological Review*, 6(4): 453–859.

Abelson, R.P. (1973); "The Structure of Belief Systems," pp. 287–339 in: *Computer Models of Thought and Action*. Schnak, R.C. and Colby, K.M. (eds.). San Francisco: Freeman.

Adomeit, H. (1982); *Soviet Risk-Taking and Crisis Behavior: A Theoretical and Empirical Analysis*. London: Allen and Unwin.

Alker, H.A. and Hermann, M.G. (1971); "Are Bayesian Decisions Artificially Intelligent? The Effects of Task and Personality on Conservatism in Processing Information," *Journal of Personality and Social Psychology*, 19(1): 31–41.

Allais, M. (1953); "Le Comportement de l'homme rationnel devant le risque: critique des postulates et axiomes de l'Ecole Américaine," *Econometrica*, 21(4): 503–546.

Allan, P. (1983); *Crisis Bargaining and the Arms Race*. Cambridge, Mass.: Ballinger.

Allison, G.T. (1971); *Essence of Decision*. Boston: Little Brown.

Allison, G.T. and Halperin, M.H. (1972); "Bureaucratic Politics: A Paradigm and Some Policy Implications," pp. 40–79 in: *Theory and Policy in International Relations*. Tanter, R. and Ullman, R. (eds.). Princeton: Princeton University Press.

Almond, G.A. and Genco, S. (1977); "Clocks, Clouds, and the Study of Politics," *World Politics*, 29(2): 489–522.

Anderson, P.A. (1981); "Justification and Precedents as Constraints in Foreign Policy Decision Making," *American Journal of Political Science*, 25(4): 738–781.

Anderson, P. and McKewon, T.J. (1987); "Changing Aspirations, Limited Attention, and War," *World Politics*, 40(1): 1–29.

Antaki, C. (1982); "A Brief Introduction to Attribution and Attributional Theories," pp. 3–22 in: *Attributions and Psychological Change*. Antaki, C. and Brewin, C. (eds.). London: Academic Press.

Argote, L. (1982); "Input Uncertainty and Organizational Coordination in Hospital Emergency Units," *Administrative Science Quarterly*, 37(3): 420–434.

Arrow, K.J. (1963); *Social Choice and Individual Values* (second edition). New York: Wiley.

Art, R. (1973); "Bureaucratic Politics and American Foreign Policy: A Critique," *Policy Sciences*, 4(4): 467–490.

Ashley, R.K. (1984); "The Poverty of Neo-Realism," *International Organization*, 38(2): 225–286.

Axelrod, R. (1986); "An Evolutionary Approach to Norms," *American Political Science Review*, 80(4): 1095–1112.

(1984); *The Evolution of Cooperation*. New York: Basic Books.

(1981); "The Emergence of Cooperation Among Egoists," *American Political Science Review*, 75(2): 306–318.

(1980a); "Effective Choice in the Prisoner's Dilemma," *Journal of Conflict Resolution*, 24(1): 3–25.

(1980b); "More Effective Choice in the Prisoner's Dilemma," *Journal of Conflict Resolution*, 24(3): 379–403.

(1977); "Argumentation in Foreign Policy Settings," *Journal of Conflict Resolution*, 19(4): 727–743.

(1976); "Decision for Nonimperialism: The Deliberations of the British Eastern Committee in 1918," pp. 77–95 in *Structure of Decision: The Cognitive Maps of Political Elites*. Axelrod, R. (ed.). Princeton: Princeton University Press.

(1973); "Schema Theory: An Information Processing Model of Perception and Cognition," *American Political Science Review*, 67(4): 1,248–1,266.

(1970); *Conflict of Interest: A Theory of Divergent Goals With Applications to Politics*. Chicago: Markham.

Azar, E.E. (1980); "The Conflict and Peace Data Bank (COPDAB) Project," *Journal of Conflict Resolution*, 24(3): 379–403.

Banzhaf, J.F.III (1965); "Weighted Voting Doesn't Work: A Mathematical Analysis," *Rutgers Law Review*, 19(2): 317–343.

Barber, J.D. (1977); *The Presidential Character* (2nd edition). Englewood Cliffs, N.J.: Prentice Hall.

Barclay, S. *et al.* (1977); *Handbook of Decision Analysis*. McLean, Va.: Advanced Research Projects Agency. Decisions and Designs, Inc.

Bar-Hillel, M. (1982); "Studies of Representativeness," pp. 69–83 in: *Judgment Under Uncertainty: Heuristics and Biases*. Kahneman, D., Slovic, P., and Tversky, A. (eds.). Cambridge: Cambridge University Press.

Barlow, I. (1940); *The Agadir Crisis*. Chapell Hill: University of North Carolina Press.

Bartos, O. (1977); "Simple Model of Negotiation: A Sociological Point of View," *Journal of Conflict Resolution*, 21(4): 565–581.

Behr, R.L. (1981); "Nice Guys Finish Last – Sometimes," *Journal of Conflict Resolution*, 25(2): 289–300.

Ben-Zvi, A. (1976); "Hindsight and Foresight: A Conceptual Framework for the Analysis of Surprise Attacks," *World Politics*, 28(3): 381–395.

Betts, R.K. (1978); "Analysis, War, and Decision: Why Intelligence Failures Are Inevitable," *World Politics*, 31(1): 61–89.

Beyth-Marom, R. (1982); "How Probable is Probable? A Numerical Translation of Verbal Probability Expressions," *Journal of Forecasting*, 1(3): 257–269.

Black, D. (1958); *The Theory of Committees and Elections*. Cambridge: Cambridge University Press.

Blalock, H.M. (1964); *Causal Inference in Nonexperimental Research*. Chapel Hill: University of North Carolina Press.

Blechman, B. (1966); "The Quantitative Evaluation of Foreign Policy Alternatives, Sinai 1956," *Journal of Conflict Resolution*, 10(4): 408–426.

Bloomfield, L.P. (1974); *The Foreign Policy Process: Making Theory Relevant*. Beverly Hills, Calif.: Sage.

Bohrnstedt, G.W. and Knoke, D. (1982); *Statistics for Social Data Analysis*. Itasca, Ill.: Peacock Publishers.

Bonham, G.M. and Shapiro, M.J. (1986); "Mapping Structures of Thought," pp. 29–52 in: *Different Text Analysis Procedures for the Study of Decision Making*. Gallhofer, I.N. *et al.* (eds.), Amsterdam: Sociometric Research Foundation.

(1976); "Explanation of the Unexpected: The Syrian Intervention in Jordan in 1970," pp. 113–141 in: *Structure of Decision: The Cognitive Maps of Political Elites*. Axelrod, R. (ed.), Princeton: Princeton University Press.

Bonham, G.M., Shapiro, M.J. and Trumble, J. (1979); "The October War: Changes in Cognitive Orientations Toward the Middle East Conflict," *International Studies Quarterly*, 23(1): 3–44.

Brady, L.P. (1978); "The Situation and Foreign Policy," pp. 173–190 in: *Why Nations Act*. East, M.A. *et al.* (eds.). Beverly Hills, Calif.: Sage.

Brams, S.J. (1985a); *Superpower Games: Applying Game Theory to Superpower Conflict*. New Haven: Yale University Press.

(1985b); *Rational Politics*. Washington, D.C.: CQ Press.

(1977); "Deception in 2×2 Games," *Journal of Peace Science*, 2(1): 171–203.

(1976); *Paradoxes in Politics: An Introduction to the Nonobvious in Political Science*. New York: Free Press.

(1975); *Game Theory and Politics*. New York: Free Press.

Brams, S.J. and Affuso, P.A. (1985); "New Paradoxes of Voting Power in the EC Council of Ministers," *Electoral Studies*, 4(2): 135–139.

(1976); "Power and Size: A New Paradox," *Theory and Decision*, 7(1–2): 29–56.

Brams, S.J., Felsenthal, D.S. and Maoz, Z. (1987); 'Chairman Paradoxes Under Approval Voting," pp. 223–233 in: *Theory and Decision: Essays in Honor of Werner Leinfellner* Berghel, Hal (ed.). Dordrecht: Reidel.

(1986); "New Chairman Paradoxes," pp. 245–255 in: *Paradoxical Effects of Social Behavior: Essays in Honor of Anatol Rapoport*. Mitter, Peter and Diekman, Andreas (eds.). Vienna: Physica-Verlag.

Brams, S.J. and Hessel, M.P. (1984); "Threat Power in Sequential Games," *International Studies Quarterly*, 28(1): 15–36.

(1983); "Staying Power in 2×2 Games," *Theory and Decision*, 15(3): 279–302.

Brams, S.J. and Kilgour, D.M. (1987); "Threat, Escalation and Crisis Stability: A Game Theoretic Analysis," *American Political Science Review*, 81(3): 833–850.

Brams, S.J. and Wittman, D. (1981); "Non-Myopic Equilibria in 2×2 Games," *Conflict Management and Peace Science*, 6(3): 39–62.

Braybrook, D. and Lindbloom, C.E. (1963); *A Strategy for Decision: Policy Evaluation as a Social Process*. New York: Free Press.

Brecher, M. (1980); *Decisions in Crisis: Israel, 1967 and 1973*. Berkeley: University of California Press.

(1979a); "State Behavior in International Crises," *Journal of Conflict Resolution*, 23(3): 446–480.

(ed.) (1979b); *Studies in Crisis Behavior*. New Brunswick, N.J.: Transaction Books.

(1977a); "Toward a Theory of International Crisis Behavior," *International Studies Quarterly*, 21(2): 39–74.

(1977b); "India's Devaluation of 1966: Linkage Politics and Crisis Decision Making," *British Journal of International Studies*, 3(1): 1–25.

(1974a); *Decisions in Israel's Foreign Policy*. New Haven: Yale University Press.

(1974b); "Inputs and Decisions for War and Peace: The Israeli Experience," *International Studies Quarterly*, 18(2): 131–177.

(1973); "Images, Process, and Feedback in Foreign Policy: Israel's Decision on German Reparations," *American Political Science Review*, 67(1): 73–102.

(1972); *The Foreign Policy System of Israel: Setting, Images, Process*. London: Oxford University Press.

Brecher, M., Steinberg, B. and Stein, J. (1969); "A Framework for Research on Foreign Policy Behavior," *Journal of Conflict Resolution*, 13(1): 75–101.

Breznitz, S. (1984); *Cry Wolf: The Psychology of False Alarms*. Hillsdale, N.J.: Lawrence Erlbaum Associates.

Budescu, David V. and Wallsten, T.S. (1985); "Consistency in Interpretation of Probabilistic Phrases," *Organizational Behavior and Human Decision Processes*, 36: 391–405.

Bueno de Mesquita, B. (1985); "The 'War Trap' Revisited: A Revised Expected Utility Model," *American Political Science Review*, 79(1): 156–173.

(1973); "The Costs of War: A Rational Expectations Approach," *American Political Science Review*, 77(2): 347–358.

(1981a); *The War Trap*. New Haven: Yale University Press.

(1981b); "Risk, Power Distribution, and the Likelihood of War," *International Studies Quarterly*, 25(4): 541–567.

(1978); "Systemic Polarization and the Occurrence and Duration of War," *Journal of Conflict Resolution*, 22(2): 241–268.

(1975); "Measuring Systemic Polarity," *Journal of Conflict Resolution*, 19(2): 178–216.

Bueno de Mesquita, B. and Singer, J.D. (1973); "Alliances, Capabilities, and War: A Review and Synthesis," *Political Science Annual*, 4: 237–280.

Bull, H. (1977); *The Anarchical Society*. New York: Columbia University Press.

Bullock, A. (1952); *Hitler: A Study of Tyranny*. New York: Harper and Row.

Burnstein, E. and Berbaum, M.L. (1983); "Stages in Group Decision Making: The Decomposition of Historical Narratives," *Political Psychology*, 4(3): 531–561.

Burnstein, E. *et al.* (1971); "Risky Shift is Eminently Rational," *Journal of Personality and Social Psychology*, 20(3): 462–471.

Caldwell, D. (1977); "Bureaucratic Foreign Policy Making," *American Behavioral Scientist*, 21(1): 87–110.

Carrol, J.W. (1985); "Infinite Terminating Points and the Iterated Prisoner's Dilemma," unpublished paper. Tucson, Ariz.: University of Arizona.

Cartwright, D. (1971); "Risk Taking by Individuals and Groups: An Assessment of Research Employing Choice Dilemmas," *Journal of Personality and Social Psychology*, 20(3): 361–378.

Cartwright, D. and Zander, A. (eds.) (1968); *Group Dynamics: Research and Theory*. New York: Harper and Row.

Choucri, N. and North, R.C. (1975); *Nations in Conflict*. San Francisco: Freeman.

Churchill, W. (1948); *The Gathering Storm*. Cambridge, Mass.: Houghton Mifflin.

Cohen, J. (1972); *Psychological Probability, or the Art of Doubt*. London: George Allen and Unwin.

Cohen, R. (1983); *The Rules of the Game in International Relations*. Madison: University of Wisconsin Press.

(1979); *Threat Perception in International Crises*. Madison: University of Wisconsin Press.

Collins, B.E. and H. Guetzkow (1964); *A Social Psychology of Group Processes for Decision Making*. New York: Wiley.

Condorcet, Marquis de (1785); *Essai sur l'application de l'analyse a la probabilité des decisions rendues a la pluralité des voix*. Paris: L'Imprimerie Royale.

Converse, P.E. (1964); "The Nature of Belief Systems in Mass Publics," pp. 206–261 in: *Ideology and Discontent*. Apter, D.E. (ed.). London: The Free Press of Glencoe.

Coombs, C.H., Dawes, R.M. and Tversky, A. (1970); *Mathematical Psychology: An Elementary Introduction*. Englewood Cliffs, N.J.: Prentice Hall.

Crecine, J.P. (1967); "A Computer Simulation of Municipal Budgeting," *Management Science*, 13(3): 786–815.

Cross, J. (1969); *The Economics of Bargaining*. New York: Basic Books.

Cyret, R.M. and March, J.G. (1963); *A Behavioral Theory of the Firm*. Englewood Cliffs, N.J.: Prentice Hall.

Dacey, R. and Pendegraft, N. (1987); "The Impact of Election Frequency and Crises Upon the Arms Race," Paper presented at the annual meeting of the International Studies Association, Washington, D.C., April 14–18.

(1986); "The Optimality of TIT-FOR-TAT," Paper presented at the annual meeting of the International Studies Association, Anaheim, Calif., March 25–29.

Davis, O., Dempster, M.A.H. and Wildavski, A. (1966); "A Theory of the Budgetary Process," *American Political Science Review*, 60(3): 529–547.

Davis, J.H. (1973); "Group Decision and Social Interaction: A Theory of Social Decision Schemes," *Psychological Review*, 80(1): 92–135.

Davis, M. (1983); *Game Theory: A Non Technical Introduction* (2nd edition). New York: Basic Books.

Dawes, R.M. (1979); "The Robust Beauty of Improper Linear Models," *American Psychologist*, 34(7): 571–582.

(1971); "A Case Study of Graduate Admissions: Application of Three Principles of Human Decision Making," *American Psychologist*, 26(2): 180–188.

Deegan, J. and E.W. Packel (1982); "To the (Minimally Winning) Victors Go the (Equally Divided) Spoils: A New Power Index for Simple N-Person Games," pp. 239–255 in *Modules in Applied Mathematics: Political and Related*

Models. Brams, S.J., Lucas, W.F., and Straffin, P.D. (eds.). New York: Springer Verlag.

De Rivera, J. (1968); *The Psychological Dimension of Foreign Policy*. Columbus, Ohio: Bobbs-Merrill.

Destler, I.M. (1972); *Presidents, Bureaucrats, and Foreign Policy*. Princeton: Princeton University Press.

Deutsch, K.W. and Singer, J.D. (1964); "Multipolar Systems and International Stability," *World Politics*, 16(3): 390–406.

Dougherty, J.E. and Pfaltzgraff, R.L. (1971); *Contending Theories of International Politics*. Philadelphia: J.B. Lippincott.

Dowty, A. (1984); *Middle East Crisis: U.S. Decision Making in 1958, 1970, and 1973*. Berkeley and Los Angeles: University of California Press.

Druckman, D. (1968); "Dogmatism, Pre-Negotiation Experience, and Simulated Group Representation as Determinants of Dyadic Behavior in a Bargaining Situation," *Journal of Personality and Social Psychology*. 6(2): 279–290.

Dummett, M. (1984); *Voting Procedures*. Oxford: Oxford University Press.

Dupuy, T.N. and Martell, P. (1986); *Flawed Victory: The Arab–Israeli Conflict and the 1982 War in Lebanon*. Fairfax, Va.: Hero Books.

Duval, S. and Duval, V.H. (1983); *Consistency and Cognition: A Theory of Causal Attribution*. Hillsdale, N.J.: Lawrence Erlbaum Associates.

East, M.H., Salmore, S.A. and Hermann, C.F. (eds.) (1978); *Why Nations Act*. Beverly Hills, Calif.: Sage.

Easton, D. (1965); *The Political System* (2nd edition). New York: A.A. Knopf.

Eban, A. (1983); *The New Diplomacy: International Politics in the Nuclear Age*. New York: Random House.

Ebert, R.J. and Kurse, T.E. (1978); "Bootstraping the Security Analyst," *Journal of Applied Psychology*, 63(1): 110–119.

Eddy, D.M. (1982); "Probabilistic Reasoning in Clinical Medicine: Problems and Opportunities," pp. 249–267 in: *Judgment Under Uncertainty: Heuristics and Biases*. Kahneman, D., Slovic, P., and Tversky, A. (eds.). Cambridge: Cambridge University Press.

Einhorn, Hillel J. and Hogarth, R.M. (1978); "Confidence in Judgment: Persistence of the Illusion of Validity," *Psychological Review*, 85: 395–416.

Eldrige, A.F. (1979); *Images of Conflict*. New York: St Martin's Press.

Elster, J. (1979); *Ulysses and the Sirens: Studies of Rationality and Irrationality*. Cambridge: Cambridge University Press.

Endler, N.S. and Edwards, J. (1982); "Stress and Personality," pp. 36–48 in: *Handbook of Stress: Theoretical and Clinical Aspects*. Golberger, L. and Breznitz, S. (eds.). New York: Free Press.

Ethredge, L.C. (1978); "Personality Effects on American Foreign Policy, 1898–1968: A Test of Interpersonal Generalization Theory," *American Political Science Review*, 72(2): 434–451.

(1977); *A World of Men: The Private Sources of American Foreign Policy*. Cambridge, Mass.: MIT Press.

Farquharson, R. (1969); *Theory of Voting*. New Haven: Yale University Press.

Felsenthal, D.S. and Maoz, Z. (1988); "A Comparative Analysis of Sincere and

Sophisticated Voting Under the Plurality and Approval Voting Procedures," *Behavioral Science*, 33(2): 116–130.

Felsenthal, D.S., Rapoport, A., and Maoz, Z. (1988); "Tacit Cooperation in Three-Alternative Non-Cooperative Games: A New Model of Sophisticated Behavior Under the Plurality Procedure," *Electoral Studies*, 7(2): 143–161.

Fischoff, B. (1982); "Debiasing," pp. 422–444 in: *Judgment Under Uncertainty: Heuristics and Biases*. Kahneman, D., Slovic, P., and Tversky, A. (eds.). Cambridge: Cambridge University Press.

Fischoff, B., Slovic, P., and Lichtenstein, S. (1977); "Knowing With Certainty: The Appropriateness of Extreme Confidence," *Journal of Experimental Psychology (Human Perception and Performance)*, 3: 552–564.

Fisher, B.A. (1974); *Small Groups Decision Making: Communication and the Group Process*. New York: McGraw-Hill.

Frankel, J. (1963); *The Making of Foreign Policy: An Analysis of Decision Making*. London: Oxford University Press.

Fraser, N.M. and Hipel, K.W. (1984); *Conflict Analysis: Models and Resolutions*. New York and Amsterdam: North-Holland.

Fraser, N.M. and Kilgour, D.M. (1986); *General Ordinal 2×2 Games*. Technical Report No. 172 (April). Waterloo, Ont.: Department of Management Sciences, University of Waterloo.

Friedlander, S. and Cohen, R. (1975); "The Personality Correlates of Belligerence in International Conflict," *Comparative Politics*, 7(2): 156–186.

Gaenseln, F. (1980); "Democracy vs. Efficiency: Some Arguments from the Small Group," *Political Psychology*, 2(1): 15–29.

Gallhofer, I.N., Saris, W.E., and Melman, M. (1986); "The Empirical Decision Analysis Procedure," pp. 53–68 in: *Different Text Analysis Procedures for Political Decision Making*. Gallhofer, I.N., Saris, W.E., and Melman, M. (eds.). Amsterdam: Sociometric Research Foundation.

(1979); "Strategy Choices and Foreign Policy Decision Makers: The Netherlands,1914," *Journal of Conflict Resolution*, 23(3): 425–445.

George, A.L. (1980); *Presidential Decisionmaking in Foreign Policy: The Effective Use of Information and Advice*. Boulder, Colo.: Westview Press.

(1979); "The Causal Nexus Between Cognitive Beliefs and Decision Making," pp. 95–124 in: *Psychological Models of International Relations*. Falkowski, L. (ed.). Boulder, Colo.: Westview Press.

(1972); "The Case for Multiple Advocacy in Making Foreign Policy," *American Political Science Review*, 66(3): 751–794.

(1969); "The 'Operational Code': A Neglected Approach to the Study of Political Leaders and Decision Making," *International Studies Quarterly*, 8(2): 190–222.

(1968); "Comments on Allison's Thesis," unpublished paper. Stanford, Calif.: Stanford University.

(1955); "American Policy Making and the North Korean Aggression," *World Politics*, 7(2): 209–232.

George, A.L. and George, G.L. (1956); *Woodrow Wilson and Colonel House: A Personality Study*. New York: John Day.

George, A.L. and Smoke, R. (1974); *Deterrence in American Foreign Policy: Theory and Practice*. New York: Columbia University Press.

George, A.L. *et al.* (1975); *Towards a More Soundly Based Foreign Policy: Making Better Use of Information*. Commission on the Organization of the Government for the Conduct of Foreign Policy. Washington, D.C.: U.S. Government Printing Office.

Gibbard, A. (1973); "Manipulation of Voting Schemes: A General Result," *Econometrica*, 41(4): 587–601.

Gilpin, R. (1984); "The Richness of the Tradition of Political Realism," *International Organization*. 38(2): 287–304.

(1981); *War and Change in World Politics*. Cambridge: Cambridge University Press.

Golan, M. (1976); *The Secret Conversations of Henry Kissinger*. Tel Aviv: Shoken. (Hebrew)

Goldberg, L.R. (1970); "Man Versus Model of Man: A Rationale, Plus Some Evidence on a Method for Improving on Clinical Inferences," *Psychological Review*, 73(6): 422–432.

Greenstein, F.I. (1969); *Personality and Politics: Problems of Inference, Evidence, and Conceptualization*. Chicago: Markham.

Guetzkow, H. (1968); "Differentiation of Roles in Task-Oriented Groups," pp. 512–526 in: *Group Dynamics: Research and Theory*. Cartwright, D. and Zander, A. (eds.). New York: Harper and Row.

Haan, N. (1982); "The Assessment of Coping, Defense, and Stress," pp. 254–269 in: *Handbook of Stress: Theoretical and Clinical Aspects*. Golberger, L. and Breznitz, S. (eds.). New York: Free Press.

Halberstam, D. (1972); *The Best and The Brightest*. New York: Random House.

Halperin, M.A. (1974); *Bureaucratic Politics and Foreign Policy*. Washington, D.C.: Brookings.

(1972); "The Decision to Deploy the ABM," *World Politics*, 25(1): 62–95.

Halperin, M.A. and Kanter, A. (eds.) (1973); *Readings in American Foreign Policy: A Bureaucratic Perspective*. Boston: Little Brown.

Handel, M. (1981); *The Diplomacy of Surprise*. Cambridge, Mass.: Harvard University Press.

(1976); *Perception, Deception, and Surprise: The Case of the Yom Kippur War*. Jerusalem: Leonard Davis Institute of International Relations.

Hart, J. (1977); "Cognitive Maps of Three Latin American Policy Makers," *World Politics*, 30(1): 115–140.

(1976a); "Comparative Cognition: Politics of International Control of the Oceans," pp. 180–217 in: *Structure of Decision*. Axelrod, R. (ed.). Princeton: Princeton University Press.

(1976b); "Three Approaches to the Measurement of Power in International Relations," *International Organization*, 30(2): 299–305.

Heikal, H. (1975); *The Road to Ramadan*. New York: Penguin.

Hempel, C. (1965); *Aspects of Scientific Explanation*. New York: Free Press.

Heradsveit, D. and Bonham, G.M. (1986); "Decision Making in the Face of Uncertainty: Attribution of Norwegian and American Officials," *Journal of Peace Research*, 23(4): 339–356.

Herbig, D. and Herbig, C. (1982); "On Military Deception," pp. 3–30 in:

Strategic Military Deception. Herbig, D. and C. (eds.). New York: Pergamon.

Herek, G.M., Janis, I.L., and Huth, P. (1987); "Decision Making During International Crises: Is Quality of Process Related to Outcome?" *Journal of Conflict Resolution*, 31(2): 203–226.

Hermann, C.F. (1972); "Threat, Time, and Surprise: A Simulation of International Crises," pp. 187–211 in: *International Crises: Insights from Behavioral Research*. Hermann, C.F. (ed.). New York: Free Press.

(1969a); *Crises in Foreign Policy: A Simulation Analysis*. New York: Bobbs-Merrill.

(1969b); "International Crisis as a Situational Variable," pp. 409–421 in: *International Politics and Foreign Policy* (2nd edition). Rosenau, J.N. (ed.). New York: Free Press.

Hermann, M.G. (1980); "Explaining Foreign Policy Behavior Using the Personal Characteristics of Political Leaders," *International Studies Quarterly*, 24(1): 7–46.

(1979); "Who Becomes A Political Leader? Some Societal and Regime Influences on the Selection of a Head of State," pp. 15–48 in: *Psychological Models in International Relations*. Falkowski, L. (ed.). Boulder, Colo.: Westview.

(1978); "Effects of Personal Characteristics of Political Leaders on Foreign Policy," pp. 140–172 in: *Why Nations Act*. East, M.A., Salmore, S.A., and Hermann, C.F. (eds.). Beverly Hills, Calif.: Sage.

(1976); "Some Personal Characteristics Related to Foreign-Aid Voting of Congressmen," pp. 313–334 in: *A Psychological Examination of Political Leaders*. Hermann, M.G. (ed.). New York: Free Press.

(1974); "Leader Personality and Foreign Policy Behavior," pp. 201–234 in: *Comparing Foreign Policies: Theories, Findings, and Methods*. J.N. Rosenau (ed.). New York: Sage-Halsted.

Hermann, M.G. and Kogan, N. (1977); "Effects of Negotiators' Personalities on Negotiation Behavior," in: *Negotiations: Social Psychological Perspectives*. Druckman, D. (ed.). Beverly Hills, Calif.: Sage.

Heuer, R.J. (ed.) (1978); *Quantitative Approaches to Political Intelligence*. Boulder, Colo.: Westview Press.

Hildebrand, D., Liang, J., and Rosenthal, H. (1977); *The Analysis of Ordinal Data*. New York: Wiley.

Hilsman, R. (1964); *To Move A Nation: The Politics of Foreign Policy in the Administration of John F. Kennedy*. New York: Delta.

Hirshleifer, J. and Martinez-Coll, J.C. (1988); "What Strategies Support the Evolutionary Emergence of Cooperation?" *Journal of Conflict Resolution*, 32(2): 367–398.

Hoffmann, S. (1978); *Primacy or World Order*. New York: McGraw-Hill.

Holroyd, K.A. and Lazarus, R.S. (1982); "Stress, Coping, and Somatic Adaptation," pp. 21–35 in: *Handbook of Stress: Theoretical and Clinical Aspects*. Goldberger, L. and Breznitz, S. (eds.). New York: Free Press.

Holsti, K.J. (1988); *International Politics: A Framework for Analysis* (5th edition). Englewood Cliffs, N.J.: Prentice Hall.

(1970); "National Role Conceptions in the Study of Foreign Policy," *International Studies Quarterly*, 14(2): 233–309.

Holsti, O.R. (1979); "Theories of Crisis Decision Making," pp. 99–136 in: *Diplomacy: New Approaches in History, Theory and Policy*. Lauren, P.G. (ed.). New York: Free Press.

(1977); "The 'Operational Code' as an Approach to the Analysis of Belief Systems," Final NSF Report, Grant No. SOC 75–15–368. Durham, N.C.: Duke University.

(1976); "Foreign Policy Making Viewed Cognitively," pp. 18–54 in: *Structure of Decision*. Axelrod, R. (ed.). Princeton: Princeton University Press.

(1972a); *Crisis, Escalation, War*. Montreal: McGill University Press.

(1972b); "Time, Alternatives, and Communications: The 1914 and Cuban Missile Crisis," pp. 58–80 in: *International Crises: Insights from Behavioral Research*. Hermann, C.F. (ed.). New York: Free Press.

(1967); "Cognitive Dynamics and Images of the Enemy," pp. 25–96 in: *Enemies in Politics*. Finlay, D. *et al.* (eds.). Chicago: Rand McNally.

(1962); "The Belief System and National Images: A Case Study," *Journal of Conflict Resolution*, 6(2): 244–252.

Holsti, O.R. and George, A.L. (1975); "The Effects of Stress on Foreign Policy Makers," pp. 255–319 in: *Political Science Annual*. C.P. Cotter (ed.). Indianapolis: Bobbs-Merrill.

Holsti, O.R., North, R.C., and Brody, R.A. (1969); "The Management of International Crisis: Affect and Action in American-Soviet Relations," in: *Theory and Research on the Causes of War*. Pruitt, D.G. and Snyder, R.G. (eds.). Englewood Cliffs: Prentice Hall.

(1968); "Perception and Action in the 1914 Crisis," pp. 123–158 in: *Quantitative International Politics*. Singer, J.D. (ed.). New York: Free Press.

Hopple, G.W. (1980); *Political Psychology and Biopolitics*. Boulder, Colo.: Westview Press.

Horelick, A.L., Johnson, A.R., and Steinbruner, J.D. (1975); *The Study of Soviet Foreign Policy: Decision-Theory Related Approaches*. Beverly Hills, Calif.: Sage.

Howard, N. (1971); *Paradoxes of Rationality: Theory of Metagames and Political Behavior*. Cambridge, Mass.: MIT Press.

Hsiung, J.C. (1985); "Sino–U.S.–Soviet Relations in a Triadic Game Perspective," pp. 107–131 in: *Beyond China's Independent Foreign Policy*. Hsiung, J.C. (ed.). New York: Praeger.

Huth, P. and Russett, B.M. (1984); "What Makes Deterrence Work: Cases from 1900 to 1960," *World Politics*, 36(4): 496–526.

Iklé, C.F. (1964); *How Nations Negotiate*. New York: Harper.

Janis, I.L. (1982); *Groupthink* (2nd edition). Boston: Houghton and Mifflin.

Janis, I.L. and L. Mann (1977); *Decision Making: A Psychological Analysis of Conflict, Choice, and Commitment*. New York: Free Press.

Jervis, R. (1986); "Representativeness in Foreign Policy Decisions," *Political Psychology* 7(3): 278–301.

(1980); "Political Decision Making: Recent Contributions," *Political Psychology*, 2(2): 86–101.

(1978); "Cooperation Under the Security Dilemma," *World Politics*, 30(2): 167–214.

(1976); *Perception and Misperception in International Politics*. Princeton: Princeton University Press.

(1970); *The Logic of Images in International Relations*. Princeton: Princeton University Press.

(1969); "The Costs of the Quantitative Study of International Relations," pp. 177–217 in: *Contending Approaches to International Relations*. Knorr, K. and Rosenau, J.N. (eds.). Princeton: Princeton University Press.

Jervis, R., Lebow, R.N. and Stein, J.G. (1985); *Psychology and Deterrence*. Baltimore: John Hopkins University Press.

Jewell, L.N. and Reitz, H.J. (1981); *Group Effectiveness in Organizations*. Glenview, Ill.: Scott, Foresman, and Co.

Kahneman, D., Slovic, P., and Tversky, A. (eds.) (1982); *Judgment Under Uncertainty: Heuristics and Biases*. Cambridge: Cambridge University Press.

Kahneman, D. and Tversky, A. (1982); "Intuitive Prediction: Biases and Corrective Procedures," pp. 414–421 in: *Judgment Under Uncertainty: Heuristics and Biases*. Kahneman, D., Slovic, P., and Tversky, A. (eds.). Cambridge: Cambridge University Press.

(1979); "Prospect Theory: An Analysis of Decision Under Risk," *Econometrica*, 47(2): 263–291.

(1973); "On the Psychology of Prediction," *Psychological Review*, 80(4): 237–251.

Kalb, M. and Kalb, B. (1974); *Kissinger*. Boston: Little Brown.

Kaplan, A. (1964); *The Conduct of Inquiry*. San Francisco: Chandler.

Kaplan, M.A. (1957); *System and Process in International Relations*. New York: Wiley.

Kaplan, M.F. (1977); "Discussion Polarization Effects on Modified Jury Decision Paradigm: Informational Influences," *Sociometry*, 40(3): 262–271.

Kaplan, M.F. and Miller, C.E. (1977); "Judgment and Group Discussion: Effects of Presentation and Memory Factors on Polarization," *Sociometry*, 40(4): 337–342.

Kaplan, S.S. (1981); *Diplomacy of Power: Soviet Armed Forces as a Political Instrument*. Washington, D.C.: Brookings.

Kelley, H.H. (1973); "The Processes of Causal Attribution," *American Psychologist*, 28: 107–128.

Kelley, H.H. and Michela, J.L. (1980); "Attribution Theory and Research," *Annual Review of Psychology*, 31: 457–501.

Kennan, G.F. (1947); "The Sources of Soviet Conduct," *Foreign Affairs*, 25(2): 566–582.

Keohane, R.O. (1986); "Realism, Neorealism, and the Study of World Politics," pp. 1–26 in: *Neorealism and Its Critics*. Keohane, R.O. [ed.]. New York: Columbia University Press.

(1984); *After Hegemony: Cooperation and Discord in the World Political Economy*. Princeton: Princeton University Press.

(1983); "Theory of World Politics: Structural Realism and Beyond," pp. 503–540 in: *Political Science: The State of the Discipline*. Finifter, A. (ed.). Washington, D.C.: American Political Science Association.

Keohane, R.O. and Nye, J. (1977); *Power and Interdependence: World Politics in Transition*. Boston: Little Brown.

Kickert, W.J. (1978); *Fuzzy Theories of Decision Making*. Leiden: Martinus Nijhoff.

Kilgour, D.M. (1985); "Anticipation and Stability in Two-Person Non-Cooperative Games," pp. 26–51 in: *Dynamic Models of International Conflict*. Luterbacher, U. and Ward, M. (eds.). Boulder, Colo.: Lynne Reiner Publishers.

(1974); "A Shapley Value for Cooperative Games With Quarreling," pp. 193–206 in: *Game Theory as a Theory of Conflict Resoluton*. Rapoport, A. (ed.). Boston: D. Riedel.

Kissinger, H.A. (1979); *White House Years*. Boston: Little Brown.

(1974); "Detente with the Soviet Union: The Reality of Competition and the Imperative of Cooperation," *U.S. Department of State Bulletin*, 62 (1842): 505–519.

(1966); "Domestic Structure and Foreign Policy," *Daedalus*, 95(2): 503–529.

Krasner, S. (1972); "Are Bureaucrats Important? Or, Allison's Wonderland," *Foreign Policy*, 7(2): 159–179.

Kuhn, T. (1970); *The Logic of Scientific Revolutions* (2nd edition). Chicago: University of Chicago Press.

Lakatos, I. (1970); "Falsification and the Methodology of Scientific Research Programmes," pp. 154–177 in: *Criticism and the Growth of Knowledge*. Lakatos, I. and Mursgrave, A. (eds.). Cambridge: Cambridge University Press.

Langer, W.C. (1972); *The Mind of Adolf Hitler*. New York: Signet Books.

Lanir, Z. (1983); *Strategic Surprise in the Yom Kippur War*. Tel Aviv: Am Oved. (Hebrew)

Lanzetta, G.T. (1965); "Group Behavior Under Stress," pp. 212–219 in: *Human Behavior and International Politics*. Singer, J.D. (ed.). Chicago: Markham.

Larson, D. (1986); "Game Theory and the Psychology of Reciprocity," unpublished paper. New York: Columbia University.

Lave, C.A. and March, J.G. (1975); *Introduction to Models in the Social Sciences* New York: Harper and Row.

Lazarus, R.S. (1968); *Psychological Stress and the Coping Process*. New York: McGraw-Hill.

Lebow, R.N. (1981); *Between Peace and War: The Nature of International Crisis*. Baltimore: Johns Hopkins University Press.

Leites, N. (1951); *The Operational Code of the Soviet Politburo*. New York: McGraw-Hill.

Leng, R.J. (1988); "Crisis Learning Games," *American Political Science Review*, 82(1): 179–194.

(1983); "When Will They Ever Learn? Coercive Bargaining in Recurrent Crises," *Journal of Conflict Resolution*, 27(3): 379–419.

(1980); "Influence Strategies and Interstate Conflict," pp. 124–160 in: *The Correlates of War, II*. Singer, J.D. (ed.). New York: Free Press.

Levi, A. and Tetlock, P.E. (1980); "A Cognitive Analysis of Japan's 1940 Decision for War," *Journal of Conflict Resolution*, 24(2): 195–211.

Levy, J. (1986); "Organizational Routines and the Causes of War," *International Studies Quarterly*, 30(2): 193–222.

(1985); "Theories of General War," *World Politics*, 37(3): 344–374.

(1983); *War in the Great Power System*. Lexington, Ky.: University Press of Kentucky.

Lewin, K. (1948); *Resolving Social Conflicts: Selected Papers on Group Dynamics*. New York: Harper.

Li, Y. and Thompson, W. (1977); "The Stochastic Process of Alliance Formation Behavior," *American Political Science Review*, 72(4): 1,288–1,303.

Lichtenstein, S., Fischoff, B., and Phillips, C.D. (1982); "Calibration of Probabilities: The State of the Art to 1980," pp. 312–340 in: *Judgment Under Uncertainty: Heuristics and Biases*. Kahneman, D., Slovic, P., and Tversky, A. (eds.). Cambridge: Cambridge University Press.

Lipson, C. (1986); "Banker's Dilemma," pp. 200–225 in: *Cooperation Under Anarchy*. Oye, K. (ed.). Princeton: Princeton University Press.

Lockhart, C. (1979); *Bargaining in International Crises*. New York: Columbia University Press.

Lowi, T.J. (1964); "American Business, Public Policy, Case Studies, and Public Policy," *World Politics*, 16(4): 677–715.

Luce, R. and Raiffa, H. (1957); *Games and Decisions*. New York: Wiley.

Maersheimer, J. (1983); *Conventional Deterrence*. Ithaca: Cornell University Press.

Majeski, S.J. (1984); "Arms Races as Iterated Prisoners' Dilemmas," *Mathematical Social Science*, 7(3): 253–266.

Mandel, R. (1987); *Irrationality in International Confrontation*. New York: Greenwood Press.

Mandler, G. (1982); "Stress and Thought Processes," pp. 88–104 in: *Handbook of Stress: Theoretical and Clinical Aspects*. Golberger, L. and Breznitz, S. (eds.). New York: Free Press.

Mangusson, D. (1982); "Situational Determinants of Stress: An Interactional Perspective," pp. 231–253 in: *Handbook of Stress: Theoretical and Clinical Aspects*. Golberger, L. and Breznitz, S. (eds.). New York: Free Press.

Mansbach, R.W. and Vasquez, J. (1981); *In Search of Theory: A New Paradigm for Global Politics*. New York: Columbia University Press.

Maoz, Z. (1989); *Paradoxes of War: On the Art of National Self-Entrapment*. Boston: Unwin Hyman.

(1986); "Multiple Paths to Choice: An Approach for the Analysis of Foreign Policy Decisions," pp. 69–96 in: *Different Text Analysis Procedures for the Study of Decision Making*. Gallhofer, I.N., Saris, W.E., and Melman, M. (eds.). Amsterdam: Sociometric Research Foundation.

(1984a); "Scientific Logic and Intuition in Intelligence Forecasts," pp. 77–123 in: *Quantitative Indicators in World Politics*. Singer, J.D. and Stoll, R.J. (eds.). New York: Praeger.

(1984b); "The Expected Utility of International Conflict: Some Logical Traps and Empirical Surprises in 'The War Trap'," unpublished paper. Haifa: University of Haifa.

(1983); "Resolve, Capabilities, and the Outcomes of Interstate Disputes, 1816–1976," *Journal of Conflict Resolution*, 27(2): 195–229.

(1982a); *Paths to Conflict: International Dispute Initiation, 1816–1976*. Boulder, Colo.: Westview Press.

(1982b); "Crisis Initiation: A Theoretical Exploration of a Neglected Topic in International Crisis Theory," *Review of International Studies*, 8(4): 215–232.

——— (1981); "The Decision to Raid Entebbe: Decision Analysis Applied to Crisis Behavior," *Journal of Conflict Resolution*, 23(4): 677–707.

Maoz, Z. and Abdolali, N. (1989); "Regime Types and International Conflict," *Journal of Conflict Resolution*, 34(1): 3–35.

Maoz, Z. and Felsenthal, D.S. (1987); "Self-Binding Commitments, The Inducement of Trust, Social Choice, and the Theory of International Cooperation," *International Studies Quarterly*, 31(2): 177–200.

Maoz, Z. and Shayer, A. (1987); "The Cognitive Structure of Peace and War Argumentation: Israeli Prime Ministers Versus the Knesset," *Political Psychology*, 8(4): 575–604.

Maoz, Z. and Yaniv, A. (1989); "Game, Supergame and Compound Escalation: Israel–Syrian Confrontations, 1948–1984," unpublished paper. Haifa: University of Haifa.

Martel, R. (ed.) (1986); *The Origins of the Second World War Reconsidered*. Boston: Allen and Unwin.

May, E.R. (1973); *"Lessons" of the Past: The Uses and Misuses of History in American Foreign Policy*. New York: Oxford University Press.

McClelland, C.A. (1968); "Access to Berlin: The Quantity and Variety of Events," pp. 159–186 in: *Quantitative International Politics: Insights and Evidence*. Singer, J.D. (ed.). New York: Free Press.

McClosky, H. (1967); "Personality and Attitude Correlates of Foreign Policy Orientation," pp. 51–110 in: *Domestic Sources of Foreign Policy*. Rosenau, J.N. (ed.). New York: Free Press.

——— (1962); "Concerning Strategies for a Science of International Politics," pp. 186–205 in: *Foreign Policy Decision Making*. Snyder, R.C., Bruck, H.W., and Sapin, B. (eds.). New York: Free Press.

McGowan, P.J. and H.B. Shapiro (1973); *The Comparative Study of Foreign Policy: A Survey of Scientific Findings*. Beverly Hills, Calif.: Sage.

McGuire, W.J. (1966); "The Current Status of Consistency Theory," pp. 1–46 in: *Cognitive Consistency: Motivational Antecedents and Behavioral Consequences*. Feldman, S. (ed.). New York: Academic Press.

McLean, A.A. (1979); *Work Stress*. Reading, Mass.: Addison Wesley.

Michles, R. (1962); *Political Parties*. New York: Free Press.

Miller, G.A. (1956); "The Magical Number Seven Plus or Minus Two: Some Limits on Our Capacity for Processing Information," *Psychological Review*, 63(1): 81–97.

Mintzberg, H., Raisinghani, D., and Theoret, A. (1976); "The Structure of 'Unstructured' Decision Processes," *Administrative Studies Quarterly*, 21(2): 246–275.

Mongar, T. (1969); "Personality and Decision Making: John F. Kennedy in Four Crisis Decisions," *Canadian Journal of Political Science*, 2(2): 200–225.

Moon, D.J. (1975); "The Logic of Political Inquiry," pp. 131–228 in: *Handbook of Political Science* (vol. 1). Greenstein, F.I. and Polsby, N.W. (eds.). Menlo Park, Calif.: Addison Wesley.

Morgan, P. (1977); *Deterrence*. Beverly Hills: Sage.

Morgenthau, H.J. (1973); *Politics Among Nations*. (Fifth edition.) New York: Knopf.

Morrow, J.D. (1988); "Social Choice and System Structure in International Politics," *World Politics*, 41(1): 75–97.

Nagel, J. (1975); *The Descriptive Analysis of Power*. New Haven: Yale University Press.

Nash, J. (1951); "Non-Cooperative Games," *Annals of Mathematics*, 54: 286–295. (1950); "The Bargaining Problem," *Econometrica*, 18(2): 155–162.

Neudstadt, R.E.(1970); *Alliance Politics*. New York: Columbia University Press. (1964); *Presidential Power: The Politics of Leadership*. New York: Wiley.

Niou, E.M.S. and Ordeshook, P.C. (1987); "Preventive War and the Balance of Power," *Journal of Conflict Resolution*, 31(3): 387–419.

(1986); "Balance of Power in International Systems," *Journal of Conflict Resolution*, 30(4): 685–715.

Nisbett, R.E. and Ross, L. (1980); *Human Inference: Strategies and Shortcomings of Social Judgment*. Englewood Cliffs, N.J.: Prentice Hall.

North, R.C. (1969); "Research Pluralism and the International Elephant," pp. 218–242 in: *Contending Approaches to International Politics*. Knorr, K. and Rosenau, J. (eds.). Princeton: Princeton University Press.

Nurmi, H. (1983); "Voting Procedures: A Summary Analysis," *British Journal of Political Science*, 13(2): 181–208.

O'Donnell, T. (1979); "Organizational Influences on Cognitive Structures: Foreign Service Officers and the Arab–Israeli Dispute," paper delivered at the annual meeting of the American Political Science Association, Washington, D.C. August 30 – September 3.

Ordeshook, P.C. (1986); *Game Theory and Political Theory*. Cambridge: Cambridge University Press.

Organski, A.F.K. and Kugler, J. (1980); *The War Ledger*. Chicago: University of Chicago Press.

Paige, G.D. (1977); "On Values and Science: The Korean Decision Reconsidered," *American Political Science Review*, 71(4): 1063–1069.

(1968); *The Korean Decision*. New York: Free Press.

Phillips, L.D. and Edwards, W. (1966); "Conservatism in a Simple Probability Inference Task," *Journal of Experimental Psychology*, 72(2): 346–354.

Pillar, P. (1983); *Negotiating Peace: War Termination as a Bargaining Process*. Princeton: Princeton University Press.

Popper, K.W. (1968); *Conjectures and Refutations: On the Growth of Scientific Knowledge*. (Second edition.) New York: Basic Books.

(1957); *The Logic of Scientific Discovery*. London: Routledge and Kegan Paul.

Pruitt, D.G. (1981); *Negotiation Behavior*. New York: Academic Press.

(1971a); "Choice Shifts in Group Discussion: An Introductory Review," *Journal of Personality and Social Psychology*, 20(3): 339–360.

(1971b); "Conclusions: Toward an Understanding of Choice Shifts in Group Discussion," *Journal of Personality and Social Psychology*, 20(3): 495–510.

(1965); "Definition of the Situation as a Determinant of International Action," pp. 391–432 in: *International Behavior: A Social-Psychological Analysis*. Kelman, H.C. (ed.). New York: Holt, Reinhart and Winston.

Raiffa, H. (1982); *The Art and Science of Negotiation*. Cambridge: Harvard University Press.

580

(1968); *Decision Analysis: Introductory Lectures on Choices Under Uncertainty*. Menlo Park: Addison Wesley.

Rapoport, Am., Felsenthal, D.S., and Maoz, Z. (1988a); "Microscosms and Macrocosms: Seat Allocation in Proportional Representation Systems," *Theory and Decision*, 28(1): 11–33.

(1988b); "Proportional Representation in Israel's General Federation of Labor: An Empirical Evaluation of a New Scheme," *Public Choice*, 59(3): 151–165.

Rapoport, Am. and Golan, E. (1985); "An Assessment of Political Power in the Israeli Knesset," *American Political Science Review*, 79(3): 673–692.

Rapoport, An. (1970); *N-Person Game Theory*. Ann Arbor: University of Michigan Press.

(1966); *Two-Person Game Theory: The Essential Ideas*. Ann Arbor: University of Michigan Press.

(1960); *Fights, Games, and Debates*. Ann Arbor: University of Michigan Press.

Rapoport, An. and Chammah, A. (1965); *The Prisoners' Dilemma: A Study in Conflict and Cooperation*. Ann Arbor: University of Michigan Press.

Rapoport, An., Guyer, M. and Gordon, D. (1976); *The 2×2 Game*. Ann Arbor: University of Michigan Press.

Rasler, K.A., Thompson, W.R. and Chester, K.M. (1980); "Foreign Policy Decision Makers, Personality Attributes, and Interviews: A Note on Reliability Problems," *International Studies Quartery*, 24(1): 47–66.

Ray, J.L. and Singer, J.D. (1973); "Measuring the Concentrating of Power in the International System," *Sociological Methods and Research*, 1(4): 403–437.

Richardson, L.F. (1960); *Arms and Insecurity*. Chicago: Quadrangle.

Riker, W. (1986); *The Art of Political Manipulation*. New Haven: Yale University Press.

(1962); *The Theory of Political Coalitions*. New Haven: Yale University Press.

Riker, W. and Ordeshook, P. (1973); *An Introduction to Positive Political Theory*. Englewood Cliffs, N.J.: Prentice Hall.

Roberts, F.S. (1976); "Strategy for the Energy Crisis: The Case of Commuter Policy," pp. 142–179 in: *Structure of Decision*. Axelrod, R. (ed.). Princeton: Princeton University Press.

Robinson, J.A. and Snyder, R.C. (1965); "Decision Making in International Politics," pp. 433–463 in: *International Behavior: A Social-Psychological Analysis*. Kelman, H.C. (ed.). New York: Holt, Rinehart and Winston.

Rogow, A. (1963); *James Forrestal: A Study of Personality, Politics, and Policy*. New York: Macmillan.

Rokeach, M. (1960); *The Open and Closed Mind: Investigations into the Nature of Belief Systems and Personality Systems*. New York: Basic Books.

Rosati, J.A. (1980); "Developing a Systematic Decision Making Framework: Bureaucratic Politics in Perspective," *World Politics*, 33(2): 234–252.

Rosecrance, R.N. (1966); "Bipolarity, Multipolarity, and the Future," *Journal of Conflict Resolution*, 10(3): 314–327.

(1963); *Action and Reaction in World Politics*. Boston: Little, Brown.

Rosenau, J.N. (1968); "Private Preference and Political Responsibilities: The Relative Potency of Individual and Role Variables in the Behavior of United States Senators," pp. 17–50 in: *Quantitative International Politics*. Singer, J.D. (ed.). New York: Free Press.

(1967a); "The Premises and Promises of Decision Making Analysis," pp. 189–211 in: *Contemporary Political Analysis*. Charlesworth, J.C. (ed.). New York: Free Press.

(1967b); "Foreign Policy as an Issue-Area," pp. 11–50 in: *Domestic Sources of Foreign Policy*. Rosenau, J.N. (ed.). New York: Free Press.

(1966); "Pre-Theories and Theories of Foreign Policy," pp. 27–92 in: *Approaches to Comparative and International Politics*. Farrel, R.B. *et al.* (eds.). Evanston, Ill.: Northwestern University Press.

Rosenau, J.N. and Hoggard, G. (1974); "Foreign Policy Behavior in Dyadic Relationships: Testing a Pre-Theoretical Extension," in: *Comparing Foreign Policies: Theories, Findings, and Methods*. Rosenau, J.N. (ed.). Beverly Hills, Calif.: Sage.

Rosenau, J.N. and Ramesy, G.H. (1975); "External and Internal Typologies of Foreign Policy Behavior," pp. 245–262 in: *Sage International Yearbook of Foreign Policy Studies*. McGowan, P.G. (ed.). Beverly Hills, Calif.: Sage.

Ross, S. (1976); "Complexity and the Presidency: Gouverneur Morris in the Constitutional Convention," pp. 96–112 in: *Structure of Decision*. Axelrod, R. (ed.). Princeton: Princeton University Press.

Rubin, J.Z. (ed.) (1981); *The Dynamics of Third Party Intervention* New York: Praeger.

Rubin, J.Z. and Brown, B.R. (1975); *The Social Psychology of Bargaining and Negotiation*. New York: Academic Press.

Rummel, R.J. (1963); "Dimensions of Conflict Behavior Within and Between Nations," *General Systems*, 8(1): 1–50.

Russett, B.M. (1983); *The Prisoners of Insecurity*. San Francisco: Freeman.

Russett, B.M. and Starr, H. (1984); *World Politics: The Menu for Choice* (second edition). San Francisco: Freeman.

Saaty, T.L. (1980); *The Analytic Hierarchy Process*. New York: McGraw-HIill.

(1977); "A Scaling Method for Priorities in Hierarchical Structures," *Journal of Mathematical Psychology*, 15(2): 234–281.

Sadat, A. (1978); *In Search of Identity*. New York: Harper and Row.

Saris, W.E. and Gallhofer, I.N. (1984); "Formulations of Real-Life Decisions: A Study of Foreign Policy Decisions," *Acta Psychologica*, 56(2): 247–265.

Schelling, T.C. (1984); *Choice and Consequences*. Cambridge: Harvard University Press.

(1978); *Micromotives and Macrobehavior*. New York: Norton.

(1966); *Arms and Influence* New Haven: Yale University Press.

(1960); *The Strategy of Conflict*. Cambridge, Mass.: Harvard University Press.

Schelsinger, A. Jr.(1965); *A Thousand Days: John F. Kennedy in the White House*. Boston: Houghton Mifflin.

Schiff, Z. and Ya'ari, E. (1984); *Israel's Lebanon War*. New York: Simon and Schuster.

Semmel, A.K. and Minix, D.G. (1979); "Small Group Dynamics and Foreign Policy Decision Making," in *Psychological Models in International Politics*. Falkowski, L. (ed.). Boulder, Colo.: Westview.

Shapiro, M.J. and Bonham, G.M. (1973); "Cognitive Processes and Foreign Policy Decision Making," *International Studies Quarterly*, 17(1): 147–174.

Shapley, L.S. and Shubik, M. (1954); "A Method for Evaluating the Distribution of Power in a Committee System," *American Political Science Review*, 48(3): 787–792.

Shaw, M.E. (1976); *Group Dynamics: The Psychology of Small Group Behavior*. New York: McGraw-Hill.

(1964); "Communication Networks," in: *Advances in Experimental Social Psychology*. Berkowitz, L. (ed.). New York: Academic Press.

Shirer, W.L. (1960); *The Rise and Fall of the Third Reich*. New York: Simon and Schuster.

Shlaim, A. (1976); "Failures in National Intelligence Estimates: The Case of the Yom Kippur War," *World Politics*, 28(3): 348–380.

Shlaim, A. and R. Tanter (1978); "Decision Process, Choice, and Consequences: Israel's Deep Penetration Bombing in Egypt, 1970," *World Politics*, 30(4): 483–516.

Shubik, M. (1982); *Game Theory in the Social Sciences: Concepts and Solutions*. Cambridge, Mass.: MIT Press.

Siegman, A.W. (1982); "Nonverbal Correlates of Anxiety and Stress," pp. 306–319 in: *Handbook of Stress: Theoretical and Clinical Aspects*. Golberger, L. and Breznitz, S. (eds.). New York: Free Press.

Simon, H.A. (1976); *Administrative Behavior* (third edition). New York: Free Press. (1957); *Models of Man: Social and Rational*. New York: Wiley.

Simowitz, R. (1982); *The Logical Consistency and Soundness of the Balance of Power Theory*. Denver, Colo.: Monograph Series in World Affairs, University of Denver.

Singer, J.D. (1961); "The Level-of-Analysis Problem in International Relations," *World Politics*, 13(1): 77–92.

Singer, J.D., Bremer, S., and Stuckey, J. (1972); "Capability Distribution, Uncertainty, and Major Power War, 1820–1965," pp. 19–48 in: *Peace, War, and Numbers*. Russett, B.M. (ed.). Beverly Hills, Calif.: Sage.

Snidal, D. (1985); "Coordination Versus Prisoner's Dilemma: Implications for International Cooperation and Regimes," *American Political Science Review*, 79(4): 923–942.

Snyder, G. and P. Diesing (1977); *Conflict Among Nations*. Princeton: Princeton University Press.

Snyder, J.L. (1978); "Rationality at the Brink: The Role of Cognitive Processes in Failure of Deterrence," *World Politics*, 30(3): 345–365.

Snyder, R.C. (1955); "Toward Greater Order in the Study of International Politics," *World Politics*, 7(3): 461–478.

Snyder, R.C., Bruck, H.W., and Sapin, B. (1962); *Foreign Policy Decision Making: An Approach to the Study of International Politics*. New York: Free Press. (1954); *Decision Making as an Approach to the Study of International Politics*. Princeton, N.J.: Foreign Policy Analysis Project, Princeton University.

Snyder, R.C. and Paige, G.D. (1958); "The United States' Decision to Resist Aggression in Korea: The Application of an Analytic Scheme," *Administrative Science Quarterly*, 3(3): 341–378.

Sorensen, T. (1965); *Kennedy*. New York: Harper and Row.

Starr, H. (1984); *Henry Kissinger: Perceptions of International Politics*. Lexington, Ky.: University Press of Kentucky.

Staw, B.M. *et al.* (1981); "Threat-Rigidity Effects in Organizational Behavior: A Multilevel Analysis," *Administrative Science Quarterly*, 26(4): 501–524.

Steers, R.M. (1981); *Introduction to Organizational Behavior*. Santa Monica, Calif.: Goodyear.

Stein, A. (1982); "When Misperception Matters," *World Politics*, 34(4): 505–526.

Stein, A. and Russett, B. (1980); "The Consequences of International Conflict," pp. 399–422 in: *Handbook of International Conflict*. Gurr, T.R. (ed.). New York: Free Press.

Stein, J.G. (1985); "Calculation, Miscalculation, and Conventional Deterrence II: The View From Jerusalem," .pp. 60–88 in: *Psychology and Deterrence*, Jervis, R., Lebow, R.N., and Stein, J.G. (eds.). Baltimore: Johns Hopkins University Press.

(1978); "Can Decision Makers Be Rational and Should They Be? Evaluating the Quality of Decisions," *Jerusalem Journal of International Relations*, 3(2–3): 316–339.

Stein, J.G. and Tanter, R. (1980); *Rational Decision Making: Israel's Security Choices, 1967*. Columbus, Ohio: Ohio State University Press.

Steinbruner, J.D. (1974); *The Cybernetic Theory of Decision*. Princeton: Princeton University Press.

Stewart, R. (1972); *Contrasts in Management*. New York: McGraw-Hill.

Straffin, P.D. (1982); "Power Indices in Politics," pp. 256–321 in: *Modules in Applied Mathematics: Political and Related Models*. Brams, S.J., Lucas, W.F., and Straffin, P.D. (eds.). New York: Springer Verlag.

Strauss, A. (1978); *Negotiations: Varieties, Contexts, Processes, and Social Order*. San Francisco: Jossey-Bass.

Stuart, D. and Starr, H. (1981–82); "The 'Inherent Bad Faith' Model Reconsidered: Dulles, Kennedy, and Kissinger," *Political Psychology*, 3(1): 1–33.

Tanter, R. (1978); "International Crisis Behavior: An Appraisal of the Literature," *Jerusalem Journal of International Relations*, 3(2–3): 340–374.

(1974); *Modeling and Managing International Conflicts: The Berlin Crises*. Beverly Hills, Calif.: Sage.

(1966); "Dimensions of Conflict Behavior Within and Between Nations," *Journal of Conflict Resolution*, 10(1): 41–64.

Taylor, A.J.P. (1963); *The Origins of the Second World War*. New York: Penguin.

Taylor, M. (1976); *Anarchy and Cooperation*. London: Wiley.

Tetlock, P.E. (1985); "Integrative Complexity of American and Soviet Foreign Policy Rhetoric: A Time-Series Analysis," *Journal of Personality and Social Psychology*, 46(4): 1,565–1,585.

(1984); "Cognitive Style and Political Belief Systems in the British House of Commons," *Journal of Personality and Social Psychology*, 46(2): 365–375.

(1983a); "Accountability and the Complexity of Thought," *Journal of Personality and Social Psychology*, 45(1): 74–83.

(1983b); "Cognitive Style and Political Ideology," *Journal of Personality and Social Psychology*, 45(1): 118–126.

Tetlock, P.E. and Levi, A. (1982); "Attribution Bias: On the Inconclusiveness of the Cognition-Motivation Debate," *Journal of Experimental Social Psychology*, 18(1): 66–88.

Tetlock, P.E. and McGuire, C. Jr (1986); "Cognitive Perspectives on Foreign Policy," pp. 255–273 in: *Political Behavior Annual*, Long, S. (ed.). Boulder, Colo.: Westview Press.

Thakur, R.C. (1982); "Tacit Deception Re-Examined: The Geneva Conference of 1954," *International Studies Quarterly*, 26(1): 127–139.

Thompson, J.D. (1967); *Organizations in Action: Social Science Bases of Administrative Theory*. New York: McGraw-Hill.

Touval, S. (1982); *The Peace Brokers: Intermediaries in the Arab–Israeli Conflict*. Princeton: Princeton University Press.

Truman, H.S. (1964); *Memoirs: Years of Trial and Hope*. Garden City, N.Y.: Doubleday.

Tuchman, B.W. (1962); *The Guns of August*. New York: Macmillan.

Tversky, A. (1972); "Elimination by Aspects: A Theory of Choice," *Psychological Review*, 79(2): 207–232.

Tversky, A. and D. Kahneman (1986); "Rational Choice and the Framing of Decisions," *The Journal of Business*, 59(4–S): S225–S250.

(1981); "The Framing of Decisions and the Psychology of Choice," *Science*, 211: 453–458.

(1974); "Judgment Under Uncertainty: Heuristics and Biases," *Science*, 185: 1124–1130.

(1973); "Availability: A Heuristic for Judging Frequency and Probability," *Cognitive Psychology*, 5(2): 207–232.

Tversky, A. and Sattath, S. (1979); "Preference Trees," *Psychological Review*, 86(6): 542–573.

Vasquez, J.A. (1983); *The Power of Power Politics*. New Brunswick: Rutgers University Press.

Verba, S. (1961); "Assumptions of Rationality and Non-Rationality in Models of the International System," pp. 93–117 in: *The International System: Theoretical Essays*. Knorr, K. and Verba, S. (eds.). Princeton: Princeton University Press.

Vertzberger, Y. (1986); "Foreign Policy Decisionmakers as Practical-Intuitive Historians: Applied History and its Shortcomings," *International Studies Quarterly*, 30(2): 223–247.

(1978); "India's Border Crisis With China, 1962," *Jerusalem Journal of International Relations*, 3(2–3): 117–142.

Vinokur, A. and Burnstein, E. (1974); "Effects of Partially Shared Persuasive Arguments on Group Induced Shifts," *Journal of Personality and Social Psychology*, 29(3): 305–315.

von Neuman, J. and Morgenstern, O. (1944); *Theory of Games and Economic Behavior*. Princeton: Princeton University Press.

Wagner, A. (1974); *Crisis Decision Making: Israel's Experience in 1967 and 1973*. New York: Praeger.

Wagner, R.H. (1986); "The Theory of Games and Balance-of-Power," *World Politics*, 38(4): 546–576.

(1984); "War and Expected Utility Theory," *World Politics*, 36(3): 407–423.

(1983); "The Theory of Games and the Problem of International Cooperation," *American Political Science Review*, 77(2): 230–248.

Walker, S.G. (1987); "Role Theory and the Origins of Foreign Policy," pp. 269–284 in: *New Directions in the Study of Foreign Policy*. Hermann, C.F., Kegley, C.W. Jr., and Rosenau, J.N. (eds.). Boston: Allen and Unwin.

(1986); "Operational Codes and Content Analysis: The Case of Henry Kissinger," pp. 13–28 in: *Different Text Analysis Procedures for the Study of Decision Making*. Gallhofer, I.N., Saris, W.E. and Melman, M. (eds.), Amsterdam: Sociometric Research Foundation.

(1983); "The Motivational Foundation of Political Belief Systems," *International Studies Quarterly*, 27(2): 179–201.

(1977): "The Interface Between Beliefs and Behavior: Henry Kissinger's Operational Code and the Vietnam War," *Journal of Conflict Resolution*, 21(1): 129–168.

Wallace, M.D. (1973); "Alliance Polarization, Cross-Cutting, and International War, 1815–1964," *Journal of Conflict Resolution*, 17(4): 575–604.

Wallsten, Thomas, S. and David V. Budescu (1983); "Encoding Subjective Probabilities: A Psychological and Psychometric Review," *Management Science*, 29(1): 151–173.

Walton, R.E. and R. McKersie (1965); *A Behavioral Theory of Labor Negotiations*. New York: Wiley.

Waltz, K.E. (1986); "Reply to My Critics," pp. 322–346 in: *Neorealism and Its Critics*. Keohane, R.O. (ed.). New York: Columbia University Press.

(1979); *Theory of International Relations*. Menlo Park, Calif.: Addison Wesley.

(1964); "The Stability of a Bipolar World," *Daedalus*, 93: 892–927.

(1958); *Man, the State, and War*. New York: Columbia University Press.

Ward, M.D. (1984); "Differential Paths to Parity: A Study of the U.S.–Soviet Arms Race," *American Political Science Review*, 63(2): 297–317.

Weinberg, G.L. (1980); *The Foreign Policy of Hitler's Germany: Starting World War II, 1937–1939*. Chicago: University of Chicago Press.

(1970); *The Foreign Policy of Hitler's Germany: Diplomatic Revolution in Europe, 1933–1936*. Chicago: University of Chicago Press.

Weiner, B. (1986); *An Attributional Theory of Motivation and Emotion*. New York: Springer-Verlag.

(1972); *Theories of Motivation: From Mechanism to Cognition*. Chicago: Markham.

Whaley, B. (1973); *Codeword Barbarossa*. Cambridge, Mass.: MIT Press.

Wheeler, D.D. and Janis, I.L. (1980); *A Practical Guide for Making Decisions*. New York: Free Press.

Weiegele, T.C. (1979); "Signal Leakage and the Remote Psychological Assessment of Foreign Policy Elites," in: *Psychological Models in International Politics*. Falkowski, L. (ed.). Boulder, Colo.: Westview.

(1973); "Decision Making in International Crisis: Some Biological Factors," *International Studies Quarterly*, 17(3): 295–335.

Wilkenfeld, J. (1968); "Domestic and Foreign Policy Conflict Behavior of Nations," *Journal of Peace Research*, 3(1): pp. 56–69.

Wilkenfeld, J. et al. (1980); *Foreign Policy Behavior*. Beverly Hills, Calif.: Sage.

Williamson, S.R. (1969); *The Politics of Grand Strategy*. Cambridge, Mass.: Harvard University Press.

Withey, S.B. (1962); "Reaction to Uncertain Threat," in: *Man and Society in*

Disaster. Baker, G.W. and Chapman, D.W. (eds.). New York: Basic Books.

Wohlstetter, R. (1962); *Pearl Harbor: Warning and Decision*. Stanford: Stanford University Press.

Yaniv, A. (1987); *Dilemmas of Security: Politics, Strategy, and the Israeli Experience in Lebanon*. New York: Oxford University Press.

(1985); "Syria and Israel: The Politics of Escalation," pp. 157–179 in: *Syria Under Assad*. Maoz, M. and Yaniv, A. (eds.), London: Croom Helm.

Yaniv, A. and Katz, E. (1980); "MAD, Detente, and Peace: A Hypothesis on the Evolution of International Conflicts and Its Mathematico-Deductive Extension," *International Interactions*, 7(2): 223–239.

Yaranella, E.J. (1977); "Tensions and Ambiguities in the Decision Making Approach: From Snyder, Bruck, and Sapin to Allison," *International Interactions*, 2(2): 101–106.

Young, H.P. (1974); "An Axiomatization of Borda's Rule," *Journal of Economic Theory*, 9(1): 43–52.

Young, O. (1968); *The Politics of Force: Bargaining in International Crises*. Princeton: Princeton University Press.

(1967); *The Intermediaries*. Princeton: Princeton University Press.

Zagare, F.C. (1987); *The Dynamics of Deterrence*. Chicago: University of Chicago Press.

(1985); "Toward a Reformulation of the Theory of Mutual Deterrence," *International Studies Quarterly*, 29(2): 155–169.

(1984a); "Limited Move Equilibria in 2×2 Games," *Theory and Decision*, 16(1): 1–19.

(1984b); *Game Theory: Concepts and Applications*. Beverly Hills, Calif.: Sage.

(1983); "A Game-Theoretic Evaluation of the 1973 Cease-Fire Alert Decision," *Journal of Peace Research*, 20(1): 73–86.

(1982); "Competing Game-Theoretic Explanations: The Geneva Converence of 1954," *International Studies Quarterly*, 26(1): 141–147.

(1979); 'The Geneva Conference of 1954: A Case of Tacit Deception," *International Studies Quarterly*, 23(3): 390–411.

(1977); "A Game-Theoretic Analysis of the Vietnam Negotiations," *Journal of Conflict Resolution*, 21(4): 663–684.

Zartman, I.W. (1977); "Negotiations as a Joint Decision Making Process," *Journal of Conflict Resolution*, 21(4): 619–638.

Zartman, I.W. and Berman, M. (1982); *The Practical Negotiator*. New Haven: Yale University Press.

Zehuten, F. (1932). *Problems of Monopoly and Economic Warfare*. London: Routledge and Kegan Paul.

Zimmer, A.C. (1983). "Verbal Versus Numerical Processing of Subjective Probabilities," pp. 159–182 in: *Decision Making Under Uncertainty*. R.W. Scholz (ed.). Amsterdam: North Holland.

Zimmerman, W. (1973). "Issue-Areas and Foreign Policy Processes: A Research Note in Search for a General Theory," *American Political Science Review*, 67(4): 1,204–1,212.

Zinnes, D.A. (1980). "Three Puzzles in Search of a Researcher," *International Studies Quarterly*, 24(3): 315–342.

(1976). *Contemporary Research in International Relations*. New York: Free Press.

NAME INDEX

SUBJECT INDEX

Entries with capital letters in parentheses denote terms which have formal measures in the text, or which have special abbreviations used in the text.